Klaus von Heusinger, Claudia Maienborn and Paul Portner (Eds.,
Semantics – Foundations, History and Methods

This volume is part of a larger set of handbooks to Semantics

1 **Semantics: Foundations, History and Methods**
  Klaus von Heusinger, Claudia Maienborn, Paul Portner (eds.)

2 **Semantics: Lexical Structures and Adjectives**
  Claudia Maienborn, Klaus von Heusinger, Paul Portner (eds.)

3 **Semantics: Theories**
  Claudia Maienborn, Klaus von Heusinger, Paul Portner (eds.)

4 **Semantics: Noun Phrases and Verb Phrases**
  Paul Portner, Klaus von Heusinger, Claudia Maienborn (eds.)

5 **Semantics: Sentence and Information Structure**
  Paul Portner, Claudia Maienborn, Klaus von Heusinger (eds.)

6 **Semantics: Interfaces**
  Claudia Maienborn, Klaus von Heusinger, Paul Portner (eds.)

7 **Semantics: Typology, Diachrony and Processing**
  Klaus von Heusinger, Claudia Maienborn, Paul Portner (eds.)

Semantics
Foundations, History and Methods

Edited by
Klaus von Heusinger
Claudia Maienborn
Paul Portner

DE GRUYTER
MOUTON

ISBN 978-3-11-037373-8
e-ISBN (PDF) 978-3-11-036850-5
e-ISBN (EPUB) 978-3-11-039334-7

Library of Congress Cataloging-in-Publication Data
Names: Heusinger, Klaus von, editor. | Maienborn, Claudia, editor. | Portner,
   Paul, editor.
Title: Semantics : foundations, history and methods / edited by Klaus von Heusinger,
   Claudia Maienborn, Paul Portner
Description: Berlin ; Boston : De Gruyter, [2019] | Series: Mouton reader |
   Includes bibliographical references and index.
Identifiers: LCCN 2018030925 (print) | LCCN 2018049527 (ebook) | ISBN
   9783110368505 (electronic Portable Document Format (pdf) | ISBN
   9783110373738 (print : alk. paper) | ISBN 9783110368505 (e-book pdf) |
   ISBN 9783110393347 (e-book epub)
Subjects: LCSH: Semantics.
Classification: LCC P325 (ebook) | LCC P325 .S37994 2019 (print) | DDC
   401/.43--dc23
LC record available at https://lccn.loc.gov/2018030925

Bibliographic information published by the Deutsche Nationalbibliothek
The Deutsche Nationalbibliothek lists this publication in the Deutsche Nationalbibliografie;
detailed bibliographic data are available in the Internet at http://dnb.dnb.de.

© 2019 Walter de Gruyter GmbH, Berlin/Boston
Cover image: alxpin/iStock / Getty Images Plus
Typesetting: Integra Software Services Pvt. Ltd.
Printing and binding: CPI books GmbH, Leck

www.degruyter.com

Contents

1 Claudia Maienborn, Klaus von Heusinger and Paul Portner
   Meaning in linguistics —— 1

2 Pierre Jacob
   Meaning, intentionality and communication —— 14

3 Mark Textor
   (Frege on) Sense and reference —— 33

4 Barbara Abbott
   Reference: Foundational issues —— 62

5 Georgia M. Green
   Meaning in language use —— 94

6 Peter Pagin and Dag Westerståhl
   Compositionality —— 122

7 Stefan Engelberg
   Lexical decomposition: Foundational issues —— 156

8 Stephan Meier-Oeser
   Meaning in pre-19th century thought —— 182

9 Brigitte Nerlich
   The emergence of linguistic semantics in the 19th and early 20th century —— 217

10 Albert Newen and Bernhard Schröder
   The influence of logic on semantics —— 242

11 Ruth Kempson
   Formal semantics and representationalism —— 273

12 Manfred Krifka
   Varieties of semantic evidence —— 306

Lisa Matthewson
13   **Methods in cross-linguistic semantics —— 340**

Alice G.B. ter Meulen
14   **Formal methods in semantics —— 362**

Oliver Bott, Sam Featherston, Janina Radó and Britta Stolterfoht
15   **The application of experimental methods in semantics —— 387**

Index —— 409

Claudia Maienborn, Klaus von Heusinger and Paul Portner
1 Meaning in linguistics

1 Introduction —— 1
2 Truth —— 2
3 Compositionality —— 5
4 Context and discourse —— 10
5 Meaning in contemporary semantics —— 12
6 References —— 13

Abstract: The article provides an introduction to the study of meaning in modern semantics. Major tenets, tools, and goals of semantic theorizing are illustrated by discussing typical approaches to three central characteristics of natural language meaning: truth conditions, compositionality, and context and discourse.

1 Introduction

Meaning is a key concept of cognition, communication and culture, and there is a diversity of ways to understand it, reflecting the many uses to which the concept can be put. In the following we take the perspective on meaning developed within linguistics, in particular modern semantics, and we aim to explain the ways in which semanticists approach, describe, test and analyze meaning. The fact that semantics is a component of linguistic theory is what distinguishes it from approaches to meaning in other fields like philosophy, psychology, semiotics or cultural studies. As part of linguistic theory, semantics is characterized by at least the following features:

1. Empirical coverage: It strives to account for meaning in all of the world's languages.
2. Linguistic interfaces: It operates as a subtheory of the broader linguistic system, interacting with other subtheories such as syntax, pragmatics, phonology and morphology.
3. Formal expliciteness: It is laid out in an explicit and precise way, allowing the community of semanticists to jointly test it, improve it, and apply it to new theoretical problems and practical goals.

Claudia Maienborn, Tübingen, Germany
Klaus von Heusinger, Cologne, Germany
Paul Portner, Washington, DC, USA

4. Scientific paradigm: It is judged on the same criteria as other scientific theories, viz. coherence, conceptual simplicity, its ability to unify our understanding of diverse phenomena (within or across languages), to raise new questions and open up new horizons for research.

In the following we exemplify these four features on three central issues in modern semantic theory that define our understanding of meaning: truth conditions, compositionality, and context and discourse.

2 Truth

If one is to develop an explicit and precise scientific theory of meaning, the first thing one needs to do is to identify some of the data which the theory will respond to, and there is one type of data which virtually all work in semantics takes as fundamental: truth conditions. At an intuitive level, truth conditions are merely the most obvious way of understanding the meaning of a declarative sentence. If I say *It is raining outside*, I have described the world in a certain way. I may have described it correctly, in which case what I said is true, or I may have described it incorrectly, in which case it is false. Any competent speaker knows to a high degree of precision what the weather must be like for my sentence to count as true (a correct description) or false (an incorrect description). In other words, such a speaker knows the truth conditions of my sentence. This knowledge of truth conditions is extremely robust – far and wide, English speakers can make agreeing judgments about what would make my sentence true or false – and as a result, we can see the truth conditions themselves as a reliable fact about language which can serve as part of the basis for semantic theory.

While truth conditions constitute some of the most basic data for semantics, different approaches to semantics reckon with them in different ways. Some theories treat truth conditions not merely as the data which semantics is to deal with, but more than this as the very model of sentential meaning. This perspective can be summarized with the slogan "meaning is truth conditions", and within this tradition, we find statements like the following:

(1) $[\![\textit{It is raining outside}]\!]^{t,s}$ = TRUE iff it is raining outside of the building where the speaker s is located at time t, and = FALSE otherwise.

The double brackets $[\![X]\!]$ around an expression X names the semantic value of X in the terms of the theory in question. Thus, (1) indicates a theory which takes the semantic value of a sentence to be its truth value, TRUE or FALSE. The meaning of the sentence, according to the truth conditional theory, is then captured by the entire statement (1).

Although (1) represents a truth conditional theory according to which semantic value and meaning (i.e., the truth conditions) are distinct (the semantic value is a crucial component in giving the meaning), other truth conditional theories use techniques which allow meaning to be reified, and thus identified with semantic value, in a certain sense. The most well-known and important such approach is based on possible worlds:

(2) a. [[*It is raining outside*]]^{w,t,s} = TRUE iff it is raining outside of the building where the speaker *s* is located at time *t* in world *w*, and = FALSE otherwise.
b. [[*It is raining outside*]]^{t,s} = the set of worlds {w : it is raining outside of the building where the speaker *s* is located at time *t* in world *w*}

A possible world is a complete way the world could be. (Other theories use constructs similar to possible worlds, such as situations.) The statement in (2a) says virtually the same thing as (1), making explicit only that the meaning of *It is raining outside* depends not merely on the actual weather outside, but whatever the weather may turn out to be. Crucially, by allowing the possible world to be treated as an arbitrary point of evaluation, as in (2a), we are able to identify the truth conditions with the set of all such points, as in (2b). In (2), we have two different kinds of semantic value: the one in (2a), relativized to world, time, and speaker, corresponds to (1), and is often called the *extension* or *reference*. That in (2b), where the world point of evaluation has been transferred into the semantic value itself, is then called the *intension* or *sense*. The sense of a full sentence, for example given as a set of possible worlds as in (2b), is called a *proposition*. Specific theories differ in the precise nature of the extension and intension: The intension may involve more or different parameters than *w*, *t*, *s*, and several of these may be gathered into a set (along with the world) to form the intension. For example, in tense semantics, we often see intensions treated as sets of pairs of a world and a time.

The majority of work in semantics follows the truth conditional approach to the extent of making statements like those in (1)–(2) the fundamental fabric of the theory. Scholars often produce explicit fragments, i.e. mini-theories which cover a subset of a language, which are actually functions from expressions of a language to semantic values, with the semantic values of sentences being truth conditional in the vein of (1)–(2). But not all semantic research is truth conditional in this explicit way. Descriptive linguistics, functional linguistics, typological linguistics and cognitive linguistics frequently make important claims about meaning (in a particular language, or crosslinguistically). For example, Wolfart (1973: 25), a descriptive study of Plains Cree states: "Semantically, direction serves to specify actor and goal. In sentence (3), for instances, the direct theme sign /ā/ indicates the noun *atim* as goal, whereas the inverse theme sign /ekw/ in (4) marks the same noun as actor."

(3) nisēkih**ā**nān   atim
    scare(1p-3)   dog(3)
    'We scare the dog.'

(4) nisēkih**iko**nān   atim
    scare(3-1p)   dog(3)
    'The dog scares us.'

Despite not being framed as such, this passage is implicitly truth conditional. Wolfart is stating a difference in truth conditions which depends on the grammatical category of direction using the descriptions "actor" and "goal", and using the translations of cited examples. This example serves to illustrate the centrality of truth conditions to any attempt to think about the nature of linguistic meaning.

As a corollary to the focus on truth conditions, semantic theories typically take relations like entailment, synonymy, and contradiction to provide crucial data as well. Thus, the example sentence *It is raining outside* entails (5), and this fact is known to any competent speaker.

(5) It is raining outside or the kids are playing with the water hose.

Obviously, this entailment can be understood in terms of truth conditions (the truth of the one sentence guarantees the truth of the other), a fact which supports the idea that the analysis of truth conditions should be a central goal of semantics. It is less satisfying to describe synonymy in terms of truth conditions, as identity of truth conditions doesn't in most cases make for absolute sameness of meaning, in an intuitive sense – consider *Mary hit John* and *John was hit by Mary*; nevertheless, a truth conditional definition of synonymy allows for at least a useful concept of synonymy, since people can indeed judge whether two sentences would accurately describe the same circumstances, whereas it's not obvious that complete intuitive synonymy is even a useful concept, insofar as it may never occur in natural language.

The truth conditional perspective on meaning is intuitive and powerful where it applies, but in and of itself, it is only a foundation. It doesn't, at first glance, say anything about the meanings of subsentential constituents, the meanings or functions of non-declarative sentences, or non-literal meaning, for example. Semantic theory is responsible for the proper analysis of each of these features of language as well, and we will see in many of the articles in this handbook how it has been able to rise to these challenges, and many others.

3 Compositionality

A crucial aspect of natural language meaning is that speakers are able to determine the truth conditions for infinitely many distinct sentences, including sentences they have never encountered before. This shows that the truth conditions for sentences (or whatever turns out to be their psychological correlate) cannot be memorized. Speakers do not associate truth conditions such as the ones given in (1) or (2) holistically with their respective sentences. Rather, there must be some principled way to compute the meaning of a sentence from smaller units. In other words, natural language meaning is essentially combinatorial. The meaning of a complex expression is construed by combining the meaning of its parts in a certain way. Obviously, syntax plays a significant role in this process. The two sentences in (6), for instance, are made up of the same lexical material. It is only the different word order that is responsible for the different sentence meanings of (6a) and (6b).

(6) a. Caroline kissed a boy.
    b. A boy kissed Caroline.

In a similar vein, the ambiguity of a sentence like (7) is rooted in syntax. The two readings paraphrased in (7a) and (7b) correspond to different syntactic structures, with the PP being adjoined either to the verbal phrase or to the direct object NP.

(7) Caroline observed the boy with the telescope.
    a. Caroline observed the boy with the help of the telescope.
    b. Caroline observed the boy who had a telescope.

Examples such as (6) and (7) illustrate that the semantic combinatorial machinery takes the syntactic structure into account in a fairly direct way. This basic insight lead to the formulation of the so-called "principle of compositionality", attributed to Gottlob Frege (1892), which is usually formulated along the following lines:

(8) Principle of compositionality:
    The meaning of a complex expression is a function of the meanings of its parts and the way they are syntactically combined.

According to (8), the meaning of, e.g., *Caroline sleeps* is a function of the meanings of *Caroline* and *sleeps* and the fact that the former is the syntactic subject of the latter. There are stronger and weaker versions of the principle of compositionality, depending on what counts as "parts" and how exactly the semantic combinatorics is determined by the syntax. For instance, adherents of a stronger version of the principle of compositionality typically assume that the parts that constitute the meaning of a complex expression are only its immediate constituents. According to this view, only the NP [Caroline] and the VP [kissed a boy] would count as parts when computing the sentence meaning for (6a), but not (directly) [kissed] or [a boy].

Modern semantics explores many different ways of implementing the notion of compositionality formally. One particularly useful framework is based on the mathematical concept of a function. It takes the meaning of any complex expression as being the result of applying the meaning of one of its immediate parts (= the functor) to the meaning of its other immediate part (= the argument). With functional application as the basic semantic operation that is applied stepwise, mirroring the binary branching of syntax, the function-argument approach allows for a straightforward syntax-semantics mapping.

Although there is wide agreement among semanticists that, given the combinatorial nature of linguistic meaning, some version of the principle of compositionality must certainly hold, it is also clear that, when taking into account the whole complexity and richness of natural language meaning, compositional semantics is faced with a series of challenges. As a response to these challenges, semanticists have come up with several solutions and amendments. These relate basically to (A) the syntax-semantics interface, (B) the relationship between semantics and ontology, and (C) the semantics-pragmatics interface.

A Syntax-Semantics Interface

One way to cope with challenges to compositionality is to adjust the syntax properly. This could be done, e.g., by introducing possibly mute, i.e. phonetically empty, functional heads into the syntactic tree that nevertheless carry semantic content, or by relating the semantic composition to a more abstract level of syntactic derivation – Logical Form – that may differ from surface structure due to invisible movement. That is, the syntactic structure on which the semantic composition is based may be more or less directly linked to surface syntax, such that it fits the demands of compositional semantics. Of course, any such move should be independently motivated.

B Semantics – Ontology

Another direction that might be explored in order to reconcile syntax and semantics is to reconsider the inventory of primitive semantic objects the semantic fabric is assumed to be composed of. A famous case in point is Davidson's (1967) plea for an ontological category of events. A crucial motivation for this move was that the standard treatment of adverbial modifiers at that time was insufficient insofar as it failed to account properly for the combinatorial behavior and entailments of adverbial expressions. By positing an additional event argument introduced by the verb, Davidson laid the grounds for a theory of adverbial modification that would overcome these shortcomings. Under this assumption Davidson's famous sentence (9a) takes a semantic representation along the lines of (9b):

(9) a. Jones buttered the toast in the bathroom with the knife at midnight.
　　b. $\exists e$ [butter (jones, the toast, e) & in (e, the bathroom) & instr (e, the knife) & at (e, midnight)]

According to (9b), there was an event e of Jones buttering the toast, and this event was located in the bathroom. In addition, it was performed by using a knife as an instrument, and it took place at midnight. That is, Davidson's move enabled standard adverbial modifiers to be treated as simple first-order predicates that add information about the verb's hidden event argument. The major merits of such a Davidsonian analysis are, first, that it accounts for the typical entailment patterns of adverbial modifiers directly on the basis of their semantic representation. That is, the entailments in (10) follow from (9b) simply by virtue of the logical rule of simplification.

(10) a. Jones buttered the toast in the bathroom at midnight.
　　　b. Jones buttered the toast in the bathroom.
　　　c. Jones buttered the toast at midnight.
　　　d. Jones buttered the toast.

And, secondly, Davidson paved the way for treating adverbial modifiers on a par with adnominal modifiers. In the meantime, researchers working within the Davidsonian paradigm have discovered more and more fundamental analogies between the verbal and the nominal domain, attesting to the fruitfulness of Davidson's move.

　　In short, by enriching the semantic universe with a new ontological category of events, Davidson solved the compositionality puzzle of adverbials and arrived at a semantic theory superior to its competitors in both conceptual simplicity and empirical coverage. Of course once again, such a solution does not come without costs. With Quine's (1958) dictum "No entity without identity!" in mind, any ontological category a semantic theory makes use of requires a proper ontological characterization and legitimization. In the case of events, this is still the subject of ongoing debates among semanticists.

C Semantics-Pragmatics Interface

Finally, challenges to compositionality might also be taken as an invitation to reconsider the relationship between semantics and pragmatics by asking how far the composition of sentential meaning goes, and what the principles of pragmatic enrichment and pragmatic licensing are. One notorious case in point is the adequate delineation of linguistic knowledge and world knowledge. To give an example, when considering the sentences in (11), we know that each of them refers to a very different kind of opening event. Obviously, the actions underlying, for instance, the opening of a can differ substantially from those of opening one's eyes or opening a file on a computer.

(11) a. She opened the can.
 b. She opened her eyes.
 c. She opened the electronic file.

To a certain extent, this knowledge is of linguistic significance, as can be seen when taking into account the combinatorial behavior of certain modifiers:

(11) a. She opened the can {with a knife, *abruptly, *with a double click}.
 b. She opened her eyes {*with a knife, abruptly, *with a double click}.
 c. She opened the electronic file {*with a knife, *abruptly, with a double click}.

A comprehensive theory of natural language meaning should therefore strive to account for these observations. Nevertheless, incorporating this kind of world knowledge into compositional semantics would be neither feasible nor desireable. A possible solution for this dilemma lies in the notion of *semantic underspecification*. Several proposals have been developed which take the lexical meaning that is fed into semantic composition to be of an abstract, context neutral nature. In the case of *to open* in (11), for instance, this common meaning skeleton would roughly say that some action of an agent x on an object y causes a change of state such that y is accessible afterwards. This would be the verb's constant meaning contribution that can be found in all sentences in (11a–c) and which is also present, e.g., in (11d), where we don't have such clear intuitions about how x acted upon y, and which is therefore more liberal as to adverbial modification.

(11) d. She opened the gift {with a knife, abruptly, with a double click}.

That is, underspecification accounts would typically take neither the type of action performed by x nor the exact sense of accessibility of y as part of the verb's lexical meaning. To account for this part of the meaning, compositional semantics is complemented by a procedure of pragmatic enrichment, by which the compositionally derived meaning skeleton is pragmatically specified according to the contextually available world knowledge.

Semantic underspecification/pragmatic enrichment accounts provide a means for further specifying a compositionally well-formed, underspecified meaning representation. A different stance towards the semantics-pragmatics interface is taken by so-called "coercion" approaches. These deal typically with the interpretation of sentences that are strictly speaking ungrammatical but might be "rescued" in a certain way. An example is given in (12).

(12) The alarm clock stood intentionally on the table.

The sentence in (12) does not offer a regular integration for the subject-oriented adverbial *intentionally*, i.e, the subject NP *the alarm clock* does not fulfill the adverbial's request for an intentional subject. Hence, a compositional clash results and the sentence is ungrammatical. Nevertheless, although deviant, there seems to be a way to rescue the sentence so that it becomes acceptable and interpretable anyway. In the case of (12), a possible repair strategy would be to introduce an actor, who is responsible for the fact that the alarm clock stands on the table. This move would provide a suitable anchor for the adverbial's semantic contribution. Thus, we understand (12) as saying that someone put the alarm clock on purpose on the table. That is, in case of a combinatorial clash, there seems to be a certain leeway for non-compositional adjustments of the compositionally derived meaning. The defective part is "coerced" into the right format. The exact mechanism of coercion and its grammatical and pragmatic licensing conditions are still poorly understood.

In current semantic research many quite different directions are being explored with respect to the issues A–C. What version of the principle of compositionality ultimately turns out to be the right one and how compositional semantics interacts with syntax, ontology, and pragmatics is, in the end, an empirical question. Yet, the results and insights obtained so far in this endeavor are already demonstrating the fruitfulness of reckoning with compositionality as a driving force in the constitution of natural language meaning.

4 Context and discourse

Speakers do not use sentences in isolation, but in the context of an utterance situation and as part of a longer discourse. The meaning of a sentence depends on the particular circumstances of its utterances, but also on the discourse context in which it is uttered. At the same time the meaning of linguistic expression changes the context, e.g., the information available to speaker and hearer. The analysis of the interaction of context, discourse and meaning provides new and challenging issues to the research agenda in the semantics-pragmatics interface as described in the last section. In the following we focus on two aspects of these issues to illustrate how the concept of meaning described above can further be developed by theorizing on the interaction between sentence meaning, contextual parameters and discourse structure.

So far we have characterized the meaning of a sentence by its truth conditions and, as a result, we have "considered semantics to be the study of propositions" (Stalnaker 1970: 273). It is justified by the very clear concept that meaning describes "how the world is". However, linguistic expressions often need additional information to form propositions as sentences contain indexical elements, such as *I, you, she, here, there, now* and the tenses of verbs. Indexical expressions cannot be interpreted according to possible worlds, i.e. how the conditions might be, but they are interpreted according to the actual utterance situation. Intensive research into this kind of context dependency led to the conclusion that the proposition itself depends on contextual parameters like *speaker, addressee, location, time* etc. This dependency is most prominently expressed in Kaplan's (1977) notion *character* for the meaning of linguistic expressions. The character of an expression is a function from the context of utterance c, which includes the values for the speaker, the hearer, the time, the location etc. to the proposition. Other expressions such as *local, different, a certain, enemy, neighbor* may contain "hidden" indexical parameters. They express their content dependent on one or more reference points given by the context. Thus meaning is understood as an abstract concept or function from contexts to propositions, and propositions themselves are described as functions from possible worlds into truth conditions.

The meaning of a linguistic expression is influenced not only by such relatively concrete aspects of the situation of use as speaker and addressee, but also by intentional factors like the assumptions of the speaker and hearer about the world, their beliefs and their goals. This type of context is continuously updated by the information provided by each sentence in a discourse. We see that linguistic expressions are not only "context-consumers", but also "context-shifters". This can be illustrated by examples from anaphora, presuppositions and various discourse relations.

(13) a. A man walks in the park. He smokes.
     b. #He smokes. A man walks in the park.

(14) a. Rebecca married Thomas. She regrets that she married him.
     b. Rebecca regrets that she married Thomas. ?She married him.

(15) a. John left. Ann started to cry.
     b. Ann started to cry. John left.

In (13) the anaphoric pronoun needs an antecedent, in other words it is a context-consumer as it takes the information provided in the context for fixing its meaning. The indefinite noun *a man* however is a context-shifter. It changes the context by introducing a discourse referent into the discourse or discourse structure such that the pronoun can be linked to it. In (13a) the indefinite introduces the referent and the anaphoric pronoun can be linked to it, in (13b) the pronoun in the first sentence has no antecedent and if the indefinite noun phrase in the second clause should refer to the same discourse referent it must not be indefinite. In (14) we see the contribution of presupposition to the context. (14b) is odd, since one can regret only something that is known to have happened. To assert this again makes the contribution of the second sentence superfluous and the small discourse incoherent. (15) provides evidence that we always assume some relation between sentences above a simple conjunction of two propositions. The relation could be a sequence of events or a causal relation between the two events, and this induces different meanings on the two small discourses as a whole. These and many more examples have led to the development of dynamic semantics, i.e. the view that meaning is shifting a given information status to a new one.

There are different ways to model the context dependency of linguistic expressions and the choice among them is still an unresolved issue and a topic of considerable contemporary interest. We illustrate this by presenting one example from the literature. Stalnaker proposes to represent the context as a set of possible worlds that are shared by speaker and hearer, his "common ground". A new sentence is interpreted with respect to the common ground, i.e. to a set of possible worlds. The interpretation of the sentence changes the common ground (given that the hearer does not reject the content of the sentence) and the updated common ground is the new context for the next sentence. Kamp (1988) challenges this view as problematic, as possible worlds do not provide enough linguistically relevant information, as the following example illustrates (due to Barbara Partee, first discussed in Heim 1982: 21).

(16) Exactly one of the ten balls is not in the bag. It is under the sofa.

(17) Exactly nine of the ten balls are in the bag. #It is under the sofa.

Both sentences in (16) and (17) have the same truth conditions, i.e. in exactly all possible circumstances in which (16) is true (17) is true, too; still the continuation with the second sentence is only felicitous in (16), but not in (17). (16) explicitly introduces an antecedent in the first sentence, and the pronoun in the second sentence can be anaphorically linked to it. In (17), however, no explicit antecedent is introduced and therefore we cannot resolve the anaphoric reference of the pronoun. Extensive research on these issues has proven very fruitful for the continuous developing of our methodological tools and for our understanding of natural language meaning in context and its function for discourse structure.

5 Meaning in contemporary semantics

Meaning is a notion investigated by a number of disciplines, including linguistics, philosophy, psychology, artificial intelligence, semiotics as well as many others. The definitions of meaning are as manifold and plentiful as the different theories and perspectives that arise from these disciplines. We have argued here that in order to use meaning as a well-defined object of investigation, we must perceive facts to be explained and have tests to expose the underlying phenomena, and we must have a well-defined scientific apparatus which allows us to describe, analyze and model these phenomena. This scientific apparatus is contemporary semantics: It possesses a clearly defined terminology, it provides abstract representations and it allows for formal modeling that adheres to scientific standards and renders predictions that can be verified or falsified. We have illustrated the tenets, tools and goals of contemporary semantics by discussing typical approaches to three central characteristics of meaning: truth conditionality, compositionality, and context and discourse.

Recent times have witnessed an increased interest of semanticists in developing their theories on a broader basis of empirical evidence, taking into account crosslinguistic data, diachronic data, psycho- and neurolinguistic studies as well as corpus linguistic and computational linguistic resources. As a result of these efforts, contemporary semantics is characterized by a continuous explanatory progress, an increased awareness of and proficiency in methodological issues, and the emergence of new opportunities for interdisciplinary cooperation. Along these lines, the articles of this handbook develop an integral, many-faceted and yet well-rounded picture of this joint endeavour in the linguistic study of natural language meaning.

6 References

Davidson, Donald 1967. The logical form of action sentences. In: N. Resher (ed.). *The Logic of Decision and Action*. Pittsburgh, PA: University of Pittsburgh Press, 81–95. Reprinted in: D. Davidson (ed.), *Essays on Actions and Events*. Oxford: Clarendon Press, 1980, 105–148.
Frege, Gottlob 1892/1980. Über Sinn und Bedeutung. *Zeitschrift für Philosophie und philosophische Kritik* 100, 25–50. English translation in: P. Geach & M. Black (eds.). *Translations from the Philosophical Writings of Gottlob Frege*. Oxford: Blackwell, 1980, 56–78.
Heim, Irene 1982. *The Semantics of Definite and Indefinite Noun Phrases*. Ph.D. dissertation. University of Massachusetts, Amherst, MA. Reprinted: Ann Arbor, MI: University Microfilms.
Kaplan, David 1977/1989. Demonstratives. An Essay on the Semantics, Logic, Metaphysics, and Epistemology of Demonstratives and Other Indexicals. Ms. Los Angeles, CA, University of California. Printed in: J. Almog & J. Perry & H. Wettstein (eds.). *Themes from Kaplan*. Oxford: Oxford University Press, 1989, 481–563.
Kamp, Hans 1988. Belief attribution and context & Comments on Stalnaker. In: R.H. Grimm & D.D. Merrill (eds.). *Contents of Thought*. Tucson, AZ: The University of Arizona Press, 156–181, 203–206.
Quine, Willard van Orman 1958. Speaking of Objects. *Proceedings and Addresses of the American Philosophical Association* 31, 5–22.
Stalnaker, Robert 1970. Pragmatics. *Synthese* 22, 272–289.
Wolfart, H. Christoph 1973. *Plains Cree: A Grammatical Study*. Transactions of the American Philosophical Society, New Series, vol. 63, pt. 5. Philadelphia, PA: The American Philosophical Society.

Pierre Jacob
2 Meaning, intentionality and communication

1   Introduction —— 14
2   Intentionality: Brentano's legacy —— 15
3   Early pragmatics: ordinary language philosophy and speech act theory —— 18
4   Grice on speaker's meaning and implicatures —— 21
5   The emergence of truth-conditional pragmatics —— 25
6   Concluding remarks: pragmatics and cognitive science —— 29
7   References —— 30

Abstract: This article probes the connections between the metaphysics of meaning and the investigation of human communication. It first argues that contemporary philosophy of mind has inherited most of its metaphysical questions from Brentano's puzzling definition of intentionality. Then it examines how intentionality came to occupy the forefront of pragmatics in three steps. (1) By investigating speech acts, Austin and ordinary language philosophers pioneered the study of intentional actions performed by uttering sentences of natural languages. (2) Based on his novel concept of speaker's meaning and his inferential view of human communication as a cooperative and rational activity, Grice developed a three-tiered model of the meaning of utterances: (i) the linguistic meaning of the uttered sentence; (ii) the explicit truth-conditional content of the utterance; (iii) the implicit content conveyed by the utterance. (3) Finally, the new emerging truth-conditional trend in pragmatics urges that not only the implicit content conveyed by an utterance but its explicit content as well depends on the speaker's communicative intention.

1 Introduction

This article lies at the interface between the scientific investigation of human verbal communication and metaphysical questions about the nature of meaning. Words and sentences of natural languages have meaning (or semantic properties) and they are used by humans in tasks of verbal communication. Much of

Pierre Jacob, Paris, France

https://doi.org/10.1515/9783110368505-002

twentieth-century philosophy of mind has been concerned with metaphysical questions raised by the perplexing nature of meaning. For example, what is it about the meaning of the English word "dog" that enables a particular token used in the USA in 2008 to latch onto hairy barking creatures that lived in Egypt four thousand years earlier (cf. Horwich 2005)?

Meanwhile, the study of human communication in the twentieth century can be seen as a competition between two models, which Sperber & Wilson (1986) call the "code model" and the "inferential model." A decoding process maps a signal onto a message associated to the signal by an underlying code (i.e., a system of rules or conventions). An inferential process maps premises onto a conclusion, which is warranted by the premises. When an addressee understands a speaker's utterance, how much of the content of the utterance has been coded into, and can be decoded from, the linguistic meaning of the utterance? How much content does the addressee retrieve by his ability to infer the speaker's communicative intention? These are the basic scientific questions in the investigation of human verbal communication.

Much philosophy of mind in the twentieth century devoted to the metaphysics of meaning sprang from Brentano's puzzling definition of the medieval word "intentionality" (section 2). Austin, one of the leading ordinary language philosophers, emphasized the fact that by uttering sentences of some natural language, a speaker may perform an action, i.e., a speech act (section 3). But he espoused a social conventionalist view of speech acts, which later pragmatics rejected in favor of an inferential approach. Grice instead developed an inferential model of verbal communication based on his concept of speaker's meaning and his view that communication is a cooperative and rational activity (section 4). However, many of Grice's insights have been further developed into a non-Gricean truth-conditional pragmatics (section 5). Finally, the "relevance-theoretic" approach pioneered by Sperber & Wilson (1986) fills part of the gap between the study of meaning and the cognitive sciences (section 6).

2 Intentionality: Brentano's legacy

Brentano (1874) made a twofold contribution to the philosophy of mind: he provided a puzzling definition of intentionality and he put forward the thesis that intentionality is "the mark of the mental." Intentionality is the power of minds to be about things, properties, events and states of affairs. As the meaning of its Latin root (*tendere*) indicates, "intentionality" denotes the mental tension whereby the human mind aims at so-called "intentional objects."

The concept of intentionality should not be confused with the concept of intention. Intentions are special psychological states involved in the planning and execution of actions. But on Brentano's view, intentionality is a property of all psychological phenomena. Nor should "intentional" and "intentionality" be confused with the predicates "intensional" and "intensionality," which mean "non-extensional" and "non-extensionality": they refer to logical features of sentences and utterances, some of which may describe (or report) an individual's psychological states. "Creature with a heart" and "creature with a kidney" have the same extension: all creatures with a heart have a kidney and conversely (cf. Quine 1948). But they have different intensions because having a heart and having a kidney are different properties. This distinction mirrors Frege's (1892) distinction between sense and reference (cf. article 3 [this volume] (Textor) *Sense and reference* and article 4 [this volume] (Abbott) *Reference*). In general, a linguistic context is non-extensional (or intensional) if it fails to license both the substitution of coreferential terms *salva veritate* and the application of the rule of existential generalization.

As Brentano defined it, intentionality is what enables a psychological state or act to represent a state of affairs, or be directed upon what he called an "intentional object." Intentional objects exemplify the property which Brentano called "intentional inexistence" or "immanent objectivity," by which he meant that the mind may aim at targets that do not exist in space and time or represent states of affairs that fail to obtain or even be possible. For example, unicorns do not exist in space and time and round squares are not possible geometrical objects. Nonetheless thinking about either a unicorn or a round square is not thinking about nothing. To admire Sherlock Holmes or to love Anna Karenina is to admire or love something, i.e., some intentional object. Thus, Brentano's characterization of intentionality gave rise to a gap in twentieth-century philosophical logic between intentional-objects theorists (Meinong 1904; Parsons 1980; Zalta 1988), who claimed that there must be things that do not exist, and their opponents (Russell 1905; Quine 1948), who denied it and rejected the distinction between being and existence. (For further discussion, cf. Jacob 2003.)

Brentano (1874) also held the thesis that intentionality is constitutive of the mental: all and only psychological phenomena exhibit intentionality. Brentano's second thesis that only psychological (or mental) phenomena possess intentionality led him to embrace a version of the Cartesian ontological dualism between mental and physical things. Chisholm (1957) offered a linguistic version of Brentano's second thesis, according to which the intensionality of a linguistic report is a criterion of the intentionality of the reported psychological state (cf. Jacob 2003). He further argued that the contents of sentences describing an agent's psychological states cannot be successfully paraphrased into the behaviorist idiom of sentences describing the agent's bodily movements and behavior.

Quine (1960) accepted Chisholm's (1957) linguistic version of Brentano's second thesis which he used as a premise for an influential dilemma: if the intentional idiom is not reducible to the behaviorist idiom, then the intentional idiom cannot be part of the vocabulary of the natural sciences and intentionality cannot be "naturalized." Quine's dilemma was that one must choose between a physicalist ontology and intentional realism, i.e., the view that intentionality is a real phenomenon. Unlike Brentano, Quine endorsed physicalism and rejected intentional realism.

Some of the physicalists who accept Quine's dilemma (e.g., Churchland 1989) have embraced eliminative materialism and denied the reality of beliefs and desires. The short answer to this proposal is that it is difficult to make sense of the belief that there are no beliefs. Others (such as Dennett 1987) have taken the "instrumentalist" view that, although the intentional idiom is a useful stance for predicting a complex physical system's behavior, it lacks an explanatory value. But the question arises how the intentional idiom could make useful predictions if it fails to describe and explain anything (cf. Jacob 1997, 2003 and Rey 1997).

As a result of the difficulties inherent to both eliminative materialism and interpretive instrumentalism, several physicalists have chosen to deny Brentano's thesis that only non-physical things exhibit intentionality, and to challenge Quine's dilemma according to which intentional realism is not compatible with physicalism. Their project is to "naturalize" intentionality and account for the puzzling features of intentionality (e.g., the fact that the mind may aim at non-existing objects and represent non-actual states of affairs), using only concepts recognizable by natural scientists (cf. section 3 on Grice's notion of non-natural meaning).

In recent philosophy of mind, the most influential proposals for naturalizing intentionality have been versions of the so-called "teleosemantic" approach championed by Millikan (1984), Dretske (1995) and others, which is based on the notion of biological function (or purpose). Teleosemantic theories are so-called because they posit an underlying connection between teleology (design or function) and content (or intentionality): a representational device is endowed with a function (or purpose). Something whose function is to indicate the presence of some property may fail to fulfill its function. If and when it does, then it may generate a false representation or represent something that fails to exist.

Brentano's thesis that only mental phenomena exhibit intentionality seems also open to the challenge that expressions of natural languages, which are not mental things, have intentionality in virtue of which they too can represent things, properties, events and states of affairs. In response, many philosophers of mind, such as Grice (1957, 1968), Fodor (1987), Haugeland (1981) and Searle (1983, 1992), have endorsed the distinction between the underived intentionality of a speaker's psychological states and the derived intentionality (i.e., the conventional meaning) of the sentences by the utterance of which she expresses her mental states. On their view, sentences of natural languages would lack meaning unless humans used them for some purpose. (But for dissent, see Dennett 1987.)

Some philosophers go one step further and posit the existence of an internal "language of thought:" thinking, having a thought or a propositional attitude is to entertain a token of a mental formula realized in one's brain. On this view, like sentences of natural languages, mental sentences possess syntactic and semantic properties. But, unlike sentences of natural languages, they lack phonological properties. Thus, the semantic properties of a complex mental sentence systematically depend upon the meanings of its constituents and their syntactic combination. The strongest arguments for the existence of a language of thought are based on the productivity and systematicity of thoughts, i.e., the facts that there is no upper limit on the complexity of thoughts and that a creature able to form certain thoughts must be able to form other related thoughts. On this view, the intentionality of an individual's thoughts and propositional attitudes derives from the meanings of symbols in the language of thought (cf. Fodor 1975, 1987).

3 Early pragmatics: ordinary language philosophy and speech act theory

Unlike sentences of natural languages, utterances are created by speakers, at particular places and times, for various purposes, including verbal communication. Not all communication, however, need be verbal. Nor do people use language solely for the purpose of communication; one can use language for clarifying one's thoughts, reasoning and making calculations. Utterances, not sentences, can be shouted in a hoarse voice and tape-recorded. Similarly, the full meaning of an utterance goes beyond the linguistic meaning of the uttered sentence, in two distinct aspects: both its representational content and its so-called "illocutionary force" (i.e., whether the utterance is meant as a prediction, a threat or an assertion) are underdetermined by the linguistic meaning of the uttered sentence.

Prior to the cognitive revolution of the 1950's, the philosophy of language was divided into two opposing approaches: so-called "ideal language" philosophy (in the tradition of Frege, Russell, Carnap and Tarski) and so-called "ordinary language" philosophy (in the tradition of Wittgenstein, Austin, Strawson and later Searle). The word "pragmatics," which derives from the Greek word *praxis* (which means *action*), was first introduced by ideal language philosophers as part of a threefold distinction between syntax, semantics and pragmatics (cf. Morris 1938 and Carnap 1942). Syntax was defined as the study of internal relations among symbols of a language. Semantics was defined as the study of the relations between symbols and their denotations (or designata). Pragmatics was defined as the study of the relations between symbols and their users (cf. article 11 [Semantics: Interfaces] (Jaszczolt) *Semantics and pragmatics*).

Ideal language philosophers were interested in the semantic structures of sentences of formal languages designed for capturing mathematical truths. The syntactic structure of any "well-formed formula" (i.e., sentence) of a formal language is defined by arbitrary rules of formation and derivation. Semantic values are assigned to simple symbols of the language by stipulation and the truth-conditions of a sentence can be mechanically determined from the semantic values of its constituents by the syntactic rules of composition. From the perspective of ideal language philosophers, such features of natural languages as their context-dependency appeared as a defect. For example, unlike formal languages, natural languages contain indexical expressions (e.g., "now", "here" or "I") whose references can change with the context of utterance.

By contrast, ordinary language philosophers were concerned with the distinctive features of the meanings of expressions of natural languages and the variety of their uses. In sharp opposition to ideal language philosophers, ordinary language philosophers stressed two main points, which paved the way for later work in pragmatics. First, they emphasized the context-dependency of the descriptive content expressed by utterances of sentences of natural languages (see section 4). Austin (1962a: 110–111) denied that a sentence *as such* could ever be ascribed truth-conditions and a truth-value: "the question of truth and falsehood does not turn only on what a sentence is, nor yet on what it means, but on, speaking very broadly, the circumstances in which it is uttered." Secondly, they criticized what Austin (1962b) called the "descriptive fallacy," according to which the sole point of using language is to state facts or describe the world (cf. article 5 [this volume] (Green) *Meaning in language use*).

As indicated by the title of Austin's (1962b) book, *How to Do Things with Words*, they argued that by uttering sentences of some natural language, a speaker performs an action, i.e., a speech act: she performs an "illocutionary act" with a particular illocutionary force. A speaker may give an order, ask a question, make a threat, a promise, an entreaty, an apology, an assertion and so on. Austin (1962b) sketched a new framework for the description and classification of speech acts. As Green (2007) notes, speech acts are not to be confused with acts of speech: "one can perform an act of speech, say by uttering words in order to test a microphone, without performing a speech act." Conversely, one can issue a warning without saying anything, by producing a gesture or a "minatory facial expression."

Austin (1962b) identified three distinct levels of action in the performance of a speech act: the "locutionary act," the "illocutionary act," and the "perlocutionary act," which stand to one another in the following hierarchical structure. By uttering a sentence, a speaker performs the locutionary act of saying something by virtue of which she performs an illocutionary act with a given illocutionary force (e.g., giving an order). Finally, by performing an illocutionary act endowed with a specific illocutionary force, the speaker performs a perlocutionary act, whereby she achieves some psychological or behavioral effect upon her audience, such as frightening him or convincing him.

Before he considered this threefold distinction within the structure of speech acts, Austin had made a distinction between so-called "constative" and "performative" utterances. The former is supposed to describe some state of affairs and is true or false according to whether the described state of affairs obtains or not. Instead of being a (true or false) description of some independent state of affairs, the latter is supposed to constitute (or create) a state of affairs of its own. Clearly, the utterance of a sentence in either the imperative mood ("Leave this room immediately!") or the interrogative mood ("What time is it right now?") is performative in this sense: far from purporting to register any pre-existing state of affairs, the speaker either gives an order or asks a question. By drawing the distinction between constative and performative utterances, Austin was able to criticize the descriptive fallacy and emphasize the fact that many utterances of declarative sentences are performative (not constative) utterances.

In particular, Austin was interested in explicit performative utterances ("I promise I'll come," "I order you to leave" or "I apologize"), which include a main verb that denotes the very speech act that the utterance performs. Austin's attention was drawn towards explicit performatives, whose performance is governed, not merely by linguistic rules, but also by social conventions and by what Searle (1969: 51) called "institutional facts" (as in "I thereby pronounce you husband and wife"), i.e., facts that (unlike "brute facts") presuppose the existence of human institutions. Specific bodily movements count as a move in a game, as an act of e.g., betting, or as part of a marriage ceremony only if they conform to some conventions that are part of some social institutions. For a performative speech act to count as an act of baptism, of marriage, or an oath, the utterance must meet some social constraints, which Austin calls "felicity" conditions. Purported speech acts of baptism, oath or marriage can fail some of their felicity conditions and thereby "misfire" if either the speaker lacks the proper authority or the addressee fails to respond with an appropriate uptake – in response to e.g., an attempted bet sincerely made by the speaker. If a speaker makes an insincere promise, then he is guilty of an "abuse."

Austin came to abandon his former distinction between constative and performative utterances when he came to realize that some explicit performatives can be used to make true or false assertions or predictions. One can make an explicit promise or an explicit request by uttering a sentence prefixed by either "I promise" or "I request." One can also make an assertion or a prediction by uttering a sentence prefixed by either "I assert" or "I predict." Furthermore, two of his assumptions led Austin to embrace a social conventionalist view of illocutionary acts. First, Austin took explicit performatives as a general model for illocutionary acts. Secondly, he took explicit performatives, whose felicity conditions include the satisfaction of social conventions, as a paradigm of all explicit performatives. Thus Austin (1962b: 103) was led to embrace a social conventionalist view of illocutionary acts according to which the illocutionary force of a speech act is "conventional in the sense that it could be made explicit by the performative formula."

Austin's social conventionalist view of illocutionary force was challenged by Strawson (1964: 153–154) who pointed out that the assumption that no illocutionary act could be performed unless it conformed to some social convention would be "like supposing that there could not be love affairs which did not proceed on lines laid down in the *Roman de la Rose*." Instead, Strawson argued, what confers to a speech act its illocutionary force is that the speaker intends it to be so taken by her audience. By uttering "You will leave," the speaker may make a prediction, a bet or order the addressee to leave. Only the context, not some socially established convention, may help the audience determine the particular illocutionary force of the utterance.

Also, as noted by Searle (1975) and by Bach & Harnish (1979), speech acts may be performed indirectly. For example, by uttering "I would like you to leave," a speaker directly expresses her desire that her addressee leave. But in so doing, she may indirectly ask or request her addressee to do so. By uttering "Can you pass the salt?" – which is a direct question about her addressee's ability – , the speaker may indirectly request him to pass the salt. As Recanati (1987: 92–93) argues, when a speaker utters an explicit performative such as "I order you to leave," her utterance has the direct illocutionary force of a statement. But it may also have the indirect force of an order. There need be no socially established convention whereby a speaker orders her audience to leave by means of an utterance with a verb that denotes the act performed by the speaker.

4 Grice on speaker's meaning and implicatures

In his 1957 seminal paper, Grice did three things: he drew a contrast between "natural" and "non-natural" meaning; he offered a definition of the novel concept of speaker's meaning; and he sketched a framework within which human communication is seen as a cooperative and rational activity (the addressee's task being to infer the speaker's meaning on the basis of her utterance, in accordance with a few principles of rational cooperation). In so doing, Grice took a major step towards an "inferential model" of human communication, and away from the "code model" (cf. article 11 [Semantics: Interfaces] (Jaszczolt) *Semantics and pragmatics*).

As Grice (1957) emphasized, smoke is a natural sign of fire: the former naturally means the latter in the sense that not unless there was a fire would there be any smoke. By contrast, the English word "fire" (or the French word "feu") non-naturally means fire: if a person erroneously believes that there is a fire (or wants to intentionally mislead another into wrongly thinking that there is a fire) when there is none, then she can produce a token of the word "fire" in the absence of a fire. (Thus, the notion of non-natural meaning is Grice's counterpart of Brentano's intentionality.)

Grice (1957, 1968, 1969) further introduced the concept of speaker's meaning, i.e., of someone meaning something by exhibiting some piece of behavior that can, but need not, be verbal. For a speaker S to mean something by producing some utterance x is for S to intend the utterance of x to produce some effect (or response r) in an audience A by means of A's recognition of this very intention. Hence, the speaker's meaning is a communicative intention, with the peculiar feature of being reflexive in the sense that part of its content is that an audience recognize it.

Strawson (1964) turned to Grice's concept of speaker's meaning as an intentionalist alternative to Austin's social conventional account of illocutionary acts (section 2). Strawson (1964) also pointed out that Grice's complex analysis of speaker's meaning or communicative intention requires the distinction between three complementary levels of intention. For S to mean something by an utterance x is for S to intend:

(i) S's utterance of x to produce a response r in audience A;
(ii) A to recognize S's intention (i);
(iii) A's recognition of S's intention (i) to function at least as part of A's reason for A's response r.

This analysis raises two opposite problems: it is both overly restrictive and insufficiently so. First, as Strawson's reformulation shows, Grice's condition (i) corresponds to S's intention to perform what Austin (1962b) called a perlocutionary act. But for S to successfully communicate with A, it is not necessary that S's intention to perform her perlocutionary act be fulfilled (cf. Searle 1969: 46–48). Suppose that S utters: "It is raining," intending (i) to produce in A the belief that it is raining. A may recognize S's intention (i); but, for some reason, A may mistrust *S* and fail to acquire the belief that it is raining. *S* would have failed to convince *A* (that it is raining), but *S* would nonetheless have successfully communicated what she meant to *A*. Thus, fulfillment of *S*'s intention (i) is not necessary for successful communication. Nor is the fulfillment of *S*'s intention (iii), which presupposes the fulfillment of *S*'s intention (i). All that is required for *S* to communicate what she meant to *A* is *A*'s recognition of *S*'s intention (ii) that *S* has the higher-order intention to inform *A* of her first-order intention to inform *A* of something.

Secondly, Strawson (1964) pointed out that his reformulation of Grice's definition of speaker's meaning is insufficiently restrictive. Following Sperber & Wilson (1986: 30), suppose that *S* intends *A* to believe that she needs his help to fix her hair-dryer, but she is reluctant to ask him openly to do so. *S* ostensively offers *A* evidence that she is trying to fix her hair-dryer, thereby intending *A* to believe that she needs his help. *S* intends *A* to recognize her intention to inform him that she needs his help. However, *S* does not want *A* to know that she knows that he is watching her. Since *S* is not openly asking *A* to help her, she is not communicating with *A*. Although *S* has the second-order intention that *A* recognizes her first-order intention to inform him that she needs his help, she does not want *A* to recognize her second-order intention. To deal with such a case, Strawson (1964) suggested that the analysis of Grice's speaker's meaning include *S*'s third-order intention to have her second-order intention recognized by her audience. But as Schiffer (1972) pointed out, this opens the way to an infinity of higher-order intentions. Instead, Schiffer (1972) argued that for *S* to have a communicative intention, *S*'s intention to inform *A* must be mutually known to *S* and *A*. But as pointed out by Sperber & Wilson (1986: 18–19), people who share mutual knowledge know that they do. So the question arises: how do speaker and hearer know that they do? (We shall come back to this issue in the concluding remarks.)

Grice (1968) thought of his concept of speaker's meaning as a basis for a reductive analysis of semantic notions such as sentence- or word-meaning. But most linguists and philosophers have expressed skepticism about this aspect of Grice's program (cf. Chomsky 1975, 1980). By contrast, many assume that some amended version of Grice's concept of speaker's meaning can serve as a basis for an inferential model of human communication. In his 1967 William James Lectures, Grice argued that what enables the hearer to infer the speaker's meaning on the basis of her utterance is that he rationally expects all utterances to meet the "Cooperative Principle" and a set of nine maxims or norms organized into four main categories which, by reference to Kant, he labeled maxims of Quantity (informativeness), Quality (truthfulness), Relation (relevance) and Manner (clarity).

As ordinary language philosophers emphasized, in addition to what is being said by an assertion – what makes the assertion true or false – , the very performance of an illocutionary act with the force of an assertion has pragmatic implications. For example, consider Moore's paradox: by uttering "It is raining but I do not believe it," the speaker is not expressing a logical contradiction, as there is no logical contradiction between the fact that it is raining and the fact that the speaker fails to believe it. Nonetheless, the utterance is pragmatically paradoxical because by asserting that it is raining, the speaker thereby expresses (or displays) her belief that it is raining, but her utterance explicitly denies that she believes it.

Grice's (1967/1975) third main contribution to an inferential model of communication was his concept of conversational implicature, which he introduced as "a term of art" (cf. Grice 1989: 24). Suppose that Bill asks Jill whether she is going out and Jill replies: "It's raining." For Jill's utterance about the weather to constitute a response to Bill's question, additional assumptions are required, such as, for example, that Jill does not like rain (i.e., that if it is raining, then Jill is not going out) which, together with Jill's response, may entail that she is not going out.

Grice's approach to communication, based on the Cooperative Principle and the maxims, offers a framework for explaining how, from Jill's utterance, Bill can retrieve an implicit answer to his question by supplying some additional assumptions. Bill must be aware that Jill's utterance is not a direct answer to his question. Assuming that Jill does not violate (or "flout") the maxim of relevance, she must have intended Bill to supply the assumption that e.g., she does not enjoy rain, and to infer that she is not going out from her explicit utterance. Grice (1967/1975) called the additional assumption and the conclusion "conversational" implicatures. In other words, Grice's conversational implicatures enable a hearer to reconcile a speaker's utterance with his assumption that the speaker conforms to the Principle of Cooperation. Grice (1989: 31) insisted that "the presence of a conversational implicature must be capable of being worked out; for even if it can in fact be intuitively grasped, unless the intuition is replaceable by an argument, the implicature (if present at all) will not count as a conversational implicature." (Instead, it would count as a so-called "conventional" implicature, i.e., a conventional aspect of meaning that makes no contribution to the truth-conditions of the utterance.) Grice further distinguished "generalized" conversational implicatures, which are generated so to speak "by default," from "particularized" conversational implicatures, whose generation depends on special features of the context of utterance.

Grice's application of his cooperative framework to human communication and his elaboration of the concept of (generalized) conversational implicature were motivated by his concern to block certain moves made by ordinary language philosophers. One such move was exemplified by Strawson's (1952) claim that, unlike the truth-functional conjunction of propositional calculus, the English word "and" makes different contributions to the full meanings of the utterances of pairs of conjoined sentences. For example, by uttering "John took off his boots and got into bed" the speaker may mean that the event first described took place first.

In response, Grice (1967/1975, 1981) argued that, in accordance with the truth-table of the logical conjunction of propositional calculus, the utterance of any pair of sentences conjoined by "and" is true if and only if both conjuncts are true and false otherwise. He took the view that the temporal ordering of the sequence of events described by such an utterance need not be part of the semantic content (or truth-conditions) of the utterance. Instead, it arises as a conversational implicature retrieved by the hearer through an inferential process guided by his expectation that the speaker is following the Cooperative Principle and the maxims, e.g., the sub-maxim of orderliness (one of the sub-maxims of the maxim of Manner), according to which there is some reason why the speaker chose to utter the first conjunct first.

Also, under the influence of Wittgenstein, some ordinary language philosophers claimed that unless there are reasons to doubt whether some thing is really red, it is illegitimate to say "It looks red to me" (as opposed to "It is red"). In response, Grice (1967/1975) argued that whether an utterance is true or false is one thing; whether it is odd or misleading is another (cf. Carston 2002a: 103; but see Travis 1991 for dissent).

5 The emergence of truth-conditional pragmatics

Grice's seminal work made it clear that verbal communication involves three layers of meaning: (i) the linguistic (conventional) meaning of the sentence uttered, (ii) the explicit content expressed (i.e., "what is said") by the utterance, and (iii) the implicit content of the utterance (its conversational implicatures). Work in speech act theory further suggests that each layer of meaning also exhibits a descriptive dimension (e.g., the truth conditions of an utterance) and a pragmatic dimension (e.g., the fact that a speech act is an assertion). Restricting itself to the descriptive dimension of meaning, the rest of this section discusses the emergence of a new truth-conditional pragmatic approach, whose core thesis is that what is said (not just the conversational implicatures of an utterance) depends on the speaker's meaning. By further extending the inferentialist model of communication, this pragmatic approach to what is said contravenes two deeply entrenched principles in the philosophy of language: literalism and minimalism.

Ideal language philosophers thought of indexicality and other context-sensitive phenomena as defective features of natural languages. Quine (1960: 193) introduced the concept of an eternal sentence as one devoid of any context-sensitive or ambiguous constituent so that its "truth-value stays fixed through time and from speaker to speaker." An instance of an eternal sentence might be: "Three plus two equals five." Following Quine, many philosophers (see e.g., Katz 1981) subsequently accepted literalism, i.e., the view that for any statement made in some natural language, using a context-sensitive sentence in a given context, there is some eternal sentence in the same language that can be used to make the same statement in any context. Few linguists and philosophers nowadays subscribe to literalism because they recognize that indexicality is an ineliminable feature of natural languages. However, many subscribe to minimalism.

Grice urged an inferential model of the pragmatic process whereby a hearer infers the conversational implicatures of an utterance from what is said. But he embraced the minimalist view that what is said departs from the linguistic meaning of the uttered sentence *only* as is necessary for the utterance to be truth-evaluable (cf. Grice 1989: 25). If a sentence contains an ambiguous phrase (e.g., "He is in the grip of a vice"), then it must be disambiguated. If it contains an indexical, then it cannot be assigned its proper semantic value except by relying on contextual information. But according to minimalism, appeal to contextual information is always mandated by some linguistic constituent (e.g., an indexical) within the sentence. In order to determine what is said by the utterance of a sentence containing e.g., the indexical pronoun "I," the hearer relies on the rule according to which any token of "I" refers to the speaker who used that token. As Stanley (2000: 391) puts it, "all truth-conditional effects of extra-linguistic context can be traced to logical form" (i.e., the semantic information that is grammatically encoded).

Unlike the reference of a pure indexical like "I," however, the reference of a demonstratively used pronoun (e.g., "he") can only be determined by representing the speaker's meaning, not by a semantic rule. So does understanding the semantic value of "here" or "now." A person may use a token of "here" to refer to a room, a street, a city, a country, the Earth, and so forth. Similarly, a person may use a token of "now" to refer to a millisecond, an hour, a day, a year, a century, and so forth. One cannot determine the semantic value of a token of either "here" or "now" without representing the speaker's meaning.

According to truth-conditional pragmatics, what is said by an utterance is determined by pragmatic processes, which are not necessarily triggered by some syntactic constituent of the uttered sentence (e.g., an indexical). By contrast, minimalists reject truth-conditional pragmatics and postulate, in the logical form of the sentence uttered, the existence of hidden variables whose semantic values must be contextually determined for the utterance to be truth-evaluable (see the controversy between Stanley 2000 and Recanati 2004 over whether the logical form of an utterance of "It's raining" contains a free variable for locations).

The rise of truth-conditional pragmatics may be interpreted (cf. Travis 1991) as vindicating the view that an utterance's truth-conditions depend on what Searle (1978, 1983) calls "the Background," i.e., a network of practices and unarticulated assumptions (but see Stalnaker 1999 and cf. article 12 [Semantics: Theories] (Dekker) *Dynamic semantics* for a semantic approach). Although the verb "to cut" is unambiguous, what counts as cutting grass differs from what counts as cutting a cake. Only against alternative background assumptions will one be able to discriminate the truth-conditions of "John cut the grass" and of "John cut the cake." However, advocates of minimalism argue that if, instead of using a lawn mower, John took out his pocket-knife and cut each blade lengthwise, then by uttering "John cut the grass" the speaker would speak the truth (cf. Cappelen & Lepore 2005).

Three pragmatic processes involved in determining what is said by an utterance have been particularly investigated by advocates of truth-conditional pragmatics: free enrichment, loosening and transfer.

5.1 Free enrichment

Grice (1967/1975, 1981) offered a pragmatic account according to which the temporal or causal ordering between the events described by the utterance of a conjunction is conveyed as a conversational implicature. But consider Carston's (1988) example: "Bob gave Mary his key and she opened the door." Carston (1988) argues that part of what is said is that "she" refers to whoever "Mary" refers to and that Mary opened the door with the key Bob gave her. If so, then the fact that Bob gave Mary his key before Mary opened the door is also part of what is said. Following Sperber & Wilson (1986: 189), suppose a speaker utters "I have had breakfast," as an indirect way of declining an offer of food. By minimalist standards, what the speaker said was that she has had breakfast at least once in her life prior to her utterance. According to Grice, the hearer must be able to infer a conversational implicature from what the speaker said. However, the hearer could not conclude that the speaker does not wish any food from the truism that she has had breakfast at least once in her life before her utterance. Instead, for the hearer to infer that the speaker does not wish to have food in response to his question, what the speaker must have said is that she has had breakfast just prior to the time of utterance.

5.2 Loosening

Cases of free enrichment are instances of strengthening the concept linguistically encoded by the meaning of the sentence – for example, strengthening of the concept encoded by "the key" into the concept expressible by "the key Bob gave to Mary". However, not all pragmatic processes underlying the generation of what is said from the linguistic meaning of the sentence are processes of conceptual strengthening or narrowing. Some are processes of conceptual loosening or broadening. For example, imagine a speaker's utterance in a restaurant of "My steak is raw" whereby what she says is not that her steak is literally uncooked but rather that it is undercooked.

5.3 Transfer

Strengthening and loosening are cases of modification of a concept linguistically encoded by the meaning of a word. Transfer is a process whereby a concept encoded by the meaning of a word is mapped onto a related but different concept. Transfer is illustrated by examples from Nunberg (1979, 1995): "The ham sandwich left without paying" and "I am parked out back." In the first example, the property expressed by the predicate "left without paying" is being ascribed to the person who ordered the sandwich, not to the sandwich itself. In the second example, the property of being parked out back is ascribed not to the speaker, but to the car that stands in the ownership relation to her.

The gist of truth-conditional pragmatics is that speaker's meaning is involved in determining both the conversational implicatures of an utterance and what is said. As the following example shows, however, it is not always easy to decide whether a particular assumption is a conversational implicature of an utterance or part of what is said. Consider "The picnic was awful. The beer was warm." For the second sentence to offer a justification (or explanation) of the truth expressed by the first, the assumption must be made that the beer was part of the picnic. According to Carston (2002b), the assumption that the beer was part of the picnic is a conversational implicature (an implicated premise) of the utterance. According to Recanati (2004), the concept linguistically encoded by "the beer" is strengthened into the concept expressible by "the beer that was part of the picnic" and part of what is said.

6 Concluding remarks: pragmatics and cognitive science

Sperber & Wilson's (1986) relevance-theoretic approach squarely belongs to truth-conditional pragmatics: it makes three contributions towards bridging the gap between pragmatics and the cognitive sciences. First, it offers a novel account of speaker's meaning. As Schiffer (1972) pointed out, not unless S's intention to inform A is mutually known to S and A could S's intention count as a genuine communicative intention (cf. section 3). But how could S and A know that they mutually know S's intention to inform A of something? Sperber & Wilson (1986) argue that they cannot and urge that the mutual knowledge requirement be replaced by the idea of mutual manifestness. An assumption is manifest to S at t if and only if S is capable of representing and accepting it as true at t. A speaker's informative intention is an intention to make (more) manifest to an audience a set of assumptions {I}. A speaker's communicative intention is her intention to make it mutually manifest that she has the above informative intention. Hence, a communicative intention is a second-order informative intention.

Secondly, relevance theory is so-called because Sperber & Wilson (1986) accept a Cognitive principle of relevance according to which human cognition is geared towards the maximization of relevance. Relevance is a property of an input for an individual at t: it depends on both the set of contextual effects and the cost of processing, where the contextual effect of an input might be the set of assumptions derivable from processing the input in a given context. Other things being equal, the greater the set of contextual effects achieved by processing an input, the more relevant the input. The greater the effort required by the processing, the lower the relevance of the input. They further accept a Communicative principle of relevance according to which every ostensively produced stimulus conveys a presumption of its own relevance: an ostensive stimulus is optimally relevant if and only if it is relevant enough to be worth the audience's processing effort and it is the most relevant stimulus compatible with the communicator's abilities and preferences.

Finally, the relevance-theoretic approach squarely anchors pragmatics into what cognitive psychologists call "third-person mindreading," i.e., the ability to represent others' psychological states (cf. Leslie 2000). In particular, it emphasizes the specificity of the task of representing an agent's communicative intention underlying her (communicative) ostensive behavior. The observer of some non-ostensive intentional behavior (e.g., hunting) can plausibly ascribe an intention to the agent on the basis of the desirable outcome of the latter's behavior, which can be identified (e.g., hit his target), whether or not the behavior is successful.

However, the desirable outcome of a piece of communicative behavior (i.e., the addressee's recognition of the agent's communicative intention) cannot be identified unless the communicative behavior succeeds (cf. Sperber 2000; Origgi & Sperber 2000 and Wilson & Sperber 2002). Thus, the development of pragmatics takes us from the metaphysical issues about meaning and intentionality inherited from Brentano to the cognitive scientific investigation of the human mindreading capacity to metarepresent others' mental representations.

Thanks to Neftalí Villanueva Fernández, Paul Horwich and the editors for comments on this article.

7 References

Austin, John L. 1962a. *Sense and Sensibilia*. Oxford: Oxford University Press.
Austin, John L. 1962b. *How to Do Things with Words*. Oxford: Clarendon Press.
Bach, Kent & Robert M. Harnish 1979. *Linguistic Communication and Speech Acts*. Cambridge, MA: The MIT Press.
Brentano, Frantz 1874/1911/1973. *Psychology from an Empirical Standpoint*. London: Routledge & Kegan Paul.
Cappelen, Herman & Ernie Lepore 2005. *Insensitive Semantics*. Oxford: Blackwell.
Carnap, Rudolf 1942. *Introduction to Semantics*. Chicago, IL: The University of Chicago Press.
Carston, Robyn 1988. Implicature, explicature and truth-theoretic semantics. In: R. Kempson (ed.). *Mental Representations: The Interface between Language and Reality*. Cambridge: Cambridge University Press, 155–181.
Carston, Robyn 2002a. *Thoughts and Utterances. The Pragmatics of Explicit Communication*. Oxford: Blackwell.
Carston, Robyn 2002b. Linguistic meaning, communicated meaning and cognitive pragmatics. *Mind & Language* 17, 127–148.
Chisholm, Robert M. 1957. *Perceiving: A Philosophical Study*. Ithaca, NY: Cornell University Press.
Chomsky, Noam 1975. *Reflections on Language*. New York: Pantheon Books.
Chomsky, Noam 1980. *Rules and Representations*. New York: Columbia University Press.
Churchland, Paul M. 1989. *A Neurocomputational Perspective: The Nature of Mind and the Structure of Science*. Cambridge, MA: The MIT Press.
Dennett, Daniel C. 1987. *The Intentional Stance*. Cambridge, MA: The MIT Press.
Dretske, Fred 1995. *Naturalizing the Mind*. Cambridge, MA: The MIT Press.
Fodor, Jerry A. 1975. *The Language of Thought*. New York: Crowell.
Fodor, Jerry A. 1987. *Psychosemantics: The Problem of Meaning in the Philosophy of Mind*. Cambridge, MA: The MIT Press.
Frege, Gottlob 1892/1980. Über Sinn und Bedeutung. *Zeitschrift für Philosophie und philosophische Kritik* 100, 25–50. English translation in: P. Geach & M. Black (eds.). *Translations from the Philosophical Writings of Gottlob Frege*. Oxford: Blackwell, 1980, 56–78.
Green, Mitchell 2007. Speech acts. *Stanford Encyclopedia of Philosophy*, http://plato.stanford.edu/entries/speech-acts, July 20, 2008.

Grice, H. Paul 1957. Meaning. *The Philosophical Review* 64, 377–388. Reprinted in: H. P. Grice. *Studies in the Way of Words*. Cambridge, MA: Harvard University Press, 1989, 212–223.

Grice, H. Paul 1967/1975. Logic and conversation. In: P. Cole & J. Morgan (eds.). *Syntax and Semantics 3: Speech Acts*. New York: Academic Press, 41–58. Reprinted in: H.P. Grice. *Studies in the Way of Words*. Cambridge, MA: Harvard University Press, 1989, 22–40.

Grice, H. Paul 1968. Utterer's meaning, sentence meaning and word meaning. *Foundations of Language* 4, 225–242. Reprinted in: H.P. Grice. *Studies in the Way of Words*. Cambridge, MA: Harvard University Press, 1989, 117–137.

Grice, H. Paul 1969. Utterer's meaning and intentions. *Philosophical Review* 78, 147–177. Reprinted in: H.P. Grice. *Studies in the Way of Words*. Cambridge, MA: Harvard University Press, 1989, 86–116.

Grice, H. Paul 1978. Further notes on logic and conversation. In: P. Cole (ed.). *Syntax and Semantics 9: Pragmatics*. New York: Academic Press, 113–128. Reprinted in: H. P. Grice. *Studies in the Way of Words*. Cambridge, MA: Harvard University Press, 1989, 41–57.

Grice, H. Paul 1981. Presuppositions and conversational implicatures. In: P. Cole (ed.). *Radical Pragmatics*. New York: Academic Press, 183–198. Reprinted in: H. P. Grice. *Studies in the Way of Words*. Cambridge, MA: Harvard University Press, 1989, 269–282.

Grice, H. Paul 1989. *Studies in the Way of Words*. Cambridge, MA: Harvard University Press.

Haugeland, John 1981. Semantic engines: An introduction to mind design. In: J. Haugeland (ed.). *Mind Design, Philosophy, Psychology, Artificial Intelligence*. Cambridge, MA: The MIT Press, 1–34.

Horwich, Paul 2005. *Reflections on Meaning*. Oxford: Oxford University Press.

Jacob, Pierre 1997. *What Minds Can Do*. Cambridge: Cambridge University Press.

Jacob, Pierre 2003. Intensionality. *Stanford Encyclopedia in Philosophy*, http://plato.Stanford.edu/intensionality/, June 15, 2006.

Katz, Jerry J. 1981 *Language and Other Abstract Objects*. Oxford: Blackwell.

Leslie, Alan 2000. 'Theory of Mind' as a mechanism of selective attention. In: M. Gazzaniga (ed.). *The New Cognitive Neuroscience*. Cambridge, MA: The MIT Press, 1235–1247.

Meinong, Alexis 1904. Über Gegenstandstheorie. In: A. Meinong (ed.). *Untersuchungen zur Gegenstandstheorie und Psychologie*. Leipzig: Barth, 1–50. English translation in: R. M. Chisholm (ed.). *Realism and the Background of Phenomenology*. Glencoe: The Free Press, 1960, 76–117.

Millikan, Ruth G. 1984. *Language, Thought and Other Biological Objects*. Cambridge, MA: The MIT Press.

Morris, Charles 1938. *Foundations of the Theory of Signs*. Chicago, IL: The University of Chicago Press.

Nunberg, Geoffrey 1979. The non-uniqueness of semantic solutions: Polysemy. *Linguistics & Philosophy* 3, 143–184.

Nunberg, Geoffrey 1995. Transfers of meaning. *Journal of Semantics* 12, 109–132.

Origgi, Gloria & Dan Sperber 2000. Evolution, communication and the proper function of language. In: P. Carruthers & A. Chamberlain (eds.). *Evolution and the Human Mind: Language, Modularity and Social Cognition*. Cambridge: Cambridge University Press, 140–169.

Parsons, Terence 1980. *Nonexistent Objects*. New Haven, CT: Yale University Press.

Quine, Willard van Orman 1948. On what there is. Reprinted in: W.V.O. Quine. *From a Logical Point of View*. Cambridge, MA: Harvard University Press, 1953, 1–19.

Quine, Willard van Orman 1960. *Word and Object*. Cambridge, MA: The MIT Press.

Recanati, François 1987. *Meaning and Force*. Cambridge: Cambridge University Press.
Recanati, François 2004. *Literal Meaning*. Cambridge: Cambridge University Press.
Rey, Georges 1997. *Contemporary Philosophy of Mind: A Contentiously Classical Approach*. Oxford: Blackwell.
Russell, Bertrand 1905. On denoting. *Mind* 14, 479–493. Reprinted in: R. C. Marsh (ed.). *Bertrand Russell, Logic and Knowledge, Essays 1901–1950*. New York: Capricorn Books, 1956, 41–56.
Schiffer, Stephen 1972. *Meaning*. Oxford: Oxford University Press.
Searle, John R. 1969. *Speech Acts*. Cambridge: Cambridge University Press.
Searle, John R. 1975. Indirect speech acts. In: P. Cole & J. Morgan (eds.). *Syntax and Semantics 3: Speech Acts*. New York: Academic Press, 59–82.
Searle, John R. 1978. Literal meaning. *Erkenntnis* 13, 207–224.
Searle, John R. 1983. *Intentionality*. Cambridge: Cambridge University Press.
Searle, John R. 1992. *The Rediscovery of the Mind*. Cambridge, MA: The MIT Press.
Sperber, Dan 2000. Metarepresentations in an evolutionary perspective. In: D. Sperber (ed.). *Metarepresentations: A Multidisciplinary Perspective*. Oxford: Oxford University Press, 117–137.
Sperber, Dan & Deirdre Wilson 1986. *Relevance, Communication and Cognition*. Cambridge, MA: Harvard University Press.
Stalnaker, Robert 1999. *Context and Content*. Oxford: Oxford University Press.
Stanley, Jason 2000. Context and logical form. *Linguistics & Philosophy* 23, 391–434.
Strawson, Peter F. 1952. *Introduction to Logical Theory*. London: Methuen.
Strawson, Peter F. 1964. Intention and convention in speech acts. *The Philosophical Review* 73, 439–460. Reprinted in: P.F. Strawson. *Logico-linguistic Papers*. London: Methuen, 1971, 149–169.
Travis, Charles 1991. Annals of analysis: *Studies in the Way of Words*, by H.P. Grice. *Mind* 100, 237–264.
Wilson, Deirdre & Dan Sperber 2002. Truthfulness and relevance. *Mind* 111, 583–632.
Zalta, Edward N. 1988. *Intensional Logic and the Metaphysics of Intentionality*. Cambridge, MA: The MIT Press.

Mark Textor
3 (Frege on) Sense and reference

1 Sense and reference: a short overview —— 33
2 Introducing sense and reference —— 35
3 Extending and exploring sense and reference —— 39
4 Criticising sense and reference —— 49
5 Summary —— 58
6 References —— 59

Abstract: Gottlob Frege argues in *Über Sinn und Bedeutung* that every intuitively meaningful expression has a sense. He characterises the main ingredient of sense as a 'mode of presentation' of at most one thing, namely the referent. Theoretical development of sense and reference has been a fundamental task for the philosophy of language. In this article I will reconstruct Frege's motivation for the distinction between sense and reference (section 2). I will then go on to discuss how the distinction can be applied to predicates, sentences and context-dependent expressions (section 3). The final section 4 shows how discussions of Frege's theory lead to important proposals in semantics.

1 Sense and reference: a short overview

Gottlob Frege argues in *Über Sinn und Bedeutung* that every intuitively meaningful expression has a sense ("Sinn"). The main ingredient of sense is suggestively characterised as a 'mode of presentation' of at most one thing, namely the referent ("Bedeutung"). Frege's theory of sense and reference has been at the centre of the philosophy of language in the 20th century. The discussion about it is driven by the question whether an adequate semantic theory needs to or even can coherently ascribe sense and reference to natural language expressions. On the side of Frege's critics are, among others, Russell and Kripke.

Russell (1905) argues that the introduction of sense creates more problems than it solves. If there are senses, one should be able to speak about them. But according to Russell, every attempt to do so leads to an 'inextricable tangle'. Russell goes on to develop his theory of definite descriptions to avoid the

---

Mark Textor, London, United Kingdom

https://doi.org/10.1515/9783110368505-003

problems Frege's theory seems to create. How and whether Russell's argument works is still a matter of dispute. (For recent discussions see Levine 2004 and Makin 2000.)

More recently, Kripke (1972) has marshalled modal and epistemic arguments against what he called the "The Frege-Russell picture". "Neo-Millians" or "Neo-Russellians" are currently busy closing the holes in Kripke's arguments against Frege.

Frege's friends have tried to develop and defend the distinction between sense and reference. In *Meaning and Necessity* Carnap (1956) takes Frege to task for multiplying senses beyond necessity and therefore proposes to replace sense and reference with intension and extension. I will return to Carnap's view in section 4.1.

Quine (1951) has criticised notions like sense and intension as not being definable in scientifically acceptable terms. Davidson has tried to preserve Frege's insights in view of Quine's criticism. According to Davidson, "a theory of truth patterned after a Tarski-type truth definition tells us all we need to know about sense. Counting truth in the domain of reference, as Frege did, the study of sense thus comes down to the study of reference" (Davidson 1984: 109). And reference is, even by Quinean standards, a scientifically acceptable concept. Davidson's proposal to use theories of truth as theories of sense has been pursued by in recent years and lead to fruitful research into the semantics of proper names. (See McDowell 1977 and Sainsbury 2005. See also Wiggins 1997.)

Dummett has criticised Davidson's proposal (see Dummett 1993, essay 1 and 2). A theory of sense should be graspable by someone who does not yet master a language and a theory of truth does not satisfy this constraint. A theory of meaning (sense) should be a theory of understanding and a theory of understanding should take understanding to consist in the possession of an ability, for example, the ability to recognise the bearer of a name.

The jury is still out on the question whether the distinction between sense and reference should be preserved or abandoned. The debate has shed light on further notions like compositionality, co-reference and knowledge of meaning. In this article I want to introduce the basic notions, sense and reference, and the problems surrounding them.

A note of caution. Frege's theory is not clearly a descriptive theory about natural language, but applies primarily to an ideal language like the *Begriffsschrift* (see Frege, *Philosophical and Mathematical Correspondence* (PMC): 101). If a philosopher of language seeks inspiration in the work of Frege, he needs to consider the question whether the view under consideration is about natural language or a language for inferential thought.

2 Introducing sense and reference

2.1 Conceptual content and cognitive value

Frege starts his logico-philosophical investigations with judgement and inference. (See Burge 2005: 14f). An inference is a judgement made "because we are cognizant of other truths as providing a justification for it." (*Posthumous Writings* (PW): 3). The premises of an inference are not sentences, but acknowledged truths.

In line with this methodology, Frege introduces in BS the conceptual content of a judgement as an abstraction from the role the judgement plays in inference:

> Let me observe that there are two ways in which the contents of two judgements can differ: it may, or it may not, be the case that all inferences that can be drawn from the first judgement when combined with certain other ones can always be drawn from the second when combined with the same judgements. [...] Now I call the part of the content that is the same in both the conceptual content.
>
> (BS, §3: 2–3)

Frege's 'official' criterion for sameness of conceptual content is:

> s has the same conceptual content as s* iff
>
> given truths t_1 to t_n as premises, the same consequences can be inferred from s and s* together with t_1 to t_n.
>
> (See, BS, §3)

Frege identifies the conceptual content of a sentence with a complex of the things for which the sentence constituents stand (BS §8). This raises problems for the conceptual content of identity sentences. In identity sentences the sign of identity is flanked by what Frege calls 'proper names'. What is a proper name?

For Frege, every expression that can be substituted for a genuine proper name *salva grammaticale* and *salva veritate* qualifies as a proper name. Fregean proper names include genuine proper names, complex demonstratives ('That man') when completed by contextual features and definite descriptions ('the negation of the thought that 2 = 3'). Following Russell (1905), philosophers and linguists have argued that definite descriptions do not belong on this list. Definite descriptions do not stand for objects, but for properties of properties. For example, 'The first man on the moon is American' asserts that (the property) being a first man on the moon is uniquely instantiated and that whatever uniquely has this property has also the property of being American. The discussion about the semantics of definite descriptions is ongoing, but we can sidestep this issue by focusing on genuine proper names. (For an overview of the recent discussion about definite descriptions see Bezuidenhout & Reimer 2004.)

Equations figure as premises in inferences that extend our knowledge. How can this be so? In BS Frege struggles to give a convincing answer. If one holds that "=" stands for the relation of identity, the sentences

(S1) The evening star = the evening star

and

(S2) The evening star = the morning star.

have the same conceptual content CC:

CC(S1): <Venus, Identity, Venus> = CC(S2): <Venus, Identity, Venus>.

But although (S1) and (S2) stand for the same complex, they differ in inferential potential. For example, if we combine the truth that (S1) expresses with the truth that the evening star is a planet we can derive nothing new, but if we combine the latter truth we can derive the truth that the morning star is a planet.

Prima facie, (i) Frege's sameness criteria for conceptual content are in conflict with (ii) his claim that expressions are everywhere merely placeholders for objects. In BS Frege responds by restricting (ii): in a sentence of the form "a = b" the signs "a" and "b" stand for themselves; the sentence says that "a" and "b" have the same conceptual content. The idea that designations refer to themselves in some contexts helps to explain the difference in inferential potential. It can be news to learn that "Dr. Jekyll" stands for the same person as "Mr. Hyde". Although promising, we will see in a moment that this move *alone* does not distinguish (S1) and (S2) in the way required.

Treating identity statements as the exception to the rule that every expression just stands for an object allows Frege to keep his identification of the conceptual content of a sentence with a complex of objects and properties. The price is that the reference of a non-ambiguous and non-indexical term will shift from one sentence to another. Consider a quantified statement like:

$$(\forall x)(\forall y)((x = y \,\&\, Fx) \rightarrow Fy)$$

If signs stand for themselves in identity-statements, one can neither coherently suppose that the variables in the formula range over signs, nor over particulars. (See Furth 1964: xix, and Mendelsohn 1982: 297f.)

These considerations prime us for the argument that motivates Frege's introduction of the distinction between sense and reference. Frege's new argument uses the notion of cognitive value ("Erkenntniswert"). For the purposes of Frege's argument it is not important to answer the question "What is cognitive value?": more important is the question "When do two sentences s and s* differ in cognitive value?" Answer: If the justified acceptance of s puts one in a position to come to know something that one neither knew before nor could infer from what one knew before, while the justified acceptance of s* does not do so (or the other way around). Frege hints at this notion of cognitive value in a piece of self-criticism in *The Foundations of Arithmetic* (FA). If a true equation connected two terms that refer to the same thing in the same way

> [a]ll equations would then come down to this, that whatever is given to us in the same way is to be recognized as the same. But this is so self-evident and so unfruitful that it is not worth stating. Indeed, *no conclusion could ever be drawn here that was different from any of the premises.*
>
> (FA, §67: 79. My emphasis)

If a rational and minimally logically competent person accepts what "The evening star is a planet" says, and she comes also to accept the content of "The evening star = the morning star", she is in a position to acquire the knowledge that the morning star is a planet. This new knowledge was not inferable from what she already knew. Things are different if she has only reason to accept the content of "The evening star = the evening star". Exercising logical knowledge won't take her from this premise to a conclusion that she was not already in a position to know on the basis of the other premise or her general logical knowledge.

On the basis of this understanding of cognitive value, Frege's argument can now be rendered in the following form:

(P1) (S1) "The evening star = the evening star" differs in cognitive value from (S2) "The evening star = the morning star".
(P2) The difference in cognitive value between (S1) and (S2) cannot be constituted by a difference in reference of the signs composing the sentence.
(P3) "If the sign 'a' is distinguished from the sign 'b' only as object (here by means of its shape), not *as sign* (i.e., *not by the manner in which it designates something*) the cognitive value of a = a becomes essentially equal to the cognitive value of a = b."
(P4) "A difference can only arise if the difference between the signs corresponds to a difference between the mode of presentation of that which is designated."
(C1) The difference in cognitive value between (S1) and (S2) is constituted by the fact that different signs compose (S1) and (S2) AND that the different signs designate something in different ways.

We have now explained (P1) and Frege has already given convincing reasons for holding (P2) in BS. Let us look more closely at the other premises.

2.2 Sense, sign and logical form

In *On Sense and Reference* (S&R) Frege gives several reasons for the rejection of the *Begriffsschrift* view of identity statements. The most compelling one is (P3). Frege held in BS that (S1) has a different cognitive value from (S2) because (i) in (S2) different singular terms flank the identity sign that (ii) stand for themselves. If this difference is to ground the difference in cognitive value, Frege must provide an answer to the question "When do *different* signs and when does the *same* sign (tokens of the same sign) flank the identity sign?" that is adequate for this purpose. (P3) says that the individuation of signs in terms of their form alone is not adequate. Frege calls signs that are individuated by their form 'figures'. The distinctive properties of a figure are geometrical and physical properties. There are identity-statements that contain two tokens of the same figure ("Paderewski = Paderewski"), which have the same cognitive value as identity statements that contain two tokens of different figures ("Paderewski = the prime minister of Poland between 1917 and 1919"). There are also identity-statements that contain tokens of different figures ("Germany's oldest bachelor is Germany's oldest unmarried eligible male") that have the same cognitive value as identity statements that contain two tokens of the same figure ("Germany's oldest bachelor is Germany's oldest bachelor").

If sameness (difference) of figure does not track sameness (difference) of cognitive value, then the *Begriffsschrift* view needs to be supplemented by a method of sign individuation that is not merely form-based. Frege's constructive suggestion is (P4). Let us expand on (P4). I will assume that I have frequently seen what I take to be the brightest star in the evening sky. I have given the star the name "the evening star". I will apply "the evening star" to an object if and only if it is the brightest star in the evening sky. I am also fascinated by what I take to be the brightest star in the morning sky. I have given this star the name "the morning star" and I will apply "the morning star" to an object if and only if it is the brightest star in the morning sky.

Now if the difference in form between "the evening star" and "the morning star" indicates a difference in mode of designation, one can explain the difference in cognitive value between (S1) and (S2). (S1) and (S2) contain different figures AND the different figures refer to something in a different way (they are connected in my idiolect to different conditions of correct reference).

Frege assumes also that a difference in cognitive value can *only* arise if different terms designate in different ways. But (S1) and (S2) would be translated differently into the language of first-order logic with identity: (S1) as "$a = a$", (S2) as "$a = b$". Why not hold with Putnam (1954) that the difference in logical form grounds the difference in cognitive value?

This challenge misses the point of (P3). How can we determine the logical form of a statement independently of a method of individuating signs? As we have already seen, if "b" is a mere stylistic alternative for "a" (the difference in form indicates no difference in mode of presentation), the logical form of "a = b" is $a = a$. If difference of cognitive value is to depend on differences of logical form, logical form cannot merely be determined by the form of the signs contained in the sentence. Logical form depends on sense. The appeal to logical form cannot make the notion of sense superfluous.

If Frege's argument is convincing, it establishes the conclusion that the sense of an expression is distinct from its reference. The argument tells us what sense is not, it does not tell us what it is. The premises of the argument are compatible with every assumption about the nature of sense that allows the sense of an expression to differ from its reference.

3 Extending and exploring sense and reference

3.1 The sense and reference of predicates and sentences

Not only proper names have sense and reference. Frege extends the distinction to concept-words (predicates) and sentences. A letter to Husserl contains a diagram that outlines the complete view (PMC: 63):

Proper Name	Sentence	Concept-word
↓	↓	↓
Sense	Thought	Sense concept-word
↓	↓	↓
Referent	Truth-Value	Concept → Object that falls under it.

Fig. 3.1: Frege's diagram

The sense of a complete assertoric sentence is a thought. The composition of the sentence out of sentence-parts mirrors the composition of the thought it expresses. If (i) a sentence S is built up from a finite list of simple parts e_1 to e_n according to a finite number of modes of combination, (ii) e_1 to e_n express senses, and (iii) the thought expressed by S contains the senses of e_1 to e_n arranged in a way that corresponds to the arrangement of e_1 to e_n in S, we can express new thoughts by re-combining sentence-parts we already understand. Since, we can express new thoughts, we should accept (i) to (iii). (See Frege, *Collected Papers* (CP): 390 and PMC: 79.)

Compositionality is the property of a language L that the meaning of its complex expressions is determined by the meaning of their parts and their mode of combination. (See article 6 [this volume] (Pagin & Westerståhl) *Compositionality*.) According to Frege, natural language and his formal language have a property that is *like* compositionality, but not the same.

First, the claim that the composition of a sentence *mirrors* the composition of the thought expressed implies that the sense of the parts and their mode of combination *determine* the thought expressed, but the determination thesis does not imply the mirroring thesis.

Second, Fregean thoughts are not meanings. The meaning of an indexical sentence ("I am hungry") does not vary with the context of utterance, the thought expressed does.

Third, the assertoric sentence that expresses a thought often contains constituents that are not words, while compositionality is usually defined in terms of expression parts that are themselves expressions. For example, Frege takes pointings, glances and the time of utterance to be part of the sign that expresses a thought. (See T, CP: 358 (64). For discussion see Künne 1992 and Textor 2007.)

If the thought expressed by a sentences s consists of the senses expressed by the parts of s in an order, a sentence s expresses a different thought from a sentence s^* if s and s^* are not composed from parts with the same sense in the same order. (See Dummett 1981a: 378–379.) Hence, the Mirror Thesis implies that only isomorphic sentences can express the same thought. This conclusion contradicts Frege's view that the same thought can be decomposed differently into different parts, and that no decomposition can be selected on independent grounds as identifying the thought. Frege argues, for example, that 'There is at least one square root of 4' and 'The number 4 has the property that there is something of which it is the square' express the same thought, but the wording of the sentence suggests different decompositions of the thought expressed. (See CP: 188 (199–200).) Progress in logic often consists in discovering that different sentences express the same thought. (See PW: 153–154.) Hence, there is not *the* structure of a thought. *A fortiori*, the sentence structure cannot be isomorphic with the structure of the thought expressed.

The Mirror and Multiple Decomposition Thesis are in conflict. Dummett (1989) and Rumfitt (1994) want to preserve the Mirror View that has it that thoughts are complex entities, Geach (1975), Bell (1987) and Kemmerling (1990) argue against it. Textor (2009) tries to integrate both.

Does an assertoric sentence have a referent, and, if it has one, what is it? Frege introduces the concept of a function into semantic analysis. Functional signs are incomplete. In '1 + ξ' the Greek letter simply marks an argument place. If we complete the functional expression '1 + ξ' with '1', we 'generate' a complex designator for the value of the function for the argument 1, the number 2. The analysis of the designator '1 + 1' into functional expressions and completing expressions mirrors the determination of its referent. Frege extends the analysis to equations like '1 + 1' to '$2^2 = 4$'. In order to do so, he assumes (i) that the equation can be decomposed into functional (for example '$ξ^2 = 4$') and non-functional expressions (for example '2'). The functional expression stands for a function, the non-functional one for an argument. Like '1 + 1', the equation '$2^2 = 4$' shall stand for the value the concept $x^2 = 4$ assumes for the argument 2. Frege identifies the values of these functions as truth-values: the True and the False (CP: 144 (13)).

To generalise: An assertoric sentence *s* expresses a thought and refers to a truth-value. It can be decomposed into functional expressions (*concept-words*) that stand for functions from arguments to truth-values (*concepts*). The truth-value of *s* is the value which the concept referred to by the concept-word distinguishable in *s* returns for the argument referred to by the proper name(s) in *s*. In this way the semantics of sentences and their constituents interlock. The plausibility of the given description depends crucially on the assumption that talk of truth-values is more than a stylistic variant of saying that what a sentence says is true (false). Frege's arguments for this assumption are still under scrutiny. (See Burge 2005, essay 3 and Ricketts 2003.)

3.2 Sense determines reference

The following argument is valid: Hesperus is a planet; Hesperus shines brightly. Therefore, something is a planet and shines brightly. By contrast, this argument isn't: Hesperus is a planet; Phosphorus shines brightly. Therefore, something is a planet and shines brightly. Why?

A formally valid argument is an argument whose logical form guarantees its validity. All arguments of the form "Fa, Ga, Therefore: (∃x) (Fx & Gx)" are valid, i.e. if the premises are true, the conclusion must also be true. If the first argument is formally valid, the "Hesperus" tokens must have the same sense and reference. If the sense were different, the argument would be a fallacy of equivocation. If the reference could be different, although the sense was the same, the argument could take us from true premises to a false conclusion, because the same sense could determine different objects in the premises and the conclusion. This consideration makes a thesis plausible that is frequently attributed to Frege, although never explicitly endorsed by him:

> *Sense-Determines-Reference*: Necessarily, if α and β have the same sense, α and β have the same referent.

Sense-Determines-Reference is central to Frege's theory. But isn't it refuted by Putnam's (1975) twin earth case? My twin and I may connect the same mode of presentation with the syntactically individuated word "water", but the watery stuff in my environment is H_2O, in his XYZ. While I refer to H_2O with "water", he refers to XYZ with "water".

It is far from clear that this is a convincing counterexample to Sense-Determines-Reference. If we consider context-dependent expressions, it will be necessary to complicate to *Sense-determines-Reference* to *Sense-determines-Reference in context of utterance*. But this complication does not touch upon the principle. Among other things, Putnam may be taken to have shown that "water" is a context-dependent expression.

3.3 Transparency and homogeneity

In the previous section we were concerned with the truth-preserving character of formally valid arguments. In this section the knowledge-transmitting character of such arguments will become important: a formally valid argument enables us to come to know the conclusion on the basis of our knowledge of the premises and the logical laws (See Campbell 1994, chap. 3.1 and 3.2). Formally valid arguments can only have this epistemic virtue if sameness of sense is transparent in the following way:

> *Transparency-of-Sense-Sameness*: Necessarily, if α and β have the same sense, everyone who grasps the sense of α and β, thereby knows that α and β have the same sense, *provided that there is no difficulty in grasping the senses involved*.

Assume for reduction that sameness of sense is not transparent in the first argument in section 3.2. Then you might understand and accept "Hesperus is a planet" (first premise) and understand and accept "Hesperus shines brightly" (second premise), but fail to recognise that the two "Hesperus" tokens have the same sense. Hence, your understanding of the premises does not entitle you to give them the form "Fa" and "Ga" and hence, you cannot discern the logical form that ensures the formal validity of the argument. Consequently, you are not in a position to come to know the conclusion on the basis of your knowledge of the premises alone. The argument would be formally valid, but one could not come to know its conclusion without adding the premise

Hesperus mentioned in premise 1 is the same thing as Hesperus mentioned in premise 2.

Since we take some arguments like the one above to be complete and knowledge transmitting, sameness of sense must be transparent.

If we assume in addition to *Transparency-of-Sense-Sameness*:

Competent speakers know that synonymous expressions co-refer, if they refer at all,

we arrive at:

Sense-Determines-Reference: Necessarily, if α and β have the same sense, and α refers to *a* and β refers to *b*, everyone who grasps the sense of α and β knows that *a* = *b*.

Frege makes use of Sense-Reference in *Thoughts* to argue for the view that an indexical and a proper name, although co-referential, differ in sense.

Transparency-of-Sense-Sameness has further theoretical ramifications. Russell wrote to Frege:

I believe that in spite of all its snowfields Mont Blanc itself is a component part of what is actually asserted in the proposition 'Mont Blanc is more than 4000 meters high'.

(PMC: 169)

If Mont Blanc is part of the thought expressed by uttering "Mont Blanc is a mountain", every piece of rock of Mont Blanc is part of this thought. To Frege, this conclusion seems absurd (PMC: 79). Why can a part of Mont Blanc that is unknown to me not be part of a sense I apprehend? Because if there were unknown constituents of the sense of "Mont Blanc" I could not know whether the thought expressed by one utterance of "Mont Blanc is a mountain" is the same as that expressed by another merely by grasping the thought. Hence, Frege does not allow Mont Blanc to be a constituent of the thought that Mont Blanc is a mountain. He endorses the Homogeneity Principle that a sense can only have other senses as constituents (PMC: 127).

How plausible is *Transparency-of-Sense-Sameness*? Dummett (1975: 131) takes it to be an 'undeniable feature of the notion of meaning'. Frege's proviso to *Transparency-of-Sense-Sameness* shows that he is aware of difficulties. Many factors (the actual wording, pragmatic implicatures, background information) can bring about that one assents to *s* while doubting *s**, although these sentences express the same thought. Frege has not worked out a reply to these difficulties. However, he suggests that two sentences express the same thought if one can explain away appearances to the contrary by appeal to pragmatics etc.

Recently, some authors have argued that it is not immediate knowledge of co-reference, but the entitlement to 'trade on identity' which is the basic notion in a theory of sense (see Campbell 1994: 88). For example, if I use the demonstrative pronoun repeatedly to talk about an object that I visually track ("That bird is a hawk. Look, now that bird pursues the other bird"), I am usually not in a position to know immediately that I am referring to the same thing. But the fact that I am tracking the bird gives me a defeasible right to presuppose that the same bird is in question. There is no longer any suggestion that the grasp of sense gives one a privileged access to sameness of reference.

3.4 Sense without reference

According to Frege, the conditions for having a sense and the conditions for having a referent are different. Mere grammaticality is sufficient for an expression that can stand in for (genuine) proper names ("the King of France") to have a sense, but it is not sufficient for it to have a referent (S&R: 159 (28)).

What about genuine proper names? The name 'Nausikaa' in Homer's *Odyssee* is probably empty. "But it behaves as if it names a girl, and it is thus assured of a sense." (PW: 122). Frege's message is:

> If α is a well-formed expression that can take the place of a proper name or α is a proper name that purports to refer to something, α has a sense.

An expression purports to refer if it has some of the properties of an expression that does refer and the possession of these properties entitles the uninformed speaker to treat it like a referring expression. For instance, in understanding "Nausikaa" I will bring information that I have collected under this name to bear upon the utterance.

It is very plausible to treat (complex) expressions and genuine proper names differently when it comes to significance. We can ask a question like "Does *a* exist?" or "Is *a* so-and-so"?, even if "*a*" does not behave as if it to refers to something. "The number which exceeds itself" does not behave as if it names something. Yet, it seems implausible to say that "The number which exceeds itself cannot exist" does not express a thought. What secures a sense for complex expressions is that they are composed out of significant expressions in a grammatically correct way. Complex expressions need not behave as if they name something, simple ones must.

Since satisfaction of the sufficient conditions for sense-possession does not require satisfaction of the sufficient conditions for referentiality, there can be sense without reference:

> *Sense-without-Reference*: If the expression α is of a type whose tokens can stand for an object, the sense of α determines *at most one* referent.

If *Sense without Reference* is true, the mode of presentation metaphor is misleading. For there can be no mode of presentation without something that is presented. Some Neo-Fregeans take the mode of presentation metaphor to be so central that they reject *Sense without Reference* (see Evans 1982: 26). But one feels that what has to give here is the mode of presentation metaphor, not the idea of empty but significant terms. Are there more convincing reasons to deny that empty singular terms are significant?

The arguments pro and contra *Sense without Reference* are based on existence conditions for thoughts. According to Evans, a thought must either be either true or false, it cannot lack a truth-value (Evans 1982: 25). Frege is less demanding:

> The being of a thought may also be taken to lie in the possibility of different thinkers grasping the same thought as one and the same thought. (CP: 376 (146))

A thought is the sense of a complete propositional question. One grasps the thought expressed by a propositional question iff one knows when the question deserves the answer "Yes" and when it deserves the answer "No". Frege aims above for the following existence condition:

> (E!) The thought that p exists if the propositional question "p?" can be raised and addressed by different thinkers in a rational way.

There is a mere illusion of a thought if different thinkers cannot rationally engage with the same question. On the basis of (E!), Frege rejects the view that false thoughts aren't thoughts. It was rational to ask whether the circle can be squared and different thinkers could rationally engage with this question. Hence, there is a thought and not merely a thought illusion, although the thought is necessarily false.

The opposition to *Sense-without-Reference* is also fuelled by the idea that (i) a thought expressed by a sentence *s* is what one grasps when one understands (an utterance of) *s* and (ii) that one cannot understand (an utterance of) a sentence with an empty singular term. A representative example of an argument against *Sense without Reference* that goes through understanding is Evans argument from diversity (Evans 1982: 336). He argues that the satisfaction of the conditions for understanding a sentence *s* with a proper name *n* requires the existence of the referent of *n*. Someone who holds *Sense without Reference* can provide a communication-allowing relation in the empty case: speaker and audience grasp the same mode of presentation. But Evans rightly insists that this proposal is *ad hoc*. For usually, we don't require exact match of mode of presentation. The Fregean is challenged to provide a common communication-allowing relation that is present in the case where the singular term is empty and the case where it is referential.

Sainsbury (2005, chapter 3.6) proposes that the common communication-allowing relation is causal: exact match of mode of presentation is not required, only that there is a potentially knowledge-transmitting relation between the speaker's use and the audience episode of understanding the term.

3.5 Indirect sense and reference

If we assume that the reference of a sentence is determined by the reference of its parts, the substitution of co-referential terms of the same grammatical category should leave the reference of the sentence (e.g. truth-value) unchanged. However, Frege points out that there are exceptions to this rule:

> Gottlob said (believes) that the evening star shines brightly in the evening sky.
> The evening star = the morning star.
> Gottlob said (believes) that the morning star shines brightly in the evening sky.

Here the exchange of co-referential terms changes the truth-value of our original statement. (In order to keep the discussion simple I will ignore propositional attitude ascriptions in which the singular terms are not within the scope of 'S believes that ...', see Burge (2005: 198). For a more general discussion of these issues see article 16 [Semantics: Noun Phrases and Verb Phrases] (Swanson) *Propositional attitudes*.)

Frege takes these cases to be exceptions of the rule that the reference of a sentence is determined by the referents of its constituents. What the exceptions have in common is that they involve a shift of reference:

> In reported speech one talks about the sense, e.g. of another person's remarks. It is quite clear that in this way of speaking words do not have their *customary* reference but designate what is usually their sense. In order to have a short expression, we will say: In reported speech, words are used *indirectly* or have their *indirect* reference. We distinguish accordingly the *customary* sense from its *indirect* sense.

(S&R: 159 (28))

Indirect speech is a defect of natural language. In a language that can be used for scientific purposes the same sign should everywhere have the same referent. But in indirect discourse the same words differ in sense and reference from normal discourse. In a letter to Russell Frege proposes a small linguistic reform to bring natural language closer to his ideal: "we ought really to have special signs in indirect speech, though their connection with the corresponding signs in direct speech should be easy to recognize" (PMC: 153).

Let us implement Frege's reform of indirect speech by introducing indices that indicate sense types. The index 0 stands for the customary sense expressed by an unembedded occurrence of a sign, 1 for the sense the sign expresses when embedded under one indirect speech operator like "S said that ...". By iterating indirect speech operators we can generate an infinite hierarchy of senses:

Direct speech:	The-evening-star$_0$ shines$_0$ brightly$_0$ in$_0$ the-evening-sky$_0$.
Indirect speech:	Gottlob$_0$ believes$_0$ that the-evening-star$_1$ shines$_1$ brightly$_1$ in$_1$ the-evening-sky$_1$.
Doubly indirect speech:	Bertrand$_0$ believes$_0$ that Gottlob$_1$ believes$_1$ that the-evening-star$_2$ shines$_2$ brightly$_2$ in$_2$ the-evening-sky$_2$.
Triply indirect speech:	Ludwig$_0$ believes$_0$ that Bertrand$_1$ believes$_1$ that Gottlob$_2$ believes$_2$ that the-evening-star$_3$ shines$_3$ brightly$_3$ in$_3$ the-evening-sky$_3$.

....

"The evening star$_0$" refers to the planet Venus and expresses a mode of presentation of it; "the evening star$_1$" refers to the customary sense of "the evening star", a mode of presentation of the planet Venus. "The evening star$_2$" refers to a mode of presentation of the mode of presentation of Venus and expresses a mode of presentation of a mode of presentation of a mode of presentation of Venus.

Let us first attend to an often made point that requires a conservative modification of Frege's theory. It seems natural to say that the name of a thought ("that the evening star shines brightly in the evening sky") is composed of the nominaliser "that" and the names of the thought constituents in an order ("that" + "the evening star" + "shines" ...). If "the evening star" names a sense in "Gottlob said that the evening star shines brightly in the evening sky", then "Gottlob said that the evening star shines brightly in the evening sky and it does shine brightly in the evening sky" should be false (the sense of "the evening star" does not shine brightly). But the sentence is true!

Does this refute Frege's reference shift thesis? No, for can't one designator refer to two things? The designator "the evening star$_1$" refers to the sense of "the evening star$_0$" AND to the evening star. Since such anaphoric back reference seems always possible, we have no reference shift, but a systematic increase of referents. Fine (1989: 267f) gives independent examples of terms with multiple referents.

Frege himself should be sympathetic to this suggestion. In S&R he gives the following example:

John fancies that *London is the biggest city in the world*.

According to Frege, the italicised sentence 'counts double' ("ist doppelt zu nehmen" S&R: 175, (48)). Whatever the double count exactly is, the sentence above will be true iff

John believes *that London is the biggest city in the world*
AND
It is not the case *that London is the biggest city in the world*.

Instead of doubly counting the same 'that'-designator, we can let it stand for a truth-value and the thought that determines the truth-value. Reference increase seems more adequate than reference shift.

Philosophers have been skeptical of Frege's sense hierarchy. What is so bad about an infinite hierarchy of senses and references? If there is such a hierarchy, the language of propositional attitude ascriptions is unlearnable, argues Davidson. One cannot provide a finitely axiomatised theory of truth for propositional attitude ascriptions if a "that"-clause is infinitely ambiguous (Davidson 1984: 208). The potentially infinitely many meanings of "that p" would have to be learned one by one. Hence, we could not understand propositional attitude ascriptions we have not heard before, although they are composed of words we already master.

This argument loses its force if the sense of a "that" designator is determined by the sense of the parts of the sense named and their mode of combination (see Burge 2005: 172). One must learn that "that" is a name forming operator that takes a sentence s and returns a designator of the thought expressed by s. Since one can iterate the name forming operator one can understand infinitely many designations for thoughts on the basis of finite knowledge.

But is there really an infinite hierarchy of senses and references? We get an infinite hierarchy of sense and references on the following assumptions:

(P1) Indirect reference of w in n embeddings = sense of w in n-1 embeddings
(P2) Indirect sense of w in n embeddings ≠ sense of w in n embeddings
(P3) Indirect sense of w in n embeddings ≠ indirect sense of w in m embeddings if $n \neq m$.

Dummett has argued against (P2) that "the replacements of an expression in double *oratio obliqua* which will leave the truth-value of the whole sentence unaltered are -- just as in single *oratio obliqua* -- those which have the same sense" (Dummett 1981a: 269). Assume for illustration that "bachelor" is synonymous with "unmarried eligible male". Dummett is right that we can replace "bachelor" *salva veritate* in (i) "John believes that all bachelors are dirty" and (ii) "John believes that Peter believes that all bachelors are dirty" with "unmarried eligible male". But this does not show that "bachelor" retains its customary sense in multiple embeddings. For Frege argues that the sense of "unmarried eligible male" also shifts under the embedding. No wonder they can be replaced *salva veritate*.

However, if singly and doubly embedded words differ in sense and reference, one should expect that words with the same sense cannot be substituted *salva veritate* in different embeddings. The problem is that it is difficult to check in a convincing way for such failures. If we stick to the natural language sentences, substitution of one token of the same word will not change anything; if we switch to the revised language with indices, we can no longer draw on intuitions about truth-value difference.

In view of a lack of direct arguments one should remain agnostic about the Fregean hierarchy. I side here with Parsons that the choice between a theory of sense and reference with or without the hierachy "must be a matter of taste and elegance" (Parsons 1997: 408). The reader should consult the Appendix of Burge's (2005) essay 4 for attempts to give direct arguments for the hierarchy, Peacocke (1999: 245) for arguments against and Parsons (1997: 402ff) for a diagnosis of the failure of a possible Fregean argument for the hierarchy.

4 Criticising sense and reference

4.1 Carnap's alternative: extension and intension

Carnap's *Meaning and Necessity* plays an important role in the reception of Frege's ideas. However, as Carnap himself emphasizes he does not have the same explanatory aims as Frege. Carnap himself aims to explicate and extend the distinction between denotation and connotation, while he ascribes to Frege the goal of explicating the distinction between the object named by a name and its meaning (Carnap 1956: 127). This description of Frege does not bear closer investigation. Frege argues that predicates ("$\xi > 1$") don't name their referents, yet they have a sense that determines a referent. Predicates refer, although they are not names.

Carnap charges Frege for multiplying senses without good reason (Carnap 1956: 157 and 137). If every name has exactly one referent and one sense, and the referent of a name must shift in propositional attitude contexts, Frege must have names for senses which in turn must have new senses that determine senses and so on. Whether this criticism is convincing is, as we have seen in the previous section, still an open issue.

Carnap lays the blame for the problem at the door of the notion of naming. Carnap's method of intension and extension avoids using this notion. Carnap takes equivalence relations between sentences and subsentential expressions as given. In a second step he assigns to all equivalent expressions an object. For example, if s is true in all state descriptions in which $s*$ is true, they have the same intension. If s and $s*$ have the same truth-value, they have the same extension. Expressions have intension and extension, but they don't name either. It seems however unclear how Carnap can avoid appeal to naming when it comes to equivalence relations between names. 'Hesperus' and 'Phosphorus' have the same extension because they *name* the same object (see Davidson 1962: 326f).

An intension is a function from a possible world w (a state-description) to an object. The intension of a sentence s is, for example, a function that maps a possible world w onto the truth value of s in w; the intension of a singular term is a function that maps a possible world w onto an object in w. Carnap states that the intension of every expression is the same as its (direct) sense (Carnap 1956: 126). Now, intensions are more coarsely individuated than Fregean senses. The thought that 2 + 2 = 4 is different from the thought that 123 + 23 = 146, but the intension expressed by "2 + 2 = 4" and "123 + 23 = 146" is the same. Every true mathematical statement has the same intension: the function that maps every possible world to the True.

Although Carnap's criticism does not hit its target, his method of extension and intension has been widely used. Lewis (1970), Kaplan (1977/1989) and Montague (1973) have refined and developed it to assign intensions and extensions to a variety of natural language expressions.

4.2 Rigidity and sense

What, then, is the sense of a proper name? Frege suggests, but does not clearly endorse, the following answer: The sense of a proper name (in the idiolect of a speaker) is given by a definite description that the speaker would use to distinguish the proper name bearer from all other things. For example, *my* sense of "Aristotle" might be given by the definite description "the inventor of formal logic". I will now look at two of Kripke's objections against this idea that have figured prominently in recent discussion.

First, the modal objection (for a development of this argument see Soames 1998):
1. Proper names are rigid designators.
2. The descriptions commonly associated with proper names by speakers are non-rigid.
3. A rigid designator and a non-rigid one do not have the same sense.

Therefore:
4. No proper name has the same sense as a definite description speakers associate with it.

A singular term α is a rigid designator if, and only if, α refers to x in every possible world *in which x exists* (Kripke 1980: 48–49). One can make sense of rigid designation without invoking a plurality of possible worlds. If the sentence which results from uniform substitution of singular terms for the dots in the schema

> ... might not have been ...

expresses a proposition which we intuitively take to be false, then the substituted term is a rigid designator, if not, not.

Why accept (3)? If "Aristotle" had the same sense as "the inventor of formal logic", we should be able to substitute "the inventor of formal logic" in all sentences without altering the truth-value (*salva veritate*). But

> Aristotle might not have been the inventor of formal logic. (Yes!)

and

> Aristotle might not have been Aristotle. (No!)

But in making this substitution we go from a true sentence to a false one. How can this be? Kripke's answer is: Even if everyone would agree that Aristotle is the inventor of formal logic, the description "the inventor of formal logic" is not synonymous with "Aristotle". The description is only used to *fix the reference of the proper name*. If someone answers the question "Who is Aristotle?" by using the description, he gives no information about the sense of "Aristotle". He just gives you advice how to pick out the right object.

The modal argument is controversial for several reasons. Can the difference between sentences with (non-rigid) descriptions and proper names not be explained without positing a difference in sense? Dummett gives a positive answer that explains the difference in terms of a difference in scope conventions between proper names and definite descriptions (see Dummett 1981a: 127ff; Kripke 1980, Introduction: 11ff replies; Dummett 1981b Appendix 3 replies to the reply).

Other authors accept the difference, but argue that there are rigid definite descriptions that are associated with proper names. (See, for example, Jackson 2005.) The debate about this question is ongoing.

Second, the epistemic objection: Most people associate with proper names only definite descriptions that are not satisfied by only one thing ("Aristotle is the great Greek philosopher") or by the wrong object ("Peano is the mathematician who first proposed the axioms for arithmetic"). The 'Peano' axioms were first proposed by Dedekind (see Kripke 1972: 84).

These objections do not refute Frege's conclusion that co-referential proper names can differ in something that is more finely individuated than their reference. What the objections show to be implausible is the idea that the difference between co-referential proper names consists in a difference of associated definite descriptions. But arguments that show that a proper name does not have the same sense as a particular definite description do not show the more general thesis that a proper name has a sense that is distinct from its referent to be false. In order to refute the general thesis an additional argument is needed. The constraint that the sense of an expression must be distinct from its reference leaves Frege ample room for manoeuvre. Consider the following two options:

The sense of "Aristotle" might be conceptually primitive: it is not possible to say what this sense is without using the same proper name again. This is not implausible. We usually don't define a proper name. This move of course raises the question how the sense of proper names should be explained if one does not want to make it ineffable. More soon.

The sense of "Aristotle" in my mouth is identical with a definite description, but not with a famous deeds description like "the inventor of bi-focals". Neo-Descriptivists offer a variety of meta-linguistic definite descriptions ("the bearer of 'N'") 'to specify the sense of the name (see, for example, Forbes 1990: 536ff and Jackson 2005).

4.3 Too far from the ideal?

Frege has provided a good reason to distinguish sense from reference. The expressions composing an argument must be distinguished by form and mode of presentation, if the form of an argument is to reveal whether it is formally valid or not. If figures that differ in form also differ in sense, the following relations obtain between sign, sense and reference:

> The regular connection between a sign, its sense, and its reference is of such a kind that to the sign there corresponds a definite sense and to that in turn a definite referent, while to a given referent (an object) there does not belong only a single sign.
>
> (S&R: 159 (27))

The "no more than one" requirement is according to Frege the most important rule that logic imposes on language. (For discussion see May 2006.) A language that can be used to conduct proofs must be unambiguous. A proof is a series of judgements that terminates in the logically justified acknowledgement that a thought stands for the True. If "2 + 2 = 4" expressed different thoughts, the designation *that 2 + 2 = 4* would not identify the thought one is entitled to judge on the basis of the proof (CP: 316, Fn. 3).

Frege is under no illusion: there is, in general, no such regular connection between sign, sense and reference in natural language:

> To every expression belonging to a complete totality of signs [Ganzes von Bezeichnungen], there should certainly correspond a definite sense; but natural languages often do not

satisfy this condition, and one must be content if the same word has the same sense in the same context [Zusammenhänge]. (S&R: 159 (27–28))

In natural language, the same shape-individuated sign may have more than one sense ("Bank"), and different occurrences of the same sign with the same reference may vary in sense ("Aristotle" in my mouth and your mouth). Similar things hold for concept-words. In natural language some concept-words are incompletely defined, others are vague. The concept-word "is a natural number" is only defined for numbers, the sense of the word does not determine its application to flowers, "is bald" is vague, it is neither true nor false of me. Hence, some sentences containing such concept-words violate the law of excluded middle: they are neither true nor false. To prevent truth-value gaps Frege bans vague and incompletely defined concept-words from the language of inference. Even the language of mathematics contains complex signs with more than one referent ("√2").

Natural language doesn't comply with the rule that every expression has in all contexts exactly one sense. Different speakers associate different senses with the figure "Aristotle" referring to the same person at the same time and/or the same speaker associates different senses with the same proper name at different times. Frege points out that different speakers can *correctly* use the same proper name for the same bearer on the basis of different definite descriptions (S&R: 27, fn. 2). More importantly, such a principle seems superfluous, since differences in proper name sense don't prevent speakers of natural language from understanding each other's utterances. Hence, we seem to be driven to the consequence that differences in sense between proper names and other expressions don't matter, what matters is that one talks about the same thing:

> So long as the reference remains the same, such variations of sense may be tolerated, although they are to be avoided in the theoretical structure of a demonstrative science ("beweisende Wissenschaft") and ought not to occur in a perfect language.
> (S&R: 158, & fn. 4 (27))

Why is variation of sense tolerable outside demonstrative sciences? Frege answers:

> The task of vernacular languages is essentially fulfilled if people engaged in communication with one another connect the same thought, or approximately the same thought, with the same sentence For this it is not at all necessary that the individual words should have a sense and reference of their own, provided that only the whole sentence has a sense.
> (PMC: 115. In part my translation)

Frege makes several interesting points here, but let us focus on the main one: if you and I connect approximately the same thought with "Aristotle was born in Stagira", we have communicated successfully. What does 'approximately the same' amount to? What is shared when you understand my question "Is Aristotle a student of Plato?" is not the thought I express with "Aristotle is a student of Plato". If one wants to wax metaphysically, what is shared is a complex consisting of Aristotle (the philosopher) and Plato (the Philosopher) standing in the relation of being a student connected in such a way that the complex is true iff Aristotle is a student of Plato. There are no conventional, community-wide senses for ordinary proper names, there is only a conventional community wide reference. Russell sums this up nicely when he writes to Frege:

> In the case of a simple proper name like "Socrates" I cannot distinguish between sense and reference; I only see the idea which is something psychological and the object. To put it better: I don't acknowledge the sense, only the idea and the reference.
> (Letter to Frege 12.12.1904. PMC: 169)

If we go along with Frege's use of "sign" for a symbol individuated in terms of the mode of presentation expressed, we must say that often we don't speak the same Fregean language, but that it does not matter for communication. If we reject it, we will speak the same language, but proper names turn out to be ambiguous. (Variations of this argument can be found in Russell 1910/11: 206–207; Kripke 1979: 108; Evans 1982: 399f and Sainsbury 2005: 12ff)

This line of argument makes the *Hybrid View* plausible (see Heck 1995: 79). The Hybrid View takes Frege to be right about the content of beliefs expressed by sentences containing proper names, but wrong about what atomic sentences literally say. "Hesperus is a planet" and "Phosphorus is a planet" have the same content, because the proper name senses are too idiosyncratic to contribute to what one literally says with an utterance containing the corresponding name. Grasping what an assertoric utterance of an atomic sentence literally says is, in the basic case, latching on to the right particulars and properties combined in the right way. The mode in which they are presented does not matter. By contrast, "S believes that Phosphorus is a planet" and "S believes that Hesperus is a planet" attribute *different beliefs* to S.

The argument for the Hybrid View requires the Fregean to answer the question "Why is it profitable to think of natural language in terms of the Fregean ideal in which every expression has one determinate sense?" (see Dummett 1981a: 585).

Dummett himself answers that we will gradually approximate the Fregean ideal because we can only rationally decide controversies involving proper names ("Did Napoleon really exist?") when we agree about the sense of these names (Dummett 1981a: 100f). Evans' reply is spot on: "[I]t is the actual practice of using the name 'a', not some ideal substitute, that interests us [...]" (Evans 1982: 40). The semanticist studies English, not a future language that will be closer to the Fregean ideal.

Heck has given another answer that is immune to the objection that the Fregean theory is not a theory for a language anyone (already) speaks. Proponents of the Hybrid View assume (i) that one has to know to which thing "Hesperus" refers in order to understand it and (ii) that there is no constraint on the ways or methods in which one can come to know this. But if understanding your utterance of "George Orwell wrote 1984" consists at least in part in coming to *know* of George Orwell that the utterance is about him, one cannot employ any mode of presentation of George Orwell. The speaker will assume that his audience can come to know what he is talking about on the basis of his utterance and features of the context. If the audience's method of finding out who is talked about does not draw on these reasons, they still might get it right. But it might easily have been the case that the belief they did actually acquire was false. In this situation they would not know who I am talking about with "George Orwell". Hence, the idea that in understanding an assertoric utterance one acquires knowledge limits the ways in which one may think of something in order to understand an utterance about it (Heck 1995: 102).

If this argument for the application of the sense/reference distinction to natural language is along the right lines, the bearers of sense and reference are no longer form-individuated signs. The argument shows at best that the constraints on understanding an *utterance* are more demanding than getting the references of the uttered words and their mode of combination right. This allows different utterances of the same form-individuated sentence to have different senses. There is no requirement that the audience and the speaker grasp the same sense in understanding (making) the utterance. The important requirement is that they all know what they are referring to.

There is another line of argument for the application of the sense/reference distinction to natural language. Frege often seems to argue that one only needs sense AND reference in languages 'designed' for inferential thinking. But of course we also make inferences in natural languages. Communication in natural language is often *joint* reasoning. Take the following argument:

You: Hegel was drunk.

Me: And Hegel is married.

We both: Hegel was drunk and is married.

Neither you nor I know both premises independently of each other; each person knows one premise and transmits knowledge of this premise to the other person via testimony. Together we can come to know the conclusion by deduction from the premises. But the argument above can only be valid and knowledge-transferring if you and I are entitled to take for granted that "Hegel" in the first premise names the same person as "Hegel" in the second premise without further justification.

Otherwise the argument would be incomplete; its rational force would rest on implicit background premises. According to Frege, whenever coincidence in reference is obvious, we have sameness of sense (PMC: 234). Every theory that wants to account for inference must acknowledge that sometimes we are entitled to take co-reference for granted. Hence, we have a further reason to assume that utterances of natural language sentences have senses.

4.4 Sense and reference for context-dependent expressions

Natural language contains unambiguous signs, tokens of which stand for different things in different utterances *because the sign means what it does*. Among such context-dependent expressions are:
- personal pronouns: 'I', 'you', 'my', 'he', 'she', 'it'
- demonstrative pronouns: 'that', 'this', 'these' and 'those'
- adverbs: 'here', 'now', 'today', 'yesterday', 'tomorrow'
- adjectives: 'actual', 'present' (a rather controversial entry)

An expression has a use as a context-dependent expression if it is used in a way that its reference in that use can vary with the context of utterance while its linguistic meaning stays the same.

Context-dependent expressions are supposed to pose a major problem for Frege. Perry (1977) has started a fruitful discussion about Frege's view on context-dependent expressions. Let us use the indexical 'now' to make clear what the problem is supposed to be:
1. If tokens of the English word 'now' are produced at different times, the tokens refer to different times.
2. If two signs differ in reference, they differ in sense.

Hence,
3. Tokens of the English word 'now' that are produced at different times differ in sense.
4. It is not possible that two tokens of 'now' co-refer if they are produced at different times.

Hence,
5. It is not possible that two tokens of 'now' that are produced at different times have the same sense.

Every token of 'now' that is produced at time t differs in sense from all other tokens of 'now' not produced at t. Now one will ask what is the particular sense of a token of 'now' at t? Perry calls this 'the completion problem'. Is the sense of a particular token of 'now' the same as the sense of a definite description of the time t at which 'now' is uttered? No, take any definite description d of the time t that does not itself contain 'now' or a synonym of 'now'. No statement of the form 'd is now' is trivial. Take as a representative example, 'The start of my graduation ceremony is now'. Surely, it is not self-evident that the start of my graduation ceremony is now. Hence, Perry takes Frege to be settled with the unattractive conclusion that for each time t there is a primitive and particular way in which t is presented to us at t, which gives rise to thoughts accessible only at t, and expressible then with 'now' (Perry 1977: 491). Perry (1977) and Kaplan (1977/1989) have argued that one should, for this and further reasons, replace Fregean thoughts with two successor notions: character and content. The character of an indexical is, roughly, a rule that fixes the referent of the context-dependent expression in a context; the content is, roughly, the referent that has been so fixed. This revision of Frege has now become the orthodox theory.

4.5 The mode of presentation problem

Frege's theory of sense and reference raises the question "What are modes of presentation?" If modes of presentation are not the meanings of definite descriptions, what are they? This question can be understood as a request to reduce modes of presentation to scientifically more respectable things. I have no argument that one cannot reduce sense to something more fundamental and scientifically acceptable, but there is inductive evidence that there is no such reduction: many people have tried very hard for a long time, none of them has succeeded (see Schiffer 1990 and 2003). Modes of presentation may simply be modes of presentation and not other things (see Peacocke 1992: 121).

Dummett has tried to work around this problem by making a theory of sense a theory of understanding:

> [T]here is no obstacle to our saying what it is that someone can do when he grasps that sense; and that is all that we need the notion of sense for. (Dummett 1981a: 227)

If this is true, we can capture the interesting part of the notion of sense by explaining what *knowledge of sense* consists in. Does *knowledge of sense* reduce to something scientifically respectable? Dummett proposes the following conditions for *knowing the sense* of a proper name:

> S knows the sense of a proper name N iff
>
> S has a criterion for recognising for any given object whether it is the bearer of N.
> (Dummett 1981a: 229)

Does your understanding "Gottlob Frege" consist in a criterion for recognising him when he is presented to you? (See Evans 1982, sec. 4.2.) No, he can no longer be presented to you in the way he could be presented to his contemporaries. Did the sense of "Gottlob Frege" change when he died?

The real trouble for modes of presentation seems not to be their irreducibility, but the problem to say, in general, what the difference between two modes of presentation consists in. Consider Fine's (2007: 36) example. You live in a symmetrical universe. At a certain point you are introduced to two identical twins. Perversely you give them simultaneously the same name 'Bruce'. Even in this situation it is rational to assert the sentence "Bruce is not the same person as Bruce".

The Fregean description of this case is that the figure "Bruce" expresses in one idiolect two modes of presentation. But what is the difference between these modes of presentation? The difference cannot be specified in purely qualitative terms. The twins have all their qualitative properties in common. Can the difference be specified in indexical terms? After all, you originally saw one Bruce over there and the other over here. This solution seems *ad hoc*. For, in general, one can forget the features that distinguished the bearer of a name when one introduced the name and yet continue to use the name. Can the difference in mode of presentation be specified in terms of the actual position of the two Bruce's? Maybe, but this difference cannot ground the continued use of name and it raises the question of what makes the current distinction sustain the use of the name originally introduced on the basis of other features. As long as these and related questions are not answered, alternatives to sense and reference merit a fair hearing.

5 Summary

Frege's work on sense and reference has set the agenda for over a century of research. The main challenge for Frege's friends is to find a plausible way to apply his theoretical apparatus to natural languages. Whether one believes that the challenge can be met or not, Frege has pointed us to a pre-philosophical datum, the fact that true identity statements about the same object can differ in cognitive value, that is a crucial touchstone for philosophical semantics.

I want to thank Sarah-Jane Conrad, Silvan Imhof, Laura Mercolli, Christian Nimtz, the Editors and an anonymous referee for helpful suggestions.

6 References

Works by Frege

Begriffsschrift (BS, 1879). Reprinted: Darmstadt: Wissenschaftliche Buchgesellschaft, 1977.
The Foundations of Arithmetic (FA, 1884). Oxford: Blackwell, 1974. (C. Thiel (ed.). *Die Grundlagen der Arithmetik*. Hamburg: Meiner, 1988.)
Nachgelassene Schriften (NS), edited by Hans Hermes, Friedrich Kambartel & Friedrich Kaulbach. 2nd rev. edn. Hamburg: Meiner Verlag 1983. 1st edn. translated by Peter Long & Roger White as *Posthumous Writings* (PW). Oxford: Basil Blackwell, 1979.
Wissenschaftlicher Briefwechsel (BW), edited by Gottfried Gabriel, Hans Hermes, Friedrich Kambartel, Christian Thiel & Albert Veraart. Hamburg: Meiner Verlag, 1976. Abridged by Brian McGuinness and translated by Hans Kaal as *Philosophical and Mathematical Correspondence* (PMC). Oxford: Basil Blackwell, 1980.
McGuinness, Brian (ed.) 1984: *Gottlob Frege: Collected Papers on Mathematics, Logic and Philosophy* (CP). Oxford: Basil Blackwell.
'Über Sinn und Bedeutung'. *Zeitschrift für Philosophie und philosophische Kritik* 100, 25–50. Translated as 'On Sense and Meaning' (S&R), in: McGuinness 1984, 157–177.
'Der Gedanke'. *Beiträge zur Philosophie des deutschen Idealismus* 1, 58–77. Translated as 'Thoughts' (T), in: McGuinness 1984, 351–373.

Other Works

Bell, David 1987. Thoughts. *Notre Dame Journal of Philosophical Logic* 28, 36–51.
Bezuidenhout, Anne & Marga Reimer (eds.) 2004. *Descriptions and Beyond*. Oxford: Oxford University Press 2004.
Burge, Tyler 2005. *Truth, Thought, Reason: Essays on Frege*. Oxford: Clarendon Press.
Campbell, John 1994. *Past, Space and Self*. Cambridge, MA: The MIT Press.
Carnap, Rudolf 1956. *Meaning and Necessity*. 2nd edn. Chicago, IL: The University of Chicago Press.
Church, Alonzo 1951. A formulation of the logic of dense and denotation. In: P. Henle, H. M. Kallen & S. K. Langer (eds.). *Structure, Method and Meaning. Essays in Honour of Henry M. Sheffer*. New York: Liberal Arts Press, 3–24.
Church, Alonzo 1973. Outline of a revised formulation of the logic of sense and denotation (Part I). *Noûs* 7, 24–33.
Church, Alonzo 1974. Outline of a revised formulation of the logic of sense and denotation (Part II). *Noûs* 8, 135–156.
Davidson, Donald 1962. The method of extension and intension. In: P. A. Schilpp (ed.). *The Philosophy of Rudolf Carnap*. La Salle, IL: Open Court, 311–351.
Davidson, Donald 1984. *Inquiries into Truth and Interpretation*. Oxford: Oxford University Press.
Dummett, Michael 1975. Frege's distinction between sense and reference [Spanish translation under the title 'Frege']. *Teorema* V, 149–188. Reprinted in: M. Dummett. *Truth and Other Enigmas*. London: Duckworth, 1978, 116–145.
Dummett, Michael 1981a. *Frege: Philosophy of Language*. 2nd edn. London: Duckworth.
Dummett, Michael 1981b. *The Interpretation of Frege's Philosophy*. London: Duckworth.

Dummett, Michael 1989. More about thoughts. *Notre Dame Journal of Philosophical Logic* 30, 1–19.
Dummett, Michael 1993. *The Seas of Language*. Oxford: Oxford University Press.
Evans, Gareth 1982. *Varieties of Reference*. Oxford: Oxford University Press.
Fine, Kit 1989. The problem of de re modality. In: J. Almog, J. Perry & H. K. Wettstein (eds.). *Themes from Kaplan*. Oxford: Oxford University Press, 197–272.
Fine, Kit 2007. *Semantic Relationism*. Oxford: Blackwell.
Forbes, Graeme 1990. The indispensability of *Sinn*. *The Philosophical Review* 99, 535–563.
Furth, Montgomery 1964. Introduction. In: M. Furth (ed.). *The Basic Laws of Arithmetic: Exposition of the System*. Berkeley, CA: University of California Press, v–lix.
Geach, Peter T. 1975. Names and identity. In: S. Guttenplan (ed.). *Mind and Language*. Oxford: Clarendon Press, 139–158.
Heck, Richard 1995. The sense of communication. *Mind* 104, 79–106.
Jackson, Frank 2005. What are proper names for? In: J. C. Marek & M. E. Reicher (eds.). *Experience and Analysis. Proceedings of the 27th International Wittgenstein Symposium.* Vienna: hpt-öbv, 257–269.
Kaplan, David 1989. Demonstratives. In: J. Almog, J. Perry & H. K. Wettstein (eds.). *Themes from Kaplan*. Oxford: Oxford University Press, 481–563.
Kripke, Saul 1980. *Naming and Necessity*. Cambridge, MA: Harvard University Press. (Separate reissue of: S. Kripke. Naming and necessity. In: D. Davidson & G. Harman (eds.). *Semantics of Natural Language*. Dordrecht: Reidel, 1972, 253–355 and 763–769.)
Kripke, Saul 1979. A puzzle about belief. In: A. Margalit (ed.). *Meaning and Use*. Dordrecht: Reidel, 239–283. Reprinted in: N. Salomon & S. Soames (eds.). *Propositions and Attitudes*. Oxford: Oxford University Press, 1989, 102–148.
Kemmerling, Andreas 1990. Gedanken und ihre Teile. *Grazer Philosophische Studien* 37, 1–30.
Künne, Wolfgang 1992. Hybrid proper names. *Mind* 101, 721–731.
Levine, James 2004. On the 'Gray's elegy' argument and its bearing on Frege's theory of sense. *Philosophy and Phenomenological Research* 64, 251–295.
Lewis, David 1970. General semantics. *Synthese* 22, 18–67.
Makin, Gideon 2000. *The Metaphysicians of Meaning*. London: Routledge.
May, Robert 2006. The invariance of sense. *The Journal of Philosophy* 103, 111–144.
McDowell, John 1977. On the sense and reference of a proper name. *Mind* 86, 159–185.
Mendelsohn, Richard L. 1982. Frege's *Begriffsschrift* Theory of identity. *The Journal for the History of Philosophy* 20, 279–299.
Montague, Richard 1973. The proper treatment of quantification in ordinary English. In: J. Hintikka, J. Moravcsik & P. Suppes (eds.). *Approaches to Natural Language*. Dordrecht: Reidel, 221–242. Reprinted in: R. Thomason (ed.). *Formal Philosophy. Selected Papers of Richard Montague*. New Haven, CT: Yale University Press, 1974, 247–270.
Parsons, Terence 1997. Fregean theories of truth and meaning. In: M. Schirn (ed.). *Frege: Importance and Legacy*. Berlin: de Gruyter, 371–409.
Peacocke, Christopher 1992. *A Study of Concepts*. Cambridge, MA: The MIT Press.
Peacocke, Christopher 1999. *Being Known*, Oxford: Oxford University Press.
Perry, John 1977. Frege on demonstratives. *The Philosophical Review* 86, 474–497.
Putnam, Hilary 1954. Synonymy and the analysis of belief sentences. *Analysis* 14, 114–122.
Putnam, Hilary 1975. The meaning of 'meaning'. In: K. Gunderson (ed.). *Language, Mind and Knowledge*. Minneapolis, MN: University of Minnesota Press. Reprinted in: H. Putnam.

Mind. Language and Reality: Philosophical Papers, Volume 2. Cambridge: Cambridge University Press, 1975, 215–271.

Quine, Willard van Orman 1951. Two dogmas of empiricism. *The Philosophical Review* 60, 20–43. Reprinted in: W.V.O. Quine. *From a Logical Point of View*. Harvard: Harvard University Press, 1953, 20–47.

Ricketts, Thomas 2003. Quantification, sentences, and truth-values. *Manuscrito: Revista International de Filosofia* 26, 389–424.

Rumfitt, Ian 1994. Frege's theory of predication: An elaboration and defense, with some new applications. *The Philosophical Review* 103, 599–637.

Russell, Bertrand 1905. On denoting. *Mind* 14, 479–493.

Russell, Bertrand 1910/11. Knowledge by acquaintance and knowledge by description. *Proceedings of the Aristotelian Society New Series* 11, 108–128. Reprinted in: B. Russell. *Mysticism and Logic*. London: Unwin, 1986, 201–221.

Sainsbury, Mark R. 2005. *Reference without Referents*. Oxford: Oxford University Press.

Schiffer, Stephen 1990. The mode of presentation problem. In: A. C. Anderson & J. Owens (eds.). *Propositional Attitudes*. Stanford, CA: CSLI Publications. 249–269.

Schiffer, Stephen 2003. *The Things We Mean*. Oxford: Oxford University Press.

Soames, Scott 1998. The modal argument: Wide scope and rigidified descriptions. *Noûs* 32, 1–22.

Textor, Mark 2007. Frege's theory of hybrid proper names developed and defended. *Mind* 116, 947–982.

Textor, Mark 2009. A repair of Frege's theory of thoughts. *Synthese* 167, 105–123.

Wiggins, David 1997. Meaning and truth conditions: From Frege's grand design to Davidson's. In: B. Hale & C. Wright (eds.). *A Companion to the Philosophy of Language*. Oxford: Blackwell, 3–29.

Barbara Abbott
4 Reference: Foundational issues

1 Introduction —— 62
2 Direct reference —— 65
3 Frege's theory of sense and reference —— 67
4 Reference vs. quantification and Russell's theory of descriptions —— 71
5 Strawson's objections to Russell —— 76
6 Donnellan's attributive-referential distinction —— 77
7 Kaplan's theory of indexicality —— 80
8 Proper names and Kripke's return to Millian nondescriptionality —— 82
9 Propositional attitude contexts —— 86
10 Indefinite descriptions —— 88
11 Summary —— 91
12 References —— 91

Abstract: This chapter reviews issues surrounding theories of reference. The simplest theory is the "Fido"-Fido theory – that reference is all that an NP has to contribute to the meaning of phrases and sentences in which it occurs. Two big problems for this theory are coreferential NPs that do not behave as though they were semantically equivalent and meaningful NPs without a referent. These problems are especially acute in sentences about beliefs and desires – propositional attitudes. Although Frege's theory of sense, and Russell's quantificational analysis, seem to solve these problems for definite descriptions, they do not work well for proper names, as Kripke shows. And Donnellan and Strawson have other objections to Russell's theory. Indexical expressions like "I" and "here" create their own issues; we look at Kaplan's theory of indexicality, and several solutions to the problem indexicals create in propositional attitude contexts. The final section looks at indefinite descriptions, and some more recent theories that make them appear more similar to definite descriptions than was previously thought.

1 Introduction

Reference, it seems, is what allows us to use language to talk about things and thus vital to the functioning of human language. That being said there remain

Barbara Abbott, Lake Leelanau, MI, USA

several parameters to be fixed in order to determine a coherent field of study. One important one is whether reference is best viewed as a semantic phenomenon – a relation between linguistic expressions and the objects referred to, or whether it is best viewed as pragmatic – a three-place relation among language users, linguistic expressions, and things. The ordinary everyday meaning of words like "refer" and "reference" would incline us toward the pragmatic view (we say, e.g., *Who were you referring to?*, not *Who was your phrase referring to?*). However there is a strong tradition, stemming from work in logic and early modern philosophy of language, of viewing reference as a semantic relation, so that will be the main focus of our attention at the outset, although we will turn before long to pragmatic views.

1.1 Reference vs. predication

Another parameter to be determined is what range of expressions (can be used to) refer. The traditional model sentence, e.g. *Socrates runs*, consists of a simple noun phrase (NP), a proper name in this case, and a simple verb phrase (VP). The semantic function of the NP is to pick out (i.e. refer to) some entity, and the function of the VP is to predicate a property of that entity. The sentence is true if the entity actually has that property, and false otherwise. Seen in this light, reference and predication are quite different operations. Of course many natural language sentences do not fit this simple model. In a semantics which is designed to treat the full panoply of expression types and to provide truth conditions for sentences containing them, the distinction between reference and predication may not be so clear or important. In classical Montague Grammar, for example, expressions of all categories (except determiners and conjunctions) are assigned an extension, where extension is a formal counterpart of reference (Montague 1973; (see article 11 [this volume] (Kempson) *Formal semantics and representationalism*). (In Montague Grammar expressions are also assigned an intension, which corresponds to a Fregean sense – see below, and cf. (see article 3 [this volume] (Textor) *Sense and reference.*) An expression's extension may be an ordinary type of entity, or, more typically, it may be a complex function of some kind. Thus the traditional bifurcation between reference and predication is not straightforwardly preserved in this approach. However for our purposes we will assume this traditional bifurcation, or at least that there is a difference between NPs and other types of expressions, and we will consider reference only for NPs. Furthermore our primary focus will be on definite NPs, which are the most likely candidates for referring expressions, though they may have other, non-referring uses too (see the articles in [Semantics: Noun Phrases and Verb Phrases]). The category of definite NPs includes proper names (e.g. *Amelia Earhart*), definite descriptions (e.g. *the book Sally is reading*), demonstrative descriptions (e.g. *this house*), and pronouns (e.g. *you, that*). We will have only a limited amount to say about pronouns; for the full story, (see article 1 [Semantics: Noun Phrases and Verb Phrases] (Büring) *Pronouns*). (Another important category comprises generic NPs; for these, (see article 8 [Semantics: Noun Phrases and Verb Phrases] (Carlson) *Genericity*.) Whether other types of NP, such as indefinite descriptions (e.g. *a letter from my mother*), can be properly said to be referring expressions is an issue of some dispute – see below, section 10.

1.2 The metaphysical problem of reference

Philosophers have explored the question of what it is, in virtue of which an expression has a reference – what links an expression to a reference and how did it come to do that? Frege (1892) argued that expressions express a sense, which is best thought of as a collection of properties. The reference of an expression is that entity which possesses exactly the properties contained in the sense. Definite descriptions are the clearest examples for this theory; *the inventor of bifocals* specifies a complex property of having been the first to think up and create a special type of spectacles, and that NP refers to Benjamin Franklin because he is the one who had that property. One problem with this answer to the question of what determines reference is the mysterious nature of senses. Frege insisted they were not to be thought of as mental entities, but he did not say much positive about what they are, and that makes them philosophically suspect. (see article 3 [this volume] (Textor) *Sense and reference*.) Another answer, following Kripke (1972), is what is usually referred to as a "causal (or historical) chain". The model in this case is proper names, and the idea is that there is some initial kind of naming event whereupon an entity is bestowed with a name, and then that name is passed down through the speech community as a name of that entity. In this article we will not be so much concerned with the metaphysical problem of what determines reference, but instead the linguistic problem of reference – determining what it is that referring expressions contribute semantically to the phrases and sentences in which they occur.

1.3 The linguistic problem of reference

The two answers to the metaphysical problem of reference correlate with two answers to the linguistic question of what it is that NPs contribute to the semantic content of phrases and sentences in which they appear. Frege's answer to the linguistic question is that expressions contribute their reference to the reference of the phrases in which they occur, and they contribute their sense to the sense of those phrases. But there are complications to this simple answer that we will review below in section 3. The other answer is that expressions contribute only their reference to the semantic content of the phrases and sentences in which they occur. Since this is a simpler answer, we will begin by looking at it in some more detail, in section 2, in order to able to understand why Frege put forward his more complex theory.

2 Direct reference

The theory according to which an NP contributes only its reference to the phrases and sentences in which it occurs is currently called the "direct reference" theory (the term was coined by Kaplan 1989). It is also sometimes called the "*Fido*-Fido" theory, the idea being that you have the name *Fido* and its reference is the dog, Fido, and that's all there is to reference and all there is to the meaning of such phrases. One big advantage of this simple theory is that it does not result in the postulation of any suspect entities. However there are two serious problems for this simple theory: one is the failure of coreferential NPs to be fully equivalent semantically, and the other is presented by seemingly meaningful NPs which do not have a reference – so called "empty NPs". We will look more closely at each of these problems in turn.

2.1 Failure of substitutivity

According to the direct reference theory, coreferential NPs – NPs which refer to the same thing – should be able to be substituted for each other in any sentence without a change in the semantics of the sentence or its truth value. (This generalization about intersubstitutivity is sometimes referred to as "Leibniz' Law".) If all that an NP has to contribute semantically is its reference, then it should not matter how that reference is contributed. However almost any two coreferential NPs will not seem to be intersubstitutable – they will seem to be semantically different. Frege (1892) worried in particular about two different kinds of sentence that showed this failure of substitutivity.

2.1.1 Identity sentences

The first kind are identity sentences – sentences of the form $a = b$, or (a little more colloquially) *a is (the same entity as) b*. If such a sentence is true, then the NPs *a* and *b* are coreferential so, according to the direct reference theory, it shouldn't matter which NP you use, including in identity sentences themselves! That is, the two sentences in (1) should be semantically equivalent (these are Frege's examples).

(1) a. The morning star is the morning star.
    b. The morning star is the evening star.

However, as Frege noted, the two sentences are very different in their cognitive impact. (1a) is a trivial sentence, whose truth is known to anyone who understands English (it is analytic). (1b) on the other hand gives the results of a major astronomical finding. Thus even though the only difference between (1a) and (1b) is that we have substituted coreferential NPs (*the evening star* for *the morning star*), there is still a semantic difference between them.

2.1.2 Propositional attitude sentences

The other kind of sentence that Frege worried about was sentences about propositional attitudes – the attitudes of sentient beings about situations or states of affairs. Such sentences will have a propositional attitude verb like *believe, hope, know, doubt, want,* etc. as their main verb, plus a sentential complement saying what the subject of the verb believes, hopes, wants, etc. Just as with identity statements, coreferential NPs fail to be intersubstitutable in the complements of such sentences. However the failure is more serious in this case. Intersubstitution of coreferential NPs in identity sentences always preserves truth value, but in propositional attitude sentences the truth value may change. Thus (2a) could be true while (2b) was false.

(2) a. Mary knows that the morning star is a planet.
    b. Mary knows that the evening star is a planet.

We can easily imagine that Mary has learned the truth about the morning star, but not about the evening star.

2.2 Empty NPs

The other major problem for the direct reference theory is presented by NPs that do not refer to anything – NPs like *the golden mountain* or *the round square*. The direct reference theory seems to make the prediction that sentences containing such NPs should be semantically defective, since they contain a part which has no reference. Yet sentences like those in (3) do not seem defective at all.

(3) a. Lee is looking for the golden mountain.
     b. The philosopher's stone turns base metals into gold.

Sentences about existence, especially those that deny existence, pose special problems here. Consider (4):

(4) The round square does not exist.

Not only is (4) not semantically defective, it is even true! So this is the other big problem for the *Fido*-Fido direct reference theory.

3 Frege's theory of sense and reference

As noted above, Frege proposed that referring expressions have semantic values on two levels, reference and sense. Frege was anticipated in this by Mill (1843), who had proposed a similar distinction between denotation (reference) and connotation (sense). (Mill's use of the word "connotation" must be kept distinct from its current use to mean hints or associations connected with a word or phrase. Mill's connotations functioned like Frege's senses – to determine reference (denotation).) One important aspect of Frege's work was his elegant arguments. He assumed two fundamental principles of compositionality. At the level of senses he assumed that the sense of a complex expression is determined by the senses of its component parts plus their syntactic mode of combination. Similarly at the level of reference, the reference of a complex expression is determined by the references of its parts plus their mode of combination. (Following Frege, it is commonly assumed today that meanings, whatever they are, are compositional. That is thought to be the only possible explanation of our ability to understand novel utterances. (see article 6 [this volume] (Pagin & Westerståhl) *Compositionality*.) Using these two principles Frege argued further that the reference of a complete sentence is its truth value, while the sense of a sentence is the proposition it expresses.

3.1 Solution to the problem of substitutivity

Armed with senses and the principles of compositionality, plus an additional assumption that we will get to shortly, Frege was able to solve most, though not all, of the problems pointed out above.

3.1.1 Identity sentences

First, for the problem of failure of substitutivity of coreferential NPs in identity statements Frege presents a simple solution. Recall example (1) repeated here.

(1) a. The morning star is the morning star.
　　b. The morning star is the evening star.

Although *the morning star* and *the evening star* have the same reference (making (1b) a true sentence), the two NPs differ in sense. Thus (1b) has a different sense from (1a) and so we can account for the difference in cognitive impact.

3.1.2 Propositional attitude sentences

Turning to the problem of substitutivity in propositional attitude contexts, Frege again offers us a solution, although the story is a bit more complicated in this case. Here are the examples from (2) above.

(2) a. Mary knows that the morning star is a planet.
　　b. Mary knows that the evening star is a planet.

Simply observing that *the evening star* has a different sense from *the morning star* will account for why (2b) has a different sense from (2a), but by itself does not yet account for the possible change in truth value. This is where the extra piece of machinery mentioned above comes in. Frege pointed out that expressions can sometimes shift their reference in particular contexts. When we quote expressions, for example, those expressions no longer have their customary reference, but instead refer to themselves. Consider the example in (5)

(5) "The evening star" is a definite description.

The phrase *the evening star* as it occurs in (5) does not refer to the planet Venus any more, but instead refers to itself. Frege argued that a similar phenomenon occurs in propositional attitude contexts. In such contexts, Frege argued, expressions also shift their reference, but here they refer to their customary sense. This means that the reference of (2a) (its truth value) involves the customary sense of the phrase *the morning star* rather than its customary reference, while the reference/truth value of (2b) involves instead the customary sense of the phrase *the evening star*. Since we have two different components, it is not unexpected that we could have two different references – truth values – for the two sentences.

3.2 Empty NPs

NPs that have no reference were the other main problem area for the direct reference theory. One problem was the apparent meaningfulness of sentences containing such NPs. It is easy to see how Frege's theory solved this problem. As long as such NPs have a sense, the sentences containing them can have a well-formed sense as well, so their meaningfulness is not a problem. We should note, though, that Frege's theory predicts that such sentences will not have a truth value. That is because the truth value, as we have noted, is determined by the references of the constituent expressions in a sentence, and if one of those expressions doesn't have a reference then the whole sentence will not have one either. This means that true negative existential sentences, such as (4) repeated here:

(4) The round square does not exist.

remain a problem for Frege. Since the subject does not have a reference, the whole sentence should not have a truth value, but it does.

3.3 Further comments on Frege's work

Several further points concerning Frege's work will be relevant in what follows.

3.3.1 Presupposition

As we have just observed, Frege's principle of compositionality at the level of reference, together with his conclusion that the reference of a sentence is its truth value, means that a sentence containing an empty NP will fail to have a truth value. Frege held that the use of an NP involves a presupposition, rather than an assertion, that the NP in question has a reference. (see article 14 [Semantics: Interfaces] (Beaver & Geurts) *Presupposition*.) Concerning example (6)

(6) The one who discovered the elliptical shape of the planetary orbits died in misery.

Frege said that if one were to hold that part of what one asserts in the use of (6) is that there is a person who discovered the elliptical shape of the planetary orbits, then one would have to say that the denial of (6) is (7).

(7) Either the one who discovered the elliptical shape of the planetary orbits did not die in misery, or no one discovered the elliptical shape of the planetary orbits.

But the denial of (6) is not (7) but rather simply (8).

(8) The one who discovered the elliptical shape of the planetary orbits did not die in misery.

Instead, both (6) and (8) presuppose that the definite description *the one who discovered the elliptical shape of the planetary orbits* has a reference, and if the NP were not to have a reference, then neither sentence would have a truth value.

3.3.2 Proper names

It was mentioned briefly above that Mill's views were very similar to Frege's in holding that referring expressions have two kinds of semantic significance – both sense and reference, or in Mill's terms, connotation and denotation. Mill, however, made an exception for proper names, which he believed did not have connotation but only denotation. Frege appeared to differ from Mill on that point. We can see that, given Frege's principle of compositionality of sense, it would be important for him to hold that proper names do have a sense, since sentences containing them can clearly have a sense, i.e. express a proposition. His most famous comments on the subject occur in a footnote to "On sense and reference" in which he appeared to suggest that proper names have a sense which is similar to the sense which a definite description might have, but which might vary from person to person. The name Aristotle, he seemed to suggest, could mean 'the pupil of Plato and teacher of Alexander the Great' for one person, but 'the teacher of Alexander the Great who was born in Stagira' for another person (Frege 1892, fn. 2).

3.3.3 Propositions

According to Frege, the sense of a sentence is the proposition it expresses, but it has been very difficult to determine what propositions are. Frege used the German word "Gedanke" ('thought'), and as we have seen, for Frege (as for many others) propositions are not only what sentences express, they are also the objects of propositional attitudes. Subsequent formalizations of Frege's ideas have used the concept of possible worlds to analyze them. Possible worlds are simply alternative ways things (in the broadest sense) might have been. E.g. I am sitting in my office at this moment, but I might instead have gone out for a walk; there might have been only 7 planets in our solar system, instead of 8 or 9. Using this notion, propositions were analyzed as functions from possible worlds to truth values (or equivalently, as sets of possible worlds). This meshes nicely with the idea that the sense of a sentence combined with facts about the way things are (a possible world) determine a truth value. However there are problems with this view; for example, all mathematical truths are necessarily true, and thus true in every possible world, but the sentences expressing them do not seem to have the same meaning (in some pre-theoretic sense of meaning), and it seems that one can know the truth of one without knowing the truth of all of them – e.g. someone could know that two plus two is four, but not know that there are an infinite number of primes. (For continued defense of the possible worlds view of the objects of thought, see Stalnaker 1984, 1999.) Following Carnap (1956), David Lewis (1972) suggested that sentence meanings are best viewed as entities with syntactic structure, whose elements are the senses (intensions) of the constituent expressions. We will see an additional proposal concerning what at least some propositions are shortly, in section 4 on Russell.

3.4 Summary comments on Frege

Frege's work was neglected for some time, both within and outside Germany. Eventually it received the attention it deserved, especially during the development of formal semantic treatments of natural language by Carnap, Kripke, Montague, and others (see article 10 [this volume] (Newen & Schröder) *Logic and semantics*), (see article 11 [this volume] (Kempson) *Formal semantics and representationalism*). Although the distinction between sense and reference (or intension and extension) is commonly accepted, Frege's analysis of propositional attitude contexts has fallen out of favor; Donald Davidson has famously declared Frege's theory of a shift of reference in propositional attitude contexts to be "plainly incredible" (Davidson 1968/1984: 108), and many others seem to have come to the same conclusion.

4 Reference vs. quantification and Russell's theory of descriptions

In his classic 1905 paper "On denoting", Bertrand Russell proposed an alternative to Frege's theory of sense and reference. To understand Russell's work it helps to know that he was fundamentally concerned with knowledge. He distinguished knowledge by acquaintance, which is knowledge we gain directly via perception, from knowledge by description (cf. Russell 1917), and he sought to analyze the latter in terms of the former. Russell was a direct reference theorist, and rejected Frege's postulation of senses (though he did accept properties, or universals, as the semantic content of predicative expressions). The only genuine referring expressions, for Russell, were those that could guarantee a referent, and the propositions expressed by sentences containing such expressions are singular propositions, which contain actual entities. If I were to point at Mary, and utter (9a), I would be expressing the singular proposition represented in (9b).

(9) a. She is happy.
    b. <Mary, happiness>

Note that the first element of (9b) is not the name Mary, but Mary herself. Any NP which is unable to guarantee a referent cannot contribute an entity to a singular proposition. Russell's achievement in "On denoting" was to show how such NPs could be analyzed away into the expression of general, quantificational propositions.

4.1 Quantification

In traditional predicate logic, overtly quantificational NPs like *every book, no chair* do not have an analysis per se, but only in the context of a complete sentence. (In logics with generalized quantifiers, developed more recently, this is not the case; (see article 4 [Semantics: Noun Phrases and Verb Phrases] (Keenan) *Quantifiers*.) Look at the examples in (10) and (11).

(10) a. Every book is blue.
     b. $\forall x[book(x) \supset blue(x)]$

(11) a. No table is sturdy.
     b. $\sim\exists x[table(x) \& sturdy(x)]$

(10b), the traditional logical analysis of (10a), says (when translated back into English) *For every x, if x is a book then x is blue*. We can see that *every*, the quantificational element in (10a), has been elevated to the sentence level, in effect, so that it expresses a relationship between two properties – the property of being a book and the property of being blue. Similarly (11b) says, roughly, *It is not the case that there is an x such that x is a table and x is sturdy*. It can be seen that this has the same truth conditions as *No table is sturdy*, and once again the quantificational element (*no* in this case) has been analyzed as expressing a relation between two properties, in this case the properties of being a table and being sturdy.

4.2 Russell's analysis of definite descriptions

Russell's analysis of definite descriptions was called "the paradigm of philosophy" (by Frank Ramsey), and if analysis is the heart of philosophy then indeed it is that. One of the examples Russell took to illustrate his method is given in (12a), and its analysis is in (12b).

(12) a. The present king of France is bald.
 b. $\exists x[\text{king-of-France}(x) \, \& \, \forall y[\text{king-of-France}(y) \supset y=x] \, \& \, \text{bald}(x)]$

The analysis in (12b) translates loosely into the three propositions expressed by the sentences in (13).

(13) a. There is a king of France.
 b. There is at most one king of France.
 c. He is bald.

(*He*, in (13c) must be understood as bound by the initial *There is a...* in (13a).) As can be seen, the analysis in (12b) contains no constituent that corresponds to *the present king of France*. Instead *the* is analyzed as expressing a complex relation between the properties of being king of France and being bald. Let us look now at how Russell's analysis solves the problems for the direct reference theory.

4.3 Failure of substitutivity

4.3.1 Identity sentences

Although Russell was a direct reference theorist, we can see that, under his analysis, English definite descriptions have more to contribute to the sentences in which they occur than simply their reference. In fact they no longer contribute their reference at all (because they are no longer referring expressions, and do not have a reference). Instead they contribute the properties expressed by each of the predicates occurring in the description. It follows that two different definite descriptions, such as *the morning star* and *the evening star*, will make two different contributions to their containing sentences. And thus it is no mystery why the two identity sentences from (1) above, repeated here in (14), have different cognitive impact.

(14) a. The morning star is the morning star.
b. The morning star is the evening star.

The meaning of the second sentence involves the property of being seen in the evening as well as that of being seen in the morning.

4.3.2 Propositional attitude sentences

When we come to propositional attitude sentences the story is a little more complicated. Recall that Russell's analysis does not apply to a definite description by itself, but only in the context of a sentence. It follows that when a definite description occurs in an embedded sentence, as in the case of propositional attitude sentences, there will be two ways to unpack it according to the analysis. Thus Russell predicts that such sentences are ambiguous. Consider our example from above, repeated here as (15).

(15) Mary knows that the morning star is a planet.

According to Russell's analysis we may unpack the phrase *the morning star* with respect to either *the morning star is a planet* or *Mary knows that the morning star is a planet*. The respective results are given in (16).

(16) a. Mary knows that $\exists x[\text{morning star}(x)\ \&\ \forall y[\text{morning star}(y) \supset y=x]\ \&\ \text{planet}(x)]$
b. $\exists x[\text{morning star}(x)\ \&\ \forall y[\text{morning star}(y) \supset y=x]\ \&\ \text{Mary knows that planet}(x)]$

The unpacking in (16a) is what is called the *narrow scope* or *de dicto* (roughly, about the words) interpretation of (15). The proposition that Mary is said to know involves he semantic content that the object in question is the star seen in the morning. The unpacking in (16b) is called the *wide scope* or *de re* (roughly, about the thing) interpretation of (15). It attributes to Mary knowledge concerning a certain entity, but not under any particular description of that entity. The short answer to the question of how Russell's analysis solves the problem of failure of substitutivity in propositional attitude contexts is that, since there are no referring constituents in the sentence after its analysis, there is nothing to substitute anything for. However Russell acknowledged that one could, in English, make a verbal substitution of one definite description for a coreferential one, but only on the wide scope, or *de re* interpretation. If we consider a slightly more dramatic example than (15), we can see that there seems to be some foundation for Russell's prediction of ambiguity for propositional attitude sentences. Observe (17):

(17) Oedipus wanted to marry his mother.

Our first reaction to this sentence is probably to think that it is false – after all, when Oedipus found out that he had married his mother, he was very upset. This reaction is to the narrow scope, or *de dicto* reading of the sentence which attributes to Oedipus a desire which involves being married to specifically his mother and which is false. However there is another way to take the sentence according to which it seems to be true: there was a woman, Jocasta, who happened to be Oedipus's mother and whom he wanted to marry. This second interpretation is the wide scope, or *de re*, reading of (17), according to which Oedipus has a desire concerning a particular individual, but where the individual is not identified for the purposes of the desire itself by any description.

4.4 Empty NPs

Recall our initial illustration of Russell's analysis of definite descriptions, repeated here.

(18) a. The present king of France is bald.
  b. $\exists x[\text{king-of-France}(x) \& \forall y[\text{king-of-France}(y) \supset y=x] \& \text{bald}(x)]$

The example shows Russell's solution to the problem of empty NPs. While for Frege such sentences have a failed presupposition and lack a truth value, under Russell's analysis they assert the existence of the entity in question, and are therefore simply false. Furthermore Russell's analysis of definite descriptions solves the more pressing problem of empty NPs in existence sentences. Under his analysis *The round square does not exist* would be analyzed as in (19)

(19) $\sim\exists x[\text{round}(x) \& \text{square}(x) \& \forall y[[\text{round}(y) \& \text{square}(y)] \supset y=x]]$

which is meaningful and true.

4.5 Proper names

Russell's view of proper names was very similar to Frege's view; he held that they are abbreviations for definite descriptions (which might vary from person to person) and thus that they have semantic content in addition to, or more properly in lieu of, a reference (cf. Russell 1917).

4.6 Referring and denoting

As we have seen, for Russell, definite descriptions are not referring expressions, though he did describe them as denoting. For Russell almost any NP is a denoting phrase, including, e.g. *every hat* and *nobody*. One might ask what, if any, expressions were genuine referring expressions for Russell. Ultimately he held that only a demonstrative like *this*, used demonstratively, would meet the criterion, since only such an expression could guarantee a referent. These were the only true proper names, in his view. (See Russell 1917: 216 and fn. 5.) It seems clear that we often use language to convey information about individual entities; if Russell's analysis is correct, it means that the propositions containing that information must almost always be inferred rather than being directly expressed. Russell's analysis of definite descriptions (though not of proper names) has been defended at length by Neale (1990).

5 Strawson's objections to Russell

Russell's paper "On Denoting" stood without opposition for close to 50 years, but in 1950 P.F. Strawson's classic reply "On Referring" appeared. Strawson had two major objections to Russell's analysis – his neglect of the indexicality of definite descriptions like *the king of France*, and his claim that sentences with definite descriptions in them were used to assert the existence of a reference for the description. Let us look at each of these more closely.

5.1 Indexicality

Indexical expressions are those whose reference depends in part on aspects of the utterance context, and thus may vary depending on context. Obvious examples are pronouns like *I* and *you*, and adverbs like *here*, and *yesterday*. Such expressions make vivid the difference between a sentence and the use of a sentence to make a statement – a difference which may be ignored for logical purposes (given that mathematical truths are non-indexical) but whose importance in natural language was stressed by Strawson. Strawson pointed out that a definite description like *the king of France* could have been used at different past times to refer to different people – Louis XV in 1750, but Louis XVI in 1770, for example. Hence he held that it was a mistake to speak of expressions as referring; instead we can only speak of using an expression to refer on a particular occasion. This is the pragmatic view of reference that was mentioned at the outset of this article. Russell lived long enough to publish a rather tart response, "Mr. Strawson on referring", in which he pointed out that the problem of indexicality was independent of the problems of reference which were his main concern in "On denoting". However indexicality does raise interesting and relevant issues, and we return to it below, in section 7. (see article 17 [Semantics: Noun Phrases and Verb Phrases] (Schlenker) *Indexicality and de se*.)

5.2 Empty NPs and presupposition

The remainder of Strawson's paper was primarily concerned with arguing that Russell's analysis of definite descriptions was wrong in its implication that sentences containing them would be used to assert the existence (and uniqueness) of entities meeting their descriptive content. Instead, he said, a person using such a sentence would only imply "in a special sense of 'imply' " (Strawson 1950: 330) that such an entity exists. (Two years later he introduced the term *presuppose* for this special sense of *imply*, Strawson 1952: 175.) And in cases where there is no such entity – that is for sentences with empty NPs, like *The king of France is bald* as uttered in 1950 – one could not make either a true or a false statement. The question of truth or falsity, in such cases, simply does not arise. (see article 14 [Semantics: Interfaces] (Beaver & Geurts) *Presupposition*.) We can see that Strawson's position on empty NPs is very much the same as Frege's, although Strawson did not appear to be familiar with Frege's work on the subject.

6 Donnellan's attributive-referential distinction

In 1966 Keith Donnellan challenged Russell's theory of definite descriptions, as well as Strawson's commentary on that theory. He argued that both Russell and Strawson had failed to notice that there are two distinct uses of definite descriptions.

6.1 The basic distinction

When one uses a description in the *attributive* way in an assertion, one "states something about whoever or whatever is the so-and-so" (Donnellan 1966: 285). This use corresponds pretty well to Russell's theory, and in this case, the description is an essential part of the thought being expressed. The main novelty was Donnellan's claim of a distinct *referential* use of definite descriptions. Here one "uses the description to enable his audience to pick out whom or what he is talking about and states something about that person or thing" (Donnellan 1966: 285). In this case the description used is simply a device for getting one's addressee to recognize whom or what one is talking about, and is not an essential part of the utterance. Donnellan used the example in (20) to illustrate his distinction.

(20) Smith's murderer is insane.

For an example of the attributive use, imagine the police detective at a gruesome crime scene, thinking that whoever could have murdered dear old Smith in such a brutal way would have to have been insane. For a referential use, we might imagine that Jones has been charged with the murder and that everybody is pretty sure he is the guilty party. He behaves very strangely during the trial, and an onlooker utters (20) by way of predicating insanity of Jones. The two uses involve different presuppositions: on the attributive use there is a presupposition that the description has a reference (or denotation in Russell's terms), but on the referential use the speaker presupposes more specifically of a particular entity (Jones, in our example) that it is the one meeting the description. Note though, that a speaker can know who or what a definite description denotes and still use that description attributively. For example I might be well acquainted with the dean of my college, but when I advise my student, who has a grievance against the chair of the department, by asserting (21),

(21) Take this issue to the dean of the college.

I use the phrase *the dean of the college* attributively. I mean to convey the thought that the dean's office is the one appropriate for the issue, regardless of who happens to be dean at the current time.

6.2 Contentious issues

While it is generally agreed that an attributive-referential distinction exists, there have been several points of dispute. The most crucial one is the status of the distinction – whether it is semantic or pragmatic (something about which Donnellan himself seemed unsure).

6.2.1 A pragmatic analysis

Donnellan had claimed that, on the referential use, a speaker can succeed in referring to an entity which does not meet the description used, and can make a true statement in so doing. The speaker who used (20) referentially to make a claim about Jones, for instance, would have said something true if Jones was indeed insane whether or not he murdered Smith. Kripke (1977) used this aspect to argue that Donnellan's distinction is nothing more than the difference between speaker's reference (the referential use) and semantic reference (the attributive use). He pointed out that similar kinds of misuses or errors can arise with proper names, for which Donnellan's distinction, if viewed as semantic, could not be invoked (see below, section 8). Kripke argued further that since the same kind of attributive-referential difference in use of definite descriptions would arise in a language stipulated to be Russellian – that is, in which the only interpretation for definite descriptions was that proposed by Russell in "On denoting" – the fact that it occurs in English does not argue that English is not Russellian, and thus does not argue that the distinction is semantic. (See Reimer 1998 for a reply.)

6.2.2 A semantic analysis

On the other hand David Kaplan (1978) (among others, but cf. Salmon 2004) noted the similarity of Donnellan's distinction to the *de dicto/de re* ambiguity which occurs in propositional attitude sentences. Kaplan suggested an analysis on which referential uses are involved in the expression of Russellian singular propositions. Suppose Jones is Smith's murderer; then the referential use of (20) expresses the singular proposition consisting of Jones himself plus the property of being insane. (In suggesting this analysis Kaplan was rejecting Donnellan's claim about the possibility of making true statements about misdescribed entities. Others have also adopted this revised view of the referential use, e.g. Wettstein 1983, Reimer 1998.) Kaplan's analysis of the referential understanding is similar to the analysis of the complement of a propositional attitude verb when it is interpreted *de re*, while the ordinary Russellian analysis seems to match the analysis of the complement interpreted *de dicto*. However the two understandings of a sentence like (20), without a propositional attitude predicate, always have the same truth value while, as we have seen, in the context of a sentence about someone's propositional attitude, the two interpretations can result in a difference in truth value. In explaining his analysis, Kaplan likened the referential use of definite descriptions to demonstrative NPs. This brings us back to the topic of indexicality.

7 Kaplan's theory of indexicality

A major contribution to our understanding of reference and indexicality came with Kaplan's (1989) classic, but mistitled, article "Demonstratives". The title should have been "Indexicals". Acknowledging the error, Kaplan distinguished pure indexicals like *I* and *tomorrow*, which do not require an accompanying indication of the intended reference, from demonstrative indexicals, e.g. *this*, *that book*, whose uses do require such an indication (or demonstration, as Kaplan dubbed it). The paper itself was equally concerned with both subcategories.

7.1 Content vs. character

The most important contribution of Kaplan's paper was his distinction between two elements of meaning – the content of an expression and its character.

7.1.1 Content

The content of the utterance of a sentence is the proposition it expresses. Assuming compositionality, this content is determined by the contents of the expressions which go to make up the uttered sentence. The existence of indexicals means that the content of an utterance is not determined simply by the expressions in it, but also by the context of utterance. Thus different utterances of, e.g., (22)

(22) I like that.

will determine different propositions depending who is speaking, the time they are speaking, and what they are pointing at or otherwise indicating, and would vary depending on these parameters. In each case the proposition involved would be, on Kaplan's view (following Russell), a singular proposition.

7.1.2 Character

Although on Kaplan's view the contribution of indexicals to propositional content is limited to their reference, they do have a meaning: *I*, for example, has a meaning involving the concept of being the speaker. These latter types of linguistically encoded meaning are what Kaplan referred to as "character". In general, the character of an expression is a function which, given a context of utterance, returns the content of that expression in that context. In a way Kaplan is showing that Frege's concept of sense actually needs to be subdivided into these two elements of character and content. (Cf. Kaplan 1989, fn. 26.)

7.2 An application of the distinction

Indexicals, both pure and demonstrative, have a variable character – their character determines different contents in different contexts of utterance. However the content so determined is constant (an actual entity, on Kaplan's view). Using the distinction between character and content, Kaplan is able to explain why (23)

(23) I am here now.

is in a sense necessary, but in another sense contingent. Its character is such that anyone uttering (23) would be making a true statement, but the content determined on any such occasion would be a contingent proposition. For instance if I were to utter (23) now, my utterance would determine the singular proposition containing me, my office; 2:50 pm on January 18, 2007; and the relation of being which relates an entity, a place, and a time. That proposition is true at the actual world, but false in many others.

7.3 The problem of the essential indexical

Perry (1979), following Castañeda (1968), pointed out that indexicality seems to pose a special problem in propositional attitude sentences. Suppose Mary, a ballet dancer, has an accident resulting in amnesia. She sees a film of herself dancing, but does not recognize herself. As a result of seeing the film she comes to believe, *de re*, of the person in the film (i.e. herself) that that person is a good dancer. Still she lacks the knowledge that it is she herself who is a good dancer. As of now we have no way of representing this missing piece of knowledge. Perry proposed recognizing belief states, in addition to the propositions which are the objects of belief, in order to solve this problem; Mary grasps the proposition, but does not grasp it in the first person way. Lewis (1979) proposed instead viewing belief as attribution to oneself of a property; he termed this "belief *de se*". Belief concerning a nonindexical proposition would then be self-attribution of the property of belonging to a possible world where that proposition was true. Mary has the latter kind of belief with respect to the proposition that she is a good dancer, but does not (yet) attribute to herself good dancing capability.

7.4 Other kinds of NP

As we have seen, Strawson pointed out that some definite descriptions which would not ordinarily be thought of as indexical can have an element of indexicality to them. An indexical definite description like *the (present) king of France* would, on Kaplan's analysis, have both variable character and variable content. As uttered in 1770, for example, it would yield a function whose value in any possible world is whoever is king of France in 1770. That would be Louis XVI in the actual world, but other individuals in other worlds depending on contingent facts about French history. As uttered in 1950 the definite description has no reference in the actual world, but does in other possible worlds (since it is not a necessary fact that France is a republic and not a monarchy in 1950 – the French Revolution might have failed). A nonindexical definite description like *the inventor of bifocals* has a constant character but variable content. That is, in any context of utterance its content is the function from possible worlds that picks out whoever it is who invented bifocals in that world. For examples of NPs with constant character and constant content, we must turn to the category of proper names.

8 Proper names and Kripke's return to Millian nondescriptionality

It may be said that in asserting that proper names have denotation without connotation, Mill captured our ordinary pre-theoretic intuition. That is, it seems intuitively clear that proper names do not incorporate or express any properties like having taught Alexander the Great or having invented bifocals. On the other hand we can also understand why both Frege and Russell would be driven to the view that, despite this intuition, they do express some kind of property. That is because the alternative would be the direct reference, or *Fido*-Fido view, and the two kinds of problems that we saw arising for that view arise for proper names as well as definite descriptions. Thus identity sentences of the form $a = b$ are informative with proper names as they are with definite descriptions, as exemplified in (24).

(24) a. Mark Twain is Mark Twain.
b. Samuel Clemens is Mark Twain.

Intuitively (24b) conveys information over and above that conveyed by (24a). Similarly exchanging co-referential proper names in propositional attitude sentences can seem to change truth value.

(25) a. Mary knows that Mark Twain wrote *Tom Sawyer*.
b. Mary knows that Samuel Clemens wrote *Tom Sawyer*.

We can well imagine someone named Mary for whom (25a) would be true yet for whom (25b) would seem false. Furthermore there are many proper names which are non-referential, and for which negative identity sentences like (26) would seem true and not meaningless.

(26) Santa Claus does not exist.

If proper names have a sense, or are otherwise equivalent to definite descriptions, then some or all of these problems are solved. Thus it was an important development when Kripke argued for a return to Mill's view on proper names. But before we get to that, we should briefly review a kind of weakened description view of proper names.

8.1 The 'cluster' view

Both Wittgenstein (1953) and Searle (1958) argued for a view of proper names according to which they are associated semantically with a cluster of descriptions – something like a disjunction of properties commonly associated with the bearer of the name. Wittgenstein's example used the name *Moses*, and he suggested that there is a variety of descriptions, such as "the man who led the Israelites through the wilderness", "the man who as a child was taken out of the Nile by Pharaoh's daughter", which may give meaning to the name or support its use (Wittgenstein 1953, §79). No single description is assumed to give the meaning of the name. However, as Searle noted, on this view it would be necessarily true that Moses had at least one of the properties commonly attributed to him (Searle 1958: 172).

8.2 The return to Mill's view

In January of 1970 Saul Kripke gave an important series of lectures titled "Naming and necessity" which were published in an anthology in 1972 and in 1980 reissued as a book. In these lectures Kripke argued against both the Russell-Frege view of proper names as abbreviated definite descriptions and the Wittgenstein-Searle view of proper names as associated semantically with a cluster of descriptions, and in favor of a return to Mill's nondescriptional view of proper names. Others had come to the same conclusion (e.g. Marcus 1961, Donnellan 1972), but Kripke's defense of the nondescriptional view was the most thorough and influential. The heart of Kripke's argument depends on intuitions about the reference of expressions in alternative possible worlds. These intuitions indicate a clear difference in behavior between proper names and definite descriptions. A definite description like *the student of Plato who taught Alexander the Great* refers to Aristotle in the actual world, but had circumstances been different – had Xenocrates rather than Aristotle taught Alexander the Great – then *the student of Plato who taught Alexander the Great* would refer to Xenocrates, and not to Aristotle. Proper names, on the other hand, do not vary their reference from world to world. Kripke dubbed them "rigid designators". Thus sentences like (27) seem true to us.

(27) Aristotle might not have taught Alexander the Great.

Furthermore, Kripke pointed out, a sentence like (27) would be true no matter what contingent property description is substituted for the predicate. In fact something like (28) seems to be true:

(28) Aristotle might have had none of the properties commonly attributed to him.

But the truth of (28) seems inconsistent with both the Frege-Russell definite description view of proper names and the Wittgenstein-Searle cluster view. On the other hand a sentence like (29) seems false.

(29) Aristotle might not have been Aristotle.

This supports Kripke's claim of rigid designation for proper names; since the name *Aristotle* must designate the same individual in any possible world, there is no possible world in which that individual is not Aristotle. And thus, to put things in Kaplan's terms, proper names have both constant character and constant content.

8.3 Natural kind terms

Although it goes beyond our focus on NPs, it is worth mentioning that Kripke extended his theory of nondescriptionality to at least some common nouns – those naming species of plants or animals, like *elm* and *tiger*, as well as those for well-defined naturally occurring substances or phenomena, such as *gold* and *heat*, and some adjectives like *loud*, and *red*. In this Kripke's views differed from Mill, but were quite similar to those put forward by Putnam (1975). Putnam's most famous thought experiment involved imagining a "twin earth" which is identical to our earth except that the clear, colorless, odorless substance which falls from the sky as rain and fills the lakes and rivers, and which is called *water* by twin-English speaking twin earthlings, is not H_2O but instead a complex compound whose chemical formula Putnam abbreviates XYZ. Putnam argues that although $Oscar_1$ on earth and $Oscar_2$ on twin earth are exactly the same mentally when they think "I would like a glass of water", nevertheless the contents of their thoughts are different. His famous conclusion: " 'Meanings' just ain't in the *head*" (Putnam 1975: 227; see Segal 2000 for an opposing view.)

8.4 Summary

Let us take stock of the situation. We saw that the simplest theory of reference, the *Fido*-Fido or direct reference theory, had problems with accounting for the apparent semantic inequivalence of coreferential NPs – the fact that true identity statements could be informative, and that exchanging coreferential NPs in propositional attitude contexts could even result in a change in truth value. This theory also had a problem with non-referring or empty NPs, a problem which became particularly acute in the case of true negative existence statements. Frege's theory of sense seemed to solve most of these problems, and Russell's analysis of definite descriptions seemed to solve all of them. However, though the theories of Frege and Russell are plausible for definite descriptions, as Kripke made clear they do not seem to work well for proper names, for which the direct reference theory is much more plausible. But the same two groups of problems – those involving co-referential NPs and those involving empty NPs – arise for proper names just as they do for definite descriptions. Of these problems, the one involving substituting coreferential NPs in propositional attitude contexts has attracted the most attention. (see article 16 [Semantics: Noun Phrases and Verb Phrases] (Swanson) *Propositional attitudes*.)

9 Propositional attitude contexts

Kripke's arguments for a return to Mill's view of proper names have generally been found to be convincing (although exceptions will be noted below). This appears to leave us with the failure of substitutivity of coreferential names in propositional attitude contexts. However Kripke (1979) argued that the problem was not actually one of substitutivity, but a more fundamental problem in the attribution of propositional attitudes.

9.1 The Pierre and Peter puzzles

Kripke's initial example involved a young Frenchman, Pierre, who when young came to believe on the basis of postcards and other indirect evidence that London was a beautiful city. He would sincerely assert (30) whenever asked.

(30) Londres et jolie.

Eventually, however, he was kidnapped and transported to a very bad section of London, and learned English by the direct method. His circumstances did not allow him to explore the city (which he did not associate with the city he knew as *Londres*), and thus based on his part of town, he would assert (31).

(31) London is not pretty.

The question Kripke presses us to answer is that posed in (32):

(32) Does Pierre, or does he not, believe that London is pretty?

An alternative, monolingual, version of the puzzle involves Peter, who has heard of Paderewski the pianist, and Paderewski the Polish statesman, but who does not know that they were the same person and who is furthermore inclined to believe that anyone musically inclined would never go into politics. The question is (33):

(33) Does Peter, or does he not, believe that Paderewski had musical talent?

Kripke seems to indicate that these questions do not have answers: "...our normal practices of interpretation and attribution of belief are subjected to the greatest possible strain, perhaps to the point of breakdown. So is the notion of the *content* of someone's assertion, the *proposition* it expresses" (Kripke 1979: 269; italics in original). Others, however, have not been deterred from answering Kripke's questions in (32) and (33).

9.2 Proposed solutions

Many solutions to the problem of propositional attitude attribution have been proposed. We will look here at several of the more common kinds of approaches.

9.2.1 Metalinguistic approaches

Metalinguistic approaches to the problem involve linguistic expressions as components of belief in one way or another. Quine (1956) had suggested the possibility of viewing propositional attitudes as relations to sentences rather than propositions. This would solve the problem of Pierre, but would seem to leave Peter's problem, given that we have a single name *Paderewski* in English (but see Fiengo & May 1998). Others (Bach 1987, Katz 2001) have put forward metalinguistic theories of proper names, rejecting Kripke's arguments for their nondescriptionality. The idea here is that a name N means something like "the bearer of *N*". This again would seem to solve the Pierre puzzle (Pierre believes that the bearer of *Londres* is pretty, but not the bearer of *London*), but not Peter's Paderewski problem. Bach argues that (33) would need contextual supplementation to be a complete question about Peter's beliefs (see Bach 1987: 165ff).

9.2.2 Hidden indexical theories

The remaining two groups of theories are consistent with Kripke's nondescriptional analysis of proper names. Hidden indexical theories involve postulating an unmentioned (or hidden) element in belief attributions, which is "a mode of presentation" of the proposition, belief in which is being attributed. (Cf. Schiffer 1992, Crimmins & Perry 1989.) Thus belief is viewed as a three-place relation, involving a believer, a proposition believed, and a mode of presentation of that proposition. Furthermore these modes of presentation are like indexicals in that different ones may be invoked in different contexts of utterance. The answer to (32) or (33) could be either Yes or No, depending upon which kind of mode of presentation was understood. The approach of Richard (1990) is similar, except that the third element is intended as a translation of a mental representation of the subject of the propositional attitude verb.

9.2.3 Pragmatic theories

Our third kind of approach is similar to the hidden indexical theories in recognizing modes of presentation. However the verb *believe* (like other propositional attitude verbs) is seen as expressing a two-place relation between a believer and a proposition, and no particular mode of presentation is entailed. Instead, this relation is defined in such a way as to entail only that there is at least one mode of presentation under which the proposition in question is believed. (Cf. Salmon 1986.) This kind of theory would answer either (32) or (33) with a simple Yes since there is at least one mode of presentation under which Pierre believes that London is pretty, and at least one under which Peter believes that Paderewski had musical talent. A pragmatic explanation is offered for our tendency to answer *No* to (32) on the basis of Pierre's English assertion *London is not pretty*.

10 Indefinite descriptions

We turn now to indefinite descriptions – NPs which in English begin with the indefinite article *a/an*.

10.1 Indefinite descriptions are not referring expressions

As we saw above, Russell did not view definite descriptions as referring expressions, so it will come as no surprise that he was even more emphatic about indefinite descriptions. He had several arguments for this view (cf. Russell 1919: 167ff). Consider his example in (34).

(34) I met a man.

Suppose that the speaker of (34) had met Mr. Jones, and that that meeting constituted her grounds for uttering (34). In that case, were *a man* referential, it would have to refer to Mr. Jones. Nevertheless someone who did not know Jones at all could easily have a full understanding of (34). And were the speaker of (34) to add (35) to her utterance

(35) ...but it wasn't Jones.

she would not be contradicting herself (though of course she would be lying, under the circumstances). On the other hand if it should turn out that the speaker of (34) did not meet Jones after all, but did meet some other man, it would be very hard to regard (34) as false. Russell's arguments have been reiterated and augmented by Ludlow & Neale (1991).

10.2 Indefinite descriptions are referring expressions

Since Russell's time others (e.g. Strawson 1952) have argued that indefinite descriptions do indeed have referring uses. The clearest kinds of cases are ones in which chains of reference occur, as in (36) (from Chastain 1975: 202).

(36) A man was sitting underneath a tree eating peanuts. A squirrel came by, and the man fed it some peanuts.

Both *a man* and *a squirrel* in (36) seem to be coreferential with subsequent expressions that many people would consider to be referring – if not *the man*, then at least *it*. Chastain argues that there is no reason to deny referentiality to the indefinite NPs which initiate such chains of reference, and that indeed, that is where the subsequent expressions acquired their referents. It should be noted, though, that if serving as antecedent for one or more pronouns is considered adequate evidence for referentiality, then overtly quantificational NPs should also be considered referential, as shown in (37).

(37) a. Everybody who came to my party had a good time. They all thanked me afterward.
b. Most people don't like apples. They only eat them for their health.

10.3 Parallels between indefinite and definite descriptions

Another relevant consideration is the fact that indefinite descriptions seem to parallel definite descriptions in several ways. They show an ambiguity similar to the *de dicto-de re* ambiguity in propositional attitude contexts, as shown in (38).

(38) Mary wants to interview a diplomat.

(38) could mean either that there is a particular diplomat whom Mary is planning to interview (where *a diplomat* has wide scope corresponding to the *de re* reading for definite descriptions), or that she wants to interview some diplomat or other – say to boost the prestige of her newspaper. (This reading, where *a diplomat* has narrow scope with respect to the verb *wants*, corresponds to the *de dicto* reading of definite descriptions.) Neither of these readings entails the other – either could be true while the other is false. Furthermore indefinite descriptions participate in a duality of usage, the specific-nonspecific ambiguity (see article 3 [Semantics: Noun Phrases and Verb Phrases] (von Heusinger) *Specificity*), which is very similar to Donnellan's referential-attributive ambiguity for definite descriptions. Thus while the indefinites in Chastain's example above are most naturally taken specifically, the indefinite in (39) must be taken nonspecifically unless something further is added (since otherwise the request would be infelicitous).

(39) Please hand me a pencil.

(See also Fodor & Sag 1982.) In casual speech specific uses of indefinite descriptions can be unambiguously paraphrased using non-demonstrative *this*, as in (40).

(40) This man was sitting underneath a tree eating peanuts.

However non-demonstrative *this* cannot be substituted for the non-specific *a* in (39) without causing anomaly. So if at least some occurrences of definite descriptions are viewed as referential, these parallels provide an argument that the corresponding occurrences of indefinite descriptions should also be so viewed. (Devitt 2004 argues in favor of this conclusion.)

10.4 Discourse semantics

More recently approaches to semantics have been developed which provide an interpretation for sentences in succession, or discourses. Initially developed independently by Heim (1982) and Kamp (1981), these approaches treat both definite and indefinite descriptions as similar in some ways to quantificational terms and in some ways to referring expressions such as proper names. Indefinite descriptions introduce new discourse entities, and subsequent references, whether achieved with pronouns or with definite descriptions, add information about those entities. (see article 11 [Semantics: Theories] (Kamp & Reyle) Discourse *Representation Theory*), (see article 12 [Semantics: Theories] (Dekker) *Dynamic semantics*.)

10.5 Another puzzle about belief

We noted above that indefinite descriptions participate in scope ambiguities in propositional attitude contexts. The example below in (41) was introduced by Geach (1967), who argued that it raises a new problem of interpretation.

(41) Hob thinks a witch has blighted Bob's mare, and Nob wonders whether she (the same witch) killed Cob's sow.

Neither the ordinary wide scope or narrow scope interpretation is correct for (41). The wide scope interpretation (*there is a witch such that...*) would entail the existence of a witch, which does not seem to be required for the truth of (41). On the other hand the narrow scope interpretation (*Hob thinks that there is a witch such that...*) would fail to capture the identity between Hob's witch and Nob's witch. This problem, which Geach referred to as one of "intentional identity", like many others, has remained unsolved.

11 Summary

As we have seen, opinions concerning referentiality vary widely, from Russell's position on which almost no NPs are referential to a view on which almost any NP has at least some referential uses. The differences may seem inconsequential, but they are central to issues surrounding the relations among language, thought, and communication – issues such as the extent to which we can represent the propositional attitudes of others in our speech, and even the extent to which our own thoughts are encoded in the sentences we utter, as opposed to being inferred from hints provided by our utterances.

12 References

Bach, Kent 1987. *Thought and Reference*. Oxford: Oxford University Press.
Carnap, Rudolf 1956. *Meaning and Necessity: A Study in Semantics and Modal Logic*. 2nd edn. Chicago, IL: The University of Chicago Press.
Castañeda, Hector-Neri 1968. On the logic of attributions of self knowledge to others. *Journal of Philosophy* 65, 439–456.
Chastain, Charles 1975. Reference and context. In: K. Gunderson (ed.). *Minnesota Studies in the Philosophy of Science, vol. 7: Language Mind and Knowledge*. Minneapolis, MN: University of Minnesota Press, 194–269.

Crimmins, Mark & John Perry 1989. The prince and the phone booth. *Journal of Philosophy* 86, 685–711.
Davidson, Donald 1968. On saying that. *Synthese* 19, 130–146. Reprinted in: D. L. Davidson. *Inquiries into Truth and Interpretation*. Oxford: Clarendon Press, 1984, 93–108.
Devitt, Michael 2004. The case for referential descriptions. In: M. Reimer & A. Bezuidenhout (eds.). *Descriptions and Beyond*. Oxford: Clarendon Press, 280–305.
Donnellan, Keith S. 1966. Reference and definite descriptions. *Philosophical Review* 77, 281–304.
Donnellan, Keith S. 1972. Proper names and identifying descriptions. In: D. Davidson & G. Harman (eds.). *Semantics of Natural Language*. Dordrecht: Reidel, 356–379.
Fiengo, Robert & Robert May 1998. Names and expressions. *Journal of Philosophy* 95, 377–409.
Fodor, Janet D. & Ivan Sag 1982. Referential and quantificational indefinites. *Linguistics & Philosophy* 5, 355–398.
Frege, Gottlob 1892. Über Sinn und Bedeutung. *Zeitschrift für Philosophie und philosophische Kritik*, 25–50. English Translation in: P. Geach & M. Black (eds.). *Translations from the Philosophical Writings of Gottlob Frege*. Oxford: Blackwell, 1980, 56–78.
Geach, Peter T. 1967. Intentional identity. *Journal of Philosophy* 64, 627–632.
Heim, Irene 1982. *The Semantics of Definite and Indefinite Noun Phrases*. Ph.D. dissertation. University of Massachusetts, Amherst, MA. Reprinted: Ann Arbor, MI: University Microfilms.
Kamp, Hans 1981. A theory of truth and semantic representation. In: J. Groenendijk, T. M.V. Janssen & M. Stokhof (eds.). *Formal Methods in the Study of Language*. Amsterdam: Mathematical Centre, 277–322. Reprint in: J. Groenendijk, T.M.V. Janssen & M. Stokhof (eds.). *Truth, Interpretation and information: Selected Papers from the Third Amsterdam Colloquium*. Dordrecht: Foris, 1984, 1–41.
Kaplan, David 1978. Dthat. In: P. Cole (ed.). *Syntax and Semantics 9: Pragmatics*. New York: Academic Press, 221–243.
Kaplan, David 1989. Demonstratives: An essay on the semantics, logic, metaphysics, and epistemology of demonstratives and other indexicals. In: J. Almog, J. Perry & H. Wettstein (eds.). *Themes from Kaplan*. Oxford: Oxford University Press, 481–563.
Katz, Jerrold J. 2001. The end of Millianism: Multiple bearers, improper names, and compositional meaning. *Journal of Philosophy* 98, 137–166.
Kripke, Saul 1972. Naming and necessity. In: D. Davidson & G. Harman (eds.). *Semantics of Natural Language*. Dordrecht: Reidel, 253–355 and 763–769. Reissued separately with Preface, Cambridge, MA: Harvard University Press, 1980.
Kripke, Saul 1977. Speaker's reference and semantic reference. In: P. A. French, T. E. Uehling, Jr. & H. Wettstein (eds.). *Midwest Studies in Philosophy, vol. II: Studies in the Philosophy of Language*. Morris, MN: University of Minnesota, 255–276.
Kripke, Saul 1979. A puzzle about belief. In: A. Margalit (ed.). *Meaning and Use*. Dordrecht: Reidel, 139–183.
Lewis, David 1972. General semantics. In: D. Davidson & G. Harman (eds.). *Semantics of Natural Language*. Dordrecht: Reidel, 169–218.
Lewis, David. 1979. Attitudes *de dicto* and *de se*. *Philosophical Review* 88, 513–543.
Ludlow, Peter & Stephen Neale 1991. Indefinite descriptions. *Linguistics & Philosophy* 14, 171–202.
Marcus, Ruth Barcan 1961. Modalities and intensional languages. *Synthese* 13, 303–322.
Mill, John Stuart 1843. *A System of Logic, Ratiocinative and Inductive, Being a Connected View of the Principles of Evidence, and the Methods of Scientific Investigation*. London: John W. Parker.

Montague, Richard 1973. The proper treatment of quantification in ordinary English. In: J. Hintikka, J. Moravcsik & P. Suppes (eds.). *Approaches to Natural Language: Proceedings of the 1970 Stanford Workshop on Grammar and Semantics*. Dordrecht: Reidel, 221–242. Reprinted in: R. Thomason (ed.). *Formal Philosophy: Selected Papers of Richard Montague*. New Haven, CT: Yale University Press, 1974, 247–270.
Neale, Stephen 1990. *Descriptions*. Cambridge, MA: The MIT Press.
Perry, John 1979. The problem of the essential indexical. *Noûs* 13, 3–21.
Putnam, Hilary 1975. The meaning of 'meaning'. In: K. Gunderson (ed.). *Language, Mind and Knowledge*. Minneapolis, MN: University of Minnesota Press. Reprinted in: H. Putnam. *Philosophical Papers, vol. 2: Mind, Language and Reality*. Cambridge: Cambridge University Press, 1975, 215–271.
Quine, Willard van Orman 1956. Quantifiers and propositional attitudes. *Journal of Philosophy* 53, 177–187.
Reimer, Marga 1998. Donnellan's distinction/Kripke's test. *Analysis* 58, 89–100.
Richard, Mark 1990. *Propositional Attitudes*. Cambridge: Cambridge University Press.
Russell, Bertrand 1905. On denoting. *Mind* 14, 479–493.
Russell, Bertrand 1917. Knowledge by acquaintance and knowledge by description. Reprinted in: B. Russell. *Mysticism and Logic*. Paperback edn. Garden City, NY: Doubleday, 1957, 202–224.
Russell, Bertrand 1919. *Introduction to mathematical philosophy*. London: Allen & Unwin. Reissued n.d., New York: Touchstone Books.
Russell, Bertrand 1957. Mr. Strawson on referring. *Mind* 66, 385–389.
Salmon, Nathan 1986. *Frege's Puzzle*. Cambridge, MA: The MIT Press.
Salmon, Nathan 2004. The good, the bad, and the ugly. In: M. Reimer & A. Bezuidenhout (eds.). *Descriptions and Beyond*. Oxford: Clarendon Press, 230–260.
Schiffer, Stephen 1992. Belief ascription. *Journal of Philosophy* 89, 499–521.
Searle, John R. 1958. Proper names. *Mind* 67, 166–173.
Segal, Gabriel M. 2000. *A Slim Book about Narrow Content*. Cambridge, MA: The MIT Press.
Stalnaker, Robert C. 1984. *Inquiry*. Cambridge, MA: The MIT Press.
Stalnaker, Robert C. 1999. *Context and Content*. Oxford: Oxford University Press.
Strawson, Peter F. 1950. On referring. *Mind* 59, 320–344.
Strawson, Peter F. 1952. *Introduction to Logical Theory*. London: Methuen.
Wettstein, Howard K. 1983. The semantic significance of the referential-attributive distinction. *Philosophical Studies* 44, 187–196.
Wittgenstein, Ludwig 1953. *Philosophical Investigations*. Translated into English by G.E.M. Anscombe. Oxford: Blackwell.

Georgia M. Green
5 Meaning in language use

1 Overview — 94
2 Deixis — 95
3 The Gricean revolution: The relation of utterance meaning to sentence meaning — 98
4 Implications for word meaning — 107
5 The nature of context, and the relationship of pragmatics to semantics — 112
6 Summary — 117
7 References — 118

Abstract: In a speech community, meaning attaches to linguistic forms through the ways in which speakers use those forms, intending and expecting to communicate with their interlocutors. Grice's (1957) insight that conventional linguistic meaning amounts to the expectation by members of a speech community that hearers will recognize speakers' intentions in saying what they say the way they say it. This enabled him to sketch how this related to lexical meaning and presupposition, and (in more detail) implied meaning. The first substantive section of this article briefly recapitulates the work of Bar-Hillel (1954) on indexicals, leading to the conclusion that even definite descriptions have an indexical component. Section 3 describes Grice's account of the relation of intention to intensions and takes up the notion of illocutionary force. Section 4 explores the implications of the meaning-use relationship for the determination of word meanings. Section 5 touches briefly on the consequences of the centrality of communication for the nature of context and the relation of context and pragmatic considerations to formal semantic accounts.

1 Overview

At the beginning of the 20th century a tension existed between those who took languages to be representable as formal systems with complete truth-conditional semantics (Carnap, Russell, Frege, Tarski) – and who viewed natural language as rather defective in that regard, and those who took the contextual use of language

Georgia M. Green, Urbana, IL, USA

to be determinative of the meanings of its forms (Austin, Strawson, the later Wittgenstein). (See also article 3 [this volume] (Textor) *Sense and reference*.) For a very readable account of this intellectual battleground, see Recanati (2004). The debate has been largely resolved with acceptance (not always explicitly recognized) of the views of Bar-Hillel and Grice on the character of the human use of language.

In a speech community, meaning attaches to linguistic forms through the ways in which speakers use those forms, intending and expecting to communicate with their interlocutors. This is immediately obvious in the case of the reference of indexical terms like *I* and *you*, and the determination of the illocutionary force of utterances. It extends also to matters of reference generally, implicature, coherence of texts and discourse understanding, as well as to the role of linguistic forms in maintaining social relations (politeness). Grice's (1957) insight that conventional linguistic meaning amounts to the expectation by members of a speech community that hearers will recognize speakers' intentions in saying what they say the way they say it enabled him to sketch how this related to lexical meaning and presupposition, and (in more detail) implied meaning. While the view presented here has its origins in Grice's insight, it is considerably informed by elaborations and extensions of it over the past 40 years.

2 Deixis

Bar-Hillel (1954) demonstrated that it is not linguistic forms that carry pragmatic information, but the facts of their utterance, and this notion was elaborated in Stalnaker (1972). Bar-Hillel claimed that indexicality is an inherent and unavoidable aspect of natural language, speculating that more than 90% of the declarative sentences humans utter have use-dependent meanings in that they involve implicit references to the speaker, the addressee and/or the speech time. The interpretation of first and second person pronouns, tenses, and deictic adverbials are only the tip of the iceberg. A whole host of other relational terms (not to mention deictic and anaphoric third-person references, and even illocutionary intentions) require an understanding of the speaker's frame of reference for interpretation. To demonstrate, it is an elementary observation that utterances of sentences like those in (1) require an indication of when and where the sentence was uttered to be understood enough to judge whether they are true or false.

(1) a. I am hungry.
    b. It's raining.

In fact, strictly speaking, the speaker's intention is just as important as location in space-time of the speech act. Thus, (1b) can be intended to refer to the location of the speaker at speech-time, or to some location (like the location of a sports event being viewed on television) that the speaker believes to be salient in the mind of the addressee, and will be evaluated as true or false accordingly. Of course, the reference of past and future tenses is also a function of the context in which they are uttered, referring to times that are a function of the time of utterance. Thus, if I utter (2a) at t_0, I mean that I am hungry at t_0; if I utter (2b) at t_0, I mean that I was hungry at some point before t_0, and if I say (2c) at t_0, I mean that I will be hungry at some point after t_0.

(2) a. I am hungry.
　　b. I was hungry.
　　c. I will be hungry.

Although (2a) indicates a unique time, (2b) and (2c) refer very vaguely to some time before or after t_0; nothing in the utterance specifies whether it is on the order of minutes, days, weeks, years, decades, or millenia distant. Furthermore, it is not clear whether the time indicated by (2a) is a moment or an interval of indefinite duration which includes the moment of utterance. See McCawley (1971), Dowty (1979), Partee (1973), and Hinrichs (1986) for discussion of some issues and ramifications of the alternatives.

Although Bar-Hillel never refers to the notion of intention, he seems to have recognized in discussing the deictic *this* that indexicals are multiply indeterminate, despite being linked to the context of utterance: "'This' is used to call attention to something in the centre of the field of vision of its producer, but, of course, also to something in his spatial neighborhood, even if not in his centre of vision or not in his field of vision at all, or to some thing or some event or some situation, etc., mentioned by himself or by somebody else in utterances preceding his utterance, and in many more ways" (Bar-Hillel 1954: 373). The indexical *this* can thus be intended (a) deictically to refer to something gesturally indicated, (b) anaphorically to refer to a just completed bit of discourse, (c) cataphorically, to refer to a bit of discourse that will follow directly, or (d) figuratively, to refer to something evoked by whatever is indicated and deictically referred to (e.g., to evoke the content of a book by indicating an image of its dust jacket), as in (3), where *this* refers not to a part of a photograph that is gesturally indicated, or to the dust jacket on which it appears, but to the text of the book the dust jacket was designed to protect.

(3)　Oh, I've read this!

Similarly, there is an indexical component to the interpretation of connectives and relational adverbials in that their contribution to the meaning of an utterance involves determining what bit of preceding discourse they are intended to connect whatever follows them to, as illustrated in (4).

(4) a. Therefore, Socrates is mortal.
   b. For that reason, we oppose this legislation.

In addition to such primary indexicals – linguistic elements whose interpretation is bound to the circumstances of their utterance, there are several classes of expressions whose interpretation is directly bound to the interpretation of such primary indexicals. Partee (1989) discussed covert pronominals, for example, *local* as in (5).

(5) Dan Rather went to a local bar.

Is the bar local relative to Rather's characteristic location? to his location at speech-time? to the location of the speaker at speech time? to the characteristic location of the speaker?

In addition, as has long been acknowledged in references to "the universe of discourse," interpretation of the definite article invokes indexical reference; the uniqueness presupposition associated with use of the definite article amounts to a belief by the speaker that the intended referent of the definite NP is salient to the addressee. Indeed, insofar as the interpretation of ordinary kind names varies with the expectations about the universe of discourse that the speaker imputes to the addressee (Nunberg 1978), this larger class of indexicals encompasses the immense class of descriptive terms, including *cat, mat, window, hamburger, red*, and the like as in (6).

(6) a. The blond hamburger spilled her coffee.
   b. The cat shattered next to the mat.

(Some of the conclusions of Nunberg (1978) are summarized in Nunberg (1979), but the latter work does not give an adequate representation of Nunberg's explanation of how the use of words by speakers in contexts facilitates reference. For example, Nunberg (1979) does not contain accounts of either the unextractability of interpretation from context (and the non-existence of null contexts), or the notion of a system of normal beliefs in a speech community. Yet both notions are central to understanding Nunberg's arguments for his conclusions about polysemy and interpretation.)

The important point here is that with these secondary indexicals (and in fact, even with the so-called primary indexicals, Nunberg 1993), interpretation is not a simple matter of observing properties of the speech situation (source of the speech sound, calendric time, etc.), but involves making judgements about possible mappings from signal to referent (essentially the same inferential processes as are involved in disambiguation – cf. Green (1995)). Bar-Hillel (1954) and Morgan (1978) pointed out that the interpretation of demonstratives involves choosing from among many (perhaps indefinitely many) objects the speaker may have been pointing at, as well as what distinct class or individual the speaker may have intended to refer to by indicating that object (as pointed out by Nunberg 1978). Thus, the interpretation of indexicals involves choices from the elements of a set (possibly an infinite set) that is limited differently in each speech situation. For further discussion, see also article 13 [Semantics: Interfaces] (Diessel) *Deixis and demonstratives*.

Bar-Hillel's observations on the nature of indexicals form the background for the development of context-dependent theories of semantics by Stalnaker (1970), Kamp (1981), Heim (1982) and others. See also articles 11 [Semantics: Theories] (Kamp & Reyle) *Discourse Representation Theory* and 2 [Semantics: Theories] (Dekker) *Dynamic semantics*. Starting from a very different set of considerations, Grice (1957) outlined how a speaker's act of using a linguistic form to communicate so-called literal meaning makes critical reference to speaker and hearer, with far-reaching consequences. Section 3 takes up this account in detail.

3 The Gricean revolution: The relation of utterance meaning to sentence meaning

3.1 Meaning according to Grice

Grice (1957) explored the fact that we use the same word (*mean*) for what an event entails, what a speaker intends to communicate by uttering something, and what a linguistic expression denotes. How these three kinds of meaning are related was illuminated by his later (and regrettably widely misunderstood) work on implicature (see Neale 1992 for discussion). Grice (1957) defined NATURAL MEANING (*meaning*$_N$) as natural entailment: the subject of *mean* refers to an event or state, as in (7).

(7) Red spots on your body means you have measles.

He reserved the notion NON-NATURAL MEANING (*meaning*$_{NN}$) for signification by convention: the subject refers to an agent or a linguistic instrument, as in (8).

(8) a. By "my better half", John meant his wife.
    b. In thieves' cant, "trouble and strife" means 'wife'.

Thus, Grice treated the linguistic meaning of expressions as strictly conventional. He declined to use the word *sign* for it as he equated *sign* with *symptom*, which characterizes natural meaning. He showed that non-natural meaning cannot be reduced via a behaviorist causal strategy to 'has a tendency to produce in an audience a certain attitude, dependent on conditioning,' as that would not distinguish non-natural meaning from natural meaning, and in addition, would fail to distinguish connotation from denotation. He argued that the causal account can characterize so-called "standard" meanings, but not meaning on an occasion of use, although meaning on an occasion of use is just what should explain standard meaning, especially on a causal account. Grice also rejected the notion that *X meant*$_{NN}$ *Y* is equivalent to 'the speaker S intended the expression X to make the addressee H believe Y', because that would include in addition to the conventional meaning of a linguistic expression, an agent's utterly nonconventional manipulation of states and events. Finally, he ruled out interpretations of *X meant*$_{NN}$ *Y* as 'the speaker intended X to make H believe Y, and to recognize S's intention', because it still includes in the same class as conventional linguistic meaning any intentional, nonconventional acts whose intention is intended to be recognized – such as presenting the head of St. John the Baptist on a platter. Grice supported instead a theory where *A meant*$_{NN}$ *something by X* entails that (a) an agent intended the utterance of X to induce a belief or intention in H, and (b) the agent intended X to be recognized as intended to induce that belief/intention. This formulation implies that A does not believe (a) will succeed without recognition of A's intention. Grice's argument begins by showing that in directive cases such as getting someone to leave, or getting a driver to stop a car (examples which do not crucially involve language), the intended effect must be the sort of thing that is within the control of the addressee. Thus, *X means*$_{NN}$ *something* amounts to 'people intend X to induce some belief/intention P by virtue of H taking his recognition of the intention to produce effect P as a reason to believe/intend P'. Grice pointed out that only primary intentions need to be recognized: the utterer/agent is held to intend what is normally conveyed by the utterance or a consequence of the act, and ambiguous cases are resolved with evidence from the context that bears on identifying a plausible intention.

Grice's (1975) account of communicated meaning is a natural extension of his (1957) account of meaning in general (cf. also Green 1990, Neale 1992), in that it characterizes meaning as inherently intentional: recognizing an agent's intention is essential to recognizing what act she is performing (i.e., what she meant$_{NN}$ by her act). Grice's reference to the accepted purpose or direction of the talk exchange (Grice 1975: 45) in the characterization of the Cooperative Principle implies that speaker and hearer are constantly involved (usually not consciously) in interpreting what each other's goals must be in saying what they say. Disambiguating structurally or lexically ambiguous expressions like *old men and women*, or *ear* (i.e., of corn, or to hear with), inferring what referent a speaker intends to be picked out from her use of a definite noun phrase like *the coffee place*, and inferring what a speaker meant to implicate by an utterance that might seem unnecessary or irrelevant all depend equally on the assumptions that the speaker did intend something to be conveyed by her utterance that was sufficiently specific for the goal of the utterance, that she intended the addressee to recognize this intention, and by means of recognizing the intention, to recognize what the speaker intended to be conveyed.

In semantics, as intended, the idea that the act of saying something communicates more than just what is said allowed researchers to distinguish constant, truth-conditional meanings that are associated by arbitrary convention with linguistic forms from aspects of understanding that are a function of a meaning being conveyed in a particular context (by whatever means). This in turn enabled syntacticians to abandon the hopeless quest for hidden structures whose analysis would predict non-truth-conditional meanings, and to concentrate on articulating syntactic theories that were compatible with theories of compositional semantics, articulating the details of the relation between form and conventional, truth-conditional meaning. Finally, it inspired a prodigious amount of research in language behavior (e.g., studies of rhetoric and politeness), where it has, unfortunately, been widely misconstrued.

The domain of the principles described in Grice (1975) is actually much broader than usually understood: all intentional use of language, whether literal or not, and regardless of purpose. That is, Grice intended a broad rather than a narrow interpretation of the term *conversation*. Grice's view of the overarching Cooperative Principle: "Make your conversational contribution such as is required, at the stage at which it occurs, by the accepted purpose or direction of the talk exchange in which you are engaged" (Grice 1975: 45) is in fact that it is just the linguistic reflex of a more general principle which governs, in fact, defines, rational behavior: behavior intended to accomplish or enable the achievement of some purpose or goal. Insofar as these are notions universally attributable to human beings, such a principle should be universally applicable with regard to language use. Supposed counterexamples have not held up; for discussion, see Keenan (1976), Prince (1983), Green (1990). Thus, the Cooperative Principle will figure in the interpretation of language generally, not just clever talk, and in fact, will figure in the interpretation of behavior generally, whether communicative or not. Additional facets of this perspective are discussed in articles 14 [Semantics: Interfaces] (Beaver & Geurts) *Presupposition*, and 15 [Semantics: Interfaces] (Simons) *Implicature*.

3.2 The Cooperative Principle

Since Grice was explicit about the Cooperative Principle not being restricted to linguistic acts, and because the imperative formulation has led to so much misunderstanding, it is useful to rephrase it more generally, and declaratively, where it amounts to this:

> Individuals act in accordance with their goals.

Grice described four categories (Quantity, Quality, Relevance and Manner) of special cases of this principle, that is, applications of it to particular kinds of requirements, and gave examples of their application in both linguistic and non-linguistic domains. It is instructive to translate these into general, declarative formulations as well:

An agent will do as much as is required for the achievement of the current goal. (QUANTITY I)

An agent will not do more than is required. (QUANTITY II)

Agents will not deceive co-agents. (QUALITY)
> Consequently, an agent will try to make any assertion one that is true.
> (I)   An agent will not say what she believes to be false.
> (II) An agent will not say that for which she lacks adequate evidence.

An agent's action will be relevant to and relative to an intention of the agent. (RELATION)

An agent will make her actions perspicuous to others who share a joint intention. (MANNER)
(I)   Agents will not disguise actions from co-agents. Consequently, agents will not speak obscurely in attempting to communicate.
(II) Agents will act so that intentions they intend to communicate are unambiguously reconstructible.
(III) Agents will spend no more energy on actions than is necessary.
(IV) Agents will execute sub-parts of a plan in an order that will maximize the perceived likelihood of achieving the goal.

The status of the maxims as just special cases of the Cooperative Principle implies that they are not (contra Lycan 1984: 75) logical consequences (corollaries), because they don't follow as necessary consequences in all possible worlds. Nor are they additional stipulations, or an exhaustive list of special cases. Likewise, the maxims do not constitute the Cooperative Principle, as some writers have thought (e.g., Sperber & Wilson 1986: 36). On the contrary, the Cooperative Principle is a very general principle which determines, depending on the values shared by participants, any number of maxims instantiating ways of conforming to it.

The maxims are not rules or norms that are taught or learned, as some writers would have it (e.g., Pratt 1981: 11, Brown & Yule 1983: 32, Blum-Kulka & Olshtain 1986: 175, Allwood, Anderson & Dahl 1977: 37, Ruhl 1989: 96, Sperber & Wilson 1986: 162). See Green (1990) for discussion. Rather, they are just particular ways of acting in accordance with one's goals; all other things being equal, conforming to the Cooperative Principle involves conforming to all of them. When you can't conform to all of them, as Grice discusses, you do the best you can.

The premise of the Cooperative Principle, that individuals act in accordance with their goals is what allows Grice to refer to the Cooperative Principle as a definition of what it means to be rational (Grice 1975: 45, 47, 48–49), and the maxims as principles that willy-nilly govern interpersonal human behavior. If X's goal is to get Y to do some act A, or believe some proposition P, it follows that X will want to speak in such a way that A or P is clearly identifiable (Maxims of Quality, Quantity, Manner), and X will not say things that will distract Y from getting the point (Maxim of Relevance). Furthermore, most likely, X will not want to antagonize Y (everybody's Maxim of Politeness). Cohen & Levesque (1991) suggest that their analysis of joint intention enables one to understand "the *social contract* implicit in engaging in a dialogue in terms of the conversants' jointly intending to make themselves understood, and to understand the other" (Cohen & Levesque 1991: 509), observing that this would predict the back-channel comprehension checks that pervade dialogue, as "means to attain the states of mutual belief that discharge this joint intention of understanding" (Cohen & Levesque 1991: 509).

The characterization of the Cooperative Principle as the assumption that speakers act rationally (i.e., in accordance with their goals) makes a variety of predictions about the interpretation of behavior. First of all, it predicts that people will try to interpret weird, surprising, or unanticipated behavior as serving some unexpected goal before they discount it as irrational. The tenacity with which we assume that speakers observe the Cooperative Principle, and in particular the maxim of relevance was illustrated in Green (1990). That is, speakers assume that other speakers do what they do, say what they say, on purpose, intentionally, and for a reason (cf. Brown & Levinson 1978: 63). In other words, they assume that speech behavior, and indeed, all behavior that isn't involuntary, is goal-directed.

Speakers "know" the maxims as strategies and tactics for efficiently achieving goals, especially through speech. A person's behavior will be interpreted as conforming to the maxims, even when it appears not to, because of the assumption of rationality (goal-directedness). Hearers will make inferences about the world or the speaker, or both, whenever novel (that is, previously unassumed) propositions have to be introduced into the context to make the assumption of goal-directedness and the assumption of knowledge of the strategies consistent with the behavior. Implicatures arise when the hearer additionally infers that the speaker intended those inferences to be made, and intended that intention to be recognized (cf. article 15 [Semantics: Interfaces] (Simons) *Implicature*). If no such propositions can be imagined, the speaker will be judged irrational, but irrationality will consist in believing the unbelievable, or believing something unfathomable, not in having imperfect knowledge of the maxims, or in not observing the maxims.

Only our imagination limits the goals, and beliefs about the addressee's goals, that we might attribute to the speaker. If we reject the assumption that the speaker is irrational, then we must at the very least assume that there is some goal to which his utterance is relevant in the given context, even if we can't imagine what it is.

Another illustration of the persistence of the assumption that utterances are acts executed in accordance with a plan to achieve a goal: even if we know that a sequence of sentences was produced by a computer, making choices entirely at random within the constraints of some grammar provided to it, if the sentences can be construed as connected and produced in the service of a single goal, it is hard not to understand them that way. That is why output like (9) from random sentence generators frequently produces giggles.

(9) a. Sandy called the dog.
    b. Sandy touched the dog.
    c. Sandy wanted the dog.
    d. The dog arrived.
    e. The dog asked for Kim.

One further point requires discussion here. Researchers eager to challenge or to apply a Gricean perspective have often failed to appreciate how important it is that discourse is considered purposive behavior. Grice presumes that participants have goals in participating (apparently since otherwise they wouldn't be participating). This is the gist of his remark that "each participant recognizes in [talk exchanges], to some extent, a common purpose or set of purposes, or at least a mutually accepted direction" (Grice 1975: 45). This is perhaps the most misunderstood passage in "Logic and Conversation". Grice is very vague about these purposes: how many there are, how shared they have to be. With decades of hindsight, we can see that the purposes are first of all not unique. Conversants typically have hierarchically embedded goals.

Second, goals are not so much shared or mutual, as they are mutually modelled (Cohen & Perrault 1979, Cohen & Levesque 1980, Green 1982, Appelt 1985, Cohen & Levesque 1990, Perrault 1990): for George to understand Martha's utterance of "X" to George, George must have beliefs about Martha which include Martha's purpose in uttering "X" to George, which in turn subsumes Martha's model of George, including George's model of Martha, etc. Grice's assertion (1975: 48) that "in characteristic talk-exchanges, there is a common aim even if [...] it is a second-order one, namely, that each party should, for the time being, identify himself with the transitory conversational interests of the other" is an underappreciated expression of this view. The idea that participants will at least temporarily identify with each other's interests, i.e., infer what each other is trying to do, is what allows quarrels, monologues, and the like to be included in the talk exchanges that the Cooperative Principle governs. Grice actually cited quarrels and letter-writing as instances that did not fit an interpretation of the Cooperative Principle that he rejected (Grice 1975: 48), vitiating critiques by Pratt (1981) and Schauber & Spolsky (1986). The participants may have different values and agendas, but given Grice's (1957) characterization of conventional meaning, for any communication to occur, each must make assumptions about the other's goals, at least the low-level communicative goals. This is the sense in which participants recognize a "common goal". When the assumptions participants make about each other's goals are incorrect, and this affects non-trivial beliefs about each other, we say they are "talking at cross-purposes", precisely because of the mismatch between actual goals and beliefs, and attributed goals and beliefs.

Interpreting the communicative behavior of other human beings as intentional, and as relevant, necessary, and sufficient for the achievement of some presumed goal seems to be unavoidable. As Gould (1991: 60) noted, in quite a different context, "humans are pattern-seeking animals. We must find cause and meaning in all events." This is, of course, equally true of behavior that isn't intended as communicative. Crucially, we do not seem to entertain the idea that someone might be acting for no reason. That alternative, along with the possibility that he isn't even doing what we perceive him to be doing, that it's just happening to him, is one that we seem reluctant to accept without any independent support, such as knowledge that people do that sort of thing as a nervous habit, like playing with their hair.

Thus, "cooperative" in the sense of the Cooperative Principle does not entail each party accepting all of their interlocutor's goals as their own and helping to achieve them. Rather, it is most usefully understood as meaning no more – and no less – than 'trying to understand the interaction from the other participants' 'point of view', i.e., trying to understand what their goals and assumptions must be. When Grice refers to the Cooperative Principle as "rational", it is just this assumption that actions are undertaken to accomplish goals that he has in mind.

3.3 Illocutionary intentions

The second half of the 20th century saw focussed investigation of speech acts in general, and illocutionary aspects of meaning in particular, preeminently in the work of Austin (1962), Searle (1969) and Bach & Harnish (1979). Early on, the view within linguistics was that (i) illocutionary force was indicated by performative verbs (Austin 1962) or other Illocutionary-Force-Indicating-Devices (IFIDs, Stampe 1975) such as intonation or "markers" like preverbal *please*), and that (ii) where illocutionary force was ambiguous or unclear, that was because the performative clause prefixed to the sentence (Lakoff 1968, Ross 1970, Fraser 1974, Sadock 1974) was "abstract" and invisible. This issue has not been much discussed since the mid-1970s, and Dennis Stampe's (1975) conclusion that so-called performative verbs are really constative, so that the appearance of performativity is an inference from the act of utterance may now be the default assumption. It makes performativity more a matter of the illocutionary intentions of the speaker than of the classification of visible or invisible markers of illocutionary force. The term "illocutionary intentions" is meant to include the relatively large but limited set of illocutionary forces described and classified by Austin (1962) and Searle (1969) and many others (stating, requesting, promising and the like). So, expositives are utterances which a speaker (S) makes with the intention that the addressee (A) recognize S's intention that A believe that S believes their content. Promises are made with the intention that A recognize S's intention that A believe that S will be responsible for making their content true. Interrogatives are uttered with the belief that A will recognize S's intention that A provide information which S indicates.

From the hearer's point of view such illocutionary intentions do not seem significantly different from intentions about the essentially unlimited class of possible perlocutionary effects that a speaker might intend an addressee to recognize as intended on an occasion of use. So, reminders are expositives uttered with the intention that A will recognize that S believes A has believed what S wants A to believe. Warnings are utterances the uttering of which is intended to be recognized as intended to inform A that some imminent or contingent state of affairs will be bad for A. An insult is uttered with the intention that A recognize S's intent to convey S's view of A as having properties normally believed to be bad. Both kinds of intentions figure in conditions on the use of linguistic expressions of various sorts. For example, there are a whole host of phrasal verbs (many meaning roughly 'go away') such as *butt out*, that can be described as directive-polarity expressions (instantiating, reporting, or evoking directives), as illustrated in (10), where the asterisk prefixed to an expression indicates that it is ungrammatical.

(10) a. Butt out!
　　 b. *They may butt out.
　　 c. *Why do they butt out?
　　 d. They were asked to butt out.
　　 e. They refused to butt out.
　　 f. Why don't you butt out?

But there are also expressions whose distribution depends on mental states of the speaker regarding the addressee that are not matters of illocutionary force. Often it is an intention to produce a particular perlocutionary effect, as with threat-polarity expressions like *Or else!*, exemplified in (11).

(11) a. Get out, or else!
　　 b. *I want to get out, or else!
　　 c. *Who's on first, or else?
　　 d. They said we had to get out, or else.
　　 e. They knew they had to get out, or else.
　　 f. *They were surprised that we had to get out, or else.

Sometimes, however, the relevant mental state of the speaker does not involve intentions at all. This is the case with ignorance-polarity constructions and idioms which are acceptable only in contexts where a relevant being (typically the speaker) is ignorant of the answer to an indicated question, as in (12) (cf. Horn 1972, 1978).

(12) a. Where the hell is it?
　　 b. I couldn't figure out where the hell it was.
　　 c. *We went back to the place where the hell we left it.
　　 d. *I knew where the hell it would be found.

It is possible to represent this kind of selection formally, say, in terms of conjoined and/or nested propositions representing speaker intentions and speaker and addressee beliefs about intentions, actions, existence, knowledge and values. But it is not the linguistic sign which is the indicator of illocutionary intentions, it is the act of uttering it. An utterance is a warning just in case S intends A to recognize the uttering of it as intended to cause A to recognize that some situation may result in a state which A would consider bad. In principle, such conditions could be referenced as constraints in the lexical entries for restricted forms. A threat-polarity item like *or else!* presupposes a warning context, with the additional information that the speaker intends the addressee to recognize (that the speaker intends the addressee to recognize) that if the warning is not heeded, some individual or situation will be responsible for some state of affairs that endangers the referent of the subject of the clause to which *or else* is appended.

Illocutionary force, like deixis, is an aspect of meaning that is fairly directly derivative of the use of a linguistic expression. At the other end of the spectrum, lexical meaning, which appears much more concrete and fixed, has also been argued to depend on the sort of social contract that the Cooperative Principle engenders, as explicated by Nunberg (1978, 2004). This is the topic of Section 4.

4 Implications for word meaning

In general, to the extent that we are able to understand each other, it is because we all use language in accordance with the Cooperative Principle. This entails (cf. Grice 1957) that we will only use a referential term when we believe that our addressee will be able to identify our intended referent from our reference to it by that term in that context, and will believe that we intended him to do so. But the bottom line is that the task of the addressee is to deduce what sense the speaker most likely intended, and he will use all available clues to do so, without regard to whether they come from within or outside the immediate sentence or bit of discourse at hand. This means that even so-called literal meanings have an indexical character in depending on the speaker's ability to infer correctly what an addressee will assume a term is intended to refer to on an occasion of use (cf. Nunberg 1978). Even the sense of predicative lexical items in an utterance is not fixed by or in a linguistic system, but can only be deduced in connection with assumptions about the speaker's beliefs about the knowledge and expectations of the addressee.

To illustrate, as has been often noted (cf. Ruhl 1989, Green 1998), practically any word can be used to denote an almost limitless variety of kinds of objects or functions: in addition to referring to a fruit, or a defective automobile, *lemon* might refer to the wood of the lemon tree, as in (13a), to the flavor of the juice of the fruit (13b), to the oil from the peel of the fruit (13c), to an object which has the color of the fruit (13d), to something the size of the fruit (13e), and to a substance with the flavor of the fruit (13f). These are only the most obvious uses from an apparently indefinitely large set.

(13) a. Lemon has an attractive grain, much finer than beech or cherry.
    b. I prefer the '74 because the '73 has a lemon aftertaste.
    c. Lemon will not penetrate as fast as linseed.
    d. The lemon is too stretchy, but the coral has a snag in it.
    e. Shape the dough into little lemons, and let rise.
    f. Two scoops of lemon, please, and one of Rocky Road.

The idea that what a word can be used to refer to might vary indefinitely is clearly unsettling. It makes the fact that we (seem to) understand each other most of the time something of a miracle, and it makes the familiar, comfortable Conduit Theory of communication (critiqued in Reddy 1979), according to which speakers encode ideas in words and sentences and send them to addressees to decode, quite irrational. But the conclusion that as language users we are free to use any word to refer to anything at all, any time we want is unwarranted. Lexical choice is always subject to the pragmatic constraint that we have to consider how likely it is that our intended audience will be able to correctly identify our intended referent from our use of the expression we choose. What would really be irrational would be using a word to refer to anything other than what we estimate our addressee is likely to take it to refer to, because it would be self-defeating. Thus, in spite of all the apparent freedom afforded to language users, rationality severely limits what a speaker is likely to use a term to refer to in a given context. Since people assume that people's actions are goal-directed (so that any act will be assumed to have been performed for a reason), a speaker must be assumed to believe that, all things considered, the word she chooses is the best word to further her goals in its context and with respect to her addressee.

    Speakers frequently exploit the freedom they have, within the bounds of this constraint, referring to movies as turkeys, cars as lemons, and individuals in terms of objects associated with them, as when we say that the flute had to leave to attend his son's soccer game, or that the corned beef spilled his beer. If this freedom makes communication sound very difficult to effect, and very fragile, it is important to keep in mind that we are probably less successful at it than we think we are, and generally oblivious of the work that is required as well. But it is probably not really that fragile. Believing as an operational principle in the convenient fiction that words have fixed meanings is what makes using them to communicate appear to require no effort. If we were aware of how much interpretation we depended on each other to do to understand us, we might hesitate to speak. Instead, we all act as if we believe, and believe that everyone else believes, that the denotation an individual word may have on an occasion of use is limited, somewhat arbitrarily, as a matter of linguistic convention. Nunberg (1978), extending observations made by Lewis (1969), called this sort of belief a normal belief, defined so that the relation *normally-believe* holds of a speech community and a proposition P when people in that community believe that it is normal (i.e., unremarkable, to be expected) in that community to believe P and to believe that everyone in that community believes that it is normal in that community to believe P. See also Stalnaker (1974) and Atlas (2004). (The term *speech community*, following Nunberg (1978), is not limited to geographical or political units, or even institutionalized social units, but encompasses any group of individuals with common interests. Thus, we all belong simultaneously to a number of speech communities, depending on our interests and backgrounds; we might be women and mothers and Lutherans and lawyers and football fans and racketball players, who knit and surf the internet, and are members of countless speech communities besides these.) Illustrating the relevance to traditional semantic concerns of the notion of normal belief, it is normal beliefs about cars and trucks, and about what properties of them good old boys might find relevant that would lead someone to understand the coordination in (14a) with narrow adjectival scope and that in (14b) with wider scope: for example, because of the aerodynamic properties of trucks relative to cars, *fast truck* is almost an oxymoron.

(14) a. The good ol' boys there drive fast cars and trucks.
　　　b. The good ol' boys there drive red cars and trucks.

This technical use of *normal belief* should not be confused with other notions that may have the same name. A normal belief in the sense intended is only remotely related to an individual's belief about how things normally are, and only remotely related (in a different direction) to a judgement that it is unremarkable to hold such a belief. The beliefs that are normal within a community are those that "constitute the background against which all utterances in that community are rationally made" (Nunberg 1978: 94–95).

Addressing the issue of using words to refer to things, properties, and events, what it is considered normal to use a word like *tack* or *host* or *rock* or *metal* to refer to varies with the community. These are social facts, facts about societies, and only incidentally and contingently and secondarily facts about words. More precisely, they are facts about what speakers believe other speakers believe about conventions for using words. Thus, it is normal among field archaeologists to use mesh bound in frames to sift through excavated matter for remnants of material culture, and it is normally believed among them that this is normal, and that it is normal to refer to the sieves as *screens*. Likewise, among users of personal computers, it is normally believed that the contents of a data file may be inspected by projecting representations of portions of it on an electronic display, and it is normally believed that this belief is normally held, and that it is normal to refer to the display as a *screen*. Whether *screen* is (intended to be) understood as (normally) referring to a sort of sieve or to a video display depends on assumptions made by speaker and hearer about the assumptions each makes about the other's beliefs, including beliefs about what is normal in a situation of the sort being described, and about what sort of situation (each believes the other believes) is being discussed at the moment of utterance. This is what makes word meaning irreducibly a matter of language use. Although different senses of a word may sometimes have different syntactic distributions (so-called selectional restrictions), McCawley (1968) showed that this is not so much a function of the words themselves as it is a function of properties that language users attribute to the presumed intended referents of the words.

Normal use is defined in terms of normal belief, and normal belief is an intensional concept. If everybody believes that everybody believes that it is normal to believe P, then belief in P is a normal belief, even if nobody actually believes P. In light of this, we are led to a view of word usage in which, when a speaker rationally uses a word w to indicate some intended individual or class a, she must assume that the addressee will consider it rational to use w to indicate a in that context. She must assume that if she and her addressee do not in fact have the same assumptions about what beliefs are normal in the community-at-large, and in every relevant subgroup, at least the addressee will be able to infer what relevant beliefs the speaker imputes to the addressee, or expects the addressee to impute to the speaker, and so on, in order to infer the intended referent.

If we define an additional, recursive relation *mutually-believe* as holding among two sentient beings A and B and a proposition when A believes the proposition, believes that B believes the proposition, believes that B believes that A believes the proposition, and so on (cf. Cohen & Levesque 1990), then we can articulate the notion *normal meaning* (not to be confused with 'normal referent out of context' – cf. Green 1995: 14f, Green 1996: 59 for discussion):

> some set (or property) m is a normal meaning (or denotation) of an expression w insofar as it is normally believed that w is used to indicate m.

A meaning m for an expression w is normal in a context insofar as speaker and addressee mutually believe that it is normally believed that w is used to indicate m in that context. We can then say that 'member of the species *canis familiaris*' is a normal meaning for the word *dog* insofar as speaker and addressee mutually believe that it is normally believed in their community that such entities are called *dogs*.

Some uses of referential expressions like those exemplified in (13) are not so much abnormal or less normal than others as they are normal in a more narrowly defined community. In cases of systematic polysemy, all the use-types (or senses), whether normal in broadly defined or very narrowly exclusive communities, are relatable to one another in terms of functions like 'source of', 'product of', 'part of', 'mass of', which Nunberg (1978) characterized as *referring functions* (for discussion, see Nunberg 1978, 2004, Green 1996, 1998, Pelletier & Schubert 1986, Nunberg & Zaenen 1992, Copestake & Briscoe 1995, Helmreich 1994). For example, using the word *milkshake* as in (15) to refer to someone who orders a milkshake exploits the referring function 'purchaser of', and presumes a mutual belief that it is normal for restaurant personnel to use the name of a menu item to refer to a purchaser of that item, or more generally, for sales agents to use a description of a purchase to refer to the purchaser.

(15) The milkshake claims you kicked her purse.

This is in addition, of course, to the mutual belief it presumes about what the larger class of English speakers normally use *milkshake* to refer to, and the mutual belief that the person identified as the claimant ordered a milkshake.

The assumption that people's actions are purposeful, so that any act will be assumed to have been performed for a reason, is a universal normal belief – everyone believes it and believes that everyone believes it (cf. Green 1993). The consequence of this for communicative acts is that people intend and expect that interpreters will attribute particular intentions to them, so consideration of just what intention will be attributed to speech actions must enter into rational utterance planning (cf. Green 1993, also Sperber & Wilson 1986). This is the Gricean foundation of this theory (cf. also Neale 1992).

If the number of meanings for a given lexical term is truly indefinitely extendable (as it appears to be), or even merely very large, it is impractical in the extreme to try to list them. But the usual solution to the problem of representing an infinite class in a finite (logical) space is as available here as anywhere else, at least to the extent that potential denotations can be described in terms of composable functions on other denotations, and typically, this is the case (Nunberg 1978: 29–62). It is enough to know, Nunberg argues, that if a term can be used to refer to some class X, then it can be used, given appropriate context, to refer to objects describable by a recognizable function on X. This principle can be invoked recursively, and applies to functions composed of other functions, and to expressions composed of other expressions, enabling diverse uses like those for *lemon* in (13) to be predicted in a principled manner.

Because the intended sense (and thence the intended referent) of an utterance of any referential term ultimately reflects what the speaker intends the hearer to understand from what the speaker says by recognizing that the speaker intends him to understand that, interpreting an utterance containing a polysemic ambiguity (or indeed, any sort of ambiguity) involves doping out the speaker's intent, just as understanding a speaker's discourse goals does. For additional discussion, see also articles 10 [Semantics: Lexical Structures and Adjectives] (de Swart) *Mismatches and coercion* and 11 [Semantics: Lexical Structures and Adjectives] (Tyler & Takahashi) *Metaphors and metonymies*.

5 The nature of context, and the relationship of pragmatics to semantics

5.1 Disambiguation and interpretation

Pragmatic information is information about the speaker's mental models. Consequently, such semantic issues as truth conditions and determination of ambiguity are interdependent with issues of discourse interpretation, and the relevant contexts essential to the resolution of both are not so much the surrounding words and phrases as they are abstractions from the secular situations of utterance, filtered through the minds of the participants (cf. Stalnaker 1974). As a result, it is unreasonable to expect that ambiguity resolution independent of models of those situations can be satisfactory. Linguistic pragmatics irreducibly involves the speaker's model of the addressee, and the hearer's model of the speaker (potentially recursively). For George to understand Martha's utterance of "X" to him, he must not only recognize (speech perception, parsing) that she has said "X," he must have beliefs about her which allow him to infer what her purpose was in uttering "X," which means that he has beliefs about her model of him, including her model of his model of her, and so on. Any of these beliefs is liable to be incorrect at some level of granularity. George's model of Martha (and hers of him) is more like a sketch than a photograph: there are lots of potentially relevant things they don't know about each other, and they most likely have got a few (potentially relevant) things wrong right off the bat as well. Consequently, even under the best of circumstances, whatever proposition George interprets Martha's utterance to be expressing may not exactly match the proposition she intended him to understand. The difference, which often is not detected, may or may not matter in the grand scheme of things. Since acts are interpreted at multiple levels of granularity, this holds for the interpretation of acts involved in choosing words and construction types, as well as for acts of uttering sentences containing or instantiating them. From this it follows that the distinction between pragmatic effects called "intrusive pragmatics" (Levinson 2000) or explicature (Sperber & Wilson 1986) and those described as implicature proper has little necessary significance for an information-based account of language structure. Because the computation of pragmatic effects by whatever name involves analysis of what is underspecified in the actual utterance, and how what is uttered compares to what might reasonably have been expected, it involves importing propositions, a process beyond the bounds of computation within a finite domain, even if supplemented by a finite set of functions.

When a reader or hearer recognizes that an utterance is ambiguous, resolving that ambiguity amounts to determining which interpretation was intended. When recognizing an ambiguity affects parsing, resolving it may involve grammar and lexicon, as for example, when it involves a form which could be construed as belonging to different syntactic categories (e.g., *The subdivision houses most of the officers* vs. *The subdivision* HOUSES *are very similar*, or Visiting relatives *is a lot of fun* vs. Visiting relatives *are a lot of fun*). But grammar and lexicon may not be enough to resolve such ambiguities, as in the case of familiar examples like (16).

(16) a. I saw her duck.
  b. Visiting relatives can be a lot of fun.

They will rarely suffice to resolve polysemies or attachment ambiguities like *I returned the key to the library*. In all of these cases, it is necessary to reconstruct what it would be reasonable for the speaker to have intended, given what is known or believed about the beliefs and goals of the speaker, exactly as when seeking to understand the relevance of an unambiguous utterance in a conversation – that is, to understand why the speaker bothered to utter it, or to say it the way she said it. The literature on natural language understanding contains numerous demonstrations that the determination of how an ambiguous or vague term is intended to be understood depends on identifying the most likely model of the speaker's beliefs and intentions about the interaction. Nunberg (1978: 84–87) discusses the beliefs and goals that have to be attributed to him in order for his uncle to understand what he means by *jazz* when he asks him if he likes jazz. Crain & Steedman (1985), and Altmann & Steedman (1988) offer evidence that experimentally controllable aspects of context that reflect speakers' beliefs about situations affect processing in more predictable ways than mechanistic parsing strategies. Green (1996: 119–122) describes what is involved in identifying what is meant by *IBM*, *at*, and *seventy-one* in *Sandy bought IBM at 71*.

At the other end of the continuum of grammatical and pragmatic uncertainty is Sperber & Wilson's (1986: 239–241) discussion of the process of understanding irony and sarcasm, as when one says *I love people who don't signal*, intending to convey 'I hate people who don't signal.' (A further step in the process is required to interpret *I love people who signal!* as intended to convey the same thing; the difference is subtle, because the contextual conditions likely to provoke the two utterances are in a subset relation. One might say *I love people who don't signal* to inform an interlocutor of one's annoyance at someone who the speaker noticed did not signal, but *I love people who signal* is likely to be used sarcastically only when the speaker believes that it is obvious to the addressee that someone should have signaled and did not.)

Nonetheless, it may be instructive here to examine the resolution of a salient lexical ambiguity. Understanding the officials' statement in example (17) involves comparing how different assumptions about mutual beliefs about the situation are compatible with different interpretations, in order to determine whether *plant* refers to a vegetable organism or to the production facility of a business (or perhaps just to the apparatus for controlling the climate within it, or maybe to the associated grounds, offices and equipment generally), or even to some sort of a decoy.

(17) Officials at International Seed Co. beefed up security at their South Carolina facility in the face of rumors that competitors would stop at nothing to get specimens of a newly-engineered variety, saying, "That plant is worth $5 million."

If the interpreter supposes that what the company fears is simply theft of samples of the organism, she will take the official as intending *plant* to refer to the (type of the) variety: being able to market tokens of that type represents a potential income of $5 million. On the other hand, if the interpreter supposes that the company fears damage to their production facility or the property surrounding it – say, because she knows that samples of the organism are not even located at the production facility any more, and/or that extortionists have threatened to vandalize company property if samples of the organism are not handed over, she is likely to take *plant* as intended to refer to buildings and grounds or equipment. Believing that the company believes that potential income from marketing the variety is many times greater than $5 million would have the same effect. If the interpreter believes that the statement was made in the course of an interview where a company spokesperson discussed the cost of efforts to protect against industrial espionage, and mentioned how an elaborate decoy system had alerted them to a threat to steal plant specimens, she might even take *plant* as intended to refer to a decoy. The belief that officials believe that everyone relevant believes that both the earnings potential of the organism, and the value of relevant structures and infrastructure are orders of magnitude more or less than $5 million would contribute to this conclusion, and might even suffice to induce it on its own.

Two points are relevant here. First, depending on how much of the relevant information is salient in the context in which the utterance is being interpreted, the sentence might not even be recognized as ambiguous. This is equally true in the case of determining discourse intents. For example, identifying sarcastic intent is similar to understanding the reference of an expression in that it depends on attributing to the speaker intent to be sarcastic. (Such an inference is supported by finding a literal meaning to be in conflict with propositions assumed to be mutually believed, but this is neither necessary nor sufficient for interpreting an utterance as sarcastic.) Being misled in the attribution of intent is a common sort of misunderstanding, indeed, a sort that is likely to go undetected. These issues are discussed at length in articles 8 [Semantics: Lexical Structures and Adjectives] (Kennedy) *Ambiguity and vagueness*, 12 [Semantics: Theories] (Dekker) *Dynamic semantics*, 11 [Semantics: Interfaces] (Jaszczolt) *Semantics and pragmatics*, 12 [Semantics: Interfaces] (Zimmermann) *Context dependency* and 17 [Semantics: Interfaces] (Potts) Conventional implicature and expressive content.

Second, there is nothing linguistic about the resolution of the lexical ambiguity in (17). All of the knowledge that contributes to the identification of a likely intended referent is encyclopedic or contextual knowledge of (or beliefs about) the relevant aspects of the world, including the beliefs of relevant individuals in it (e.g., the speaker, the (presumed) addressees of the quoted speech, the reporter of the quoted speech, and the (presumed) addressees of the report). That disambiguation of an utterance in its context may require encyclopedic knowledge of a presumed universe of discourse is hardly a new observation; it has been a commonplace in the linguistics and Artificial Intelligence literature for decades. Its pervasiveness and its significance sometimes seem to be surprisingly underappreciated.

A similar demonstration could be made for many structural ambiguities, including some of the ones mentioned at the beginning of this section. Insofar as language users resolve ambiguities that they recognize by choosing the interpretation most consistent with their model of the speaker and of the speaker's model of the world, modelling this ability of theirs by means of probability-based grammars and lexicons (e.g., Copestake & Briscoe 1995) is likely to provide an arbitrarily limited solution. When language users fail to recognize ambiguities in the first place, it is surely because beliefs about the speaker's beliefs and intentions in the context at hand which would support alternative interpretations are not salient to them.

This view treats disambiguation, at all levels, as indistinct from interpretation, insofar as both involve comparing an interpretation of a speaker's utterance with goals and beliefs attributed to that speaker, and rejecting interpretations which in the context are not plausibly relevant to the assumed joint goal for the discourse. This is a conclusion that is unequivocally based in Grice's seminal work (Grice 1957, 1975), and yet it is one that he surely did not anticipate. See also Atlas (2004).

5.2 Computational modelling

Morgan (1973) showed that determining the presuppositions of an utterance depends on beliefs attributed to relevant agents (e.g., the speaker, and agents and experiencers of propositional attitude verbs) and is not a strictly linguistic matter. Morgan's account, and Gazdar's (1979) formalization of it, show that the presuppositions associated with lexical items are filtered in being projected as presuppositions of the sentence of which they form a part, by conversational implicature, among other things. (See also articles 11 [Semantics: Theories] (Kamp & Reyle) *Discourse Representation Theory*, 14 [Semantics: Interfaces] (Beaver & Geurts) *Presupposition* and 15 [Semantics: Interfaces] (Simons) *Implicature*.) Conversational implicature, as discussed in section 3 of this article is a function of a theory of human behavior generally, not something specifically linguistic, because it is based on inference of intentions for actions generally, not on properties of the artifacts that are the result of linguistic actions: conversational implicatures arise from the assumption that it is reasonable (under the particular circumstances of the speech event in question) to expect the addressee A to infer that the speaker S intended A to recognize S's intention from the fact that the speaker uttered whatever she uttered. It would be naive to expect that the filtering in the projection of presuppositions could be represented as a constraint or set of constraints on values of any discrete linguistic feature, precisely because conversational implicature is inherently indeterminate (Grice 1975, Morgan 1973, Gazdar 1979).

Despite the limitations on the computation and attribution of assumptions, much progress has been made in recent years on simultaneous disambiguation and parsing of unrestricted text. To take only the example that I am most familiar with, Russell (1993) describes a system which unifies syntactic and semantic information from partial parses to postulate (partial) syntactic and semantic information for unfamiliar words. This progress suggests that a promising approach to the problem of understanding unrestricted texts would be to expand the technique to systematically include information about contexts of utterance, especially since it can be taken for granted that words will be encountered which are being used in unfamiliar ways. The chief requirement for such an enterprise is to reject (following Reddy 1979) the simplistic view of linguistic expressions as simple conduits for thoughts, and model natural language use as action of rational agents who treat the exchange of ideas as a joint goal, as Grice, Cohen, Perrault, and Levesque have suggested in the articles cited. This is a nontrivial task, and if it does not offer an immediate payoff in computational efficiency, ultimately it will surely pay off in increased accuracy, not to mention in understanding the subtlety of communicative and interpretive techniques.

6 Summary

Some of the conclusions outlined here are surely far beyond what Bar-Hillel articulated in 1954, and what Grice may have had in mind in 1957 or 1968, the date of the William James Lectures in which the Cooperative Principle was articulated. Nonetheless, our present understanding rests on the shoulders of their work. Bar-Hillel (1954) demonstrated that it is not linguistic forms that carry pragmatic information, but the facts of their utterance. The interpretation of first and second person pronouns, tenses, and deictic adverbials are only the most superficial aspect of this. Bar-Hillel's observations on the nature of indexicals form the background for the development of context-dependent theories of semantics by Stalnaker (1970), Kamp (1981), Heim (1982) and others. Starting from a very different set of considerations, Grice (1957) outlined how a speaker's act of using a linguistic form to communicate so-called literal meaning makes critical reference to speaker and hearer, with far-reaching consequences. Grice's (1957) insight that conventional linguistic meaning depends on members of a speech community recognizing speakers' intentions in saying what they say the way they say it enabled him to sketch how this related to lexical meaning and presupposition, and (in more detail) implied meaning. While the view presented here has its origins in Grice's insight, it is considerably informed by elaborations and extensions of it over the past 40 years. The distinction between natural meaning (entailment) and non-natural meaning (conventional meaning) provided the background against which his theory of the social character of communication was developed in the articulation of the Cooperative Principle. While the interpersonal character of illocutionary acts was evident from the first discussions, it was less obvious that lexical meaning, which appears much more concrete and fixed, could also be argued to depend on the sort of social contract that the Cooperative Principle engenders. Subsequent explorations into the cooperative aspects of action generally make it reasonable to anticipate a much more integrated understanding of the interrelations of content and context, of meaning and use, than seemed likely forty years ago.

7 References

Allwood, Jens, Lars-Gunnar Anderson & Östen Dahl 1977. *Logic in Language*. Cambridge: Cambridge University Press.
Altmann, Gerry & Mark Steedman 1988. Interaction with context during sentence processing. *Cognition* 30, 191–238.
Appelt, Douglas E. 1985. *Planning English Sentences*. Cambridge: Cambridge University Press.
Atlas, Jay David 2004. Presupposition. In: L. R. Horn & G. Ward (eds.). *The Handbook of Pragmatics*. Oxford: Blackwell, 29–52.
Austin, John L. 1962. *How to Do Things with Words*. Cambridge, MA: Harvard University Press.
Bach, Kent & Robert M. Harnish 1979. *Linguistic Communication and Speech Acts*. Cambridge, MA: The MIT Press.
Bar-Hillel, Yehoshua 1954. Indexical expressions. *Mind* 63, 359–379.
Blum-Kulka, Shoshana & Elite Olshtain 1986. Too many words: Length of utterance and pragmatic failure. *Studies in Second Language Acquisition* 8, 165–180.
Brown, Gillian & George Yule 1983. *Discourse Analysis*. Cambridge: Cambridge University Press.
Brown, Penelope & Stephen Levinson 1978. Universals in language usage: Politeness phenomena. In: E. Goody (ed.). *Questions and Politeness: Strategies in Social Interaction*. Cambridge: Cambridge University Press, 56–311. (Expanded version published 1987 in book form as *Politeness*, by Cambridge University Press.)
Cohen, Philip R. & Hector J. Levesque 1980. Speech acts and the recognition of shared plans. *Proceedings of the Third National Conference of the Canadian Society for Computational Studies of Intelligence*. Victoria, BC: University of Victoria, 263–271.
Cohen, Philip R. & Hector J. Levesque 1990. Rational interaction as the basis for communication. In: P. Cohen, J. Morgan & M. Pollack (eds.). *Intentions in Communication*. Cambridge, MA: The MIT Press, 221–256.
Cohen, Philip R. & Hector J. Levesque 1991. Teamwork. *Noûs* 25, 487–512.
Cohen, Philip R. & C. Ray Perrault 1979. Elements of a plan based theory of speech acts. *Cognitive Science* 3, 177–212.
Copestake, Ann & Ted Briscoe 1995. Semi-productive polysemy and sense extension. *Journal of Semantics* 12, 15–67.
Crain, Stephen & Mark Steedman 1985. On not being led up the garden path: The use of context by the psychological parser. In: D. R. Dowty, L. Karttunen & A. M. Zwicky (eds.). *Natural Language Parsing*. Cambridge: Cambridge University Press, 320–358.
Dowty, David 1979. *Word Meaning and Montague Grammar*. Dordrecht: Reidel.
Fraser, Bruce 1974. An examination of the performative analysis. *Papers in Linguistics* 7, 1–40.
Gazdar, Gerald 1979. *Pragmatics, Implicature, Presupposition, and Logical Form*. New York: Academic Press.
Gould, Stephen J. 1991. *Bully for Brontosaurus*. New York: W. W. Norton.
Green, Georgia M. 1982. Linguistics and the pragmatics of language use. *Poetics* 11, 45–76.
Green, Georgia M. 1990. On the universality of Gricean interpretation. In: K. Hall et al. (eds.). *Proceedings of the 16th Annual Meeting of the Berkeley Linguistics Society*. Berkeley, CA: Berkeley Linguistics Society, 411–428.
Green, Georgia M. 1993. *Rationality and Gricean Inference*. Cognitive Science Technical Report UIUC-BI-CS-93-09. Urbana, IL, University of Illinois.

Green, Georgia M. 1995. Ambiguity resolution and discourse interpretation. In: K. van Deemter & S. Peters (eds.). *Semantic Ambiguity and Underspecification*. Stanford, CA: CSLI Publications, 1–26.

Green, Georgia M. 1996. *Pragmatics and Natural Language Understanding*. 2nd edn. Hillsdale, NJ: Lawrence Erlbaum Associates.

Green, Georgia M. 1998. Natural kind terms and a theory of the lexicon. In: E. Antonsen (ed.). *Studies in the Linguistic Sciences* 28. Urbana, IL: Department of Linguistics, University of Illinois, 1–26.

Grice, H. Paul 1957. Meaning. *Philosophical Review* 66, 377–388.

Grice, H. Paul 1975. Logic and conversation. In: P. Cole & J. L. Morgan (eds.). *Syntax and Semantics 3: Speech Acts*. New York: Academic Press, 41–58.

Heim, Irene 1982. *The Semantics of Definite and Indefinite Noun Phrases*. Ph.D. dissertation, University of Massachusetts, Amherst, MA. Reprinted: Ann Arbor, MI: University Microfilms.

Helmreich, Stephen 1994. *Pragmatic Referring Functions in Montague Grammar*. Ph.D. dissertation. University of Illinois, Urbana, IL.

Hinrichs, Erhard 1986. Temporal anaphora in discourses of English. *Linguistics & Philosophy* 9, 63–82.

Horn, Laurence R. 1972. *On the Semantic Properties of Logical Operators in English*. Ph.D. dissertation, University of California, Los Angeles, CA. Reprinted: Bloomington, IN: Indiana University Linguistics Club, 1976.

Horn, Laurence R. 1978. Some aspects of negation. In: J. Greenberg, C. Ferguson & E. Moravcsik (eds.). *Universals of Human Language, vol. 4, Syntax*. Stanford, CA: Stanford University Press, 127–210.

Kamp, Hans 1981. A theory of truth and semantic representation. In: J. Groenendijk, T. M. V. Janssen & M. Stokhof (eds.). *Formal Methods in the Study of Language*. Amsterdam: Mathematical Centre, 277–321.

Keenan, Elinor O. 1976. The universality of conversational implicature. *Language in Society* 5, 67–80.

Kripke, Saul 1972. Naming and necessity. In: D. Davidson & G. Harman (eds.). *Semantics of Natural Language*. Dordrecht: Reidel, 253–355 and 763–769.

Lakoff, Robin L. 1968. *Abstract Syntax and Latin Complementation*. Cambridge, MA: The MIT Press.

Levinson, Stephen C. 2000. *Presumptive Meanings: The Theory of Generalized Conversational Implicature*. Cambridge, MA: The MIT Press.

Lewis, David 1969. *Convention: A Philosophical Study*. Cambridge, MA: Harvard University Press.

Lycan, William G. 1984. *Logical Form in Natural Language*. Cambridge, MA: The MIT Press.

McCawley, James D. 1968. The role of semantics in a grammar. In: E. Bach & R. T. Harms (eds.). *Universals in Linguistic Theory*. New York: Holt, Rinehart & Winston, 124–169.

McCawley, James D. 1971. Tense and time reference in English. In: C. Fillmore & D. T. Langendoen (eds.). *Studies in Linguistic Semantics*. New York: Holt, Rinehart & Winston, 97–113.

Morgan, Jerry L. 1973. *Presupposition and the Representation of Meaning: Prolegomena*. Ph.D. dissertation. University of Chicago, Chicago, IL.

Morgan, Jerry L. 1978. Two types of convention in indirect speech acts. In: P. Cole (ed.). *Syntax and Semantics 9: Pragmatics*. New York: Academic Press, 261–280.

Neale, Stephen 1992. Paul Grice and the philosophy of language. *Language and Philosophy* 15, 509–559.
Nunberg, Geoffrey 1978. *The Pragmatics of Reference*. Ph.D. dissertation. CUNY, New York. Reprinted: Bloomington, IN: Indiana University Linguistics Club. (Also published by Garland Publishing, Inc.)
Nunberg, Geoffrey 1979. The non-uniqueness of semantic solutions: Polysemy. *Linguistics & Philosophy* 3, 145–185.
Nunberg, Geoffrey 1993. Indexicality and deixis. *Linguistics & Philosophy* 16, 1–44.
Nunberg, Geoffrey 2004. The pragmatics of deferred interpretation. In: L. R. Horn & G. Ward (eds.). *The Handbook of Pragmatics*. Oxford: Blackwell, 344–364.
Nunberg, Geoffrey & Annie Zaenen 1992. Systematic polysemy in lexicology and lexicography. In: H. Tommola, K. Varantola, & J. Schopp (eds.). *Proceedings of Euralex 92. Part II*. Tampere: The University of Tampere, 387–398.
Partee, Barbara 1973. Some structural analogues between tenses and pronouns in English. *Journal of Philosophy* 70, 601–609.
Partee, Barbara 1989. Binding implicit variables in quantified contexts. In: C. Wiltshire, B. Music & R. Graczyk (eds.). *Papers from the 25th Regional Meeting of the Chicago Linguistic Society*. Chicago, IL: Chicago Linguistic Society, 342–365.
Pelletier, Francis J. & Lenhart K. Schubert 1986. Mass expressions. In: D. Gabbay & F. Guenthner (eds.). *Handbook of Philosophical Logic, vol. 4*. Dordrecht: Reidel, 327–407.
Perrault, Ray 1990. An application of default logic to speech act theory. In: P. Cohen, J. Morgan & M. Pollack (eds.). *Intentions in Communication*. Cambridge, MA: The MIT Press, 161–186.
Pratt, Mary L. 1981. The ideology of speech-act theory. *Centrum* (N.S.) I:1, 5–18.
Prince, Ellen 1983. *Grice and Universality*. Ms. Philadelphia, PA. University of Pennsylvania. http://www.ling.upenn.edu/~ellen/grice.ps, August 3, 2008.
Putnam, Hilary 1975. The meaning of 'meaning.' In: K. Gunderson (ed.). *Language, Mind, and Knowledge*. Minneapolis, MN: University of Minnesota Press, 131–193.
Recanati, Francois 2004. Pragmatics and semantics. In: L. R. Horn & G. Ward (eds.). *The Handbook of Pragmatics*. Oxford: Blackwell, 442–462.
Reddy, Michael 1979. The conduit metaphor – a case of frame conflict in our language about language. In: A. Ortony (ed.). *Metaphor and Thought*. Cambridge: Cambridge University Press, 284–324.
Ross, John R. 1970. On declarative sentences. In: R. Jacobs & P. S. Rosenbaum (eds.). *Readings in English Transformational Grammar*. Waltham, MA: Ginn, 222–272.
Ruhl, Charles 1989. *On Monosemy*. Albany, NY: SUNY Press.
Russell, Dale W. 1993. *Language Acquisition in a Unification-Based Grammar Processing System Using a Real-World Knowledge Base*. Ph.D. dissertation. University of Illinois, Urbana, IL.
Sadock, Jerrold M. 1974. *Toward a Linguistic Theory of Speech Acts*. New York: Academic Press.
Schauber, Ellen & Ellen Spolsky 1986. *The Bounds of Interpretation*. Stanford, CA: Stanford University Press.
Searle, John. 1969. *Speech Acts*. Cambridge: Cambridge University Press.
Sperber, Dan & Deirdre Wilson 1986. *Relevance: Communication and Cognition*. Cambridge, MA: Harvard University Press.
Stalnaker, Robert C. 1970. Pragmatics. *Synthese* 22, 272–289.

Stalnaker, Robert C. 1972. Pragmatics. In: D. Davidson & G. Harman (eds.). *Semantics of Natural Language*. Dordrecht: Reidel, 380–397.

Stalnaker, Robert C. 1974. Pragmatic presuppositions. In: M. K. Munitz & P. K. Unger (eds.). *Semantics and Philosophy*. New York: New York University Press, 197–214.

Stampe, Dennis 1975. Meaning and truth in the theory of speech acts. In: P. Cole & J. L. Morgan (eds.). *Syntax and Semantics 3: Speech Acts*. New York: Academic Press, 1–40.

Peter Pagin and Dag Westerståhl
6 Compositionality

1 Background —— 122
2 Grammars and semantics —— 124
3 Variants and properties of compositionality —— 126
4 Arguments in favor of compositionality —— 136
5 Arguments against compositionality —— 142
6 Problem cases —— 146
7 References —— 152

Abstract: This article is concerned with the principle of compositionality, i.e. the principle that the meaning of a complex expression is a function of the meanings of its parts and its mode of composition. After a brief historical background, a formal algebraic framework for syntax and semantics is presented. In this framework, both syntactic operations and semantic functions are (normally) partial. Using the framework, the basic idea of compositionality is given a precise statement, and several variants, both weaker and stronger, as well as related properties, are distinguished. Several arguments for compositionality are discussed, and the standard arguments are found inconclusive. Also, several arguments against compositionality, and for the claim that it is a trivial property, are discussed, and are found to be flawed. Finally, a number of real or apparent problems for compositionality are considered, and some solutions are proposed.

1 Background

Compositionality is a property that a language may have and may lack, namely the property that the meaning of any complex expression is *determined* by the meanings of its parts and the way they are put together. The language can be natural or formal, but it has to be interpreted. That is, meanings, or more generally, *semantic values* of some sort must be assigned to linguistic expressions, and compositionality concerns precisely the distribution of these values.

Peter Pagin, Stockholm, Sweden
Dag Westerståhl, Gothenburg, Sweden

Particular semantic analyses that are in fact compositional were given already in antiquity, but apparently without any corresponding general conception. For instance, in *Sophist*, chapters 24–26, Plato discusses subject-predicate sentences, and suggests (pretty much) that such a sentence is true [false] if the predicate (verb) attributes to what the subject (noun) signifies things that are [are not]. Notions that approximate the modern concept of compositionality did emerge in medieval times. In the Indian tradition, in the 4th or 5th century CE, Śabara says that

> The meaning of a sentence is based on the meaning of the words.

and this is proposed as the right interpretation of a sūtra by Jaimini from sometime 3rd–6th century BCE (cf. Houben 1997: 75–76). The first to propose a general principle of this nature in the Western tradition seems to have been Peter Abelard (2008, 3.00.8) in the first half of the 12th century, saying that

> Just as a sentence materially consists in a noun and a verb, so too the understanding of it is put together from the understandings of its parts.
> (Translation by and information from Peter King 2007: 8.)

Abelard's principle directly concerns only subject-predicate sentences, it concerns the understanding process rather than meaning itself, and he is unspecific about the nature of the putting-together operation. The high scholastic conception is different in all three respects. In early middle 14th century John Buridan (1998, 2.3, Soph. 2 Thesis 5, QM 5.14, fol. 23vb) states what has become known as the *additive principle*:

> The signification of a complex expression is the sum of the signification of its non-logical terms.
> (Translation by and information from Peter King 2001: 4).

The additive principle, with or without the restriction to non-logical terms, appears to have become standard during the late middle ages (for instance, in 1372, Peter of Ailly refers to the common view that it 'belongs to the [very] notion of an expression that every expression has parts each one of which, when separated, signifies something of what is signified by the whole'; 1980: 30). The medieval theorists apparently did not possess the general concept of a function, and instead proposed a particular function, that of summing (collecting). Mere collecting is inadequate, however, since the sentences *All A's are B's* and *All B's are A's* have the same parts, hence the same collection of part-meanings and hence by the additive principle have the same meaning.

With the development of mathematics and concern with its foundations came a renewed interest in semantics. Gottlob Frege is generally taken to be the first person to have formulated explicitly the notion of compositionality and to claim that it is an essential feature of human language (although some writers have doubted that Frege really expressed, or really believed in, compositionality; e.g. Pelletier 2001 and Janssen 2001). In "Über Sinn und Bedeutung", 1892, he writes:

> Let us assume for the time being that the sentence has a reference. If we now replace one word of the sentence by another having the same reference, this can have no bearing upon the reference of the sentence.
>
> (Frege 1892: 62)

This is (a special case of) the *substitution version* of the idea of semantic values being determined; if you replace parts by others with the same value, the value of the whole doesn't change. Note that the values here are *Bedeutungen* (referents), such as truth values (for sentences) and individual objects (for individual-denoting terms).

Both the substitution version and the function version (see below) were explicitly stated by Rudolf Carnap in (1956) (for both extension and intension), and collectively labeled 'Frege's Principle'.

The term 'compositional', was introduced by Hilary Putnam in Putnam (1975a: 77), read in Oxford in 1960 but not published until in the collection Putnam (1975b). Putnam says "[...] the concept of a compositional mapping should be so defined that the range of a complex sentence should depend on the ranges of sentences of the kinds occurring in the 'derivational history' of the complex sentence." The first use of the term in print seems to be due to Jerry Fodor (a former student of Putnam's) and Jerrold Katz (1964), to characterize meaning and understanding in a similar sense.

Today, compositionality is a key notion in linguistics, philosophy of language, logic, and computer science, but there are divergent views about its exact formulation, methodological status, and empirical significance. To begin to clarify some of these views we need a framework for talking about compositionality that is sufficiently general to be independent of particular theories of syntax or semantics and yet allows us to capture the core idea behind compositionality.

2 Grammars and semantics

The function version and the substitution version of compositionality are two sides of the same coin: that the meaning (value) of a compound expression is a *function* of certain other things (other meanings (values) and a 'mode of composition'). To formulate these versions, two things are needed: a set of *structured expressions* and a *semantics* for them.

Structure is readily taken as *algebraic* structure, so that the set E of linguistic expressions is a domain over which certain syntactic operations or rules are defined, and moreover E is *generated* by these operations from a subset A of *atoms* (e.g. words). In the literature there are essentially two ways of fleshing out this idea. One, which originates with Montague (see 1974a), takes as primitive the fact that linguistic expressions are grouped into *categories* or *sorts*, so that a syntactic rule comes with a specification of the sorts of each argument as well as of the value. This use of *many-sorted algebra* as an abstract linguistic framework is described in Janssen (1986) and Hendriks (2001). The other approach, first made precise in Hodges (2001), is one-sorted but uses *partial algebras* instead, so that rather than requiring the arguments of an operation to be of certain sorts, the operation is simply *undefined* for unwanted arguments. (A many-sorted algebra can in a straightforward way be turned into a one-sorted partial one (but not always vice versa), and under a natural condition the sorts can be recovered in the partial algebra (see Westerståhl 2004 for further details and discussion). Some theorists combine partiality with primitive sorts; for example, Keenan & Stabler 2004 and Kracht 2007.) The partial approach is in a sense simpler and more general than the many-sorted one, and we follow it here.

Thus, let a *grammar*

$$\mathbf{E} = (E, A, \Sigma)$$

be a partial algebra, where E and A are as above and Σ is a set of partial functions over E of finite arity which generate all expressions in E from A. To illustrate, the familiar rules

	NP → Det N	(NP-rule)
	S → NP VP	(S-rule)

correspond to binary partial functions, say $\alpha, \beta \in \Sigma$, such that, if *most*, *dog*, and *bark* are atoms in A, one derives as usual the sentence *Most dogs bark* in E, by first applying α to *most* and *dog*, and then applying β to the result of that and *bark*. These functions are necessarily partial; for example, β is undefined whenever its second argument is *dog*.

It may happen that one and the same expression can be generated in more than one way, i.e. the grammar may allow *structural ambiguity*. So it is not really the expressions in E but rather their *derivation histories*, or *analysis trees*, that should be assigned semantic values. These derivation histories can be represented as *terms* in a (partial) *term algebra* corresponding to **E**, and a *valuation function* is then defined from terms to surface expressions (usually finite strings of symbols). However, to save space we shall ignore this complication here, and formulate our definitions as if semantic values were assigned directly to expressions. More precisely, the simplifying assumption is that each expression is generated in a *unique* way from the atoms by the rules. One consequence is that the notion of a *subexpression* is well-defined: the subexpressions of t are t itself and all expressions used in the generation of t from atoms (it is fairly straightforward to lift the uniqueness assumption, and reformulate the definitions given here so that they apply to terms in the term algebra instead; see e.g. Westerståhl 2004 for details).

The second thing needed to talk about compositionality is a *semantics* for **E**. We take this simply to be a function μ from a subset of E to some set M of semantic values ('meanings'). In the term algebra case, μ takes grammatical terms as arguments. Alternatively, one may take *disambiguated* expressions such as phrase structure markings by means of labeled brackets. Yet another option is to have an extra syntactic level, like Logical Form, as the semantic function domain. The choice between such alternatives is largely irrelevant from the point of view of compositionality.

The semantic function μ is also allowed to be partial. For example, it may represent our partial understanding of some language, or our attempts at a semantics for a fragment of a language. Further, even a complete semantics will be partial if one wants to maintain a distinction between *meaningfulness* (being in the domain of μ) and *grammaticality* (being derivable by the grammar rules).

No assumption is made about meanings. What matters for the abstract notion of compositionality is not meanings as such, but *synonymy*, i.e. the partial equivalence relation on E defined by:

$$u \equiv_\mu t \text{ iff } \mu(u), \mu(t) \text{ are both defined and } \mu(u) = \mu(t).$$

(We use s, t, u, with or without subscripts, for arbitrary members of E.)

3 Variants and properties of compositionality

3.1 Basic compositionality

Both the function version and the substitution version of compositionality can now be easily formulated, given a grammar **E** and a semantics μ as above.

Funct(μ) For every rule $\alpha \in \Sigma$ there is a meaning operation r_α such that if $\alpha(u_1, \ldots, u_n)$ is meaningful, then

$$\mu(\alpha(u_1, \ldots, u_n)) = r_\alpha(\mu(u_1), \ldots, \mu(u_n)).$$

Note that Funct(μ) presupposes the *Domain Principle* (DP): subexpressions of meaningful expressions are also meaningful. The substitution version of compositionality is given by

Subst($\equiv_\mu$) If $s[u_1, \ldots, u_n]$ and $s[t_1, \ldots, t_n]$ are both meaningful expressions, and if $u_i \equiv_\mu t_i$ for $1 \leq i \leq n$, then $s[u_1, \ldots, u_n] \equiv_\mu s[t_1, \ldots, t_n]$.

The notation $s[u_1, \ldots, u_n]$ indicates that s contains (not necessarily immediate) disjoint occurrences of subexpressions among $u_1, \ldots, u_n$, and $s[t_1, \ldots, t_n]$ results from replacing each u_i by t_i. Restricted to immediate subexpressions Subst($\equiv_\mu$) says that $\equiv_\mu$ is a partial *congruence relation*:

If $\alpha(u_1, \ldots, u_n)$ and $\alpha(t_1, \ldots, t_n)$ are both meaningful and $u_i \equiv_\mu t_i$ for $1 \leq i \leq n$, then $\alpha(u_1, \ldots, u_n) \equiv_\mu \alpha(t_1, \ldots, t_n)$.

Under DP, this is equivalent to the unrestricted version.

Subst($\equiv_\mu$) does not presuppose DP, and one can easily think of semantics for which DP fails. However, a first observation is:

(1) Under DP, Funct(μ) and Subst($\equiv_\mu$) are equivalent.

That Rule(μ) implies Subst($\equiv_\mu$) is obvious when Subst($\equiv_\mu$) is restricted to immediate subexpressions, and otherwise proved by induction over the generation complexity of expressions. In the other direction, the operations r_α must be found. For $m_1, \ldots, m_n \in M$, let $r_\alpha(m_1, \ldots, m_n) = \mu(\alpha(u_1, \ldots, u_n))$ if there are expressions u_i such that $\mu(u_i) = m_i$, $1 \leq i \leq n$, and $\mu(\alpha(u_1, \ldots, u_n))$ is defined. Otherwise, $r_\alpha(m_1, \ldots, m_n)$ can be undefined (or arbitrary). This is enough, as long as we can be certain that the definition is independent of the choice of the u_i, but that is precisely what Subst($\equiv_\mu$) says.

The requirements of basic compositionality are in some respects not so strong, as can be seen from the following observations:

(2) If μ gives the same meaning to all expressions, then Funct(μ) holds.
(3) If μ gives different meanings to all expressions, then Funct(μ) holds.

(2) is of course trivial. For (3), consider Subst($\equiv_\mu$) and observe that if no two expressions have the same meaning, then $u_i \equiv_\mu t_i$ entails $u_i = t_i$, so Subst($\equiv_\mu$), and therefore Funct(μ), holds trivially.

3.2 Recursive semantics

The function version of compositional semantics is given by recursion over syntax, but that does not imply that the meaning operations are defined by recursion over *meaning*, in which case we have *recursive semantics*. Standard semantic theories are typically both recursive and compositional, but the two notions are mutually independent. In the recursive case we have:

Rec(μ) There is a function b and for every $\alpha \in \Sigma$ an operation r_α such that for every meaningful expression s,

$$\mu(s) = \begin{cases} b(s) \text{ if } s \text{ is atomic} \\ r_\alpha(\mu(u_1), ..., \mu(u_n), u_1, ..., u_n) \text{ if } s = \alpha(u_1, ..., u_n) \end{cases}$$

For μ to be recursive, the basic function b and the meaning composition operation r_α must themselves be recursive, but this is not required in the function version of compositionality. In the other direction, the presence of the expressions $u_1, ..., u_n$ themselves as arguments to r_α has the effect that the compositional substitution laws need not hold (cf. Janssen 1997).

If we drop the recursiveness requirement on b and r_α, Rec(μ) becomes vacuous. This is because $r_\alpha(m_1, ..., m_n, u_1, ..., u_n)$ can simply be *defined* to be $\mu(\alpha(u_1, ..., u_n))$ whenever $m_i = \mu(u_i)$ for all i and $\alpha(u_1, ..., u_n)$ is meaningful (and undefined otherwise). Since inter-substitution of synonymous but distinct expressions changes at least one argument of r_α, no counterexample is possible.

3.3 Weaker versions

Basic (first-level) compositionality takes the meaning of a complex expression to be determined by the meanings of the *immediate* subexpressions and the top-level syntactic operation. We get a weaker version – second-level compositionality – if we require only that the operations of the *two* highest levels, together with the meanings of expressions at the second level, determine the meaning of the whole complex expression. A possible example comes from constructions with quantified noun phrases where the meanings of both the determiner and the restricting noun – i.e. two levels below the head of the construction in question – are needed for semantic composition, a situation that may occur with possessives and some reciprocals. In Peters & Westerståhl (2006, ch. 7) and in Westerståhl (2008) it is argued that, in general, the corresponding semantics is second-level but not (first-level) compositional.

Third-level compositionality is defined analogously, and is weaker still. In the extreme case we have *bottom-level*, or *weak* functional compositionality, if the meaning of the complex term is determined only by the meanings of its atomic constituents and the entire syntactic construction (i.e. the derived operation that is extracted from a complex expression by knocking out the atomic constituents). A function version of this becomes somewhat cumbersome (but see Hodges 2001, sect. 5), whereas the substitution version becomes simply:

AtSubst($\equiv_\mu$) Just like Subst($\equiv_\mu$) except that the u_i and t_i are all atomic.

Although weak compositionality is not completely trivial (a language could lack the property), it does not serve the language users very well: the meaning operation r_α that corresponds to a complex syntactic operation α cannot be predicted from its build-up out of simpler syntactic operations and their corresponding meaning operations. Hence, there will be infinitely many complex syntactic operations whose semantic significance must be learned one by one.

It may be noted here that terminology concerning compositionality is somewhat fluctuating. David Dowty (2007) calls (an approximate version of) weak functional compositionality *Frege's Principle*, and refers to Funct(μ) as *homomorphism compositionality*, or *strictly local compositionality*, or *context-free semantics*. In Larson & Segal (1995), this is called *strong compositionality*. The labels *second-level compositionality*, *third-level*, etc. are not standard in the literature but seem appropriate.

3.4 Stronger versions

We get stronger versions of compositionality by enlarging the domain of the semantic function, or by placing additional restrictions on meaningfulness or on meaning composition operations. An example of the first is Zoltán Szabó's (2000) idea that the same meaning operations define semantic functions in all possible human languages, not just for all sentences in each language taken by itself. That is, whenever two languages have the same syntactic operation, they also associate the same meaning operation with it.

An example of the second option is what Wilfrid Hodges has called the *Husserl property* (going back to ideas in Husserl 1900):

(Huss) Synonymous expressions belong to the same (semantic) category.

Here the notion of category is defined in terms of substitution; say that $u \sim_\mu t$ if, for every s in E, $s[u] \in dom(\mu)$ iff $s[t] \in dom(\mu)$. So (Huss) says that synonymous terms can be inter-substituted without loss of meaningfulness. This is often a reasonable requirement (though Hodges 2001 mentions some putative counter-examples). (Huss) also has the consequence that Subst($\equiv_\mu$) can be simplified to Subst$_1$($\equiv_\mu$), which only deals with replacing *one* subexpression by another. Then one can replace *n* subexpressions by applying Subst$_1$($\equiv_\mu$) *n* times; (Huss) guarantees that all the 'intermediate' expressions are meaningful.

An example of the third kind is that of requiring the meaning composition operations to be computable. To make this more precise we need to impose more order on the meaning domain, viewing meanings too as given by an algebra M = (M, B, Ω), where B ⊆ M is a finite set of *basic meanings*, Ω is a finite set of elementary operations from *n*-tuples of meanings to meanings, and M is generated from B by means of the operations in Ω. This allows the definition of meaning operations by recursion over M. The semantic function μ is then defined simultaneously by recursion over syntax and by recursion over the meaning domain. Assuming that the elementary meaning operations are computable in a sense relevant to cognition, the semantic function itself is computable.

A further step in this direction is to require that the meaning operations be *easy* to compute, thereby reducing or minimizing the complexity of semantic interpretation. For instance, meaning operations that are either elementary or else formed from elementary operations by function composition and function application would be of this kind (cf. Pagin 2011 for work in this direction).

Another strengthening, also introduced in Hodges (2001), concerns Frege's so-called Context Principle. A famous but cryptic saying by Frege (1884, x) is: "Never ask for the meaning of a word in isolation, but only in the context of a sentence". This principle has been much discussed in the literature (for example, Dummett 1973, Dummett 1981, Janssen 2001, Pelletier 2001), and sometimes taken to *conflict* with compositionality. However, if not seen as saying that words somehow lose their meaning in isolation, it can be taken as a *constraint* on meanings, in the form of what we might call the Contribution Principle:

(CP) The meaning of an expression is the contribution it makes to the meanings of complex expressions of which it is a part.

This is vague, but Hodges notes that it can be made precise with an additional requirement on the synonymy $\equiv_\mu$. Assume (Huss), and consider:

InvSubst$_\exists$($\equiv_\mu$) If $u \not\equiv_\mu t$, there is an expression s such that either exactly one of s[u] and s[t] is meaningful, or both are and s[u] $\not\equiv_\mu$ s[t].

So if two expressions of the same category are such that no complex expression of which the first is a part changes meaning when the first is replaced by the second, they are synonymous. That is, if they make the *same* contribution to *all* such complex expressions, their meanings cannot be distinguished. This can be taken as one half of (CP), and compositionality in the form of $\text{Subst}_1(\equiv_\mu)$ as the other.

Remark: Hodges' main application of these notions is to what has become known as the *extension problem*: given a partial compositional semantics μ, under what circumstances can μ be extended to a larger fragment of the language? Here (CP) can be used as a requirement, so that the meaning of a new word w, say, must respect the (old) meanings of complex expressions of which w is a part. This is especially suited to situations when all new items are parts of expressions that already have meanings (cofinality). Hodges defines a corresponding notion of *fregean extension* of μ, and shows that in the situation just mentioned, and given that μ satisfies (Huss), a *unique* fregean extension always exists. Another version of the extension problem is solved in Westerståhl (2004). An abstract account of compositional extension issues is given in Fernando (2005). *End of remark*

We can take a step further in this direction by requiring that replacement of expressions by expressions with *different* meanings *always* changes meaning:

$\text{InvSubst}_v(\equiv_\mu)$ If for some i, $0 \leq i \leq n$, $u_i \not\equiv_\mu t_i$, then for every expression s, either exactly one of $s[u_1, \ldots, u_n]$ and $s[t_1, \ldots, t_n]$ are meaningful, or both are and $s[u_1, \ldots, u_n] \not\equiv_\mu s[t_1, \ldots, t_n]$.

This disallows synonymy between complex expressions transformable into each other by substitution of constituents at least some of which are non-synonymous, but it does allow synonymous expressions with different structure. Carnap's principle of synonymy as *intensional isomorphism* forbids this, too. With the concept of *intension* from possible-worlds semantics it can be stated as

(RC) $t \equiv_\mu u$ iff
   i) t, u are atomic and co-intensional, or
   ii) for some α, $t = \alpha(t_1, \ldots, t_n)$, $u = \alpha(u_1, \ldots, u_n)$, and $t_i \equiv_\mu u_i$, $1 \leq i \leq n$

(RC) entails both $\text{Subst}(\equiv_\mu)$ and $\text{InvSubst}_v(\equiv_\mu)$, but is very restrictive. It disallows synonymy between *brother* and *male sibling* as well as between *John loves Susan* and *Susan is loved by John*, and allows different expressions to be synonymous only if they differ at most in being transformed from each other by substitution of synonymous atomic expressions.

(RC) seems too strong. We get an intermediate requirement as follows. First, define *μ-congruence*, $\simeq_\mu$ in the following way:

($\simeq_\mu$) $t \simeq_\mu u$ iff
     i) t or u is atomic, $t \equiv_\mu u$, and neither is a constituent of the other, *or*
     ii) $t = \alpha(t_1, \ldots, t_n)$, $u = \beta(u_1, \ldots, u_n)$, $t_i \simeq u_i$, $1 \leq i \leq n$, and for all $s_1, \ldots, s_n$, $\alpha(s_1, \ldots, s_n) \equiv_\mu \beta(s_1, \ldots, s_n)$, if either is defined.

Then require synonymous expressions to be congruent:

(Cong)   If $t \equiv_\mu u$, then $t \simeq_\mu u$.

By (Cong), synonymous expressions cannot differ much syntactically, but they may differ in the two crucial respects forbidden by (RC). (Cong) does not hold for natural language if logically equivalent sentences are taken as synonymous. That it holds otherwise remains a conjecture (but see Johnson 2006).

It follows from (Cong) that meanings are (or can be represented as) structured entities: entities uniquely determined by how they are built, i.e. entities from which constituents can be extracted. We then have projection operations:

(Rev)   For every meaning operation $r: E^n \to E$ there are projection operations $s_{r,i}$ such that $s_{r,i}(r(m_1, \ldots, m_n)) = m_i$.

Together with the fact that the operations r_i are meaning operations for a compositional semantic function μ, (Rev) has semantic consequences, the main one being a kind of *inverse* functional compositionality:

InvFunct(μ)   The syntactic expression of a complex meaning m is determined, up to μ-congruence, by the composition of m and the syntactic expressions of its parts.

For the philosophical significance of inverse compositionality, see sections 4.6 and 5.2 below. For ($\simeq_\mu$), (Cong), InvFunct(μ), and a proof that (Rev) is a consequence of (Cong) (really of the equivalent statement that the meaning algebra is a *free algebra*), see Pagin (2003a). (Rev) seems to be what Jerry Fodor understands by 'reverse compositionality' in e.g. Fodor (2000: 371).

3.5 Direct and indirect compositionality

Pauline Jacobson (2002) distinguishes between *direct* and *indirect* compositionality, as well as between *strong direct* and *weak direct* compositionality. This concerns how the analysis tree of an expression maps onto the expression itself, an issue we have avoided here, for simplicity. Informally, in strong direct compositionality, a complex expression *t* is built up from sub-expressions (corresponding to subtrees of the analysis tree for *t*) simply by means of concatenation. In weak direct compositionality, one expression may wrap around another (as *call up* wraps around *him* in *call him up*). In indirect compositionality, there is no such simple correspondence between the composition of analysis trees and elementary operations on strings.

Even under our assumption that each expression has a unique analysis, our notion of compositionality here is indirect in the above sense: syntactic operations may delete strings, reorder strings, make substitutions and add new elements. Strictly speaking, however, the direct/indirect distinction is not a distinction between kinds of semantics, but between kinds of syntax. Still, discussion of it tends to focus on the role of compositionality in linguistics, e.g. whether to let the choice of syntactic theory be guided by compositionality (cf. Dowty 2007 and Kracht 2007. For discussion of the general significance of the distinction, see Barker & Jacobson 2007).

3.6 Compositionality for "interpreted languages"

Some linguists, among them Jacobson, tend to think of grammar rules as applying to *signs*, where a sign is a triple $\langle e, k, m \rangle$ consisting of a string, a syntactic category, and a meaning. This is formalized by Marcus Kracht (see 2003, 2007), who defines an *interpreted language* to be a set L of signs in this sense, and a *grammar G* as a set of partial functions from signs to signs, such that L is generated by the functions in G from a subset of atomic (lexical) signs. Thus, a meaning assignment is built into the language, and grammar rules are taken to apply to meanings as well.

This looks like a potential strengthening of our notion of grammar, but is not really used that way, partly because the grammar is taken to operate independently (though in parallel) at each of the three levels. Let p_1, p_2, and p_3 be the projection functions on triples yielding their first, second, and third elements, respectively. Kracht calls a grammar *compositional* if for each *n*-ary grammar rule α there are three operations $r_{\alpha,1}$, $r_{\alpha,2}$, and $r_{\alpha,3}$ such that for all signs $\sigma_1, \ldots, \sigma_n$ for which α is defined,

$$\alpha(\sigma_1, \ldots, \sigma_n) =$$
$$\langle r_{\alpha,1}(p_1(\sigma_1), \ldots, p_1(\sigma_n)), r_{\alpha,2}(p_2(\sigma_1), \ldots, p_2(\sigma_n)), r_{\alpha,3}(p_3(\sigma_1), \ldots, p_3(\sigma_n)) \rangle$$

and moreover $\alpha(\sigma_1, \ldots, \sigma_n)$ is defined if and only if each $r_{\alpha,i}$ is defined for the corresponding projections.

In a sense, however, this is not really a variant of compositionality but rather another way to organize grammars and semantics. This is indicated by (4) and (5) below, which are not hard to verify. First, call G *strict* if $\alpha(\sigma_1, \ldots, \sigma_n)$ defined and $p_i(\sigma_i) = p_i(\tau_i)$ for $1 \leq i \leq n$ entails $\alpha(\tau_1, \ldots, \tau_n)$ defined, and similarly for the other projections. All compositional grammars are strict.

(4) Every grammar G in Kracht's sense for an interpreted language L is a grammar (E, A, Σ) in the sense of section 2 (with $E = L$, A = the set of atomic signs in L, and Σ = the set of partial functions of G). Provided G is strict, G is compositional (in Kracht's sense) iff each of p_1, p_2, and p_3, seen as assignments of values to signs (so p_3 is the meaning assignment), is compositional (in our sense).

(5) Conversely, if $\mathbf{E} = (E, A, \Sigma)$ is a grammar and μ a semantics for $\mathbf{E}$, let $L = \{\langle u, u, \mu(u)\rangle : u \in dom(\mu)\}$. Define a grammar G for L (with the obvious atomic signs) by letting

$$\alpha(\langle u_1, u_1, \mu(u_1)\rangle, \ldots, \langle u_n, u_n, \mu(u_n)\rangle) = \langle \alpha(u_1, \ldots, u_n), \alpha(u_1, \ldots, u_n),$$
$$\mu(\alpha(u_1, \ldots, u_n))\rangle$$

whenever $\alpha \in \Sigma$ is defined for $u_1, \ldots, u_n$ and $\alpha(u_1, \ldots, u_n) \in dom(\mu)$ (undefined otherwise). Provided μ is closed under subexpressions and has the Husserl property, μ is compositional iff G is compositional.

3.7 Context dependence

In standard possible-worlds semantics the role of meanings are served by *intensions*: functions from possible worlds to extensions. For instance, the intension of a sentence returns a truth value, when the argument is a world for which the function is defined. Montague (1968) extended this idea to include not just worlds but arbitrary *indices i* from some set I, as ordered tuples of contextual factors relevant to semantic evaluation. Speaker, time, and place of utterance are typical elements in such indices. The semantic function μ then assigns a meaning $\mu(t)$ to an expression t, which is itself a function such that for an index $i \in I$, $\mu(t)(i)$ gives an extension as value. Kaplan's (1989) *two-level* version of this first assigns a function (*character*) to t taking certain parts of the index (the *context*, typically including the speaker) to a *content*, which is in turn a function from selected parts of the index to extensions.

In both versions, the usual concept of compositionality straightforwardly applies. The situation gets more complicated when semantic functions themselves take contextual arguments, e.g. if a meaning-in-context for an expression t in context c is given as $\mu(t, c)$. The reason for such a change might be the view that the contextual meanings are contents in their own right, not just extensional fallouts of the standing, context-independent meaning. But with context as an additional argument we have a new source of variation. The most natural extension of compositionality to this format is given by

C-Funct(μ) For every rule $\alpha \in \Sigma$ there is a meaning operation r_α such that for every context c, if $\alpha(u_1, \ldots, u_n)$ has meaning in c, then

$$\mu(\alpha(u_1, \ldots, u_n), c) = r_\alpha(\mu(u_1, c), \ldots, \mu(u_n, c)).$$

C-Funct(μ) seems like a straightforward extension of compositionality to a contextual semantics, but it can fail in a way non-contextual semantics cannot, by a *context-shift failure*. For we can suppose that although $\mu(u_i, c) = \mu(u_i, c')$, $1 \leq i \leq n$, we still have $\mu(\alpha(u_1, \ldots, u_n), c) \neq \mu(\alpha(u_1, \ldots, u_n), c')$. One might see this as a possible result of so-called *unarticulated constituents*. Maybe the meaning of the sentence

(6) It rains.

is sensitive to the location of utterance, while none of the *constituents* of that sentence (say, *it* and *rains*) is sensitive to location. Then the contextual meaning of the sentence at a location l is different from the contextual meaning of the sentence at another location l', even though there is no such difference in contextual meaning for any of the parts. This may hold even if substitution of *expressions* is compositional.

There is therefore room for a weaker principle that cannot fail in this way, where the meaning operation *itself* takes a context argument:

C-Funct(μ)$_c$ For every rule $\alpha \in \Sigma$ there is a meaning operation r_α such that for every context c, if $\alpha(u_1, \ldots, u_n)$ has meaning in c, then $\mu(\alpha(u_1, \ldots, u_n), c) = r_\alpha(\mu(u_1, c), \ldots, \mu(u_n, c), c)$.

The only difference is the last argument of r_α. Because of this argument, C-Funct(μ)$_c$ is not sensitive to the counterexample above, and is more similar to non-contextual compositionality in this respect.

This kind of semantic framework is discussed in Pagin (2005); a general format, and properties of the various notions of compositionality that arise, are presented in Westerståhl (2011). For example, it can be shown that (weak) compositionality for contextual meaning entails compositionality for the corresponding standing meaning, but the converse does not hold.

So far, we have dealt with extra-linguistic context, but one can also extend compositional semantics to dependence on *linguistic context*. The semantic value of some particular *occurrence* of an expression may then depend on whether it is an occurrence in, say, an extensional context, or an intensional context, or a hyperintensional context, a quotation context, or yet something else.

A framework for such a semantics needs a set C of *context types*, an initial *null* context type $\theta \in C$ for unembedded occurrences, and a ternary function ψ from context types, syntactic operators and argument place numbers to context types. If $\alpha(t_1, \ldots, t_n)$ occurs in context type c, then $t_1, \ldots, t_n$ will occur in context types $\psi(c, \alpha, 1), \ldots, \psi(c, \alpha, n)$ respectively. The context type for a particular occurrence t_i^o of an expression t_i in a host expression t is then determined by its immediately embedding operator α_1 and the argument place, *its* immediately embedding operator and the argument place, and so on until the topmost operator occurrence.

The semantic function μ takes an expression t and a context type c into a semantic value. The only thing that will differ for *linguistic* context from C-Funct$(\mu)_c$ above is that the context of the subexpressions may be different (according to the function ψ) from the context of the containing expression:

LC-Funct$(\mu)_c$ For every $\alpha \in \Sigma$ there is an operation r_α such that for every context $c \in C$, if $\alpha(u_1, \ldots, u_n)$ has meaning in c, then

$$\mu(\alpha(u_1, \ldots, u_n), c) = r_\alpha(\mu(u_1, c_1), \ldots, \mu(u_n, c_n), c),$$

where $c_i = \psi(c, \alpha, i)$, $1 \leq i \leq n$.

4 Arguments in favor of compositionality

4.1 Learnability

Perhaps the most common argument for compositionality is the argument from *learnability*: A natural language has infinitely many meaningful sentences. It is impossible for a human speaker to learn the meaning of each sentence one by one. Rather, it must be possible for a speaker to learn the entire language by learning the meaning of a finite number of expressions, and a finite number of construction forms. For this to be possible, the language must have a compositional semantics. The argument was to some extent anticipated already in Sanskrit philosophy of language. During the first or second century BCE Patañjali writes:

> … Bṛhaspati addressed Indra during a thousand divine years going over the grammatical expressions by speaking each particular word, and still he did not attain the end. … But

then how are grammatical expressions understood? Some work containing general and particular rules has to be composed ...
> (Cf. Staal 1969: 501–502. Thanks to Brendan Gillon for the reference.)

A modern classical passage plausibly interpreted along these lines is due to Donald Davidson:

> It is conceded by most philosophers of language, and recently by some linguists, that a satisfactory theory of meaning must give an account of how the meanings of sentences depend upon the meanings of words. Unless such an account could be supplied for a particular language, it is argued, there would be no explaining the fact that we can learn the language: no explaining the fact that, on mastering a finite vocabulary and a finite set of rules, we are prepared to produce and understand any of a potential infinitude of sentences. I do not dispute these vague claims, in which I sense more than a kernel of truth. Instead I want to ask what it is for a theory to give an account of the kind adumbrated.
> (Davidson 1967: 17)

Properly spelled out, the problem is not that of learning the meaning of infinitely many meaningful sentences (given that one has command of a syntax), for if I learn that they all mean that *snow is white*, I have already accomplished the task. Rather, the problem is that there are infinitely many propositions that are each expressed by some sentence in the language (with contextual parameters fixed), and hence infinitely many equivalence classes of synonymous sentences.

Still, as an argument for compositionality, the learnability argument has two main weaknesses. First, the premise that there are infinitely many sentences that have a determinate meaning although they have never been used by any speaker, is a very strong premise, in need of justification. That is, at a given time t_0, it may be that the speaker or speakers employ a semantic function μ defined for infinitely many sentences, or it may be that they employ an alternative function μ_0 which agrees with μ on all sentences that have in fact been used but is simply *undefined* for all that have not been used. On the alternative hypothesis, when using a new sentence s, the speaker or the community gives some meaning to s, thereby extending μ_0 to μ_1, and so on. Phenomenologically, of course, the new sentence seemed to the speakers to come already equipped with meaning, but that was just an illusion. On this alternative hypothesis, there is no infinite semantics to be learned. To argue that there is a learnability problem, we must first justify the premise that we employ an infinite semantic function. This cannot be justified by induction, for we cannot infer from finding sentences meaningful that they were meaningful before we found them, and exactly that would have to be the induction base.

The second weakness is that even with the infinity premise in place, the conclusion of the argument would be that the semantics must be computable, but computability does not entail compositionality, as we have seen.

4.2 Novelty

Closely related to the learnability argument is the argument from *novelty*: speakers are able to understand sentences they have never heard before, which is possible only if the language is compositional.

When the argument is interpreted so that, as in the learnability argument, we need to explain how speakers reliably *track* the semantics, i.e. assign to new sentences the meaning that they independently have, then the argument from novelty shares the two main weaknesses with the learnability argument.

4.3 Productivity

According to the pure argument from *productivity*, we need an explanation of why we are able to *produce* infinitely many meaningful sentences, and compositionality offers the best explanation. Classically, productivity is appealed to by Noam Chomsky as an argument for generative grammar. One of the passages runs

> The most striking aspect of linguistic competence is what we may call the 'creativity of language', that is, the speaker's ability to produce new sentences that are immediately understood by other speakers although they bear no physical resemblance to sentences that are 'familiar'. The fundamental importance of this creative aspect of normal language use has been recognized since the seventeenth century at least, and it was the core of Humboldtian general linguistics.
>
> (Chomsky 1971: 74)

This passage does not appeal to pure productivity, since it makes an appeal to the understanding by other speakers (cf. Chomsky 1980: 76–78). The pure productivity aspect has been emphasized by Fodor (e.g. 1987: 147–148), i.e. that natural language can *express* an open-ended set of propositions.

However, the pure productivity argument is very weak. On the premise that a human speaker can think indefinitely many propositions, all that is needed is to assign those propositions to sentences. The assignment does not have to be systematic in any way, and all the syntax that is needed for the infinity itself is simple concatenation. Unless the assignment is to meet certain conditions, productivity requires nothing more than the combination of infinitely many propositions and infinitely many expressions.

4.4 Systematicity

A related argument by Fodor (1987: 147–150) is that of systematicity. It can be stated either as a property of speaker understanding or as an expressive property of a language. Fodor tends to favor the former (since he is ultimately concerned with the mental). In the simplest case, Fodor points out that if a language user understands a sentence of the form *tRu*, she will also understand the corresponding sentence *uRt*, and argues that this is best explained by appeal to compositionality.

Formally, the argument is to be generalized to cover the understanding of any new sentence that is formed by recombination of constituents that occur, and construction forms that are used, in sentences already understood. Hence, in this form it reduces to one of three different arguments; either to the argument from *novelty*, or to the *productivity* argument, or finally, to the argument from intersubjectivity (below), and only spells out a bit the already familiar idea of old parts in new combinations.

It might be taken to add an element, for it not only aims at explaining the understanding of new sentences that is in fact manifested, but also predicts what new sentences will be understood. However, Fodor himself points out the problem with this aspect, for if there is a sentence *s* formed by a recombination that we do *not* find meaningful, we will not take it as a limitation of the systematicity of our understanding, but as revealing that the sentence *s* is not in fact meaningful, and hence that there is nothing to understand. Hence, we cannot come to any other conclusion than that the systematicity of our understanding is maximal.

The systematicity argument can alternatively be understood as concerning natural language itself, namely as the argument that sentences formed by grammatical recombination are meaningful. It is debatable to what extent this really holds, and sentences (or so-called sentences) like Chomsky's *Colorless green ideas sleep furiously* have been used to argue that not all grammatical sentences are meaningful.

But even if we were to find meaningful all sentences that we find grammatical, this does not in itself show that compositionality, or any kind of systematic semantics, is needed for explaining it. If it is only a matter of assigning some meaning or other, without any further condition, it would be enough that we can think new thoughts and have a disposition to assign them to new sentences.

4.5 Induction on synonymy

We can observe that our synonymy intuitions conform to Subst($\equiv_\mu$). In case after case, we find the result of substitution synonymous with the original expression, if the new part is taken as synonymous with the old. This forms the basis of an *inductive generalization* that such substitutions are always meaning preserving. In contrast to the argument from *novelty*, where the idea of tracking the semantics is central, this induction argument may concern our habits of assigning meaning to, or reading meaning into, new sentences: we tend to do it compositionally.

There is nothing wrong with this argument, as far as it goes, beyond what is in general problematic with induction. It should only be noted that the conclusion is weak. Typically, arguments for compositionality aim at the conclusion that there is a systematic pattern to the assignment of meaning to new sentences, and that the meaning of new sentences can be computed somehow. This is not the case in the *induction* argument, for the conclusion is compatible with the possibility that substitutivity is the *only* systematic feature of the semantics. That is, assignment to meaning of new sentences may be completely random, except for respecting substitutivity. If the substitutivity version of compositionality holds, then (under DP) so does the function version, but the semantic function need not be computable, and need not even be finitely specifiable. So, although the argument may be empirically sound, it does not establish what arguments for compositionality usually aim at.

4.6 Intersubjectivity and communication

The problems with the idea of tracking semantics when interpreting new sentences can be eliminated by bringing in intersubjective agreement in interpretation. For by our common sense standards of judging whether we understand sentences the same way or not, there is overwhelming evidence (e.g. from discussing broadcast news reports) that in an overwhelming proportion of cases, speakers of the same language interpret new sentences *similarly*. This convergence of interpretation, far above chance, does not presuppose that the sentences heard were meaningful before they were used. The phenomenon needs an explanation, and it is reasonable to suppose that the explanation involves the hypothesis that the meaning of the sentences are computable, and so it isn't left to guesswork or mere intuition what the new sentences mean.

The appeal to intersubjectivity disposes of an unjustified presupposition about semantics, but two problems remain. First, when encountering new sentences, these are almost invariably produced by a speaker, and the speaker has intended to convey something by the sentence, but the speaker hasn't *interpreted* the sentence, but fitted it to an antecedent thought. Secondly, we have an argument for computability, but not for compositionality.

The first observation indicates that it is at bottom the success rate of linguistic communication with new sentences that gives us a reason for believing that sentences are systematically mapped on meanings. This was the point of view in Frege's famous passage from the opening of 'Compound Thoughts':

> It is astonishing what language can do. With a few syllables it can express an incalculable number of thoughts, so that even a thought grasped by a terrestrial being for the very first

time can be put into a form of words which will be understood by someone to whom the thought is entirely new. This would be impossible, were we not able to distinguish parts in the thoughts corresponding to the parts of a sentence, so that the structure of the sentence serves as the image of the structure of the thought.

(Frege 1923: 55)

As Frege depicts it here, the speaker is first entertaining a new thought, or proposition, finds a sentence for conveying that proposition to a hearer, and by means of that sentence the hearer comes to entertain the same proposition as the speaker started out with. Frege appeals to semantic structure for explaining how this is possible. He claims that the proposition has a structure that mirrors the structure of the sentence (so that the semantic relation may be an isomorphism), and goes on to claim that without this structural correspondence, communicative success with new propositions would not be possible.

It is natural to interpret Frege as expressing a view that entails that compositionality holds as a consequence of the isomorphism idea. The reason Frege went beyond compositionality (or homomorphism, which does not require a one-one relation) seems to be an intuitive appeal to symmetry: the speaker moves from proposition to sentence, while the hearer moves from sentence to proposition. An isomorphism is a one-one relation, so that each relatum uniquely determines the other.

Because of synonymy, a sentence that expresses a proposition in a particular language is typically not uniquely determined within that language by the proposition expressed. Still, we might want the speaker to be able to *work out* what expression to use, rather searching around for suitable sentences by interpreting candidates one after the other. The inverse functional compositionality principle, InvFunct(μ), of section 3.4, offers such a method. Inverse compositionality is also connected with the idea of structured meanings, or thoughts, while compositionality by itself isn't, and so in this respect Frege is vindicated (these ideas are developed in Pagin 2003a).

4.7 Summing up

Although many share the feeling that there is "more than a kernel of truth" (cf. section 4.1) in the usual arguments for compositionality, some care is required to formulate and evaluate them. One must avoid question-begging presuppositions; for example, if a presupposition is that there is an infinity of propositions, the argument for *that* had better not be that standardly conceived natural or mental languages allow the generation of such an infinite set. Properly understood, the arguments can be seen as inferences to the best explanation, which is a respectable but somewhat problematic methodology. (One usually hasn't really tried many other explanations than the proposed one.)

Another important (and related) point is that virtually all arguments so far only justify the principle that the meaning is computable or recursive, and the principle that up to certain syntactic variation, an expression of a proposition is computable from that proposition. Why should the semantics also be compositional, and possibly inversely compositional? One reason could be that compositional semantics, or at least certain simple forms of compositional semantics, is very *simple*, in the sense that a minimal number of processing steps are needed by the hearer for arriving at a full interpretation (or, for the speaker, a full expression, cf. Pagin 2011), but these issues of complexity need to be further explored.

5 Arguments against compositionality

Arguments against compositionality of natural language can be divided into four main categories:
a) arguments that certain constructions are counterexamples and make the principle false,
b) arguments that compositionality is an empirically vacuous, or alternatively trivially correct, principle,
c) arguments that compositional semantics is not *needed* to account for actual linguistic communication,
d) arguments that actual linguistic communication is not *suited* for compositional semantics.

The first category, that of counterexamples, will be treated in a separate section dealing with a number of problem cases. Here we shall discuss arguments in the last three categories.

5.1 Vacuity and triviality arguments

Vacuity. Some claims about the vacuity of compositionality in the literature are based on mathematical arguments. For example, Zadrozny (1994) shows that for every semantics μ there is a compositional semantics ν such that $\nu(t)(t) = \mu(t)$ for every expression t, and uses this fact to draw a conclusion of that kind. But note that the mathematical fact is itself trivial: let $\nu(t) = \mu$ for each t and the result is immediate from (2) in section 3.1 above (other parts of Zadrozny's results use non-wellfounded sets and are less trivial).

Claims like these tend to have the form: for any semantics μ there is a compositional semantics ν from which μ can be easily recovered. But this too is completely trivial as it stands: if we let $v(t) = \langle \mu(t), t \rangle$, v is 1-1, hence compositional by (3) in section 3.1, and μ is clearly recoverable from v.

In general, it is not enough that the old semantics can be computed from the new compositional semantics: for the new semantics to have any interest it must *agree* with the old one in some suitable sense. As far as we know there are no mathematical results showing that such a compositional alternative can always be found (see Westerståhl 1998 for further discussion).

Triviality. Paul Horwich (e.g. in 1998) has argued that compositionality is not a substantial property of a semantics, but is *trivially* true. He exemplifies with the sentence *dogs barks*, and says (1998: 156–157) that the meaning property

(7) *x* means DOGS BARK

consists in the so-called construction property

(8) *x* results from putting expressions whose meanings are DOG and BARK, in that order, into a schema whose meaning is NS V.

As far as it goes, the compositionality of the resulting semantics is a trivial consequence of Horwich's conception of meaning properties. Horwich's view here is equivalent to Carnap's conception of synonymy as intensional isomorphism. Neither allows that an expression with different structure or composed from parts with different meanings could be synonymous with an expression that means DOGS BARK. However, for supporting the conclusion that compositionality is trivial, these synonymy conditions must themselves hold trivially, and that is simply not the case.

5.2 Superfluity arguments

Mental processing. Stephen Schiffer (1987) has argued that compositional semantics, and public language semantics altogether, is superfluous in the account of linguistic communication. All that is needed is to account for how the hearer maps his mental representation of an uttered sentence on a mental representation of meaning, and that is a matter of a syntactic transformation, i.e. a translation, rather than interpretation. In Schiffer's example (1987: 192–200), the hearer Harvey is to infer from his belief that

(9) Carmen uttered the sentence 'Some snow is white'.

the conclusion that

(10) Carmen said that some snow is white.

Schiffer argues that this can be achieved by means of transformations between sentences in Harvey's neural language M. M contains a counterpart α to (9), such that α gets tokened in Harvey's so-called belief box when he has the belief expressed by (9). By an inner mechanism the tokening of α leads to the tokening of β, which is Harvey's M counterpart to (10). For this to be possible for any sentence of the language in question, Harvey needs a translation mechanism that implements a recursive translation function f from sentence representations to meaning representations. Once such a mechanism is in place, we have all we need for the account, according to Schiffer.

The problem with the argument is that the translation function f by itself tells us nothing about communicative success. By itself it just correlates neural sentences of which we know nothing except for their internal correlation. We need another recursive function g that maps the uttered sentence *Some snow is white* on α, and a third recursive function h that maps β on the proposition *that some snow is white*, in order to have a complete account. But then the composed function $h(f(g(\ldots)))$ seems to be a recursive function that maps sentences on meanings (cf. Pagin 2003b).

Pragmatic composition. According to François Recanati (2004), word meanings are put together in a process of *pragmatic* composition. That is, the hearer takes word meanings, syntax and contextual features as his input, and forms the interpretation that best corresponds to them. As a consequence, semantic compositionality is not needed for interpretation to take place.

A main motivation for Recanati's view is the ubiquity of those pragmatic operations that Recanati calls *modulations*, and which intuitively contribute to "what is said", i.e. to communicated content before any conversational implicatures. (Under varying terms and conceptions, these phenomena have been described e.g. by Sperber & Wilson 1995, Bach 1994, Carston 2002 and by Recanati himself.) To take an example from Recanati, in reply to an offer of something to eat, the speaker says

(11) I have had breakfast.

thereby saying that she has had breakfast in the morning of *the day of utterance*, which involves a modulation of the more specific kind Recanati calls *free enrichment*, and implicating by means of what she says that she is not hungry. On Recanati's view, communicated contents are always or virtually always pragmatically modulated. Moreover, modulations in general do not operate on a complete semantically derived proposition, but on conceptual constituents. For instance, in (11) it is the property of *having breakfast* that is modulated into *having breakfast this day*, not the proposition as a whole or even the property of *having had breakfast*. Hence, it seems that what the semantics delivers does not feed into the pragmatics.

However, if meanings, i.e. the outputs of the semantic function, are *structured* entities, in the sense specified by (Rev) and InvFunct(μ) of section 3.4, then the last objection is met, for then semantics is able to deliver the arguments to the pragmatic operations, e.g. properties associated with VPs. Moreover, the modulations that are in fact made appear to be controlled by a given semantic structure: as in (11), the modulated part is of the same category and occupies the same slot in the overall structure as the semantically given argument that it replaces. This provides a reason for thinking that modulations operate on a given (syntactically induced) semantic structure, rather than on pragmatically composed material (this line of reasoning is elaborated in Pagin & Pelletier 2007).

5.3 Unsuitability arguments

According to a view that has come to be called *radical contextualism*, truth evaluable content is radically underdetermined by semantics, i.e. by literal meaning. That is, no matter how much a sentence is elaborated, something needs to be added to its semantic content in order to get a proposition that can be evaluated as true or false. Since there will always be indefinitely many different ways of adding, the proposition expressed by means of the sentence will vary from context to context. Well-known proponents of radical contextualism include John Searle (e.g. 1978), Charles Travis (e.g. 1985), and Sperber & Wilson (1995). A characteristic example from Charles Travis (1985: 197) is the sentence

(12) Smith weighs 80 kg.

Although it sounds determinate enough at first blush, Travis points out that it can be taken as true or as false in various contexts, depending on what counts as important in those contexts. For example, it can be further interpreted as being true in case Smith weighs

(12′) a. 80 kg when stripped in the morning.
 b. 80 kg when dressed normally after lunch.
 c. 80 kg after being force fed 4 liters of water.
 d. 80 kg four hours after having ingested powerful diuretic.
 e. 80 kg after lunch adorned in heavy outer clothing.

Although the importance of such examples is not to be denied, their significance for semantics is less clear. It is in the spirit of radical contextualism to minimize the contribution of semantics (literal meaning) for determining expressed content, and thereby the importance of compositionality. However, strictly speaking, the truth or falsity of the compositionality principle for natural language is orthogonal to the truth or falsity of radical contextualism. For whether the meaning of a sentence s is a proposition or not is irrelevant to the question whether that meaning is determined by the meaning of the constituents of s and their mode of composition. The meaning of s may be unimportant but still compositionally determined.

In an even more extreme version, the (semantic) meaning of sentence s in a context c is what the speaker uses s to express in c. In that case meaning itself varies from context to context, and there is no such thing as an invariant literal meaning. Not even the extreme version need be in conflict with compositionality (extended to context dependence), since the substitution properties may hold within each context by itself. Context shift failure, in the sense of section 3.7, may occur, if e.g. word meanings are invariant but the meanings of complex expressions vary between contexts.

It is a further question whether radical contextualism itself, in either version, is a plausible view. It appears that the examples of contextualism can be handled by other methods, e.g. by appeal to pragmatic modulations mentioned in section 5.2 (cf. Pagin & Pelletier 2007), which does allow propositions to be semantically expressed. Hence, the case for radical contextualism is not as strong as it may *prima facie* appear. On top, radical contextualism tends to make a mystery out of communicative success.

6 Problem cases

A number of natural language constructions present apparent problems for compositional semantics. In this concluding section we shall briefly discuss a few of them, and mention some others.

6.1 Belief sentences

Belief sentences offer diffculties for compositional semantics, both real and merely apparent. At first blush, the case for a counterexample against compositionality seems very strong. For in the pair

(13) a. John believes that Fred is a child doctor.
 b. John believes that Fred is a pediatrician.

(13a) may be true and (13b) false, despite the fact that *child doctor* and *pediatrician* are synonymous. If truth value is taken to depend only on meaning and on extra-semantic facts, and the extra-semantic facts as well as the meanings of the parts and the modes of composition are the same between the sentences, then the meaning of the sentences must nonetheless be different, and hence compositionality fails. This conclusion has been drawn by Jeff Pelletier (1994).

What would be the reason for this difference in truth value? When cases such as these come up, the reason is usually that there is some kind of discrepancy in the understanding of the attributee (John) between synonyms. John may e.g. erroneously believe that *pediatrician* only denotes a special kind of child doctors, and so would be disposed to assent to (13a) but dissent from (13b) (cf. Mates 1950 and Burge 1978; Mates took such cases as a reason to be skeptical about synonymy). This is not a decisive reason, however, since it is what the words mean in the sentences, e.g. depending on what *the speaker* means, that is relevant, not what the *attributee* means by those words. The speaker contributes with words and their meanings, and the attributee contributes with his belief contents. If John's belief content matches the meaning of the embedded sentence *Fred is a pediatrician*, then (13b) is true as well, and the problem for compositionality is disposed of.

A problem still arises, however, if belief contents are more fine-grained than sentence meanings, and words in belief contexts are somehow tied to these finer differences in grain. For instance, as a number of authors have suggested, perhaps belief contents are propositions under modes of presentation (see e.g. Burdick 1982, Salmon 1986. Salmon, however, existentially quantifies over modes of presentations, which preserves substitutivity). It may then be that different but synonymous expressions are associated with different modes of presentation. In our example, John may believe a certain proposition under a mode of presentation associated with *child doctor* but not under any mode of presentation associated with *pediatrician*, and that accounts for the change in truth value.

In that case, however, there is good reason to say that the underlying form of a belief sentence such as (13a) is something like

(14) Bel(John, *the proposition that Fred is a child doctor*, M('Fred is a child doctor'))

where M(·) is a function from a sentence to a mode of presentation or a set of modes of presentation. In this form, the sentence Fred is a *pediatrician* occurs both used and mentioned (quoted), and in its used occurrence, *child doctor* may be replaced by *pediatrician* without change of truth value. Failure of substitutivity is explained by the fact that the surface form fuses a used and a mentioned occurrence. In the underlying form, there is no problem for compositionality, unless caused by quotation.

Of course, this analysis is not obviously the right one, but it is enough to show that the claim that compositionality fails for belief sentences is not so easy to establish.

6.2 Quotation

Often quotation is set aside for special treatment as an exception to ordinary semantics, which is supposed to concern *used* occurrences of expressions rather than *mentioned* ones. Sometimes, this is regarded as cheating, and quotation is proposed as a clear counterexample to compositionality: *brother* and *male sibling* are synonymous, but *'brother'* and *'male sibling'* are not (i.e. the expressions that include the opening and closing quote). Since enclosing an expression in quotes is a syntactic operation, we have a counterexample.

If quoting is a genuine syntactic operation, the syntactic rules include a total unary operator κ such that, for any simple or complex expression t,

(15) $\kappa(t) = \text{'}t\text{'}$

The semantics of quoted expressions is given simply by

(Q) $\mu(\kappa(t)) = t$

Then, since $t \equiv_\mu u$ does not imply $t = u$, substitution of u for t in $\kappa(t)$ may violate compositionality.

However, such a non-compositional semantics for quotation can be transformed into a compositional one, by adapting Frege's view in (1892) that quotation provides a special context type in which expressions refer to themselves, and using the notion of linguistically context-dependent compositionality from section 3.7 above. We shall not give the details here, only indicate the main steps.

Start with a grammar $\mathbf{E} = (E, A, \Sigma)$ (for a fragment of English, say) and a compositional semantics μ for $\mathbf{E}$. First, extend $\mathbf{E}$ to a grammar containing the quotation operator κ, allowing not only quote-strings of the form 'John', 'likes', "Mary", etc., but also things like *John likes 'Mary'* (meaning that he likes the name), whereas we disallow things like *John 'likes' Mary* or *'John likes' Mary* as ungrammatical. Let E' be the closure of E under the thus extended operations and κ, and let $\Sigma' = \{\alpha' : \alpha \in \Sigma\} \cup \{\kappa\}$. Then we have a new grammar $E' = (E', A, \Sigma')$ that incorporates quotation.

Next, extend μ to a semantics μ' for $\mathbf{E}'$, using the semantic composition operations that exist by Funct(μ), and letting (Q) above take care of κ. As indicated, the semantics μ' is *not* compositional: even if Mary is the same person as Sue, *John* likes 'Mary' doesn't mean the same as *John likes 'Sue'*. However, we can extend μ' to a semantics μ'' for **E**′ which is compositional in the sense of LC-Funct(μ)$_c$ in section 3.7. In the simplest case, there are two context types: c_u, the *use* context type, which is the default type (the null context), and the quotation context type c_q. The function ψ from context types and operators to context types is given by

$$\psi(c, \beta) = \begin{cases} c & \text{if } \beta \neq \kappa \\ c_q & \text{if } \beta = \kappa \end{cases}$$

for $\beta \in \Sigma'$ and c equal to c_u or c_q. μ'' is obtained by redefining the given composition operations in a fairly straightforward way, so that LC-Funct(μ'')$_c$ is automatically insured. μ'' then extends μ in the sense that if $t \in E$ is meaningful, $\mu''(t, c_u) = \mu(t)$, and furthermore $\mu''(\kappa(t), c_u) = \mu''(t, c_q) = t$.

So μ'' is compositional in the contextually extended sense. That $t \equiv_\mu u$ holds does not license substitution of u for t in $\kappa(t)$, since t there occurs in a quotation context, and we may have $\mu''(t, c_q) \neq \mu''(u, c_q)$. This approach is further developed in Pagin & Westerståhl (2010).

6.3 Idioms

Idioms are almost universally thought to constitute a problem for compositionality. For example, the VP *kick the bucket* can also mean 'die', but the semantic operation corresponding to the standard syntax of, say, *fetch the bucket*, giving its meaning in terms of the meanings of its immediate constituents *fetch* and *the bucket*, cannot be applied to give the idiomatic meaning of *kick the bucket*.

This is no doubt a problem of some sort, but not necessarily for compositionality. First, that a particular semantic operation fails doesn't mean that no other operation works. Second, note that *kick the bucket* is ambiguous between its literal and its idiomatic meaning, but compositionality presupposes non-ambiguous meaning bearers. Unless we take the ambiguity itself to be a problem for compositionality (see the next subsection), we should first find a suitable way to disambiguate the phrase, and only then raise the issue of compositionality.

Such disambiguation may be achieved in various ways. We could treat the whole phrase as a lexical item (an atom), in view of the fact that its meaning has to be learnt separately. Or, given that it does seem to have syntactic structure, we could treat it as formed by a different rule than the usual one. In neither case is it clear that compositionality would be a problem.

To see what idioms really have to do with compositionality, think of the following situation. Given a grammar and a compositional semantics for it, suppose we decide to give some already meaningful phrase a non-standard, idiomatic meaning. Can we then extend the given syntax (in particular, to disambiguate) and semantics in a natural way that preserves compositionality? Note that it is not just a matter of accounting for one particular phrase, but rather for all the phrases in which the idiom may occur. This requires an account of how the syntactic rules apply to the idiom, and to its parts if it has structure, as well as a corresponding semantic account.

But not all idioms behave the same. While the idiomatic *kick the bucket* is fine in *John kicked the bucket yesterday*, or *Everyone kicks the bucket at some point*, it is not good in

(16) The bucket was kicked by John yesterday.

(17) Andrew kicked the bucket a week ago, and two days later, Jane kicked it too.

By contrast, *pull strings* preserves its idiomatic meaning in passive form, and *strings* is available for anaphoric reference with the same meaning:

(18) Strings were pulled to secure Henry his position.

(19) Kim's family pulled some strings on her behalf, but they weren't enough to get her the job.

This suggests that these two idioms should be analyzed differently; indeed the latter kind is called "compositional" in Nunberg, Sag & Wasow (1994) (from which (19) is taken), and is analyzed there using the ordinary syntactic and semantic rules for phrases of this form but introducing instead idiomatic meanings of its parts (*pull* and *string*), whereas *kick the bucket* is called "non-compositional".

In principle, nothings prevents a semantics that deals differently with the two kinds of idioms from being compositional in our sense. Incorporating idioms in syntax and semantics is an interesting task. For example, in addition to explaining the facts noted above one has to prevent *kick the pail* from meaning 'die' even if *bucket* and *pail* are synonymous, and likewise to prevent the idiomatic versions of *pull* and *string* to combine illegitimately with other phrases. For an overview of the semantics of idioms, see Nunberg, Sag & Wasow (1994). Westerståhl (2002) is an abstract discussion of various ways to incorporate idioms while preserving compositionality.

6.4 Ambiguity

Even though the usual formulation of compositionality requires non-ambiguous meaning bearers, the occurrence of ambiguity in language is usually *not* seen as a problem for compositionality. This is because *lexical ambiguity* seems easily dealt with by introducing different lexical items for different meanings of the same word, whereas *structural ambiguity* corresponds to different analyses of the same surface string.

However, it is possible to argue that even though there are clear cases of structural ambiguity in language, as in *Old men and women were released first from the occupied building*, in other cases the additional structure is just an *ad hoc* way to avoid ambiguity. In particular, *quantifier scope* ambiguities could be taken to be of this kind. For example, while semanticists since Montague have had no trouble inventing different underlying structures to account for the two readings of

(20) Every critic reviewed four films.

it may be argued that this sentence in fact has just one structural analysis, a simple constituent structure tree, and that meaning should be assigned to that one structure. A consequence is that meaning assignment is no longer functional, but relational, and hence compositionality either fails or is just not applicable. Pelletier (1999) draws precisely this conclusion.

But even if one agrees with such an account of the syntax of (20), abandonment of compositionality is not the only option. One possibility is to give up the idea that the meaning of (20) is a proposition, i.e. something with a truth value (in the actual world), and opt instead for *underspecified meanings* of some kind. Such meanings can be uniquely, and perhaps compositionally, assigned to simple structures like constituent structure trees, and one can suppose that some further process of interpretation of particular utterances leads to one of the possible specifications, depending on various circumstantial facts. This is a form of context-dependence, and we saw in section 3.7 how similar phenomena can be dealt with compositionally. What was there called *standing meaning* is one kind of underspecified meaning, represented as a function from indices to 'ordinary' meanings. In the present case, where several meanings are available, one might try to use the set of those meanings instead. A similar but more sophisticated way of dealing with quantifier scope is so-called Cooper storage (see Cooper 1983). It should be noted, however, that while such strategies restore a functional meaning assignment, the compositionality of the resulting semantics is by no means automatic; it is an issue that has to be addressed anew.

Another option might be to accept that meaning assignment becomes relational and attempt instead to reformulate compositionality for such semantics. Although this line has hardly been tried in the literature, it may be an option worth exploring (For some first attempts in this direction, see Westerståhl 2007).

6.5 Other problems

Other problems than those above, some with proposed solutions, include possessives (cf. Partee 1997; Peters & Westerståhl 2006), the context sensitive use of adjectives (cf. Lahav 1989; Szabó 2001; Reimer 2002), noun-noun compounds (cf. Weiskopf 2007), *unless*+quantifiers (cf. Higginbotham 1986; Pelletier 1994), *any* embeddings (cf. Hintikka 1984), and indicative conditionals (e.g. Lewis 1976).

All in all, it seems that the issue of compositionality in natural language will remain live, important and controversial for a long time to come.

7 References

Abelard, Peter 2008. *Logica 'Ingredientibus'. 3. Commentary on Aristotele's* De Interpretatione. Corpus Christianorum Contiunatio Medievalis, Turnhout: Brepols Publishers.
Ailly, Peter of 1980. *Concepts and Insolubles*. Dordrecht: Reidel. Originally published as *Conceptus et Insolubilia*, Paris, ca. 1500.
Bach, Kent 1994. Conversational impliciture. *Mind & Language* 9, 124–162.
Barker, Chris & Pauline Jacobson (eds.) 2007. *Direct Compositionality*. Oxford: Oxford University Press.
Burdick, Howard 1982. A logical form for the propositional attitudes. *Synthese* 52, 185–230.
Burge, Tyler 1978. Belief and synonymy. *Journal of Philosophy* 75, 119–138.
Buridan, John 1998. *Summulae de Dialectica 4. Summulae de Suppositionibus*, volume 10–4 of *Artistarium*. Nijmegen: Ingenium.
Carnap, Rudolf 1956. *Meaning and Necessity*. 2nd edn. Chicago, IL: The University of Chicago Press.
Carston, Robyn 2002. *Thoughts and Utterances. The Pragmatics of Explicit Communication*. Oxford: Oxford University Press.
Chomsky, Noam 1971. Topics in the theory of Generative Grammar. In: J. Searle (ed.). *Philosophy of Language*. Oxford: Oxford University Press, 71–100.
Chomsky, Noam 1980. *Rules and Representations*. Oxford: Blackwell.
Cooper, Robin 1983. *Quantification and Syntactic Theory*. Dordrecht: Reidel.
Davidson, Donald 1967. Truth and meaning. *Synthese* 17, 304–323. Reprinted in: D. Davidson. *Inquiries into Truth and Interpretation*. Oxford: Clarendon Press, 1984, 17–36. Page reference to the reprint.
Dowty, David 2007. Compositionality as an empirical problem. In: C. Barker & P. Jacobson (eds.). *Direct Compositionality*. Oxford: Oxford University Press, 23–101.
Dummett, Michael 1973. *Frege. Philosophy of Language*. London: Duckworth.

Dummett, Michael 1981. *The Interpretation of Frege's Philosophy*. London: Duckworth.
Fernando, Tim 2005. Compositionality inductively, co-inductively and contextually. In: E. Machery, M. Werning & G. Schurz (eds.). *The Compositionality of Meaning and Content: Foundational Issues, vol. I*. Frankfurt/M.: Ontos, 87–96.
Fodor, Jerry 1987. *Psychosemantics*. Cambridge, MA: The MIT Press.
Fodor, Jerry 2000. Reply to critics. *Mind & Language* 15, 350–374.
Fodor, Jerry & Jerrold Katz 1964. The structure of a semantic theory. In: J. Fodor & J. Katz (eds.). *The Structure of Language*. Englewood Cliffs, NJ: Prentice Hall, 479–518.
Frege, Gottlob 1884. *Die Grundlagen der Arithmetik: eine logisch-mathematische Untersuchung über den Begriff der Zahl*. Breslau: W. Koebner. English translation in: J. Austin. *The Foundations of Arithmetic: A logico-mathematical enquiry into the concept of number*. 1st edn. Oxford: Blackwell, 1950.
Frege, Gottlob 1892. Über Sinn und Bedeutung. *Zeitschrift für Philosophie und philosophische Kritik* 100, 25–50. English translation in: P. Geach & M. Black (eds.). *Translations from the Philosophical Writings of Gottlob Frege*. Oxford: Blackwell, 1980, 56–78.
Frege, Gottlob 1923. Logische Untersuchungen. Dritter Teil: Gedankengefüge. *Beiträge zur Philosophie des deutschen Idealismus III* (1923–1926), 36–51. English translation in: P. Geach (ed.). *Logical Investigations*. Oxford: Blackwell, 1977, 55–77.
Hendriks, Herman 2001. Compositionality and model-theoretic interpretation. *Journal of Logic, Language and Information* 10, 29–48.
Higginbotham, James 1986. Linguistic theory and Davidson's program in semantics. In: E. Lepore (ed.). *Linguistic Theory and Davidson's Program in Semantics*. Oxford: Blackwell, 29–48.
Hintikka, Jaakko 1984. A hundred years later: The rise and fall of Frege's influence in language theory. *Synthese* 59, 27–49.
Hodges, Wilfrid 2001. Formal features of compositionality. *Journal of Logic, Language and Information* 10, 7–28.
Horwich, Paul 1998. *Meaning*. Oxford: Oxford University Press.
Houben, Jan 1997. The Sanskrit tradition. In: W. van Bekkum et al. (eds.). *The Sanskrit Tradition*. Amsterdam: Benjamins, 49–145.
Husserl, Edmund 1900. *Logische Untersuchungen II/1*. Translated by J. N. Findlay as *Logical Investigations*. London: Routledge & Kegan Paul, 1970.
Jacobson, Pauline 2002. The (dis)organisation of the grammar: 25 years. *Linguistics & Philosophy* 25, 601–626.
Janssen, Theo 1986. *Foundations and Applications of Montague Grammar*. Amsterdam: CWI Tracts 19 and 28.
Janssen, Theo 1997. Compositionality. In: J. van Benthem & A. ter Meulen (eds.). *Handbook of Logic and Language*. Amsterdam: Elsevier, 417–473.
Janssen, Theo 2001. Frege, contextuality and compositionality. *Journal of Logic, Language and Information* 10, 115–136.
Johnson, Kent 2006. On the nature of reverse compositionality. *Erkenntnis* 64, 37–60.
Kaplan, David 1989. Demonstratives. In: J. Almog, J. Perry & H. Wettstein (eds.). *Themes from Kaplan*. Oxford: Oxford University Press, 481–563.
Keenan, Edward & Edward Stabler 2004. *Bare Grammar: A Study of Language Invariants*. Stanford, CA: CSLI Publications.
King, Peter 2001. Between logic and psychology. John Buridan on mental language. Paper presented at the conference *John Buridan and Beyond*, Copenhagen, September 2001.

King, Peter 2007. Abelard on mental language. *American Catholic Philosophical Quarterly* 81, 169–187.

Kracht, Marcus 2003. *The Mathematics of Language*. Berlin: Mouton de Gruyter.

Kracht, Marcus 2007. The emergence of syntactic structure. *Linguistics & Philosophy* 30, 47–95.

Lahav, Ran 1989. Against compositionality: The case of adjectives. *Philosophical Studies* 57, 261–279.

Larson, Richard & Gabriel Segal 1995. *Knowledge of Meaning. An Introduction to Semantic Theory*. Cambridge, MA: The MIT Press.

Lewis, David 1976. Probabilities of conditionals and conditional probabilities. *The Philosophical Review* 85, 297–315.

Mates, Benson 1950. Synonymity. *University of California Publications in Philosophy* 25, 201–226. Reprinted in: L. Linsky (ed.). *Semantics and the Philosophy of Language*, Urbana, IL: University of Illinois Press, 1952, 111–136.

Montague, Richard 1968. Pragmatics. In: R. Klibanski (ed.). *Contemporary Philosophy: A Survey I: Logic and foundations of Mathematics*. La Nuove Italia Editice, Florence, 1968, 102–122. Reprinted in: R. Thomason (ed.). *Formal Philosophy. Selected Papers of Richard Montague*. New Haven, CT: Yale University Press, 1974, 95–118.

Nunberg, Geoffry, Ivan Sag & Thomas Wasow 1994. Idioms. *Language* 70, 491–538.

Pagin, Peter 2003a. Communication and strong compositionality. *Journal of Philosophical Logic* 32, 287–322.

Pagin, Peter 2003b. Schiffer on communication. *Facta Philosophica* 5, 25–48.

Pagin, Peter 2005. Compositionality and context. In: G. Preyer & G. Peter (eds.). *Contextualism in Philosophy*. Oxford: Oxford University Press, 303–348.

Pagin, Peter 2011. Communication and the complexity of semantics. In: W. Hinzen, E. Machery & M. Werning (eds.). *The Oxford Handbook of Compositionality*. Oxford: Oxford University Press.

Pagin, Peter & Francis J. Pelletier 2007. Content, context and communication. In: G. Preyer & G. Peter (eds.). *Context-Sensitivity and Semantic Minimalism. New Essays on Semantics and Pragmatics*. Oxford: Oxford University Press, 25–62.

Pagin, Peter & Dag Westerståhl 2010. Pure Quotation and general Compositionality. *Linguistics & philosophy* 33, 381–415.

Partee, Barbara H. 1997. The genitive. A case study. In: J. van Benthem & A. ter Meulen (eds.). *Handbook of Logic and Language*. Amsterdam: Elsevier, 464–470.

Pelletier, Francis J. 1994. The principle of semantic compositionality. *Topoi* 13, 11–24. Expanded version reprinted in: S. Davis & B. Gillon (eds.), *Semantics: A Reader*. Oxford: Oxford University Press, 2004, 133–157.

Pelletier, Francis J. 1999. Semantic compositionality: Free algebras and the argument from ambiguity. In: M. Faller, S. Kaufmann & M. Pauly (eds.). *Proceedings of the Seventh CSLI Workshop on Logic, Language and Computation*. Stanford, CA: CSLI Publications, 207–218.

Pelletier, Francis J. 2001. Did Frege believe Frege's Principle? *Journal of Logic, Language and Information* 10, 87–114.

Peters, Stanley & Dag Westerståhl 2006. *Quantifiers in Language and Logic*. Oxford: Oxford University Press.

Putnam, Hilary 1975a. Do true assertions correspond to reality? In: H. Putnam. *Mind, Language and Reality. Philosophical Papers vol. 2*. Cambridge: Cambridge University Press, 70–84.

Putnam, Hilary 1975b. *Mind, Language and Reality. Philosophical Papers vol. 2.* Cambridge: Cambridge University Press.
Recanati, François 2004. *Literal Meaning.* Cambridge: Cambridge University Press.
Reimer, Marga 2002. Do adjectives conform to compositionality? *Noûs* 16, 183–198.
Salmon, Nathan 1986. *Frege's Puzzle.* Cambridge, MA: The MIT Press.
Schiffer, Stephen 1987. *Remnants of Meaning.* Cambridge, MA: The MIT Press.
Searle, John 1978. Literal meaning. *Erkenntnis* 13, 207–224.
Sperber, Dan & Deirdre Wilson 1995. *Relevance. Communication & Cognition.* 2nd edn. Oxford: Blackwell.
Staal, J. F. 1969. Sanskrit philosophy of language. In: T. A. Sebeok (ed.). *Linguistics in South Asia.* The Hague: Mouton, 499–531.
Szabó, Zoltán 2000. Compositionality as supervenience. *Linguistics & Philosophy* 23, 475–505.
Szabó, Zoltán 2001. Adjectives in context. In: R. M. Harnich & I. Kenesei (eds.). *Adjectives in Context.* Amsterdam: Benjamins, 119–146.
Travis, Charles 1985. On what is strictly speaking true. *Canadian Journal of Philosophy* 15, 187–229.
Weiskopf, Daniel 2007. Compound nominals, context, and compositionality. *Synthese* 156, 161–204.
Westerståhl, Dag 1998. On mathematical proofs of the vacuity of compositionality. *Linguistics & Philosophy* 21, 635–643.
Westerståhl, Dag 2002. On the compositionality of idioms: An abstract approach. In: J. van Benthem, D. I. Beaver & D. Barker-Plummer (ed.). *Words, Proofs, and Diagrams.* Stanford, CA: CSLI Publications, 241–271.
Westerståhl, Dag 2004. On the compositional extension problem. *Journal of Philosophical Logic* 33, 549–582.
Westerståhl, Dag 2007. Remarks on scope ambiguity. In: E. Ahlsén et al. (eds.). *Communication – Action – Meaning. A Festschrift to Jens Allwood.* Göteborg: Department of Linguistics, University of Gothenburg, 43–55.
Westerståhl, Dag 2008. Decomposing generalized quantifiers. *Review of Symbolic Logic* 1:3, 355–371.
Westerståhl, Dag 2011. Compositionality in Kaplan style semantics. In: W. Hinzen, E. Machery & M. Werning (eds.). *The Oxford Handbook of Compositionality.* Oxford: Oxford University Press.
Zadrozny, Wlodek 1994. From compositional to systematic semantics. *Linguistics & Philosophy* 17, 329–342.

Stefan Engelberg
7 Lexical decomposition: Foundational issues

1   The purpose of lexical decomposition —— 156
2   The early history of lexical decomposition —— 159
3   Theoretical aspects of decomposition —— 165
4   Conclusion —— 177
5   References —— 178

Abstract: Theories of lexical decomposition assume that lexical meanings are complex. This complexity is expressed in structured meaning representations that usually consist of predicates, arguments, operators, and other elements of propositional and predicate logic. Lexical decomposition has been used to explain phenomena such as argument linking, selectional restrictions, lexical-semantic relations, scope ambiguites, and the inference behavior of lexical items. The article sketches the early theoretical development from noun-oriented semantic feature theories to verb-oriented complex decompositions. It also deals with a number of theoretical issues, including the controversy between decompositional and atomistic approaches to meaning, the search for semantic primitives, the function of decompositions as definitions, problems concerning the interpretability of decompositions, and the debate about the cognitive status of decompositions.

1 The purpose of lexical decomposition

1.1 Composition and decomposition

The idea that the meaning of single lexical units is represented in the form of lexical decompositions is based on the assumption that lexical meanings are complex. This complexity is expressed as a structured representation often involving predicates, arguments, operators, and other elements known from propositional and predicate logic. For example, the noun *woman* is represented as a

Stefan Engelberg, Mannheim, Germany

https://doi.org/10.1515/9783110368505-007

predicate that involves the conjunction of the properties of being human, female, and adult, whereas the verb *empty* can be thought of as expressing a causal relation between x and the becoming empty of y.

(1) a. *woman*:   λx[HUMAN(x) & FEMALE(x) & ADULT(x)]
    b. *to empty*:   λyλx[CAUSE(x, BECOME(EMPTY(y)))]

The structures involved in lexical decompositions resemble semantic structures on the phrasal and sentential level. There is of course an important difference between semantic decomposition and semantic composition; semantic complexity on the phrasal and sentential level mirrors the syntactic complexity of the expression while the assumed semantic complexity on the lexical level – at least as far as non-derived words are concerned – need not correspond to any formal complexity of the lexical expression.

Next, we give an overview of the main linguistic phenomena treated within decompositional approaches (section 1.2). Section 2 looks at the origins of the idea of lexical decomposition (section 2.1) and sketches some early formal theories on the lexical decomposition of nouns (sections 2.2, 2.3) and verbs (section 2.4). Section 3 is devoted to a discussion of some long-standing theoretical issues of lexical decomposition, the controversy between decompositional and non-decompositional approaches to lexical meaning (section 3.1), the location of decompositions within a language theory (section 3.2), the status of semantic primitives (section 3.3), the putative role of decompositions as definitions (section 3.4), the semantic interpretation of decompositions (section 3.5), and their cognitive plausibility (section 3.6). The discussion relies heavily on the overview of frameworks of lexical decomposition of verbs given in article 2 [Semantics: Lexical Structures and Adjectives] (Engelberg) *Frameworks of decomposition* that can be consulted for a more detailed description of the theories mentioned in the present article.

1.2 The empirical coverage of lexical decompositions

Which phenomena lexical decompositions are supposed to explain varies from approach to approach. The following have been tackled fairly often in decompositional theories:
(i) Argument linking: One of the main purposes for decomposing verbs has been the attempt to form generalizations about the relationship between semantic arguments and their syntactic realization. In causal structures like those given for *empty* (1b) the first argument of a CAUSE relation becomes the subject of the sentence and is marked with nominative in nominative-accusative

languages or absolutive in ergative-absolutive languages. Depending on the linking theory pursued, this can be expressed in different kinds of generalizations, for example, by simply claiming that the first argument of CAUSE always becomes the subject in active sentences or – more general – that the least deeply embedded argument of the decomposition is associated with the highest function in a corresponding syntactic hierarchy.

(ii) Selectional restrictions: Lexical decompositions account for semantic co-occurrence restrictions. The arguments selected by a lexical item are usually restricted to particular semantic classes. If the item filling the argument position is not of the required class, the resulting expression is semantically deviant. For instance, the verb *preach* selects an argument filler denoting a human being for its first argument slot. The decompositional features of *woman* (1a) account for the fact that *the woman preached* is semantically unobtrusive while *the hope / chair / tree preached* is not.

(iii) Ambiguity resolution: Adverbs often lead to a kind of sentential ambiguity that was attempted to be resolved by reference to lexical decompositions. In a scenario where Rebecca is pointing a gun at Jamaal, sentence (2a) may describe three possible outcomes.

(2) a. Rebecca almost killed Jamaal.
b. kill: $\lambda y \lambda x[\text{DO}(x, \text{CAUSE}(\text{BECOME}(\text{DEAD}(y))))]$

Assuming a lexical decomposition for *kill* as in (2b), ambiguity resolution is achieved by attaching *almost* to different predicates within the decomposition, yielding a scenario where Rebecca almost pulled the trigger (ALMOST DO …), a scenario where she pulled the trigger but missed Jamaal (ALMOST CAUSE …), and a scenario where she pulled the trigger, hit him but did not wound him fatally (ALMOST BECOME DEAD …).

(iv) Lexical relations: Lexical decompositions have also been employed in the analysis of semantic relations like hyperonymy, complementarity, synonymy, etc. (cf. Bierwisch 1970: 170). For example, assuming that a lexeme A is a hyperonym of a lexeme B iff the set of properties conjoined in the lexical decomposition of lexeme A is a proper part of the set of properties conjoined in the lexical decomposition of lexeme B, we derive that *child* (3a) is a hyperonym of *girl* (3b).

(3) a. *child*: $\lambda x[\text{HUMAN}(x) \& \neg \text{ADULT}(x)]$
b. *girl*: $\lambda x[\text{HUMAN}(x) \& \neg \text{ADULT}(x) \& \text{FEMALE}(x)]$

(v) Lexical field structure: Additionally, lexical decompositions have been used in order to uncover the structure of lexical fields (cf. section 2.2).

(vi) Inferences: Furthermore, lexical decompositions allow for semantic inferences that can be derived from the semantics of primitive predicates. For example, a predicate like BECOME, properly defined, allows for the inference that Jamaal in (2a) was not dead immediately before the event.

2 The early history of lexical decomposition

2.1 The roots of lexical decomposition

The idea that a meaning of a word can be explained by identifying it with the meaning of a more complex expression is deeply rooted not only in linguistics but also in our common sense understanding of language. When asked to explain to a non-native speaker what the German word *Junggeselle* means, one would probably say that a *Junggeselle* is an *unmarried man*. A decompositional way of meaning explanation is also at the core of the Aristotelian conception of word meaning in which the meaning of a noun is sufficiently explained by its genus proximum (here *man*) and its differentia specifica (here *unmarried*). Like the decompositions in (1), this conception attempts to define the meaning of a word. However, the distinction between genus proximum and differentia specifica is not explicitly expressed in lexical decompositions: From a logical point of view, each predicate in a conjunction as in (1a) qualifies as a genus proximum.

The Aristotelian distinction is also an important device in lexicographic meaning explanations as in (4a), where the next superordinate concept (*donkey*) of the lexical item in question (*jackass*) and one or more distinctive features (*male*) are given (cf. e.g., Svensén 1993: 120ff). Interestingly, meaning explanations based on genus proximum and differentia specifica have provoked some criticism within lexicography (Wiegand 1989) as well, and a closer look into standard monolingual dictionaries reveals that many meaning explanations are not of the Aristotelian kind represented in (4a): They involve near-synonyms (4b), integration of encyclopaedic (4c) and pragmatic information (4d), extensional listings of members of the class denoted by the lexeme (4e), pictorial illustrations (cf. numerous examples, e.g., in Harris 1923), or any combinations thereof.

(4) a. **jackass** [...] 1. male donkey [...] (Thorndike 1941: 501)
　　b. **grumpy** [...] surly; ill-humoured; gruff. [...] (Thorndike 1941: 413)

c. **scimitar** [...] A saber with a much-curved blade with the edge on the convex side, used chiefly by Mohammedans, esp. Arabs and Persians. [...] (Webster's, Harris 1923: 1895)
d. **Majesty** [...] title used in speaking to or of a king, queen, emperor, empress, etc.; as, Your Majesty, His Majesty, Her Majesty. [...] (Thorndike 1941: 562)
e. **cat** [...] 2. Any species of the family Felidae, of which the domestic cat is the type, including the lion, tiger, leopard, puma, and various species of tiger cats, and lynxes, also the cheetah. [...] (Webster's, Harris 1923: 343)

This foreshadows some persistent problems of later approaches to lexical decomposition.

2.2 Semantic feature theories and the semantic structure of nouns

As we have seen, the concept of some kind of decomposition has been around ever since people began to systematically think about word meanings. Yet, it was not until the advent of Structural Semantics that lexical decompositions have become part of more restrictive semantic theories. Structural Semantics emerged in the late 1920s as a reaction to the semantic mainstream, which, at the time, was oriented towards psychological explanations of idiolectal variation and the diachronic change of single word meanings. It conceived of lexical semantics as a discipline that revealed the synchronic structure of the lexicon from a non-psychological perspective. The main tenet was that the meaning of a word can only be captured in its relation to the meaning of other words.

Within Structural Semantics, lexical decompositions developed in the form of breaking down word meanings into semantic features (depending on the particular approach also called 'semantic components', 'semantic markers', or 'sememes'). An early analysis of this sort can be found in Hjelmslev's Prolegomena from 1943 (Hjelmslev 1963: 70) who observed that systematic semantic relationships can be traced back to shared semantic components (cf. Tab. 7.1). He favored a strict decompositional approach in that (i) he explicitly conceived of decompositions like the ones in Tab. 7.1 as definitions of words and (ii) assumed that content-entities like 'ram', 'woman', 'boy' have to be eliminated from the inventory of content-entities if they can be defined by decompositions (Hjelmslev 1963: 72ff).

Following the Prague School's feature-based approach to phonology, it was later assumed that semantic analyses should be based on a set of functional oppositions like [±human], [±male], etc. (cf. also article 1 [Semantics: Lexical Structures

Tab. 7.1: Semantic components (after Hjelmslev 1963: 70)

	'he'	'she'
'sheep'	'ram'	'ewe'
'human being'	'man'	'woman'
'child'	'boy'	'girl'
'horse'	'stallion'	'mare'

and Adjectives] (Bierwisch) Semantic features and primes). Semantic feature theories developed along two major lines. In Europe, structuralists like Pottier (1963, 1964), Coseriu (1964), and Greimas (1966) employed semantic features to reveal the semantic structure of lexical fields. A typical example for a semantic feature analysis in the European structuralist tradition is Pottier's (1963) analysis of the lexical field of sitting furniture with legs (French siège) that consists of the lexemes chaise, fauteuil, tabouret, canapé, and pouf (cf. Tab. 7.2). Six binary features serve to define and structure the field: s^1 = avec dossier 'with back', s^2 = sur pied 'on feet', s^3 = pour 1 personne 'for one person', s^4 = pour s'asseoir 'for sitting', s^5 = avec bras 'with armrest', and s^6 = avec matériau rigide 'with rigid material'.

Tab. 7.2: Semantic feature analysis of the lexical field siège ('seat with legs') in French (Pottier 1963: 16)

	s^1	s^2	s^3	s^4	s^5	s^6
chaise	+	+	+	+	–	+
fauteuil	+	+	+	+	+	+
tabouret	–	+	+	+	–	+
canapé	+	+	–	+	+	+
pouf	–	+	+	+	–	–

In North America, Katz, Fodor, and others tried to develop a formal theory of the lexicon as a part of so-called Interpretive Semantics that constituted the semantic component of the Standard Theory of Generative Grammar (Chomsky 1965). In this tradition, semantic features served, for example, as targets for selectional restrictions (Katz & Fodor 1963). The semantic description of lexical items consists of two types of features, 'semantic markers' and 'distinguishers', by which the meaning of a lexeme is decomposed exhaustively into its atomic concepts: "The semantic markers assigned to a lexical item in a dictionary entry are intended to reflect whatever systematic semantic relations hold between that item and the rest of the vocabulary of the language. On the other hand, the distinguishers assigned to a lexical item are intended to reflect what is idiosyncratic about its meaning." (Katz & Fodor 1963: 187). An example entry is given in Tab. 7.3.

Tab. 7.3: Readings of the english noun *bachelor* distinguished by semantic markers (in parentheses) and distinguishers (in square brackets) (Katz, after Fodor 1977: 65)

bachelor, [+N, ...],
-- (Human), (Male), [who has never married]
-- (Human), (Male), [young knight serving under the standard of another knight]
-- (Human), [who has the first or lowest academic degree]
-- (Animal), (Male), [young fur seal when without a mate during the breeding time]

Besides this feature-based specification of the meaning of lexical items, Interpretive Semantics assumed recursive rules that operate over syntactic deep structures and build up meaning specifications for phrases and sentences out of lexical meaning specifications (Katz & Postal 1964).

As we have seen, semantic feature theories make it possible to tackle phenomena in the area of lexical fields and selectional restrictions (cf. also article 6 [Semantics: Lexical Structures and Adjectives] (Cann) *Sense relations*). They can also be used in formal accounts of lexical-semantic relations. For example, expression *A* is incompatible with expression *B* iff *A* and *B* have different values for at least one of their semantic features: *boy* [+HUMAN, -ADULT, -FEMALE] is incompatible with *woman* [+HUMAN, +ADULT, +FEMALE]. Expression *A* is complementary to expression *B* iff *A* and *B* have different values for exactly one of their semantic features: for instance, *girl* [+HUMAN, -ADULT, +FEMALE] is complementary to *boy*. Expression *A* is hyperonymous to expression *B* iff the set of feature-value assignments for *A* is included in the set of feature-value assignments for *B*: thus, *child* [+HUMAN, -ADULT] is hyperonymous to *boy*.

In European structuralism, the status of semantic features was a matter of debate. They were usually conceived of as part of a descriptive, language-independent semantic metalanguage, but were also treated as cognitive entities. In Generative Grammar, Katz conceived of semantic features as derived from a universal conceptual structure: "Semantic markers must [...] be thought of as theoretical constructs introduced into semantic theory to designate language invariant but language linked components of a conceptual system that is part of the cognitive structure of the human mind." (Katz 1967: 129). In a similar vein, Bierwisch (1970: 183) assumed that the basic semantic components "are not learned in any reasonable sense of the term, but are rather an innate predisposition for language acquisition." Thus, language-specific semantic structures come about by the particular combination of semantic features that yield a lexical item.

2.3 Some inadequacies of semantic feature analyses

Semantic feature theories considerably stimulated research in lexical semantics. Beyond that, semantic features had found their way into contemporary generative syntax as a target for selectional restrictions (cf. Chomsky 1965). Yet, a number of empirical weaknesses have quickly become evident.

(i) Relational lexemes: The typical cases of semantic feature analyses seem to presuppose that all predicates are one-place predicates. Associating *woman* with the feature bundle [+HUMAN, +ADULT, +FEMALE] means that the referent of the sole argument of *woman*(x) has the three properties of being human, adult, and female. Simple feature bundles cannot account for relational predicates like *mother*(x,y) or *devour*(x,y), because the argument to which a semantic feature attaches has to be specified. With *mother*(x,y), the feature [+FEMALE] applies to the first, but not to the second argument.

(ii) Structure of verb decompositions: Semantic feature analyses usually represent word meanings as unordered sets of features. However, in particular with verbal predicates, the decomposition cannot be adequately formulated as a flat structure (cf. section 2.4).

(iii) Undecomposable words: It has been criticized that cohyponyms in larger taxonomies, such as *lion, tiger, puma*, etc. as cohyponyms of *cat* (cf. 4e) or *rose, tulip, daffodil, carnation*, etc. as cohyponyms of *flower*, cannot be differentiated by semantic features in a non-trivial way. If one of the semantic features of *rose* is [+FLOWER], then what is its distinguishing feature? This feature should abstract from a rose being a flower since [+FLOWER] has already been added to the feature list. Moreover, it should not be unique for the entry of *rose* or else the number of features threatens to surpass the number of lexical entries. In other words, there does not seem to be any plausible candidate for P that would make $\forall x[\text{ROSE}(x) \leftrightarrow (P(x) \,\&\, \text{FLOWER}(x))]$ a valid definition (cf. Fodor 1977: 150; Roelofs 1997: 46ff for arguments of this sort). Besides cohyponymy in large taxonomies, there are other lexical relations as well that cannot be adequately captured by binary feature descriptions, for instance the scalar nature of antonymy and lexical rows like *hot > warm > tepid > cool > cold*. In general, it is simply unclear for many lexical items what features might be used to distinguish them from near-synonyms (cf. *grumpy* in (4b)).

(iv) Exhaustiveness: For most lexical items, it seems to be impossible to give an exhaustive lexical analysis, that is, one that provides the features that are necessary and sufficient to distinguish the item from all other lexical items of the language without introducing features that are used solely for the description of this one particular item. Katz's distinction between markers and distinguishers does not solve the problem. Apart from the fact that the difference between 'markers' as targets for selectional restrictions and 'distinguishers' as lexeme-specific idiosyncratic features is not supported by the data (cf. Bierwisch 1969: 177ff; Fodor 1977: 144ff), this concession to semantic diversity weakens the explanatory value of semantic feature theories considerably since no restrictions are provided for what can occur as a distinguisher.

(v) Finiteness: Only rarely have large inventories of features been assembled (e.g., by Lorenz & Wotjak 1977). Moreover, semantic feature theory has not succeeded in developing operational procedures by which semantic features can be discovered. Thus, it has not become evident that there is a finite set of semantic features that allows a description of the entire vocabulary of a language, in particular that this set is smaller than the set of lexical items.

(vi) Universality: Another point of criticism has been that the alleged universality of a set of features has not been convincingly demonstrated. As Lyons (1968: 473) stated, cross-linguistic semantic comparisons of semantic structures rather point to the contrary. However, the search for a universal semantic metalanguage has continued and has become a major topic in particular among the proponents of Natural Semantic Metalanguage (cf. article 2 [Semantics: Lexical Structures and Adjectives] (Engelberg) *Frameworks of decomposition*, section 8).

(vii) Theoretical status: The often unclear theoretical status of semantic features has drawn some criticism as well. Among other things, it has been argued that in order to express that a mare is a female horse it is not necessary to enrich the metalanguage by numerous features. The relation can equally well be expressed on the level of object language by assuming a meaning postulate in form of a biconditional: $\Box \forall x[mare(x) \leftrightarrow horse(x) \& female(x)]$.

2.4 Lexical decomposition and the semantic structure of verbs

The rather complex semantic structure of many verbs could not be adequately captured by semantic feature approaches for two reasons: They focused on one-place lexemes, and they expressed lexical meaning in flat structures, that is, by simply conjoining semantic features. Instead, hierarchical structures were needed. Katz (1971) tackled this problem in the form of decompositions that also included aspectually relevant features such as 'activity' (cf. Tab. 7.4).

While this form of decomposition never caught on, other early verb decompositions (cf. Bendix 1966, Fillmore 1968, Bierwisch 1970) look more familiar to semantic representations still employed in many theories of verb semantics (5).

Tab. 7.4: Decomposition of *chase* (after Katz 1971: 304)

chase → Verb, Verb transitive, ...;
(((Activity) (Nature: (Physical)) of *X*), ((Movement) (Rate: Fast)) (Character: Following)), (Intention of *X*: (Trying to catch ((*Y* ((Movement) (Rate: Fast)))))); (SR).

(5) a. *give*(x,y,z):   X CAUSE (y HAVE z)   (after Bendix 1966: 69)
    b. *persuade*(x,y,z): X CAUSE (y BELIEVE z)   (after Fillmore 1968: 377)

It was the rise of Generative Semantics in the late 1960s that caused a shift in interest from decompositional structures of nouns to lexical decompositions of verbs. The history of lexical decompositions of verbs that emerged from these early approaches is reviewed in article 2 [Semantics: Lexical Structures and Adjectives] (Engelberg) *Frameworks of decomposition*. Starting from early generative approaches, verb decompositions have been employed in theories as different as Conceptual Semantics (cf. also article 4 [Semantics: Theories] (Jackendoff) *Conceptual Semantics*), Natural Semantic Metalanguage, and Distributed Morphology (cf. also article 5 [Semantics: Interfaces] (Harley) *Semantics in Distributed Morphology*).

3 Theoretical aspects of decomposition

3.1 Decompositionalism versus atomism

Directly opposed to decompositional approaches to lexical meaning stands a theory of lexical meaning that is known as lexical atomism or holism and whose main proponent is Jerry A. Fodor (1970, 1998, Fodor et al. 1980). According to a decompositional concept of word meaning, knowing the meaning of a word involves knowing its decomposition, that is, the linguistic or conceptual entities and relations it consists of. Fodor's atomistic conception of word meaning rejects this view and assumes instead that there is a direct correspondence between a word and the mental particular it stands for. A lexical meaning does not have constituents, and – in a strict formulation of atomism – knowing it does not involve knowing the meaning of other lexical units.

Fodor (1998: 45) observes in favor of his atomistic, anti-definitional approach that there are practically no words whose definition is generally agreed upon – an argument that cannot be easily dismissed. Atomists are also skeptical about the claim that decompositions/definitions are simpler than the words they are attached to: "Does anybody present really think that thinking BACHELOR is harder than thinking UNMARRIED? Or that thinking FATHER is harder than thinking PARENT?" (Fodor 1998: 46).

Discussing Jackendoff's (1992) decompositional representation of *keep*, Fodor (1998: 55) comments on the relation that is expressed in examples as different as *someone kept the money* and *someone kept the crowd happy*: "I would have thought, saying what relation they both instance is precisely what the word 'keep' is for; why on earth do you suppose that you can say it 'in other words'?" And he adds: "I can't think of a better way to say what 'keep' means than to say that it means *keep*. If, as I suppose, the concept KEEP is an atom, it's hardly surprising that there's no better way to say what 'keep' means than to say that it means *keep*." More detailed arguments for and against atomistic positions will appear throughout this article.

The controversy between decompositionalists and atomists is often connected to the question whether decompositions or meaning postulates should be employed to characterize lexical meaning. Meaning postulates are used to express analytic knowledge concerning particular semantic expressions (Carnap 1952: 67). Lexical meaning postulates are necessarily true. They consist of entailments where the antecedent is an open lexical proposition (6a).

(6) a. $\Box \forall x[\text{BACHELOR}(x) \rightarrow \text{MAN}(x)]$
    $\Box \forall x[\text{BACHELOR}(x) \rightarrow \neg \text{MARRIED}(x)]$
  b. $\Box \forall x[\text{BACHELOR}(x) \leftrightarrow (\text{MAN}(x) \& \neg \text{MARRIED}(x))]$
  c. *bachelor*: $\lambda x[\text{MAN}(x) \& \text{UNMARRIED}(x)]$

Meaning postulates can also express bidirectional entailments as in (6b) where the biconditional expresses a definition-like equivalence between a word and its decomposition. I will assume that in the typical case on a pure lexical level of meaning description decompositional approaches like (6c) conceive of word meanings as bidirectional entailments as in (6b) while atomistic approaches involve monodirectional entailments as in (6a) (cf. similarly Chierchia & McConnell-Ginet 1990: 360ff). Thus, meaning postulates do not per se characterize atomistic approaches to meaning, but it is rather the kind of meaning postulate that serves to distinguish the two basic stances on word meaning. Informally, one might say that bidirectional meaning postulates provide definitions, monodirectional ones single aspects of word meaning in form of relations to other semantic elements. Three caveats are in order here: (i) Semantic reconstruction on the basis of meaning postulates is not uniformly accepted either in the decompositional or in the atomistic camp. Some proponents of decompositional approaches do not adhere to a definitional view of decompositions; they claim that their decompositions do not cover the whole meaning of the lexical item (cf. section 3.4). At the same time, some radical approaches to atomism reject lexical meaning postulates completely (Fodor 1998). (ii) Decompositions and bidirectional meaning postulates are only equivalent on the level of meaning explanation (cf. Chierchia & McConnell-Ginet 1990: 362). They differ, however, in that in decompositional approaches the word defined (*bachelor* in (6c)) is not accessible within the semantic derivation while the elements of the decomposition (MAN(x) & UNMARRIED(x)) are. This can have an effect, for example, on the explanation of scope phenomena. (iii) Furthermore, decompositions as in (6c) and bidirectional meaning postulates as in (6b) can give rise to different predictions with respect to language processing (cf. section 3.6).

3.2 Decompositions and the lexicon

One of the most interesting differences in the way verb decompositions are used in different language theories concerns their location within the theory. Some approaches locate decompositions and the principles and rules that build them up in syntax (e.g., Generative Semantics, Distributed Morphology), some in semantics (e.g., Dowty's Montague-based theory, Lexical Decomposition Grammar, Natural Semantic Metalanguage), and others in conceptual structure (e.g., Conceptual Semantics) (cf. article 2 [Semantics: Lexical Structures and Adjectives] (Engelberg) *Frameworks of decomposition*). Decompositions are sometimes constrained by interface conditions as well. These interface relations between linguistic levels of representation are specified to a different degree in different theories. Lexical Decomposition Grammar has put some effort into establishing interface conditions between syntactic, semantic, and conceptual structure. In syntactic approaches to decomposition (Lexical Relational Structures, Distributed Morphology), however, the relation between syntactic decompositions and semantic representations often remains obscure – one of the few exceptions being von Stechow's (1995) analysis of the scope properties of German *wieder* 'again' in syntactic decompositions (cf. article 2 [Semantics: Lexical Structures and Adjectives] (Engelberg) *Frameworks of decomposition*).

The way decompositions are conceived has an impact on the structure of the lexicon and its role within the architecture of the language theory pursued. While some approaches advocate rather rich meaning representations (e.g., Natural Semantic Metalanguage, Conceptual Semantics), others downplay semantic representation and reduce it to a rather unstructured domain of encyclopaedic knowledge (Distributed Morphology) (cf. the overview in Ramchand 2008). Meaning representation itself can occur on more than one level. Sometimes the distinction is between semantics proper and some sort of conceptual representation (e.g., Lexical Decomposition Grammar); sometimes different levels of conceptual representation are distinguished such as Jackendoff's (2002) Conceptual Structure and Spatial Structure. Theories also differ in how much the lexicon is structured by rules and principles. While syntactic approaches often conceive of the lexicon as a mere inventory, other approaches (e.g. Levin & Rappaport Hovav's Lexical Conceptual Structures, Wunderlich's Lexical Decomposition Grammar, Pustejovsky's Event Structures) assume different kinds of linking principles, interface conditions and structure rules for decompositions (for references, cf. article 2 [Semantics: Lexical Structures and Adjectives] (Engelberg) *Frameworks of decomposition*).

3.3 Decompositions and primitives

Decompositional approaches to lexical meaning usually claim that all lexical items can be completely reduced to their component parts; that is, they can be defined. This requires certain conditions on decompositions in order to avoid infinite regress: (i) The predicates used in the decompositions are either semantic primitives or can be reduced to semantic primitives by definitions. It is necessary that the primitives are not reduced to other elements within the vocabulary, but are grounded elsewhere. (ii) Another condition is that the set of primitives be notably smaller than the lexicon (cf. Fodor et al. 1980: 268). (iii) Apart from their primitivity, it is often required that predicates within decompositions be general, that is, distinctive for a large number of lexemes, and universal, that is, relevant to the description of lexemes in all or most languages (cf. Löbner 2002: 132ff) (cf. also the discussion in article 4 [Semantics: Lexical Structures and Adjectives] (Levin & Rappaport Hovav) *Lexical Conceptual Structure*).

The status of these primitives has been a constant topic within decompositional semantics. Depending on the particular theories, the vocabulary of semantic primitives is located on different levels of linguistic structure. Theories differ as to whether these predicates are elements of the object language (e.g., Natural Semantic Metalanguage), of a semantic metalanguage (e.g., Montague Semantics) or of some set of conceptual entities (e.g., Lexical Conceptual Semantics). A finite set of primitives is rarely given, the notable exception being Natural Semantic Metalanguage. Most theories obviously assume a core of the decompositional vocabulary, including such items as CAUSE, BECOME, DO, etc., but they also include many other predicates like ALIVE, BELIEVE, IN, MOUTH, WRITE. Since they are typically not concerned with all subtleties of meaning, most theories often do not bother about the status of these elements. They might be conceived of as definable or not. While in Dowty's (1979) approach CAUSE gets a counterfactual interpretation in the vein of Lewis (1973), Lakoff (1972: 615f) treats CAUSE as a primitive universal and, similarly, in Natural Semantic Metalanguage BECAUSE is taken as a primitive.

However, no matter how many primitives a theory assumes, something has to be said about how these elements can be grounded. Among the possible answers are the following: (i) Semantic primitives are innate (or acquired before language acquisition) (e.g., Bierwisch 1970). To my knowledge, no evidence from psycholinguistics or neurolinguistics has been obtained for this claim. (ii) Semantic primitives can be reduced to perceptual features. Considering the abstract nature of some semantic features, a complete reduction to perception seems unlikely (cf. Jackendoff 2002: 339). (iii) Semantic primitives are conceptually grounded (e.g., Natural Semantic Metalanguage, Conceptual Semantics). This is often claimed but rarely pursued empirically (but cf. Jackendoff 1983, Engelberg 2006).

3.4 Decompositions and definitions

If lexical decompositions are semantically identified with biconditional meaning postulates, they can be regarded as definitions: They provide necessary and sufficient conditions. It has been questioned whether word meaning can be captured this way. The non-equivalence of *kill* and *cause to die* had been a major argument against Generative Semantics (cf. article 2 [Semantics: Lexical Structures and Adjectives] (Engelberg) *Frameworks of decomposition*, section 2). It has been observed that the definitional approach simply fails on a word-by-word basis: "There are practically no defensible examples of definitions; for all the examples we've got, practically all words (/concepts) are undefinable. And, of course, if a word (/concept) doesn't have a definition, then its definition can't be its meaning." (Fodor 1998: 45) Given what was said about lexicography in section 2.1, we must concede that even by a less strict view on semantic equivalence, the definitional approach can only be applied to a subgroup of lexical items. Atomistic and prototype-based approaches to lexical meaning thrive on these observations. Decompositionalist approaches to word meaning have reacted differently to these problems. Some have just denied them: Natural Semantic Metalanguage claims that based on a limited set of semantic primitives and their combinatorial potential a complete decomposition is possible. Other approaches, in particular Conceptual Semantics, point to the particular descriptive level of their decompositions. They claim that CAUSE does not have the same meaning as *cause*, the former being a conceptual entity. This allows Jackendoff (2002: 335f) to state that decompositions are not definitions since no equation between a word and a synonymous phrasal expression is attempted. However, the meanings of the decompositional predicates employed are all the more in need of explanations since our intuition about the meaning of natural language lexemes does not account for them anymore. As Pulman (2005) puts it in a discussion of Jackendoff's approach: "[...] if your intuition is that part of the meaning of 'drink' is that liquid should enter a mouth, then unless there is some explicit connection between the construct MOUTH and the meaning of the English word 'mouth', that intuition is not accounted for." Finally, some researchers assume that decompositions only capture the core meaning of a word (e.g., Kornfilt & Correra 1993: 83). Thus, decompositions do not exhaust a word's meaning, and they are not definitions. This, of course, poses the questions what they are decompositions of and by what semantic criteria core aspects of lexical meaning can be identified. In any case, a conception of decompositions as incomplete meaning descriptions weakens the approach considerably. "It is, after all, not in dispute that some aspects of lexical meanings can be represented in quite an exiguous vocabulary; some aspects of anything can be represented in quite an exiguous vocabulary," Fodor (1998: 48) remarks and adds: "It is supposed to be the main virtue of definitions that, in all sorts of cases, they reduce problems about the defined concepts to corresponding problems about its primitive parts. But that won't happen unless each definition has the very same content as the concept it defines." (Fodor 1998: 49) In some approaches the partial specification of meaning in semantic decompositions results from a distinction between semantic and conceptual representation (e.g., Bierwisch 1997). Semantic decompositions are underspecified and are supplemented on the utterance level with information from a conceptual representation.

The completeness question is sometimes tied to the attempt to distinguish those aspects of meaning that are grammatically relevant from those that are not. This is done in different ways. Some assume that decompositions are incomplete and represent only what is grammatically relevant. Others differentiate between levels of representation; Lexical Decomposition Grammar distinguishes Semantic Form, which includes the grammatically relevant information, from Conceptual Structure. Finally, some assume one level of representation in which only particular parts are grammatically relevant; in Rappaport Hovav & Levin (1998), general decompositional templates contain the grammatically relevant information whereas idiosyncratic aspects are reflected by lexeme-specific constants that are inserted into these templates.

However, the distinction between grammatically relevant and irrelevant properties within a semantic representation raises a serious theoretical question. It is a truism that not all subtleties of lexical meaning show grammatical effects. With *to eat*, the implied aspect of intentional agentivity is grammatically relevant in determining which argument becomes the subject while the implied aspect of biological food processing is not. However, distinguishing the grammatically relevant from the irrelevant by assigning them different locations in representations is not more than a descriptive convention unless one is able to show that grammatically relevant meaning is a particular type of meaning that can be distinguished on *semantic* grounds from grammatically irrelevant meaning. But do all the semantic properties that have grammatical effects (intentional agentivity and the like) form one natural semantic class and those that do not (biological food processing and the like) another? As it stands, it seems doubtful that such classes will emerge. As Jackendoff (2002: 290) notes, features with grammatical effects form a heterogeneous set. They include well-known distinctions such as those between agent and experiencer or causation and non-causation but also many idiosyncratic properties such as the distinction between emission verbs where the sound can be associated with an action of moving and which therefore allow a motion construction (*the car squealed around the corner*) and those where this is not the case (**the car honked around the corner*) (cf. Levin & Rappaport Hovav 1996).

3.5 Decompositions and their interpretation

It is evident that in order to give empirical content to theoretical claims on the basis of lexical semantic representations, the meaning of the entities and configurations of entities in these semantic representations must be clear. This is a major problem not only for decompositional approaches to word meaning. To give an example from Distributed Morphology (DM), Harley & Noyer (2000: 368) notice that *cheese* is a mass noun and sentences like *I had three cheeses for breakfast* are unacceptable. The way DM is set up requires deriving the mass noun restriction from encyclopaedic knowledge (cf. article 2 [Semantics: Lexical Structures and Adjectives] (Engelberg) *Frameworks of decomposition*, section 10). Thus, it is listed in the encyclopaedia that "cheese does not typically come in discrete countable chunks or types". However, to provide a claim like that with any empirical content, we need a methodology for determining what the encyclopaedic knowledge for *cheese* looks like. As we will see, lexical-semantic representations often exhibit a conflict when it comes to determining what a word actually means. If we use its syntactic behaviour as a guideline for its meaning, the semantic representation is not independently motivated but circularly determined by the very structures it purports to determine. If we use our naive everyday conception of what a word means, we lack an objective methodology of determining lexical meaning. Moreover, the two paths lead to different results. If we take a naive, syntax-independent look at the encyclopaedic semantics of *cheese*, a visit to the next supermarket will tell us that – contrary to what Harley & Noyer claim – all cheese comes in chunks or slices, so does all sausage and some of the fruit. Thus, it seems that the encyclopaedic knowledge in DM is not arrived at by naively watching the world around you. If it were, the whole architecture of Distributed Morphology would probably break down since, as corpus evidence shows, the German words for 'cheese' *Käse*, 'sausage' *Wurst*, and 'fruit' *Obst* are different with respect to the count/mass distinction although their supermarket appearance with respect to chunks and slices is very similar: *Wurst* can be freely used as a count and a mass noun; *Käse* is a mass noun that can be used as a count noun, especially, but not only, when referring to types of cheese, and *Obst* is obligatorily a mass noun. Thus, the encyclopaedic knowledge about *cheese* in Distributed Morphology seems to be forced by the fact that *cheese* is grammatically a mass noun. This two-way dependency between grammar and encyclopaedia immunizes DM against falsification and, thus, renders a central claim of DM empirically void.

The neglect of semantic methodology and theory particularly in those approaches that advocate a semantically constrained but otherwise free syntactic generation of argument structures has of course been pointed out before: "Although lip service is often paid to the idea that a verb's meaning must be compatible with syntactically determined meaning [...], it is the free projection of arguments that is stressed and put to work, while the explication of compatibility is taken to be trivial." (Rappaport Hovav & Levin 2005: 275). It has to be emphasized that it is one thing to observe differences in the syntactic behaviour of words in order to build assumptions about hitherto unnoticed semantic differences between them but it is a completely different matter to justify the existence of a particular semantic property of a word on the basis of a syntactic construction it occurs in and then use this property to predict its occurrence in this construction. The former is a useful heuristic method for tracing semantic properties that would then need to be justified independently; the latter is a circular construction of explanations that can rob a theory of most of its empirical value (cf. Engelberg 2006). This becomes particularly obvious in approaches that distinguish grammatically relevant from grammatically irrelevant meaning. For example, Grimshaw (2005: 75f) claims that "some meaning components have a grammatical life" ('semantic structure') while "some are linguistically inert" ('semantic content'). Only the former have to be linguistically represented. She then discusses Jackendoff's (1990: 253) representation of *eat* as a causative verb, which according to Jackendoff means that x causes y to go into x's mouth. While she agrees that Jackendoff's representation captures what *eat* "pretheoretically" means, she does not consider causation as part of the representation of *eat* since *eat* differs from other causatives (e.g., *melt*) in lacking an inchoative variant (Grimshaw 2005: 85f). Thus, we are confronted with a concept of grammatically relevant causation and a concept of grammatically irrelevant causation, which apart from their grammatical relevance seem to be identical. The result is a theory that pretends to explain syntactic phenomena on the basis of lexical meaning but actually just maps syntactic distinctions onto distinctions on a putatively semantic level, which, however, is not semantically motivated.

Further problems arise if decompositions are adapted to syntactic structures: There is consensus among semanticists and philosophers that causation is a binary relation with both relata belonging to the same type. Depending on the theory, the relation holds either between events or proposition-like entities. In decompositional approaches, the causing argument is often represented as an individual argument, CAUSE(x,p), since purportedly causative verbs only allow agent-denoting NPs in subject position. When this conflict is discussed, it is usually suggested that the first argument of CAUSE is reinterpreted as 'x does something' or 'that x does something'. Although such a reinterpretation can be formally implemented, it raises the question why decomposition is done at all. One could as well stay with simple predicate-argument structures like $dry(x,y)$ and reinterpret them as 'something that x does causes y to become dry'. Furthermore, the decision to represent the first argument of CAUSE as an individual argument is not motivated by the meaning of the lexical item but, in a circular way, by the same syntactic structure that it claims to explain. Finally, the assumption that all causative verbs require an agentive NP in subject position is wrong. While it holds for verbs like German *trocknen* 'to dry' it does not hold for verbs like *vergrößern* 'enlarge' that allow sentential subjects. In any case, the asymmetrical representation of causation raises the problem that two CAUSE predicates need to be introduced where one is reinterpreted in terms of the other. The problem is even bigger in approaches like Distributed Morphology that have done away with a mediating lexicon. If we assume that the bi-propositional (or bi-eventive) nature of causation is part of the encyclopaedic knowledge of vocabulary items that express causation, then causative verbs that only allow agentive subjects should be excluded from transitive verb frames completely.

Even if the predicates used in decompositions are characterized in semantic terms, the criteria are not always sufficiently precise to decide whether or not a verb has the property expressed. Levin & Rappaport Hovav (1996) observe that there are counterexamples to the wide-spread assumption that telic intransitive verbs are unaccusative and agentive intransitive verbs are unergative, namely, verbs of sound, which are unergative but not necessarily agentive nor telic (*beep, buzz, creak, gurgle*). Therefore they propose that verbs that refer to "internally caused eventualities" are unergative, which is the case if "[...] some property of the entity denoted by the argument of the verb is responsible for the eventuality" (Levin & Rappaport Hovav 1996: 501). If we want to apply this idea to the unaccusative German *zerbrechen* 'break' and the unergative *knacken* 'creak', which they do not discuss, we have to check whether it is true that some property of the twig is responsible for the creaking in *der Zweig hat geknackt* 'the twig creaked' while there is no property of the twig that is responsible for the breaking in *der Zweig ist zerbrochen* 'the twig broke'. In order to do that, we must know what 'internal causation' is; that is, we have to answer questions like: What is 'causation'? What is 'responsibility'? What is 'eventuality'? Is 'responsibility', contrary to all assumptions of theories of action, a predicate that applies to properties of twigs? What property of twigs are we talking about? Is (internal) 'causation', contrary to all theories of causation, a relation between properties and eventualities? As long as these questions are not answered, proponents of the theory will agree that the creaking of the twig but not the breaking is internally caused while opponents will deny it. And there is no way to resolve this (cf. Engelberg 2001).

Similar circularities have been noticed by others. Fodor (1998: 51, 60ff), citing work from Pinker (1989) and Higginbotham (1994), criticizes that claims about linking based on interminably vague semantic properties elude any kind of evaluation. This is all the worse since the predicates involved in decompositions are not only expressions in the linguist's metalanguage but are concepts that are attributed to the speaker and his or her knowledge about language (Fodor 1998: 59).

Stipulations about the structure of decompositions can diminish the empirical value of the theory, too. Structural aspects of decompositions concern the way embedded predicates are combined as well as the argument structure of these predicates. For example, predicates like CAUSE or POSS are binary because we conceive of causation and possession as binary relations. Their binarity is a structural aspect that is deeply rooted in our understanding of these concepts. However, it is just by convention that most approaches represent the causing entity and the possessor as the first argument of CAUSE and POSS, respectively. Which argument of multi-place predicates stands for which entity is determined by the truth conditions for this predicates. Thus, the difference between POSS($x^{POSSESSOR}, y^{ENTITY\text{-}POSSESSED}$) and POSS($x^{ENTITIY\text{-}POSSESSED}, y^{POSSESSOR}$) is just a notational one. Whenever explanations rely on this difference, they are not grounded in semantics but in notational conventions. This is, for example, the case in Lexical Decomposition Grammar where the first argument of POSS falls out as the higher one – with all its consequences for Theta Structure and linking principles (Wunderlich 1997: 39).

In summary, the problems with interpreting the predicates used in decompositions and structural stipulations severely limit the empirical content of predictions based on these decompositions. Two ways out of this situation have been pursued only rarely. Decompositional predicates can be given precise truth conditions, as is done in Dowty (1979), or they can be linked to cognitive concepts that are independently motivated (e.g., Jackendoff 1983, Engelberg 2006).

3.6 Decompositions and cognition

Starting from the 1970s, psycholinguistic evidence has been used to argue for or against lexical decompositions. While some approaches to decompositions accepted psycholinguistic data as relevant evidence, proponents of particular lexical theories denied that their theories are about lexical processing at all. Dowty (1979: 391) emphasized that what the main decompositional operators determine is not what the speaker/listener must compute but to what he can infer. Similarly, Goddard (1998: 135) states that "there is no claim that people, in the normal course of linguistic thinking, compose their thoughts directly in terms of semantic primitives; or, conversely, that normal processes of comprehension involve real-time decomposition down to the level of semantic primitives." It has also been suggested that in theorizing about decompositional versus atomistic theories one should distinguish whether lexical concepts are definitionally primitive, computationally primitive (pertaining to language processing), and/or developmentally primitive (pertaining to language acquisition) (cf. Fodor et al. 1980: 313; Carey 1982: 350f).

When lexical decompositions are interpreted in psycholinguistic terms, the typical assumption is that the components of a decomposition are processed each time the lexical item is processed. Lexical processing efforts should emerge as a function from the complexity of the lexical decomposition to processing time: The more complex the decomposition, the longer the processing time. Most early psycholinguistic studies did not produce evidence for lexical decomposition (cf. Fodor et al. 1980; Johnson-Laird 1983). Employing a forced choice task and a rating test, Fodor et al. (1980) failed to find processing differences between causative verbs like *kill*, which are putatively decompositionally complex, and non-causative verbs like *bite*. Fodor, Fodor & Garrett (1975: 522) reported a significant difference between explicit negatives (e.g., *not married*) and putatively implicit negatives (e.g., an UNMARRIED-feature in *bachelor*) in complex conditional sentences like (7).

(7) a. If practically all men in the room are not married, then few of the men in the room have wives.
b. If practically all men in the room are bachelors, then few of the men in the room have wives.

Sentences like (7a) that contain explicit negatives gave rise to longer processing times, thus suggesting that *bachelor* does not contain hidden negatives. Measuring fixation time during reading, Rayner & Duffy (1986) did not find any differences between putatively complex words like causatives and non-causatives.

Similarly, Roelofs (1997: 48ff) discussed several models for word retrieval and argued for a non-decompositional spreading-activation model.

More recent studies display a more varied picture. Gennari & Poeppel (2003) compared eventive verbs like *build, distort, show*, which denote causally structured events, with stative verbs like *resemble, lack, love*, which do not involve complex CAUSE/BECOME structures. Controlling for differences in argument structure and thematic roles, they carried out a self-paced reading study and a visual lexical decision task. They found that semantic complexity was reflected in processing time and that elements of decomposition-like structures were activated during processing. McKoon & MacFarland (2002) adopted Rappaport Hovav & Levin's (1998) template-based approach to decomposition and their distinction between verbs denoting internal causation (*bloom*) and external causation (*break*) (Levin & Rappaport Hovav 1995, 1996). They reported longer processing times for *break*-type verbs than for *bloom*-type verbs in grammaticality judgments, reading time experiments, and lexical decision tasks. They interpreted the results as confirmation that *break*-type verbs involve more complex decompositions than *bloom*-type verbs.

Different conclusions were drawn from other experiments. Applying a "release from proactive interference" technique, Mobayyen & de Almeida (2005) investigated the processing times for lexical causatives (*bend, crack, grow*), morphological causatives (*thicken, darken, fertilize*), perception verbs (*see, hear, smell*), and repetitive perception verbs with morphological markers (e.g., *re-smell*). If verbs were represented in the form of decompositions, the semantically more complex lexical and morphological causatives should pattern together and evoke longer processing times than perception verbs. However, this did not turn out to be the case. Morphological causatives and the morphologically complex *re*-verbs required longer processing than lexical causatives and perception verbs. Similar results have been obtained in action-naming tasks carried out with Alzheimer patients (cf. de Almeida 2007). That lead Mobayyen and de Almeida to the conclusion that the latter two verb types are both semantically simple and refer to non-complex mental particulars. Another line of psycholinguistic/neurolinguistic research concerns speakers with category-specific semantic deficits due to brain damage. Data obtained from these speakers have been used to argue for semantic feature approaches as well as for approaches employing meaning postulates in the nominal domain (cf. the discussion in de Almeida 1999). However, de Almeida (2001: 483) emphasizes that so far no one has found evidence for category-specific verb concept deficits, for example, deficits concerning features like CAUSE or GO.

Evidence for decomposition theories has also been sought in data from language acquisition. If a meaning of a word is its decomposition then learning a decomposed word means learning its decomposition. The most explicit early theory of decomposition-based learning is Clark's (1973) semantic-feature based theory of word-learning. In her view, only some of the features that make up a lexical representation are present when a word is first acquired whereas the other features are learned while the word is already used. The assumption that these features are acquired only successively predicts that children overgeneralize heavily when acquiring a new word. In subsequent research, it turned out that Clark's theory did not conform to the data: (i) Overgeneralization does not occur as often as predicted; (ii) with recently acquired words, undergeneralization is more typical than overgeneralization, and (iii) at some stages of acquisition, the referents a word is applied to do not have any features in common (Barrett 1995: 375ff, cf. also the review in Carey 1982: 361ff). It has been repeatedly argued that meaning postulates are better suited to explain acquisition processes (cf. Chierchia & McConnell-Ginet 1990: 363f, Bartsch & Vennemann 1972: 22). However, even if Clark's theory of successive feature acquisition is not tenable, related data are cited in favor of decompositions to show that some kind of access to semantic features is involved in acquisition. For example, it has been argued that a meaning component CAUSE is extracted from verbs by children and used in overgeneralizations like *he falled it* (cf. the overview in Clark 2003: 233ff). Some research on the acquisition of argument structure alternations has been used to argue for particular decompositional approaches, such as Pinker (1989) for Lexical Conceptual Structures in the vein of Levin & Rappaport Hovav, and Brinkmann (1997) for Lexical Decomposition Grammar.

In summary, the question whether decompositions are involved in language processing or language acquisition remains open. Although processing differences for different classes of verbs have to be acknowledged, it is often difficult to conclude from these data what forms of lexical representation are compatible with these data.

4 Conclusion

From a heuristic and descriptive point of view, lexical decomposition has proven to be a very successful device that has made it possible to discover and to tackle numerous lexical phenomena, in particular, at the syntax-semantics interface. Yet, from a theoretical point of view, lexical decompositions have remained a problematic concept that is not always well grounded in theories of semantics and cognition:

- The basic predicates within decompositions are often elusive and lack truth conditions, definitions, or an empirically grounded link to basic cognitive concepts.
- The lack of semantic grounding of decompositions often leads to circular argumentations in linking theories.
- The cognitive status of decompositions is by and large unclear; it is not known whether and how decompositions are involved in lexical processing and language acquisition.

Thus, decompositions still raise many questions: "But even if the ultimate answers are not in sight, there is certainly a sense of progress since the primitive approaches of the 1960s." (Jackendoff 2002: 377)

5 References

de Almeida, Roberto G. 1999. What do category-specific semantic deficits tell us about the representation of lexical concepts? *Brain & Language* 68, 241–248.

de Almeida, Roberto G. 2001. Conceptual deficits without features: A view from atomism. *Behavioral and Brain Sciences* 24, 482–483.

de Almeida, Roberto G. 2007. Cognitive science as paradigm of interdisciplinarity: the case of lexical concepts. In: J. L. Audy & M. Morosini (eds.). *Interdisciplinarity in Science and at the University*. Porto Alegre: EdiPUCRS, 221–276.

Barrett, Martyn 1995. Early lexical development. In: P. Fletcher & B. MacWhinney (eds.). *The Handbook of Child Language*. Oxford: Blackwell, 362–392.

Bartsch, Renate & Theo Vennemann 1972. *Semantic Structures. A Study in the Relation between Semantics and Syntax*. Frankfurt/M.: Athenäum.

Bendix, Edward H. 1966. *Componential Analysis of General Vocabulary. The Semantic Structure of a Set of Verbs in English, Hindi, and Japanese*. Bloomington, IN: Indiana University.

Bierwisch, Manfred 1969. Certain problems of semantic representations. *Foundations of Language* 5, 153–184.

Bierwisch, Manfred 1970. Semantics. In: J. Lyons (ed.). *New Horizons in Linguistics*. Harmondsworth: Penguin, 166–184.

Bierwisch, Manfred 1997. Lexical information from a minimalist point of view. In: C. Wilder, H.-M. Gärtner & M. Bierwisch (eds.). *The Role of Economy Principles in Linguistic Theory*. Berlin: Akademie Verlag, 227–266.

Brinkmann, Ursula 1997. *The Locative Alternation in German. Its Structure and Acquisition*. Amsterdam: Benjamins.

Carey, Susan 1982. Semantic development: The state of the art. In: E. Wanner & L. R. Gleitman (eds.). *Language Acquisition. The State of the Art*. Cambridge: Cambridge University Press, 347–389.

Carnap, Rudolf 1952. Meaning postulates. *Philosophical Studies* 3, 65–73.

Chierchia, Gennaro & Sally McConnell-Ginet 1990. *Meaning and Grammar. An Introduction to Semantics*. Cambridge, MA: The MIT Press.

Chomsky, Noam 1965. *Aspects of the Theory of Syntax*. Cambridge, MA: The MIT Press.
Clark, Eve V. 1973. What's in a word? On the child's acquisition of semantics in his first language. In: T. E. Moore (ed.). *Cognitive Development and the Acquisition of Language*. New York: Academic Press, 65–110.
Clark, Eve V. 2003. *First Language Acquisition*. Cambridge: Cambridge University Press.
Coseriu, Eugenio 1964. Pour une sémantique diachronique structurale. *Travaux de Linguistique et de Littérature* 2, 139–186.
Dowty, David R. 1979. *Word Meaning and Montague Grammar. The Semantics of Verbs and Times in Generative Semantics and in Montague's PTQ*. Dordrecht: Reidel.
Engelberg, Stefan 2001. Immunisierungsstrategien in der lexikalischen Ereignissemantik. In: J. Dölling & T. Zybatov (eds.). *Ereignisstrukturen*. Leipzig: Institut für Linguistik der Universität Leipzig, 9–33.
Engelberg, Stefan 2006. A theory of lexical event structures and its cognitive motivation. In: D. Wunderlich (ed.). *Advances in the Theory of the Lexicon*. Berlin: de Gruyter, 235–285.
Fillmore, Charles J. 1968. Lexical entries for verbs. *Foundations of Language* 4, 373–393.
Fodor, Janet D. 1977. *Semantics: Theories of Meaning in Generative Grammar*. New York: Crowell.
Fodor, Janet D., Jerry A. Fodor & Merrill F. Garrett 1975. The psychological unreality of semantic representations. *Linguistic Inquiry* 6, 515–531.
Fodor, Jerry A. 1970. Three reasons for not deriving 'kill' from 'cause to die'. *Linguistic Inquiry* 1, 429–438.
Fodor, Jerry A. 1998. *Concepts. Where Cognitive Science Went Wrong*. Oxford: Clarendon Press.
Fodor, Jerry A., Merrill F. Garrett, Edward C. T. Walker & Cornelia H. Parkes 1980. Against definitions. *Cognition* 8, 263–367.
Gennari, Silvia & David Poeppel 2003. Processing correlates of lexical semantic complexity. *Cognition* 89, B27–B41.
Goddard, Cliff 1998. *Semantic Analysis. A Practical Introduction*. Oxford: Oxford University Press.
Greimas, Algirdas Julien 1966. *Sémantique structurale*. Paris: Larousse.
Grimshaw, Jane 2005. *Words and Structure*. Stanford, CA: CSLI Publications.
Harley, Heidi & Rolf Noyer 2000. Formal versus encyclopedic properties of vocabulary: Evidence from nominalizations. In: B. Peeters (ed.). *The Lexicon-Encyclopedia Interface*. Amsterdam: Elsevier, 349–375.
Harris, William T. (ed.) 1923. *Webster's New International Dictionary of the English Language*. Springfield, MA: Merriam.
Higginbotham, James 1994. Priorities of thought. *Supplementary Proceedings of the Aristotelian Society* 68, 85–106.
Hjelmslev, Louis 1963. Omkring sprogteoriens grundlæggelse. *Festskrift udgivet af Københavns Universitet i anledning af Universitetets Aarsfest*. København: E. Munksgaard, 1943, 3–113. English translation: *Prolegomena to a Theory of Language*. Madison, WI: The University of Wisconsin Press, 1963.
Jackendoff, Ray 1983. *Semantics and Cognition*. Cambridge, MA: The MIT Press.
Jackendoff, Ray 1990. *Semantic Structures*. Cambridge, MA: The MIT Press.
Jackendoff, Ray 1992. *Languages of the Mind. Essays on Mental Representation*. Cambridge, MA: The MIT Press.
Jackendoff, Ray 2002. *Foundations of Language. Brain, Meaning, Grammar, Evolution*. Oxford: Oxford University Press.

Johnson-Laird, Philip N. 1983. *Mental Models. Towards a Cognitive Science of Language, Inference, and Consciousness.* Cambridge, MA: Harvard University Press.

Katz, Jerrold J. 1967. Recent issues in semantic theory. *Foundations of Language* 3, 124–194.

Katz, Jerrold J. 1971. Semantic theory. In: D. D. Steinberg & L. A. Jakobovits (eds.). *Semantics. An Interdisciplinary Reader in Philosophy, Linguistics, and Psychology.* Cambridge: Cambridge University Press, 297–307.

Katz, Jerrold J. & Jerry A. Fodor 1963. The structure of a semantic theory. *Language* 39, 170–210.

Katz, Jerrold J. & Paul M. Postal 1964. *An Integrated Theory of Linguistic Descriptions.* Cambridge, MA: The MIT Press.

Kornfilt, Jaklin & Nelson Correa 1993. Conceptual structure and its relation to the structure of lexical entries. In: E. Reuland & W. Abraham (eds.). *Knowledge and Language, vol. II: Lexical and Conceptual Structure.* Dordrecht: Kluwer, 79–118.

Lakoff, George 1972. Linguistics and natural logic. In: D. Davidson & G. Harman (eds.). *Semantics of Natural Language.* Dordrecht: Reidel, 545–655.

Levin, Beth 1993. *English Verb Classes and Alternations. A Preliminary Investigation.* Chicago, IL: The University of Chicago Press.

Levin, Beth & Malka Rappaport Hovav 1995. *Unaccusativity. At the Syntax-Lexical Semantics Interface.* Cambridge, MA: The MIT Press.

Levin, Beth & Malka Rappaport Hovav 1996. Lexical semantics and syntactic structure. In: S. Lappin (ed.). *The Handbook of Contemporary Semantic Theory.* Oxford: Blackwell, 487–507.

Lewis, David 1973. Causation. *The Journal of Philosophy* 70, 556–567.

Löbner, Sebastian 2002. *Understanding Semantics.* London: Arnold.

Lorenz, Wolfgang & Gerd Wotjak 1977. *Zum Verhältnis von Abbild und Bedeutung. Überlegungen im Grenzfeld zwischen Erkenntnistheorie und Semantik.* Berlin: Akademie Verlag.

Lyons, John 1968. *Introduction to Theoretical Linguistics.* Cambridge: Cambridge University Press.

McKoon, Gail & Talke MacFarland 2002. Event templates in the lexical representations of verbs. *Cognitive Psychology* 45, 1–44.

Mobayyen, Forouzan & Roberto G. de Almeida 2005. The influence of semantic and morphological complexity of verbs on sentence recall: Implications for the nature of conceptual representation and category-specific deficits. *Brain and Cognition* 57, 168–175.

Pinker, Steven 1989. *Learnability and Cognition. The Acquisition of Argument Structure.* Cambridge, MA: The MIT Press.

Pottier, Bernard 1963. *Recherches sur l'analyse sémantique en linguistique et en traduction mécanique.* Nancy: Publications Linguistiques de la Faculté de Lettres.

Pottier, Bernard 1964. Vers une sémantique moderne. *Travaux de Linguistique et de Littérature* 2, 107–137.

Pulman, Stephen G. 2005. Lexical decomposition: For and against. In: J. I. Tait (ed.). *Charting a New Course: Natural Language Processing and Information Retrieval: Essays in Honour of Karen Sparck Jones.* Dordrecht: Kluwer, 155–174.

Ramchand, Gillian C. 2008. *Verb Meaning and the Lexicon. A First-Phase Syntax.* Cambridge: Cambridge University Press.

Rappaport Hovav, Malka & Beth Levin 1998. Building verb meanings. In: M. Butt & W. Geuder (eds.). *The Projection of Arguments: Lexical Compositional Factors.* Stanford, CA: CSLI Publications. 97–134.

Rappaport Hovav, Malka & Beth Levin 2005. Change-of-state verbs: Implications for theories of argument projection. In: N. Erteschik-Shir & T. Rapoport (eds.). *The Syntax of Aspect. Deriving Thematic and Aspectual Interpretation.* Oxford: Oxford University Press, 274–286.

Rayner, Keith & Susan A. Duffy 1986. Lexical complexity and fixation times in reading: Effects of word frequency, verb complexity, and lexical ambiguity. *Memory & Cognition* 14, 191–201.

Roelofs, Ardi 1997. A case for nondecomposition in conceptually driven word retrieval. *Journal of Psycholinguistic Research* 26, 33–67.

von Stechow, Arnim 1995. Lexical decomposition in syntax. In: U. Egli et al. (eds.). *Lexical Knowledge in the Organisation of Language*. Amsterdam: Benjamins, 81–177.

Svensén, Bo 1993. *Practical Lexicography. Principles and Methods of Dictionary-Making*. Oxford: Oxford University Press.

Thorndike, Edward L. 1941. *Thorndike Century Senior Dictionary*. Chicago, IL: Scott, Foresman and Company.

Wiegand, Herbert E. 1989. Die lexikographische Definition im allgemeinen einsprachigen Wörterbuch. In: F. J. Hausmann et al. (eds.). *Wörterbücher. Dictionaries. Dictionnaires. Ein internationales Handbuch zur Lexikographie. An International Encyclopedia of Lexicography. Encyclopédie internationale de lexicographie* (HSK 5.1). Berlin: de Gruyter, 530–588.

Wunderlich, Dieter 1997. Cause and the structure of verbs. *Linguistic Inquiry* 28, 27–68.

Stephan Meier-Oeser
8 Meaning in pre-19th century thought

1   Introduction —— 182
2   Semantic theories in classical antiquity —— 184
3   Hellenistic theories of meaning (ca. 300 B.C.–200 A.D.) —— 189
4   Late classical sources of medieval semantics —— 192
5   Concepts of meaning in the scholastic tradition —— 194
6   Concepts of meaning in modern philosophy —— 203
7   References —— 213

Abstract: The article provides a broad survey of the historical development of western theories of meaning from antiquity to the late 18th century. Although it is chronological and structured by the names of the most important authors, schools, and traditions, the focus is mainly on the theoretical content relevant to the issue of linguistic meaning, or on doctrines that are directly related to it. I attempt to show that the history of semantic thought does not have the structure of a continuous ascent or progress; it is rather a complex multilayer process characterized by several ruptures, such as the decline of ancient or the expulsion of medieval learning by Renaissance Humanism, each connected with substantial losses. Quite a number of the discoveries of modern semantics are therefore in fact rediscoveries of much older insights.

1 Introduction

Although it is commonly agreed that semantics as a discipline emerged in the 19th and 20th centuries, the history of semantic theories is both long and rich. In fact semantics started with a rather narrow thematic scope, since it focused, like Reisig, on the "development of the meaning of certain words, as well as the study of their use", or, like Bréal, on the "laws which govern changes in meaning, the choice of new expressions, the birth and death of phrases" (see article 9 [this volume] (Nerlich) *Emergence of semantics*), but many of the theoretical issues that were opened up by this flourishing discipline during the 20th century were already traditional issues of philosophy, especially of logic.

Stephan Meier-Oeser, Berlin, Germany

https://doi.org/10.1515/9783110368505-008

The article aims to give an overview of the historical development of western theories of meaning from antiquity to the late 18th century. The attempt to condense more than 2000 years of intense intellectual labor into 25 pages necessarily leads to omissions and selections which are, of course, to a certain degree subjective. The article should not therefore be read with the expectation that it will tell the whole story. Quite a lot of what could or should have been told is actually not even mentioned. Still it is, I think, a fair sketch of the overall process of western semantic thought.

The oldest known philosophical texts explicitly concerned with the issue of linguistic meaning evolved out of more ancient reflexions on naming and on the question whether, and in what sense, the relation between words and things is conventional or natural. Plato and Aristotle were fairly aware that word meaning needs to be discussed together with sentence meaning (see sections 2.2., 2.3.). The Stoic logicians later on were even more aware of this (see section 3.), but Aristotle's approach in his most influential book *Peri hermeneias* was more influential than them. His account of the relation between linguistic expressions (written and spoken), thoughts and things, combining linguistics (*avant la lettre*), epistemology, and ontology, (see section 4.2.) brought about a long-lasting tendency within the scholastic tradition of Aristotle commentaries to focus on word meaning and to center semantics on the question whether words signify mental concepts or things. The numerous theories that have been designed to answer to this question (see section 5.2.) have strengthened the insight, shared by modern conceptual semantics, that linguistic signs do not refer to the world per se, but rather to the world as conceptualized by language users (see article 4 [Semantics: Theories] (Jackendoff) *Conceptual Semantics*). The way in which the question was put and answered in the scholastic tradition, however, in some respects fell short of its own standards. For ever since Abelard (see section 5.3.) there existed a propositional approach to meaning in scholastic logic fleshed out especially in the terminist logic (see section 5.4.) whose elaborate theories of syncategorematic terms and supposition suggested that by no means every word is related to external things, and that the reference of terms is essentially determined by the propositional context.

Medieval philosophy gave birth to a number of innovative doctrines such as Roger Bacons 'use theory' of meaning (see section 5.5.), the speculative grammar, functionally distinguishing the word classes according to their different modes of signifying (see section 5.6.), or the late medieval mentalist approach, exploring the relations between spoken utterances and the underlying mental structures of thought (see section 5.7.).

Compared to the abundance of semantic theories produced particularly within the framework of scholastic logic, the early modern contribution to semantics in the narrow sense is fairly modest (see section 6.1.). The philosophy of the 17th and 18th centuries, however, disconnecting semantics from logic and centering language theory on epistemology, opened up important new areas of interest, and reopened old ones. So, the idea of a universal grammar underlying all natural languages was forcefully reintroduced by the rationalists in the second half of the 17th century independently from the medieval *grammatica speculativa* (see section 6.4.). One of the new issues, or issues that were discussed in a new way, was the question of the function of language, or of signs in general, in the process of thinking. The fundamental influence of language on thought and knowledge became widely accepted, particularly, though not exclusively, within the empirist movement (see sections 6.2., 6.3., 6.5., 6.6.). Another innovation: from the late 17th century the philosophy of language showed a growing consciousness of and interest in the historical dimension of language (see section 6.7.).

2 Semantic theories in classical antiquity

2.1 The preplatonic view of language

Due to the fragmentary survival of textual relics from the preplatonic period the very beginnings of semantic thought are withdrawn from our sight. Though some passages in the preserved texts as well as in several later sources might prompt speculations about the earliest semantic reflexions, the textual material available seems to be insufficient for a reliable reconstruction of a presocratic semantic theory in the proper sense. The case of the so-called Sophists (literally: 'wise-makers') of the 5th century B.C. is somewhat different: they earned their living mainly by teaching knowledge and skills that were thought to be helpful for gaining private and political success. Their teachings largely consisted of grammar and rhetoric as resources or the command of language and argumentation. One of their standard topics was the 'correctness of names' (*orthotes onomaton*) which was seemingly treated by all the main sophists in separate books, such as Protagoras (ca. 490–420 B.C.), Hippias (ca. 435 B.C.), and Prodicus (ca. 465–415 B.C.), the temporary teacher of Socrates (Schmitter 2001).

2.2 Plato (427–347 B.C.)

The problem of the correctness of names, spelled out as the question whether the relation between names and things is natural or conventional, also makes up the main topic of Plato's dialogue *Cratylus* (ca. 388 B.C.), the earliest known philosophical text on language theory.

The position of naturalism is represented by Cratylus, claiming that "everything has a right name of its own, which comes by nature, and that a name is not whatever people call a thing by agreement, ... but that there is a kind of inherent correctness in names, which is the same for all men, both Greeks and barbarians." (*Cratylus* 383a–b).

The opposite view of conventionalism is advanced by Hermogenes who denies that "there is any correctness of name other than convention (*syntheke*) and agreement (*homologia*)" and holds that "no name has been generated by nature for any particular thing, but rather by the custom and usage (*thesei*) of those who use the name and call things by it" (384c–d). Democritus (ca. 420 B.C.) had previously argued against naturalism by pointing to semantic phenomena such as homonymy, synonymy, and name changes. The position represented by Hermogenes, however, goes beyond the conventionalism of Democritus insofar as he does not make any difference between the various natural languages and an arbitrary individual name-giving (*Cratylus* 385d–e) resulting in autonomous idiolects or private language.

Plato's dialogue expounds with great subtlety the problems connected to both positions. Plato advocates an organon theory of language, according to which language is a praxis and each name is functioning as "an instrument (*organon*) of teaching and of separating (i.e. classifying) reality" (388b–c). He is therefore on the one hand showing, contrary to Hermogenes's conventionalism, that names, insofar as they stand for concepts of things, have to be well defined and to take into account the nature of things in order to carve reality at the joints. On the other hand he demonstrates against Cratylus's overdrawn naturalism the absurdities one can encounter in trying to substantiate the correctness of names etymologically, by tracing all words to a core set of primordial or 'first names' (*prota onomata*) linked to the objects they denote on grounds of their phonological qualities.

Even if Plato's own position is more on the side of a refined naturalism (Sedley 2003), the dialogue, marking the strengths and shortcomings of both positions, leaves the question undecided. Its positive results rather consist (1) in underlining the difference between names and things and (2) in the language critical warning that "no man of sense should put himself or the education of his mind in the power of names" (440c).

Plato in his *Cratylus* (421d–e, 424e, 431b–c) draws, for the first time, a distinction between the word-classes of noun (*onoma*) and verb (*rhema*). In his later Dialogue *Sophistes* he shows that the essential function of language does not consist in naming things but rather in forming meaningful propositions endowed with a truth-value (*Soph.* 261c–262c; Baxter 1992). The question of truth is thus moved from the level of individual words and their relation to things to the more adequate level of propositions. No less important, however, is the fact that Plato uses this as the basis for what can be seen as the first account of propositional attitudes (see article 60 [Semantics: Noun Phrases and Verb Phrases] (Swanson) *Propositional attitudes*). For in order to claim that "thought, opinion, and imagination … exist in our minds both as true and false" he considers it necessary to ascribe a propositional structure to them. Hence Plato defines "forming opinion as talking and opinion as talk which has been held, not with someone else, nor yet aloud, but in silence with oneself" (*Theaetet* 190a), and claims, more generally, that "thought and speech (are) the same, with this exception, that what is called thought is the unuttered conversation of the soul with herself", whereas "the stream of thought which flows through the lips and is audible is called speech" (*Soph.* 263e).

Even if this view is suggested already by the Greek language itself in which *logos* means (inter alia) both speech or discourse and thought, it is in the *Sophistes* where the idea that thought is a kind of internal speech is explicitly stated for the first time. Thus, the *Sophistes* marks the point of departure of the long tradition of theories on the issue of mental speech or language of thought.

2.3 Aristotle (384–322 B.C.)

Aristotle's book *Peri hermeneias* (*De interpretatione*, *On interpretation*), especially the short introductory remarks (*De int.* 16a 3–8), can be seen as "the most influential text in the history of semantics" (Kretzmann 1974: 3). In order to settle the ground for his attempt to explain the logico-semantic core notions of name, verb, negation, affirmation, statement and sentence, Aristotle delineates the basic coordinate system of semantics, comprising the four elements he considers to be relevant for giving a full account of linguistic signification: i.e. (1) written marks, (2) spoken words, (3) mental concepts, and (4) things. This system, which under labels like 'order of speech' (*ordo orandi*) or 'order of signification' (*ordo significationis*, see 5.2.), became the basic framework for most later semantic theories (see Tab. 8.1.) does not only determine the interrelation of these elements but also gives some hints about the connection of semantics and epistemology. According to Aristotle (*De int.* 16a 3–8),

> spoken words (*ta en te phone*; literally: 'those which are in the voice') are symbols (*symbola*) of affections (*pathemata*) in the soul (i.e. mental concepts (*noemata*) according to *De int.* 16a 10), and written marks symbols of spoken words. And just as written marks are not

the same for all men, neither are spoken sounds. But what these are in the first place signs (*semeia*) of – affections of the soul – are the same for all; and what these affections are likenesses (*homoiomata*) of – actual things – are also the same.

Though the interpretation of this passage is highly controversial, the most commonly accepted view is that Aristotle seems to claim that the four elements mentioned are interrelated such that spoken words which are signified by written symbols are signs of mental concepts which in turn are likenesses (or images) of things (Weidemann 1982). This passage presents at least four assumptions that are fundamental to Aristotle's semantic theory:

1. Mental concepts are natural and therefore intersubjectively the same for all human beings.
2. Written or spoken words are, in contrast, conventional signs, i.e. sounds significant by agreement (*kata syntheken*, *De int.* 16a 19–27).
3. Mental concepts which are both likenesses (*homoiomata*) and natural effects of external things are directly related to reality and essentially independent from language.
4. Words and speech are at the same time sharply distinguished from the mental concepts and closely related to them, insofar as they refer to external things only through the mediation of concepts. Aristotle's description of the relation between words, thoughts, and things can therefore be seen as an anticipation of the so called 'semantic triangle' (Lieb 1981).

All four tenets played a prominent role in philosophy of language for a long time and yet, each of them, at one time or another, came under severe attack. The tenet that vocal expressions signify things trough the mediation of concepts, which the late ancient commentators saw as the core thesis of Aristotle's semantics (Ebbesen 1983), leads, if spelled out, to the distinction of intension and extension (Graeser 1996: 39). For it seem to be just an abbreviated form of expressing that for each word to signify something (*semainei ti*) depends upon its being connected to an understanding or a formula (*logos*) which can be a definition, a description or a finite set of descriptions (*Metaphysics* 1006a 32–1006b 5) picking out a certain thing or a certain kind of things by determining what it is to be a such and such thing (*Met.* 1030a 14–17).

Due to the prominency of the *order of signification* it may seem as if Aristotle were focusing on word semantics. There is, however, good reason to maintain that Aristotle's primary intention was a semantics of propositions. Sedley (1996: 87) has made the case that for Aristotle, just as for other teleologists like Plato and the Stoics, "who regard the whole as ontologically prior to the part … the primary signifier is the sentence, and individual words are considered only secondarily, in so far as they contribute to the sentence's function." In face of this he characterizes *De interpretatione*, which is usually seen as a specimen of word semantics as "the most seriously misunderstood text in ancient semantics" (Sedley 1996: 88). This may hold for most of the modern interpretations but not so for the medieval commentators. For quite a number of them were well aware that the somewhat cryptic formulation "those which are in the voice" does not necessarily stand for nouns and verbs exclusively but was likely meant to include also propositions and speech in general. That the treatment of words is tailored to that of propositions is indicated already by the way in which Aristotle distinguishes *onomata* (nouns) and *rhemata* (predicative expressions) not as word classes as such but rather as word classes regarding their function in sentences. For when, as Aristotle remarks, predicative expressions "are spoken alone, as such, they are nouns (*onomata*) that signify something – for the one who utters them forms the notion [or: arrests the thought], and the hearer pauses" (*De int.* 16a 19–21).

The two classes of nouns and predicative expressions, the members of which are described as the smallest conventionally significant units, are complemented by the 'conjunctions' (*syndesmoi*) which include conjunctions, the article, and pronouns and are the direct ancestors of Priscian's *syncategoremata* that became a major topic in medieval logical semantics (see section 4.5.).

Although the natural/conventional distinction separates mental concepts from spoken language, Aristotle describes the performance of thinking, just like Plato, in terms of an internal speaking. He distinguishes between an externally spoken logos and a logos or "speech in the soul" (*Met.* 1009a 20) the latter of which provides the fundament of signification, logical argumentation and demonstration (*Posterior analytics* 76b 24; Panaccio 1999: 34–41), and is at the same time the place where truth and falsehood are located properly (Meier-Oeser 2004: 314). Thus, when in *De interpretatione* (17a 2–24) it is said that the fundamental logical function of declarative sentences to assert or deny something of something presupposes a combination of a name and a verb or an inflection of a verb, this interconnection of truth or falsity and propositionality only seemingly refers primarily to spoken language. For in other passages, as *Met.* 1027b 25–30, or in the last chapter of *De interpretatione*, Aristotle emphasizes that combination and separation and thus truth "are in thought" properly and primarily. How this internal discourse which should be 'the same for all' precisely relates to spoken language remains unclear in Aristotle.

The close connection Aristotle has seen between linguistic signification and thought becomes evident in his insistence on the importance of an unambiguous and well-defined use of language the neglect of which must result in a destruction of both communication and rational discourse; for, as he claimed (*Met.* 1006b 7–12): not to signify one thing is to signify nothing, and if words do not signify anything there is an end of discourse with others, and even, strictly speaking, with oneself; because it is impossible to think of anything if we do not think of one thing.

Noticing that the normal way of speaking does not conform to the ideal of unambiguity, Aristotle is well aware about the importance of a detailed analysis of the semantic issues of homonymy, synonymy, paronymy etc. (*Categories* 1a; *Sophistical refutations* 165f) and devotes the first two books of his *Topics* to the presentation of rules for detecting, and strategies for avoiding ambiguitiy.

3 Hellenistic theories of meaning (ca. 300 B.C.–200 A.D.)

It is uncontroversial that a fully fledged theory of language, considering all the different phonetic, syntactic, semantic, and pragmatic aspects of language as its essential subject matter, is the invention of the Stoic philosophers (Pohlenz 1939). However, since hardly any authentic Stoic text has come down to us, it is still true that "the nature of the Stoics' philosophy of language is the most tantalizing problem in the history of semantics" (Kretzmann 1967: 363). After a long period of neglect and contempt, the Stoic account of semantics is today generally seen as superior even to Aristotle's, which was historically more influential (Graeser 1978: 77). For it has become a current conviction that central points of Stoic semantics are astonishingly close to some fundamental tenets that have paved the way for modern analytical philosophy.

According to Sextus Empiricus (*Adv. math.* 8.11–12; Long & Sedley 1987 [=L&S] 33B) the principal elements of Stoic semantics are:

1. the *semainon*, i.e. that which signifies, or the signifier, which is a phoneme or grapheme, i.e. the material configuration that makes up a spoken word or rather – because Stoic semantics is primarily a sentence semantics – a spoken or written sentence;
2. the *tynchanon* (or: 'name-bearer'), i.e the external material object or event referred to; and
3. the *semainomenon*, i.e. that which is signified. This is tantamount to the core concept and the most characteristic feature of the Stoic propositionalist semantics, the *lekton* (which can be translated both as 'that which is said' and 'that which can be said', i.e. the 'sayable'). The lekton proper or the 'complete lekton' (*lekton autoteles*) is the meaning of a sentence, whereas the meaning of a word is characterized as an 'incomplete lekton' (*lekton ellipes*). Even though questions and demands may have a certain kind of

lekton, the prototype of the Stoic lekton corresponds to what in modern terminology would be classified as the propositional content of a declarative sentence.

Whereas the semainon and the tynchanon are corporeal things or events, the lekton is held to be incorporeal. This puts it in an exceptional position within the materialist Stoic ontology, which considered almost everything – even god, soul, wisdom, truth, or thought – as material entities. Hence the lekton "is not to be identified with any thoughts or with any of what goes on in one's head when one says something" (Annas 1992: 76). This is evident also from the fact that the lekton corresponds to the Stoic notion of *pragma* which, however, in Stoic terminology does not stand for an external thing, as it does for Aristotle, but rather for a fact or something which is the case. The Stoic complement of the Aristotelian notion of mental concept (*noema*), is the material *phantasia logike*, i.e. a rational or linguistically expressible presentation in the soul. The phantasia logike is a key feature in the explanation of how incorporeal meaning is connected to the physical world, since the Stoics maintained "that a lekton is what subsists in accordance with a phantasia logike" (*Adv. math.* 8.70; L&S 33C). It should be clearly distinguished from the lekton or meaning as such. The phantasia logike makes up the 'internal discourse' (*logos endiathetos*) and is thus part of the subjective act of thinking, in contrast to the lekton, which is the "objective content of acts of thinking (*noeseis*)" (Long 1971: 82). The semainon and the tynchanon more or less correspond to the written or spoken signs and the things in the Aristotelian order of signification, but it has no equivalent of the lekton (see Tab. 8.1.). Meaning, as the Stoics take it, is neither some thing nor something in the head. Nor is the Stoic lekton a quasi-Platonic entity that would exist in some sense independent of whether or not one thinks of it, unlike Frege's notion of *Gedanke* (thought) (Graeser 1978: 95; Barnes 1993: 61). Whitin the context of logical inference and demonstration a lekton may function as a sign (*semeion*, not to be mistaken with *semainon*!), i.e. as a "leading proposition in a sound conditional, revelatory of the consequent" (Sextus Empiricus, *Outlines of Pyrrhonism*, L&S 35C).

Besides the notion of propositional content, one of the most interesting and innovative elements of Stoic semantics is the discovery that to take into account propositional content alone might be not in any case sufficient in order to make explicit what a sentence means. This discovery, pointing in the direction of modern speech act theory, is indicated when Plutarch (with critical intention) reports that the Stoics maintain "that those who forbid say one thing, forbid another, and command yet another. For he who says 'do not steal' says just this, 'do not steal', forbids stealing and commands not stealing" (Plutarch, *On Stoic self-contradictions* 1037d–e). In this case there are three different lekta associated to a single sentence, corresponding to the distinct linguistic functions this sentence can perform. Thus, the Stoics seem to have been well aware that the explication of meaning "involves not only the things we talk about and the thoughts we express but also the jobs we do by means of language alone" (Kretzmann 1967: 365a).

A semantic theory which is significantly different from both the Aristotelian and the Stoic is to be found in the Epicurean philosophers who, as Plutarch (*Against Colotes*; L&S 19K) reports, "completely abolish the class of sayables …, leaving only words and name-bearers" (i.e. external things), so that words refer directly to the objects of sensory perception. This referential relation still presupposes a mental 'preconception' (*prolepsis*) or a schematic presentation (*typos*) of the thing signified, for we would not "have named something if we had not previously learnt its delineation (typos) by means of preconception (*prolepsis*)" (Diogenes Laërtius, *Lives and Opinions of eminent Philosophers* L&S 17E), but signification itself remains formally a two-term relation. It is true, the semantic relation between words and things is founded on a third; but this intermediate third, the prolepsis or typos, unlike the passiones or concepts in the Aristotelian account, does not enter the class of what is signified (see Tab. 8.1.).

Tab. 8.1: The *ordo significationis*

	I	1	II	2	III	3	IV
Aristotle	graphomena	symbola	ta en te phone	semeia	pathemata	homoiomata	pragmata
Boethius	litterae written	notae	voces spoken	notae	passiones thought	similitudines	res things
~1250 +		signa		signa		signa	
Augustinus	litterae	signa	dictiones	signa	dicibile, verbum mentis	similitudo	res
~1270 +	propositio scripta	signum	propositio vocalis	signum	propositio in mente	signum	propositio in re (= state of affairs)
Ockham	scripta	signa	voces	signa	conceptus	signa	res
Epicureans	phone				prolepsis semainei		tynchanon
Stoa	semainon				phantasia logike semainei	semainomenon = lekton = pragma (= fact)	tynchanon

Labeled **grey fields** stand for elements (I, II, III) being signifiers and/or signified. Labeled **white fields** stand for semantic relations (1, 2, 3) characterizing the element on the left in regard to the one on the right. Labeled **light grey fields** stand for elements involved in the process of signification though neither being signifiers nor signified.

4 Late classical sources of medieval semantics

4.1 Augustinus (354–430)

Whereas Aristotelian logic and semantics was transmitted to the Middle Ages via Boethius, the relevant works of Augustinus provide a complex compound of modified Stoic, Skeptic and Neoplatonic elements, together with some genuinely new ideas. Probably his most important and influential contribution to the history of semantics and semiotics consists of (1) the explicit definition of words as signs, and (2) his definition of the sign which, for the first time, included both the natural indexical sign and the conventional linguistic sign as species of an all-embracing generic notion of sign. Augustinus thus opened a long tradition in which the theory of language is viewed as a special branch of the more comprehensive theory of signs.

The sign, in general, is defined as "something which, offering itself to the senses, conveys something other to the intellect" (Augustinus 1963: 33). This triadic sign conception provides the general basis for Augustinus's communicative approach to language, which holds that a word is a "sign of something, which can be understood by the hearer when pronounced by the speaker" (Augustinus 1975: 86). In contrast to natural signs which "apart from any intention or desire of using them as signs, do yet lead to the knowledge of something else", words are conventional signs "living beings mutually exchange in order to show ..., the feelings of their minds, or their perceptions, or their thoughts" (Augustinus 1963: 34). The preeminent position of spoken words among the different sorts of signs used in human communication, some of which "relate to the sense of sight, some to that of hearing, a very few to the other senses", does not result from their quantitative preponderance but rather from their significative universality, i.e. from the fact that, as Augustinus sees it, everything which can be indicated by nonverbal signs could be put into words but not vice versa (Augustinus 1963: 35).

The full account of linguistic meaning entails four elements (Augustinus 1975: 88f): (1) the word itself, as an articulate vocal sound, (2) the *dicibile*, i.e. the sayable or "whatever is sensed in the word by the mind rather than by the ear and is retained in the mind", (3) the *dictio*, i.e. the word in its ordinary significative use in contrast to the same word just being mentioned. It "involves both the word itself and that which occurs in a mind as the result of the word" (i.e. the dicibile or meaning), and (4) the thing signified (res) in the broadest sense comprising anything "understood, or sensed, or inapprehensible".

Even if the notion of dicibile obviously refers to the Stoic lekton, Augustinus has either missed or modified the essential point. For describing it as "what happens in the mind by means of the word" implies nothing less than the rejection of the Stoic expulsion of meaning (lekton) from the mind. It is as if he mixed up the lekton with the phantasia logike, which was characterized as a representation whose content "can be expressed in language" (Sextus Empiricus, *Adv. math.* 8.70; L&S 33C).

Augustinus's emphasis on the communicative and pragmatic aspects of language is manifest in his concept of the 'force of word' (*vis verbi*) which he describes as the "efficacy to the extent of which it can affect the hearer" (Augustinus 1975: 100). The import spoken words have on the hearer is not confined to their bare signification but includes a certain value and some emotive moments resulting from their sound, their familiarity to the hearer or their common use in language – aspects which Frege called *Färbungen* (colorations).

In his later theory of *verbum mentis* (mental word), especially in *De trinitate*, Augustinus advocates the devaluation of the spoken word against the internal sphere of mental cognition. It is now the mental or 'interior word' (verbum interius), i.e., the mental concept, that is considered as word in its most proper sense, whereas the spoken word appears as a mere sign or voice of the word (*signum verbi*, *vox verbi*; Augustinus 1968: 486). In line with the old concept of an internal speech, Augustinus claims that thoughts (*cogitationes*) are performed in mental words. The verbum mentis however, corresponding to what later was called the *conceptus mentis* or *intellectus*, is by no means a linguistic entity in the proper sense, for it is "nullius linguae", i.e. it does not belong to any spoken language like Latin or Greek.

Between mental and spoken words there is a further level of speech, consisting of imaginative representations of spoken words, or, as he calls them, *imagines sonorum* (images of sounds), closely corresponding to Saussure's notion of *image accoustique*. In Augustin's theory of language this internalized version of uttered words does not seem to play a major role, but it will gain importance in late medieval and early modern reflections on the influence of language on thought.

4.2 Boethius (480–528)

Boethius' translations of and comments on parts of the Aristotelian Organon (especially *De Interpretatione*) are for a long time the only available source texts for the semantics of Aristotle and his late ancient Neoplatonic commentators for the medieval world. The medieval philosophers thus first viewed Aristotle's logic through the eyes of Boethius, who made some influential decisions on semantic terminology, as well as on the interpretation of the Aristotelian text. What they learned through his writings were inter alia the conventional character of language, the view that meaning is established by an act of 'imposition', i.e., name-giving or reference-setting, and the influential idea that to 'signify' (*significare*) is to "establish an understanding" (*intellectum constituere*).

Especially in his more elaborate second commentary on *De interpretatione*, Boethius discusses at length Aristotle's four elements of linguistic semeiosis (*scripta, voces, intellectus, res*), which he calls the 'order of speaking' (*ordo orandi*) (Magee 1989: 64–92). The ordo orandi determines the direction of linguistic signification: written characters signify spoken words, whereas spoken words primarily signify mental concepts and, by means of the latter, secondarily denote the things, or, in short: words signify things by means of concepts (Boethius 1880: 24, 33).

The first step of the process of homogenizing or systematizing the semantic relations between these four elements, later continued in the Middle Ages (see 5.2.), is to be seen in Boethius's translation of Aristotle's *De interpretatione* (*De int.* 16a 3–8) (Meier-Oeser 2009). For whereas Aristotle characterizes these relations with the three terms of symbola, semeia, and homoiomata, Boethius translates both symbola and semeia as *notae* (signs; see Tab. 8.1.).

Boethius makes an additional distinction in the work of late classical Aristotle commentators: he distinguishes three levels of speech: besides - or rather, at the basis of - written and spoken discourse there is a mental speech (oratio mentis) in which thinking is performed. This mental speech is, just like Augustinus's mental word, not made up of words of any national language but rather of transidiomatic or even non-linguistic mental concepts (Boethius 1880: 36) which are, as Aristotle had claimed, "the same for all".

5 Concepts of meaning in the scholastic tradition

The view that semantic issues are not only *a* subject matter of logic but its primary and most fundamental one is characteristic for the scholastic tradition. This tradition was not confined to the Middle Ages but continued, after a partial interruption in the mid-16th century, during the 17th and 18th centuries. Because it is the largest and most elaborate tradition in the history of semantics, it seems advisable to begin with an overview of some basic aspects of medieval semantics, such as the use and the definition of the pivotal term of significatio (see 5.1.), and the most fundamental medieval debate on that subject (see 5.2.).

5.1 The use and definition of *significatio* in the scholastic tradition

The problematic vagueness or ambiguity that has frequently been pointed out regarding the notion of meaning holds, at least partly, for the Latin term of *significatio* as well. There is, however, evidence that some medieval authors were aware of this terminological difficulty. Robert Kilwardby (1215–1279) for instance noted that *significatio* can designate either the 'act or form of the signifier' (*actus et forma significantis*), the 'signified' (*significatum*), or the relation between the two (*comparatio signi ad significatum*; Lewry 1981: 379). A look at the common scholastic use of the term *significatio* does not only verify this diagnosis but reveals a number of further variants (Meier-Oeser 1996: 763–765) which mostly resulted from debates on the appropriate ontological description of significatio as some sort of quality, form, relation, act etc. The scholastic definitions of significatio and *significare* (to signify), however, primarily took up the question what signification is in the sense of 'what it is for a word or sign to signify'.

There is a current misconception: the medieval notions of sign and signification are often described in terms of what Bühler (1934: 40) called the "famous formula of *aliquid stat pro aliquo*" (something stands for something). This description, confusing signification with *supposition* (see 5.4.), falls short by reducing signification to a two-term relation between a sign and its significate, whereas in scholastic logic the relation to a cognitive faculty of a sign recipient is always a constitutive element of signification. In this vein, the most widely spread scholastic definition (Meier-Oeser 1996: 765–768), based on Boethius's translation of Aristotle's *De interpretatione* (*De int.* 16b 20), characterizes signification or the act of signifying as "to establish an understanding" (*constituere intellectum*) of some thing, or "to evoke a concept in the intellect of the hearer". The relation to the sign recipient remains pivotal when in the later Middle Ages the act of signifying is primarily defined as "to represent something to an intellect" (*aliquid intellectui repraesentare*). The common trait of the definitions mentioned (and all the others not mentioned) is (1) to describe signification – in contrast to *meaning* – not as something a word has, but rather as an act of signifying which is – in contrast to the *stare pro* – involved in a triadic relation including both the significate and a cognitive faculty.

5.2 The *order of signification* and the *great altercation* about whether words are signs of things or concepts

The introductory remarks of Aristotle's *De interpretatione* have been described as "the common starting point for virtually all medieval theories of semantics"

(Magee 1989: 8). They did at least play a most important role in medieval semantics. In the late 13th and early 14th centuries the order of the four principal elements of linguistic signification (i.e. written and spoken words, mental concepts, and things) is characterized as *ordo significationis* (order of signification; Aquinas 1989: 9a), or *ordo in significando* (order in signifying; Ockham 1978: 347). The coinage of these expressions is the terminological outcome of the second step in the process mentioned above of homogenizing the relations between these four elements. It took place in the mid-13th century, when mental concepts began to be described as signs. The Boethian pair of *notae* and *similitudines* was thus further reduced to the single notion of *sign* (signum, see Tab. 8.1.), so that the entire order of signification was then uniformly described in terms of sign relations, or, as Antonius Andreas (ca. 1280–1320) said: "written words, vocal expressions, concepts in the soul and things are coordinated according to the notion of sign and significate" (Andreas 1508: fol. 63va).

From the second half of the 13th century on, most scholastic logicians shared the view that mental concepts were signs, which provided new options for solving the "difficult question of whether a spoken word signifies the mental concept or the thing" (Roger Bacon 1978: 132). This question made up the subject matter of the most fundamental scholastic debate on semantic issues. John Duns Scotus (1265/66–1308) labeled it "the great altercation" (*magna altercatio*). The simple alternative offered in the formulation of the question is, however, by no means exhaustive, but only marks the extreme positions within a highly differentiated spectrum of possible answers (Ashworth 1987; Meier-Oeser 1996: 770–777).

The various theories of word meaning turn out to be most inventive in producing variants of the coordination of linguistic signs, concepts and things. For example (1) while especially some early authors held the mental concept to be the only proper significate of a spoken word, (2) Roger Bacon (ca. 1214 or 1220 – ca. 1292) as well as most of the so-called late medieval nominalists favored an extensionalist reference semantics according to which words signify things. (3) Especially Thomist authors took up the formula that words signify things by the mediation of concepts (*voces significant res mediantibus conceptibus*) and answered the question along the lines of the semantic triangle (Aquinas 1989: 11a). Some later authors put it the other way round and maintained (4) that words signify concepts only by the mediation of their signification of things (*voces significant conceptus mediante significatione rerum*). For "if I do not know which things the words signify I shall never learn by them which concepts the speaker has in his mind" (Smiglecius 1634: 437). Sharing the view that concepts were signs of things, (5) Scotus referred to the principle of semantic transitivity, claiming that "the sign of a sign is [also] the sign of the significate" (*signum signi est signum signati*), and held that words signify both concepts and things by one and the same act of signifying (1891: 451f). Others, in contrast, maintained (6) that there had to be two simultaneous but distinguishable acts of signification (Conimbricenses 1607: 2.39f). And still others tried to solve the problem by introducing further differentiations. Some of them were related to the *mediantibus conceptibus*-formula by the claim (7) that this formula does not imply that concepts were the immediate significates of words but rather that they were a prerequisite condition for words to signify things (Henry of Ghent 1520: 2.272v). Others were related to the notion of things, taking (8) the 'thing conceived' (*res concepta*; *res ut intelligitur*) as the proper significate of words (Scotus 1891: 543). Further approaches tried to decide the question either (9) by distinguishing senses of the term *significare* (significare suppositive – manifestative), claiming that spoken words stand for the thing but manifest the concepts (Rubius 1605: 21), or (10) by differentiating between things being signified and thoughts being expressed (Soto 1554: fol. 3 rb–va), or again (11) by taking into account the different roles of the discourse participants, so that words signify concepts for the speaker and things for the hearer (Versor 1572: fol. 8 r), or lastly (12) by distinguishing between different types of discourse, maintaining that in familiar speech words primarily refer to concepts whereas in doctrinal discourse to things (Nicolaus a S. Iohanne Baptista 1687: 40. 43ff). No matter how subtle the semantic doctrines behind these positions may have been in detail; it is still true that most of the contributions to the 'great altercation' were focusing primarily on word semantics. Scholastic semantics, however, was by no means confined to this approach.

5.3 Peter Abelard (1079–1142) and the meaning of the proposition

As early as Peter Abelard a shift in the primary interest of scholastic logic became apparent. His treatment of logic and semantics is determined by a decidedly propositional approach; all distinctions he draws and all discussions he conducts are guided by his concentration on propositions (Jacobi 1983: 91). In a conceptual move comparable to the one in Frege's famous *Über Sinn und Bedeutung*, Abelard transposes the distinction between the signification of things (which is akin to Frege's *Bedeutung*) and concepts (Frege's *Sinn*) to the level of propositions. On the one hand, and in line with Frege's *principle of compositionality*, the signification of a proposition is the complex comprehension of the sentence as it is integrated from the meanings of its components (see article 6 [this volume] (Pagin & Westerståhl) *Compositionality*). On the other hand, it corresponds to Frege's *Gedanke*, i.e. to the propositional content of a sentence. Abelard calls this, in accordance with the Stoic lekton, *dictum propositionis* ('what is said by the proposition') or *res propositionis* ('thing of the proposition', i.e. the Stoic *pragma*). These similarities do not concern only terminology, but also the ontological interpretation. For the res propositionis is characterized as being essentially nothing (*nullae penitus essentiae*; Abelard 1927: 332, 24) or as entirely nothing (*nil omnino*; 366: 1). And yet the truth value or the modal state of a proposition depends on the *res propositionis* being either true or false, necessary or possible etc. (367: 9–16).

In the logical textbooks of the late 12th and 13th centuries Abelard's notion of *dictum propositionis* is present under the name of *enuntiabile* ('what can be stated') (de Rijk 1967 2/2.208: 15ff). In the 14th century it has its analog in the theory of the 'complexly signifiable' (*complexe significabile*) developed by Adam Wodeham (ca. 1295–1358), Gregory of Rimini (ca. 1300–1358), and others in the context of intense discussions on the immediate object of knowledge and belief (Tachau 1987).

These conceptions of the significance of propositions correspond in important points to Frege's notion of 'thought' (*Gedanke*) or Bolzano's 'sentences as such' (*Sätze an sich*), and, of course, to the Stoic lekton. In contrast, Walter Burley (ca. 1275–1344) answered the question about the ultimate significance of vocal and mental propositions by advocating the notion of a *propositio in re* (proposition in reality) or a proposition composed of things, which points more in the direction of Wittgensteins notion of *Sachverhalte* (cases) or *Tatsachen* (facts; or better: states of affairs) as described in his *Tractatus logico-philosophicus* ("1. The world is all that is the case. 1.1. The world is the totality of facts, not of things."). Whereas the advocates of the *complexe significabile* project propositionality onto a Fregian-like 'third realm' of propositional content, Burley and some other authors project it onto the real world, maintaining that what makes our propositions true (or false) are not the things as such but rather the states of affairs, i.e. the things relating (or not relating) to each other in the way our propositions say they do (Meier-Oeser 2009: 503f).

5.4 The theory of *supposition* and the propositional approach to meaning

The propositional approach to meaning is also characteristic of the so-called 'terminist' or 'modern logic' (*logica moderna*), emerging in the late 12th and 13th centuries with a rich and increasingly sophisticated continuation from the 14th to the early 16th century. Most of what is genuinely novel in medieval logic and semantics is to be found in this tradition whose two most important theoretical contributions are (1) the theory of syncategorematic terms and (2) the theory of the properties of terms (*proprietates terminorum*).

1. The theory of syncategorematic terms is concerned with the semantic and logical functions of those parts of speech that have been missed out in the ordo significationis since they are neither nouns nor verbs and thus have neither a proper meaning nor a direct relation to any part of reality (Meier-Oeser 1998). Even if syncategorematic terms (i.e. quantifiers, prepositions, adverbs, conjunctions etc. like 'some', 'every', 'besides', 'necessarily', or the copula 'est') do not signify 'something' (*aliquid*) but only, as was later said, 'in some way' (*aliqualiter*), they perform semantic functions that are determinative for the meaning and the truth-value of propositions.

Since the late 12th century the syncategorematic terms became the subject matter of a special genre of logical textbooks, the *syncategoremata* tracts. They also played an important role in the vast literature on *sophismata*, i.e. on propositions like "every man is every man" or "Socrates twice sees every man besides Plato", which, due to a syncategorematic term contained in them, need further analysis in order to make explicit their unterlying logical form as well as the conditions under which they can be called true or false (Kretzmann 1982).

2. The second branch of terminist semantics was concerned with those properties of terms that are relevant for explaining truth, inference and fallacy. While signification was seen as the most fundamental property of terms, the one to which they devoted most attention was *suppositio*. Whereas any term, due to its imposition, has signification or lexical meaning on its own, it is only within the context of a proposition that it achieves the property of supposition or the function of standing for (*supponere pro*) a certain object or a certain number or kind of objects. Thus it is the propositional context that determines the reference of terms.

The main feature of supposition theory is the distinction of different kinds of suppositions. The major distinction is that between 'material supposition' (*suppositio materialis*, when a term stands for itself as a token, e.g. 'I write donkey', or a type; e.g. 'donkey is a noun'), 'simple supposition' (*s. simplex*, when a term stands for the universal form or a concept; e.g. 'donkey is a species'), and 'personal supposition' (*s. personalis*; when a term stands for ordinary objects, e.g. 'some donkey is running'). This last most important type of supposition is further divided and subdivided depending whether the truth conditions of the proposition in which the term appears require a particular quantification of the term (all x, every x, this x, some x, a certain x, etc). While supposition theory in general provides a set of rules to determine how the terms in a given propositional context have to be understood in order to render the proposition true or an inference valid, the treatment of suppositio personalis and its subclasses, which are at the center of this logico-semantic approach, focuses on the extension of the terms in a given proposition.

The characteristic feature of terminist logic, as it is exemplified both in the theory of syncategorematic terms and in the theory of supposition, is commonly described as a contextual approach (de Rijk 1967: 123–125), or, more precisely, as a propositional approach to meaning (de Rijk 1967: 552).

5.5 Roger Bacon's theory of the foundation and the change of reference

Roger Bacons theory of linguistic meaning is structured around two dominant features: (1) his semiotic approach, according to which linguistic signification is considered in connection to both conventional and natural sign processes, and (2) his original and inventive interpretation of the doctrine of the 'imposition of names' (*impositio nominum*) as the basis of word meaning. Bacon accentuates the arbitrariness of meaning (Fredborg 1981: 87ff). But even though the first namegiver is free to impose a word or sign on anything whatsoever, he or she performs the act of imposition according to the paradigm of baptizing a child, so that Bacon in this respect might be seen as an early advocate of what today is known as causal theory of reference (see article 4 [this volume] (Abbott) *Reference*). This approach, if taken seriously, has important consequences for the concept of signification. For: "all names which we impose on things we impose inasmuch as they are present to us, as in the case of names of people in baptism" (Bacon 1988: 90). Contrary to the tradition of Aristotelian or Boethian semantics (Ebbesen 1983), Bacon favors the view that words according to their imposition immediately and properly signify things rather than mental concepts of things. Thus, his account of linguistic signification abandons the model of the semantic triangle and marks an important turning point on the way from the traditional intensionalist semantics to the extensionalist reference semantics as it became increasingly accepted in the 14th century (Pinborg 1972: 58f).

With regard to mental concepts, spoken words function just as natural signs, which indicates that the speaker possesses some concept of the object the word refers to, for this is a prerequisite for any meaningful use of language (Bacon 1978: 85f, 1988: 64).

When Bacon treats the issue of linguistic meaning as a special case of sign relations, he considers the sign relation after the model of real relations presupposing both the distinction of the terms related (so that nothing can be a sign of itself) and their actual existence (so that there can be no relation to a non-existent object). As a consequence of this account, words lose their meaning, or, as Bacon says, "fall away from their signification" (*cadunt a significatione*) if their significate ceases to exist (1978: 128).

But even if the disappearance of the thing signified annihilates the sign relation and therefore must result in the corruption of the sign itself, Bacon is well aware that the use of names and words in general is not restricted to the meaning endowed during the first act of imposition (the term *homo* does not only denote those men who were present when the original act of its imposition took place); nor do words cease to be used when their name-bearers no longer physically exist (Bacon 1978: 128). As a theoretical device for solving the resulting difficulties regarding the continuity of reference, Bacon introduced a distinction of two modes of imposition that can be seen as "his most original contribution to grammar and semantics" (Fredborg 1981: 168). Besides the 'formal mode of imposition', conducted by an illocutionary expression like "I call this ..." (*modus imponendi sub forma impositionis vocaliter expressa*), there is a kind of 'secondary imposition', taking place tacitly (*sine forma imponendi vocaliter expressa*) whenever a term is applied (*transumitur*) to any object other than that which the first name-giver 'baptized' (Bacon 1978: 130). Whereas the formal mode of imposition refers to acts of explicitly coining a new word, the second mode describes what happens in the everyday use of language. Bacon (1978: 130) states:

> We notice that infinitely many expressions are transposed in this way; for when a man is seeing for the first time the image of a depicted man he does not say that this image shall be called 'man' in the way names are given to children, he rather transposes the name of man to the picture. In the same way he who for the first time says that god is just, does not say beforehand 'the divine essence shall be called justice', but transposes the name of human justice to the divine one because of the similitude. In this way we act the whole day long and renew the things signified by vocal expressions without an explicit formula of vocal imposition.

In fact this modification of the meaning of words is constantly taking place even without the speaker or anyone else being actually aware of it. For by simply using language we "all day long impose names without being conscious of when and how" (*nos tota die imponimus nomina et non advertimus quando et quomodo*; Bacon 1978: 100, 130f). Thus, according to Roger Bacon, who in this respect is playing off a use theory of meaning against the causal approach, the common mode of language use is too complex and irregular as to be sufficiently described solely by the two features of a primary reference-setting and a subsequent causal chain of reference-borrowing.

5.6 Speculative grammar and its critics

The idea, fundamental already for Bacon, that grammar is a formal science rather than a propaedeutic art, is shared by the school of the so-called 'modist' grammarians (*modistae*) emerging around 1270 in the faculty of arts of the university of Paris and culminating in the *Grammatica Speculativa* of Thomas of Erfurt (ca. 1300). The members of this school who took it for granted that the objective of any formal science was to explain the facts by giving reasons for them rather than to simply describe them, made it their business to deduce the 'modes of signifyng' (*modi significandi*), i.e. grammatical features common to all languages, from universal 'modes of being' (*modi essendi*) by means of corresponding 'modes of understanding' (*modi intelligendi*).

Thus the tradition of 'speculative grammar' (*grammatica speculativa*) adopted Aristotle's commonly accepted claim that mental concepts, just as things, are the same for all men, and developed it further to the thesis of a universal grammar based on the structural analogy between the 'modes of being' (*modi essendi*), the 'modes of understanding' (*modi intelligendi*), and the 'modes of signifying' (*modi significandi*) that are the same for all languages (Bursill-Hall 1971). Thus, Boethius Dacus (1969: 12): one of the most important theoreticians of speculative grammar, states that

> ... all national languages are grammatically identical. The reason for this is that the whole grammar is borrowed from the things ... and just as the natures of things are similar for those who speak different languages, so are the modes of being and the modes of understanding; and consequently the modes of signifying are similar, whence, so are the modes of grammatical construction or speech. And therefore the whole grammar which is in one language is similar to the one which is in another language.

Even though the words are arbitrarily imposed (whence arise the differences between all languages), the modes of signifying are uniformly related to the modes of being by means of the modes of understanding (whence arise the grammatical similarities among all languages). Soon after 1300 the modistic approach came under substantial criticism. The main point that critics like Ockham oppose is not the assumption of a basic universal grammar, for such a claim is implied in Ockham's concept of mental grammar too, but rather two other aspects of modism: (1) the assertion of a close structural analogy between spoken or mental language and external reality (William of Ockham 1978: 158), and (2) the inadmissible reification of the modus significandi, which is involved in its description as some quality or form added to the articulate voice (*dictioni superadditum*) through the act of imposition. To say that vocal expressions 'have' different modes of signifying is, as Ockham points out, just a metaphorical manner of speaking; for what is meant is simply the fact that different words signify whatever they signify in different ways (Ockham 1974: 798).

According to John Aurifaber (ca. 1330), a vocal term is significative, or is a sign, solely by being used significatively, not on grounds of something inherent in the sound. In order to assign signification a proper place in reality, it must be ascribed to the intellect rather than to the vocal sound (Pinborg 1967: 226). This criticism of modist grammar is connected to a process that might be described as a progressive 'mentalization' of signification.

5.7 The late medieval mentalist approach to signification

The idea behind this process is the contention that without some sort of 'intentionality' the phenomena of sign, signification, and semiosis in general must remain inconceivable. The tendency to relocate the notions of sign and signification from the sphere of spoken words to the sphere of the mind is characteristic for the mentalist logic, emerging in the early 14th century and remaining dominant throughout the later Middle Ages.

The signification of spoken words and external signs in general is founded on the natural signification instantiated in the mental concepts. The cognitive mental act as that which makes any signification possible is now conceived as a sign or an act of signification in its most proper sense. The introduction of the notion of *formal signification* (*significatio formalis*), identical with the mental concept (Raulin 1500: d3vb), is the result of a fundamental change in the conception of signification. The mental concept does not *have* but rather *is* signification. This, however, does not imply that it is the signified of a spoken word but, quite the contrary: the mental concept, as Ockham (1974: 7f) claimed, is the primary signifier in subordination to which a spoken word (to which again is subordinate the corresponding written term) takes up the character of a sign (see Tab. 8.1.). Thus the significative force of mental concepts is seen as the point at which the analysis of signification necessarily must find its end. It is an ultimate fact for which no further rationale can be given (Meier-Oeser 1997: 141–143).

6 Concepts of meaning in modern philosophy

Whereas in Western Europe, under the growing influence of humanism, the scholastic tradition of terminist logic and semantics came to an end in the third decade of the 16th century, it continued vigourously on the Iberian Peninsula until the 18th century. It was then reimported from there into central Europe in the late 16th and early 17th century and dominated, though in a somewhat simplified form, academic teaching in Catholic areas for more than a century. In what is commonly labeled 'modern philosphy', however, logic, the former center of semantic theory, lost many of its medieval attainments and subsided into inactivity until the middle of the 19th century. In early modern philosophy of language the logico-semantic approach of the scholastic tradition is displaced by an epistemological approach, so that in this context the focus is not on the issue of meaning but rather on the cognitive function of language.

6.1 The modern redefinition of meaning

In early modern philosophy (outside the scholastic discourse) the "difficult question of whether a spoken word signifies the mental concept or the thing" (see 5.2.) which once had stimulated a rich variety of distinctly elaborated semantic theories was unanimously considered as definitively answered. Due to the prevalent persuasion that the primary function of speech was to express one's thoughts, most of the non-scholastic early modern authors took up the view that words signify concepts rather than things which, from a scholastic point of view, had been classified as the "more antiquated" one (Rubius 1605: 2.18). Given, however, that concepts, ideas, or thoughts are the primary meaning of words, the thesis that language has a formative influence on thought, which became increasingly widely accepted during the 18th century, turns out to be a thesis of fundamental importance to semantics.

6.2 The influence of conventional language on thought processes

Peter of Ailly (1330–1421) claimed that there is such a habitually close connection between the concept of the thing and the concept of its verbal expression that by stimulating one of these concepts the other is always immediately stimulated as well (Kaczmarek 1988: 403ff). Still closer is the correlation of language and thought in Giovanni Battista Giattini's (1601–1672) account of language acquisition. Upon hearing certain words frequently and in combination with the sensory perception of their significata, a 'complex species' is generated, and this species comprises, just like the Saussurean sign, the sound-image as well as the concept of its correlate object ("... generantur ... species complexae talium vocum simul et talium obiectorum ex ipsa consuetudine"; Giattini 1651: 431). In this vein, Jean de Raey (1622–1702) sees the "union of the external vocal sound and the inner sense" as the "immediate fundament of signification" and holds that sound (*sonus*) and meaning or sense (*sensus*) make up "one and the same thing rather than two things" (Raey 1692: 29). Thinking, therefore, "seems to be just some kind of internal speech or *logos endiathetos* without which there would be no reasoning" (30).

Even if de Reay refers to the old tradition of describing the process of thinking in terms of internal speech (see 2.2.), a fundamental difference becomes apparent when he claims that "both the speaker and the hearer have in mind primarily the sound rather than the meaning and often the sound without meaning but never the meaning without sound" (29). Until then, internal speech had generally been conceived as being performed in what Augustinus had called *verba nullius linguae* (see 4.1.), but from de Raey (and other authors of that time) inner speech is clearly intimately linked to spoken language.

The habitual connection of language and thought was the theoretical foundation for the thesis of an influence of language on thinking in the 17th century. As the introduction to the Port-Royal logic notes: "this custom is so strong, that even when we think alone, things present themselves to our minds only in connection with the words to which we have been accustomed to recourse in speaking to others." (Arnauld & Nicole 1662: 30). Because most 17th century authors adhered to the priority of thought over language they considered this custom just a bad habit. While this critical attitude remained a constant factor in the philosophical view of language during the following centuries, a new and alternative perspective, taking into account also its positive effects, was opened with Hobbes, Locke and Leibniz.

6.3 Thomas Hobbes (1588–1679)

In his Logic (*Computatio sive logica*), which makes up the first part (*De Corpore*) of his *Elementa Philosophiae* (1655, English 1656), Thomas Hobbes draws a parallel between reasoning and a mathematical calculus, the basic operations of which can be described as an addition or subtraction of ideas, thoughts, or concepts (Hobbes 1839a: 3–5). Because thoughts are volatile and fleeting (*fluxae et caducae*) they have to be fixed by means of *marks* (*notae*) which, in principle, everyone can arbitrarily choose for himself (1839a: 11f). Because the progress of science, however, can be obtained only in form of a collective accumulation of knowledge, it is necessary that "the same notes be made common to many" (Hobbes 1839b: 14). So, in addition to these marks, *signs* (*signa*) as a means of communication are required. In fact, both functions are obtained by words: "The nature of a name consists principally in this, that it is a mark taken for memory's sake; but it serves also by accident to signify and make known to others what we remember ourselves" (Hobbes 1839b: 15).

Hobbes adopts the scholastic practice of viewing linguistic signs in light of the general notion of sign. His own concept of sign, however, according to which signs in general can be described as "the antecedents of their consequents, and the consequents of their antecedents", is from the outset confined to the class of indexical signs (Hobbes 1839b: 14). Words and names ordered in speech must therefore be indexical signs rather than expressions of conceptions, just as they cannot be "signs of the things themselves; for that the sound of this word stone should be the sign of a stone, cannot be understood in any sense but this, that he that hears it collects that he that pronounces it thinks of a stone" (Hobbes 1839b: 15). It is true, from Roger Bacon onwards we find in scholastic logic the position that words are indexical signs of the speaker's concepts. Connected to this, however, was always the assumption, explicitly denied by Hobbes, that the proper significate of words are the things talked about.

Names, according to Hobbes, "though standing singly by themselves, are marks, because they serve to recall our own thoughts to mind, ... cannot be signs, otherwise than by being disposed and ordered in speech as parts of the same" (Hobbes 1839b: 15). As a result of the distinction between marks and signs, any significative function of words can be realized only in the framework of communication. These rudiments of a sentence semantics (Hungerland & Vick 1973), however, were not elaborated any further by Hobbes.

6.4 The 'Port-Royal Logic' and 'Port-Royal Grammar'

The so called *Port-Royal Logic (Logique ou l'art de penser)*, published in 1662 by Antoine Arnauld (1612–1694) and Pierre Nicole (1625–1695), is not only one of the most influential early modern books on the issue of language but in some respect also the most symptomatic one. For "it marks, better than any other, the abandonment of the medieval doctrine of an essential connection between logic and semantics", and treats the "most fundamental questions ... with the kind of inattention to detail that came to characterize most of the many semantic theories of the Enlightenment" (Kretzmann 1967: 378a).

The most influential, though actually quite modest, semantic doctrine of this text is the distinction between *comprehension* and *extension* which is commonly seen as a direct ancestor of the later distinction between *intension* and *extension*. And yet it is different: Whereas the comprehension of an idea is tantamount to "the attributes it comprises in itself that cannot be removed from it without destroying it", extension is described as "the subjects with which that idea agrees, which are also called the inferiors of the general term, which in relation to them, is called superior; as the idea of triangle is extended to all the various species of triangle" (Arnauld & Nicole 1662: 61f). It is manifest that Arnauld in this passage unfolds his doctrine along the lines of the relation of genus and species, so that the idea of a certain species would be part of the extension of the idea of the superior genus, which does not match with the current use of the intension/extension distinction. The extension of a universal idea, however, does not consist of species alone; for Arnauld also notices that the extention of a universal idea can be restricted in two different modes: either (1) "by joining another distinct or determinate idea to it" (e.g. "right-angled" to "triangle") which makes it the idea of a certain subclass of the universal idea (= extension 1), or (2) by "joining to it merely an indistinct and indeterminate idea of a part" (e.g. the quantifying syncategoreme "some") which makes it the idea of an undetermined number of individuals (= extension 2) (Arnauld & Nicole 1662: 62). What Arnauld intends to convey is simply that the restriction of a general idea can be achieved either by specification or by quantification – which, however, result in two different and hardly combinable notions of extension.

While empirism, according to which sense experience is the ultimate source of all our concepts and knowledge, was prominently represented by Hobbes, the Port-Royal Logic, taking a distinct Cartesian approach, is part of the rationalist philosophy acknowledging the existence of innate ideas or, at least, of predetermined structures of rational thought. This also holds for the *Port-Royal Grammar* (1660) (Arnauld & Lancelot 1667/1966) that opened the modern tradition of *universal grammar* which dominated linguistic studies in the 17th and 18th centuries (Schmitter 1996). The universal grammarians aimed to reduce, in a Chomskian-style analysis, the fundamental structures of language to universally predetermined mental structures. The distinction of deep and surface structure seems to be heard when Nicolas Beauzée (1717–1789) claims that since all languages are founded on an identical "méchanisme intellectuel" the "différences qui se trouvent d'une langue à l'autre ne sont, pour ainsî dire, que superficielles." (Beauzée 1767: viiif).

Whereas the rationalist grammarians took language as "the exposition of the analysis of thought" (Beauzée 1767: xxxiiif) and thus as a means of detecting the rules of thought, empirists like Locke or Condillac saw language as a means of forming and analyzing complex ideas, thus showing a pronounced tendency to ascribe a certain influence of language on thought.

6.5 John Locke (1632–1704)

Locke's *Essay Concerning Human Understanding* (1690/1975) is the most influential early modern text on language, even if the third book, which is devoted to the issue "of words", hardly offers more than a semantics of names, differentiating between names of *simple ideas*, of *mixed modes*, and of *natural substances*.

In this context Locke focuses on the question of how names and the ideas they stand for are related to external reality. With regard to simple ideas the answer is simple as well. For their causation by external object shows such a degree of regularity that our simple ideas can be considered as "very near and undiscernably alike" (389). Error and dissent, therefore, turn out to be primarily the result of inconsiderate use of language: "Men, who well examine the Ideas of their own Minds, cannot much differ in thinking; however, they may perplex themselves with words" (180).

Locke places emphasis on the priority of ideas over words in some passages (437; 689) and distinguishes between a language-independent mental discourse and its subsequent expression in words (574ff). However, the thesis that thought is at least in principle independent of language is counterbalanced by Locke's account of individual language acquisition and the actual use of language. Even if the idea is logically prior to the corresponding word, this relation is inverted in language learning. For in most cases the meaning of words is socially imparted (Lenz 2010), so that we learn a word before being acquainted with the idea customarily connected to it (Locke 1975: 437). This habitual connection of ideas with words does not only effect an excitation of ideas by words but quite often a substitution of the former by the latter (408). Thus, the *mental proposition* made up of ideas actually turns out to be a marginal case, for "most Men, if not all, in their Thinking and Reasoning within themselves, made use of Words instead of Ideas" (575). Even if clear and distinct knowledge were best achieved by "examining and judging of Ideas by themselves their Names being quite laid aside", it is, as Locke conceeds, "through the prevailing custom of using Sounds for Ideas ... very seldom practised" (579).

Locke's theory of meaning is often characterized as vague or even incoherent (Kretzmann 1968; Landesman 1976). For, on the one hand, Locke states that "Words in their primary or immediate Signification, stand for nothing, but the Ideas in the Mind of him he uses them" (Locke 1975: 405f, 159, 378, 402, 420, 422) so that words "can be Signs of nothing else" (408). On the other hand, like most scholastic authors unlike the contempora trend of the 17th and 18th centuries, he considers ideas as signs of things, and advocates the view that words "ultimately ... represent Things" (Locke 1975: 520) in accordance with the scholastic *mediantibus conceptibus*-thesis (see 5.2.; Ashworth 1984).

Whereas in the late 19th century it was considered "one of the glories of Locke's philosophy that he established the fact that names are not the signs of things but in their origins always the signs of concepts" (Müller 1887: 77), it is precisely for this view that Locke's semantic theory is often criticized as a paradigm case of private-language philosophy and semantic subjectivism. But if there is something like semantic subjectivism in Locke then it is more in the sense of a problem that he is pointing to than something that his theory tends to result in. For one of his main points regarding our use of language is that we should keep it consistent with the use of others (Locke 1975: 471), since words are "no Man's private possession, but the common measure of Commerce and Communication" (514).

Locke saw sensualism as supported by an interesting observation regarding meaning change (see article 6 [Semantics: Typology, Diachrony and Processing] (Fritz) *Theories of meaning change*) of words. Many words, he noticed, "which are made use of to stand for actions and notions quite removed from sense, have their rise from ... obvious sensible ideas and are transferred to more abstruse significations" (Locke 1975: 403). Therefore large parts of our vocabulary are "metaphorical" concepts in the sense that metaphor is defined by the modern cognitive account (see article 11 [Semantics: Lexical Structures and Adjectives] (Tyler & Takahashi) *Metaphors and metonymies*). That is, thinking about a concept from one knowledge domain in terms of another domain, as is exemplified by terms like "imagine, apprehend, comprehend, adhere, conceive, instil, disgust, disturbance, tranquillity".

This view was substantiated by Leibniz's comments on the epistemic function of the "analogie des choses sensibles et insensibles", as it becomes manifest in language. It would be worthwile, Leibniz maintained, to consider "l'usage des prepositions, comme à, avec, de, devant, en, hors, par, pour, sur, vers, qui sont toutes prises du lieu, de la distance, et du mouvement, et transferées depuis à toute sorte de changemens, ordres, suites, différences, convenances" (Leibniz 1875–1890: 5.256). Kant, too, agreed in the famous §59 of his *Critique of Judgement* that this symbolic function of language would be "worthy of a deeper study". For "... the words ground (support, basis), to depend (to be held up from above), to flow from (instead of to follow), substance ... and numberless others, are ... symbolic hypotyposes, and express concepts without employing a direct intuition for the purpose, but only drawing upon an analogy with one, i.e., transferring the reflection upon an object of intuition to quite a new concept, and one with which perhaps no intuition could ever directly correspond."

Thus, according to Locke, Leibniz and Kant, metaphor is not simply a case of deviant meaning but rather, as modern semantics has found out anew, an ubiquitous feature of language and thought.

6.6 G. W. Leibniz (1646–1716) and the tradition of symbolic knowledge

While Hobbes and Locke, at least in principle and to a certain degree, still acknowledged the possibility of a non-linguistic mental discourse or mental proposition,

Gottfried Wilhelm Leibniz emphazised the dependency of thinking on the use of signs: "thinking can take place without words ... but not without other signs" (1875–1890: 7.191). For "all our reasoning is nothing but a process of connecting and substituting characters which may be words or other signs or images" (7.31). This view became explicit and later extremely influential under the label of *cognitio symbolica* (symbolic knowledge, symbolic cognition), a term Leibniz coined in his *Meditationes de cognitione, veritate et ideis* (1684; 1875–1890: 4.423). Symbolic knowledge is opposed to intuitive knowledge (*cognitio intuitiva*) which is defined as a direct and simultaneous conception of a complex notion together with all its partial notions.

Because the limited human intellect cannot comprehend more complex concepts other than successively, the complex concept of the thing itself must be substituted by a sensible sign in the process of reasoning always supposing that a detailed explication of its meaning could be given if needed. Leibniz, therefore, maintains that the knowledge or cognition of complex objects or notions is always symbolic, i.e. performed in the medium of signs (1875–1890: 4.422f). The possibility and validity of symbolic knowledge is based on the principle of proportionality according to which the basic signs used in symbolic knowledge may be choosen arbitrarily, provided that the internal relations between the signs are analogous to the relations between the things signified (7.264). In his *Dialogue* (1677) Leibniz remarks that "even if the characters are arbitrary, still the use and interconnection of them has something that is not arbitrary - viz. a certain proportionality between the characters and the things, and the relations among different characters expressing the same things. This proportion or relation is the foundation of truth." (Leibniz 1875–1890: 7.192).

The notion of cognitio symbolica provides the epistemological foundation of both his project of a *characteristica universalis* or universal language of science and his philosophy of language. For the basic principle of analogy is also realized in natural languages to a certain extent. Leibniz therefore holds that "languages are the best mirror of the human mind and that an exact analysis of the signification of words would make known the operations of the understanding better than would anything else" (5.313).

Especially through its reception by Christian Wolff (1679–1654) and his school the doctrine of symbolic knowledge became one of the main epistemological issues of the German Enlightenment. In this tradition it is a common conviction that the use of signs in general and of language in particular provides an indispensable function for any higher intellectual operation. Hence Leibniz's proposal of a characteristica universalis has been massively taken up, even though mostly in a somewhat altered form. For what the 18th century authors are generally aiming at is not the invention of a sign system for obtaining general knowledge, but rather a general science of sign systems. The general doctrine of signs, referred to with names like *Characteristica, Semiotica,* or *Semiologia,* was considered as a most important desideratum. In 1724 Wolff's disciple Georg Bernhard Bilfinger (1693–1750) suggested the name *Ars semantica* for this, as he saw it, until then neglected discipline, the subject matter of which would be the knowledge of all sorts of signs in general as well as the theory about the invention, right use, and assessment of linguistic signs in particular (Bilfinger 1724: 298f).

The first extended attempt to fill this gap was made by Johann Heinrich Lambert (1728–1777) with his *Semiotik, oder die Lehre von der Bezeichnung der Gedanken und Dinge* (Semiotics, or the doctrine of the signification of thoughts and things), published as the second part of his *Neues Organon* (1764). The leading idea of this work is Leibniz's principle of proportionality which guarantees, as Lambert claims, the interchangeability of "the theory of the signs" and "the theory of the objects" signified. (Lambert 1764: 3.23–24).

Besides the theory of sign invention, the *hermeneutica*, the theory of sign interpretation, made up an essential part of the characteristica. Within the framework of 'general hermeneutics' (*hermeneutica generalis*), originally designed by Johann Conrad Dannhauer (1603–1666) as a complement to Aristotelian logic, the reflections on linguistic meaning focused on sentence meaning. Due to Dannhauer's influential *Idea boni interpretis* (Presentation of the good interpreter, 1630), some relics of scholastic semantics were taken up by hermeneutical theory, for which particularly the theory of supposition (see 5.4.), which provided the "knowledge about the modes in which the signification of words may vary according to their connection to others" (Reusch 1734: 266) had to be of pivotal interest. The developing discipline of hermeneutics as "the science of the very rules in compliance of which the meanings can be recognized from their signs" (Meier 1757: 1), shows a growing awareness of several important semantic doctrines, as for instance the methodological necessity of the *principle of charity* in form of a presumption of consistency and rationality (Scholz 1999: 35–64), the distinction between *language meaning* and *contextual meaning*, as it is present in Christian August Crusius's (1747: 1080) distinction between *grammatic meaning* (grammatischer Verstand), i.e. "the totality of meanings a word may ever have in one language", and *logic meaning*, i.e. the "totality of what a word can mean at a certain place and in a certain context", or the *principle of compositionality* (see article 6 [this volume] (Pagin & Westerståhl) *Compositionality*), as it appears in Georg Friedrich Meier's claim that "the sense of a speech is the sum total of the meanings of the words that make up this speech and which are connected to and determining each other" (Meier 1757: 57).

6.7 Condillac (1714–1780)

One of the most decisive features of 18th century science is its historical approach. In linguistics this resulted in a great number of works on the origin and development of language (Gessinger & von Rahden 1989). The way in which the historic-genetic point of view opened new perspectives on the relation between language and thought is most clearly reflected in Etienne Bonnot de Condillac's *Essai sur l'origine des connaissances humaines* (1746). Already in the early 18th century it was widely accepted that linguistic signs provide the basis for virtually any intellectual knowledge. Christian Thomasius (1655–1728) had argued that the use of language plays a decisive role in the ontogenetic development of each individual's cognitive faculties (Meier-Oeser 2008). Condillac goes even further and argues that the same holds for the phylogenetic development of mankind as well. Language, therefore, is not only essentially involved in the formation of thoughts or abstract ideas but also in the formation of the subject of thought, viz. of man as an intellectual being.

According to Condillac all higher cognitive operations are nothing but 'transformed sensation' (*sensation transformé*). The formative principle that effects this transformation is language or, more generally, the use of signs (*l'usage des signes*). Condillac reconstructs the historical process of language development as a process leading from a primordial natural language of actions and gestures (*langage d'action*), viewed as a language of simultaneous ideas (*langage des idées simultanées*), to the language of articulate voice (*langage des sons articulés*), viewed as a language of successive ideas (*langage des idées successives*).

We are so deeply accustomed to spoken language with its sequential catenation of articulate sounds, he notices, that we believe our ideas would by nature come to our mind one after another, just as we speak words one after another. In fact, however, the discursive structure of thinking is not naturally given but rather the result of our use of linguistic signs. The main effect of articulate language consists in the gradual analysis of complex and indistinct sensations into abstract ideas that are connected to and make up the meaning of words. Since language is a necessary condition of thought and knowledge, Locke was mistaken to claim that the primary purpose of language is to communicate knowledge (Condillac 1947–1951: 1.442a):

> The primary purpose of language is to analyze thought. In fact we cannot exhibit the ideas that coexist in our mind successively to others except in so far as we know how to exhibit them successively to ourselves. That is to say, we know how to speak to others only in so far as we know how to speak to ourselves.

It was therefore Locke's adherence to the scholastic idea of mental propositions that prevented him "to realize how necessary the signs are for the operations of the soul" (1.738a). Every language, Condillac claims, "is an analytic method". Due to his comprehensive notion of language this also holds vice versa: "every analytic method is a language" (2.119a), so that Condillac, maintaining that sciences are analytical methods by essence, comes to his provocative and controversial thesis that "all sciences are nothing but well-made languages" (2.419a).

Condillac's theory of language and its epistemic function became the core topic of the so-called school of 'ideology' (*idéologie*) that dominated the French scene in early 19th century. Although most authors of this school rejected the absolute necessity of signs and language for thinking, they adhered to the subjectivistic consequences of sensualism and considered it impossible "that one and the same sign should have the same value for all of those who use it and even for each of them at different moments of time" (Destutt de Tracy 1803: 405).

7 References

7.1 Primary Sources

Abelard, Peter 1927. *Logica ingredientibus, Glossae super Peri ermenias*. Ed. B. Geyer. Münster: Aschendorff.
Andreas, Antonius 1508. *Scriptum in arte veteri*. Venice.
Aquinas, Thomas 1989. *Expositio libri peryermenias*. In: Opera omnia I* 1. Ed. Commissio Leonina. 2nd edn. Rome.
Arnauld, Antoine & Pierre Nicole 1965. *La logique ou l'art de penser*. Paris.
Arnauld, Antoine & Claude Lancelot 1667/1966. *Grammaire générale et raisonnée ou La Grammaire de Port-Royal*. Ed. H. E. Brekle, t. 1, reprint of the 3rd edn. Stuttgart-Bad Cannstatt: Frommann, 1966.
Augustinus 1963. De doctrina Christiana. In: W. M. Green (ed.). *Sancti Augustini Opera* (CSEL 80). Vienna: Österreichische Akademie der Wissenschaften.
Augustinus 1968. De trinitate. In: W. J. Mountain & F. Glorie (eds.). *Aurelii Augustini Opera* (CCSL 50). Turnhout: Brepols.
Augustinus 1975. *De dialectica*. Ed. Jan Pinborg, translation with introduction and notes by B. Darrel Jackson. Dordrecht: Reidel.
Bacon, Roger 1978. De signis. Ed. K.M. Fredborg, L. Nielsen & J. Pinborg. *Traditio* 34, 75–136.
Bacon, Roger 1988. *Compendium Studii Theologiae*. Ed. Th. S. Maloney. Leiden: Brill.
Bilfinger, Georg Bernhard 1724. De Sermone Sinico. In: *Specimen doctrinae veterum Sinarum moralis et politicae*, Frankfurt/M.
Beauzée, Nicolas 1767. *Grammaire générale*. Paris.
Boethius, Anicius M. T. S. 1880. In Perihermeneias editio secunda. Ed. C. Meiser. Leipzig: Teubner.
Boethius Dacus 1969. *Modi significandi*. Ed. J. Pinborg & H. Roos. Copenhagen: C. E. C. Gad.
Condillac, Etienne Bonnot de 1947–1951. *Oeuvres philosophiques*. Ed. G. Le Roy. Paris: PUF.

Conimbricenses 1607. *Commentaria in universam Aristotelis dialectica*. Cologne.
Crusius, Christian August 1747. *Weg zur Gewiß/heit und Zuverlässigkeit der menschlichen Erkenntnis*. Leipzig.
Dannhauer, Johann Conrad 1630. *Idea boni interpretis*. Strasburg.
Destutt de Tracy, Antoine 1803. *Éléments d'idéologie. Vol. 2*. Paris.
Giattini, Johannes Baptista 1651. *Logica*. Rome.
Henry of Ghent 1520. *Summa quaestionum ordinarium*. Paris.
Hobbes, Thomas 1839a. *Opera philosophica quae scripsit omnia*. Ed. W. Molesworth, vol. 1. London.
Hobbes, Thomas 1839b. *The English Works*. Ed. W. Molesworth, vol. 1. London.
Hoffbauer, Johannes Christoph 1789. *Tentamina semiologica sive quaedam generalem theoriam signorum spectantia*. Halle.
Lambert, Johann Heinrich 1764. *Neues Organon oder Gedanken über die Erforschung und Bezeichnung des Wahren. Vol. 2*. Leipzig.
Leibniz, Gottfried Wilhelm 1875–1890. *Die philosophischen Schriften*. Ed. C. I. Gerhardt. Berlin. Reprinted: Hildesheim: Olms, 1965.
Locke, John 1975. *An Essay concerning Human Understand*. Ed. P. H. Nidditch. Oxford: Clarendon Press.
Meier, Georg Friedrich 1757. *Versuch einer allgemeinen Auslegungskunst*. Halle.
Nicolaus a S. Iohanne Baptista 1687. *Philosophia augustiniana*. Genova.
Ockham, William of 1974. Summa logicae. Ed. Ph. Boehner, G. Gál & S. Brown. In: *Opera philosophica* 1. St. Bonaventure, NY: The Franciscan Institute.
Ockham, William of 1978. Expositio in librum Perihermeneias Aristotelis. Ed. A. Gambatese & S. Brown. In: *Opera philosophica* 2. St. Bonaventure, NY: The Franciscan Institute.
Raey, Jean de 1692. *Cogitata de interpretatione*. Amsterdam.
Raulin, John 1500. *In logicam Aristotelis commentarium*. Paris.
Reusch, Johann Peter 1734. *Systema logicum*. Jena.
Rubius, Antonius 1605. *Logica mexicana*. Cologne.
Scotus, John Duns 1891. In primum librum perihermenias quaestiones. In: *Opera Omnia*. Ed. L. Vivès, vol. 1. Paris.
Smiglecius, Martin 1634. *Logica*. Oxford.
de Soto, Domingo 1554. *Summulae*. Salamanca.
Versor, Johannes 1572. *Summulae logicales*. Venice.

7.2 Secondary Sources

Annas, Julia E. 1992. *Hellenistic Philosophy of Mind*. Berkeley, LA: University of California Press.
Ashworth, E. Jennifer 1984. Locke on language. *Canadian Journal of Philosophy* 14, 45–74.
Ashworth, E. Jennifer 1987. Jacobus Naveros on the question: 'Do spoken words signifiy concepts or things?'. In: L. M. de Rijk & C. A. G. Braakhuis (eds.). *Logos and Pragma*. Nijmegen: Ingenium Publishers, 189–214.
Barnes, Jonathan 1993. Meaning, saying and thinking. In: K. Döring & T. Ebert (eds.). *Dialektiker und Stoiker. Zur Logik der Stoa und ihrer Vorläufer*. Stuttgart: Steiner, 47–61.
Baxter, Timothy M. S. 1992. *The Cratylus: Plato's Critique of Naming*. Leiden: Brill.
Bühler, Karl 1934. *Sprachtheorie*. Jena: Fischer.

Bursill-Hall, G. E. 1971. *Speculative Grammars of the Middle Ages*. The Hague: Mouton.
Ebbesen, Sten 1983. The odyssey of semantics from the Stoa to Buridan. In: A. Eschbach & J. Trabant (eds.). *History of Semiotics*. Amsterdam: Benjamins, 67–85.
Fredborg, Karen Margareta 1981. Roger Bacon on 'Impositio vocis ad significandum'. In: H. A. G. Braakhuis, C. H. Kneepkens & L. M. de Rijk (eds.). *English Logic and Semantics*. Nijmegen: Ingenium Publishers, 167–191.
Gessinger, Joachim & Wolfert von Rahden 1989 (eds.). *Theorien vom Ursprung der Sprache*. Berlin: de Gruyter.
Graeser, Andreas 1978. The Stoic theory of meaning. In: J. M. Rist (ed.). *The Stoics*. Berkeley, CA: University of California Press, 77–100.
Graeser, Andreas 1996. Aristoteles. In: T. Borsche (ed.). *Klassiker der Sprachphilosophie*, München: C. H. Beck, 33–47.
Hungerland, Isabel C. & George R. Vick 1973. Hobbes's theory of signification. *Journal of the History of Philosophy* 11, 459–482.
Jacobi, Klaus 1983. Abelard and Frege. The semanics of words and propositions. In: V.M. Abrusci, E. Casari & M. Mugnai (eds.). *Atti del Convegno Internazionale di storia della logica*, San Gimignano 1982. Bologna: CLUEB, 81–96.
Kaczmarek, Ludger 1988. 'Notitia' bei Peter von Ailly. In: O. Pluta (ed.). *Die Philosophie im 14. und 15. Jahrhundert*. Amsterdam: Grüner, 385–420.
Kretzmann, Norman 1967. Semantics, history of. In: P. Edwards (ed.). *The Encyclopedia of Philosophy. Vol. 7*. New York: The Macmillan Company, 358b–406a.
Kretzmann, Normann 1968. The main thesis of Locke's semantic theory. *Philosophical Review* 78, 175–196.
Kretzmann, Norman 1974. Aristotle on spoken sound significant by convention. In: J. Corcoran (ed.). *Ancient Logic and its Modern Interpretation*. Dordrecht: Kluwer, 3–21.
Kretzmann, Norman 1982. Syncategoremata, exponibilia, sophismata. In: N. Kretzmann, A. Kenny & J. Pinborg (eds.). *The Cambridge History of Later Medieval Philosophy*. Cambridge: Cambridge University Press, 211–245.
Landesman, Charles 1976. Locke's theory of meaning. *Journal of the History of Philosophy* 14, 23–35.
Lenz, Martin 2010. *Lockes Sprachkonzeption*. Berlin: de Gruyter.
Lewry, Osmund 1981. Robert Kilwardby on meaning. A Parisian course on the logica vetus. *Miscellanea mediaevalia* 13, 376–384.
Lieb, Hans-Heinrich 1981. Das 'semiotische Dreieck' bei Ogden und Richards: Eine Neuformulierung des Zeichenmodells von Aristoteles. In: H. Geckeler et al. (eds.). *Logos Semantikos. Studia Linguistica in Honorem Eugenio Coseriu, vol. 1*. Berlin: de Gruyter/Madrid: Gredos, 137–156.
Long, Anthony A. & David N. Sedley 1987. *The Hellenistic Philosophers*. Cambridge: Cambridge University Press.
Long, Anthony A. 1971. Language and thought in Stoicism. In: A. A. Long (ed.). *Problems in Stoicism*. London: The Athlone Press, 75–113.
Magee, John 1989. *Boethius on Signification and Mind*. Leiden: Brill.
Meier-Oeser, Stephan 1996. Signifikation. In: J. Ritter & K. Gründer (eds.). *Historisches Wörterbuch der Philosophie 9*. Basel: Schwabe, 759–795.
Meier-Oeser, Stephan 1997. *Die Spur des Zeichens. Das Zeichen und seine Funktion in der Philosophie des Mittelalters und der frühen Neuzeit*. Berlin: de Gruyter.

Meier-Oeser, Stephan 1998. Synkategorem. In: J. Ritter & K. Gründer (eds.). *Historisches Wörterbuch der Philosophie* 10. Basel: Schwabe, 787–799.

Meier-Oeser, Stephan 2004. Sprache und Bilder im Geist. *Philosophisches Jahrbuch* 111, 312–342.

Meier-Oeser, Stephan 2008. Das Ende der Metapher von der 'inneren Rede'. Zum Verhältnis von Sprache und Denken in der deutschen Frühaufklärung. In: H. G. Bödecker (ed.). *Strukturen der deutschen Frühaufklärung 1680–1720*. Göttingen: Vandenhoeck & Ruprecht, 195–223.

Meier-Oeser, Stephan 2009. Walter Burley's propositio in re and the systematization of the ordo significationis. In: S. F. Brown, Th. Dewender & Th. Kobusch (eds.). *Philosophical Debates at Paris in the Early Fourteenth Century*. Leiden: Brill, 483–506.

Müller, Max 1887. *The Science of the Thought*. London: Longmans, Green & Co.

Panaccio, Claude 1999. *Le Discours Intérieure de Platon à Guillaume Ockham*. Paris: Seuil.

Pinborg, Jan 1967. *Die Entwicklung der Sprachtheorie im Mittelalter*. Münster: Aschendorff.

Pinborg, Jan 1972. *Logik und Semantik im Mittelalter. Ein Überblick*. Ed. H. Kohlenberger. Stuttgart-Bad Cannstatt: Frommann-Holzboog.

Pohlenz, Max 1939. Die Begründung der abendländischen Sprachlehre durch die Stoa. (Nachrichten von der Gesellschaft der Wissenschaften, Göttingen. Philologisch-historische Klasse, N.F. 3). Göttingen: Vandenhoeck & Ruprecht, 151–198.

Rijk, Lambertus Maria de 1967. *Logica modernorum*, vol. II/1. Assen: Van Gorcum.

Schmitter, Peter (ed.) 1996. *Sprachtheorien der Neuzeit II. Von der Grammaire de Port-Royal zur Konstitution moderner linguistischer Disziplinen*. Tübingen: Narr.

Schmitter, Peter (2001). The emergence of philosophical semantics in early Greek antiquity. *Logos and Language* 2, 45–56.

Scholz, Oliver R. 1999. *Verstehen und Rationalität*. Frankfurt/M.: Klostermann.

Sedley, David 1996. Aristotle's de interpretatione and ancient semantic. In: G. Manetti (ed.). *Knowledge Through Signs*. Turnhout: Brepols, 87–108.

Sedley, David 2003. *Plato's Cratylus*. Cambridge: Cambridge University Press.

Tachau, Katherine H. 1987. Wodeham, Crathorn and Holcot: The development of the complexe significabile. In: L. M. de Rijk & H. A. G. Braakhuis (eds.). *Logos and Pragma*. Nijmegen: Ingenium Publishers, 161–189.

Weidemann, Hermann 1982. Ansätze zu einer semantischen Theorie bei Aristoteles. *Zeitschrift für Semiotik* 4, 241–257.

Brigitte Nerlich
9 The emergence of linguistic semantics in the 19th and early 20th century

1   Introduction: The emergence of linguistic semantics in the
    context of interdisciplinary research in the 19th century —— 218
2   Linguistic semantics in Germany —— 221
3   Linguistic semantics in France —— 228
4   Linguistic semantics in Britain —— 232
5   Conclusion —— 238
6   References —— 238

Abstract: This chapter deals with the 19th-century roots of current cognitive and pragmatic approaches to the study of meaning and meaning change. It demonstrates that 19th-century linguistic semantics has more to offer than the atomistic historicism for which 19th-century linguistics became known and for which it was often criticised. By contrast, semanticists in Germany, France and Britain in particular sought to study meaning and change of meaning from a much more holistic point of view, seeking inspiration from philosophy, biology, geology, psychology, and sociology to study how meaning is 'made' in the context of social interaction and how it changes over time under pressure from changing linguistic, societal and cognitive needs and influences.

> The subject in which I invite the reader to follow me is so new in kind that it has not even been given a name. The fact is that most linguists have directed their attention to the forms of words: the laws which govern changes in meaning, the choice of new expressions, the birth and death of phrases, have been left behind or have been noticed only in passing. Since this subject deserves a name as much as does phonetics or morphology, I shall call it semantics [...], the science of meaning.
>
> (Bréal 1883/1991:137)

In memory of Peter Schmitter who first helped me to explore the history of semantics

Brigitte Nerlich, Nottingham, United Kingdom

https://doi.org/10.1515/9783110368505-009

1 Introduction: The emergence of linguistic semantics in the context of interdisciplinary research in the 19th century

The history of semantics as a reflection on meaning is potentially infinite, starting probably with Greek or Hindu philosophers of language and embracing more than two thousand years of the history of mankind. It is spread over numerous disciplines, from ancient philosophy (Schmitter 2001a), to modern cognitive science. The history of semantics as a *linguistic* discipline is somewhat shorter and has been well explored (Nerlich 1992b, 1996a, 1996b). This chapter therefore summarizes results from research dealing with the history of semantics from the 1850s onwards and I shall follow the standard view that semantics as a linguistic discipline began with Christian Karl Reisig's lectures on Latin semasiology or *Bedeutungslehre*, given in the 1820s (Schmitter 1990, 2004).

As one can see from the motto cited above, another central figure in the history of linguistic semantics in the 19th century is undoubtedly Michel Bréal, the author of the famous *Essai de sémantique*, published in 1897, the cumulative product of work started as early as 1866 (Bréal 1883/1991). When this seminal book was translated into English in 1900, the name of the discipline that studied linguistic meaning and changes of meaning became 'semantics', and other terms, such as semasiology, or sematology were sidelined in the 20th century.

Although the focus is here on linguistic semantics, it should not be forgotten that the study of 'meaning' also preoccupied philosophers and semioticians. Two seminal figures in the 19th century that should be mentioned in this context are Charles Sanders Peirce in the United States who worked in the tradition of American pragmatism (Nerlich & Clarke 1996) and Gottlob Frege who helped found mathematical logic and analytic philosophy (see article 10 [this volume] (Newen & Schröder) *Logic and semantics*) and (see article 3 [this volume] (Textor) *Sense and reference*). Although Peirce exerted enormous influence on the developments of semantics, pragmatics and semiotics in the late 19th and early 20th century, his main interest can be said to have been in epistemology. Frege too exerted great influence on the development of formal semantics (see article 11 [this volume] (Kempson) *Formal semantics and representationalism*) and (see article 14 [this volume] (ter Meulen) *Formal methods*), truth-conditional semantics, feature semantics and so on, especially through his distinction between *Sinn* and *Bedeutung* or sense and reference. However, his main interest lay in logic, arithmetic and number theory. Neither Frege nor Peirce were widely discussed in the treatises on linguistic semantics which will be presented below, except for the philosophical and psychological reflections of meaning around the tradition of 'significs'. Frege was a logician, not a linguist and he himself pointed out that "[t]o a mind concerned with the beauties of language, what is trivial to the logician may seem to be just what is important" (Frege 1977: 10). The linguists discussed below were all fascinated with the beauty of language.

This chapter focuses on linguistic semantics in Germany, France, and Britain, thus leaving aside Eastern Europe, Russia, Scandinavia, and our closer neighbours, Italy, Spain, the Benelux countries and many more. However, the work carried out in these countries was, as far as I know, strongly influenced by, if not dependent on the theories developed in Germany, France, and Britain. Terminologically, German linguists initially wrote about *Semasiologie*, French ones about *la sémantique*, and some English ones about *sematology*. In the end the term *semantics* was universally adopted.

In general terms one can say that linguistic semantics emerged from a dissatisfaction with traditional grammar on the one hand, which could not deal adequately with questions of meaning, and with traditional lexicography and etymology on the other, which did not give a satisfactory account of the evolution of meaning, listing the meanings of words in a rather arbitrary fashion, instead of looking for a logical, natural or inner order in the succession of meanings. To redefine grammar, scholars looked for inspiration in the available traditions of philosophy; to redefine lexicography they grasped the tools provided by rhetoric, that is the figures of speech, especially metaphor and metonymy (Nerlich 1998). The development of the field was however not only influenced by internal factors relating to the study of language but also by developments in other fields such as geology and biology, for example, from which semantics imported concepts such as 'uniformitarianism', 'transformation', 'evolution', 'organism' and 'growth'. After initial enthusiasm about ways to give semantics 'scientific' credibility in this way, a debate about whether framing the development and change of meaning in such terms was legitimate would preoccupy semanticists in the latter half of the 19th century.

The different traditions in the field of semantics were influenced by different philosophical traditions on the one hand, by different sciences on the other. In the case of German semasiology, the heritage of Kantian philosophy, idealism, the romantic movement, and the new type of philology, or to quote some names, the works of Immanuel Kant, especially his focus on the 'active subject', Wilhelm von Humboldt and his concept of 'ergon' and 'energeia' (Schmitter 2001b) and Franz Bopp and his research into comparative grammar were of seminal importance. German semasiology after Reisig was very much attached to the predominant paradigm in linguistic science, that is, to historical-comparative philology. This might be the reason why the term 'semasiology', as designating one branch of a prospering and internationally respected discipline, was at first so successful in English speaking countries where an autonomous approach to semantics was missing. This was not the case in France, where Bréal, from 1866 onwards, used semantic research as a way to challenge the German supremacy in linguistics. Later on, however, German *Semasiologie*, just like the French tradition of *la sémantique*, began to be influenced by psychology, and thus these two traditions moved closer together.

French semantics, especially the Bréalian version, was influenced by the French philosophy of language which was rooted in the work of Etienne Bonnot de Condillac and his followers, the *Idéologues*, on words as signs. But Bréal was also an admirer of Bopp and of Humboldt. Bréal first expressed his conviction that semantics should be a psychological and historical science in his review of the seminal book, *La Vie des mots*, written in 1887 by Arsène Darmesteter (first published in English, in 1886, based on lectures given in London) and advocated caution in adopting terms and concepts from biology, such as organism and transformation (Bréal 1887).

Darmesteter had derived his theory of semantic change from biological models, such as Charles Darwin's theory of evolution and August Schleicher's model of language as an evolving organism and of languages as organised into family trees, transforming themselves independently from the speakers of the language. Darmesteter applied this conception to words themselves. It is therefore not astonishing to find that Darmesteter's booklet contains a host of biological metaphors about the birth, life and death of words, their struggle for survival, etc. This metaphorical basis of Darmesteter's theory was noted with skepticism by his colleagues who agreed however that Darmesteter's book was the first really sound attempt at analysing how and why words change their meanings. To integrate Darmesteter's insights into his own theoretical framework, Bréal had only to replace the picture of the autonomous change of a language by the axiom that words change their meaning because the speakers and hearers use them in different ways, in different situations (Delesalle 1987, Nerlich 1990). In parallel with Reisig, Darmesteter used figures of speech, such as metaphor, metonymy and synecdoche to describe the transitions between the meanings of words (Darmesteter 1887), being inspired by the achievements of French rhetoric, especially the work of César Chesneau Du Marsais (1757) on tropes as being used in ordinary language.

The English tradition of semantics emerged from philosophical discussions about language and mind in the 17th and 18th centuries (John Locke), and about etymology and the search for 'true' and original meaning (John Horne Tooke). Philosophical influences here were utilitarianism and a certain type of materialism. Semantics in its broadest sense was also used at first to underpin religious arguments about the divine origin of language. The most famous figure in what one might call religious semantics, was Richard Chenevix Trench, an Anglican ecclesiast, bishop of Dublin and later Dean of Westminster, who wrote numerous books on the history of the English language and the history of English words. His new ideas about dictionaries led the Philological Society in London to the creation of the *New English Dictionary*, later called the *Oxford English Dictionary*, which is nowadays the richest source-book for those who want to study semantic change in the English language.

After the turn of the 19th to the 20th century one can observe in Britain a rapid increase in books on 'words' – the trivial literature of semantics, so to speak (Nerlich 1992a) –, but also a more thoroughly philosophical reflection on meaning, as well as the start of a new tradition of contextualism in the work of (Sir) Alan Henderson Gardiner and John Rupert Firth, mainly influenced by the German linguist Philipp Wegener and the anthropologist Bronislaw Malinowski (see Nerlich & Clarke 1996).

Many of those interested in semantics tried to establish classifications of types or causes of semantic change, something that became in fact one of the main preoccupations for 19th-century semanticists. The classifications of types of semantic change were mostly based on logical principles, that is a typology according to the figures of speech, such as metaphor, metonymy, and extension and restriction, specifying the type of relation or transition between the meanings of a word; the typologies of causes of semantic change were mostly based on psychological principles, specifying human drives and instincts; and finally some classifications applied historical or cultural principles; but most frequently these enterprises used a mixture of all three approaches. Later on in the century, when the issue of phonetic laws reverberated through linguistics, semanticists tried not only to classify semantic changes, but to find laws of semantic change that would be as strict as the sound laws were then believed to be and in doing so, some believed to turn linguistics into a 'science' in the sense of natural science.

After this preliminary sketch I shall now deal with the three traditions of semantics one by one, the German, the French, and the British one. However, the reader of the following sections has to keep in mind that the three traditions of semantics are not as strictly separable as it might appear. There were numerous links of imitation, influence, cross-fertilization, and collaboration.

2 Linguistic semantics in Germany

It has become customary to distinguish two main periods in German semantics: (1) a logico-historical or historico-descriptive one, and (2) a psychologico-explanatory one. The father of the first tradition is Reisig, the father of the second Steinthal.

Christian Karl Reisig (Schmitter 1987, 2004) was, like many other early semanticists, a classical philologist. In his lectures on Latin grammar given in the 1820s, and first published by his student Friedrich Haase in 1839 (2nd edition 1881–1890), he tried to reform the standard view of traditional grammar by adding to it a new discipline: semasiology or *Bedeutungslehre*, that is the study of meaning in language. Grammar was normally considered to consist in the study of syntax and etymology (which then meant approximately the same as morphology or *Formenlehre*). Reisig claims that the word should not only be studied with regard to its form (etymology) and in its relation to other words (syntax), but as having a certain meaning. He points out that there are words whose meaning is neither determined by their form alone nor by their place in the sentence, and that the meaning of these words has to be studied by semasiology. More specifically semasiology is the study of the development of the meaning of certain words, as well as the study of their use, both phenomena that were covered by neither etymology nor syntax.

Reisig puts forward thirteen principles of semantics, according to which language precedes grammar, languages are the products of nations, not of single human beings, language comes into being through imagination and enthusiasm in the social interaction of people. We shall see that this dynamic view of language and semantic change became central to historical semantics at the end of the 19th century when it was also linked to a more contextual approach. According to Reisig the evolution of a particular language is determined by free language-use within the limits set by the general laws of language. These general laws of language are Kant's laws of pure intuition (space and time), and his categories. This means that language and language change are brought about by a dynamic interplay of several forces which Reisig derived from his knowledge of German idealism on the one side and the romantic movement on the other. In line with German idealistic philosophy, he wanted to find the general principles of semantic change, assumed to be based on general laws of the human mind. In tune with the romantic movement, he saw that every language has, however, its individuality, based on the history of the nation and he recognized that speakers too have certain degrees of freedom in their creative use of language. This freedom is however constrained by certain habitual associations between ideas which had already been discussed in rhetoric, but which semasiology should, he claims, take account of, namely synecdoche, metonymy and metaphor. Whereas rhetoric focuses on their aesthetic function, semasiology focuses on the way these figures have come to structure language use in a particular language.

The recognition of rhetorical figures, such as metaphor and metonymy, as habitual cognitive associations and also as procedures of semantic innovation and change was a very important step in the constitution of semantics as an autonomous discipline. The figures of speech were reinterpreted in two ways and thus emancipated from their definitions in philosophical and literary discourse: they were no longer regarded as mere abuses of language, but as necessary for the life of language, that is, the continuous use of it; and they were not mere ornaments of speech, but essential instruments of mind and language to cope with ever new communicative needs – an insight deepened in various contributions to the 19th and early 20th-century philosophy of metaphor and rediscovered in modern cognitive semantics (Nerlich & Clarke 2000; (see also article 7 [Semantics: Typology, Diachrony and Processing] (Geeraerts) *Cognitive approaches to diachronic semantics*).

To summarize: Reisig's approach to semantics is philosophical with regard to the general laws of the mind, as inherited from Kant, but it is also historical, because Reisig stressed the necessity of always studying the Latin texts very closely. One can also claim that his semantics is to some degree influenced by psychology, in as much as Reisig adds to Kant's purely philosophical principles of intuition and reason a third source of human language: sensations or feelings. It is also rhetorical and stylistic, a perspective later rejected by his followers Heerdegen and Hey.

The theory of the sign that underlies his semantics is very traditional, that is representational: the sign signifies an idea/concept (*Begriff*) or a feeling (*Empfindung*); language represents thought, a thought that itself represents the external world. For Reisig thoughts and feelings exist independently of the language that represents them, a view that Humboldt tried to destroy in his conception of language as constitutive of thought. The study of semantic change can therefore only be the study of the development of ideas or thoughts as reflected in the words that signify them. This development of thought can run along the following ('logical') lines, called metaphor (the interchange of ideas, II: 6), metonymy (the interchange of representations, II: 4), or synecdoche (II: 4). To these he adds the use of originally local prepositions to designate temporal relations, based on the interchange of the forms of intuition, time and space, again an insight that was rediscovered in modern cognitive semantics. Semasiology has to show how the different meanings of a word have emerged from the first meaning (logically and historically, II: 2), that is, how thought has unfolded itself in the meaning of words. This kind of 'Vorstellungssemantik' (Knobloch 1988: 271) would dominate German semasiology until 1930 approximately. It was then challenged and eventually overthrown by Leo Weisgerber in linguistics and by Karl Bühler in psychology. 19th-century diachronic and psychological semantics was replaced by 20th-century synchronic and structural semantics.

However, Reisig does not leave it at the narrow view of semantics sketched above. He points out that the meaning of a word is not only constituted by its function of representing ideas, but that it is determined as well by the state of the language in general and by the use of a word according to a certain style or register (Schmitter 1987: 126). In fact, in dealing with the 'stylistic' problem of choosing a word from a series of words with 'the same' meaning, he reshapes his unidimensional definition of the sign as signifying one concept. Reisig deals here with synonyms, either complete or quasi synonyms; he even indicates the importance of a new kind of study: synonymology.

This rather broad conception of semantics, including word semantics, but also stylistics and synonymology, is very similar to the one later advocated by Bréal. However, Reisig's immediate followers in Germany gradually changed Reisig's initial conception of semasiology in the following ways: they dropped the philosophical underpinnings and narrowed the scope of Reisig's semasiology by abandoning the study of words in their stylistic context, reducing semasiology more and more to a purely atomistic study of changes in word-meaning. In this new shape and form, semasiology flowered in Germany, especially after the new edition of Reisig's work in the 1880s. Up to the end of the century a host of treatises on the subject were published by philologists but also by a number of 'schoolmen' (Nerlich 1992a).

A new impetus to the study of meaning came from the rise of psychological thought in Germany, especially under the influence of Johann Friedrich Herbart, Heymann Steinthal, Moritz Lazarus, and Wilhelm Wundt, the latter three fostering a return to Humboldt's philosophy of language. At the time when Steinthal tried to reform linguistic thought through the application of psychological principles, even the most hard-nosed linguists, the neogrammarians themselves, were forced to turn to psychology. This was due to the introduction of analogy as the second most important principle of language change, apart from sound laws.

As early as 1855 Steinthal had written a book where he tried to refute the belief held by many of his fellow linguists that language is based on logical principles and that grammar is based on logic. According to Steinthal, language is plainly based on psychological principles, and these principles are largely of a semantic nature. Criticizing the view inherited from Reisig that grammar has three parts, etymology, semasiology, and syntax, he claims that there is meaning (what he calls after Humboldt an 'inner form') in etymology as well as syntax. In short, semasiology should be part of etymology and syntax, not be separated from them (1855: xxi–xxii). Using the Humboldtian dichotomy of inner and outer form, he wants to study grammar (etymology and syntax) from two points of view: semasiology and phonetics. For him language is 'significant sound', that is, sound and meaning can not be artificially separated.

In 1871 Steinthal wrote his *Abriss der Sprachwissenschaft*. Volume I was intended to be an Introduction into psychology and linguistics. In this work, he wants to explain the origin of language as meaningful sound. His theory of the emergence of language can be compared to modern symbolic interactionism (Nerlich & Clarke 1998). The principle axiom is that when we emit a sound which is understood by the other in a certain way, we understand not only the sound we made, but we understand ourselves, attain consciousness. The origin of language and of consciousness thus lies in understanding. This principle became very important to Philipp Wegener who fostered a new approach to semantics, no longer a mere word-semantics, but a semantics of communication and understanding (Wegener 1885/1991). Steinthal's conception of psychology was the basis of an influential book on semantic change in the Greek language by Max Hecht, which appeared in 1888 and was extensively quoted by the classical philologists among the semanticists.

Hermann Paul is often regarded as one of the leading figures in the neogrammarian movement and his book, the *Prinzipien der Sprachgeschichte*, first published in 1880, is regarded by some as the bible of the neogrammarians. It is true that Paul intended his book at first to be just that. But already in the second edition (1886) he extensively elaborated his at first rather patchy thoughts on semantic topics, such that Bréal – normally rather critical of neogrammarian thought, especially their phonetic bias – could say in his review of the second edition (Bréal 1887) that Paul's book constituted a major contribution to semantics (Bréal 1897: 307).

How had this change of emphasis from sound change to semantic change come about? In 1885 Wegener, like Paul a follower of Steinthal, had published his *Untersuchungen über die Grundfragen des Sprachlebens* (Wegener 1885/1991) where he had devoted a long chapter to semantic change, especially its origin in human communication and interaction. Paul had read (and reviewed) this book (just as Wegener had read and reviewed Paul's). In doing so, Paul must have discovered many affinities between his ideas and those of Wegener, and he must have been inspired to devote more thought to semantic questions. What were the affinities? The most direct resemblance was their insistence on the interaction between speaker and hearer; here again their debt to Steinthal is clear, as clear as their opposition to another very influential psychologist of language, namely Wundt.

Paul's intention was to get rid of abstractions or 'hypostasiations' such as the soul of a people or a language, ghosts that Wundt, and even Steinthal, still tried to catch. These entities, if indeed they are entities, escape, according to Paul, the grasp of any science that wants to be empirical. What can be observed, from a psychological and historical perspective, are only the psychological activities of individuals, but individuals that interact with others. This social and psychological interaction is a mediated one; it is mediated by physiological factors: the production and reception of sounds. Historical linguistics (and all linguistics should be historical in Paul's eyes) as a science based on principles is therefore closely related to two other disciplines: physiology and the psychology of the individual. From this perspective, language use does not change autonomously as it had been believed by a previous generation of linguists, but neither can it be changed by an individual act of the will. It evolves through the cumulative changes occurring in the speech activity of individuals. This speech activity normally proceeds unconsciously – we are only conscious of what we want to say, not of how we say it or how we change what we use in our speech activity: the sounds and the meanings. Accordingly, Paul devotes one chapter to sound change, one to semantic change, and one to analogy (more concerned with the changes in word-forms).

The most important dichotomy that Paul introduced into the study of semantics is that of usual and occasional meaning (*usuelle und okkasionelle Bedeutung*) (Paul 1920/1975: 75), a distinction that exerted lasting influence on semantics and also the psychology and philosophy of meaning (Stout 1891, for example). The usual signification is the accumulated sedimentation of occasional significations, the occasional signification, based on the usual signification is imbued with the intention of the speaker and reshaped by being embedded in the situation of discourse. This context-dependency of the occasional signification can have three forms: it depends on a certain perceptual background shared by speaker and hearer; it depends on what has preceded the word in the discourse; and finally it depends on the shared location of discourse. "Put the plates in the kitchen" is understood because we know that we are speaking about that kitchen here and now and no other. These contextual clues facilitate especially the understanding of words which are ambiguous or polysemous in their usual signification (but Paul does not use term 'polysemy', which had been introduced by Bréal in 1887; Nerlich & Clarke 1997, 2003). A much more radical view of the situation as a factor in meaning construction was put forward by Wegener in 1885 (Nerlich 1990).

Like so many linguists of the 19th century, Paul tries to state the main types of changes of meaning, but he insists that they correspond to the possibilities we have to modify the meaning of words on the level of occasional signification. The first type is the specialization of meaning (what Reisig and Darmesteter would have called 'synecdoche'), which he defines as the restriction of the extension of a word (the set of all actual things the word describes) and enrichment of its intension (the set of all possible things a word or phrase could describe). This type of semantic change is very common. Paul gives the example of German *Schirm*, which can be used to designate any object employed as a 'screen'. In its occasional usage it may signify a 'fire-screen', a 'lamp-screen', a 'screen' for the eyes, an 'umbrella', a 'parasol', etc. But normally, on hearing the word *Schirm* we think of a 'Regenschirm', an umbrella – what cognitive semanticists would now call its prototypical meaning. This meaning has somehow separated itself from the general meaning of 'screen' and become independent. A second basic means to extend (and restrict) word meaning is metaphor. A third type of semantic change is the transfer of meaning upon that which is connected with the usual meaning in space, time or causally (what would later be called via 'contiguity'). Astonishingly, Paul does not use the term 'metonymy' to refer to this type of semantic change.

One of the most important contributions to linguistics in general and semantics in particular was made by Wegener in his *Untersuchungen über die Grundfragen des Sprachlebens*, published in 1885. Although Wegener can to some extent be called a neogrammarian, he never accepted their strict distinction between physiology and psychology, as advocated for example by Hermann Osthoff. For Wegener language is a phenomenon based on the whole human being, their psyche and their body, of a human being who is an integral part of a communicative situation. Paul was influenced by Wegener and so was Gardiner, the Egyptologist and general linguist who dedicated his book *The Theory of Speech and Language* (Gardiner 1932/1951) to Wegener.

So much for some major contributions to German semantics. As one could easily devote an entire book to each of the three national trends in semantic thought, of which the German tradition was by far the most prolific, I can only indicate very briefly the major lines of development that semantics took in Germany after Paul. Many classical philologists continued the tradition started by Reisig. Others took Paul's achievements as a starting point for treatises on semantic change that wanted to illustrate Paul's main types of semantic change by more and more examples. Others still, such as Johan Stöcklein tried to develop Paul's core theory further by stressing, for instance, the importance of the context of the sentence for semantic change (Stöcklein 1898).

But most importantly, the influence of psychology on semantics increased strongly. Apart from Herbart's psychology of mechanical association which had had a certain influence on Steinthal and hence Paul and Wegener, and apart from some more incidental influences such as that of Sigmund Freud and Carl Gustav Jung on Hans Sperber, for example, the most important development in the field of psychology was Wundt's *Völkerpsychologie*. Two volumes of his monumental work on the psychology of such collective phenomena as language, myth and custom were devoted to language (Wundt 1900), and of these a considerable part was concerned with semantic change (on the psychology of language in Germany see Knobloch 1988).

Wundt distinguished between regular semantic change based on social processes or, as he said, the psyche of the people, and singular semantic change, based on the psyche of the individual. He divided the first class into assimilative change and complicative change, the second into name-making according to individual (or singular) associations, individual (or singular) transfer of names, and metaphorically used words. In short, the different types of semantic change were mainly based on different types of association processes (similar to Reisig in this way).

However, Wundt's work attracted a substantial body of criticism, especially from the psychologist Karl Bühler (see Nerlich & Clarke 1998) and the philosopher and general linguist Anton Marty who developed a descriptive semasiology in opposition to Wundt's historical approach (Marty 1908), in this comparable to Raoul de La Grasserie in France (de La Grasserie 1908).

Two other developments in German linguistics have at least to be mentioned: the new focus on words and things, that is on designation (*Bezeichnung*), and not so much on meaning (*Bedeutung*) and the new focus on lexical and semantic fields instead of single words. After the introduction of this first new perspective, the term 'semasiology' itself changed its meaning, standing now in opposition to 'onomasiology'. The second new perspective lead to the flourishing new field of field semantics (Nerlich & Clarke 2000).

3 Linguistic semantics in France

After this sketch of the evolution of semasiology in Germany we now turn to France, where a rather different doctrine was being developed by Michel Bréal, the most famous of French semanticists.

But Bréal was by no means the only one interested in semantic questions. Lexicographers, such as Emile Littré (1880) and later Darmesteter and Adolphe Hatzfeld, contributed to the discussion on semantic questions from a 'naturalist' point of view, applying insights of Darwin's theory of evolution, of Lamarckian transformationism and, in the case of Littré, of Auguste Comte's positivism to the problems of etymology. Littré was one of the first to advocate uniformitarian principles in linguistics, which became so important for Darmesteter and Bréal in France and William Dwight Whitney in the United States (Nerlich 1990). According to the uniformitarian view, inherited from geology (Lyell 1830–1833), the laws of language change now in operation, and which can therefore be 'observed' in living languages, were the same that structured language change in the past. Hence, one can explain past changes by laws now in operation.

Darmesteter was indeed the first to put forward a program for semantics which resembles in its broad scope that of Reisig before him and Bréal after him and in his emphasis on history that of Paul. He contended that the philosophy of language should focus on the history of languages, the transformations of syntax, grammatical forms and word meanings, as a contribution to the history of the human mind and he also claims that these figures of speech also structure changes in grammatical forms and syntactic constructions.

However, as early as the 1840s, before Littré and Darmesteter, the immediate predecessors of Bréal, another group of linguists had started to do 'semantics' under the heading of *idéologie*, or as one of its members later called it *fonctologie*, a term obviously influenced by Schleicher's distinction between form, function and relation (Schleicher 1860). French semantics of this type focused, like the later German semasiology, on the isolated word, but even more on the idea it incarnates, and excluded from its investigation the sentential or other contexts. Later on de La Grasserie (1908) proposed an 'integral semantics' based on this framework. He was (with Marty) the first to point out the difference between synchronic and diachronic semantics, or as he called it 'la sémantique statique' and 'la sémantique dynamique'.

As we shall see in part 4 of this chapter, as early as 1831 the English philosopher Benjamin Humphrey Smart was aware of the dangers of that type of 'ideology' and wanted to replace it by his type of 'sematology', stressing heavily the importance of the context in the production and understanding of meaning – that is replacing mental association by situational embeddedness (Smart 1831: 252).

However, the real winner in this 'struggle for survival' between opposing approaches to semantics, was the new school surrounding Bréal. Language was no longer regarded as an organism, nor did words 'live and die'. The focus was now on the language users, their psychological make-up and the process of mutual understanding. It was in this process that 'words changed their meanings'. Hence the laws of semantic change were no longer regarded as 'natural' or 'logical' laws, but as intellectual laws (Bréal 1883), or what one would nowadays call cognitive laws. This new psychological approach to semantic problems resembled that advocated in Germany by Steinthal, Paul and Wegener. Paul, Wegener, Darmesteter, and Bréal all stressed that the meaning of a word is not so much determined by its etymological ancestry, but by the value it has in current usage, a point of view that moved 19th-century semantics slowly from a purely diachronic to a more synchronic and functional perspective.

Although Bréal and Wegener seem not to have known each other's work, their conceptions of language and of semantics are in some ways astonishingly similar (they also overlap with theories of language developed by Whitney in the United States and Johan Nicolai Madvig (1875) in Denmark, see Hauger 1994). Brought up in the framework of traditional German comparative linguistics, both objected to the reification of language as an autonomous self-evolving system, both saw in psychology a valuable help to get an insight into how people speak and understand each other and change the language as they go along, both made fruitful use of the form-function distinction, where the function drives the evolution of the linguistic form, both assumed that to understand a sentence the hearer had much more to do than to decode it word by word – s/he has to draw inferences from the context of the sentence as a whole, as well as from the context of its use or its function in discourse –, and, finally, they both had a much broader conception of historical semantics than their contemporaries, especially some of the semasiologists in Germany and the 'ideologists' in France. In their eyes semantic change is a phenomenon not only of the word or idea, but must be observed at the morphological and syntactical level, too. The evolution of grammar or of syntax is thus an integral part of semantics.

Bréal's thoughts on semantics, gathered and condensed in the *Essai de sémantique* (*Science des significations*) (1897), had evolved over many years. The stages in the maturation of his semantic theory were, briefly stated, the following: 1866 - lecture on the form and function of words; 1868 - lecture on latent ideas; 1883 - introduction of the term *sémantique* for the study of semantic change and more particularly for the search of the intellectual laws of language change in general; 1887 – review of Darmesteter's book on the life of words, a review called quite intentionally 'history of words'. Bréal rejected all talk about the life of words. For him words do not live and die, they change according to the use speakers make of them. But postulating the importance of the speaker was not enough for him, he went so far as to proclaim that the will or consciousness of the speaker are the ultimate forces of language change. This made him very unpopular among those French linguists who still adhered to the biological paradigm of language change, based on Schleicher's views on the transformation of language. But Bréal was also criticised by some of his friends such as Antoine Meillet. Meillet stressed the role of collective forces, such as social groups, over and above the individual will of the speaker, and became as such important for a new trend in 20th-century French semantics: sociosemantics (Meillet 1904–1905).

As mentioned before, Bréal was not the only one who wrote a review of Darmesteter's book. Two of his friends and colleagues had done the same: Gaston Paris and Victor Henry, and they had basically adopted the same stand as Bréal. Henry should be remembered for his criticism of Bréal's insistence on consciousness, or at least certain degrees of consciousness, as factors in language change. Henry held the view that all changes in language are the result of unconsciously applied procedures, a view he defended in his booklet on linguistic antinomies (1896) and in his study of a case of glossolalia (1901).

How was Bréal received in Germany, a country where a long tradition of 'semasiology' already existed? It is not astonishing to find that the psychologically oriented Bréal was warmly applauded by Steinthal in his 1868 review of Bréal's lecture on latent ideas. He was also mentioned approvingly by Paul (1920/1975:

78 fn. 2). Bréal's division of linguistics into phonetics and semantics as the study of meaning at the level of the lexicon, morphology and syntax also corresponds to some extent to Steinthal's conception outlined above. It did, however, disturb those who, after Ferdinand Heerdegen's narrowing of the field of semasiology, practiced the study of semantic change almost exclusively on the level of the word, excluding morphology and syntax. This difference between French semantics and German semasiology was noted by Oskar Hey in his review of the *Essai* (1898: 551). Hey comes to the conclusion that if Bréal had not entirely ignored the German achievements in the field of semasiology, he would have noticed that everything he has to say about semantic change had already been said. He concedes, however, that etymologists, morphologists and syntacticians may have a different view on some parts of Bréal's work than he has as a classical philologist and semasiologist (see p. 555). From this it is clear that Hey had not really grasped the implications of Bréal's novel approach to semantics. Bréal tried to open up the field of historical semantics from a narrow study of changes in word-meaning to the analysis of language change in general based on the assumption that meaning and change of meaning are a function of discourse.

If one had to answer the question: where did Bréal's thoughts on semantics come from, if not from German semasiology (but Bréal had read Reisig, whom he mentions in the context of a discussion on pronouns, see 1897: 207 fn. 1), one would have to look more closely at 18th-century philosophy of language, specifically the work of the philosopher Etienne Bonnot de Condillac on words as signs and about the progress of knowledge going hand in hand with the progress of language. From this point of view words are not 'living beings' and the fate of language is not mere decay. However, Bréal did not accept Condillac's use of etymology as the instrument to find the real, original meanings of words and to get insights into the constitution of the human mind (a view also espoused in Britain by Tooke, see below). For Bréal the progress of language is linked to the progressive forgetting of the original etymological meaning, it is based on the liberation of the mind from its etymological burden.

The red thread that runs through Bréal's semantic work is the following insight: To understand the evolution and the structure of languages we should not focus so much on the forms and sounds but on the functions and meanings of words and constructions, used and built up by human beings under the influence of their will and intelligence, on the one hand, and the influence of the society they live and talk in, on the other. Unlike some of his contemporaries, Bréal therefore looked at how ideas, how our knowledge of a language and our knowledge of the world, shape the words we use. However, he was also acutely aware of the fact that this semantic and cognitive side of language studies was not yet on a par with the advances made in the study of phonetics, of the more physiological side of language, and had much to learn from the emerging experimental sciences of the human mind (Bréal 1883/1991: 151).

Bréal's most famous contribution to semantics as a discipline was probably his discussion of polysemy, a term he invented in 1887. For him, as for Elisabeth Closs Traugott today, all semantic change arises by polysemy, i.e., new meanings coexist with earlier ones, typically in restricted contexts (Traugott 2005).

French semantics had its peak between 1870 and 1900. Ironically, when the term 'semantics' was created through the translation of Bréal's *Essai*, the interest in semantics faded slightly in France. However, there were some continuations of 19th-century semantics, as for example in the work of Meillet who focused on the social aspects of semantic change. There was also, just as in Germany, a trend to study affective and emotional meaning, a trend particularly well illustrated by the work of the Swiss linguist and student of Ferdinand de Saussure, Charles Bally, on 'stylistics' (1951), followed finally by a period of syntheses, of which the work of the Belgian writer Albert Joseph Carnoy is the best example (1927).

4 Linguistic semantics in Britain

In Britain the study of semantic change was linked for a long time to a kind of etymology that had also prevailed in 18th-century France, that is the use of etymology as the instrument to find the real, original meanings of words and so to get insights into the constitution of the human mind. Genuinely philological considerations only came to dominate the scene by the middle of the century with the creation of the *Philological Society* in 1842, and its project to create a *New English Dictionary*.

The influence of Locke's *Essay Concerning Human Understanding* (1689) on English thinking had been immense, strengthened by John Horne Tooke's widely read *Diversions of Purley* (Tooke 1786–1805). Tooke's theory of meaning can be summarised in the slogan "one word - one meaning". Etymology has to find this meaning, and any use that deviates from it is regarded as 'wrong' - linguistically and morally - this also has religious implications. Up to the 1830s Tooke was much in vogue. His doctrine was, however, challenged by two philosophers: the Scottish common sense philosopher Dugald Stewart and, following him to some extent, Benjamin Humphrey Smart. In his 1810 essay "On the Tendency of some Late Philological Speculations", "Stewart attacked", as Aarsleff points out, "what might be called the atomistic theory of meaning, the notion that each single word has a precise idea affixed to it and that the total meaning of a sentence is, so to speak, the sum of these meanings." He "went to the heart of the matter, asserting that words gain meaning only in context, that many have none apart from it" (Aarsleff 1967/1983: 103). According to Stewart, words which have multiple meanings in the dictionary, or as Bréal would say, polysemous words, are easily understood in context.

This contextual view of meaning is endorsed by Smart in his anonymously published book entitled *An Outline of Sematology or an Essay towards establishing a new theory of grammar, logic and rhetoric* (1831), which was followed by a sequel to this book published in 1851, and finally by his 1855 book on thought and language. In both his 1831 and 1855 books Smart quotes the following lines from Stewart:

> (...) our words, when examined separately, are often as completely insignificant as the letters of which they are composed, deriving their meaning solely from the connection or relation in which they stand to others. (Stewart 1810: 208–209)

The *Outline* is based on Locke's *Essay*, but goes far beyond it. Smart takes up Locke's threefold division of knowledge into (1) physicology or the study of nature, (2) practology or the study of human action, and (3) sematology, the study of the use of signs for our knowledge or in short the doctrine of signs (Smart 1831: 1–2). This study deals with signs "which the mind invents and uses to carry on a train of reasoning independently of actual existences" (1831: 2, note carried over from 1).

In the first chapter of his book, which is devoted to grammar, Smart tries "to imagine the progress of speech upwards as from its first invention" (Smart 1831: 3). It starts with natural cries which have 'the same' meaning as a 'real' sentence composed of different parts, and this because "if equally understood for the actual purpose, [it] is, for this purpose, quite adequate to the artificially compounded sign", the sentence (Smart 1831: 8). But as it is impossible to have a (natural) sign for every occasion or for every purpose (to signify a perception or conception), it was necessary to find an expedient. This expedient was to put together several signs, which each had served a particular purpose, in such a way that they would modify each other, and could, united, serve the new purpose, signify something new (see Smart 1831: 9–10), From these rudest beginnings language developed gradually as an artificial instrument of communication. I cannot go into Smart's presentation of the evolution of the different parts of speech, but it is important to point out that Smart, like Stewart, rejected the notion that words have meaning in isolation. Words have only meaning in the sentence, the sentence has only meaning inside a paragraph, the paragraph only inside a text (see Smart 1831: 54–55). Signs in isolation signify notions, or what the mind knows on the level of abstraction. Signs in combination signify perceptions, conceptions and passions (see Smart 1831: 10–12). Words have thus a double force "by which they signify at the same time the actual thought, and refer to knowledge necessary perhaps to come at it" (Smart 1831: 16). This knowledge is not God-given. "It is by frequently hearing the same word in context with others, that a full knowledge of its meaning is at length obtained; but this implies that the several occasions on which it is used, are observed and compared; it implies in short, a constant enlargement of our knowledge by the use of language as an instrument to attain it" (Smart 1831: 18–19). And thus, as only words give access to ideas, ideas do not exist antecedently to language. As language does not represent notions, the understanding of language is not as simple as one might think, it cannot be used to transfer notions from the head of the speaker to the head of the hearer. Instead we use words in such a way that we adapt them to what the hearer already knows (see Smart 1831: 191).

It is therefore not astonishing to find a praise of tropes and figures of speech in the third chapter of the *Outline*, devoted to rhetoric. Smart claims that they are "essential parts of the original structure of language; and however they may sometimes serve the purpose of falsehood, they are, on most occasions, indispensable to the effective communication of truth. It is only by [these] expedients that mind can unfold itself to mind; - language is made up of them; there is no such thing as an express and direct image of thought." (Smart 1831: 210). Tropes and figures of speech "are the original texture of language and that from which whatever is now plain at first arose. All words are originally tropes; that is expressions turned (...) from their first purpose, and extended to others." (Smart 1831: 214, Nerlich & Clarke 2000).

In his 1855 book Smart wants to correct and extend Locke's thought even further, in particular get rid of the mistake according to which there is a one to one relationship between ideas and words. According to Smart, we do not add meaning to meaning to make sense of a sentence or a text, on the contrary: we subtract (Smart 1855: 139). As an example Smart gives the syntagm *old men*. Just as the French *vieillards*, the English *old men* does not mean the same thing as *vieux* added to *hommes*. To understand a whole sentence, we step down from what he calls premise to premise until we reach the conclusion.

Unfortunately, Smart's conception of the construction of meaning seems to have had little influence on English linguistic thought in the 19th century. He left, however, an impression on philosophers and psychologists of language, such as Victoria Lady Welby (1911) and George Frederick Stout who had also read Paul's work for example. Stout picked up Paul's distinction between usual and occasional meaning for example, but points out that it "must be noticed, however, that the usual signification is, in a certain sense, a fiction" (Stout 1891: 194) and that: "Permanent change of meaning arises from the gradual shifting of the limits circumscribing the general significations. This shifting is due to the frequent repetition of the same kind of occasional application" (Stout 1891: 196).

What James A.H. Murray later called 'sematology' (in a different sense to Smart's use of the term), that is the use of semantics in lexicography, received its impulses from the progress in philology and dictionary writing in Germany and from the dissatisfaction with English dictionary writing. This dissatisfaction was first expressed most strongly by Richard Garnett in 1835 when he attacked English dictionaries for overlooking the achievements of historical-comparative philology. Garnett even went as far as to call some of his countrymen's lexicographical attempts "etymological trash" (Garnett 1835: 306).

The next to point out certain deficiencies in dictionaries was the man who became much more popular for his views on semantic matters: Trench. He used his knowledge of language to argue against the 'Utilitarians', against the biological transformationists and those who held 'uniformitarian' or evolutionary views of language change. For him language is a divine gift, insofar as God has given us the power of reason, and thus the power to name things. His most popular book was *On the Study of Words* (1851), used here in its 21st edition of 1890. The difference between Trench and the up to then prevailing philosophy of language is summarized by Aarsleff in the following way:

> (...) by making the substance of language – the words – the object of inquiry, Trench placed himself firmly in the English tradition, which had its beginning in Locke. There was one important difference, however. Trench shared with the Lockeian school, Tooke and the Utilitarians, the belief that words contained information about thought, feeling, and experience, but unlike them he did not use this information to seek knowledge of the original, philosophical constitution of the mind, but only as evidence of what had been present to the conscious awareness of the users of words within recent centuries; this interest was not in etymological metaphysics, not in conjectural history; not in material philosophy, but in the spiritual and moral life of the speakers of English.
> (Aarsleff 1967/1983: 238)

He studied semantic change at one and the same time as historical records and a lessons in changing morals and history. This is best expressed in this chapter-title: "On the Morality of Words"; the chapter contains 'records of sin' and 'records of good and evil in language'. Despite these moralizing overtones, Trench's purely historical approach to etymology became slowly dominant in Britain and it found its ultimate expression in the *New English Dictionary*.

However, Trench's book contains some important insights into the nature of language and semantic change which would later on be treated more fully by Darmesteter and Bréal. It is also surprising to find that language is for Trench as it was for Smart "a collection of faded metaphors" (Trench 1851/1890: 48), that words are for him fossilized poetry (for very similar views, see Jean Paul 1962–1977 [1804]). Trench also writes about what we would nowadays call the amelioration or pejoration of word-meaning, about the changes in meaning due to politics, commerce, the influence of the church, on the rise of new words according to the needs and thoughts of the speakers, and finally we find a chapter "On the Distinction of Words", which deals with a phenomenon called by Hey, Bréal and Paul the differentiation of synonyms. The study of synonyms deals with the essential (but not entire) resemblance between word-meanings (Trench 1851/1890: 248–249). For Trench there can never be perfect synonyms, and this for the following reason:

> Men feel, and rightly, that with a boundless world lying around them and demanding to be catalogued and named [...], it is a wanton extravagance to expend two or more signs on that which could adequately be set forth by one – an extravagance in one part of their expenditure, which will be almost sure to issue in, and to be punished by, a corresponding scantness and straitness in another. Some thought or feeling or fact will wholly want one adequate sign, because another has two. Hereupon that which has been well called the process of 'desynonymizing' begins – that is, of gradually discriminating in use between words which have hitherto been accounted perfectly equivalent, and, as such, indifferently employed. (...) This may seem at first sight only as a better regulation of old territory; for all practical purposes it is the acquisition of new.
> (Trench 1851/1890: 258–259)

Trench's books, which became highly popular, must have sharpened every educated Englishman's and Englishwoman's awareness for all kinds and sorts of semantic changes.

On a more scientific level Trench's influence was even more profound. As Murray wrote in the Preface to the first volume of the *New English Dictionary* the "scheme [for the NED] originated in a resolution of the Philological Society, passed in 1857, at the suggestion of the late Archbishop Trench, then Dean of Westminster" (Murray 1884: v). In this dictionary the new historical method in philology was for the first time applied to the "life and use of words" (ibid.). The aim was "to furnish an adequate account of the meaning, origin, and history of English words now in general use, or known to have been in use at any time during the last seven hundred years." (ibid.). The dictionary endeavoured

> (1) to show, with regard to each individual word, when, how, in what shape, and with what signification, it became English; what development of form and meaning it has since received; which of its uses have, in the course of time, become obsolete, and which still survive; what new uses have since arisen, by what processes, and when: (2) to illustrate these facts by a series of quotations ranging from the first known occurrence of the word to the latest, or down to the present day; the word being thus made to exhibit its own history and meaning: and (3) to treat the etymology of each word strictly on the basis of historical fact, and in accordance with the methods and results of modern philological science.
> (Murray 1884: vi)

Etymology was no longer seen as an instrument used to get insights into the workings of the human mind, as philosophers in France and Britain had believed at the end of the 18th century, or to discover the truly original meaning of a word. It was now put on a purely scientific, i.e. historical, footing.

But, as we have seen, by then a new approach to semantics, fostered by Steinthal and Bréal under the influence of psychological thought, brought back considerations of the human mind, of the speaker, and of communication, opening up semantics from the study of the history of words in and for themselves to the study of semantic change in the context of psychology and sociology. One Cambridge philosopher, who knew Scottish common sense philosophy just as well as Kantianism, and studied meaning in the context of communication was John Grote. In the 1860s, he developed a theory of meaning as use and of thinking as a social activity based on communication (Gibbins 2007). His focus on 'living meaning' as opposed to 'fossilised' or historical meaning had parallels with the theory of meaning developed by Bréal at the same time and can be regarded as a direct precursor of ordinary language philosophy.

Influenced by Wegener, Ferdinand de Saussure (and his distinction between speech and language) and the anthropologist Malinowski (and his claim that language can only be studied as part of action), Gardiner and then Firth tried to develop a new *contextualist* approach to semantics and laid the foundation for the London School of Linguistics.

However, by the 1960s Britain, like the rest of Europe, began to feel the influence of structuralism (Pottier 1964). Gustav Stern (1931) in Denmark tried to synthesise achievements in semantics, especially with reference to the English language. Stephen Ullmann in Oxford attempted to bridge the gap between the old (French and German) type of historical-psychological and the new type of structural semantics in his most influential books on semantics written in 1951 and 1962. Although brought up in the tradition of Gardiner and Firth, Sir John Lyons finally swept away the old type of semantics and advocated the new 'structural semantics' in 1963 (Lyons 1963). The focus was now both on how meanings are shaped by their mutual relations in a system, rather than by their evolution over time and on the way meanings are constituted internally by semantic features which were, by some thought to be invariant (see Matthews 2001; for more information (see article 1 [Semantics: Lexical Structures and Adjectives] (Bierwisch) *Semantic features and primes*). Variation and change, discourse and society, mind and metaphor which had so fascinated earlier linguists were sidelined but later rediscovered inside frame semantics (see article 3 [Semantics: Theories] (Gawron) *Frame Semantics*), prototype semantics (see article 2 [Semantics: Theories] (Taylor) *Prototpye theory*), cognitive semantics (see article 1 [Semantics: Theories] (Talmy) *Cognitive Semantics*) and studies of grammaticalisation (see article 8 [Semantics: Typology, Diachrony and Processing] (Eckardt) *Grammaticalization and semantic reanalysis*).

5 Conclusion

One of the pioneers in the history of semantics, Dirk Geeraerts has, in the past, distinguished between five stages in the history of lexical semantics, namely pre-structuralist diachronic semantics, structuralist semantics, lexical semantics as practiced in the context of generative grammar, logical semantics, and cognitive semantics (Geeraerts 1997). Geeraerts himself has now provided a masterly overview of the history of semantics from its earliest beginnings up to the present (Geeraerts 2010), with chapters on historical-philological semantics, structuralist semantics, generativist semantics, neostructuralist semantics and cognitive semantics. His first chapter is at the same time broader and narrower than the history of early (pre-structuralist) semantics provided here. It provides an overview of speculative etymology in antiquity as well as of the rhetorical tradition, which I do not cover in this chapter; and when Geeraerts focuses on developments between 1830 and 1930 he mainly focuses on Bréal and Paul. So I hope that by examining discussions of what words mean and how meaning is achieved as a process between speaker and hearer, author and reader and so on in three national traditions, the French, the British and the German in early semantics, between around 1830 and 1930, and by focusing more on context than cognition, I supplement Geeraerts' work to some extent.

6 References

Aarsleff, Hans 1967/1983. *The Study of Language in Britain 1780–1860*. 2nd edn. London: Athlone Press, 1983.
Bally, Charles 1951. *Traité de Stylistique Française*. 3rd edn. Genève: George Klincksieck.
Bréal, Michel 1883. Les lois intellectuelles du langage. Fragment de sémantique. *Annuaire de l'Association pour l'encouragement des études grecques en France* 17, 132–142.
Bréal, Michel 1883/1991. *The Beginnings of Semantics: Essays, Lectures and Reviews*. Translated and introduced by George Wolf. Reprinted: Stanford, CA: Stanford University Press, 1991.
Bréal, Michel 1887. L'histoire des mots. *Revue des Deux Mondes* 1, 187–212.
Bréal, Michel 1897. *Essai de Sémantique (Science des Significations)*. Paris: Hachette.
Carnoy, Albert J. 1927. *La Science du Mot. Traité de Sémantique*. Louvain: Editions 'Universitas'.
Darmesteter, Arsène 1887. *La Vie des Mots Étudiée d'après leurs Significations*. Paris: Delagrave.
Delesalle, Simone 1987. Vie des mots et science des significations: Arsène Darmesteter et Michel Bréal *(DRLAV)*. *Revue de Linguistique* 36–37, 265–314.
Firth, John R. 1935/1957. The technique of semantics. *Transactions of the Philological Society for 1935*, 36–72. Reprinted in: J.R. Firth, *Papers in Linguistics 1934–1951*. London: Oxford University Press, 1957, 7–33.

Frege, Gottlob 1977. Thoughts. In: P. Geach (ed.). *Logical Investigations. Gottlob Frege*. New Haven, CT: Yale University Press, 1–30.
Gardiner, Alan H. 1932/1951. *The Theory of Speech and Language*. 2nd edn., with additions. Oxford: Clarendon Press, 1951.
Garnett, Richard 1835. English lexicography. *Quarterly Review* 54, 294–330.
Geeraerts, Dirk 1997. *Diachronic Prototype Semantics. A Contribution to Historical Lexicology*. Oxford: Oxford University Press.
Geeraerts, Dirk 2010. *Theories of Lexical Semantics: A Cognitive Perspective*. Oxford: Oxford University Press.
de la Grasserie, Raoul 1908. *Essai d'une Sémantique Intégrale*. Paris: Leroux.
Gibbins, John R. 2007. *John Grote, Cambridge University and the Development of Victorian Thought*. Exeter: Imprint Academic.
Hauger, Brigitte 1994. *Johan Nicolai Madvig. The Language Theory of a Classical Philologist*. Münster: Nodus.
Hecht, Max 1888. *Die griechische Bedeutungslehre: Eine Aufgabe der klassischen Philologie*. Leipzig: Teubner.
Henry, Victor 1896. *Antinomies Linguistique*. Paris: Alcan.
Henry, Victor 1901. *Le Langage Martien*. Paris: Maisonneuve.
Hey, Oskar 1898. Review of Bréal (1897). *Archiv für Lateinische Lexicographie und Grammatik* 10, 551–555.
Jean Paul [Johann Paul Friedrich Richter] 1962–1977[1804]. *Vorschule der Ästhetik*. [Introduction to Aesthetics]. In: *Werke* [Works]. Edited by Norbert Miller. Abt. 1, Vol. 5. Darmstadt: Wissenschaftliche Buchgesellschaft, 7–330.
Knobloch, Clemens 1988. *Geschichte der psychologischen Sprachauffassung in Deutschland von 1850 bis 1920*. Tübingen: Niemeyer.
Littré, Emile 1880. Pathologie verbale ou lésion de certains mots dans le cours de l'usage. *Etudes et Glanures pour Faire Suite à l'Histoire de la Langue Française*. Paris: Didier, 1–68.
Locke, John 1975/1689. *Essay on Human Understanding*. Oxford: Oxford University Press. 1st edn. 1689.
Lyell, Charles 1830–1833. *Principles of Geology, Being an Attempt to Explain the Former Changes of the Earth's Surface by Reference to Causes now in Operation*. London: Murray.
Lyons, John 1963. *Structural Semantics*. Oxford: Blackwell.
Madvig, Johann N. 1875. *Kleine philologische Schriften*. Leipzig: Teubner. Reprinted: Hildesheim: Olms, 1966.
Du Marsais, César de Chesneau 1757. *Des Tropes ou des Différens Sens dans lesquels on Peut Prendre un Même Mot dans une Même Langue*. Paris: chez David.
Matthews, Peter 2001. *A Short History of Structural Linguistics*. Cambridge: Cambridge University Press.
Marty, Anton 1908. *Untersuchungen zur Grundlegung der allgemeinen Grammatik und Sprachphilosophie* 1. Halle/Saale: Niemeyer.
Meillet, Antoine 1904–1905. Comment les mots changent de sens. *Année Sociologique* 1904–1905, 230–271. Reprinted in: *Linguistique historique et linguistique générale* I, 230–271.
Murray, James A. (ed.) 1884. *A New English Dictionary. On Historical Principles; Founded Mainly on the Materials Collected by The Philological Society* 1(a). Oxford: Clarendon Press.
Nerlich, Brigitte 1990. *Change in Language. Whitney, Bréal and Wegener*. London: Routledge.
Nerlich, Brigitte 1992a. La sémantique: 'Éducation et Récréation'. *Cahiers Ferdinand de Saussure* 46, 159–171.

Nerlich, Brigitte 1992b. *Semantic Theories in Europe, 1830–1930. From Etymology to Contextuality*. Amsterdam: Benjamins.

Nerlich, Brigitte 1996a. Semantics in the XIXth Century. In: P. Schmitter (ed.). *Geschichte der Sprachtheorie 5*. Tübingen: Narr, 395–426.

Nerlich, Brigitte 1996b. Un chaînon manquant entre la rhétorique et la sémantique: L'oeuvre d'Auguste de Chevallet. *Travaux de Linguistique* 33, 115–131.

Nerlich, Brigitte 1998. La métaphore et le métonymie: Aux sources rhétoriques des théories sémantiques modernes. *Sémiotiques* 14, 143–170.

Nerlich, Brigitte & David D. Clarke. 1996. *Language, Action, and Context: The Early History of Pragmatics in Europe and America, 1780–1930*. Amsterdam: Benjamins.

Nerlich, Brigitte & David D. Clarke 1997. Polysemy: Patterns in meaning and patterns in history. *Historiographia Linguistica* 24, 359–385.

Nerlich, Brigitte & David D. Clarke, 1998. The linguistic repudiation of Wundt. *History of Psychology* 1, 179–204.

Nerlich, Brigitte & David D. Clarke 2000. Semantic fields and frames: Historical explorations of the interface between language, action and cognition. *Journal of Pragmatics* 32, 125–150.

Nerlich, Brigitte & David D. Clarke, 2003. Polysemy and flexibility: Introduction and overview. In: B. Nerlich et al. (eds.). *Polysemy: Flexible Patterns of Meaning in Mind and Language*. Berlin: de Gruyter, 3–30.

Paul, Hermann 1880. *Principien der Sprachgeschichte*. 5th edn. Halle/Saale: Niemeyer, 1920.

Paul, Hermann 1920/1975. *Prinzipien der Sprachgeschichte*. Reprint of the 5th edn. 1920. Tübingen: Niemeyer, 1975.

Pottier, Bernard 1964. Vers une sémantique moderne. *Travaux de Linguistique et de Littérature* 2, 107–137.

Reisig, Christian K. 1839. Vorlesungen über lateinische Sprachwissenschaft. In: F. Haase (ed.). Ch. K. Reisig: *Vorlesungen über lateinische Sprachwissenschaft*. Leipzig: Lehnhold.

Schleicher, August 1860. *Die Deutsche Sprache*. Stuttgart: Cotta.

Schmitter, Peter 1987. Die Zeichen- und Bedeutungstheorie Leo Weisgerbers als Grundlage semantischen Analyse. In: P. Schmitter (ed.). *Das sprachliche Zeichen*. Münster: Nodus, 176–202.

Schmitter, Peter (ed.) 1990. *Essays Towards a History of Semantics*. Münster: Nodus.

Schmitter, Peter 2001a. The emergence of philosophical semantics in early Greek Antiquity. *Logos and Language* 2, 45–56.

Schmitter, Peter 2001b. Zur Rolle der Semantik in Humboldts linguistischem Forschungsprogramm. In: K. Adamzik & H. Christen (eds.). *Sprachkontakt, Sprachvergleich, Sprachvariation. Festschrift für Gottfried Kolde zum 65. Geburtstag*. Tübingen: Niemeyer, 307–323.

Schmitter, Peter 2004. Die Wortbildungstheorie der frühen Semasiologie. Ein weißer Fleck in den Geschichtsatlanten der Linguistik. *Beiträge zur Geschichte der Sprachwissenschaft* 14, 107–134.

Smart, Benjamin H. 1831. *An Outline of Sematology: Or an Essay Towards Establishing a New Theory of Grammar, Logic, and Rhetoric*. London: Richardson.

Smart, Benjamin H. 1855. *Thought and Language: An Essay Having in View the Revival, Correction, and Exclusive Establishment of Locke's Philosophy*. London: Longman, Brown, Green & Longmans.

Steinthal, Heymann 1855. *Grammatik, Logik und Psychologie: Ihre Prinzipien und ihr Verhältnis zueinander*. Berlin: Dümmler.

Steinthal, Heymann 1871. *Abriss der Sprachwissenschaft 1*. Berlin: Dümmler.

Stern, Gustav 1931. *Meaning and Change of Meaning. With Special Reference to the English Language*. Göteborg: Elanders Boktryckeri Aktiebolag. Reprinted: Bloomington, IN: Indiana University Press, 1968.
Stewart, Dugald 1810. *Philosophical Essays*. Edinburgh: Creech.
Stöcklein, Johann 1898. *Bedeutungswandel der Wörter. Seine Entstehung und Entwicklung*. München: Lindauer.
Stout, George Frederick 1891. Thought and language. *Mind* 16, 181–197.
Tooke, John H. 1786–1805. *Epea ptepoenta; or, the Diversions of Purley*. 2nd edn. London: printed for the author.
Traugott, Elizabeth C. 2005. Semantic change In: K. Brown (ed.). *Encyclopedia of Language and Linguistics*. Amsterdam: Elsevier.
Trench, Richard C. 1851/1890. *On the Study of Words*. 21st edn. London: Kegan Paul, Trench, Trübner & Co., 1890.
Ullmann, Stephen 1951. *The Principles of Semantics. A Linguistic Approach to Meaning*. 2nd edn. Glasgow: Jackson, 1957.
Ullmann, Stephen 1962. *Semantics*. Oxford: Blackwell.
Wegener, Philipp 1885/1991. *Untersuchungen über die Grundfragen des Sprachlebens*. Halle/Saale: Niemeyer.
Welby, Victoria Lady 1911. *Significs and Language. The Articulate Form of our Expressive and Interpretative Resources*. London: Macmillan & Co.
Wundt, Wilhelm 1900. *Völkerspsychologie I: Die Sprache*. Leipzig: Engelmann.

Albert Newen and Bernhard Schröder

10 The influence of logic on semantics

1. Overview —— 243
2. Pre-Fregean logic —— 244
3. Gottlob Frege's progress —— 247
4. Bertrand Russell's criticism and his theory of definite descriptions —— 251
5. Rudolf Carnap's theory of extension and intension: Relying on possible worlds —— 252
6. Willard V. O. Quine: Logic, existence and propositional attitudes —— 253
7. Necessity and direct reference: The two-dimensional semantics —— 256
8. Montague-Semantics: Compositionality revisited —— 257
9. Generalized quantifiers —— 261
10. Intensional theory of types —— 264
11. Dynamic logic —— 265
12. References —— 270

Abstract: The aim of this contribution is to investigate the influence of logical tools on the development of semantic theories and vice versa. Pre-19th-century logic was limited to a few sentence forms and their logical interrelations. Modern predicate logic and later type logic, both inspired by investigating the meaning of mathematical sentences, widened the view for new sentence forms and thereby made logic relevant for a wider range of expressions in natural language. In a parallel course of developments the problem of different levels of meaning like sense and reference, or intension and extension were studied and initiated a shift to modal contexts in natural language. Montague bundled in his intensional type-theoretical framework a great part of these development in a unified formal framework which had strong impact on the formal approaches in natural language semantics. While the logical developments mentioned so far could be seen as direct answers to natural language phenomena, the first approaches to dynamic logic did not get their motivation from natural language, but from the semantics of computer programming. Here, a logical toolset was adapted to specific problems of natural language semantics.

Albert Newen, Bochum, Germany
Bernhard Schröder, Essen, Germany

https://doi.org/10.1515/9783110368505-010

1 Overview

The aim of this contribution is to investigate the influence of logical tools on the development of semantic theories and vice versa. The article starts with an example of Pre-Fregean logic, i.e. Aristotelian syllogistic. This traditional frame of logic has severe limits for a theory of meaning (e.g. no possibility for multiple quantification, no variety of scope). These limitations have been overcome by Frege's predicate logic which is the root of standard modern logic and the basis for the first developments in a formal philosophy of language: We will present Frege's analysis of mathematical sentences and his transfer to the analysis of natural language sentences by introducing a theory of sense and reference. The insufficient treatment of singular terms in Frege's logic is one reason for Russell's theory of definite descriptions. Furthermore, Russell tries to organize semantics without a difference between sense and reference. Carnap introduces the first logical framework for a semantics of possible worlds and shows how one can keep the Fregean semantic intuitions without using the problematic tool of "senses". Carnap develops a systematic theory of intension and extension defining the intension of an expression as a function from possible worlds to the relevant extension. An important formal step was then the invention of modal logic by Kripke. This is the framework for the theory of direct reference of proper names and for the so-called two-dimensional semantics which is relevant to receive an adequate treatment of names, definite descriptions, and especially indexicals. Tarski's formal theory of truth is used by Davidson to argue that truth-conditions are the adequate tool to characterize the meaning of assertions. Although the idea of a truth-conditional semantics is already in the background since Frege, with Davidson's work it became the leading idea for modern semantics.

  The second part of the article (starting with section 8) will concentrate on important progresses made in this overall framework of truth-conditional semantics. Montague presented a compositional formal semantics including quantifiers, intensional contexts and the phenomenon of deixis. His ideal was to offer an absolute truth-condition for any sentence. In the next step new formal tools were invented to account not only for the extralinguistic environment but also for the discourse as a core feature of the meaning of utterances. Context-dependency in this sense is considered in approaches of dynamic semantics. Formal tools are nowadays not only used to answer the leading question "What is the meaning of a natural language expression?" In recent developments new logic formalisms are used to answer questions like "How is a convention established?" and "How can we account for the pragmatics of the utterance?" It has become clear that truth-conditional semantics has to be completed by aspects of the environment, social conventions and speaker's intentions to receive an adequate account of meaning. Therefore the latest trend is to offer new formal tools that can account for these features.

2 Pre-Fregean logic

The first system of logic was grounded by Aristotle (see 1992). He organized inferences according to a syllogistic schema which consists of two premises and a conclusion. Each sentence of such a syllogistic schema contains two predicates (F, G), a quantifier in front of the first predicate (some, every) and a negation (not) could be added in front of the second predicate. Each syllogistic sentence has the following structure "Some/every F is/is not G". Then we receive four possible types of sentences: A sentence is universal if it starts with "every" and particular if it starts with "some". A sentence is affirmative if it does not contain a negation in front of the second predicate otherwise it is negative. We receive Tab. 10.1.

Tab. 10.1: Syllogistic types of sentences

NAME	FORM	TITLE
a	Every F is G	Universal Affirmative
i	Some F is G	Particular Affirmative
e	Every F is not G	Universal Negative
o	Some F is not G	Particular Negative

The name of the affirmative syllogistic sentences is due to the Latin word "affirmo". The first vowel represents the universal sentence while the second vowel represents the particular. The name of the negative syllogistic sentences is due to the Latin word "nego" again with the same convention concerning the use of the first and second vowel. As we will see the sequence of vowels is also used to represent the syllogistic inferences. If we introduce the further quantifier "no" we can find equivalent representations but no new propositions. The sentence "No F is G" is equivalent to (e) "Every F is not G" and "No F is not G" is equivalent to (a) "Every F is G". The proposition (e) is intuitively more easily to grasp in the form "No F is G" while proposition (a) is better understandable in the original format "Every F is G". So we continue with these formulations. On the basis of these sentences we can systematically arrange the typical syllogistic inferences, e.g. the inference called "barbara" because it contains three sentences of the form (a).

Tab. 10.2: Barbara

Premise 1 (a):	Every G is H.	abbreviation: GaH
Premise 2 (a):	Every F is G.	abbreviation: FaG
Conclusion (a):	Every F is H.	abbreviation: FaH

Now we can start with systematic variations of the four types of sentences (a, i, e, o). The aim of Aristotle was to select all and only those inferences which are valid. Given the same structure of the predicates in the premises and the conclusion only varying the kind of sentence we receive e.g. the valid inferences of Tab. 10.3.

Tab. 10.3: Same predicate structure, varying types of sentences

Barbara	Darii	Ferio	Celarent
Every M is H	Every M is H	No M is H	No M is H
Every F is M	Some F are M	Some F is M	Every F is M
Every F is H	Some F are H	Some F is not H	No F is H

To present the complete list of possible syllogistic inferences we have to account for different kinds of predicate positions in the inference. We can distinguish four general schemata including the one we already had presented so far. Our first schema has the general structure (I) and we also receive the other structures (II to IV) in Tab. 10.4.

Tab. 10.4: Predicate structures

I.	M	H	II.	H	M	III.	M	H	IV.	H	M
	F	M		F	M		M	F		M	F
	F	H		F	H		F	H		F	H

For each general format we can vary the kinds of sentences that are involved in the way presented above. This leads to all possible syllogistic inferences in the Aristotelian logic. While making this claim we are ignoring the fact that Aristotle already worked out a modal logic, cf. Nortmann (1996). Concentrating on non-modal logic we have presented the core of the Aristotelian system. Although it was an ingenious discovery in ancient times, the Aristotelian system has its strong limitations: Strictly speaking, there is no space in syllogistic inferences for (a) singular terms, (b) existence claims (like "Trees exist") and there are only very limited possibilities for quantification (see section on Frege's progress). Especially, there is no possibility for multiple uses of quantifiers in one sentence. This is the most important progress which is due to the predicate logic essentially developed by Gottlob Frege. Before we present this radical step into modern logic, we shortly describe some core ideas of G. W. Leibniz, who invented already some influential ideas on the way to modern logic.

Leibniz is well-known for introducing the idea of a *calculus of logical inferences*. He introduced the idea that the syntax of the sentences mirrors the logical structure of the thoughts expressed and that there can be defined a purely syntactic procedure of proving a sentence. This leads to the modern understanding of a syntactic notion of proof which ideally allows for all sentences to decide simply on the basis of syntactic transformations whether they are provable or not. The logic systems developed by Leibniz are essentially advanced compared to the Aristotelian syllogistic. It has been shown that his logic is equivalent to the Boolean logic, i.e. the monadic predicate logic, see Lenzen (1990). Furthermore, Leibniz introduced a calculus of concepts defining concept identity, inclusion, containment and addition, see Zalta (2000) and Lenzen (2000). He reserved a special place for individual concepts. Since his work had almost no influence on the general development of logic the main ideas are only mentioned here. Ignoring a lot of interesting developments (e.g. modal systems) we can characterize a great deal of the logical systems initiated by Aristotle until the 19th century by the square of opposition (cf. article 8 [this volume] (Meier-Oeser) *Meaning in pre 19th-century thought*).

The square of opposition (see Fig. 10.1) already involves the essential distinction between different understandings of "oppositions": A contradiction of a sentence is an external negation of sentence "It is not the case that ..." while the contrary involves an "internal" negation. What is meant by an "internal" negation can only be illustrated by transforming the syllogistic sentences into modern predicate logic. The most important general features in the traditional understanding are the following: (i) From two contradictory sentences one must be false

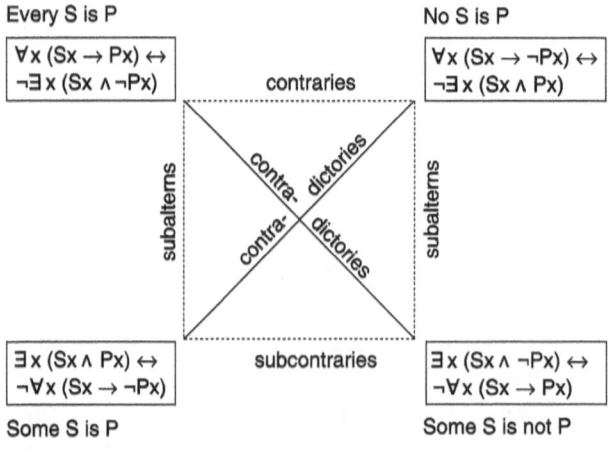

Fig. 10.1: Square of oppositions

and one be true. (ii) For two contrary sentences holds that they cannot both be true (but they can both be false). (iii) For two subcontrary sentences holds that they cannot both be false (but they can both be true).

A central problem pointed out by Abelard in the Dialectica (1956) is *presupposition of existential import:* According to one understanding of the traditional square of opposition it presupposes that sentences like "Every F is G" or "Some F is G" imply "There is at least one thing which is F". This is the so-called existential import condition which leads into trouble. The modern transformation of the syllogistic sentences into predicate logic, as included into the figure above, does not involve the existential presupposition. Let us use an example: On the one hand, "Some man is black" implies that at least one thing is a man, namely the man who has to be black if "Some man is black" is true. On the other hand, "Some man is not black" also implies that something is a man, namely the man who is not black if "Some man is not black" is true. But these are two subcontrary sentences, i.e. according to the traditional view they cannot both be false; one has to be true. Therefore (since both imply that there is a thing which is a man) it follows that men exist. In such a logic the use of a predicate F in a sentence "Some F..." presupposes that F is non-empty (simply given the meaning of F and the traditional square of opposition), i.e. there are no empty predicates. But of course (as Abelard points out) surely men might not exist. This observation leads to the modern square of opposition which uses the reading of sentences in predicate logic and leaves out the relations of contraries and subcontraries and only keeps the relation of the contradictories. The leading intuition to avoid the problematic consequence mentioned above is the claim that meaningful universal sentences like "Every man is mortal" do not imply that men exist. The existential import is denied for both predicates in universal sentences. Relying on the interpretation of particular sentences like "Some men are mortal" according to modern predicate logic, the truth of the particular sentences just means that there is at least one man which is mortal. If we want to allow nonempty predicates then we receive the modern square of opposition.

3 Gottlob Frege's progress

Frege was a main figure from two points of view: He introduced a modern predicate logic and he also developed the first systematic modern philosophy of language by transferring his insights in logic and mathematics into a philosophy of language. His logic was first developed in the "Begriffsschrift" (1879, in the following shortly:

BS), see Frege (1977). He used a special notation to characterize the content of a sentence by a horizontal line (the content line) and the act of judging the content by a vertical line (the judgement line).

$$\vdash A$$

This distinction is a clear precursor of the distinction between illocution (the type of speech act) and proposition (the content of the speech act) in Searle's speech act theory.

Frege's main aim was to clarify the status of arithmetic sentences. Dealing with a mathematical expression like „3^2" Frege analyzes it into the functional expression „$(\ )^2$" and the argument expression „3". The functional expression refers to the function of squaring something while the argument expression refers to the number 3. An essential feature of the functional expression is its being unsaturated, i.e. it has an empty space that needs to be filled by an argument expression to constitute a complete sentence. The argument expression is saturated, i.e. it has no space for any addition. Frege transferred this observation into the philosophy of language: Predicates are typical expressions which are unsaturated, while proper names and definite descriptions are typical examples for saturated expressions. Predicates refer to concepts while proper names and definite descriptions refer to objects. Since predicates are unsaturated expressions which need to be completed by a saturated expression, Frege defines concepts (as the reference of predicates) as functions which – completed by objects (as the referents of proper names and other singular terms) – always have a truth value (Truth or Falsity) as result. The truth-value is the reference of the sentence composed of the proper name and the predicate. By analogy from mathematical sentences Frege starts to analyze sentences of natural language and develops a systematic theory of meaning. Before outlining some basic aspects of this project, we first introduce the idea of a modern system of logic. Frege developed the following propositional calculus (for a detailed reconstruction of Frege's logic see von Kutschera 1989, chap. 3):

AXIOMS:

(1) a. $A \rightarrow (B \rightarrow A)$
    b. $(C \rightarrow (B \rightarrow A)) \rightarrow ((C \rightarrow B) \rightarrow (C \rightarrow A))$
    c. $(D \rightarrow (B \rightarrow A)) \rightarrow (B \rightarrow (D \rightarrow A))$
    d. $(B \rightarrow A) \rightarrow (\neg A \rightarrow \neg B)$
    e. $\neg\neg A \rightarrow A$
    f. $A \rightarrow \neg\neg A$

A RULE OF INFERENCE, which allows to derive theorems by starting with two axioms or theorems:

(2) $A \rightarrow B, A \vdash B$

If we add an axiom and a rule we receive a system of predicate logic that is complete and consistent. Frege suggested the following axiom:

(3) $\forall x A[x] \rightarrow A[a]$ (BS: 51).

The additionally relevant rule of inference was not explicitly marked by Frege but presupposed implicitly:

(4) $A \rightarrow B[a] \vdash A \rightarrow \forall x B[x]$, if „a" is not involved in the conclusion (BS: 21).

Frege tried to show the semantic consistency of the predicate calculus (which was then intensely debated) but he did not try to prove the completeness since he lacked the notion of interpretation to develop such a proof (von Kutschera 1989: 34). A formal system of axioms and rules is complete for first-order predicate logic (FOPL) if all sentences logically valid in FOPL are derivable in the formal system. The completeness proof was for the first time worked out by Kurt Gödel (1930). Frege already included second-order predicates into his system of logic. The interesting fact that second-order predicate logic is incomplete was for the first time shown by Kurt Gödel (1931).

One of the central advantages of modern predicate logic for the development of semantics is the fact that we can now use as much quantifiers in sequence as we want. We have of course to take care of the meaning of quantifiers given the sequence. The following sentences which cannot be expressed in the system of Aristotelian syllogism can be nicely expressed by the modern predicate logic using "L" as a shorthand for the two-place predicate "( ) loves ( )".

(5) Everyone loves everyone: $\forall x \forall y L(x, y)$

Using mixed quantifiers their sequence becomes relevant:

(6) a. Someone loves everyone: $\exists x \forall y L(x, y)$

    b. Everyone loves someone: $\forall x \exists y L(x, y)$
       [This can be a different person for everyone]

    c. Someone is loved by everyone: $\exists y \forall x L(x, y)$
       [There is (at least) one specific human being who is loved by all human beings]

d. Everyone is loved by someone: $\forall y \exists x L(x, y)$

e. Someone loves someone: $\exists x \exists y L(x, y)$
[There is (at least) one human being who loves (at least) one human being]

Frege's philosophy of language is based on a principle of compositionality (cf. article 6 [this volume] (Pagin & Westerståhl) *Compositionality*), i.e. the principle that the value of a complex expression is determined by the values of the parts plus its composition. He developed a systematic theory of sense and reference (cf. article 3 [this volume] (Textor) *Sense and reference*). The reference of a proper name is the designated object and the reference of a predicate is a concept while both determine the reference of the sentence, i.e. the truth-value. Given this framework of reference it follows that the sentences

(7) The morning star is identical with the morning star.

and

(8) The morning star is identical with the evening star.

have the same reference, i.e. the same truth-value: The truth-value is determined by the reference of the name and the predicate. Each token of the predicate refers to the same concept and the two names refer to the same object, the planet Venus. But sentence (7) is uninformative while sentence (8) is informative. Therefore, we need a new aspect of meaning to account for the informativity: the sense of an expression. The sense of a proper name is a mode of presentation of the designated object, i.e. "the evening star" expresses the mode of presentation characterized as the brightest star in the evening sky. Furthermore the sense of a sentence is a thought. The latter (in the case of simple sentences like "Socrates is a philosopher") is constituted by the sense of a predicate "( ) is a philosopher" and the sense of the proper name "Socrates". Frege defines the sense of an expression in general as the mode of presentation of the reference. To develop a consistent theory of sense and reference Frege introduced different senses for one and the same expression in different linguistic contexts, e.g. indirect speech (propositional attitude ascriptions) or quotations are contexts in which the sense of an expression changes. Frege's philosophy of language has at least two major problems: (1) the necessity of an infinite hierarchy of senses to account for the recursive syntactic structure (John believes that Mary believes that Karl believes .....) and (2) the problem of indexical expressions (it is accounted for in two-dimensional semantics and dynamic semantics, see below).

4 Bertrand Russell's criticism and his theory of definite descriptions

Russell (1903, partly in cooperation with Whitehead (Russell & Whitehead 1910–1913)) also developed himself both a system of logic and a philosophy of language in contrast to Frege such that we nowadays speak of Neo-Fregean and Neo-Russellian theories of meaning. Let us first have a look at Russell's logical considerations. Russell developed his famous paradox which was a serious problem for Frege because Frege presupposes in his system that he could produce sets of sets in an unconstrained manner. But if there are no constraints we run into Russell's paradox: Let R be the set of all sets which are not members of themselves. Then R is neither a member of itself nor not a member of itself. Symbolically, let $R := \{x : x \notin x\}$. Then $R \in R$ iff $R \notin R$. To illustrate the consideration: If R is a member of itself it must fulfill the definition of its members, i.e. it must not be a member of itself. If R is not a member of itself then it should not fulfill the definition of its members, i.e. it must be a member of itself. When Russell wrote his discovery in a letter to Frege who was just completing *Grundlagen der Arithmetik* Frege was despaired because the foundations of his system were undermined. Russell himself developed a solution by introducing a *theory of types* (1908). The leading idea is that we always have to clarify those objects to which the function will apply before a function can be defined exactly. This leads to a strict distinction between object language and meta-language: We can avoid the paradox by avoiding self-references and this can be done by arranging all sentences (or, equivalently, all propositional functions) into a hierarchy. The lowest level of this hierarchy will consist of sentences about individuals. The next lowest level will consist of sentences about sets of individuals. The next lowest level will consist of sentences about sets of sets of individuals, and so on. It is then possible to refer to all objects for which a given condition (or predicate) holds only if they are all at the same level, i.e. of the same type. The theory of types is a central element in modern theory of truth and thereby also for semantic theories. Russell's contribution to the philosophy of language is essentially connected with his analysis of definite descriptions (Russell 1905). The meaning of the sentence "The present King of France is bald" is analyzed as follows:
1. there is an x such that x is the present King of France ($\exists x(Fx)$)
2. for every x that is the present King of France and every y that is the present King of France, x equals y (i.e. there is at most one present King of France) ($\forall x(Fx \rightarrow \forall y (Fy \rightarrow y = x)))$
3. for every x that is the present King of France, x is bald. ($\forall x(Fx \rightarrow Bx)$)

Since France is no longer a kingdom, assertion 1. is plainly false; and since our statement is the conjunction of all three assertions, our statement is false.

Russell's analysis of definite descriptions involves a strategy to develop a purely extensional semantics, i.e. a semantic theory that can characterize the meaning of sentences without introducing the distinction between sense and reference or any related distinction of intensional and extensional meanings. Definite descriptions are analyzed such that there remains no singular term in the reformulation and ordinary proper names are according to Russell's theory hidden definite descriptions. His strategy eliminates singular terms with only one exception: He needs the basic singular term "this/that" to account for our speech about sense-data (Russell 1910). Since he takes an acquaintance relation with sense-data (and also with universals) including a sense-data ontology as a basic presupposition of his specific semantic approach, the only core idea that survived in modern semantics is his logical analysis of definite descriptions.

5 Rudolf Carnap's theory of extension and intension: Relying on possible worlds

Since Russell's project was idiosyncratically connected with a sense-data theory it was for the great majority of scientists not acceptable as a purely extensional project. The extensional semantics had to wait until Davidson used Tarski's theory of truth as a framework to characterize a new extensional semantics. Meanwhile it was Rudolf Carnap who introduced the logic of extensional and intensional meanings to modernize Frege's twofold distinction of semantics. The central progress was made by introducing the idea of possible worlds into logics and semantics: The actual world is constituted by a combination of states of affaires which are constituted by objects (properties, relations etc.). If at least one state of affairs is changed we speak of a new possible world. If the world consists of basic elements which constitute states of affaires then the possible combinations of these elements allow us to characterize all possible states of affaires. Thereby we can characterize all possible worlds since a possible world can be characterized by a class of states of affaires that is realized in this world. Using this new instrument of possible worlds Carnap introduces a systematic theory of intension. His notion of intension should substitute Frege's notion of sense and thereby account for the informational content of a sentence. His notion of extension is closely connected to Frege's notion of reference: The extension of a singular term is the object referred to by the use of the term, the extension of a predicate is the property referred to and the extension of a complete assertive sentence is its truth-value. The intension which has to account for the informational content is characterized as a function from possible worlds to the relevant extensions. In the case of a singular term the intension is a function from possible worlds (p.w.) to the object referred to in the relevant possible world. In the same line you receive the intension of predicates (as function from p.w. to sets or n-tuples) and of sentences (as functions from p.w. to truth-values) as shown in Tab. 10.5.

Tab. 10.5: Carnap's semantics of possible worlds

	Extension	Intension
singular terms	objects	individual concepts
predicates	sets of objects and n-tuples of objects	properties
sentences	truth-values	propositions

A principle limitation of a semantic of possible worlds is that you cannot account for so-called hyperintensional phenomena, i.e. one cannot distinguish the meaning of two sentences which are necessarily true (e.g. two different mathematical claims) because they are simply characterized by the same intension (matching each p.w. onto the value "true").

6 Willard V. O. Quine: Logic, existence and propositional attitudes

How should we relate quantifiers with our ontology? Quine (1953) is famous for his slogan "To be is to be the value of a bound variable". Quantifiers "there is (at least) an x ($\exists x$)", "for all x ($\forall x$)" are the heart of modern predicate logic which was already introduced by Frege (s. above). For Quine the structure of the language determines the structure of the world: If the language which is necessary to receive the best available complete description of the world contains several existential and universal quantifications then these quantifications at the same time determine the objects, properties etc. we have to presuppose. Logic, language and ontology are essentially connected according to this view. Although Quine's special views about connecting logic, language and world are very controversial nowadays the core of the idea of combining quantificational and ontological claims is widely accepted.

Another problem that is essentially inspired by the development of logic is the analysis of propositional attitude ascriptions. Quine established the following standard story:

There is a certain man in a brown hat whom Ralph has glimpsed several times under questionable circumstances on which we need not enter here; suffice it to say that Ralph suspects he is a spy. Also there is a gray-haired man, vaguely known to Ralph as rather a pillar of the community, whom Ralph is not aware of having seen except once at the beach. Now Ralph does not know it, but the men are one and the same. Can we say of this man (Bernard J. Ortcutt, to give him a name) that Ralph believes him to be a spy? If so, we find ourselves accepting a conjunction of the type:

(9) w sincerely denies '.....' . w believes that .....

as true, with one and the same sentence in both blanks. For, Ralph is ready enough to say, in all sincerity, 'Bernard J. Ortcutt is no spy.' If, on the other hand, with a view to disallowing situations of the type (9), we claim simultaneously that

(10) Ralph believes that the man in the brown hat is a spy.

(11) Ralph does not believe that the man seen at the beach is a spy.

then we cease to affirm any relationship between Ralph and any man at all.[...] 'believes that' becomes, in a word, referentially opaque.

(Quine 1956: 179, examples renumbered)

In line with Russell, Quine starts to analyze the cognitive situation of Ralph by distinguishing two readings of the sentence

(12) Ralph believes that someone is a spy.

namely:

(13) Ralph believes $[\exists x(x \text{ is a spy})]$

(14) $\exists x(\text{Ralph believes } [x \text{ is a spy}])$

Quine calls (13) the notional and (14) the relational reading of the original sentence which is at the first glance parallel to the traditional distinction between *de dicto* (13) and *de re* (14) reading. But he shows that the difference of these two readings is not sufficient to account for Ralph's epistemic situation as characterized with the sentences (10) and (11). Intuitively Ralph has a *de re* reading in both cases, one of the man on the beach and the other of a person wearing a brown hat. The transformation into *de re* readings leads to:

(15) $\exists x(\text{Ralph believes } [x \text{ is a spy}])$ (out of (10))

(16) ∃x(Ralph does not believe [x is a spy]) (out of (11))

Since both extensional quantifications are about the same object, we receive the combined sentence which explicitly attributes contradictory beliefs to Ralph:

(17) ∃x(Ralph believes [x is a spy] ∧ Ralph does not believe [x is a spy])

To avoid this unacceptable consequence Quine suggests that the ambiguity of the belief sentences cannot be accounted for by a distinction of the scopus of the quantifier (leading to *de re* and *de dicto* readings) but by a systematic ambiguity of the belief predicate: He suggests to distinguish a two-place predicate "Believe^2 (subject, proposition)" and a three-place predicate "believe^3 (subject, object-of-belief, property)".

(18) Believe^2 (Ralph, that the man with the brown hat is a spy)

(19) believe^3 (Ralph, the man with the brown hat, spy-being)

This distinction is the basis for Quine's further famous claim: We are not allowed to quantify into propositional attitudes (i.e. implying (14) from (18)): if we have interpreted a sentence such that the 'believe' predicate is used intensionally (as a two-place predicate) then we cannot ignore that and we are not allowed to change the reading to the sentence into one using a three-place predicate. We are not allowed to change from a notional reading (18) into a relational reading (19) and vice versa. This line of strategy was further improved e.g. by Kaplan (1969) and Loar (1972). It definitely made clear that we cannot always understand the belief expressed by a belief sentence simply as a relation between a subject and a proposition. Sometimes it has to be understood differently. Quine's consequence is a systematic ambiguity of the predicate "believe". This is problematic since it leads also to four-place, five-place predicates etc. (Haas-Spohn 1989: 66): for each singular term which is used in the scopus of the belief ascription we have to distinguish a notional and a relational reading. Therefore Cresswell & von Stechow (1982) suggested an alternative view which only needs to presuppose a two-place predicate "believe" but therefore changes the representation of a proposition: A proposition is not completely characterized by a set of possible worlds (according to which the relevant state of affaires is true) but in addition by a structure of the components of the proposition. Structured propositions are the alternative to a simple possible world semantics to account for propositional attitude ascriptions.

7 Necessity and direct reference: The two-dimensional semantics

The development of modal logic essentially put forward by Saul A. Kripke had strongly influenced the semantical theories. The basic intuition the modal logic started with is rather straightforward: Each entity is necessarily identical with itself (and necessarily different from anything else). Kripke (1972) shows that there are sentences which express a necessary truth but nevertheless are *a posteriori*: "Mark Twain is identical with Samuel Clemens". Since "Samuel Clemens" is the civil name of Mark Twain the sentence expresses a self-identity but it is not known *a priori* since knowing that both names refer to the same object is not part of standard linguistic knowledge. There are also sentences which express contingent facts but which can be known to be true a priori, e.g. "I am speaking now". If I utter the sentence it is *a priori* graspable that it is true but it is not a necessary truth since otherwise I would be a necessary speaker at this timepoint (but of course I could have been silent). To account for the new distinction between epistemic dimension of *a priori/a posteriori* and the metaphysical dimension of necessary/contingent Kripke introduced the theory of direct reference of proper names and Kaplan (1979/1989) introduced the two-dimensional semantics. Since Kaplan's theory of characters is nowadays a standard framework to account for names and indexicals we shortly introduce the core idea: We have to distinguish the utterance context which determines a proposition which is expressed by uttering a sentence and the circumstance of evaluation which is the relevant possible world according to which this proposition will be evaluated as true or false. We can illustrate this two-step approach as in Fig. 10.2:

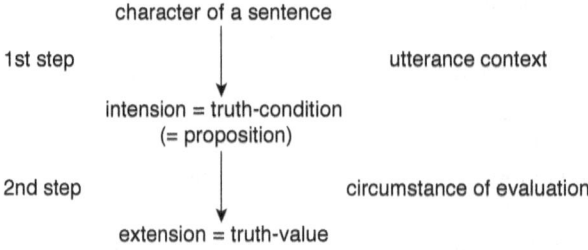

Fig. 10.2: Two-dimensional semantics

A character of a sentence is a function from possible utterance contexts to truth-conditions (propositions) and these truth-conditions are then evaluated relative to the circumstances of evaluation. Especially in the cases of indexicals we can demonstrate the two-dimensional semantics: Let us investigate the sentence

"I am a philosopher" according to three different utterance contexts w_0, w_1 und w_2 while in each world there is a different speaker: in w_0 Cicero is the speaker of the utterance, in w_1 Caesar and in w_2 Augustus. Furthermore it is in w_0 the case that Cicero is a philosopher while Caesar and Augustus are not. In w_1 Caesar and Augustus are philosophers while Cicero isn't. In w_2 no one is a philosopher (poor world!). The three worlds function both as utterance contexts and as circumstances of evaluation but of course different facts are relevant in the two different functions. Now the utterance contexts are represented veritically while the circumstances of evaluation are represented horizontally. Then the sentence "I am a philosopher" receives the character shown in Tab. 10.6.

Tab. 10.6: Character of "I am a philosopher"

Utterance Contexts	Circumstances of evaluation			Truth conditions
	w_0	w_1	w_2	
w_0	w	f	f	⟨Cicero; being a philosopher⟩
w_1	f	w	f	⟨Caesar; being a philosopher⟩
w_2	f	w	f	⟨Augustus; being a philosopher⟩

Each line represents the proposition that is determined by the sentence relative to the utterance contexts and this proposition receives a truth-value for each circumstance of evaluation. The character of the sentences has in principle to be represented for all possible worlds not only for the three ones selected above. This instrument of a "character" of a sentence is useable for all expressions of a natural language. Such it is a principle improvement and enlargement in the formal semantics that contains Carnap's theory of intensions as a special case.

8 Montague-Semantics: Compositionality revisited

Frege claimed in his principle of compositonality that the meaning of a complex expression is a function of the meanings of the expression parts and their way of composition (see section 3.). He regarded every complex expression as composed of a saturated part and a non-saturated part. The semantic counterparts are objects and functions. Frege transfers the syntactic notion of an expression which needs some complement to be a complete and well-formed expression to the semantic realm: Functions are regarded as incomplete and non-saturated. This leads him to the ontological view that functions are not "objects" ("Gegenstände").

This is Frege's term for any entitity that can be a value of a meaning function mapping expressions to their extensions. Functions, however, can be reified as "Werthverläufe" (courses-of-values), e.g. by combining their expressions with the expression *the function*, but in Frege's ontology, the "Werthverläufe" are distinct from the functions themselves.

Successors of Frege did not follow him in this ontological respect of his semantics. In Tarskian semantics one-place predicates are usually mapped to sets of individuals, two-place predicates to sets of pairs of individuals etc. N-place functions are regarded as special kinds of (n-1)-place relations. This approach allowed to make explicit the meaning of Frege's non-saturated expressions and to give a precise compositional account of the meanings of expressions of predicate logic in form of a recursive definition. But for every type of composition, like connecting formulae, applying a predicate to its arguments, or prefixing a quantifier to a formula, distinct forms of meaning composition were needed.

The notion of compositionality could be radically simplified by two developments: The application of type theory and lambda abstraction. Type theory goes back to Russell and was developed to avoid paradoxical notions as sets not containing themselves, see above sec. 4. There are a lot of versions of type theory, but in natural language semantics usually a variant is used which starts with a number of basic types, e.g. the type of objects (entities) e and the type of truth values t for an extensional language, and provides a type of functions $\langle T_1, T_2 \rangle$ for every type T_1 and every type T_2, i.e. the type of functions from entities of type T_1 to entities of type T_2. Sometimes the set of types is extended to types composed of more than two types. But any such system can easily be reduced to this binary system. Predicates can now be viewed as expressions of type $\langle e, t \rangle$, i.e. as functions from objects to truth values, because they yield a true sentence if an argument is filled in that refers to an instance of the predicate, otherwise they yield a false sentence. That just means that we take the characteristic function of the predicate extension as its meaning. A characteristic function of a set maps its members to the truth value true, its non-members to false.

In the same sense the negation operator is of type $\langle t, t \rangle$, i.e. a function from a truth-value to a truth-value (namely to the opposite one); binary sentence connectives are of type $\langle t, \langle t, t \rangle \rangle$, i.e. a function taking the first argument and yielding a function which takes the second argument and then results in a truth value.

Frege had already recognized that first-order quantifiers (as the existential quantifier *something*) are just second-order predicates, i.e. predicates applicable to first-order predicates. The application of an existential quantifier to a one-place first-order predicate is true if the predicate is non-empty. Therefore the existential quantifier can be regarded as a second-order predicate which has non-empty first-order predicates as instances, it is of type $\langle \langle e, t \rangle, t \rangle$. The semantics of the universal quantifier is analoguous: It yields the truth value true for a first-order predicate which has the whole universe of discourse as its extension.

A type problem arises with this view for predicates of arity greater than one: Their type does not fit to the quantifier. The predicate *love*, e.g. is of type ⟨e, ⟨e, t⟩⟩ because if we add one object as an argument we receive a one-place predicate as introduced above. In the sentence

(20) Everybody loves someone.

one of the two quantifiers has to be composed with *love* in a compositional approach. Let us assume *someone* is this quantifier. Then its meaning of type ⟨⟨e, t⟩, t⟩ has to be applied to the meaning of *love*, leading to a type clash, because the quantifier needs a type ⟨e, t⟩ as its argument while the predicate *love* is of a different type. Analoguous problems arise for complex formulae. How can the meaning of the two-place predicate love be transformed into the type required?

The type theory needs an extension by the introduction of a lambda-operator, borrowed from Alonzo Church's lambda calculus which was developed in Church (1936). The lambda operator is used to transform a type t expression into an expression of ⟨T_1, t⟩ depending on the variable type T_1. Let e.g. x be a variable of type e and P be of type t, then $\lambda x[P]$ has type ⟨e, t⟩, i.e. is a one-place first-order predicate. If we consider *love* as a two-place first-order predicate and love(x, y) as an expression of type t with two free variables, then $\lambda x[\text{love}(x, y)]$ is an expression of type ⟨e, t⟩. This is the type required by the quantifier. The variable x is bound to the lambda operator and y is free in this expression. If we now take *someone* as a first-order quantifier, which has type ⟨⟨e, t⟩, t⟩, then someone($\lambda x[\text{love}(x, y)]$) is an expression of type t again with free variable y. This can be made a predicate of type ⟨e, t⟩ by using the same procedure again: $\lambda y[\text{someone}(\lambda x[\text{love}(x, y)])]$, which can be used as an argument of a further quantifier *everybody*. We receive the following new analysis of (20):

(21) everybody($\lambda y[\text{someone}(\lambda x[\text{love}(x, y)])]$)

The semantics of a lambda expression $\lambda x[P]$ is defined as the characteristic function which yields *true* for all arguments which would make P true, if they were taken as assignments to x, false for the others. With this semantics we get the following logical equivalences which we used implicitly in the above formalizations:

α-CONVERSION

(22) $\lambda x[P] \equiv \lambda y[P[y/x]]$

where $P[y/x]$ is the same as P besides the fact that all occurences of x which are free in P are changed into y. α-conversion is just a formal renaming of variables.

β-REDUCTION

(23) $\lambda x[P](a) \equiv P[a/x]$

where $P[a/x]$ is the same as P besides the fact that all occurences of x which are free in P are changed into a. This, however, may be false in some non-extensional contexts, if a is a non-rigid designator. If we take

(24) Ralph believes that x is a spy.

as P then the *de re* reading of (10) is $\lambda x[P](a)$. a is interpreted outside the non-extensional context of P and its factual denotation is taken as its extension. $P[a/x]$, however, is the *de dicto* reading because a is interpreted within the belief-context. For intensional contexts these differences are treated in the intensional theory of types, see section 10 below.

η-CONVERSION

(25) $\lambda x[P(x)] \equiv P$

where x does not occur as a free variable in P. η-conversion is needed for the conversion between atomic predicates and λ-expressions.

In this type-theoretical view, a lot of other linguistic expression types can easily be integrated. Adjectives, which are applied to nouns of type $\langle e, t \rangle$, can be seen as type $\langle \langle e, t \rangle, \langle e, t \rangle \rangle$, e.g. *tasty* is a modifier which takes predicates, expressed by nouns, like *apple* and yields new predicates, like *tasty apple*.

Modifiers in general, like adverbs, prepositional phrases and relative and adverbial clauses, are regarded as type $\langle T_1, T_1 \rangle$, because they modify the meaning of their argument, but this results in an expression of the same type. This also mirrors that modifiers can be applied in an iterated manner, as *red tasty apple*, where *red* further modifies the predicate *tasty apple*.

The compositionality of meaning got a very strict interpretation in Montague's work. The type-theoretic semantics was accompanied by a syntactic formalism whose expression categories could be directly mapped onto semantic types, called categorial grammar, which was based on ideas by Kasimierz Ajdukiewicz in the mid-1930s and Yehoshua Bar-Hillel (1953).

Complex semantic types, i.e. semantic types needing some complemetation, like $\langle T_1, T_2 \rangle$ for some types T_1 and T_2, have their counterpart in complex syntactic categories like S_2/S_1 and $S_2\backslash S_1$ which need a complementation by S_1 to yield the syntactic category S_2. Given a syntactic category S_2/S_1 a complement of type S_1 has to be added to the right, in case of $S_2\backslash S_1$ to the left. Let e.g. N be the syntactic category of a noun and DP be the category of a determiner phrase, then DP/N is the category of the determiner in the examples above. The interaction of Montague's syntactic and semantic conception results in the requirement that the meaning of a complex expression can be recursively decomposed into function-argument-pairs which are always expressed by syntactically immediately adjacent constituents.

Categorial grammars describe the same class of languages as context free grammars, and they are subject to the same problems when applied to natural languages. Although most phenomena in natural languages can in principle be represented by a context free grammar, and therefore by a categorial grammar, too, both formalisms lead to quite unintuitive descriptions when applied to a realistic fragment of natural language. Especially with regard to semantic compositionality discontinous constituents require a quite unintuitive multiplication of categories.

The type theoretic view of nouns and noun phrases has also consequences for the semantic concept of quantifying expressions. Determiners like *all* or *two* as parts of determiner phrases will have to be assigned a suitable type of meaning.

9 Generalized quantifiers

As mentioned above, already Frege regarded quantifiers as second- or higher-order predicates. But Frege himself did not go the step from this insight to the consideration of other quantifiers than the universal and the existential ones. Without being aware of Frege's concept of quantifiers the generalized view on quantifiers by Mostowski (1957) and Lindström (1966) pathed the way to a generalized theory of quantifiers in linguistics around 1980. This allowed for a proper treatment of syntactically first-order quantifying expressions whose semantics was not expressible in first-order logic. e.g. *most*.

Furthermore, now, noun phrases which had no mere anaphoric function, could be interpreted as a quantifier, consisting of the determiner, e.g. *all*, which specifies the basic quantifier semantics, and the noun, e.g. *women*, or a noun-like expression which restricts the quantification. The determiner is a function of type $\langle\langle e, t\rangle, \langle\langle e, t\rangle, t\rangle\rangle$ taking the restrictor as argument and resulting in a generalized quantifier, e.g. all(woman) for the noun phrase *all women*. This generalized quantifier is (the characteristic function of) a second-order predicate which has all (charateristic functions of) first-order predicates as its instances which are true for all women. As the determiner designates the principle function in such a noun phrase some linguists prefer the term *determiner phrase*.

Generalized quantifiers can be studied with respect to their monotonicity properties. Let Q be a generalized quantifier and $Q(P)$ be true. Then it can be the case – depending on Q's semantics – that $Q(P')$ is always true if

(A) the extension of P' is a subset of the extension of P or
(B) the extension of P is a subset of the extension of P'

In the first case, we call Q *monotone decreasing* or *downward entailing*, in case (B) *monotone increasing* or *upward entailing*. An example of the first quantifier type is *no women*, an example of the second type *(at least) two women*, cf. e.g. the entailment relations between sentences the following. (26a) entails (26b), and (27a) entails (27b).

(26) a. At least two women worked as extremely successful CEOs.
b. At least two women worked as CEOs.

(27) a. No women worked as CEOs.
b. No women worked as extremely successful CEOs.

While quantifiers also expressible in first-order logic, like those in the examples above, always show one of the monotonicity properties, there are other generalized quantifiers which do not. Numerical expressions providing a lower and an upper bound for a quantity, like exact numbers, are examples for non-monotonic quantifiers. If we replace *at least two women* with *exactly two women* in the examples above, the entailment relations between the sentences disappear.

Mononicity of quantifiers seems to play an important role in natural language although not all quantifiers are monotonic themselves. But it is claimed that all simple quantifiers, i.e. one-word quantifiers or quantifiers of the form determiner + noun, are expressible as conjunctions of monotonic quantifiers. E.g. *exactly three Ps* is equivalent to the conjunction *at least three Ps and no more than three Ps*, the first conjunct (at least three Ps) being upward monotonic and the latter (no more than three Ps) being downward monotonic. There are, of course, quantifiers not bearing this property, and they are expressible in natural language, cf. *an even number of Ps*, but there does not seem to be any natural language which reserves a simple lexical item for such a purpose. The theory of generalized quantifiers therefore raises empirical questions about language universals.

Similar considerations on entailment conditions can be applied to the first argument of the determiner. For some determiners D it might be the case that $D(R)(P)$ entails $D(R')(P)$ always if

(A') the extension of R' is a subset of the extension of R or
(B') the extension of R is a subset of the extension of R'.

In the second case the determiner is called persistent, while in the first it is called antipersistent. Consider the entailment relations between the sentences below. Here, (28a) entails (28b), and (29a) entails (29b).

(28) a. Some extremely successful female CEOs smoke.
     b. Some female CEOs smoke.

(29) a. All female CEOs smoke.
     b. All extremely successfull female CEOs smoke.

It is easy to see that *some* is persistent while *all* is antipersistent. All combinations of monotonicity and persistence/antipersistence are realized in natural languages. Tab. 10.7 shows some examples. Note that the quantifiers of the square of opposition are part of this scheme.

Tab. 10.7: Monotonicity and (anti-)persistence of quantifiers

	upward monotonic	downward monotonic
antipersistent	all, every	no, at most three
persistent	some, (at least) three	not all

And the relations of being contradictory and (sub-)contrary (see sec. 2) in the square of oppositions are mirrored by negations of the whole determiner-governed sentence or the second argument: $\neg D(R, P)$ is contradictory to $D(R, P)$, while $D(R, \neg P)$ is (sub-)contrary to $D(R, P)$ (we use $\neg P$ as short for $\lambda x[\neg P(x)]$.).

Analyzing quantified expressions as structures consisting of a determiner, a restrictor and a quantifier scope provides us with a relational view of quantifiers. The determiner type $\langle\langle e, t\rangle, \langle\langle e, t\rangle, t\rangle\rangle$ is that of a second-order two-place relation. Besides the logical properties of the argument positions discussed above, there are a number of interesting properties regarding the relation of the two arguments. One of them is conservativity. A determiner is conservative iff it is always the case that

$$D(R, P) \equiv D(R, P \wedge R)$$

(where we use $P \wedge R$ as the conjunction of the predicates P and R, more precisely $\lambda x\, [P(x) \wedge R(x)]$). It is quite evident that determiners in general fulfill this condition. E.g. from

(30) Most CEOs are incompetent.

follows

(31) Most CEOs are incompetent CEOs.

But are really all determiners conservative? *Only* is an apparent counterexample:

(32) Only CEOs are incompetent.

cannot be paraphrased as

(33) Only CEOs are incompetent CEOs.

(32) being contingent, (33) tautological. But besides this observation there are syntactical reasons to doubt the classification of *only* as a determiner. Other quantifying items whose conservativity is questioned are e.g. *many* and *few*.

The foundation for the generalization of quantifiers was in principle laid in Montague's work, but he himself did not refer to other quantifiers than the classical existential and universal quantifier. The theory of generalized quantifiers was recognized in linguistics in the earley 1980s, cf. Barwise & Cooper (1980) and article 4 [Semantics: Noun Phrases and Verb Phrases] (Keenan) *Quantifiers*.

10 Intensional theory of types

Montague developed his semantics as an intensional semantics, taking into account the non-extensional aspects of natural languages as alethic-modal, temporal and deontic operators. The intensional theory of types builds on Carnap's concept of intensions as functions from possible worlds to extensions. These functions are built into the type system by adding a new functional type from possible worlds s to the other types. Type s differs from the other types insofar as there are no expressions – constants or variables – directly denoting objects of this type, i.e. no specific possible worlds besides the contextually given current one can be addressed.

The difference between an extensional sentential operator like negation and an intensional like *necessarily* is reflected by their respective types: The meaning of the negation operator has type ⟨t, t⟩ while *necessarily* needs ⟨⟨s, t⟩, t⟩ because not only the truth value of an argument *p* in the current world has impact on the truth value of *necessarily p*, but also the truth values in the alternative worlds.

In Montague (1973) he does not directly define a model-theoretic mapping for expressions of English, although this should be feasible in principle, but he gives a translation of English expressions into a logical language. Besides the usual ingredients of modal predicate logic, the lambda operator as well as variables and constants of the various types, he introduces the intensor ^ and extensor ˅ of type ⟨T, ⟨s, T⟩⟩ and ⟨⟨s, T⟩, T⟩ respectively for arbitrary types T. ^ transforms a given meaning into a Carnapian intension, i.e. ^*a* means the function from possible worlds to *a*'s extensions in these worlds. In contrast, if *b* means an intension then ˅*b* refers to the extension in the current world. The intensor is used if a usually extensionally interpreted expression is used in an intensional context. E.g. *a unicorn* and *a centaur* mean generalized quantifiers, say Q_1 and Q_2, which extensionally are false for any argument. This may be different for other possible worlds. Therefore the intensions ^Q_1 and ^Q_2 may differ. This accounts for the fact that e.g. the intensional verb *seek* applied to ^Q_1 and ^Q_2 may result in different values, as

(34) John seeks a unicorn.

may be true while

(35) John seeks a centaur.

may be false at the same time. With the intensional extension of type logic, natural language semantics gets a powerful tool to account for the interaction of intensions and extensions in compositional semantics.

The same machinery which is applicable in alethic modal logic – i.e. the logic of possibility and necessity – is transferable to other branches of intensional semantics, as e.g. the semantics of tense and temporal expressions, cf. article 13 [Semantics: Noun Phrases and Verb Phrases] (Ogihara) *Tense*.

11 Dynamic logic

Natural language expresssions not only refer to time-dependent situations, but their interpretation also is dependent on time-dependent contexts. A preceding sentence may introduce referents for later anaphoric expressions (cf. article see article 12 [Semantics: Theories] (Dekker) *Dynamic semantics* and article 12 [Semantics: Interfaces] (Zimmermann) *Context dependency*).

(36) A man walks in the park. He whistles.

Among the anaphoric expressions are – of course – nominal anaphora, like pronouns and definite descriptions. Antecedents are typically indefinite noun phrases. But possible antecedents can also be introduced in a less obvious way, e.g. by propositions expressing events. The event time can then be referenced by a temporal anaphora like *at the same time*.

(37) The CEO lighted her cigarette. At the same time the health manager came in.

The anaphora *at the same time* refers to the time when the event described in the first proposition happens.

Anaphorical relations are not necessarily realized by overt expressions, they can be implicit, too, or they may be indicated by morphological means, e.g. by the choice of a grammatical tense. Anaphora poses a problem for compositional approaches to semantics based on predicate or type logic. (36) can be formalized by an expression headed by an existential quantifier like

(38) $\exists x[\text{man}(x) \wedge \text{w-i-t-p}(x) \wedge \text{whistle}(x)]$

But the man mentioned here can be referred to anywhere in the following discourse. Therefore the quantifier scope cannot be closed at any particular position in the discourse.

The semantics of anaphora, however, is not just a matter of the scope of existential quantifiers. Expressions, like indefinite noun phrases, usually meaning an existential quantifier can in certain contexts introduce discourse referents with a universal reading. This fact was described by Geach (1962).

(39) If a farmer owns a donkey he feeds it.

means

(40) $\forall x[\forall y[\text{farmer}(x) \wedge \text{donkey}(y) \wedge \text{own}(x, y) \rightarrow \text{feed}(x, y)]]$

This kind of anaphora is a further challenge for compositional semantics as it has to deal with the fact that an expression which is usually interpreted existentially gets a universal reading here. The challenge is addressed by dynamic semantics. Pre-compositional versions were developed independently by Hans Kamp and Irene Heim as Discourse Representation Theory and File Change Semantics respectively (cf. article 11 [Semantics: Theories] (Kamp & Reyle) *Discourse Representation Theory*). In both approaches structures representing the truth-conditional content of the parts of a discourse as well as the entities which are addressable anaphorically are manipulated by the meaning of discourse constituents. The answer to the question how the meaning of a discourse constituent is to be construed is simply: as a function from given discourse representing structures to new structures of the same type, cf. Muskens (1996).

This view is made explicit in dynamic logics. This kind of logics was developed in the 1970er by David Harel and others, cf. Harel (2000), and has been primarily used for the formal interpretation of procedural programming languages.

(41) $\langle a \rangle q$

means that statement a possibly leads to a state where q is true, while

(42) $[a]q$

means that statement a necessarily leads to a state where q is true. Regarding states as possible worlds we arrive at a modal logic with as many modalities as there are (equivalence classes of) statements a, for a recursive language usually infinitely many. For many purposes the consideration can be constrained to such modalities where from each state exactly one successor state is accessible. For such modalities with functional accessibility relation the weak ($\langle ... \rangle$) and the strong operator ($[...]$) collapse semantically into one operator. If we further agree that

(43) $s_1 \wedge [a]s_2$

can be rewritten as

(44) $s_1[a]s_2$

then this notation has the intuitive reading that state s_1 is mapped by the meaning of a into s_2. A simplistic application is the following: Assume that s_1 is a characterization of the knowledge state of a recipient before receiving the information given by assertion a. Then s_2 is a characterization of the knowledge state of the recipient after being informed. If you identify knowledge states with those sets of possible worlds which are consistent with the current knowledge, and if you consider s_1 and s_2 as descriptions of sets W_1 and W_2 of possible worlds, then they differ in exactly that respect that W_2 is the intersection of W_1 and the set W_a of possible worlds in which a is true, i.e. $W_2 = W_1 \cap W_a$.

The notion of an informative utterance a can be defined by the condition that $W_2 \neq W_1$. And in order to be consistent with the previous context, it must be true that $W_2 \neq \emptyset$. The treatment of discourse states or contexts in dynamic logics is not limited to truth-conditionally characterizable knowledge. In principle any kind of linguistic context parameters can be part of the states, among these the anaphorically accessible antecedents of a sentence.

In their Dynamic Predicate Logic, as developed in Groenendijk & Stokhof (1991), Groenendijk and Stokhof model the anaphoric phenomena accounted for in Kamp's Discourse Representation Theory and Heim's File Change Semantics in a fully compositional fashion. This is mainly achieved by a dynamic interpretation of the existential quantifier:

(45) $\exists x[P(x)]$

is semantically characterized by the usual truth conditions but has the additional effect that free occurrences of the variable x have to be kept assigned to the same object in subsequent expressions which are connected appropriately. The dynamic effect is limited by the scopes of certain operators like the universal quantifier, negation, disjunction, and implication. So x is bound to the same object ouside the syntactic scope of the existential quantifier as in

(46) $\exists x[\text{man}(x) \wedge \text{w-i-t-p}(x)] \wedge \text{whistle}(x)$

although the syntactic scope of the existential quantifier ends after w-i-t-p(x). This propsosition is true, only if there is an object x which verifies all three predicates man, w-i-t-p, and whistle.

If we characterize the dynamic dimension, the sentences (36) and (39) can be formalized in Dynamic Predicate Logic as

(47) $\exists x[\text{man}(x) \wedge \text{w-i-t-p}(x)] \wedge \text{whistle}(x)$

and

(48) $\exists x[\text{farmer}(x) \wedge \exists y[\text{donkey}(y) \wedge \text{own}(x, y)]] \rightarrow \text{feed}(x, y)$

respectively. It can easily be seen, how the usual meanings of the discourse sentences

(49) A man walks in the park.

and

(50) A farmer has a donkey.

enter into the composed meaning of the discourse without any changes. In order to get the intended truth conditions for implications, it is required as truth condition that the second clause can be verified for any assigment to x verifying the first clause.

Putting together the filtering effect of propositions on possible worlds and the modifying effect on assignment functions, we can consider propositions in Dynamic Predicate Logic as functions on sets of world-assigment pairs. The empty context can be characterized by the Cartesian product of the set of possible worlds and the set of assigments. Each proposition of a discourse filters out certain world-assignment pairs. In some respects Dynamic Predicate Logic deviates from standard dynamic logic approaches, as Groenendijk & Stokhof (1991, sec. 4.3) point out, but it still can be seen as a special case of a logic in this framework.

The dynamic view of semantics can be used to model other contextual dependencies than just anaphora. Groenendijk (1999) shows another application in the Logic of Interrogation. Questions add felicity conditions for a subsequent answer to the discourse context. To a great extent, these conditions can be characterized semantically. In the Logic of Interrogation the effect of a question is understood as a partitioning of the current set of possible worlds. Each partition stands for some alternative exhaustive answer, e.g. a yes-no question partitions the set of possible worlds into one subset consistent with the positive answer and a complementary subset compatible with the negative answer.

Let us e.g. take the question (51).

(51) Does a man walk in the park?

According to the formalism of Groenendijk (1999) (51) can be formalized as (52).

(52) $?\exists x\, [\text{man}(x) \wedge \text{w-i-t-p}(x)]$

(52) partitions the set of possible worlds in two subsets W^+ and W^-, such that (53) is true for every world in W^+ and false for every world in its complement subset W^-. An appropriate answer selects exactly one of these subsets.

(53) $\exists x[\text{man}(x) \wedge \text{w-i-t-p}(x)]$

Wh-questions like (54) partition the sets of possible worlds in more partitions than yes-no questions.

(54) Who walks in the park?

Each partition corresponds to an exhaustive answer, which provides the full information who walks in the park and who does not. An assertion answers the question partially if it eliminates at least one partition. If it furthermore eliminates all partitions but one, it answers the question exhaustively.

This chapter has given a short overview how logic provided the tools for treating linguistic phenomena. Each logical system has its characteristic strength and its limits. The limits of a logical system sometimes inspired the development of new formal tools (e.g. the step from Aristotelian syllogistic to modern predicate logic) which inspired a new semantics. Sometimes a change in the focus of linguistic phenomena inspired a systematic search for new logical tools (e.g. modal logic) or a reinterpretation of already available logical tools (e.g. dynamic logic). We hope to have illustrated the main developments of the bi-directional influences of logical systems and semantics.

12 References

Abaelardus, Petrus 1956. *Dialectica*. Ed. L.M. de Rijk. Assen: van Gorcum.
Almog, Joseph, John Perry & Howard Wettstein (eds.) 1989. *Themes from Kaplan*. Oxford: Oxford University Press.
Aristoteles 1992. *Analytica priora. Die Lehre vom Schluß oder erste Analytik*. Ed. E. Rolfes. Hamburg: Meiner.
Bar-Hillel, Yehoshua 1953. A quasi-arithmetical notation for syntactic description. *Language* 29, 47–58.
Barwise, Jon & Robin Cooper 1980. Generalized quantifiers and natural language. *Linguistics & Philosophy* 4, 159–218.
Carnap, Rudolf 1947. *Meaning and Necessity*. Chicago, IL: The University of Chicago Press.
Church, Alonzo 1936. An unsolvable problem of elementary number theory. *American Journal of Mathematics* 58, 354–363.
Cresswell, Maxwell & Arnim von Stechow 1982. De re belief generalized. *Linguistics & Philosophy* 5, 503–535.
Davidson, Donald 1967. Truth and meaning. *Synthesis* 17, 304–323.
Frege, Gottlob 1966. *Grundgesetze der Arithmetik*. Hildesheim: Olms.
Frege, Gottlob 1977. *Begriffsschrift und andere Aufsätze*. Ed. I. Angelelli. Darmstadt: Wissenschaftliche Buchgesellschaft.
Frege, Gottlob 1988. *Die Grundlagen der Arithmetik. Eine logisch mathematische Untersuchung über den Begriff der Zahl*. Ed. Chr. Thiel. Hamburg: Meiner.

Frege, Gottlob 1994. *Funktion, Begriff, Bedeutung. Fünf logische Studien.* Göttingen: Vandenhoeck & Ruprecht.
Geach, Peter 1962. *Reference and Generality: An Examination of Some Medieval and Modern Theories.* Ithaca, NY: Cornell University Press.
Gödel, Kurt 1930. Die Vollständigkeit der Axiome des logischen Funktionenkalküls. *Monatshefte für Mathematik und Physik* 37, 349–360.
Gödel, Kurt 1931. Über formal unentscheidbare Sätze der Principia Mathematica und verwandter Systeme. *Monatshefte für Mathematik und Physik* 38, 173–198.
Groenendijk, Jeroen 1999. *The Logic of Interrogation.* Research report, ILLC Amsterdam.
Groenendijk, Jeroen & Martin Stokhof 1991. Dynamic Predicate Logic. *Linguistics & Philosophy* 14, 39–100.
Haas-Spohn, Ulrike 1989. Zur Interpretation der Einstellungszuschreibungen. In: E. Falkenberg (ed.). *Wissen, Wahrnehmen, Glauben. Epistemische Ausdrücke und propositionale Einstellungen.* Tübingen: Niemeyer, 50–94.
Harel, David 2000. Dynamic logic. In: D. Gabbay & F. Guenthner (eds.). *Handbook of Philosophical Logic*, vol. II: *Extensions of classical logic*, chap. II.10. Dordrecht: Reidel, 497–604.
Hodges, Wilfried 1991. *Logic.* London: Penguin.
Kaplan, David 1969. Quantifying in. In: D. Davidson & J. Hintikka (eds.). *Words & Objections. Essays on the Work of W.V.O. Quine.* Dordrecht: Reidel, 206–242.
Kaplan, David 1979. On the logic of demonstratives. *Journal of Philosophical Logic* 8, 81–98.
Kaplan, David 1989. Demonstratives. In: J. Almog, J. Perry & H. Wettstein (eds.). *Themes from Kaplan.* Oxford: Oxford University Press, 481–563.
Kripke, Saul 1972. Naming and necessity. In: D. Davidson & G. Harman (eds.). *Semantics of Natural Language.* Dordrecht: Reidel, 253–233 and 763–769.
von Kutschera, Franz 1989. *Gottlob Frege. Eine Einführung in sein Werk.* Berlin: de Gruyter.
Leibniz, Gottfried Wilhelm 1992. *Schriften zur Logik und zur philosophischen Grundlegung von Mathmatik und Naturwissenschaft.* Ed. H. Herring. Darmstadt: Wissenschaftliche Buchgesellschaft.
Lenzen, Wolfgang 1990. *Das System der Leibnizschen Logik.* Berlin: de Gruyter.
Lenzen, Wolfgang 2000. Guilielmi Pacidii Non plus ultra oder: Eine Rekonstruktion des Leibnizschen Plus-Minus-Kalküls. *Philosophiegeschichte und logische Analyse* 3, 71–118.
Lindström, Per 1966. First order predicate logic with generalized quantifiers. *Theoria* 32, 186–195.
Loar, Brian 1972. Reference and propositional attitudes. *The Philosophical Review* 81, 43–62.
Montague, Richard 1973. The proper treatment of quantification in ordinary English. In: J. Hintikka, J. Moravcsik & P. Suppes (eds.). *Approaches to Natural Language.* Dordrecht: Reidel, 221–242. Reprinted in: R. Thomason (ed.). *Formal Philosophy. Selected Papers of Richard Montague.* New Haven, CT: Yale University Press, 1974, 247–270.
Mostowski, Andrzej 1957. On a generalization of quantifiers. *Fundamenta Mathematicae* 44, 12–36.
Muskens, Reinhard 1996. Combining Montague Semantics and Discourse Representation. *Linguistics & Philosophy* 19, 143–186.
Nortmann, Ulrich 1996. *Modale Syllogismen, mögliche Welten, Essentialismus. Eine Analyse der aristotelischen Modallogik.* Berlin: de Gruyter.
Quine, Willard van Orman 1953. *From a Logical Point of View.* Cambridge, MA: Harvard University Press.

Quine, Willard van Orman 1956. Quantifiers and propositional attitudes. *The Journal of Philosophy* 53, 177–187.
Russell, Bertrand 1903. *The Principles of Mathematics*. Cambridge: Cambridge University Press.
Russell, Bertrand 1905. On denoting. *Mind* 14, 479–493.
Russell, Bertrand 1908. Mathematical logic as based on the theory of types. *American Journal of Mathematics* 30, 222–262.
Russell, Bertrand 1910. Knowledge by acquaintance and knowledge by description. *Proceedings of the Aristotelian Society* 11, 108–128.
Russell, Bertrand & Alfred N. Whitehead 1910–1913. *Principia Mathematica*. Cambridge: Cambridge University Press.
Tarski, Alfred 1935. Der Wahrheitsbegriff in den formalisierten Sprachen. *Studia Philosophica* 1, 261–405.
Zalta, Edward 2000. Leibnizian theory of concepts. *Philosophiegeschichte und logische Analyse* 3, 137–183.

Ruth Kempson
11 Formal semantics and representationalism

1 Logic, formal languages, and the grounding of linguistic methodologies —— 274
2 Natural languages as formal languages: Formal semantics —— 281
3 The challenge of context-dependence —— 284
4 Dynamic Semantics —— 286
5 The shift towards proof-theoretic perspectives —— 291
6 Ellipsis: A window on context —— 295
7 Summary —— 302
8 References —— 303

Abstract: This paper shows how formal semantics emerged shortly after the explosion of interest in formally characterising natural language in the fifties, swiftly replacing all advocacy of semantic representations within explanations of natural-language meaning. It then charts how advocacy of such representations has progressively re-emerged in formal semantic characterisations through the need to model the systemic dependency on context of natural language construal. First, the logic concepts on which subsequent debates depend are introduced, as is the formal-semantics (model-theoretic) framework in which meaning in natural language is defined as a reflection of a direct language-world correspondence. The problem of context dependence is then set out which has been the primary motivation for introducing semantic representation, with sketched accounts of pronoun construal relative to context. It is also shown how, in addition to such arguments, proof-theoretic (hence structural) concepts have been increasingly used in semantic modelling of natural languages. Finally, ellipsis is introduced as a novel window on context providing additional evidence for the need to advocate representations in semantic explanation. The paper concludes with reflections on how the goal of modelling the incremental dynamics of natural language interpretation forges a much closer link between competence and performance models than has hitherto been envisaged.

Ruth Kempson, London, United Kingdom

https://doi.org/10.1515/9783110368505-011

1 Logic, formal languages, and the grounding of linguistic methodologies

The meaning of natural-language (NL) expressions, of necessity, is wholly invisible; and one of the few supposedly reliable ways to establish the interpretation of expressions is through patterns of inference. Inference is the relation between two pieces of information such that one can be wholly inferred from the other (if for example I assert that I discussed my analysis with at least two other linguists, then I imply I have an analysis, that I have discussed it with more than one linguist, and that I am myself a linguist). Inference alone is not however sufficient to pinpoint the interpretation potential of NL expressions. Essential to NL interpretation is the pervasive dependence of expressions on context for how they are to be understood, a problem which has been a driving force in the development of formal semantics. This article surveys the emergence of formal semantics following growth of interest in the formal characterisation of NL grammars (Chomsky 1955, Lambek 1958). It introduces logic concepts on which subsequent debates depend and the formal-semantics framework (the formal articulation of what has been called *truth-conditional semantics*), in which NL is claimed to be a logic. It then sets out the problem of context dependence with its apparent need to add a level of semantic representation over and above whatever is needed for syntax, and shows how semanticists have increasingly turned to tools of proof theory (the syntactic mechanisms for defining inference in logic) to project compositionality of content in natural language. Ellipsis data are introduced as an additional basis for evaluating the status of representations specific to characterising NL construal; and the paper concludes with reflections on how modelling the incremental dynamics of the step-by-step way in which information is built up in discourse forges a much closer link between competence and performance models than has hitherto been envisaged.

During the sixties, with emergence of the new Chomskian framework (Chomsky 1965), inquiry into the status of NL semantics within the grammar of a language was inevitable. There were two independent developments: articulation of semantics as part of the broadly Chomskian philosophy (Katz & Fodor 1963, Katz 1972), and Montague's extension of formal-language semantic tools to NL (Thomason (ed.) 1974). The point of departure for both Chomskian and formal semantics paradigms was the inspiration provided by the formal languages of logic, though, as we shall see, they make rather different use of this background.

Logics are defined for the formal study of inference irrespective of subject matter, with individual formal languages defined to reflect specific forms of reasoning, *modal logic* to reflect modal reasoning, *temporal logic* to reflect temporal reasoning, etc. *Predicate logic*, as its name implies, is defined to reflect forms of reasoning that turn on subsentential structure, involving quantification, names, and predicates: it is the logic arguably closest to natural languages. In *predicate logic*, the grammar defines a system for inducing an infinite set of propositional formulae with internal predicate-argument structure over which semantic operations can be defined to yield a compositional account of meaning for these formulae. Syntactic rules involve mappings from (sub)-formulae to (sub)-formulae making essential reference to structural properties; semantic rules assign interpretations to elementary parts of such formulae and then compute interpretations by mapping interpretations onto interpretations from bottom to top ('bottom-up') as dictated by the structures syntactically defined. With co-articulation of syntax and semantics, inference as necessary, truth dependence is then defined syntactically and semantically, the former making reference solely to properties of structure of the formulae in question, the latter solely to truth-values assigned to such formulae (relative to some so-called *model*). The syntactic characterisation of inference is defined by rules which map one propositional structure into another, the interaction of this small set of rules (the *proof rules*) predicting all and only the infinite set of valid inferences. We can use this pattern to define what we mean by *representationalism*, as follows. A *representationalist* account is one that involves essential attribution of structure in the characterisation of the phenomenon under investigation. Any account of natural language which invokes syntactic structure of natural language strings is providing a representationalist account of language. More controversially, representationalist accounts of meaning are those in which the articulation of structure is an integral part of the account of NL interpretation in addition to whatever characterisation is provided of syntactic properties of sentence-strings.

1.1 The Chomskian methodology

In the Chomskian development of a linguistic philosophy for NL grammar, it was the methodology of grammar-writing for these familiar logics which was adapted to the NL case. By analogy, NL grammars were defined as a small number of rules inducing an infinite set of strings, success in characterising a language residing in whether all and only the wellformed sentences of the language are characterised by the given rule set. Grammars were to be evaluated not by data of language use or corpus analysis, but by whether the grammar induces the set of strings judged by a speaker to be grammatical. In this, Chomsky was universally followed: linguists generally agreed that there should be no grounding of grammars directly in evidence from what is involved in producing or parsing a linguistic string. Models of language were logically prior to consideration of performance factors; so data relevant to grammar construction had to be intuitions of grammaticality as made by individuals with capacity in the language. This commitment to complete separation of competence-based grammars from all performance considerations has been the underpinning to almost all linguistic theorising since then, though as we shall see, this assumption is being called into question.

Following the Chomskian methodology, Katz and colleagues set out analogous criteria of adequacy for semantic theories of NL: that they should predict relations between word meaning and sentence meaning as judged by speakers of the language; synonymy for all expressions having the same meaning; entailment (equivalently, inference) for all clausal expressions displaying a (possibly asymmetric) dependence of meaning; ambiguity for expressions with more than one interpretation. The goal was to devise rule specifications that yield these results, with candidate theories evaluated solely by relative success in yielding the requisite set of semantic relations/properties. Much of the focus was on exploring appropriate *semantic representations* in some internalised *language of thought* to assign to words to secure a basis for predicting such entailment relations as *John killed Bill, Bill died*, or *John is a bachelor, John is an unmarried man* (Katz 1972, Fodor 1981, 1983, 1998, Pustejovsky 1995, Jackendoff 2002). There was no detailed mapping defined from such constructs onto the objects/events which the natural language expression might be presumed to depict.

1.2 Language as logic: The formal-semantic methodology

It was Montague and the program of formal semantics that defined a truth-theoretic grounding for natural language interpretation. Montague took as his point of departure both the methodology and formal tools of logic (cf. article 10 [this volume] (Newen & Schröder) *Logic and semantics*). He argued that by extending the syntactic and semantic systems of modal/temporal predicate logic with techniques defined in the lambda calculus, the extra flexibility of natural language could be directly captured, with each individual natural language defined to be a formal language no different in kind from a suitably enriched variant of predicate logic (see Montague 1970 reprinted in Thomason (ed.) 1974). In predicate logic, inference is definable from the strings of the language, with invocation of syntax as an independent level of representation essentially eliminable in being no more than a way of describing semantic combinatorics; and, in applying this concept to natural languages, many formal semanticists adopt similar assumptions (in particular categorial grammar: Morrill 1994). Their theoretical assumptions are thus unlike Chomskian NL grammars in which syntax, hence representations of structure, is central. Since these two paradigms made such distinct use of these formal languages in grounding their NL grammars, an essential background to appreciating the debate is a grasp of predicate logic as a language.

1.3 Predicate logic: Syntax, semantics and proof theory

The remit of predicate logic is to express inference relations that make essential reference to sub-propositional elements such as quantifiers and names, extending propositional logic (with its connectives ∧ ('and'), → ('if-then', the *conditional* connective), ∨ ('or'), ¬ ('not'). The language has a lexicon, syntax and semantics (Gamut 1991). There is a finite stock of primitive expressions, and a small set of operators licensed by the grammar: the propositional connectives and the quantifiers ∀ (*universal*), ∃ (*existential*). Syntactic rules define the properties of these operators, mapping primitive expressions onto progressively more complex expressions; and for each such step, there is a corresponding semantic rule so that meanings of individual expressions can be defined as recursively combining to yield a formal specification of necessary and sufficient truth-conditions for propositional formulae in which they are contained.

There are a number of equivalent ways of defining such semantics. In the Montague system, the semantics is defined with respect to a *model* defined as (i) a set of stipulated individuals as the *domain of discourse*, (ii) appropriate assignment of a *denotation* (equivalently *extension*) for the primitive expressions from that set: individuals from the domain of discourse for names, sets of individuals for one-place predicate expressions, and so on. Semantic rules map these assignments onto denotations for composite expressions. Such denotations are based exclusively on assignments given to their parts and their mode of combination as defined by the syntax, yielding a truth value (True, False) with respect to the model for each propositional formula. There is a restriction on the remit of such semantics. Logics are defined to provide the formal vehicle over which inference independent of subject matter can be defined. Accordingly, model-theoretic semantics for the expressions of predicate logic takes the denotation of terminal expressions as a primitive, hence without explanation: all it provides is a formal way of expressing compositionality for the language, given an assumption of a stipulated language-denotation relation for the elementary expressions. With such semantics, relationships of inference between propositional formulae are definable. There are two co-extensive characterisations of inference. One, more familiar to linguists, is a semantic characterisation (*entailment*). A proposition ϕ entails a distinct proposition ψ if in all models in which ϕ is true ψ is true (explicitly a characterisation in terms of truth-dependence). Synonymy, or equivalence, $\equiv$, is when this relation is two-way. The other characterisation of inference is syntactic, i.e. proof-theoretic, defined as the deducibility of one propositional formula from another using *proof rules*: all such derivations (proofs) involve individual steps that apply strictly in virtue of structural properties of the formulae. Bringing syntax and semantics together, a logic is *sound* if the proof rules derive only inferences that are true in the intended models, and *complete* if it can derive all the true statements according to the models. Thus, in logic, syntax and semantics are necessarily in a tight systematic relation.

These proof rules constitute some minimal set, and it is interaction between them which determines all and only the correct inferences expressible in the language. In *natural deduction systems* (Fitch 1951, Prawitz 1965), defined to reflect individual local steps in any such derivation, each operator has an associated introduction and elimination rule. Elimination rules map complex formulae onto simpler formulae: introduction rules map simpler formulae onto a more complex formula. For example, there is *Conditional Elimination* (*Modus Ponendo Ponens*), which given premises of the form ϕ and $\phi \rightarrow \psi$ licenses the deduction of ψ; there is *Conditional Introduction*, which, conversely, from the demonstration of a proof of ψ on the basis of some assumption ϕ enables the assumption of ϕ to be removed, and a weaker conclusion $\phi \rightarrow \psi$ to be derived. Of the predicate-logic rules, *Universal Elimination* licenses the inference of $\forall x F(x)$ to $F(a)$, simplifying the formula by removing the quantifying operator and replacing its variable with a constructed *arbitrary name*. *Universal Introduction* enables the universal quantifier to be re-introduced into a formula replacing a corresponding formula containing such a name, subject to certain restrictions. In rather different spirit, *Existential Elimination* involves a move from $\exists x F(x)$ by assumption to $F(a)$ (a an arbitrary name) to derive some conclusion ϕ that crucially does not depend on any properties associated with the particular name a.

A sample proof (Fig.11.1) with annotations as metalevel comment detailing the rules used, illustrates a characteristic proof pattern. Early steps of the proof involve eliminating the quantificational operators and the structure they impose, revealing the propositional structure simpliciter with names in place of variables; central steps of inference (here just one) involve rules of propositional calculus; late steps of the proof re-introduce the quantificational structure with suitable quantifier-variable binding. ($\vdash$ is the proof sign for valid inference.)

These rules provide a full characterisation of inference, in that their interaction yields all and only the requisite inference relations as valid proofs of the system, with semantic definitions grounding the syntactic rules appropriately. In sum, inference in logical systems is characterisable both semantically, in terms of denotations, and syntactically, in proof-theoretic terms; and, in these defined languages, the semantic and syntactic characterisations are co-extensive, defined to yield the same results.

1.4 Predicate logic and natural language

Bringing back into the picture the relation between such formal languages and natural languages, what first strikes a student of NL is that predicate logic is really rather UNlike natural languages. In NL, quantifying expressions occur in just the same places as other noun phrases, and not, as in predicate logic, in some position adjoined to fully defined sentential units (see $\forall x(F(x) \to G(x))$ in Fig. 11.1. Nonetheless, there is parallelism between predicate logic and NL structure in the mechanisms defined for such quantified formulae. The *arbitrary names* involved in proofs for quantified formulae display a pattern similar to NL quantifying expressions. In some sense then, NL quantifying expressions can be seen as closer to the constructs used to model the dynamics of inferential action than to the predicate-logic language itself.

$\forall x(F(x) \to G(x)), \forall xF(x) \vdash \forall xG(x)$

1. $\forall x(F(x) \to G(x))$ Assumption
2. $\forall x.F(x)$ Assumption
3. $F(a) \to G(a)$ Universal-Elim, 1
4. $F(a)$ Universal-Elim, 2
5. $G(a)$ Modus Ponens, 3, 4
6. $\forall xG(x)$ Universal-Intro, 5

Fig. 11.1: Sample proof by universal elimination/introduction

Confirming this, there is tantalising parallelism between NL quantifiers and terms of the epsilon calculus (Hilbert & Bernays 1939), the logic defining the properties of these arbitrary names. In this logic, the *epsilon term* that corresponds to an arbitrary name carries a record of the mode of combination of the propositional formula within which it occurs:

(1) $\exists xF(x) \equiv F(\varepsilon xF(x))$

The formula on the right hand side of the equivalence sign is a predicate-argument sequence and within the argument of this sequence, there is a required second token of the predicate F as the restrictor for that argument term (ε is the variable-binding term operator that is the analogue of the existential quantifier). The effect is that the term itself replicates the content of the overall formula. As we shall see, this internal complexity to epsilon terms corresponds directly to so-called *E-type pronouns* (Geach 1972, Evans 1980), in which the pronoun appears to reconstruct the whole of some previous propositional formula, despite only coreferring to an indefinite term. In (2), that is, it is the woman that was sitting on the steps that the pronoun *she* is used to refer to:

(2) A woman was sitting on the steps. She was sobbing.

So there is interest in exploring links between construal of NL quantifiers and epsilon terms (see von Heusinger 1997, Kempson, Meyer-Viol & Gabbay 2001, von Heusinger & Kempson (eds.) 2004). There is also, more generally, as we shall see, growth of interest in exploring links between NL interpretation processes and proof-theoretic characterisations of inference.

In the meantime, what should be remembered is that predicate logic, with its associated syntax-semantics correspondence, is taken as the starting point for all formal-semantic modelling of a truth-conditional semantics for NL; and this leads to very different assumptions held in the conflicting Chomskian and formal-semantic paradigms about the status of representations within the overall NL grammar. For Chomskians, with the parallelism with logic largely residing in the methodology of defining a grammar yielding predictions that are consistent and complete for the phenomenon being modelled, the ontology for NL grammars is essentially representationalist. The grammar is said to comprise rules, an encapsulated body of knowledge acquired by a child (in part innate, and encapsulated from other devices controlled by the cognitive system). Whether or not semantics might depend on some additional system of representations is seen as an empirical matter, and not of great import. To the contrary in the Montague paradigm, no claims about the relation between language and the mind are made, and in particular there is no invocation of any mind-internal *language of thought*. Language is seen as an observable system of patterns similar in kind to formal languages of logic (cf. article 10 [this volume] (Newen & Schröder) *Logic and semantics*). From this perspective, syntax is only a vehicle over which semantic (model-theoretic) rules project interpretations for NL strings. If natural languages are indeed to be seen as formal languages, as claimed, the syntax will do no more in the grammar than yield the appropriate pairing of phonological sequences and denotational contents, so is not the core defining property of a grammar: it is rather the pairing of NL strings and truth-conditionally defined content that is its core. This is the stance of categorial grammar: Lambek (1958), Morrill (1994).

Not all grammars incorporating formal semantic insights are this stringent: Montague's defined grammar for English as a formal language had low-level rules ensuring appropriate morphological forms of strings licensed by the grammar rules. But even though formal semanticists might grant that structural properties of language require an independent system of structure-inducing rules said to constitute NL syntax, the positing of an additional mentalistic level of representation internal to the projection of denotational content for the structured strings of the language is debarred in principle. The core formal-semantics claim is that interpretation for NL strings is definable over the interpretation of the terminal elements of the language and their mode of combination as dictated by the syntax AND NOTHING ELSE: this is the *compositionality of meaning* principle. Positing any level of representation intermediate between the system projecting syntactic structure of strings and the projection of content for those strings is tantamount to abandoning this claim. The move to postulate a level of semantic representation as part of some supposed semantic component of NL grammar is thus hotly contested. In short, though separation of competence performance considerations as a methodological assumption is shared by all, there is not a great deal else for advocates of the Chomskian and Montague paradigms to agree about.

2 Natural languages as formal languages: Formal semantics

The early advocacy of semantic representations as put forward by Katz and colleagues (cf. Katz & Fodor 1963, Katz 1972) was unsuccessful (see the devastating critique of Lewis 1970); and from then on, research in NL semantics has been largely driven by the Montague program. Inevitably not all linguists followed this direction. Those concerned with lexical specifications tended to resist formal-semantic assumptions, retaining articulations of representationalist forms of analysis despite lack of formal-semantic underpinnings, relying on linguistic, computational, or psycho-linguistic forms of justification (Pustejovsky 1995, Fodor 1998, Jackendoff 2002).

However, there were in any case what were taken at the time to be good additional reasons for not seeking to develop a representational alternative to the model-theoretic program following the pattern of the syntactic characterisation of inference for predicate logic provided by the rules of proof (though see Hintikka 1974). For any one semantic characterisation, there are a large number of alternative proof systems for predicate and propositional calculus, with no possible means of choosing between them, the only unifying factor being their shared semantic characterisation. Hence it would seem that, if a single choice for explanation has to be made, it has to be a semantic one. Moreover, because of the notorious problems in characterising generalized quantifiers such as *most* (Barwise & Cooper 1981), it is only model-theoretic characterisations of NL content that have any realistic chance of adequate coverage.

In such debates, the putative relevance of processing considerations was not even envisaged. Yet amongst many variant proof-theoretic methods for predicate-logic proof systems, Fitch-style natural deduction is invariably cited as the closest to the observable procedural nature of natural language reasoning (Fitch 1951, Prawitz 1965). If consideration of external factors such as psycholinguistic plausibility had been taken as a legitimate criterion for determining selection between alternative candidate proof systems, this scepticism about the feasibility of selecting from amongst various proof-theoretic methodologies to construct a representationalist (proof-theoretic) model of NL inference might not have been so widespread. However, inclusion of performance-related considerations was, and largely still is, deemed to be illegitimate; and a broad range of subsequently established empirical results appear to confirm the decision to retain the NL-as-formal-language methodology. A corollary has been that vocabularies for syntactic and semantic generalisations had to be disjoint, with only the syntactic component of the grammar involving representations, semantics notably involving no more than a bottom-up characterisation of denotational content defined model-theoretically over the structures determined by the syntax, hence with a non-representationalist account of NL semantics. Nevertheless, as we shall see, representationalist assumptions within semantics have been progressively re-emerging as these formal-semantic assumptions have led to ever increasing postulations of unwarranted ambiguity, suggesting that something is amiss in the assumption that the semantics of NL expressions are directly encapsulated in their assigned denotational content.

2.1 The Lambda calculus and NL semantics

There was one critical tool which Montague utilised to substantiate the claim that natural languages can be treated as having denotational semantics read off their syntactic structure: the lambda calculus (cf. also article 7 [Semantics: Theories] (Zimmermann) *Model-theoretic semantics*).

The lambda calculus is a formal language with a function operator λ which binds variables in some open formula to yield an expression that denotes a function from the type of the variable onto the type of the formula. For example $F(x)$, an open predicate-logic formula, can be used as the basis for constructing the expression $\lambda x[F(x)]$, where the lambda-term is identical in content to the one-place predicate expression F (square brackets for lambda-binding visually distinguish lambda binding and quantifier binding). Thus the formula $\lambda x[F(x)]$ makes explicit the functional nature of the predicate term F, as does its logical type $\langle e, t \rangle$ (equivalently $e \rightarrow t$): any such expression is a predicate that explicitly encodes its denotational type mapping individual-denoting expressions onto propositional formulae. All that is needed to be able to define truth conditions over a syntactically motivated structure is to take the predicate logic analogue for any NL quantification-containing sentence, and define whatever processes of abstraction are needed over the predicate-expressions in the agreed predicate-logic representation of content to yield a match with requirements independently needed by the NL expressions making up that sentence. For example, on the assumption that $\forall x(Student(x) \rightarrow Smoke(x))$ is an appropriate point of departure for formulating the semantic content of *Every student smokes*, two steps of abstraction can be applied to that predicate-logic formula, replacing the two predicate constants with appropriately typed variables and lambda operators to yield the term $\lambda P \lambda Q[\forall x(P(x) \rightarrow Q(x))]$ as specifying the lexical content of *every*. This term can then combine first with the term *Student* (to form a noun-phrase meaning) and then with the term *Smokes* (as a verb-phrase meaning) to yield back the predicate logic formula $\forall x(Student(x) \rightarrow Smokes(x))$. This derivation can be represented as a tree structure with parallel syntactic and semantic labelling:

(3)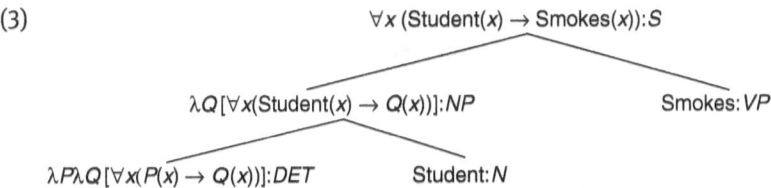

The consequence is that noun phrases are not analysed as individual-denoting expressions of type e (for individual), but as higher-type expressions $((e \rightarrow t) \rightarrow t)$. Since the higher-typed formula is deducible from the lower-typed formula, such a lifting was taken to be fully justified and applied to all noun-phrase contents, thereby in addition reinstating syntactic and semantic parallelism for these expressions. This gave rise to the generalised quantifier theory of natural language quantification (Barwise & Cooper 1981, article 4 [Semantics: Noun Phrases and Verb Phrases] (Keenan) *Quantifiers*). The surprising result is the required assumption that the content attributable to the VP is semantically the argument (despite whatever linguistic arguments there might be that the verb is the syntactic head in its containing phrase), and the subject expresses the functor that applies to it, mapping it into a propositional content, so semantic and syntactic considerations appear no longer to coincide.

This methodology of defining suitable lambda terms that express the same content as some appropriate predicate-logic formula was extended across the broad array of NL structures (with the addition of possible world and temporal indices in what was called *intensional semantics*). Hence the demonstrable claim that the formal semantic method captures a concept of compositionality for natural language sentences while retaining predicate-logic insights into the content to be ascribed, a formal analysis which also provides a basis for characterisations of entailment, synonymy, etc. With syntactic and semantic characterisations of formal languages defined in strictly separate vocabulary, albeit in tandem, the Montague methodology for natural languages imposes separation of syntactic and semantic characterisations of natural language strings, the latter being defined exclusively in terms of combinatorial operations on denotational contents, with any intermediate form of representation being for convenience of exegesis only. Montague indeed explicitly demonstrated that the mapping onto intermediate (intensional) logical forms in articulating model-theoretic meanings was eliminable.

Following predicate-logic semantics methodology, there was little concern with the concept of meaning for elementary expressions. However, relationships between word meanings were defined by imposing constraints on possible denotations as *meaning postulates* (following Carnap 1947). For example, the *be* of identity was defined so that extensions of its arguments were required to be coextensive across all possible worlds: conversely, the verbs *look for* and *find* were defined to ensure that they did NOT have equivalent denotational contents.

3 The challenge of context-dependence

Despite the dismissal by formal semanticists in the seventies of ANY form of representation within a semantic characterisation of interpretation, it was known rightaway that the model-theoretic stance as a program for natural language semantics within the grammar is not problem-free. One major problem is the inability to distinguish synonymous expressions when within propositional attitude reports (*John believes groundhogs are woodchucks* vs *John believes groundhogs are groundhogs*), indeed any necessary truths, a problem which led to invoking *structured meanings* (Cresswell 1985, Lappin & Fox 2005). Another major problem is the context-dependency of NL construal, a truth-theoretic semantics for NL expressions having to be defined relative to some concept of context (cf. article 12 [Semantics: Interfaces] (Zimmermann) *Context dependency*). This is a foundational issue which has been a recurrent concern amongst philosophers over many centuries (cf. article 9 [this volume] (Nerlich) *Emergence of semantics* for a larger perspective on the same problem).

The pervasiveness of the context-dependence of NL interpretation was not taken to be of great significance by some, in Lewis (1970) the only provision being the stipulation of an addition to the model of an open-ended set of *indices* indicating objects in the utterance context (speaker, hearer, and some finite list of individuals). Nevertheless, the problem posed by context was recognised as a challenge; and an early attempt to meet it, sustaining a core Montagovian conception of denotational semantics, while nevertheless disagreeing profoundly over details, was proposed by Barwise & Perry (1983). Their proposed enriched semantic ontology, *Situation Semantics*, included situations and an array of partial semantic constructs (*resource situations*, *infons*, etc.) with sentence meanings requiring *anchoring* in such situations in order to constitute contents with context-determined values. Inference relations were then defined in terms of relations between situations, with speakers being *attuned* to such relations between situations (see the subsequent exchange between Fodor and Barwise on such direct interpretation of NL strings: Fodor 1988, Barwise 1989).

3.1 Anaphoric dependencies

Recognition of the extent of this problem emerged in attempts to provide principled explanations for how pronouns are understood. Early on, Partee (1973) had pointed out that pronouns can be interpreted anaphorically, indexically or as a bound-variable. In (4), the pronoun is subject to apparent indexical construal (functioning like a name as referring to some intended object from the context); but in (5) it is interpreted like a predicate-logic variable with its value determined by some antecedent quantifying expression, hence not from the larger context:

(4) She is tired.

(5) Every woman student is panicking that she is inadequate.

Yet, as Kamp and others showed (Evans 1980, Kamp 1981, Kamp & Reyle 1993), this is just the tip of the iceberg, in that the phenomenon of anaphoric dependence is not restrictable to the domain provided by any one NL sentence in any obvious analogue of predicate-logic semantics. There are for example *E-type* uses of that same pronoun in which it picks up its interpretation from a quantified expression across a sentential boundary:

(6) A woman student left. She had been panicking about whether she was going to pass.

If natural languages matched predicate-logic patterns, not only would we apparently be forced to posit ambiguity as between indexical and bound-variable uses of pronouns, but one would be confronted with puzzles that do not fall into either classification: this pronoun appears to necessitate positing a term denoting some arbitrary witness of the preceding propositional formula, in (6) a name arbitrarily denoting some randomly picked individual having the properties of being a student, female, and having left. Such NL construal is directly redolent of the epsilon terms underpinning arbitrary names of natural deduction proofs, carrying a history of the compilation of content from the sentence providing the antecedent (von Heusinger 1997). But this just adds to the problem for it seems there are three different interpretations for one pronoun, hence ambiguity. Moreover, as Partee had pointed out, tense specifications display all the hallmarks of anaphora construal, able to be interpreted either anaphorically, indexically or as a bound variable, indeed with E-type effects as well, so this threat of proliferating ambiguities is not specific to pronouns.

4 Dynamic Semantics

The responses to this challenge can all be labelled *dynamic semantics* (Muskens, van Benthem & Visser 1997, Dekker 2000).

4.1 Discourse Representation Theory

Discourse Representation Theory (DRT: Kamp 1981, Kamp & Reyle 1993) was the first formal articulation of a response to the challenge of modelling anaphoric dependence in a way that enables its various uses to be integrated. Sentences of natural language were said to be interpreted by a *construction algorithm* for interpretation which takes the syntactic structure of a string as input and maps this by successive constructional steps onto a structured representation called a *Discourse Representation Structure* (DRS), which was defined to correspond to a partial model for the interpretation of the NL string. A DRS contains named entities (*discourse referents*) introduced from NL expressions, with predicates taking these as arguments, the sentence relative to which such a partial model is constructed being defined to be true as long as there is at least one embedding of the DRS into the overall model. For example, for a simple sentence-sequence such as (7), the *construction algorithm* for building discourse representation structure induces a DRS for the interpretation of the first sentence in which one discourse referent is entered into the DRS corresponding to the name and one for the quantifying expression, together with a set of predicates corresponding to the verb and nouns.

(7) John loves a woman. She is French.

(8)
x, y
John=x
loves(y)(x)
woman(y)

The DRS in (8) might then be extended, continuing the construal process for the overall discourse by applying the construction algorithm to the second sentence to yield the expanded DRS:

(9)
x, y, z
John=x
loves(y)(x)
woman(y)
z = y
French(y)

To participate in such a process, indefinite NPs are defined as introducing a new discourse referent into the DRS, definite NPs and pronouns require that the referent entered into the DRS be identical to some discourse referent already introduced, and names require a direct embedding into the model providing the interpretation. Once constructed, the DRS is evaluated by its embeddability into the model. Any such resulting DRS is true in a model if and only if there is at least one embedding of it within the overall model.

Even without investigating further complexities that license the embeddability of one DRS within another and the famous characterisation of *If a man owns a donkey, he beats it* (cf. article 11 [Semantics: Theories] (Kamp & Reyle) *Discourse Representation Theory*), an immediate bonus for this approach is apparent. The core cases of the so-called E-type pronouns fall into the same characterisation as more obvious cases of co-reference: all that is revised is the domain across which some associated quantifying expression can be seen to bind. It is notable in this account that there is no structural reflex of the syntactic properties of the individual quantifying determiner: indeed this formalism was among the first to come to grips with the name-like properties of such quantified formulae (cf. Fine 1984). It might of course seem that such a construction process is obliterating the difference between names, quantifying expressions, and anaphoric expressions, since all lead to the construction of discourse referents in a DRS. But, as we have seen, these expressions are distinguished by differences in the construction process. The burden of explanation for NL expressions is thus split: some aspect of their content is characterised by the mode of construction of the intervening DRS, some of it by the embeddability conditions of that structure into the overall model.

The particular significance of DRT lies in the Janus-faced properties of the DRS's defined. On the one hand, a DRS corresponds to a partial model (or more weakly, is a set of constraints on a model), defined as true if and only if it is embeddable in the overall model (hence is the same type of construct). On the other hand, specific structural properties of the DRS may be invoked in defining antecedent-pronoun relations, hence such a level is an essential intermediary between NL string and the denotations assigned to its expressions. Nonetheless, this level has a fully defined semantics constituting its embeddability into an overall model, so its properties are explicitly defined. There is a second sense in which DRT departs from previous theories. In providing a formal articulation of the incremental process of how interpretation is built up relative to some previously established context, there is implicit rejection of the methodology disallowing reference to performance in articulations of NL competence. Indeed the DRS construction algorithm is a formal reflection of sentence-by-sentence accumulation of content in a discourse (hence the term *Discourse Representation Theory*). So DRT not only offers a representationalist account of NL meaning, but one reflecting the incrementality of utterance processing.

4.2 Dynamic Predicate Logic

This account of anaphoric resolution sparked immediate response from proponents of the model-theoretic tradition. For example, Groenendijk & Stokhof (1991) argued that the intervening construct of DRT was both unnecessary and illicit in making compositionality of NL expressions definable not directly over the NL string but only via this intermediate structure. Part of their riposte to Kamp involved positing Dynamic Predicate Logic (DPL) with two variables for each quantifier and a new attendant semantics, so that once one of these variables gets closed off in ways familiar from predicate-logic binding, the second remains open, bindable by a quantifying mechanism introduced as part of the semantic combinatorics associated with some preceding string, hence obtaining cross-sentential anaphoric binding without any ancillary level of representation as invoked in DRT (cf. article 12 [Semantics: Theories] (Dekker) *Dynamic semantics*). Both the logic and its attendant semantics were new. Nevertheless, such a view is directly commensurate with the stringently model-theoretic view of context-dependent interpretation for natural language sentences provided by e.g. Stalnaker (1970, 1999): in these systems, progressive accumulation of interpretation across sequences of sentences in a discourse is seen exclusively in terms of intersections of sets of possible worlds progressively established, or rather, to reflect the additional complexity of formulae containing unbound variables, intersection of sets of pairs of worlds and assignments of values to variables (see Heim 1982 where this is set out in detail).

In the setting out of DPL as a putative competitor over DRT in characterising the same data without any level of representation, there was no attempt to address the challenge which Kamp had brought to the fore in articulating DRT, that of characterizing HOW anaphoric expressions contribute to the progressive accumulation of interpretation: on the DPL account, the pronoun in question was simply presumed to be coindexed with its antecedent. Notwithstanding this lack of take up of the challenge which DRT was addressing, there has been continuing debate since then as to whether any intervening level of representation is justified over and above whatever syntactic levels are posited to explain syntactic properties of natural language expressions. Examples such as (10)–(11) have been central to the debate (Kamp 1996, Dekker 2000):

(10) Nine of the ten marbles are in the bag. It is under the sofa.

(11) One of the ten marbles isn't in the bag. It is under the sofa.

According to the DRT account, the reason why the pronoun *it* cannot successfully be used with the interpretation that it picks up on the one marble not in the bag in (10) is because such an entity is only inferrable from information given by expressions in the previous sentence: no REPRESENTATION of any term denoting such an entity in (10) has been made available by the construction process projecting a discourse representation structure on the basis of which the truth conditions of the previous sentence are compiled. So though in all models validating the truth of (10) there must be a marble not in the bag described, there cannot be a successful act of reference to such an individual in using the pronoun. By way of contrast, in (11), despite its being true in all the same models that (10) is true, it is because the term denoting the marble not in the bag is specifically introduced that anaphoric resolution is successful. Hence, it is argued, the presence of an intermediate level of representation is essential.

4.3 The pervasiveness of context-dependence

Despite Kamp's early insight (Kamp 1981) that anaphora resolution was part of the construction for building up interpretation, this formulation of anaphoric dependence was set aside in the face of the charge that DRT did not provide a compositional account of natural language semantics, and alternative generalised-quantifier accounts of natural language quantification were provided reinstating compositionality of content over the NL string within the DRT framework even though positing an intermediate level of representation (van Eijck & Kamp 1997).

Despite great advances made by DRT, the issue of how to model context dependence continues to raise serious challenges to model-theoretic accounts of NL content. The different modes of interpretation available for pronouns extend far beyond a single syntactic category. Definite NPs, demonstrative NPs, and tense all present a three-way ambiguity between indexical, bound-variable and E-type forms of construal; and this ambiguity, if not reducible to some general principle, requires that the language be presumed to contain more than one such expression, with many discrete expression-denotation pairings. Such ambiguity is a direct consequence of the assumption that an articulation of meaning of an expression has to be in terms of its systematic contribution to truth conditions of the sentences in which it occurs. Such distinct uses of pronouns do indeed need to be expressed as contributing different truth conditions, whether as variable, as name, or as some analogue of an epsilon term; but the very fact that this ambiguity occurs in all context-dependent expressions in all languages indicates that something systematic is going on: this pattern is wholly unlike the accidental homonymy typical of lexical ambiguity.

Furthermore, it is the non-existence of context-dependence in interpretation of classical logic which lies at the heart of the difference between the two types of system. In predicate logic, by definition, there is no articulation of context or how interpretation is built up relative to that. The phenomenon under study is that of inference, and the formal language is defined to match such patterns (and not the way in which the formulae in question might themselves have been established). Natural languages are however not purpose-built systems; and context-dependence is essential to their success as an economical vehicle for expressing arbitrarily rich pieces of information relative to arbitrarily varying contexts. This perspective is buttressed by work in the neighbouring disciplines of philosophy of language and pragmatics. The gap between intrinsic content of words and their interpretation in use had been emphasised by the later Wittgenstein (1953), Austin (papers collected in 1961), Grice (papers collected in 1989), Sperber & Wilson (1986/1995), Carston (2002). The fact that context is essential to NL construal imposes an additional condition of adequacy on accounts of NL content: a formal characterisation of the meaning of NL expressions needs to define both the input which an individual NL expression provides to the interpretation process and the nature of contexts with which such input interacts. Answers to the problem of context formulation cannot, however, be expected to come from the semantics of logics. Rather, we need some basis for formulating specifications that UNDER-determine any assigned content. Given the needed emphasis on underspecification, on what it means to be part-way through a process whereby some content is specifiable only as output, it is natural to think in terms of representations, or, at least, in terms of constraints on assignment of content. This is now becoming common-place amongst linguists (Underspecified Discourse Representation Semantics (UDRT), Reyle 1993, van Leusen & Muskens 2003). Indeed Hamm, Kamp & van Lambalgen (2006) have argued explicitly that such linguistically motivated semantic representations have to be construed within a broadly computational, hence representationalist theory of mind.

5 The shift towards proof-theoretic perspectives

It might seem as though, with representationalism in semantics such a threat to the fruitfulness of the Montague paradigm, any such claim would be deluged with counter-arguments from the formal-semantics community (Dekker 2000, Muskens 1996). But, to the contrary, use of representationalist tools is continuing apace in both orthodox and less orthodox frameworks; and the shift towards more representational modes of explanation is not restricted to anaphora resolution.

5.1 The Curry-Howard isomorphism

An important proof-theoretic result pertaining to the compositionality of NL content came from the proof that the lambda calculus and type deduction in intuitionistic logic are isomorphic (intuitionistic logic is weaker than classical logic in that several classical tautologies do not hold). This is the so-called *Curry-Howard isomorphism*. Its relevance to linguists, which I define ostensively by illustration, is that the fine structure of how compositionality of content for NL expressions is built up can be represented proof-theoretically, making use of this isomorphism (Morrill 1994, Carpenter 1997).

The isomorphism is displayed in proofs of type deduction in which propositions are types, with a label demonstrating how that proof type as conclusion was derived. The language of the labels is none other than the lambda calculus, with functional application in the labels corresponding to type deduction on the formula side. So in the label, we might have a lambda term, e.g. $\lambda x[Sneeze(x)]$, and in the formula its corresponding type $e \to t$. The compositionality of content expressible through functional application defined over lambda terms can thus be represented as a step of natural deduction over labelled propositional formulae, with functional application on the labels and modus ponens on the typed formula. For example, a two-place predicate representable as $\lambda x\lambda y[See(x)(y)]$ can be stated as a label to a typed formula:

(12) $\lambda x\lambda y[See(x)(y)] : e \rightarrow (e \rightarrow t)$

This, when combined with a formula

(13) $Mary : e$

yields as output:

(14) $\lambda y[See(Mary)(y)] : e \rightarrow t$

And this in its turn when paired with

(15) $John : e$

yields as output by one further step of simultaneous functional application and Conditional Elimination:

(16) $See(Mary)(John) : t$

So compilation of content for the string *John sees Mary* can be expressed as a labelled deduction proof (12)–(16), reflecting the bottom-up compilation of content for the NL expression.

5.2 Proof theory as syntax: Type Logical Grammar

This method for using the fine structure of natural deduction as a means of representing NL compositionality has had very wide applicability, in categorial grammar and elsewhere (Dalrymple, Shieber & Pereira 1991, Dalrymple (ed.) 1999). In categorial grammar in particular (following Lambek 1958 who defined a simple extension of the lambda calculus with the incorporation of two order-sensitive operators indicating functional application with respect to some left/right placed argument), the Curry-Howard isomorphism is central, and with later postulation of modal operators to define syntactic domains (Morrill 1990, 1994), such systems have been shown to have expressive power sufficient to match a broad array of variation expressible in natural languages (leaving on one side the issue of context dependence). Hence the categorial-grammar claim that NL grammars are logics with attendant proof systems. These are characteristically presented either in natural-deduction format or in its meta-level analogue, the sequent calculus.

The advantage of such systems is the fine level of granularity they provide for reflecting bottom-up compositionality of content, given suitable (higher) type assignments to NL expressions. In being logics, natural languages are presumed to have syntax and semantics defined in tandem, with the proof display being no more than an elegant display of how prosodic sequences (words) are paired projected by steps of labelled type deduction onto denotational contents. In particular, no representationalist assumptions are made vis a vis either syntax or logical representations (see Morrill 1994 for a particularly clear statement of this strictly denotationalist commitment).

Nonetheless in more recent work, Morrill departs from at least one aspect of this stringent categorial grammar proof-theoretic ideology. In all categorial grammar formalisms, as indeed in many other frameworks, there is strict separation of competence and performance considerations with grammar-formalisms only evaluated in terms of their empirical predictive success; yet Morrill & Gavarró (2004) and Morrill (2010) argue that an advantage of the particular categorial-grammar characterisation adopted (with linear-logic proof derivations), is the step-wise correspondence of individual steps in the linear-logic derivation to measures of complexity in processing the NL string, this being a bonus for the account. Thus representational properties of grammar-defined derivations would seem at least evidenced by performance data, even if such proof-theoretically defined derivations are taken to be eliminable as a core property of the grammar formalism itself.

5.3 Type Theory with records

A distinct proof-theoretic equivalent of Montague's PTQ grammar was defined by Ranta (1994), who adopted as a basis for his framework the methodology of Martin-Löf's (1984) proof theory for intuitionistic type theory. By way of introducing the Martin-Löf ontology, remember how in natural deduction proofs there are meta-level annotations (section 1.4), but these are only partially explicit: many do not record dependencies between arbitrary names as they are set up. The Martin-Löf methodology to the contrary requires that all such dependencies are recorded, and duly labelled; and Ranta used this rich attendant labelling system to formulate analyses of anaphora resolution and quantification, and from these he established a structural concept of context, notably going beyond what is achievable in categorial grammar formalisms. Furthermore, such explicit representations of dependency have been used to establish a fully explicit proof-theoretic grounding for generalized quantifiers, from which an account of anaphora resolution follows incorporating E-type pronouns as a subtype (Ranta 1994, Piwek 1998, Fernando 2002).

In Cooper (2006), the Ranta framework is taken a step further, yielding the Type Theory with Records framework (TTR). Cooper uses a concept of *record* and *record-type* to set out a general framework for modelling both context-dependent interpretation and the intrinsic underspecification that NL expressions themselves contribute to the interpretation process. Echoing the DRT formulation, the interpretation to be assigned the sentence *A man owns a donkey* is set out as taking the form of the record-type (Cooper 2005) (the variables in these formulations, as labels to proof terms, are like arbitrary names, expressing dependencies between one term and another:

(17) $\begin{bmatrix} x : Ind \\ c_1 : man(x) \\ y : Ind \\ c_2 : donkey(y) \\ c_3 : own(y)(x) \end{bmatrix}$

x, y are variables of individual type,
c_1 is of the type of proof that x is a man, (hence a proof that is dependent on some proof of x),
c_2 is of the type of proof that y is a donkey, ...

A record of that record type would be some instantiation of variables e.g.:

(18) $\begin{bmatrix} x = a \\ c_1 = p_1 \\ y = b \\ c_2 = p_2 \\ c_3 = p_3 \end{bmatrix}$

p_1 a proof of 'man(a)',
p_2 a proof of 'donkey(y)',
and so on.

This is a proof-theoretic reformulation of the situation-theory concepts of infon (= situation-type) and situation. A record represents some situation that provides values that make some record-type true. The concept of record-type corresponds to sentence meanings in abstraction from any given context/record: a sentence meaning is a mapping from records to record-types. It is no coincidence that such dependency labelling has properties like that of epsilon terms, since, like them, the terms that constitute the labels to the derived types express the history of the mode of combination. The difference between this and DRT lies primarily in the grounding of records and record-types in proof-theoretic rather than model-theoretic underpinnings (Cooper 2006). Like DRT, this articulation of record theory with types as a basis for NL semantics leaves open the link with syntax. However, in recent work, Ginzburg and Cooper have extended the concept of records and record-types yet further to incorporate full details of linguistic signs (with phonological, syntactic and semantic information – a multi-level representational system Ginzburg & Cooper 2004, cf. article 10 [Semantics: Theories] (Ginzburg) *Situation Semantics*).

6 Ellipsis: A window on context

So far, the main focus has been anaphora construal, but ellipsis presents another window on context. Elliptical fragments are those where there is only a fragment of a clause: words and whole phrases can simply be omitted when the context fully determines what is needed to complete the interpretation. The intrinsic interest of such elliptical fragments is that they provide evidence that very considerable richness of labelling is required in modelling NL construal. Like pronominal anaphora, ellipsis displays a huge diversity. Superficially, the phenomenon might seem to be amenable to some more sophisticated variant of anaphora construal. There are, that is, what look like indexical construals, and also analogues of coreference and bound-variable anaphora:

(19) (Mother to a toddler stretching up to the stove above their head)
Johnny, don't.

(20) John stopped in time but I didn't.

(21) Everyone who submitted their thesis without checking it wished that the others had too.

To capture the array of effects illustrated in (20)–(21), there is a model-theoretic account of ellipsis (Dalrymple, Shieber & Pereira 1991) whose starting point is to take the model-theoretic methodology, and from the propositional content provided by the antecedent clause, to define some lambda term to isolate an appropriate predicate for combining with the NP term provided by the fragment. For (20), one might define the term $\lambda x[\text{stop-in-time}(x)]$; for (21) the term $\lambda x[\exists y(\text{thesis}(y) \wedge \text{submit}(y)(x) \wedge \neg\text{check}(y)(x))]$. However, even allowing for complexities of possible sequences of quantificational dependencies replaced at the ellipsis site as in (21), the rebinding mechanism has to be yet more complex, as what is rebound may be not merely some subject value and whatever quantified expressions are dependent on that, but cases where the subject expression is itself dependent on some expression within its restrictor, so that an even higher-order form of abstraction is required:

(22) The man who arrested Joe failed to read him his rights, as did the man who arrested Sue.

This might seem to be an echo of the debate between DRT and DPL, with the higher-order account having the formal tools to express the parallelism of construal carried over from the antecedent clause to the ellipsis site as in (20)–(21), without requiring any invocation of a representation of content. However, there are many cases of ellipsis, as syntacticians have demonstrated, where only an account which invokes details of some assigned structure to the string can explain the available interpretations (Fiengo & May 1994, Merchant 2004). For example, there are morphological idiosyncracies displayed by individual languages that surface as restrictions on licensed elliptical forms. In a case-rich language such as German, for example, the fragment has to occur with the case form it would be expected to have in a fully explicit follow-on to the antecedent clause (Greek also displays exactly the same type of requirement). English, where case is very atrophied, imposes no such requirement (Morgan 1973, Ginzburg & Cooper 2004):

(23) Hans will nach London gehen. Ich/*mich auch.

(24) Hans wants to go to London. Me too.

This is not the kind of information which a higher-order unification account can express, as its operations are defined on the model-theoretic construal of the antecedent conjunct, not over morphological sequences. There are many more such structure-particular variations indicating that ellipsis would seem to have to be defined over representations of structure, hence to be analysed as a syntactic phenomenon, in each case defined over some suitable approximate correspondent to the surface strings (there has to be this caveat as there are well-known cases of *vehicle-change* where what is reconstructed is not the linguistic form, Fiengo & May 1994):

(25) John has checked his thesis notes carefully, but I haven't.

However, there are puzzles for both types of account. Fragments may occur in dialogue for which arguably only a pragmatic enrichment process can capture the effects (not based either on structured strings or on their model-theoretic contents, Stainton 2006):

(26) A (leaving hotel): The station?
      B (receptionist): Left out of the door. Then second on the right.

For reasons such as this, ellipsis continues to receive a great deal of attention, with no single account apparently able single-handedly to match the fine-grained nature of the cross-conjunct/speaker patterning that ellipsis construal can achieve. The conclusion generally drawn is that the folk intuition about ellipsis is simply not expressible. Indeed the added richness in TTR of combining Ranta's type-logical formalism with the feature-matrix vocabulary of Head Driven Phrase Structure Grammar (HPSG: Sag, Wasow & Bender 2002) to obtain a system combining independent semantic, syntactic and morphological paradigms was at least in part driven by the observed 'fractal heterogeneity' of ellipsis (Ginzburg & Cooper 2004).

However, there is one last chance to capture such effects in an integrated way, and this is to posit a system of labelling recording individual steps of information build-up with whatever level of granularity is needed to preserve the idiosyncracies in the individual steps. Ellipsis construal can then be defined by making reference to such records. This type of account is provided in Dynamic Syntax (Kempson, Meyer-Viol & Gabbay 2001, Cann, Kempson & Marten 2005, Purver, Cann & Kempson 2006, Cann, Kempson & Purver 2007).

6.1 Dynamic Syntax: A reflection of parsing dynamics as a basis for syntax

Dynamic Syntax (DS) models the dynamics of how interpretation is incrementally built up following a parsing dynamics, with progressively richer representations of content constructed as words are processed relative to context. This articulation of the stepwise way in which interpretation is built up is claimed to be ALL that is needed for explaining NL syntax: representations constructed are simultaneously the vehicle for explaining syntactic distributions and a vehicle for representing how interpretation is built up.

The methodology adopts a representationalist stance vis a vis content (Fodor 1983). Predicate-argument structures are represented in a tree format with the assumption of progressive update of partial tree-representations of content. Context, too, is represented in the same terms, evolving in tandem with each update. This concept of structural growth totally replaces the semantically blind syntactic specifications characteristic of such formalisms as Minimalism (Chomsky 1995) and HPSG. It is seen as starting from an initial one-node tree stating the goal of the interpretation process to establish some propositional formula (the tree representation to the left of the $\mapsto$ in (27)). Then, using both parse input and information from context, some propositional formula is progressively built up (the tree representation to the right of the $\mapsto$ in (27)).

(27) Parsing *John upset Mary*

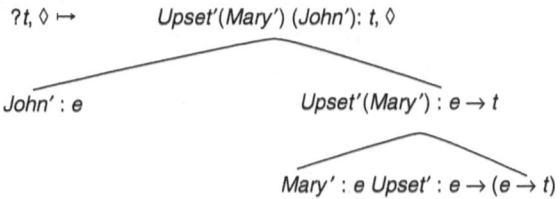

The output is a fully decorated tree whose topnode is a representation of some proposition expressed with its associated type specification, and each dominated node has a concept formula, e.g. *John'* representing some individual John, and an indication of what semantic type that concept is. The primitive types are types e and t as in formal semantics but construed syntactically as in the Curry-Howard isomorphism, labelled type deduction determining the decorations on non-terminal nodes once all terminal nodes are fixed and suitably decorated with formula values. There is invariably one node under development in any partial tree, as indicated by the pointer $\Diamond$. So a parse process for (27) would constitute a transition across partial trees, the substance of this transition turning on how the growth relation $\mapsto$ is to be determined by the word sequence. The concept of *requirement* $?X$ for any decoration X is central. Decorations on nodes such as $?t$, $?e$, $?(e \rightarrow t)$, etc. express requirements to construct formulae of the appropriate type on the nodes so decorated, and these requirements drive the subsequent tree-construction process. A string can then be said to be wellformed if and only if there is at least one derivation involving monotonic growth of partial trees licensed by computational (general), lexical and pragmatic actions following the sequence of words that yields a complete tree with no requirements outstanding.

Just as the concept of tree growth is central, so too is the concept of procedure for mapping one partial tree to another. Individual transitions from partial tree to partial tree are all defined as *procedures* for tree growth. The formal system underpinning the partial trees that are constructed is a logic of finite trees (LOFT: Blackburn & Meyer-Viol 1994). There are two basic modalities, $\langle\downarrow\rangle$ and $\langle\uparrow\rangle$, and Kleene * operators defined over these relations, e.g. $\langle\uparrow_*\rangle Tn(a)$ indicating that somewhere dominating this node is the tree-node $Tn(a)$ (a standard tree-theoretic characterisation of 'dominate'). The procedures in terms of which the tree growth processes are defined then involve such actions as make($\langle\downarrow\rangle$), go($\langle\downarrow\rangle$), make($\langle\downarrow_*\rangle$), put($X$) (for any decoration X), etc. This applies both to general constraints on tree growth (hence the syntactic rules of the system) and to specific tree update actions constituting the lexical content of words. So the contribution which a word makes to utterance interpretation is expressed in the same vocabulary as general structural growth processes, and is invariably more than just a concept specification: it is a sequence of actions developing a sub-part of a tree, possibly building new nodes, and assigning them decorations such as formula and type specifications.

Of the various concepts of underspecification, two are central. On the one hand, there is underspecification of conceptual content, with anaphoric expressions being defined as adding to a node in a tree a place-holding metavariable of a given type as a provisional formula value to be replaced by some fixed value which the immediate context makes available. This is a relatively uncontroversial approach to anaphora construal, equivalent to formulations in many other frameworks (notably DRT and TTR). On the other hand, there is underspecification and update of structural relations, in particular replacing all movement or feature-passing accounts of discontinuity effects, with introduction of an UNFIXED node, one whose structural relation is not specified at the point of construction, and whose value must be provided from the construction process. Formally the construction of a new node within a partial tree is licensed from some node requiring a propositional type, with that relation being characterised only as that of domination (weakly specified tree relations are indicated by a dashed line with $Tn(0)$ as the rootnode: this is step (i) of (28). The update to this relatively weak tree-relation for English, lacking as it does any case specifications, becomes possible only once having parsed the verb. This is the unification step (ii) of (28), an action which satisfies both type and structure update requirements:

(28) Parsing *Mary, John upset*

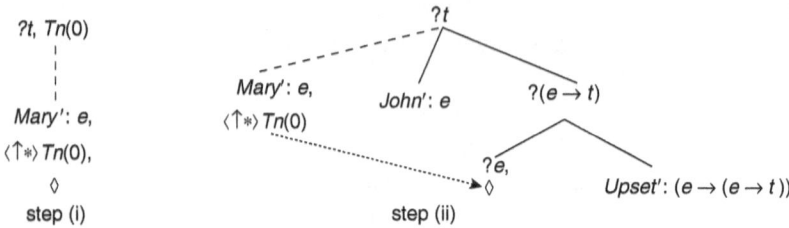

step (i)   step (ii)

This process, like the substitution operation associated with pronoun construal feeds into the ongoing process of creating a completed tree, in this case by steps of labelled type deduction.

It might seem that all such talk of (partial) trees as representations of content could not in principle simultaneously serve as both a syntactic explanation and a basis for semantic interpretation, because of the problems posed by quantification, known to necessitate a globally defined process expressing scope dependencies between quantifying expressions, and generally agreed to involve mismatch between logical and syntactic category (see section 2.1). However, quantified expressions are taken to map onto epsilon terms, hence of type *e* (Kempson, Meyer-Viol & Gabbay 2001, ch.7); and in having a restrictor which reflects the content of the proposition in which they are contained, the defining property of epsilon terms is that they grow incrementally, as additional predicates are added to the term under construction (see section 1.4). And these epsilon terms, metavariables and tree relations, all under development, all interact to yield the complex interactions more familiarly seen as scope and anaphoric sensitivities to long-distance and other discontinuity effects.

The bonus of this framework for modelling ellipsis is that by taking not merely structured representations of content as first-class citizens but the procedures used to incrementally build up such stucture, ellipsis construal is expressible in an integrated way: it is indeed definable as determined directly by context. What context comprises is the richer notion that includes some sequence of words, their assigned content, and its attendant propositional tree structure, PLUS the sequence of actions whereby that structure and its content were established. Any one of these may be used to build up interpretation of the fragment, and together they determine the range of interpretations available: recovery of some predicate content from context (19)–(20), recovery of some actions in order to create a parallel but distinct construal (21)–(22). This approach to ellipsis as building up structure by reiterating content or actions can thus replace the higher order unification account with a more general, intuitive, and yet essentially representationalist account.

A unique property of the DS grammar mechanisms is that production is expressed in the same terms as parsing, as progressive build-up of semantic structure, differing from parsing only in having also a richer representation of what the speaker is trying to express as a filter on whether appropriate semantic structure is being induced by the selected words. This provides a basis from which to expect fluent exchange of speaker/hearer roles in dialogue, in which a speaker sets out a partial structure which their interlocutor, parsing what they say, takes over:

(29) Q: Who did John upset?
    A: Himself.

(30) A: I saw John.
    B: With his mother?
    A: Yes, with Sue. In the park.

Since both lexical and syntactic actions are defined as tree-growth processes, construal of elliptical fragments both within and across speakers is expected to allow replication of any such actions following their use to build interpretation for some antecedent, predicting the mixture of semantic and syntactic factors in ellipsis. Scope dependencies are unproblematic. These are not expressed on the trees, but formulated as an incrementally collected set of constraints on the evaluation of the emergent epsilon terms. These are applied once the propositional formula is constructed, determining the resulting epsilon term. So despite the apparently global nature of scope, parallel scope dependencies can be expressed as the re-use of a sequence of actions that had earlier been used in the construal of the antecedent string, replicating scope actions but relative to the terms constructed in interpreting the fragment. Even case, defined as an output filter on the resultant tree, is unproblematic, unlike for semantic characterisations of ellipsis, as in (23). So, it is claimed, interaction of morphology, syntax, and even pragmatics in ellipsis construal is predictable given DS assumptions.

To flesh this out would involve a full account of how DS mechanisms interact to yield appropriate results. All this sketch provides is a point of departure for addressing ellipsis in an integrated manner (see also a variant of DRT: Asher & Lascarides 2002). More significantly, the DS account of context and the emergent concept of content intrinsic to NL words themselves are essentially representationalist. The ellipsis account succeeds in virtue of the fact that lexical specifications are procedures that interact with context to induce the building of representations of denotational content. Natural languages are accordingly denotationally interpretable only via a mapping onto an intermediate logical system.

And, since compositionality of denotational content is defined over the resulting trees, it is the incrementality of projection of word meaning and the attendant monotonicity of the tree growth process which constitutes compositionality definable over the words making up sentences.

7 Summary

Inevitably, issues raised by anaphora and ellipsis remain open. But, even without resolving these, research goals have strikingly shifted since early work in formal semantics and the representationalism debate it engendered. The dispute remains; but answers to the questions are very different. On the view espoused within TTR and DS formulations, a natural language is not definable as a logic in the mould of predicate logic. Rather, it is a set of mechanisms out of which truth-denoting objects can be built relative to what is available in context. To use Cooper's apt turn of phrase 'natural languages are tools for formal language construction' (Cooper & Ranta 2008): so semantic representations are central to the form of explanation.

Whatever answers individual researchers might reach to individual questions, one thing is certain: new puzzles are taking centre-stage. The data of semantic investigation are not now restricted to judgements of entailment relations between sentences. The remit includes modelling the human capacity to interpret fragments in context in conjunction with other participants in dialogue; and defining appropriate concepts of information update. Each of these challenges involves an assumption that the human capacity for natural language is a capacity for language processing in context. With this narrowing of the gap between competence and performance considerations, assumptions about the nature of such semantic representations of content can be re-evaluated. We can again pose the question of the status of representations in semantic modelling; but we can now pose this as a question of the relation of such representations to those required for modelling cognitive inference more broadly. Furthermore, such questions can be posed from a number of frameworks as starting point: categorial grammar, Type Theory with Records, DRT and its variants, Dynamic Syntax, to name but a few. And it is these new avenues of research which are creating new ways of understanding the nature of natural language and linguistic competence.

Eleni Gregoromichelaki, Ronnie Cann and two readers provided most helpful comments leading to significant improvement of this paper. However, normal disclaimers apply.

8 References

Asher, Nicholas & Alex Lascarides 2002. *Logics of Conversation*. Cambridge, MA: The MIT Press.
Austin, John 1961. *How to Do Things with Words*. Oxford: Clarendon Press.
Barwise, Jon 1989. *The Situation in Logic*. Stanford, CA: CSLI Publications.
Barwise, Jon & Robin Cooper 1981. Generalized quantifiers and natural language. *Linguistics & Philosophy* 4, 159–219.
Barwise, Jon & John Perry 1983. *Situations and Attitudes*. Cambridge, MA: The MIT Press.
Blackburn, Patrick & Wilfried Meyer-Viol 1994. Linguistic logic and finite trees. *Bulletin of the Interest Group of Pure and Applied Logics* 2, 2–39.
Cann, Ronnie, Ruth Kempson & Lutz Marten 2005. *Dynamics of Language*. Amsterdam: Elsevier.
Cann, Ronnie, Ruth Kempson & Matthew Purver 2007. Context, wellformedness and the dynamics of dialogue. *Research on Language and Computation* 5, 333–358.
Carnap, Rudolf 1947. *Meaning and Necessity. A Study in Semantics and Modal Logic*. Chicago, IL: The University of Chicago Press.
Carpenter, Robert 1997. *Type-Logical Semantics*. Cambridge, MA: The MIT Press.
Carston, Robyn 2002. *Thoughts and Utterances: The Pragmatics of Explicit Utterances*. Oxford: Blackwell.
Chomsky, Noam 1955. *Syntactic Structures*. The Hague: Mouton.
Chomsky, Noam 1965. *Aspects of the Theory of Syntax*. Cambridge, MA: The MIT Press.
Chomsky, Noam 1995. *The Minimalist Program*. Cambridge, MA: The MIT Press.
Cooper, Robin 2005. Austinian truth, attitudes and type theory. *Research on Language and Computation* 3, 333–362.
Cooper, Robin 2006. Records and record types in semantic theory. *Journal of Logic and Computation* 15, 99–112.
Cooper, Robin & Aarne Ranta 2008. Natural language as collections of resources. In: R. Cooper & R. Kempson (eds.). *Language in Flux: Dialogue Coordination, Language Variation, Change, and Evolution*. London: College Publications, 109–120.
Cresswell, Max 1985. *Structured Meaning*. Cambridge, MA: The MIT Press.
Dalrymple Mary, Stuart Shieber & Fernando Pereira 1991. Ellipsis and higher-order unification. *Linguistics & Philosophy* 14, 399–452.
Dalrymple, Mary (ed.) 1999. *Semantics and Syntax in Lexical Functional Grammar: The Resource Logic Approach*. Cambridge, MA: The MIT Press.
Dekker, Paul 2000. Coreference and representationalism. In: K. von Heusinger & U. Egli (eds.). *Reference and Anaphoric Relations*. Dordrecht: Kluwer, 287–310.
Evans, Gareth 1980. Pronouns. *Linguistic Inquiry* 11, 337–362.
Fernando, Timothy 2002. Three processes in natural language interpretation. In: W. Sieg, R. Sommer & C. Talcott (eds.). *Reflections on the Foundations of Mathematics: Essays in Honor of Solomon Feferman*. Natick, MA: Association for Symbolic Logic, 208–227.
Fiengo, Robert & Robert May 1994. *Indices and Identity*. Cambridge, MA: The MIT Press.
Fine, Kit 1984. *Reasoning with Arbitrary Objects*. Oxford: Blackwell.
Fitch, Frederic 1951. *Symbolic Logic*. New York: The Ronald Press Company.
Fodor, Jerry 1981. *Re-Presentations*. Cambridge, MA: The MIT Press.
Fodor, Jerry 1983. *Modularity of Mind*. Cambridge, MA: The MIT Press.
Fodor, Jerry 1988. A situated grandmother. *Mind & Language* 2, 64–81.
Fodor, Jerry 1998. *Concepts*. Oxford: Oxford University Press.

Gamut, L.T.F. 1991. *Logic, Language and Meaning*. Chicago, IL: The University of Chicago Press.
Geach, Peter 1972. *Logic Matters*. Oxford: Oxford University Press.
Ginzburg, Jonathan & Robin Cooper 2004. Clarification, ellipsis, and the nature of contextual updates. *Linguistics & Philosophy* 27, 297–365.
Grice, Paul 1989. *Studies in the Way of Words*. Cambridge, MA: Harvard University Press.
Groenendijk, Jeroen & Martin Stokhof 1991. Dynamic predicate logic. *Linguistics & Philosophy* 14, 39–100.
Hamm, Fritz, Hans Kamp & Michiel van Lambalgen 2006. There is no opposition between formal and cognitive semantics. *Theoretical Linguistics* 32, 1–40.
Heim, Irene 1982. *The Semantics of Definite and Indefinite Noun Phrases*. Ph.D. dissertation. University of Massachusetts, Amherst, MA. Reprinted: Ann Arbor, MI: University Microfilms.
Hilbert, David & Bernays, Paul 1939. *Grundlagen der Mathematik*. Vol. II. 2nd edn. Berlin: Springer.
Hintikka, Jaako 1974. Quantifiers vs. quantification theory. *Linguistic Inquiry* 5, 153–177.
Jackendoff, Ray 2002. *Foundations of Language: Brain, Meaning, Grammar, Evolution*. Oxford: Oxford University Press.
Kamp, Hans 1981. A theory of truth and semantic representation. In: J. Groenendijk, T. Janssen & M. Stokhof (eds.). *Formal Methods in the Study of Language*. Amsterdam: Mathematical Centre, 277–322.
Kamp, Hans 1996. Discourse Representation Theory and Dynamic Semantics: Representational and nonrepresentational accounts of anaphora. French translation in: F. Corblin & C. Gardent (eds.). *Interpréter en contexte*. Paris: Hermes, 2005.
Kamp, Hans & Uwe Reyle 1993. *From Discourse to Logic*. Dordrecht: Kluwer.
Katz, Jerrold 1972. *Semantic Theory*. New York: Harper & Row.
Katz, Jerrold & Jerry Fodor 1963. The structure of a semantic theory. *Language* 39, 170–210.
Kempson, Ruth, Wilfried Meyer-Viol & Dov Gabbay 2001. *Dynamic Syntax: The Flow of Language Understanding*. Oxford: Blackwell.
Lambek, Joachim 1958. The mathematics of sentence structure. *American Mathematical Monthly* 65, 154–170.
Lappin, Shalom & Christopher Fox 2005. *Foundations of Intensional Semantics*. Oxford: Blackwell.
van Leusen, Noor & Reinhard Muskens 2003. Construction by description in discourse representation. In: J. Peregrin (ed). *Meaning: The Dynamic Turn*, chap. 12. Amsterdam: Elsevier, 33–65.
Lewis, David 1970. General semantics. *Synthese* 22, 18–67. Reprinted in: G. Harman & D. Davidson (eds.). *Formal Semantics of Natural Language*. Dordrecht: Reidel, 1972, 169–218.
Martin-Löf, Per 1984. *Intuitionistic Type Theory*, Naples: Bibliopelis.
Merchant, Jason 2004. Fragments and ellipsis. *Linguistics & Philosophy* 27, 661–738.
Montague, Richard 1970. English as a formal language. In: Bruno Visentini et al. (eds.). *Linguaggi nella Societ à e nella Tecnica*. Milan: Edizioni di Comunità, 189–224. Reprinted in: R. Thomason (ed.). *Formal Philosophy. Selected Papers of Richard Montague*. New Haven, CT: Yale University Press, 1974, 188–221.
Morgan, Jerry 1973. Sentence fragments and the notion 'sentence'. In: H. R. Kahane, R. Kahane & B. Kachru (eds.). *Issues in Linguistics*. Urbana, IL: University of Illinois Press, 719–751.
Morrill, Glyn 1990. Intensionality and boundedness. *Linguistics & Philosophy* 13, 699–726.
Morrill, Glyn 1994. *Type Logical Grammar*. Dordrecht: Foris.

Morrill, Glyn 2010. *Categorial Grammar: Logical Syntax, Semantics, and Processing*. Oxford: Oxford University Press.

Morrill, Glyn & Anna Gavarró 2004. On aphasic comprehension and working memory load. In: *Proceedings of Categorial Grammars: An Efficient Tool for Natural Language Processing*. Montpellier, 259–287.

Muskens, Reinhard 1996. Combining Montague semantics and Discourse Representation. *Linguistics & Philosophy* 19, 143–186.

Muskens, Reinhard, Johan van Benthem & Albert Visser 1997. *Dynamics*. In: J. van Benthem & A. ter Meulen (eds.). *Handbook of Logic and Language*. Amsterdam: Elsevier, 587–648.

Partee, Barbara 1973. Some structural analogies between tenses and pronouns in English. *The Journal of Philosophy* 70, 601–609.

Piwek, Paul 1998. *Logic, Information and Conversation*. Ph.D dissertation. University of Technology, Eindhoven.

Prawitz, Dag 1965. *Natural Deduction: A Proof-Theoretical Study*. Uppsala: Almqvist & Wiksell.

Purver, Matthew, Ronnie Cann & Ruth Kempson 2006. Grammars as parsers: The dialogue challenge. *Research on Language and Computation* 4, 289–326.

Pustejovsky, James 1995. *The Generative Lexicon*. Cambridge, MA: The MIT Press.

Ranta, Aarne 1994. *Type-Theoretic Grammar*. Oxford: Clarendon Press.

Reyle, Uwe 1993. Dealing with ambiguities by underspecification: Construction, representation and deduction. *Journal of Semantics* 10, 123–179.

Sag, Ivan, Tom Wasow & Emily Bender 2002. *Head Phrase Structure Grammar: An Introduction*. 2nd edn. Stanford, CA: CSLI Publications.

Sperber, Dan & Deirdre Wilson 1986/1995. *Relevance: Communication and Cognition*. Oxford: Blackwell.

Stainton, Robert 2006. *Words and Thoughts*. Oxford: Oxford University Press.

Stalnaker, Robert 1970. Pragmatics. *Synthese* 22, 272–289.

Stalnaker, Robert 1999. *Context and Content*. Oxford: Oxford University Press.

Thomason, Richmond (ed.) 1974. *Formal Philosophy. Selected Papers of Richard Montague*. New Haven, CT: Yale University Press.

van Eijk, Jan & Hans Kamp 1997. Representing discourse in context. In: J. van Benthem & A. ter Meulen (eds.). *Handbook of Logic and Language*. Amsterdam: Elsevier, 179–239.

von Heusinger, Klaus 1997. Definite descriptions and choice functions. In: S. Akama (ed.). *Logic, Language and Computation*. Dordrecht: Kluwer, 61–92.

von Heusinger, Klaus & Ruth Kempson (eds.) 2004. *Choice Functions in Linguistic Theory*. Special issue of *Research on Language and Computation* 2.

Wittgenstein, Ludwig 1953. *Philosophical Investigations*. Translated by Gillian Anscombe. 3rd edn. Oxford: Blackwell, 1967.

Manfred Krifka
12 Varieties of semantic evidence

1. Introduction: Aspects of meaning and possible sources of evidence —— 306
2. Fieldwork techniques in semantics —— 312
3. Communicative behavior —— 323
4. Behavioral effects of semantic processing —— 325
5. Physiological effects of semantic processing —— 328
6. Corpus-linguistic methods —— 333
7. Conclusion —— 335
8. References —— 336

Abstract: Meanings are the most elusive objects of linguistic research. The article summarizes the type of evidence we have for them: various types of metalinguistic activities like paraphrasing and translating, the ability to name entities and judge sentences true or false, as well as various behavioral and physiological measures such as reaction time studies, eye tracking, and electromagnetic brain potentials. It furthermore discusses the specific type of evidence we have for different kinds of meanings, such as truth-conditional aspects, presuppositions, implicatures, and connotations.

1 Introduction: Aspects of meaning and possible sources of evidence

1.1 Why meaning is a special research topic

If we ask an astronomer for evidence for phosphorus on Sirius, she will point out that spectral analysis of the light from this star reveals bands that are characteristic of this element, as they also show up when phosphorus is burned in the lab. If we ask a linguist the more pedestrian question for evidence that a certain linguistic expression – say, the sentence The quick brown fox jumps over the lazy dog – has meaning, answers are probably less straightforward and predictable. He might point out that speakers of English generally agree that it has meaning – but how do they know? So it is perhaps not an accident that the study of meaning is the subfield

Manfred Krifka, Berlin, Germany

of linguistics that developed only very late in the 2500 years of history of linguistics, in the 19th century (cf. article 9 [this volume] (Nerlich) *Emergence of semantics*).

The reason why it is difficult to imagine what evidence for meaning could be is that it is difficult to say what *meaning* is. According to a common assumption, communication consists in putting *meaning* into a *form*, a form that is then sent from the speaker to the addressee (the conduit metaphor of communication, see Lakoff & Johnson 1980). Aspects that are concerned with the form of linguistic expressions and their material realization as studied in syntax, morphology, phonology and phonetics; they are generally more tangible than aspects concerned with their content. But semanticists in general hold that semantics, the study of linguistic meaning, indeed has an object to study that is related but distinct from the forms in which it is encoded, from the communicative intentions of the speaker and from the resulting understanding of the addressee.

1.2 Aspects of meaning

The English noun *meaning* is multiply ambiguous, and there are several readings that are relevant for semantics. One branch of investigation starts out with meaning as a notion rooted in *communication*. Grice (1957) has pointed out that we can ask what a *speaker* meant by uttering something, and what the *utterance* means that the speaker uttered. Take John F. Kennedy's utterance of the sentence *Ich bin ein Berliner* on June 26, 1963. What JFK meant was that in spite of the cold war, the USA would not surrender West Berlin – which was probably true. What the utterance meant was that JFK is a citizen of Berlin, which was clearly false. Obviously, the speaker's meaning is derived from the utterance meaning and the communicative situation in which it was uttered. The way how this is derived, however, is less obvious – cf. article 2 [this volume] (Jacob) *Meaning, intentionality and communication*, especially on particularized conversational implicatures.

A complementary approach is concerned with the meaning of linguistic forms, sometimes called literal meanings, like the meaning of the German sentence Ich bin ein Berliner which was uttered by JFK to convey the intended utterance meaning. With forms, one can distinguish the following aspects of meaning (cf. also article 3 [this volume] (Textor) *Sense and reference*, and article 4 [this volume] (Abbott) *Reference*). The character is the meaning independent from the situation of utterance (like speaker, addressee, time and location – see Kaplan 1978). The character of the sentence used by JFK is that the speaker of the utterance is a citizen of Berlin at the time of utterance. If we find a sticky note in a garbage can, reading I am back in five minutes – where we don't know the speaker, the time, or location of the utterance – we just know the character. A character, supplied with the situation of utterance, gets us the content or intension (Frege's Sinn) of a linguistic form. In the proper historical context, JFK's utterance has the content that JFK is a citizen of Berlin on June 26, 1963. (We gloss over the fact here that this first has to be decoded as a particular speech act, like an assertion.) This is a proposition, which can be true or false in particular circumstances. The extension or reference of an expression (Frege's Bedeutung) is its content when applied to the situation of utterance. In the case of a proposition, this is a truth value; in the case of a name or a referring expression, this is an entity. Sometimes meaning is used in a more narrow sense, as opposed to reference; here I have used meaning in an encompassing way.

Arguably, the communicative notion of meaning is the primary one. Meaning is rooted in the intention to communicate. But human communication crucially relies on linguistic forms, which are endowed with meaning as outlined, and for which speakers can construct meanings in a compositional way (see article 6 [this volume] (Pagin & Westerståhl) *Compositionality*). Semantics is concerned with the meaning of linguistic forms, a secondary and derived notion. But the use of these forms in communication is crucial data to re-engineer the underlying meaning of the forms. The ways how literal meanings are used in acts of communication and their effects on the participants, in general, is part of pragmatics (cf. article 11 [Semantics: Interfaces] (Jaszczolt) *Semantics and pragmatics*).

1.3 Types of access to meaning

Grounding meaning of linguistic expressions in communication suggests that there are various kinds of empirical evidence for meaning. First, we can observe the external behavior of the participants in, before and after the act of communication. Some kinds of behavior can be more directly related to linguistic meaning than others, and hence will play a more central role in discovering underlying meaning. For example, commands often lead to a visible non-linguistic reaction, and simple *yes/no*-questions will lead to linguistic reactions that are easily decodable. Secondly, we can measure aspects of the external behavior in detail, like the reaction times to questions, or the speed in which passages of text are read (cf. article 9 [Semantics: Typology, Diachrony and Processing] (Frazier) *Meaning in psycholinguistics*). Third, we can observe physiological reactions of participants in communication, like the changing size of their pupil, the saccades of the eyes reading a text, the eye gaze when presented to a visual input together with a spoken comment, or the electromagnetic field generated by their cortex (cf. article 15 (Bott, Featherston, Radó & Stolterfoht) *Experimental methods*. Fourth, we can test hypotheses concerning meaning in the output of linguistic forms itself, using statistical techniques applied to corpora (cf. article 15 [Semantics: Typology, Diachrony and Processing] (Katz) *Semantics in corpus linguistics*).

1.4 Is semantics possible?

The reader should be warned that correlations between meanings and observable phenomena like non-linguistic patterns of behavior or brain scans do not guarantee that the study of meaning can be carried out successfully. Leonard Bloomfield, a behavioralist, considered the observable effects so complex and interwoven with other causal chains that the science of semantics is impossible:

> We have defined the meaning of a linguistic form as the situation in which the speaker utters it and the response which it calls forth in the hearer. [...] In order to give a scientifically accurate definition of meaning for every form of a language, we should have to have a scientifically accurate knowledge of everything in the speaker's world. The actual extent of human knowledge is very small compared to this. [...] The statement of meanings is therefore the weak point in language-study, and will remain so until human knowledge advances very far beyond its present state.
>
> (Bloomfield 1933: 139f)

We could imagine similar skepticism concerning the science of semantics from a neuroscientist believing that meanings are activation patterns of our head. The huge number of such patterns, and their variation across individuals that we certainly have to expect, seems to preclude that they will provide the foundation for the study of meaning.

Despite Bloomfield's qualms, the field of semantics has flourished. Where he went wrong was in believing that we have to consider the whole world of the speaker, or the speaker's whole brain. There are ways to cut out phenomena that stand in relation to, and bear evidence for, meanings in much more specific ways. For example, we can investigate whether a specific sentence in a particular context and describing a particular situation is considered true or false; and derive from that hypotheses about the meaning of the sentence and the meaning of the words involved in that sentence. The usual methods of science – forming hypotheses and models, deriving predictions, making observations and constructing experiments that support or falsify the hypotheses – have turned out to be applicable to linguistic semantics as well.

1.5 Native semantic activities

There are many native activities that directly address aspects of meaning. When Adam named the animals of paradise he assigned expressions to meanings, as we do today when naming things or persons or defining technical terms. We explain the meaning of words or idioms by paraphrasing them – that is, by offering different expressions with the same or at least similar meanings. We can refer to aspects of meaning: We say that one expression *means* the same as another one, or its opposite; we say that one expression *refers* to a subcase of another. As for speaker's meanings, we can elaborate on what someone meant by such-and-such words, and can point out differences between that and what the words actually meant or how they were understood by the addressee. Furthermore, for human communication to work it is crucial that untruthful use of language can be detected, and liars can be identified and punished. For this, a notion of what it means for a sentence or text to be true or false is crucial. Giving a statement at court means to know what it means to speak the truth, and the whole truth. Hence, it seems that meanings are firmly established in the pre-scientific ways we talk about language.

We can translate, that is, rephrase an expression in one language by an expression in another while keeping the meaning largely constant. We can teach the meaning of words or expressions to second language learners or to children acquiring their native language – even though both groups, in particular children in first language acquisition, will acquire meanings to a large part implicitly, by contextual clues. The sheer possibility of translation has been enormously important for the development of humankind. We find records of associated practices, like the making of dictionaries, dating back to Sumerian-Akkadian glossaries of 2300 BC.

These linguistic activities show that meaning is a natural notion, not a theoretical concept. They also provide important source of evidence for meaning. For example, it would be nearly impossible to construct a dictionary in linguistic field work without being able to ask for what a particular word means, or how a particular object is called. As another example, it would be foolish to dismiss the monumental achievements of the art of dictionary writing as evidence for the meaning of words.

But there are problems with this kind of evidence that one must be aware of. Take dictionary writing. Traditional dictionaries are often unsystematic and imprecise in their description of meaning. They do not distinguish systematically between contextual (or "occasional") meaning and systematic meaning, nor do they keep ambiguity and polysemy apart in a rigorous way. They often do not distinguish between linguistic aspects and more general cultural aspects of the meaning and use of words. Weinreich (1964) famously criticized the 115 meanings of the verb *to turn* that can be found in Webster's Third Dictionary. Lexicography has greatly improved since then, with efforts to define lexical entries by a set of basic words and by recognizing regularities like systematic variations between word meanings (e.g. the intransitive use of transitive verbs, or the polysemy triggered in particular contexts of use).

1.6 Talking about meanings

Pre-scientific ways to address meanings rely on an important feature of human language, its *self reference* – we can use language to talk about language. This feature is so entrenched in language that it went unnoticed until logicians like Frege, Russell and Tarski, working with much more restricted languages, pointed out the importance of the metalanguage / object language distinction. It is only quite recently that we distinguish between regular language, reference to expressions, and reference to meanings by typographical conventions and write things like "*XXX* means 'YYY'".

The possibility to describe meanings may be considered circular – as when Tarski states that *'Snow is white' is true if and only if snow is white*. However, it does work under certain conditions. First, the meaning of an unknown word can be described, or at least delimited, by an expression that uses known words; this is the classical case of a definition. If we had only this procedure available as evidence for meaning, things would be hopeless because we have to start somewhere with a few expressions whose meanings are known; but once we have those, they can act as bootstraps for the whole lexicon of a language. The theory of Natural Semantic Metalanguage even claims that a small set of concepts (around 200) and a few modes of combining them are sufficient to achieve access to the meanings of all words of a language (Goddard 1998).

Second, the meanings of an ambiguous word or expression can be paraphrased by expressions that have only one or the other meaning. This is common practice in linguistic semantics, e.g. when describing the meaning of *He saw that gasoline can explode* as (a) 'He saw an explosion of a can of gasoline' and (b) 'He recognized the fact that gasoline is explosive'. Speakers will generally agree that the original sentence has the two meanings teased apart by the paraphrases. There are variations on this access to meaning. For example, we might consider a sentence in different linguistic contexts and observe differences in the meaning of the sentence by recognizing that it has to be paraphrased differently. For the paraphrases, we can use a language that has specific devices that help to clarify meanings, like variables. For example, we can state that a sentence like *Every man likes a woman that likes him* has a reading 'Every man x likes a woman y that likes x', but not 'There is a woman y that every man x likes and that likes x'. The disadvantage of this is that the paraphrases cannot be easily grasped by naïve native speakers. In the extreme case, we can use a fully specified formal language to specify such meanings, such as first-order predicate logic; the existing reading of our example then could be specified as $\forall x[\text{man}(x) \rightarrow \exists y[\text{woman}(y) \wedge \text{likes}(x, y) \wedge \text{likes}(y, x)]]$.

Talking about meanings is a very important source of evidence for meanings. However, it is limited not only by the problem mentioned above, that it describes meanings with the help of other meanings. There are many cases where speakers cannot describe the meanings of expressions because this task is too complex – think of children acquiring their first language, or aphasics loosing the capacity of language. And there are cases in which the description of meanings would be too complex for the linguist. We may think of first fieldwork sessions in a research project on an unknown language. Somewhat closer to home, we may also think of the astonishingly complex meanings of natural language determiners such as *a, some, a certain, a particular, a given* or indefinite *this* in *there was this man standing at the door* whose meanings had to be teased apart by careful considerations of their acceptability in particular contexts.

2 Fieldwork techniques in semantics

In this section we will discuss various techniques that have been used in linguistic fieldwork, understood in a wide sense as to include work on one's own language and on language acquisition, for example. There are a variety of sources that reflect on possible procedures; for example, the authors in McDaniel, McKee & Cairns (eds.) (1996) discuss techniques for the investigation of syntax in child language, many of which also apply to semantic investigations, and Matthewson (2004) is concerned with techniques for semantic research in American languages which, of course, are applicable for work on other languages as well (cf. also article 13 [this volume] (Matthewson) *Methods in cross-linguistic semantics*, and article 10 [Semantics: Typology, Diachrony and Processing] (Crain) *Meaning in first language acquisition*).

2.1 Observation, transcription and translation

The classical linguistic fieldwork method is to record conversations and texts in natural settings, transcribe them, and assign translations, ideally with the help of speakers that are competent in a language that they share with the investigator. In classical American structuralism, this has been the method *de rigueur*, and it is certainly of great importance when we want to investigate natural use of language.

However, this technique is also severely limited. First, even large text collections may not provide the evidence that distinguishes between different hypothesis. Consider superlatives in English; is *John is the tallest student* true if John and Mary both are students that are of the same height and taller than any other student? Competent English speakers say no, superlatives must be unique – but it might be impossible to find out on the basis of a corpus of non-elicited text.

Secondly, there is the problem of translation. Even when we grant that the translation is competent according to usual standards, it is not clear how we should deal with distinctions in the object language that are not easily made in the meta language. For example, Matthewson (2004) shows that in Menominee (Algonquian, Northern Central United States of America), inalienable nouns can have a prefix *me-* indicating an arbitrary owner, as contrasted with a prefix *o-* indicating a specific 3rd person owner. This difference could not be derived from simple translations of Menominee texts into English, as English does not make this distinction. There is also the opposite problem of distinctions that are forced on us by the meta language; for example, pronouns in English referring to humans distinguish two genders, which may not be a feature of the object language. Hence, as Matthewson puts it, translations should be seen as clues for semantic analysis, rather as its result.

Translations, or more generally paraphrases, are problematic for more fundamental reasons as evidence for meaning, as they explain the meaning of an expression α by way of the meaning of an expression β, hence it presupposes the existence and knowledge of meanings, and a judgment of similarity of meaning. However, it appears that without accepting this type of hermeneutic circle the study of semantics could not get off the ground. But there are methods to test hypotheses that have been generated first with the help of translations and paraphrases by independent means.

2.2 Pointing

Pointing is a universal non-linguistic human behavior that aligns with aspects of meanings of certain types of linguistic expressions (cf. also article 13 [Semantics: Interfaces] (Diessel) *Deixis and demonstratives*). Actually, pointing may be as characteristic for humans as language, as humans appear to be the only apes that point (cf. Tomasello 2008).

Pointing is most relevant for referring expressions, with names as the prototypical example (cf. article 4 [this volume] (Abbott) *Reference*). These expressions denote a particular entity that is also identified by the pointing gesture, and hence pointing is independent evidence for the meaning of such expressions. For example, if in a linguistic fieldwork situation an informant points to a person and utters *Max*, this might be taken to be the name of that person. We can conclude that *Max* denotes that person, in other words, that the meaning of *Max* is the person pointed at.

Simple as this scenario is, there are certain prerequisites for it to work. For example, the pointing gesture must be recognized as such; in different cultures, the index finger, the stretched-out hand, or an upward movement of the chin may be used, and in some cultures there may be a taboo against pointing gestured when directed at humans. Furthermore, there must be one most salient object in the pointing cone (cf. Kranstedt et al. 2006) that will then be identified. This presupposes a pre-linguistic notion of objects, and of saliency. This might work well when persons or animals are pointed at, who are cognitively highly salient. But mistakes can occur when there is more than one object in the pointing cone that are equally salient. When Captain Cook on his second voyage visited an island in the New Hebrides with friendly natives and tried to communicate with them, he pointed to the ground. What he heard was *tanna*, which he took as the name of the island, which is still known under this name. Yet the meaning of *tana* in all Melanesian languages is simply "earth". The native name for Tanna is reported to be *parei* (Gregory 2003); it is not in use anymore.

Pointing gestures may also help to identify the meaning of common nouns, adjectives, or verbs – expressions that denote sets of entities or events. The pointing is directed towards a specimen, but reference is at entities of the same type as the one pointed at. There is an added source of ambiguity or vagueness here: What is "the same type as"? On his first voyage, Captain Cook made landfall in Australia, and observed creatures with rabbit-like ears hopping on their hind legs. When naturalist Joseph Banks asked the local Guugu Yimidhirr people how they are called, presumably with the help of some pointing gesture, he was the first to record the word *kangaroo*. But the word *gangurru* actually just refers to a large species of black kangaroo, not to the marsupial family in general (cf. Haviland 1974).

Quine (1960: ch. II), in an argument to discount the possibility of true translation, famously described the problems that even a simple act like pointing and naming might involve. Assume a linguist points to a white rabbit, and gets the response *gavagai* . Quine asks whether this may mean 'rabbit', or perhaps 'animal', or perhaps 'white', or perhaps even 'non-detached rabbit parts'. It also might mean 'rabbit stage', in which case repeated pointing will identify different reference objects. All these options are theoretical possibilities under the assumption that words can refer to arbitrary aspects of reality. However, it is now commonly assumed that language is build on broad cognitive commonalities about entities and classes. There is evidence that pre-linguistic babies and higher animals have concepts of objects (as contrasted to substances) and animals (as contrasted to lifeless beings) that preclude a conceptualization of a rabbit as a set of rabbit legs, a rabbit body, a rabbit head and a pair of rabbit ears moving in unison. Furthermore, there is evidence that objects are called with terms of a middle layer of a taxonomic hierarchy, the so-called "generic level", avoiding terms that are too general or too specific (cf. Berlin, Breedlove & Raven 1973). Hence a rabbit will not be called *thing* in English, or *animal*, and it will not be called *English angora* either except perhaps by rabbit breeders that work with a different taxonomy. This was the reason for Captain Cooks misunderstanding of *gangurru*; the native Guugu Yimidhirr people had a different, and more refined, taxonomic hierarchy for Australian animals, where species of kangaroo formed the generic level; for the British visitors the family itself belonged to that level.

Pointing, or related gestures, have been used to identify the meaning of words. For example, in the original study of Berlin & Kay (1969) on color terms subjects were presented with a two-dimensional chart of 320 colors varying according to spectral color and saturation. The task was to identify the best specimen for a particular color word (the focal color) and the extent to which colors fall under a particular color word. Similar techniques have been used for other lexical fields, for example for the classification of vessels using terms like *cup*, *mug* or *pitcher* (cf. Kempton 1981; see Fig. 12.1).

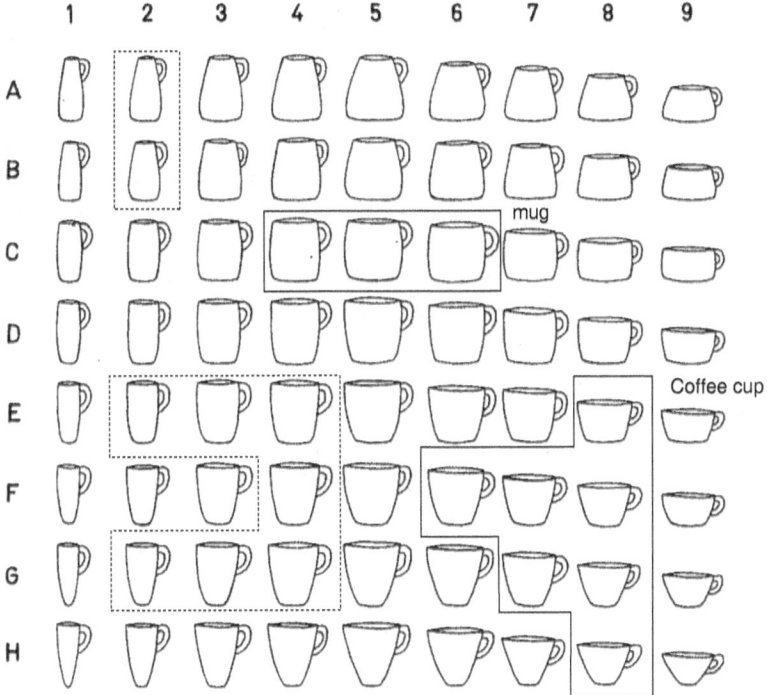

Fig. 12.1: Vessel categories after Kempton (1981: 103). Bold lines: Identification of >80% agreement between subjects for mug and coffee cup. Dotted lines: Hypothetical concept that would violate connectedness and convexity (see below)

Tests of this type have been carried out in two ways: Either subjects were presented with a field of reference objects ordered after certain dimensions; e.g. Berlin & Kay (1969) presented colors ordered after their wave length (the order they present themselves in a rainbow) and after their saturation (with white and black as the extremes). Kempton's vessels were presented as varying in two dimensions: The relation between the upper and lower diameters, and the relation between height and width. When judging whether certain items fall under a term or not, the neighboring items that already have been classified might influence the decision. Another technique, which was carried out in the World Color Survey (see Kay et al. 2008), presented color chips in random order to avoid this kind of influence.

The pointing test can be used in two ways: Either we point at an entity in order to get the term that is applicable to that entity, or we have a term and point to various objects to find out whether the term is applicable. The first approach asks an *onomasiological* question; it is concerned with the question: How is this thing called? The second approach asks the complementary *semasiological* question: What does this expression mean?

Within a Fregean theory of meaning, a distinction is made between reference and sense (cf. article 3 [this volume] (Textor) Sense and reference). With pointing to concrete entities we gain access to the reference of expressions, and not to the sense, the concept that allows us to identify the reference. But by varying potential reference objects we can form hypotheses about the underlying concept, even though we can never be certain that by a variation of reference objects we will uncover all aspects of the underlying concept. Goodman (1955) illustrated this with the hypothetical adjective grue that, say, refers to green objects when used before the year 2100 and to blue objects when used after that time; no pointing experiment executed before 2100 could differentiate grue from green. Meaning shifts like that do happen historically: The term Scotia referred to Ireland before the 11th century, and after to Scotland; the German term gelb was reduced in extension when the term orange entered the language (cf. the traditional local term Gelbe Rüben 'yellow turnips' for carrots). But these are language changes, and not meanings of items within a language. A meaning like the hypothetical grue appears as strange as a reference towards non-detached rabbit parts. We work under the hypothesis that meanings of lexical items are restricted by general principles of uniformity over time. There are other such principles that restrict possible meanings, for example connectedness and, more specifically, convexity (Gärdenfors 2000). In the vessel example above, where potential reference objects were presented following certain dimensions, we expect that concepts do not apply to discontinuous areas and have the general property that when x is an α and y is an α, then everything in between x and y is an α as well. The dotted lines in Fig. 12.1 represent an extension of a concept that would violate connectedness and convexity.

In spite of all its problems, pointing is the most elementary kind of evidence for meaning without which linguistic field work, everyday communication and language acquisition would be impossible. Yet it seems that little research has been done on pointing and language acquisition, be it first or second. Its importance, however, was recognized as early as in St. Augustin's Confessions (5th century AD), where he writes about his own learning of language:

> When they [the elders] called some thing by name and pointed it out while they spoke, I saw it and realized that the thing they wished to indicate was called by the name they then uttered. And what they meant was made plain by the gestures of their bodies, by a kind of natural language, common to all nations [...]
>
> (Confessions, Book I: 8)

2.3 Truth value judgments (TVJ)

Truth value judgments do the same job for the meaning of sentences as pointing does for referring expressions. In the classical setup, a situation is presented with non-linguistic means together with a declarative sentence, and the speaker has to indicate whether this sentence is true or false with respect to the situation. This judgement is an linguistic act by itself, so it can be doubted that this provides a way to base the study of meaning wholly outside of language. But arguably, agreeing or disagreeing are more primitive linguistic acts that may even rely on simple gestures, just as in the case of pointing.

The similarity between referential expressions – which identify objects – and declarative sentences – which identify states of affairs in which they are true – is related to Frege's identification of the reference of sentences with their truth value with respect to a particular situation (even though this was not the original motivation for this identification, cf. Frege 1892). This is reflected in the two basic extensional types assumed in sentence semantics: Type e for entities referred to by names, and type t for truth values referred to by sentences. But there is an important difference here: There are many distinct objects – D_e, the universe of discourse, is typically large; but there are just two (basic) truth values – D_t, the set of truth values, standardly is {0, 1}, falsity and truth. Hence we can distinguish referring expressions more easily by their reference than we can distinguish declarative sentences. One consequence of this is that onomasiological tests do not work. We cannot present a "truth value" and expect a declarative sentence that is true. Also, on presenting a situation in a picture or a little movie we cannot expect that the linguistic reactions are as uniform as when we, say, present the picture of an apple. But the semasiological direction works fine: We can present speakers with a declarative sentence and a situation or a set of situations and ask whether the sentence is true in those situations.

Truth values are not just an ingenious idea of language philosophers to reduce the meaning of declarative sentences to judgments whether a sentence is true or false in given situations. They are used pre-linguistically, e.g. in court procedures. Within linguistics, they are used to investigate the meaning of sentences in experiments and in linguistic field work. They have been particularly popular in the study of language acquisition because they require a rather simple reaction by the child that can be expected even from two-year olds.

The TVJ task comes in two flavors. In both, the subjects are presented with a sentence and a situation, specified by a picture, an acted-out scene with hand puppets or a movie, or by the actual world provided that the subjects have the necessary information about it. In the first version, the subjects should simply state whether the sentence is true or false. This can be done by a linguistic reaction, by a gesture, by pressing one of two buttons, or by ticking off one of two boxes. We may also record the speed of these reactions in order to get data about the processing of expressions. In the second version, there is a character, e.g. a hand puppet, that utters the sentence in question, and the subjects should reward or punish the character if the sentence is true or false with respect to the situation presented (see e.g. Crain 1991). A reward could be, for example, feeding the hand puppet a cookie. Interestingly, the second procedure taps into cognitive resources of children that are otherwise not as easily accessible.

Gordon (1998), in a description of TVJ in language acquisition, points out that this task is quite natural and easy. This is presumably so because truth value judgment is an elementary linguistic activity, in contrast to, say, grammaticality judgments. TVJ also puts less demands on answers than wh-questions (e.g. *Who chased the zebra?* vs. *Did the lion chase the zebra?*) This makes it the test of choice for children and for language-impaired persons.

But there are potential problems in carrying out TVJ tasks. For example, Crain et al. (1998) have investigated the phenomenon that children seem to consider a sentence like *Every farmer is feeding a donkey* false if there is a donkey that is not fed by the farmer. They argue that children are confused by the extra donkey and try to reinterpret the sentence in a way that seems to make sense. A setup in which attention is not drawn to a single object might be better; even adding a second unfed donkey makes the judgments more adult-like. Also, children respond better to scenes that are acted out than to static pictures. In designing TVJ experiments, one should consider the fact that positive answers are given quicker and more easily than negative ones. Furthermore, one should be aware that unconscious reactions of the experimenter may provide subtle clues for the "right" answer (the "Clever Hans" effect, named after the horse that supposedly could solve arithmetic problems). For example, when acting out and describing a scene, the experimenter may be more hesitant when uttering a false statement.

2.4 TVJ and presuppositions/implicatures

There are different aspects of meaning beyond the literal meaning, such as presuppositions, conventional implicatures, conversational implicatures and the like, and it would be interesting to know how such meaning components fare in TVJ tasks. Take presuppositions (cf. also article 14 [Semantics: Interfaces] (Beaver & Geurts) *Presupposition*). Theories such as Stalnaker (1974) that treat them as preconditions of interpretation predict that sentences cannot be interpreted with respect to situations that violate their presuppositions. The TVJ test does not seem to support this view. The sentence *The dog is eating the bone* will most likely be judged true with respect to a picture showing two dogs, where one of the dogs is eating a bone. This may be considered evidence for the ease of accommodation, which consists of restricting the context to the one dog that is eating a bone. Including a third option or truth value like "don't know" might reveal the specific meaning contribution of presuppositions

As for conversational implicature (cf. article 15 [Semantics: Interfaces] (Simons) *Implicature*) we appear to get the opposite picture. TVJ tests have been used to check the relevance of scalar implicatures. For example, Noveck (2001), building on work of Smith (1980), argued that children are "more logical" than adults because they can dissociate literal meanings from scalar implicatures. Children up to 11 years react to statements like *some giraffes have long necks* (where the picture shows that all giraffes have long necks) with an affirmative answer, while most adults find them inappropriate.

2.5 TVJ variants: Picture selection and acting out

The picture selection task has been applied for a variety of purposes beyond truth values (cf. Gerken & Shady 1998). But for the purpose of investigating sentence meanings, it can be seen as a variant to the TVJ task: The subject is exposed to a declarative sentence and two or more pictures and has to identify the picture for which the sentence is true. It is good to include irrelevant pictures as filler items, which can test the attention of the subjects. The task can be used to identify situations that fit best to a sentence. For example, for sentences with presuppositions it is expected that a picture will be chosen that does not only satisfy the assertion, but also the presupposition. So, if the sentence is *The dog is eating a bone*, and if a picture with one or two dogs is shown, then presumably the picture with one dog will be preferred. Also, sentences whose scalar implicature is satisfied will be preferred over those for which this is not the case. For example, if the sentence is *some giraffes have long necks*, a picture in which some but not all giraffes have long necks will be preferred over a picture in which all giraffes are long-necked.

Another relative of the TVJ task is the Act Out task in which the subject has to "act out" a sentence with a scene such that the sentence is true. Again, we should expect that sentences are acted out in a way as to satisfy all meaning components – assertion, presupposition, and implicature – of a sentence.

2.6 Restrictions of the TVJ methodology

One restriction of the various TVJ methodologies appears to be that they just target expressions that have a truth value, that is, sentences. However, they allow to investigate the meaning of subsentential expressions, under the assumption that the meaning of sentences is computed in a compositional way from the meanings of their syntactic parts (cf. article 6 [this volume] (Pagin & Westerståhl) *Compositionality*). For example, the meaning of spatial presuppositions like *on, on top of, above* or *over* can be investigated with scenes in which objects are arranged in particular ways.

Another potential restriction of TVJ as discussed so far is that we assumed that the situations are presented by pictures. Language is not restricted to encoding information that can be represented by visual stimuli. But we can also present sounds, movie scenes or comic strips that represent temporal developments, or even olfactory and tactile stimuli to judge the range of meanings of words (cf. e.g. Majid et al. 2006 for verbs of cutting and breaking).

TVJ is also difficult to apply when deictic expressions are involved, as they often require reference to the speaker, who is typically not part of the picture. For example, in English the sentence *The ball is in front of the tree* means that the ball is in between the speaker that faces the tree and the tree; the superficially corresponding sentence in Hausa means that the ball is behind the tree (cf. Hill 1982). In English, the tree is seen as facing the speaker, whereas in Hausa the speaker aligns with the tree (cf. article 5 [Semantics: Typology, Diachrony and Processing] (Pederson) *The expression of space*). Such differences are not normally represented in pictures, but it can be done. One could either represent the picture from a particular angle, or represent a speaker with a particular position and orientation in the picture itself and ask the subject to identify with that figure.

The TVJ technique is systematically limited for sentences that do not have truth values, such as questions, commands, or exclamatives. But we can generalize it to a judgment of appropriateness of sentences given a situation, which sometimes is done to investigate politeness phenomena and the like. There are also subtypes of declarative sentences that are difficult to investigate with TVJ, namely modal statements, e.g. *Mary must be at home*, or habituals and generics that allow for exceptions, like *Delmer walks to school*, or *Birds fly* (cf. article 8 [Semantics: Noun Phrases and Verb Phrases] (Carlson) *Genericity*). This is arguably so because those sentences require to consider different possible worlds, which cannot be easily represented graphically.

2.7 TVJ with linguistic presentation of situation

The TVJ technique can be applied for modal or generic statements if we present the situation linguistically, by describing it. For example, we could ask whether *Delmer walks to school* is true if Delmer walks every day except Fridays, when his father gives him a ride. Of course, this kind of linguistic elicitation technique can be used in nearly all the cases described so far. It has clear advantages: Linguistic descriptions are easy and cheap to produce and can focus the attention of the subject to aspects that are of particular relevance for the task. For this reason it is very popular for quick elicitations whether a sentence can mean such-and-such.

Matthewson (2004) argues that elicitation is virtually the only way to get to more subtle semantic phenomena. She also argues that it can be combined with other techniques, like TVJ and grammaticality judgments. For example, in investigating aspect marking in St'át'imcets Salish (Salishan, Southwestern Canada) the sentence *Have you been to Seattle?* is translated using an adverb *lán* that otherwise occurs with the meaning 'already'; a follow-up question could be whether it is possible to drop *lán* in this context, retaining roughly the same meaning.

The linguistic presentation of scenes comes with its own limitations. There is the foundational problem that we get at the meaning of an expression α by way of the meaning of an expression β. It cannot be applied in case of insufficient linguistic competence, as with young children or language-impaired persons.

2.8 Acceptability tests

In this type of test, speakers are given an expression and a linguistic context and/or an description of an extralinguistic situation, and are asked whether the expression is acceptable with respect to this context or the situation. With it, we can explore the felicity conditions of an expression, which often are closely related to certain aspects of its meaning.

Acceptability tests are the natural way to investigate presuppositions and conventional implicatures of expressions. For example, additive focus particles like *also* presuppose that the predication holds for an alternative to the focus item. Hence in a context like *John went to Paris*, the sentence *John also went to PRAGUE* is felicitous, but the sentence *Mary also went to PRAGUE* is not. Acceptability tests can also be used to investigate information-structural distinctions. For example, in English, different accent patterns indicate different focus structures; this can be seen when judging sentences like *JOHN went to Paris* vs. *John went to PARIS* in the context of questions like *Who went to Paris?* and *John went where?* (cf. article 5 [Semantics: Sentence and Information Structure] (Krifka) *Questions*). As another example, Portner & Yabushita (1998) discussed the acceptability of sentences with a topic-comment structure in Japanese where the topic was identified by a noun phrase with a restrictive relative clause and found that such structures are better if the relative clause corresponds to a comment on the topic in the preceding discourse. Acceptability tests can also be used to test the appropriateness of terms with honorific meaning, or various shades of expressive meaning, which have been analyzed as conventional implicatures by Potts (2005).

When applying acceptability judgments, it is natural to present the context first, to preclude that the subject first comes up with other contexts which may influence the interpretation. Another issue is whether the contexts should be specified in the object language, or can also be given in the meta-language that is used to carry out the investigation. Matthewson (2004) discusses the various advantages and disadvantages – especially if the investigator has a less-than-perfect command over the object language – and argues that using a meta-language is acceptable, as language informants generally can resist the possible influence of the metalanguage on their responses.

2.9 Elicited production

We can turn the TVJ test on its head and ask subjects to describe given situations with their own words. In language acquisition research, this technique is known as "elicited production", and encompasses all linguistic reactions to planned stimuli (cf. Thornton 1998). In this technique the presumed meaning is fixed, and controls the linguistic production; we can hypothesize about how this meaning can be represented in language. The best known example probably is the retelling of a little movie called the Pear Story, which has unearthed interesting differences in the use of tense and aspect distinctions in different languages (cf. Chafe 1980 for the original publication). Another example, which allows to study the use of meanings in interaction, is the "map task", where one person explains the configuration of objects or a route on a map to another without visual contact.

The main problem of elicited production is that the number of possible reactions by speakers is, in principle, unlimited. It might well be that the type of utterances one expects do not occur at all. For example, we could set up a situation in which person A thinks that person B thinks that person C thinks that it is raining, to test the recursivity of propositional attitude expressions, but we will have to wait long till such utterances are actually produced. So it is crucial to select cues that constrain the linguistic production in a way that ensures that the expected utterances will indeed occur.

2.10 From sentence meanings to word meanings

The TVJ technique and its variants test the meaning of sentences, not of words or subsentential expressions. Also, with elicitation techniques, often we will get sentence-like reactions. With elicited translations, it is also advisable to use whole sentences instead of single words or simpler expressions, as Matthewson (2004) argues. It is possible to elicit the basic meaning of nouns or certain verbs directly, but this is impossible for many other words. The first ten most frequent words in English are often cited as being *the, of, and, a, to, in, is, you, that*; it would be impossible to ask a naïve speaker of English what they mean or discover there meanings in other more direct ways, with the possible exception of *you*.

We can derive hypotheses about the meaning of such words by using them in sentences and judging the truth value of the sentences with respect to certain situations, and their acceptability in certain contexts. For example, we can unearth the basic uses of the definite article by presenting pictures containing one or two barking dogs, and ask to pick out the best picture for *the dog is barking*. The underlying idea is that the assignment of meanings to expressions is compositional, that is, that the meaning of the complex expression is a result of the meaning of its parts and the way they are combined.

3 Communicative behavior

Perhaps the most important function of language is to communicate, that is, to transfer meanings from one mind to another. So we should be able to find evidence for meaning by investigating communicative acts. This is obvious in a trivial sense: If A tells B something, B will often act in certain ways that betray that B understood what

A meant. More specifically, we can investigate particular aspects of communication and relate them to particular aspects of meaning. We will look at three examples here: Presuppositions, conversational implicatures and focus-induced alternatives.

Presuppositions (cf. article 14 [Semantics: Interfaces] (Beaver & Geurts) *Presupposition*) are meaning components that are taken for granted, and hence appear to be downtoned. This shows up in possible communicative reactions. For example, consider the following dialogues:

A: *Unfortunately, it is raining.*
B: *No, it isn't.*

Here, B denies that it is raining; the meaning component of *unfortunate* expressing regret by the speaker is presupposed or conventionally implicated.

A: *It is unfortunate that it is raining.*
B: *No, it isn't.*

Here, B presupposes that it is raining, and states that this is unfortunate. In order to deny the presupposed part, other conversational reactions are necessary, like *But that's not unfortunate*, or *But it doesn't rain*. Simple and more elaborate denials are a fairly consistent test to distinguish between presupposed and proffered content (cf. van der Sandt 1988).

For conversational implicatures (cf. article 15 [Semantics: Interfaces] (Simons) *Implicature*) the most distinctive property is that they are cancelable without leading to contradiction. For example, *John has three children* triggers the scalar implicature that John has exactly three children. But this meaning component can be explicitly suspended: *John has three children, if not more*. It can be explicitly cancelled: *John has three children, in fact he has four*. And it does not arise in particular contexts, e.g. in the context of *People get a tax reduction if they have three children*. This distinguishes conversational implicatures from presuppositions and semantic entailments: *John has three children, {if not two / in fact, two}* is judged contradictory.

Our last example concerns the introduction of alternatives that are indicated by focus, which in turn can be marked in various ways, e.g. by sentence accent. A typical procedure to investigate the role of focus is the question-answer test (cf. article 5 [Semantics: Sentence and Information Structure] (Krifka) *Questions*). In the following four potential question-answer pairs (A1-B1) and (A2-B2) are well-formed, but (A1-B2) and (A2-B1) are odd.

A1: *Who ate the cake?*
A2: *What did Mary eat?*

B1: *MARY ate the cake.*
B2: *Mary ate the CAKE.*

This has been interpreted as saying that the alternatives of the answer have to correspond to the alternatives of the question.

To sum up, using communicative behavior as evidence for meaning consists in evaluating the appropriateness of certain conversational interactions. Competent speakers generally agree on such judgments. The technique has been used in particular to identify, and differentiate, between different meaning components having to do with the presentation of meanings, in particular with information structure.

4 Behavioral effects of semantic processing

When discussing evidence for the meaning of expressions we have focused so far on the meanings themselves. We can also investigate how semantic information is processed, and get a handle on how the human mind computes meanings. To get information on semantic processing, judgment tasks are often not helpful, and might even be deceiving. We need other types of evidence that arguably stand in a more direct relation to semantic processing. It is customary to distinguish between behavioral data on the one hand, and neurophysiologic data that directly investigates brain phenomena on the other. In this section we will focus on behavioral approaches (cf. also article 15 [this volume] (Bott, Featherston, Radó & Stolterfoht) *Experimental methods*).

4.1 Reaction times

The judgment tasks for meanings described so far can also tap into the processing of semantic information if the timing of judgments is considered. The basic assumption is that longer reaction times, everything else being equal, are a sign for semantic processing load.

For example, Clark & Lucy (1975) have shown that indirect speech acts take longer for processing than direct ones, and attribute this to the additional inferences that they require. Noveck (2004) has shown that the computation of scalar implicature takes time; people that reacted to sentences like *Some elephants are mammals* with a denial (because all elephants and not just some are) took considerably longer. Kim (2008) has investigated the processing of *only*-sentences, showing that the affirmative content is evaluated first, and the presupposition is taken into account only after.

Reaction times are relevant for many other psycholinguistic paradigms, beyond tasks like TVJ, and can provide hints for semantic processing. One notable example is the semantic phenomenon of coercion, changes of meanings that are triggered by the particular context in which meaning-bearing expressions occur (cf. article 10 [Semantics: Lexical Structures and Adjectives] (de Swart) *Mismatches and coercion*). One well-known example is aspectual coercion: Temporal adverbials of the type *until dawn* select for atelic verbal predicates, hence *The horse slept until dawn* is fine. But *The horse jumped until dawn* is acceptable as well, under an iterative interpretation of *jump* that is not reflected overtly. This adaptation of the basic meaning to fit the requirements of the context should be cognitively costly, and there is indeed evidence for the additional semantic processing involved. Piñango et al. (2006) report on various studies and their own experiments that made use of the dual task interference paradigm: Subjects listen to sentences and, at particular points, deal with an unrelated written lexical decision task. They were significantly slower in deciding this task just after an expression that triggered coercion (e.g. *until* in the second example, as compared to the first). This can be taken as evidence for the cognitive effort involved in coercion; notice that there is not syntactic difference between the sentences to which such reaction time difference could be attributed.

4.2 Reading process: Self-paced reading and eye tracking

Another window into semantic processing is the observation of the reading process. There are two techniques that have been used: (i) Self-paced reading, where subjects are presented with a text in a word-by-word or phrase-by-phrase fashion; the subject has control over the speed of presentation, which is recorded. (ii) Eye tracking, where the reading movements of the subject are recorded by cameras and matched with the text being read. While self-paced reading is easier to handle as a research paradigm, it has the disadvantage that it might not give fine-grained data, as subjects tend to get into a rhythmical tapping habit.

Investigations of reading have provided many insights into semantic processing; however, it should be kept in mind that by their nature they only help to investigate one particular aspect of language use that lacks many features of spoken language.

For example, reading speed has been used to determine how speakers deal with semantic ambiguity: Do they try to resolve it early on, which would mean that they slow down when reading triggers of ambiguity, or do they entertain an underspecified interpretation? Frazier & Rayner (1990) have shown that reading slows down after ambiguous words, as e.g. in *The records were carefully guarded {after they were scratched / after the political takeover}*, showing evidence for an early commitment for a particular reading. However, with polysemous words, no such slowing could be detected; an example is *Unfortunately the newspaper was destroyed, {lying in the rain / managing advertising so poorly}*.

The *newspaper* example is a case of coercion, which shows effects for semantic processing under the dual task paradigm (see discussion of Piñango et al. 2006 above). Indeed, Pickering, McElree & Frisson (2006) have shown that the aspectual coercion cases do not result in increased reading times; thus different kinds of tests seem to differ in their sensitivity.

Another area for which reading behavior has been investigated is the time course of pronoun resolution: Are pronouns resolved as early as possible, at the place where they occur, or is the semantic processor procrastinating this decision? According to Ehrlich & Rayner (1983), the latter is the case. They manipulated the distance between an antecedent and its pronoun and showed that distance had an effect on reading times, but only well after the pronoun itself was encountered.

4.3 Preferential looking and the visual world paradigm

Visual gaze and eye movement can be used in other ways as windows to meaning and semantic processing.

One technique to investigate language understanding is the preferential looking paradigm, a version of the picture selection task that can be administered to young infants. Preferential looking has been used for the investigation of stimulus discrimination, as infants look at new stimuli longer than at stimuli that they are already accustomed to. For the investigation of semantic abilities, so-called "Intermodal Preferential Looking" is used: Infants hear an expression and are presented at the same time with two pictures or movie scenes side by side; they preferentially look at the one that fits the description best. Hirsh-Pasek & Golinkoff (1996) have used this technique to investigate the understanding of sentences by young children that produce only single-word utterances.

A second procedure that uses eye gaze is known as "Visual World Paradigm". The general setup is as follows: Subjects are presented with a scene and a sentence or text, and have to judge whether the sentence is true with respect to the scene. In order to perform this verification, subjects have to glance at particular aspects of the scene, which yields clues about the way how the sentence is verified or falsified, that is, how it is semantically processed.

In an early study, Eberhard et al. (1995) have shown that eye gaze tracks semantic interpretation quite closely. Listeners use information on a word-by-word basis to reduce the set of possible visual referents to the intended one. For example, when instructed to *Touch the starred yellow square*, subjects were quick to look at the target in the left-hand situation, slower in the middle situation, and slowest in the right-hand situation. Sedivy et al. (1999) have shown that there are similar effects of incremental interpretation even with non-intersective adjectives, like *tall*.

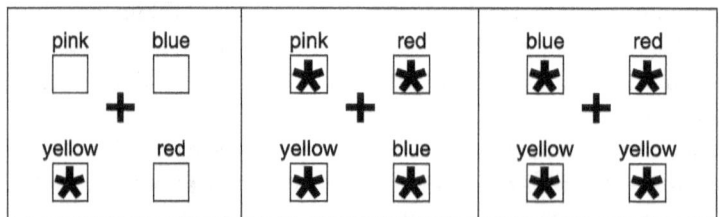

Fig. 12.2: Stimulus of eye gaze test (from Eberhard et al. 1995)

Altman & Kamide (1999) have shown that eye gaze is not just cotemporaneous with interpretation, but may jump ahead; subjects listening to *The boy will eat the...* looked preferentially at the picture of a cake than at the picture of something non-edible. In a number of studies, including Weber, Braun & Crocker (2006), the effect of contrastive accent has been studied. When listeners had already fixated one object – say, the purple scissors – and now are asked to touch *the RED scissors* (where there is a competing red vase), they gaze at the red scissors more quickly, presumably because the square property is given. This effect is also present, though weaker, without contrastive accent, presumably because the use of modifying adjectives is inherently contrastive.

For another example of this technique, see article 15 [this volume] (Bott, Featherston, Radó & Stolterfoht) *Experimental methods*.

5 Physiological effects of semantic processing

There is no clear-cut way to distinguishing physiological effects from behavioral effects. With the physiological phenomena discussed in this section it is evident that they are truly beyond conscious control, and thus may provide more immediate access to semantic processing.

Physiological evidence can be gained in a number of ways: From lesions of the brain and how they affect linguistic performance, from excitations of brain areas during surgery, from the observable metabolic processes related to brain activities, and from the electro-magnetic brain potentials that accompany the firing of bundles of neurons. There are other techniques that have been used occasionally, such as pupillary dilation, which correlates with cognitive load. For example, Krüger, Nuthmann & van der Meer (2001) show with this measure that representations of event sequences following their natural order are cognitively less demanding than when not following the time line.

5.1 Brain lesions and stimulations

Since the early discoveries of Broca and Wernicke, it has been assumed that specific brain lesions affect the relation between expressions to meanings. The classical picture of Broca's area responsible for production and Wernicke's area responsible for comprehension is now known to be incomplete (cf. Damasio et al. 2004), but it is still assumed that Broca's aphasia impedes the ability to use complex syntactic forms to encode and also to decode meanings. From lesion studies it became clear that areas outside the classical Broca/Wernicke area and the connecting Geschwind area are relevant for language production and understanding. Brain regions have been identified where lesions lead to semantic dementia (also known as anomic aphasia) that selectively affects the recognition of names of persons, nouns for manipulable objects such as tools, or nouns of natural objects such as animals. These regions are typically situated in the left temporal lobe, but the studies reported by Damasio et al. also indicate that regions of the right hemisphere play an important role.

It remains unclear, however, whether these lesions affect particular linguistic abilities or more general problems with the pre-linguistic categorization of objects. A serious problem with the use of brain lesions as source of evidence is that they are often not sufficiently locally constrained as to allow for specific inferences.

Stimulation techniques allow for more directed manipulations, and hence for more specific testing of hypothesis. There are deep stimulation techniques that can be applied during brain surgery. There is also a new technique, Transcranial Magnetic Stimulation (TMS), which affects the functioning of particular brain regions by electromagnetic fields applied from outside of the skull.

5.2 Brain imaging of metabolic effects

The last decades have seen a lively development of methods that help to locate brain activity by identifying correlated metabolic effects. Neuronal activity in certain brain regions stimulate the flow of oxygen-rich blood, which in turn can be localized by various means. While early methods like PET (Positron-

Electron Tomography) required the use of radioactive markers, the method of fMRI (functional Magnetic-Resonance Imaging) is less invasive; it is based on measuring the electromagnetic fields of water molecules excited by strong magnetic fields. A more recent method, NIRS (Near Infrared Spectroscopy), applies low-frequency laser light from outside the skull; it is currently the least invasive technique. All the procedures mentioned have a low temporal resolution, as metabolic changes are slow, within the range of a second or so. However, their spatial resolution is quite acute, especially for fMRI using strong magnetic fields.

Results of metabolic brain-image techniques often support and refine findings derived from brain lesions (cf. Damasio et al. 2004). As an example of a recent study, Tyler, Randall & Stamatakis (2008) challenge the view that nouns and verbs are represented in different brain regions; they rather argue that inflected nouns and verbs and minimal noun phrases and minimal verb phrases, that is, specific syntactic uses of nouns and verbs, are spatially differentiated. An ongoing discussion is how general the findings about localizations of brain activities are, given the enormous plasticity of the brain.

5.3 Event-related potentials

This family of procedures investigates the electromagnetic fields generated by the cortical activity. They are observed by sensors placed on the scalp that either track minute variations of the electric field (EEG) or the magnetic field (MEG). The limitations of this technique are that only fields generated by the neocortex directly under the cranium can be detected. As the neocortex is deeply folded, this applies only to a small part of it. Furthermore, the number of electrodes that can be applied on the scalp is limited (typically 16 to 64, sometimes up to 256), hence the spatial resolution is weak even for the accessible parts of the cortex. Spatial resolution is better for MEG, but the required techniques are considerably more complex and expensive. On the positive side, the temporal resolution of the technique is very high, as it does not measure slow metabolic effects of brain activity, but the electric fields generated by the neurons themselves (more specifically, the action potentials that cause neurotransmitter release at the synapses). EEG electrodes can record these fields if generated by a large number of neurons in the pyramidal bundles of neurons in which the cortex is organized, in the magnitude of at least 1000 neurons.

ERP (Event-related potentials), the correlation of EEG signals with stimuli events, has been used for thirty years in psycholinguistic research, and specifically for semantic processing since the discovery by Kutas & Hillyard (1980) of a specific brain potential, the N400. This is a frequently observed change in the potential leading to higher negativity roughly 400ms after the onset of a relevant stimulus. See Kutas, van Petten & Kluender (2006) for a review of the vast literature, and Lau, Phillips & Poeppel (2008) for a partially critical view of standard interpretations.

The N400 effect is seen when subjects are presented in an incremental way with sentences like *I like my coffee with cream and {sugar / socks}*, and the EEG signals of the first and the second variant is compared. In the second variant, with a semantically incongruous word, a negativity around 400ms after the onset of the anomalous word (here: *socks*) appears when the brain potential development is averaged over a number of trials.

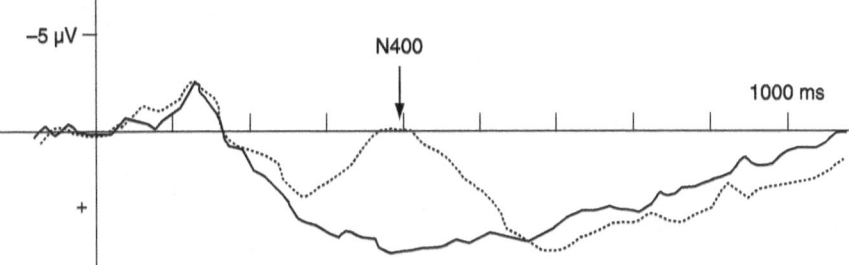

Fig. 12.3: Averaged EEG over sentences with no semantic violation (solid line) and with semantic violation (dotted line); vertical axis at the onset of the anomalous word (from Lau, Phillips & Poeppel 2008)

There are at least two interpretations of the N400 effect: Most researchers see it as a reflex of the attempt to integrate the meaning of a subexpression into the meaning of the larger expression, as constructed so far. With incongruous words, this task is hard or even fails, which is reflected by a stronger N400. The alternative view is that the N400 reflects the effort of lexical access. This is facilitated when the word is predictable by the context, but also when the word is frequent in general. There is evidence that highly frequent words lead to a smaller N400 effect. Also, N400 can be triggered by simple word priming tasks; e.g. in *coffee – {tea / chair}*, the non-primed word *chair* leads to an N400. See Lau, Phillips & Poeppel (2008) for consequences of the integration view and the lexical access view of the N400.

The spatial location of the N400 is also a matter of dispute. While Kutas, van Petten & Kluender (2006) claim that its origins are in the left temporal lobe and hence can be related to established language areas, the main electromagnetic field can be observed rather in the centroparietal region, and often on the right hemisphere. Lau, Phillips & Poeppel (2008) discuss various possible interpretations of these findings.

There are a number of other reproducible electrophysiological effects that point at additional aspects of language processing. In particular, Early Left Anterior Negativity (ELAN) has been implicated in phrase structure violations (150ms), Left Anterior Negativity (LAN) appears with morphosyntactic agreement violations (300-500ms), and P600, a positivity after 600ms, has been seen as evidence for difficulties of syntactic integration, perhaps as evidence for attempts at syntactic restructuring. It is being discussed how specific N400 is for semantics; while it is triggered by phenomena that are clearly related to the meaning aspects of language, it can be also found when subjects perform certain non-linguistic tasks, as in melody recognition. Interestingly, N400 can be masked by syntactic inappropriateness, as Hahne & Friederici (2002) have shown. This can be explained by the plausible assumption that structures first have to make syntactic sense before semantic integration can even start to take place.

There are a number of interesting specific findings around N400 or related brain potentials (cf. Kutas, van Petten & Kluender 2006 for an overview). Closed-class words generally trigger smaller N400 effects than open-class words, and the shape of their negativity is different as well – it is more drawn out up to about 700ms. As already mentioned, low-frequency words trigger greater N400 effects, which may be seen as a point in favor for the lexical access theory; however, we can also assume that low frequency is a general factor that impedes semantic integration. It has been observed that N400 is greater for inappropriate concrete nouns than for inappropriate abstract nouns. With auditory presentations of linguistic structures, it was surprising to learn that N400 effects can appear already before the end of the triggering word; this is evidence that word recognition and semantic integration sets in very early, after the first phonemes of a word.

The larger context of an expression can modulate the N400 effect, that is, the preceding text of a sentence can determine whether a particular word fits and is easy to integrate, or does not fit and leads to integration problems. For example, in a context in which piercing was mentioned, *earring* triggers a smaller N400 than *necklace*. This has been seen as evidence that semantic integration does not differentiate between lexical access, the local syntactic fit and the more global semantic plausibility; rather, all factors play a role at roughly the same time.

N400 has been used as evidence for semantic features. For example, in the triple *The pizza was too hot to* {*eat / drink / kill*}, the item *drink* elicits a smaller N400 than *kill*, which can be interpreted as showing that the expected item *eat* and the test item *drink* have semantic features in common (ingestion), in contrast to *eat* and *kill*.

Brain potentials have also been used to investigate the semantic processing of negative polarity items (cf. article 4 [Semantics: Sentence and Information Structure] (Giannakidou) *Polarity items*). Saddy, Drenhaus & Frisch (2004) and Drenhaus et al. (2006) observe that negative polarity items in inappropriate contexts trigger an N400 effect (as in {*A / no*} *man was ever happy*}. With NPIs and with positive polarity items, a P600 could be observed as well, which is indicative for an attempt to achieve a syntactic structure in which there is a suitable licensing operator in the right syntactic configuration. Incidentally, these findings favor the semantic integration view of the N400 over the lexical access view.

There are text types that require special efforts for semantic integration – riddles and jokes. With jokes based on the reinterpretation of words, it has been found that better comprehenders of jokes show a slightly higher N400 effect on critical words, and a larger P600 effect for overall integration. Additional effort for semantic integration has also been shown for metaphorical interpretations.

A negativity around 320ms has been identified by Fischler et al. (1985) for statements known to the subjects to be false, even if they were not asked to judge the truth value. But semantic anomaly clearly overrides false statements; as Kounios & Holcomb (1992) have showed, in the examples like *No dogs are {animals / fruits}*, the latter triggers an N400 effect.

More recent experiments using MEG have discovered a brain potential called AMF (Anterior Midline Field) situated in the frontal lobe, an area that is not normally implied in language understanding. The effect shows up with coercion phenomena (cf. article 10 [Semantics: Lexical Structures and Adjectives] (de Swart) *Mismatches and coercion*). Coercion does not lead to an N400 effect; there is no anomaly with *John began the book* (which has to be coerced to *read* or *write* the book). But Pylkkänen & McElree (2007) found an AMF effect about 350ms after onset. This effect is absent with semantically incongruous words, as well with words that do not require coercion. Interestingly, the same brain area has been implied for the understanding of sarcastic and ironic language in lesion studies (Shamay-Tsoory et al. 2005).

6 Corpus-linguistic methods

Linguistic corpora, the record of past linguistic production, is a valuable source of evidence for linguistic phenomena in general, and in case of extinct languages, the only kind of source (cf. article 15 [Semantics: Typology, Diachrony and Processing] (Katz) *Semantics in corpus linguistics*). This includes the study of semantic phenomena. For the case of extinct languages we would like to mention, in particular, the task of deciphering, which consists in finding a mapping between expressions and meanings.

Linguistic corpora can provide for evidence of meaning in many different ways. An important philosophical research tradition is hermeneutics, originally the art of understanding of sacred texts. Perhaps the most important concept in the modern hermeneutic tradition is the explication of the so-called hermeneutic circle (cf. Gadamer 1960): The interpreter necessarily approaches the text with a certain kind of knowledge that is necessary for an initial understanding, but the understanding of the text in a first reading will influence and deepen the understanding in subsequent readings.

With large corpora that are available electronically, new statistical techniques have been developed that can tap into aspects of meaning that might otherwise be difficult to recognize. In linguistic corpora, the analysis of word co-occurrences and in particular collocations can yield evidence for meaning relations between words.

For example, large corpora have been investigated for verb-NP collocations using the so-called Expectation Maximization (EM) algorithm (Rooth et al. 1999). This algorithms leads to the classification of verbs and nouns into clusters such that verbs of class X frequently occur with nouns of class Y. The initial part of one such cluster, developed from the British National Corpus, looks as in the following table. The verbs can be characterized as verbs that involve scalar changes, and the nouns as denoting entities that can move along such scales.

	number	rate	price	cost	level	amount	sale	value	interest	demand
increase.as:s	•	•	•	•	•	•	•	•	•	•
increase:aso:o		•	•	•	•	•	•	•	•	
fall.as:s	•	•	•	•	•	•	•	•		•
pay.aso:o	•	•	•		•	•			•	•
reduce.aso:o	•	•	•	•	•	•	•	•		•
rise.as:s	•	•	•	•	•	•	•			•
exceed.aso:o	•	•	•	•	•			•	•	•
exceed.aso:s	•	•	•	•	•	•	•	•	•	•
affect.aso:s	•	•	•	•	•		•	•	•	•
grow.as:s	•					•	•	•	•	

Fig. 12.4: Clustering analysis of nouns and verbs; dots represent pairs that occur in the corpus. "as:s" stands for subjects of intransitive verbs, "aso:s" and "aso:o" for subjects and objects of transitive verbs, respectively (from Rooth et al. 1999)

We can also look at the frequency of particular collocations within this cluster, as illustrated in the following table for the verb *increase*.

Tab. 12.1: Frequency of nouns occurring with INCREASE (from Rooth et al. 1999)

increase			
number	134.147	proportion	23.8699
demand	30.7322	size	22.8108
pressure	30.5844	rate	20.9593
temperature	25.9691	level	20.7651
cost	23.9431	price	17.9996

While pure statistical approaches as Rooth et al. (1999) are of considerable interest, most applications of large-scale corpus-based research are based on a mix between hand-coding and automated procedures. The best-known project that has turned into an important application is WordNet (Fellbaum (ed.) 1998). A good example for the mixed procedure is Gildea & Juravsky (2002), a project that attempted semi-automatic assignment of thematic roles. In a first step, thematic roles were hand-coded for a large number of verbs, where a large corpus provided for a wide variety of examples. These initial examples, together with the coding, were used to train an automatic syntactic parser, which then was able to assign thematic roles to new instances of known predicates and even to new, unseen predicates with reasonable accuracy.

Yet another application of corpus-linguistic methods involves parallel corpora, collections of texts and their translations into one or more other languages. It is presupposed that the meanings of the texts are reasonably similar (but recall the problems with translations mentioned above). Refined statistical methods can be used to train automatic translation devices on a certain corpus, which then can be extended to new texts that then are translated automatically, a method known as example based machine translation.

For linguistic research, parallel corpora have been used in other ways as well. If a language α marks a certain distinction overtly and regularly, whereas language β marks that distinction only rarely and in irregular ways, good translations pairs of texts from α into β can be used to investigate the ways and frequency in which the distinction in β is marked. This method is used, for example, in von Heusinger (2002) for specificity, using Umberto Eco's *Il nome della rosa*, and Behrens (2005) for genericity, using Sait-Exupéry's *Le petit prince*. The articles in Cysouw & Wälchli (2007) discuss the potential of the technique, and its problems, for typological research.

7 Conclusion

This article, hopefully, has shown that the elusive concept of meaning has many reflexes that we can observe, and that semantics actually stands on as firm grounds as other disciplines of linguistics. The kinds of evidence for semantic phenomena are very diverse, and not always as convergent as semanticists might wish them to be. But they provide for a very rich and interconnected area of study that has shown considerable development since the first edition of the *Handbook Semantics* in 1991. In particular, a wide variety of experimental evidence has been adduced to argue for processing of meaning. It is to be hoped that the next edition will show an even richer and, hopefully, more convergent picture.

8 References

Altmann, Gerry & Yuki Kamide 1999. Incremental interpretation at verbs: Restricting the domain of subsequent reference. *Cognition* 73, 247–264.
Behrens, Leila. 2005. Genericity from a cross-linguistic perspective. *Linguistics* 43, 257–344.
Berlin, Brent, Dennis E. Breedlove & Peter H. Raven 1973. General principles of classification and nomenclature in folk biology. *American Anthropologist* 75, 214–242.
Berlin, Brent & Paul Kay 1969. *Basic Color Terms. Their Universality and Evolution*. Berkeley, CA: University of California Press.
Bloomfield, Leonard 1933. *Language*. New York: Henry Holt and Co.
Chafe, Wallace (ed.) 1980. *The Pear Stories: Cognitive, Cultural, and Linguistic Aspects of Narrative Production*. Norwood, NJ: Ablex.
Clark, Herbert H. & Peter Lucy 1975. Understanding what is meant from what is said: A study in conversationally conveyed requests. *Journal of Verbal Learning and Verbal Behavior* 14, 56–72.
Crain, Stephen 1991. Language acquisition in the absence of experience. *Behavioral and Brain Sciences* 14, 597–650.
Crain, Stephen, Rosalind Thornton, Laura Conway & Diane Lillo-Martin 1998. Quantification without quantification. *Language Acquisition* 5, 83–153.
Cysouw, Michael & Bernhard Wälchli 2007. Parallel texts: Using translational equivalents in linguistic typology. Special issue of *Sprachtypologie und Universalienforschung* 60, 95–99.
Damasio, Hanna, Daniel Tranel, Thomas Grabowski, Ralph Adolphs & Antonio Damasio 2004. Neural systems behind word and concept retrieval. *Cognition* 92, 179–229.
Drenhaus, Heiner, Peter beim Graben, Doug Saddy & Stefan Frisch 2006. Diagnosis and repair of negative polarity constructions in the light of symbolic resonance analysis. *Brain & Language* 96, 255–268.
Eberhard, Kathleen, Michael J. Spivey-Knowlton, Judy Sedivy & Michael Tanenhaus 1995. Eye movement as a window into real-time spoken language comprehension in a natural context. *Journal of Psycholinguistic Research* 24, 409–436.
Ehrlich, Kate & Keith Rayner 1983. Pronoun assignment and semantic integration during reading: Eye movement and immediacy of processing. *Journal of Verbal Learning and Verbal Behavior* 22, 75–87.
Fellbaum, Christiane (ed.) 1998. *WordNet: An Electronic Lexical Database*. Cambridge, MA: The MIT Press.
Fischler, Ira, Donald G. Childers, Teera Achariyapaopan & Nathan W. Perry 1985. Brain potentials during sentence verification: Automatic aspects of comprehension. *Biological Psychology* 21, 83–105.
Frazier, Lyn & Keith Rayner 1990. Taking on semantic commitments: Processing multiple meanings vs. multiple senses. *Journal of Memory and Language* 29, 181–200.
Frege, Gottlob 1892. Über Sinn und Bedeutung. *Zeitschrift für Philosophie und philosophische Kritik* 100, 25–50.
Gadamer, Hans Georg 1960. *Wahrheit und Methode. Grundzüge einer philosophischen Hermeneutik*. Tübingen: Mohr.
Gärdenfors, Peter 2000. *Conceptual Spaces – The Geometry of Thought*. Cambridge, MA: The MIT Press.

Gerken, LouAnn & Michele E. Shady 1998. The picture selection task. In: D. McDaniel, C. McKee & H. S. Cairns (eds.). *Methods for Assessing Children's Syntax.* Cambridge, MA: The MIT Press, 125–146.

Gildea, Daniel & Daniel Jurafsky 2002. Automatic labeling of semantic roles. *Computational Linguistics* 28, 245–288.

Goddard, Cliff 1998. *Semantic Analysis. A Practical Introduction.* Oxford: Oxford University Press.

Goodman, Nelson 1955. *Fact, Fiction, and Forecast.* Cambridge, MA: Harvard University Press.

Gordon, Peter 1998. The truth-value judgment task. In: D. McDaniel, C. McKee & H. S. Carins (eds.). *Methods for Assessing Children's Syntax.* Cambridge, MA: The MIT Press, 211–235.

Gregory, Robert J. 2003. An early history of land on Tanna, Vanuatu. *The Anthropologist* 5, 67–74.

Grice, Paul 1957. Meaning. *The Philosophical Review* 66, 377–388.

Hahne, Anja & Angela D. Friederici 2002. Differential task effects on semantic and syntactic processes are revealed by ERPs. *Cognitive Brain Research* 13, 339–356.

Haviland, John B. 1974. A last look at Cook's Guugu-Yimidhirr wordlist. *Oceania* 44, 216–232.

von Heusinger, Klaus 2002. Specificity and definiteness in sentence and discourse structure. *Journal of Semantics* 19, 245–274.

Hill, Clifford. 1982. Up/down, front/back, left/right: A contrastive study of Hausa and English. In: J. Weissenborn & W. Klein (eds.). *Here and There: Cross-Linguistic Studies on Deixis and Demonstration.* Amsterdam: Benjamins, 11–42.

Hirsh-Pasek, Kathryn & Roberta M. Golinkoff 1996. *The Origin of Grammar: Evidence from Early Language Comprehension.* Cambridge, MA: The MIT Press.

Kaplan, David 1978. On the logic of demonstratives. *Journal of Philosophical Logic* VIII, 81–98. Reprinted in: P. French, T. Uehling & H.K. Wettstein (eds.). *Contemporary Perspectives in the Philosophy of Language.* Minneapolis, MN: University of Minnesota Press, 1979, 401–412.

Kay, Paul, Brent Berlin, Luisa Maffi & Wiliam R. Merrifield 2008. *The World Color Survey.* Stanford, CA: CSLI Publications.

Kempton, William. 1981. *The Folk Classification of Ceramics.* New York: Academic Press.

Kim, Christina 2008. Processing presupposition: Verifying sentences with 'only'. In: J. Tauberer, A. Eilam & L. MacKenzie (eds.). *Proceedings of the 31st Penn Linguistics Colloquium.* Philadelphia, PA: University of Pennsylvania.

Kounios, John & Phillip J. Holcomb 1992. Structure and process in semantic memory: Evidence from event-related brain potentials and reaction times. *Journal of Experimental Psychology. General* 121, 459–479.

Kranstedt, Alfred, Andy Lücking, Thies Pfeiffer & Hannes Rieser 2006. Deixis: How to determine demonstrated objects using a pointing cone. In: Sylvie Gibet, Nicolas Courty & Jean-François Kamp (eds.). *Gesture in Human-Computer Interaction and Simulation.* Berlin: Springer, 300–311.

Krüger, Frank, Antje Nuthmann & Elke van der Meer 2001. Pupillometric indices of the temporal order representation in semantic memory. *Zeitschrift für Psychologie* 209, 402–415.

Kutas, Marta & Steven A. Hillyard 1980. Reading senseless sentences: Brain potentials reflect semantic incongruity. *Science* 207, 203–205.

Kutas, Marta, Cyma K. van Petten & Robert Kluender 2006. Psycholinguistics electrified II 1994–2005. In: M.A. Gernsbacher & M. Traxler (eds.). *Handbook of Psycholinguistics.* New York: Elsevier, 83–143.

Lakoff, George & Mark Johnson 1980. *Metaphors we Live by*. Chicago, IL: The University of Chicago Press.

Lau, Ellen F., Colin Phillips & David Poeppel 2008. A cortical network for semantics: (de) constructing the N400. *Nature Reviews Neuroscience* 9, 920–933.

McDaniel, Dena, Cecile McKee & Helen Smith Cairns (eds.) 1996. *Methods for Assessing Children's Syntax*. Cambridge, MA: The MIT Press.

Majid, Asifa, Melissa Bowerman, Miriam van Staden & James Boster 2006. The semantic categories of cutting and breaking events: A crosslinguistic perspective. *Cognitive Linguistics* 18, 133–152.

Matthewson, Lisa 2004. On the methodology of semantic fieldwork. *International Journal of American Linguistics* 70, 369–415.

Noveck, Ira 2001. When children are more logical than adults: Experimental investigations of scalar implicatures. *Cognition* 78, 165–188.

Noveck, Ira 2004. Pragmatic inferences linked to logical terms. In: I. Noveck & D. Sperber (eds.). *Experimental Pragmatics*. Basingstoke: Palgrave Macmillan, 301–321.

Pickering, Martin J., Brian McElree & Steven Frisson 2006. Underspecification and aspectual coercion. *Discourse Processes* 42, 131–155.

Piñango, Maria M., Aaron Winnick, Rashad Ullah & Edgar Zurif 2006. Time course of semantic composition: The case of aspectual coercion. *Journal of Psycholinguistic Research* 35, 233–244.

Portner, Paul & Katsuhiko Yabushita 1998. The semantics and pragmatics of topic phrases. *Linguistics & Philosophy* 21, 117–157.

Potts, Christopher 2005. *The Logic of Conventional Implicatures*. Oxford: Oxford University Press.

Pylkkänen, Liina & Brian McElree 2007. An MEG study of silent meaning. *Journal of Cognitive Neuroscience* 19, 1905–1921.

Quine, Willard van Orman 1960. *Word and Object*. Cambridge, MA: The MIT Press, 26–79.

Rayner, Keith 1998. Eye movements in reading and information processing: 20 years of research. *Psychological Bulletin* 124, 372–422.

Rooth, Mats, Stefan Riezler, Detlef Prescher & Glenn Carroll 1999. Inducing a semantically annotated lexicon via EM-based clustering. In: R. Dale & K. Church (eds.). *Proceedings of the 37th Annual Meeting of the Association for computational Linguistics*. College Park, MD: ACL. 104–111.

Saddy, Douglas, Heiner Drenhaus & Stefan Frisch 2004. Processing polarity items: Contrastive licensing costs. *Brain & Language* 90, 495–502.

van der Sandt, Rob A. 1988. *Context and Presupposition*. London: Croom Helm.

Sedivy, Julie C., Michael K. Tanenhaus, Craig C. Chambers & Gregory N. Carlson 1999. Achieving incremental semantic interpretation through contextual representation. *Cognition* 71, 109–147.

Shamay-Tsoory, Simone, Rachel Tomer & Judith Aharon-Peretz 2005. The neuroanatomical basis of understanding sarcasm and its relationship to social cognition. *Neuropsychology* 19, 288–300.

Smith, Carlotta L. 1980. Quantifiers and question answering in young children. *Journal of Experimental Child Psychology* 30, 191–205.

Stalnaker, Robert 1974. Pragmatic presuppositions. In: M. K. Munitz & P. K. Unger (eds.). *Semantics and Philosophy*. New York: New York University Press, 197–214.

Thornton, Rosalind 1998. Elicited production. In: D. McDaniel, C. McKee & H. S. Carins (eds.). *Methods for Assessing Children's Syntax*. Cambridge, MA: The MIT Press, 77–95.

Tomasello, Michael 2008. Why don't apes point? In: R. Eckardt, G. Jäger & Tonjes Veenstra (eds.). *Variation, Selection, Development. Probing the Evolutionary Model of Language Change*. Berlin: Mouton de Gruyter, 375–394.

Tyler, Lorraine K., Billi Randall & Emmanuel A. Stamatakis 2008. Cortical differentiation for nouns and verbs depends on grammatical markers. *Journal of Cognitive Neuroscience* 20, 1381–1389.

Weber, Andrea, Bettina Braun & Matthew W. Crocker 2006. Finding referents in time: Eye-tracking evidence for the role of contrastive accents. *Language and Speech* 49, 367–392.

Weinreich, Uriel 1964. Webster's Third. A critique of its semantics. *International Journal of American Linguistics* 30, 405–409.

Lisa Matthewson
13 Methods in cross-linguistic semantics

1 Introduction —— 340
2 The need for cross-linguistic semantics —— 340
3 On semantic fieldwork methodology —— 341
4 What counts as a universal? —— 346
5 How do we find universals? —— 350
6 Semantic universals in the literature —— 354
7 Variation —— 355
8 References —— 358

Abstract: This article outlines methodologies for conducting research in cross-linguistic semantics, with an eye to uncovering semantic universals. Topics covered include fieldwork methodology, types of evidence for semantic universals, different types of semantic universals (with examples from the literature), and semantic parameters.

1 Introduction

This article outlines methodologies for conducting research in cross-linguistic semantics, with an eye to uncovering semantic universals. Section 2 briefly motivates the need for cross-linguistic semantic research, and section 3 outlines fieldwork methodologies for work on semantics. Section 4 addresses the issue of what counts as a universal, and section 5 discusses how one finds universals. Section 6 provides examples of semantic universals, and section 7 discusses variation. The reader is also referred to articles 12 [this volume] (Krifka) *Varieties of semantic evidence* and 2 [Semantics: Typology, Diachrony and Processing] (Bach & Chao) *Semantic Types across Languages*

2 The need for cross-linguistic semantics

It is by now probably uncontroversial that our field's empirical base needs to be as broad as possible. Typologists have always known this; generativists have also

Lisa Matthewson, Vancouver, Canada

https://doi.org/10.1515/9783110368505-013

mostly advanced beyond the view that we can uncover Universal Grammar by doing in-depth study of a single language. Although semantics was the last subfield of formal linguistics to undertake widespread cross-linguistic investigation, such work has been on the rise ever since the synthesis of generative syntax and Montague semantics in the 1980s. In the 20 years since Comrie (1989: 4) wrote that for a 'Chomskyist' for whom universals are abstract principles, "there is no way in which the analysis of concrete data from a wide range of languages would provide any relevant information", we have seen many instances where empirical cross-linguistic work *has* falsified abstract universal principles. Among many others, Maria Bittner's pioneering work on Kalaallisut (Eskimo-Aleut, Greenland) is worth mentioning here (e.g., Bittner 1987, 1994, 2005, 2008), as well as the papers in Bach et al.'s (1995) quantification volume, and the body of research responding to Chierchia's (1998) Nominal Mapping Parameter. It is clear that we will only come close to discovering semantic universals by looking at data from a wide range of languages.

3 On semantic fieldwork methodology

The first issue for a cross-linguistic semantic researcher is how to obtain usable data in the field. The material presented here draws on Matthewson (2004); the reader is also referred to article 12 [this volume] (Krifka) *Varieties of semantic evidence*. The techniques described here are theory-neutral; I assume that regardless of one's theoretical assumptions, similar data-collection processes are appropriate.

3.1 In support of direct elicitation

It was once widely believed that direct elicitation is an illegitimate methodology; see for example Harris & Voegelin (1953: 59). Even in this century we find statements like the following:

> The referential meaning of nouns (in terms of definiteness and specificity) is an intricate topic that is extremely hard to investigate on the basis of elicitation. In the end it is texts or connected discourse in general in the language under investigation which provide the most important clues for analysis of these grammatical domains.
> (Dimmendaal 2001: 69)

It is true that connected discourse is an indispensable part of any investigation into noun phrase semantics. However, this methodology alone is insufficient.

Within semantics, there are two main reasons why textual materials are insufficient as an empirical base. The first is shared with syntactic research, namely that one cannot obtain negative evidence from texts. One cannot claim with any certainty that any structure is impossible, if one only investigates spontaneously produced data. The second reason is specific to semantics, namely that texts provide little direct evidence about meaning. A syntactician working with a textual corpus has at least a number of sentences which may be assumed to be grammatical. But a text is paired with at most a translation – an incomplete representation of meaning. Direct elicitation results in more detailed, targeted information than a translation. (This is not to deny that examination of texts is useful; texts are good sources of information about topic-tracking devices or reference time maintenance, for example.)

3.2 Eliciting semantic judgments

The semantics of utterances or parts of utterances are not consciously accessible to native speakers. Comments, paraphrases and translations offered by consultants are all useful clues for the fieldworker (see article 12 [this volume] (Krifka) *Varieties of semantic evidence*). However, just as a syntactician does not ask a native speaker to provide a tree-structure (but rather asks for grammaticality judgments of sentences which are designed to test for constituency, etc.), so a semanticist does not ask a native speaker to conduct semantic analysis. This includes generally avoiding questions such as 'what does this word mean?', 'when is it okay to use this word?' and 'does this sentence have two meanings?' Instead, we mainly proceed by requesting judgments on the acceptability of sentences in particular discourse contexts.

A *judgment* is an acceptance or rejection of some linguistic object, and ideally reflects the speaker's native competence. (However, see Carden 1970, Schütze 1996 on the problem of speaker variability in judgments.) I assume there is only one kind of judgment within semantics, that of whether a grammatical sentence (or string of sentences) is acceptable in a given discourse context. Native speakers are not qualified to give 'judgments' about technical concepts such as entailment, tautology, ambiguity or vagueness (although of course consultants' comments can give valuable clues about these issues). All of these concepts can and should be tested for via acceptability judgment tasks.

The acceptability judgment task is similar to the truth value judgment task used in language acquisition research (cf. Crain & Thornton 1998 and much other work; see article 10 [Semantics: Typology, Diachrony and Processing] (Crain) *Meaning in first language acquisition*. The way to elicit an acceptability judgment is to first provide a discourse context to the consultant, then present an utterance, and ask whether the utterance is acceptable in that context. The consultant's answer potentially gives us information about the truth-value of the sentence in that context, and about the pragmatic felicity of the sentence in that context (e.g., whether its presuppositions are satisfied).

The relation of the acceptability judgment task to truth values derives from Grice's (1975) Maxim of Quality: we assume that a speaker will only accept a sentence S in a discourse context C if S is true in C. Conversely, if S is false in C, a speaker will reject S in C. From this it follows that acceptance of a sentence gives positive information about truth value (the sentence is true in this discourse context), but rejection of a sentence gives only partial information: the sentence *may* be false, but it may also be rejected on other grounds. Article 10 [Semantics: Typology, Diachrony and Processing] (Crain) *Meaning in first language acquisition* offers useful discussion of the influence of the Cooperative Principle on responses to acceptability judgment tasks. And see von Fintel (2004) for the claim that speakers will assign the truth-value 'false' to sentences which involve presupposition failure, and which are therefore actually infelicitous (and analyzed as having no truth value).

When conducting an acceptability judgment task, it is important to present the consultant with the discourse context before presenting the object language sentence(s). If the consultant hears the sentence in the absence of a context, s/he will spontaneously think of a suitable context or range of contexts for the sentence. If the speaker's imagined context differs from the one the researcher is interested in, false negatives can arise, particularly if the researcher is interested in a dispreferred or non-obvious reading.

The other important question is *how* to present the discourse context. In section 3.4 I will discuss the use of non-verbal stimuli when presenting contexts. Concentrating for now on verbal strategies, we have two choices: explain the context in the object language, or in a meta-language (a language the researcher is fluent in). Either method can work, and I believe that there is little danger in using a meta-language to describe a context. The context is merely background information; its linguistic features are not relevant. In fact, presenting the context in a meta-language has the advantage that the consultant is unlikely to copy structural features from the context-description to the sentence being judged. (In Matthewson 2004, I argue that even in a translation task, the influence of meta-language syntax and semantics is less than has sometimes been feared. Based on examples drawn from Salish, I argue that consultants will only copy structures up to the point allowed by their native grammar, and that any problems of cross-language influence are easily solvable by means of follow-up elicitation.) See article 12 [this volume] (Krifka) *Varieties of semantic evidence* for further discussion of issues in presenting discourse contexts.

3.3 Eliciting translations

Translations have the same status as paraphrases or additional comments about meaning offered by the consultant: they are a clue to meaning, and should be taken seriously, but they are not primary data. A translation represents the consultant's best effort to express the same truth conditions in another language – but often, there is no way to express exactly the same truth conditions in two different languages. Even if we assume effability, i.e. that every proposition expressible in one language is expressible in any language (Katz 1976), a translation task will usually fall short of pairing a proposition in one language with a truth-conditionally identical counterpart in the other language. The reasons for this include the fact that what is easily expressible in one language may be expressible only with difficulty in another, or that what is expressed using an unambiguous proposition in one language is best rendered in another language by an utterance which is ambiguous or vague. Furthermore, what serves as a good translation of a sentence in one discourse context may be a poor or inappropriate translation of the same sentence in a different discourse context. As above, the only *direct* evidence about truth conditions are acceptability judgments in particular contexts.

The problem of ambiguity is acute when dealing with a translation or paraphrase task. If an object-language sentence is ambiguous, its translation or paraphrase often only produces the preferred reading. And a consultant will often want to explicitly disambiguate; after all, Grice's Manner Maxim exhorts a cooperative speaker to avoid ambiguity. If one suspects that a sentence may be ambiguous, one should not simply give the sentence and ask what it means. Instead, present a discourse context, and elicit an acceptability judgment. Eliciting the dispreferred reading first is a good idea (or, if the status of the readings is not known, using different elicitation orders on different days). It is also a good idea to construct discourse contexts which pragmatically favour the dispreferred reading. Manipulating pragmatic plausibility can also establish the absence of ambiguity: if a situation pragmatically favours a certain possible reading, but the consultant rejects the sentence in that context, one can be pretty sure that the reading is absent.

When dealing with presuppositions, or other aspects of meaning which affect felicity conditions, translations provide notoriously poor information. Felicity conditions are usually ignored in the translation process; the reader is referred to Matthewson (2004) for examples of this.

When eliciting translations, the basic rule is only to ask for translations of complete, grammatical sentences. (See Nida 1947: 140 for this point; Harris & Voegelin 1953: 70–71, on the contrary, advise that one begin by asking for translations of single morphemes.) Generally speaking, any sub-sentential string will probably not be translatable with any accuracy by a native speaker. A sub-sentential translation task rests on the faulty assumption that the meaning which is expressed by a certain constituent in one language is expressible by a constituent in another language. Even if the syntactic structures *are* roughly parallel in the two languages, the meaning of a sub-sentential string may depend on its environment (cf. for example languages where bare noun phrases are interpreted as specific or definite only in certain positions).

The other factor to be aware of when eliciting translations is that a sentence which would result in ungrammaticality if it were translated in a structure-preserving way, will be restructured. In Matthewson (2004) I provide an example of this involving testing for Condition C violations in Salish. Due to pro-drop and free word order, the St'át'imcets (Lillooet Salish, British Columbia) sentence which translates *Mary saw her mother* is structurally ambiguous with *She saw Mary's mother*. The wrong way to test for potential Condition C-violating structures (which has been tried!) is to ask for translations of the potentially ambiguous sentence into English. Even if the object language does allow Condition C violations (i.e., does allow the structure *She$_i$ saw Mary$_i$'s mother*), the consultant will never translate the sentence into English as *She saw Mary's mother*. (See Davis 2009 for discussion of strategies for dealing with the particular elicitation problems of Condition C.)

3.4 Elicitation using non-verbal stimuli

It was once widely believed that elicitation should proceed by means of non-verbal stimuli, which are used to generate spontaneous speech in the object language, and that a meta-language should be entirely avoided (see for example Hayes 1954, Yegerlehner 1955, or Aitken 1955). It will already be clear that I reject this view, as do most modern researchers. Elicitation using only visual stimuli cannot provide negative evidence, for example.

Visual stimuli are routinely used in language acquisition experiments; see Crain & Thornton (1998), among others. The methodology is equally applicable to fieldwork with adults. The stimuli can be created using computer technologies, but they do not need to be high-tech; they can involve puppets, small toys, or line-drawings. Usually, these methodologies are not intended to replace verbal elicitation, but serve as a support and enhancement for it. For example, a picture or a video will be shown, and may be used to elicit spontaneous discourse, but is also usually followed up with judgment questions.

The advantage of visual aids is obvious: the methodology avoids potential interference from linguistic features of the context description, and it can potentially more closely approximate a real-life discourse context. This is particularly relevant for pragmatically sensitive questions, where it is almost impossible to hold cues in the meta-language (e.g., intonation) constant. This methodology also allows standardization across different elicitation sessions, different fieldworkers, and different languages. When researchers share their video clips, for example, we can be certain that the same contexts are being tested and can compare cross-linguistic results with more confidence.

Another advantage of visual stimuli concerns felicity conditions. It is quite challenging to elicit information about presupposition failure using only verbal descriptions of discourse contexts, as the necessary elements of the context include information about the interlocutors' belief or knowledge states. However, video, animation or play-acting give a potential way to represent a character's knowledge state, and if carefully constructed, the stimulus can rule out potential presupposition accommodation. The consultant can then judge the acceptability of an utterance by one of the characters in the video/play which potentially contains presupposition failure.

The main disadvantage of these methodologies is logistics: compared to verbally describing a context, visually representing it takes more time and effort. Many hours can go into planning (let alone filming or animating) a video for just one discourse context. In many cases, verbal strategies are perfectly adequate and more efficient. For example, when trying to establish whether a particular morpheme encodes past tense, it is relatively simple to describe a battery of discourse contexts for a single sentence and obtain judgments for each context. One can quickly and unambiguously explain that an event took place yesterday, is taking place at the utterance time, or will take place tomorrow, for example. In sum, verbal elicitation still remains an indispensable and versatile methodology.

The next section turns to semantic universals. We first discuss what semantic universals look like, and then how one gets from cross-linguistic data to the postulation of universals.

4 What counts as a universal?

Universals come in two main flavours: absolute/unconditional ('all languages have x'), and implicational ('if a language has x, it has y'). Examples of each type are given in (1) and (2); all of these except (1b) can be found in the Konstanz Universals Archive.

(1) Absolute/unconditional universals:
   a. Every language has an existential element such as a verb or particle (Ferguson 1972: 78–79).
   b. Every language has expressions which are interpreted as denoting individuals Article 2 [Semantics: Typology, Diachrony and Processing] (Bach & Chao) *Semantic Types across Languages*.
   c. Every language has N's and NPs of the type e → t (Partee 2000).
   d. The simple NP of any natural language express monotone quantifiers or conjunctions of monotone quantifiers (Barwise & Cooper 1981: 187).

(2) Implicational universals:
   a. If a language has adjectives for shape, it has adjectives for colour and size (Dixon 1977).
   b. A language distinguishes between count and mass nouns iff a language possesses configurational NPs (Gil 1987).
   c. There is a simple NP which expresses the [monotone decreasing] quantifier ~Q if and only if there is a simple NP with a weak non-cardinal determiner which expresses the [monotone increasing] quantifier Q (Barwise & Cooper 1981: 186).

Within the typological literature, 'universals' are often actually tendencies ('statistical universals'). Many of the entries in the Konstanz Universals Archive contain phrases like 'with more than chance frequency', 'more likely to', 'most often', 'typically' or 'tend to'. For obvious reasons, one does not find much attention paid to statistical universals in the generativist literature.

Another difference between typological and formal research relates to whether more importance is attached to implicational or unconditional universals. Typological research finds the implicational kind more interesting, and there is a strand of belief according to which it is difficult to distinguish unconditional universals from the preconditions of one's theory. For example, take (1c) above. Is this a semantic universal, or a theoretical decision under which we describe the semantic behaviour of languages? (Thanks to a reviewer for discussion of this point.)

There are certainly unconditional universals which seem to be empirically unfalsifiable. One example is semantic compositionality, which is assumed by many formal semanticists to hold universally. As discussed in von Fintel & Matthewson (2008) and references therein, compositionality is a methodological axiom which is almost impossible to falsify empirically. On the other hand, many unconditional universals *are* falsifiable; for example, Barwise and Cooper's NP-Quantifier Universal, introduced in section 5 below. Even (1c) does make a substantive claim, although worded in theoretical terms. It asserts that all languages share certain meanings; it is in a sense irrelevant if one doesn't agree that we should analyze natural language using the types e and t.

If typologists are suspicious of unconditional universals, formal semanticists may tend to regard implicational universals as merely a stepping stone to a deeper discovery. Many of the implications as they are stated are probably not primitively part of Universal Grammar. They may either have a functional explanation, or they may be descriptive generalizations which should be derivable from the theory rather than forming part of it. For example, take the semantic implicational universal in (3) (provided by a reviewer):

(3) If a language has a definite article, then a type shift from <e,t> to <<e,t>,t> is not freely available (without using the article).

(3) is ideally merely one specific instance of a general ban on type-shifting when there is an overt element which does the job. This in turn may follow from some general economy principle, and not need to be stated separately.

A final point of debate relates to level of abstractness. Formal semanticists often propose constraints which are only statable at a high level of abstractness, but some researchers believe that universals should always be surface testable. For example, Comrie (1989) argues that abstractly-stated universals have the drawback that they rely on analyses which may be faulty. And Levinson (2003: 320) argues for surface-testability because "highly abstract generalizations ... are impractical to test against a reasonable sample of languages."

Abstractness is required in the field of semantics because superficial statements almost never reveal what is really going on. This becomes clear if one considers how much reliable information about meaning can be gleaned from sources like descriptive grammars. In fact, the inadequacy of superficial studies is illustrated by the very examples cited by Levinson (2003) in support of his claim that "Whorf's (1956: 218) emphasis on the 'incredible degree of linguistic diversity of linguistic systems over the globe' looks considerably better informed than the opinions of many contemporary thinkers." Levinson's examples include variation in lexical categories, and the fact that some languages have no tense (Levinson 2003: 328). However, these are areas where examination of superficial data can lead to hasty conclusions about variation, and where deeper investigation often reveals underlying similarities.

With respect to lexical categories, Jelinek (1995) famously advanced the strong and interesting hypothesis that Straits Salish (Washington and British Columbia) lacks categorial distinctions. The claim was based on facts such as that any open-class lexical item can function as a predicate in Straits, without a copular verb.

However, subsequent research has found, among other things, that the head of a relative clause cannot be occupied by just any open-class lexical item. Instead, this position is restricted to elements which correspond to nouns in languages like English (Demirdache & Matthewson 1995, Davis & Matthewson 1999, Davis 2002; see also Baker 2003). This is evidence for categorial distinctions, and Jelinek herself has since rejected the category-neutral view of Salish (orally, at the 2002 International Conference on Salish and Neighbouring Languages; see also Montler 2003).

As for tense, while tenseless languages may exist, we cannot determine whether a language is tensed or not based on superficial evidence. I will illustrate this based on St'át'imcets; see Matthewson (2006b) for details. St'át'imcets looks like a tenseless language on the surface, as there is no obligatory morphological encoding of the distinction between present and past. (4) illustrates this for an activity predicate; the same holds for all aspectual classes:

(4) mets-cál=lhkan
 write-ACT=1SG.SUBJ
 'I wrote / I am writing.'

St'át'imcets does have obligatory marking for future interpretations; (4) cannot be interpreted as future. The main way of marking the future is with the future modal *kelh*.

(5) mets-cál=lhkan=*kelh*
 write-ACT=1SG.SUBJ=*FUT*
 'I will write.'

The analytical problem is non-trivial here: the issue is whether there is a phonologically unpronounced tense in (4). The assumption of null tense would make St'át'imcets similar to English, and therefore would be the null hypothesis (see section 5.1). The hypothesis is empirically testable language-internally, but only by looking beyond obvious data such as that in (4)–(5). For example, it turns out that St'át'imcets and English behave in a strikingly parallel manner with respect to the temporal shifting properties of embedded predicates. In English, when a stative past-tense predicate is embedded under another past tense, a simultaneous reading is possible. The same is true in St'át'imcets, as shown in (6).

(6) tsút=tu7   s=Pauline   [kw=s=guy't-ál'men=s=tu7]
 say=then   NOM=Pauline   [DET=NOM=sleep-want=3POSS=then]
 'Pauline said that she was tired.'
 OK: Pauline said at a past time t that she was tired at t

On the other hand, in English a future embedded under another future does *not* allow a simultaneous reading, but only allows a forward-shifted reading (Enç 1996, Abusch 1998, among others). The same is true of St'át'imcets, as shown in (7). Just as in English, the time of Pauline's predicted tiredness must be later than the time at which Pauline will speak.

(7) tsút=*kelh*   s=Pauline   [kw=s=guy't-ál'men=s=*kelh*]
    say=*FUT*   NOM=Pauline   [DET=NOM=sleep-want=3POSS=*FUT*]
    'Pauline will say that she will be tired.'
    *Pauline will say at a future time t that she is tired at t.
    OK: Pauline will say at a future time t that she will be tired at t' after t.

The parallel behaviour of the two languages can be explained if we assume that the St'át'imcets matrix clauses in (6)–(7) contain a phonologically covert non-future tense morpheme (Matthewson 2006b). The embedding data can then be afforded the same explanation as the corresponding facts in English (see e.g., Abusch 1997, 1998, Ogihara 1996 for suggestions).

We can see that there is good reason to believe that St'át'imcets is tensed, but the evidence for the tense morpheme is not surface-obvious. Of course, there are other languages which have been argued to be tenseless (see e.g., Bohnemeyer 2002, Bittner 2005, Lin 2006, Ritter & Wiltschko 2005, and article 4 [Semantics: Typology, Diachrony and Processing] (Smith) *Tense and aspect*. However, I hope to have shown that it is useless to confine one's examination of temporal systems to superficial data. Doing this would lead to the possibly premature rejection of core universal properties of temporal systems in human language. This in turn suggests that we cannot say that semantic universals must be surface-testable.

5 How do we find universals?

Given that we must postulate universals based on insufficient data (as data is never available for all human languages), we employ a range of strategies to get from data to universals. I will not discuss sources of evidence such as language change or cognitive-psychological factors; the reader is referred to article 6 [Semantics: Typology, Diachrony and Processing] (Fritz) *Theories of meaning change*, article 7 [Semantics: Typology, Diachrony and Processing] (Geeraerts) *Cognitive approaches to diachronic semantics*, and article 1 [Semantics: Theories] (Talmy) *Cognitive Semantics* for discussion. Article 12 [this volume] (Krifka) Varieties of semantic evidence is also relevant here.

5.1 Assume universality

One approach to establishing universals is simply to assume them, based on study of however many languages one has data from. This is actually what all universals research does, as no phenomenon has ever been tested in all of the world's languages. A point of potential debate is the number of languages which need to be examined before a universal claim should be made. This issue arises for semanticists because the nature of the fieldwork means that testing semantic universals necessarily proceeds quite slowly.

My own belief is that one should always assume universality in the absence of evidence to the contrary – and then go and look for evidence to the contrary. In earlier work I dubbed this strategy the 'No variation null hypothesis' (Matthewson 2001); see also article 2 [Semantics: Typology, Diachrony and Processing] (Bach & Chao) *Semantic Types across Languages*. The assumption of universality is a methodological strategy which tells us to begin with the strongest empirically falsifiable hypothesis. It does not entail that there is an absence of cross-linguistic variation in the semantics, and it does not mean that our analyses of unfamiliar languages must look parallel to those of English. On the contrary, work which adopts this strategy is highly likely to uncover semantic variation, and to help establish the parameters within which natural language semantics may vary.

The null hypothesis of universality is assumed by much work within semantics. In fact, some of the most influential semantic universals to have been proposed, those of Barwise & Cooper (1981), advance data only from English in support. (See also Keenan & Stavi 1986 for related work, and article 2 [Semantics: Typology, Diachrony and Processing] (Bach & Chao) *Semantic Types across Languages* for further discussion.) We saw two of Barwise and Cooper's universals above; here are two more for illustration. U1 is a universal semantic definition of the noun phrase (DP, in modern terminology):

> U1. NP-Quantifier universal (Barwise & Cooper 1981: 177)
>
> Every natural language has syntactic constituents (called noun-phrases) whose semantic function is to express generalized quantifiers over the domain of discourse.

U3 contains the well-known conservativity constraint, as well as asserting that there are no languages which lack determiners in the semantic sense.

> U3. Determiner universal (Barwise & Cooper 1981: 179)
>
> Every natural language contains basic expressions, (called determiners) whose semantic function is to assign to common count noun denotations (i.e., sets) A a quantifier that lives on A.

Barwise and Cooper do not offer data from any non-English language, yet postulate universal constraints. This methodology was clearly justified, and the fact that not all of their proposed universals have stood the test of time is largely irrelevant. By proposing explicit and empirically testable constraints, Barwise and Cooper's work inspired a large amount of subsequent cross-linguistic research, which has expanded our knowledge of quantificational systems in languages of the world. For example, several of the papers in the Bach et al. volume (1995) specifically address the NP-Quantifier Universal; see also Bittner & Trondhjem (2008) for a recent criticism of standard analyses of generalized quantifiers.

It is sometimes asserted that the strategy of postulating universals as soon as one can, or even of claiming that an unfamiliar language shares the same analysis as English, is euro-centric (see e.g., Gil 2001). But this is not correct. Since English is a well-studied language, it is legitimate to compare lesser-studied languages to analyses of English. It is our job to see whether we can find evidence for similarities between English and unfamiliar languages, especially when the evidence may not be superficially obvious. The important point here is that the null hypothesis of universality does not assign analyses of any language any priority over language-faithful analyses of any other languages. The null hypothesis is that all languages are the *same* – not that all languages are like English. Thus, it is just as likely that study of a non-Indo-European language will cause us to review and revise previous analyses of English. One example of this is Bittner's (2008) analysis of temporal anaphora. Bittner proposes a universal system of temporal anaphora which "instead of attempting to extend an English-based theory to a typologically distant language ... proceeds in the opposite direction – extending a Kalaallisut-based theory to English" (Bittner 2008: 384). Another example is the analysis of quantification presented in Matthewson (2001). I observe there that the St'át'imcets data are incompatible with the standard theory of generalized quantifiers, because St'át'imcets possesses no determiners which create a generalized quantifier by operating on a common noun denotation, as English *every* or *most* do. (The insight that Salish languages differ from English in their quantificational structures is originally due to Jelinek 1995.) I propose that the analysis suggested by the St'át'imcets data may be applicable also to English. In a similar vein, see Bar-el (2005) for the claim that the aspectual system of Sḵwx̱wú7mesh invites us to reanalyze the aspectual system of English.

The null hypothesis of universality guides empirical testing in a fruitful way; it gives us a starting hypothesis to test, and it allows us to use knowledge gained from study of one language in study of another. It inspires us to look beyond the superficial for underlying similarities, yet it does not force us to assume similarity where none exists. It also explicitly encodes the belief that there are limits on cross-linguistic variation. In contrast, an extreme non-universalist position (cf. Gil 2001) would essentially deny the idea that we have any reason to expect similarity between languages. This can lead to premature acceptance of exotic analyses.

5.2 Language acquisition and learnability

Generative linguists are interested in universals which are likely to have been provided by Universal Grammar, and clues about this can come from acquisition research and learnability theory. As argued by Crain & Pietroski (2001: 150) among others, the features which are most likely to be innately specified by UG are those which are shared across languages but which are not accessible to a child in the Primary Linguistic Data (the linguistic input available to the learner). Crain and Pietroski offer the examples of coreference possibilities for pronouns and strong crossover; the restrictions found in these areas are by hypothesis not learnable based on experience. The discussion of tense above is another case in point, as the data required to establish the existence of the null tense morpheme are not likely to be often presented to children in their first few years of life.

5.3 A typological survey

It may seem that a typological survey is at the opposite end of the spectrum from the research approaches discussed so far. However, even nativists should not discount the benefits of typological research. Such studies can help us gain perspective on which research questions are of central interest from a cross-linguistic point of view.

One example of this involves determiner semantics. A preliminary study by Matthewson (2013) (based on grammars of 33 languages from 25 language families) suggests that English is in many ways typologically unusual with respect to the syntax and semantics of determiners. For example, cross-linguistically, articles are the exception rather than the rule. Demonstratives are present in almost all languages, but rarely seem to occupy determiner position as they do in English; strong quantifiers often appear to occupy a different position again. In many languages, the only strong quantifiers are universals. While distributive universal quantifiers are frequently reduplications or affixes, non-distributive ones are not. What we see is that a broad study can lead us to pose questions that would perhaps not otherwise be addressed, such as what the reason is for the apparent correlation between the syntax of a universal quantifier and its semantics. There are many examples of typological studies which have inspired formal semantic analyses (e.g., Cusic 1981, Comrie 1985, Corbett 2000, to name a few, and see also Haspelmath et al. 2001 for a comprehensive overview of typology and universals).

6 Semantic universals in the literature

It is occasionally implied that since there is no agreed-upon set of semantic universals, they must not exist. For example, Levinson (2003: 315) claims: "There are in fact very few hypotheses about semantic universals that have any serious, cross-linguistic backing." However, I believe that the reason there is not a large number of agreed-upon semantic universals is simply that semantic universals have so far only infrequently been explicitly proposed and subjected to cross-linguistic testing. And the situation is changing: there is a growing body of work which addresses semantic variation and its limits, and the literature has reached a level of maturity where the relevant questions can be posed in an interesting way. (Some recent dissertations which employ semantic fieldwork are Faller 2002, Wilhelm 2003, Bar-el 2005, Gillon 2006, Tonhauser 2006, Deal 2010, Murray 2010, Peterson 2010, among others.) Many more semantic universals will be proposed as the field continues to conduct in-depth, detailed study of a wide range of languages.

In this section I provide a very brief overview of some universals within semantics, illustrating universals from a range of different domains.

In the area of lexical semantics we have for example Levinson's (2003: 315) proposal restricting elements encoding spatial relations. He argues that universally, there are at most three frames of reference upon which languages draw, each of which has precise characteristics that could have been otherwise. Levinson's proposals are discussed further in article 13 [Semantics: Typology, Diachrony and Processing] (Landau) Space in *semantics and cognition;* see also article 1 [Semantics: Theories] (Talmy) *Cognitive Semantics* for discussion of location.

A proposal which restricts composition methods and semantic rules is that of Bittner (1994). Bittner claims that there are no language-specific or construction-specific semantic rules. She proposes a small set of universal operations which essentially consist of functional application, type-lifting, lambda-abstraction, and a rule interpreting empty nodes. Although her proposal may seem to be worded in a theory-dependent way, claims about possible composition rules can be, and have been, challenged on at least partly empirical grounds;

see for example Heim & Kratzer (1998), Chung & Ladusaw (2003) for challenges to the idea that the only compositional rule is functional application.

Another proposal of Bittner's involves a set of universals of temporal anaphora, based on comparison of English with Kalaallisut. These include statements about the location of states, events, processes and habits relative to topical instants or periods, and restrictions on the default topic time for different event-types. The constraints are explicitly formulated independently of syntax: "Instead of aligning LF structures, this strategy aligns communicative functions" (Bittner 2008: 383).

A relatively common type of semantic universal involves constraints on semantic types. For example, Landman (2006) proposes that universally, traces and pro-forms can only be of type e. This is a purely semantic constraint: it is independent of whether the syntax of a language allows elements occupying the relevant positions to be of different categories.

A universal constraint on the syntax-semantics mapping is proposed by Gillon (2006). Gillon argues that universally, all and only elements which occupy D(eterminer) position introduce a contextual domain restriction variable (von Fintel 1994). (Gillon has to claim, contra Chierchia 1998, that languages like Mandarin have null determiners.) An interesting constructional universal is suggested by Faller (2007). She argues that the semantics of reciprocal constructions (involving plurality, distinctness of co-arguments, universal quantification and reflexivity) may be cross-linguistically uniform.

7 Variation

The search for universals is a search for limits on variation. If we assume a null hypothesis of universality, any observed variation necessitates a rejection of our null hypothesis and leads us to postulate restrictions on the limits of variation. Restrictions on variation are known in the formal literature as 'parameters', but the relation between parameters and universals is so tight that restricted sets of options from which languages choose can be classified as a type of universal (cf. article 2 [Semantics: Typology, Diachrony and Processing] (Bach & Chao) *Semantic Types across Languages*.

One prime source for semantic variation is independent syntactic variation. Given compositionality, the absence of certain structures in a language may result in the absence of certain semantic phenomena. Within the semantics proper, one well-known parameter is Chierchia's (1998) Nominal Mapping Parameter, which states that languages vary in the denotation of their NPs.

A language may allow NPs to be mapped into predicates, into arguments (i.e., kinds), or both. These choices correlate with a cluster of co-varying properties across languages. The Nominal Mapping Parameter represents a weakening of the null hypothesis that the denotations of NPs will be constant across languages. Whether or not it is correct is an empirical matter, and Chierchia's work has inspired a large amount of discussion (e.g., Cheng & Sybesma 1999, Schmitt & Munn 1999, Chung 2000, Longobardi 2001, 2005, Doron 2004, Dayal 2004, Krifka 2004, among others). As with Barwise and Cooper's universals, Chierchia's parameter has done a great deal to advance our understanding of the denotations of NPs across languages.

The Nominal Mapping Parameter also illustrates the restricted nature of the permitted variation; there are only three kinds of languages. Relevant work on restricted variation within semantics is discussed in article 3 [Semantics: Typology, Diachrony and Processing] (Doetjes) *Count/mass distinctions,* article 4 [Semantics: Typology, Diachrony and Processing] (Smith) *Tense and aspect,* and article 5 [Semantics: Typology, Diachrony and Processing] (Pederson) The expression of space.

There is often resistance to the postulation of semantic parameters. One possible ground for this resistance is the belief that semantics should be more cross-linguistically invariant than other areas of the grammar. For example, Chomsky (2000: 185) argues that "there are empirical grounds for believing that variety is more limited for semantic than for phonetic aspects of language." It is not clear to me, however, that we have empirical grounds for believing this. We are still in the early stages of research into semantic variation; we probably do not know enough yet to say whether semantics varies less than other areas of the grammar.

Another possible ground for skepticism about semantic parameters is the belief that semantic variation is not learnable. However, there is no reason why this should be so. Chierchia, for example, outlines a plausible mechanism by which the Nominal Mapping Parameter is learnable, with Chinese representing the default setting in line with Manzini & Wexler's (1987) Subset Principle (Chierchia 1998: 400–401). Chierchia argues that his parameter "is learned in the same manner in which every other structural difference is learned: through its overt morphosyntactic manifestations. It thus meets fully the reasonable challenge that all parameters must concern live morphemes."

A relatively radical semantic parameter is the proposal that some languages lack pragmatic presuppositions in the sense of Stalnaker (1974) (Matthewson 2006a, based on data from St'át'imcets). This parameter fails to be tied to specific lexical items, as it is stated globally. However, the presupposition parameter places languages in a subset-superset relation, and as such is potentially learnable, as long as the initial setting is the St'át'imcets one. A learner who assumes that her language lacks pragmatic presuppositions can learn that English possesses such presuppositions on the basis of overt evidence (such as 'Hey, wait a minute!' responses to presupposition failure, cf. von Fintel 2004).

One common way in which languages vary in their semantics is in degree of underspecification. For example, I argued above that St'át'imcets shares basic tense semantics with English. The languages differ in that the St'át'imcets tense morpheme is semantically underspecified, failing to distinguish past from present reference times. Another case of variation in underspecification involves modality. According to Rullmann, Matthewson & Davis (2008), St'át'imcets modals allow similar interpretations to English modal auxiliaries. However, the interpretations are distributed differently across the lexicon: while in English, a single modal allows a range of different conversational backgrounds (giving rise to deontic, circumstantial or epistemic interpretations, Kratzer 1991), in St'át'imcets, the conversational background is lexically encoded in the choice of modal. Conversely, while in English, the quantificational force of a modal is lexically encoded, in St'át'imcets it is not; each modal is compatible with both existential and universal interpretations.

One strong hypothesis would be that all languages possess the same functional categories, but that languages differ in the levels of underspecification in the lexical entries of the various morphemes, and in the way in which they 'bundle' the various aspects of meaning into morphemes. As an example of the latter case, Lin's (2006) analysis of Chinese involves partially standard semantics for viewpoint aspect and for tense, but a different bundling of information from that found in English (for example, the perfective aspect in Chinese includes a restriction that the reference time precedes the utterance time).

In terms of lexical aspect, there appears to be cross-linguistic variation in the semantics of basic aspectual classes. Bar-el (2005) argues that stative predicates in Skwxwú7mesh Salish include an initial change-of-state transition. Bar-el implies that while the basic building blocks of lexical entries are provided (e.g., that events can either begin or end with BECOME transitions (cf. Dowty 1979, Rothstein 2004), languages combine these in different ways to give different semantics for the various aspectual classes. Thus, the semantics we traditionally attribute to 'accomplishments' or to 'states' are not primitives of the grammar. While the Salish/English aspectual differences appear not to be reducible to underspecification or bundling, further decompositional analysis may reveal that they are.

I would like to thank Henry Davis for helpful discussion during the writing of this article, and Klaus von Heusinger and Noor van Leusen for helpful feedback on the first draft.

8 References

Abusch, Dorit 1997. Sequence of tense and temporal de re. *Linguistics & Philosophy* 20, 1–50.
Abusch, Dorit 1998. Generalizing tense semantics for future contexts. In: S. Rothstein (ed.). *Events and Grammar*. Dordrecht: Kluwer, 13–33.
Aitken, Barbara 1955. A note on eliciting. *International Journal of American Linguistics* 21, 83.
Bach, Emmon et al. (eds.) 1995. *Quantification in Natural Languages*. Dordrecht: Kluwer.
Baker, Mark 2003. *Lexical Categories: Verbs, Nouns and Adjectives*. Cambridge: Cambridge University Press.
Bar-el, Leora 2005. *Aspectual Distinctions in Skwxwú7mesh*. Ph.D. dissertation. University of British Columbia, Vancouver, BC.
Barwise, Jon & Robin Cooper 1981. Generalized quantifiers and natural language. *Linguistics & Philosophy* 4, 159–219.
Bittner, Maria 1987. On the semantics of the Greenlandic antipassive and related constructions. *International Journal of American Linguistics* 53, 194–231.
Bittner, Maria 1994. Cross-linguistic semantics. *Linguistics & Philosophy* 17, 53–108.
Bittner, Maria 2005. Future discourse in a tenseless language. *Journal of Semantics* 22, 339–388.
Bittner, Maria 2008. Aspectual universals of temporal anaphora. In: S. Rothstein (ed.). *Theoretical and Crosslinguistic Approaches to the Semantics of Aspect*. Amsterdam: Benjamins, 349–385.
Bittner, Maria & Naja Trondhjem 2008. Quantification as reference: Kalaallisut Q-verbs. In: L. Matthewson (ed.). *Quantification: A Cross-Linguistic Perspective*. Amsterdam: Emerald, 7–66.
Bohnemeyer, Jürgen 2002. *The Grammar of Time Reference in Yukatek Maya*. Munich: Lincom Europa.
Carden, Guy 1970. A note on conflicting idiolects. *Linguistic Inquiry* 1, 281–290.
Cheng, Lisa & Rint Sybesma 1999. Bare and not-so-bare nouns and the structure of NP. *Linguistic Inquiry* 30, 509–542.
Chierchia, Gennaro 1998. Reference to kinds across languages. *Natural Language Semantics* 6, 339–405.
Chomsky, Noam 2000. *New Horizons in the Study of Language and Mind*. Cambridge: Cambridge University Press.
Chung, Sandra 2000. On Reference to kinds in Indonesian. *Natural Language Semantics* 8, 157–171.
Chung, Sandra & William Ladusaw 2003. *Restriction and Saturation*. Cambridge, MA: The MIT Press.
Comrie, Bernard 1985. *Tense*. Cambridge: Cambridge University Press.
Comrie, Bernard 1989. *Language Universals and Linguistic Typology: Syntax and Morphology*. Oxford: Blackwell.
Corbett, Greville 2000. *Number*. Cambridge: Cambridge University Press.
Crain, Stephen & Paul Pietroski 2001. Nature, nurture, and universal grammar. *Linguistics & Philosophy* 24, 139–186.
Crain, Stephen & Rosalind Thornton 1998. *Investigations in Universal Grammar: A Guide to Experiments on the Acquisition of Syntax*. Cambridge, MA: The MIT Press.

Cusic, David 1981. *Verbal Plurality and Aspect.* Ph.D. dissertation. Stanford University, Stanford, CA.
Davis, Henry 2002. Categorial restrictions in St'át'imcets (Lillooet) relative clauses. In: C. Gillon, N. Sawai & R. Wojdak (eds.). *Papers for the 37th International Conference on Salish and Neighbouring Languages.* Vancouver, BC: University of British Columbia, 61–75.
Davis, Henry 2009. Cross-linguistic variation in anaphoric dependencies: Evidence from the Pacific Northwest. *Natural Language and Linguistic Theory* 27, 1–43.
Davis, Henry & Lisa Matthewson 1999. On the functional determination of lexical categories. *Révue Québecoise de Linguistique* 27, 27–67.
Dayal, Veneeta 2004. Number marking and (in)definiteness in kind terms. *Linguistics & Philosophy* 27, 393–450.
Deal, Amy Rose 2010. *Topics in the Nez Perce Verb.* Ph.D. dissertation. University of Massachusetts, Amherst, MA.
Demirdache, Hamida & Lisa Matthewson 1995. On the universality of syntactic categories. In: J. Beckman (ed.). *Proceedings of the North Eastern Linguistic Society (= NELS) 25.* Amherst, MA: GLSA, 79–93.
Dimmendaal, Gerrit 2001. Places and people: Field sites and informants. In: P. Newman & M. Ratliff (eds.). *Linguistic Fieldwork.* Cambridge: Cambridge University Press, 55–75.
Dixon, Robert M.W. 1977. Where have all the adjectives gone? *Studies in Language* 1, 19–80.
Doron, Edit 2004. Bare singular reference to kinds. In: R. Young & Y. Zhou (eds.). *Proceedings of Semantics and Linguistic Theory (= SALT) XIII.* Ithaca, NY: Cornell University, 73–90.
Dowty, David 1979. *Word Meaning in Montague Grammar.* Dordrecht: Reidel.
Enç, Murvet 1996. Tense and modality. In: S. Lappin (ed.). *The Handbook of Contemporary Semantic Theory.* Oxford: Blackwell, 345–358.
Faller, Martina 2002. *Semantics and Pragmatics of Evidentials in Cuzco Quechua.* Ph.D. dissertation. Stanford University, Los Angeles, CA.
Faller, Martina 2007. The ingredients of reciprocity in Cuzco Quechua. *Journal of Semantics* 243, 255–288.
Ferguson, Charles 1972. Verbs of 'being' in Bengali, with a note on Amharic. In: J. Verhaar (ed.). *The Verb 'Be' and its Synonyms: Philosophical and Grammatical Studies, 5.* Dordrecht: Reidel, 74–114.
von Fintel, Kai 1994. *Restrictions on Quantifier Domains.* Ph.D. dissertation. University of Massachusetts, Amherst, MA.
von Fintel, Kai 2004. Would you believe it? The king of France is back! Presuppositions and truth value intuitions. In: A. Bezuidenhout & M. Reimer (eds.). *Descriptions and Beyond.* Oxford: Oxford University Press, 261–296.
von Fintel, Kai & Lisa Matthewson 2008. Universals in semantics. *The Linguistic Review* 25, 49–111.
Gil, David 1987. Definiteness, noun phrase configurationality, and the count-mass distinction. In: E. Reuland & A. ter Meulen (eds.). *The Representation of (In)Definiteness.* Cambridge, MA: The MIT Press, 254–269.
Gil, David 2001. Escaping Euro-centrism: Fieldwork as a process of unlearning. In: P. Newman & M. Ratliff (eds.). *Linguistic Fieldwork.* Cambridge: Cambridge University Press, 102–132.
Gillon, Carrie 2006. *The Semantics of Determiners: Domain Restriction in Sḵwx̱wú7mesh.* Ph.D. dissertation. University of British Columbia, Vancouver, BC.

Grice, H. Paul 1975. Logic and conversation. In: P. Cole & J. L. Morgan (eds.). *Syntax and Semantics 3: Speech Acts.* New York: Academic Press, 41–58. Reprinted in: S. Davis (ed.). *Pragmatics.* Oxford: Oxford University Press, 1991, 305–315.

Harris, Zellig S. & Charles F. Voegelin 1953. Eliciting in linguistics. *Southwestern Journal of Anthropology* 9, 59–75.

Haspelmath, Martin et al. (eds.) 2001. *Language Typology and Language Universals: An International Handbook* (HSK 20.1–2). Berlin: de Gruyter.

Hayes, Alfred 1954. Field procedures while working with Diegueño. *International Journal of American Linguistics* 20, 185–194.

Heim, Irene & Angelika Kratzer 1998. *Semantics in Generative Grammar.* Oxford: Blackwell.

Jelinek, Eloise 1995. Quantification in Straits Salish. In: E. Bach et al. (eds.). *Quantification in Natural Languages.* Dordrecht: Kluwer, 487–540.

Katz, Jerrold 1976. A hypothesis about the uniqueness of human language. In: S. Harnad, H. Steklis & J. Lancaster (eds.). *Origins and Evolution of Language and Speech.* New York: New York Academy of Sciences, 33–41.

Keenan, Edward & Jonathan Stavi 1986. A semantic characterization of natural language determiners. *Linguistics & Philosophy* 9, 253–326.

Konstanz Universals Archiv 2002–. *The Universals Archive,* maintained by the University of Konstanz, Department of Linguistics. http://typo.uni-konstanz.de/archive/intro/, March 5, 2009.

Kratzer, Angelika 1991. Modality. In: D. Wunderlich & A. von Stechow (eds.). *Semantics: An International Handbook of Contemporary Research* (HSK 6). Berlin: de Gruyter, 639–650.

Krifka, Manfred 2004. Bare NPs: Kind-referring, indefinites, both, or neither? Empirical issues in syntax and semantics. In: R. Young & Y. Zhou (eds.). *Proceedings of Semantics and Linguistic Theory (= SALT) XIII.* Ithaca, NY: Cornell University, 180–203.

Landman, Meredith 2006. *Variables in Natural Language.* Ph.D. dissertation. University of Massachusetts, Amherst, MA.

Levinson, Stephen 2003. *Space in Language and Cognition: Explorations in Cognitive Diversity.* Cambridge: Cambridge University Press.

Lin, Jo-Wang 2006. Time in a language without tense: The case of Chinese. *Journal of Semantics* 23, 1–53.

Longobardi, Giuseppe 2001. How comparative is semantics? A unified parametric theory of bare nouns and proper names. *Natural Language Semantics* 9, 335–361.

Longobardi, Giuseppe 2005. A minimalist program for parametric linguistics? In: H. Broekhuis et al. (eds.). *Organizing Grammar: Linguistic Studies for Henk van Riemskijk.* Berlin: de Gruyter, 407–414.

Manzini, M. Rita & Kenneth Wexler 1987. Parameters, binding theory, and learnability. *Linguistic Inquiry* 18, 413–444.

Matthewson, Lisa 1998. *Determiner Systems and Quantificational Strategies: Evidence from Salish.* The Hague: Holland Academic Graphics.

Matthewson, Lisa 2001. Quantification and the nature of cross-linguistic variation. *Natural Language Semantics* 9, 145–189.

Matthewson, Lisa 2004. On the methodology of semantic fieldwork. *International Journal of American Linguistics* 70, 369–415.

Matthewson, Lisa 2006a. Presuppositions and cross-linguistic variation. In: C. Davis, A. Deal & Y. Zabbal (eds.). *Proceedings of the North Eastern Linguistic Society (= NELS)* 36. Amherst, MA: GLSA, 63–76.

Matthewson, Lisa 2006b. Temporal semantics in a superficially tenseless language. *Linguistics & Philosophy* 29, 673–713.
Matthewson, Lisa 2013. Strategies of quantification in St'át'imcets and the rest of the world. In: K. Gill, S. Harlow & G. Tsoulas (eds.). *Strategies of quantification*. Oxford: Oxford University Press, 15–38.
Montler, Timothy 2003. Auxiliaries and other categories in Straits Salishan. *International Journal of American Linguistics* 69, 103–134.
Murray, Sarah 2010. *Evidentiality and the Structure of Speech Acts*. Ph.D. dissertation. Rutgers University, New Brunswick, NJ.
Nida, Eugene 1947. Field techniques in descriptive linguistics. *International Journal of American Linguistics* 13, 138–146.
Ogihara, Toshi-Yuki 1996. *Tense, Attitudes and Scope*. Dordrecht: Kluwer.
Partee, Barbara 2000. 'Null' determiners vs. no determiners. Lecture read at the *2nd Winter Typology School*, Moscow.
Peterson, Tyler 2010. *Epistemic Modality and Evidentiality in Gitksan at the Semantics-Pragmatics Interface*. Ph.D. dissertation. University of British Columbia, Vancouver, BC.
Ritter, Elizabeth & Martina Wiltschko 2005. Anchoring events to utterances without tense. In: J. Alderete, C-h. Han & A. Kochetov (eds.). *Proceedings of the 24th West Coast Conference on Formal Linguistics (= WCCFL)*. Somerville, MA: Cascadilla Proceedings Project, 343–351.
Rothstein, Susan 2004. *Structuring Events*. Oxford: Blackwell.
Rullmann, Hotze, Lisa Matthewson & Henry Davis 2008. Modals as distributive indefinites. *Natural Language Semantics* 16, 317–357.
Schmitt, Cristina & Alan Munn 1999. Against the nominal mapping parameter: Bare nouns in Brazilian Portuguese. In: P. Tamanji, M. Hirotani & N. Hall (eds.). *Proceedings of the North Eastern Linguistic Society (=NELS) 29*. Amherst, MA: GLSA, 339–353.
Schütze, Carson 1996. *The Empirical Base of Linguistics: Grammaticality Judgments and Linguistic Methodology*. Chicago, IL: The University of Chicago Press.
Stalnaker, Robert 1974. Pragmatic presuppositions. In: M.K. Munitz & P.K. Unger (eds.). *Semantics and Philosophy*. New York: New York University Press, 197–213.
Tonhauser, Judith 2006. *The Temporal Semantics of Noun Phrases: Evidence from Guaraní*. Ph.D. dissertation. Stanford University, Stanford, CA.
Whorf, Benjamin 1956. *Language, Thought and Reality: Selected Writings of Benjamin Lee Whorf*. Edited by J. Carroll. Cambridge, MA: The MIT Press.
Wilhelm, Andrea 2003. *Telicity and Durativity: A Study of Aspect in Dene Suline (Chipewyan) and German*. Ph.D. dissertation, University of Calgary, Calgary, AL.
Yegerlehner, John 1955. A note on eliciting techniques. *International Journal of American Linguistics* 21, 286–288.

Alice G.B. ter Meulen
14 Formal methods in semantics

1   Introduction —— 362
2   First order logic and natural language —— 366
3   Formal systems, proofs and decidability —— 368
4   Semantic models, validity and completeness —— 369
5   Formalizing linguistic methods —— 372
6   Linguistic applications of syntactic methods —— 374
7   Linguistic applications of semantic methods —— 378
8   Conclusions —— 381
9   References —— 382

Abstract: Covering almost an entire century, this article reviews in general and non-technical terms how formal, logical methods have been applied to the meaning and interpretation of natural language. This paradigm of research in natural language semantics produced important new linguistic results and insights, but logic also profited from such innovative applications. Semantic explanation requires properly formalized concepts, but only provides genuine insight when it accounts for linguistic intuitions on meaning and interpretation or the results of empirical investigations in an insightful way. The creative tension between the linguistic demand for cognitively realistic models of human linguistic competence and the logicians demand for a proper and explicit account of all and only the valid reasoning patterns initially led to an interesting divergence of methods and associated research agendas. With the maturing of natural language semantics as a branch of cognitive science an increasing number of logicians trained in linguistics and linguists apt in using formal methods are developing more convergent empirical issues in interdisciplinary research programs.

1 Introduction

The scientific analysis of patterns of human reasoning properly belongs to the ancient discipline of logic, bridging more than twenty centuries from its earliest roots in the ancient Greek philosophical treatises of Plato and Aristotle on syllogisms to its contemporary developments in connecting dynamic reasoning in context to

---

Alice G.B. ter Meulen, Geneva, Switzerland

underlying neurobiological and cognitive processes. In reasoning with information from various sources available to us, we systematically exploit (i) the meaning of the words, (ii) the way they are put together in clauses, as well as (iii) the relations between these clauses and (iv) the circumstances in which we received the information in order to arrive at a conclusion (Frege 1892; Tarski 1956). The formal analysis of reasoning patterns not only offers an important window on the meaning and interpretation of logical languages, but also of ordinary, acquired, i.e. natural languages. It constitutes a core component of cognitive science, providing the proper scientific methods to model human information processing as constitutive structure and form.

Any explanatory scientific theory of the meaning and interpretation of natural language must at some level aim to characterize all and only those patterns of reasoning that guarantee to preserve in one way or another the assumed truth of the information on which the conclusions are based. In analyzing *patterns* of inferences, content and specific aspects of the interpretation can only be taken into consideration, if they can be expressed in syntactic form and constitutive structure or in the semantic meta-language. The contemporary research program of natural language semantics has significantly expanded the expressions of natural language to be subjected to such formal methods of logical analysis to cover virtually all syntactic categories, as well as relations between sentences and larger sections of discourse or text, mapping syntactic, configurational structures to sophisticated notions of semantic content or information structure (Barwise & Perry 1983; Chierchia 1995; Cresswell 1985; Davidson & Harman 1972; Dowty, Wall & Peters 1981; Gallin 1975; Partee, ter Meulen & Wall 1990).

The classical division of labor between *syntactic* and *semantic* theories of reasoning is inherited from the mathematical logical theories developed in the early twentieth century, when logical, i.e. *un*natural and purposefully designed languages were the primary subject of investigation. Syntactic theories of reasoning exploit as explanatory tools merely constitutive, configurational methods, structural, i.e. formal operations such as substitution and pure symbol manipulation of the associated proof theories. The semantic theories of reasoning require an interpretation of such constitutive, formal structure in models to characterize truth-conditions and validity of reasoning as systematic interaction between form and meaning (Boolos & Jeffrey 1980). The syntactic, proof theoretic strategy with its customary disregard for meaning as intangible, has originally been pursued most vigorously for natural language in the research paradigm of generative grammar. Its earliest mathematical foundational research in automata theory, formal grammars and their associated design languages regarded structural operations as the only acceptable formal methods. Reasoning or inference was as such not the target of their investigations, as grammars were principally limited to characterize sentence internal properties and their computational complexity

(Chomsky 1957; Chomsky 1959; Chomsky & Miller 1958, 1963; Hopcroft & Ullman 1979; Gross & Lentin 1970). The semantic, model-theoretic strategy of investigating human reasoning has been pursued most vigorously in natural language semantics, Lambek and Montague grammars and game theoretic semantics, and their 21st century successors, the various dynamic theories of meaning and interpretation founded on developments in intensional and epistemic logics of (sharing) belief and knowledge (Barwise 1989; van Benthem 1986; van Benthem & ter Meulen 1997; Cresswell 1985; Davidson & Harman 1972; Kamp 1981; Kamp & Reyle 1993; Lambek 1958; Lewis 1972, 1983; Montague 1974; Stalnaker 1999).

Formal methods deriving from logic are also applied in what has come to be known as formal *pragmatics*, where parameters other than worlds or situations, such as context or speaker/hearer, time of utterance or other situational elements may serve in the models to determine meaning and situated inference. This article will address formal methods in semantics as main topic, as formal pragmatics may be considered a further generalization of these methods to serve wider linguistic applications, but as such does not in any intrinsic way differ from the formal methods used in semantics.

In both logical and natural languages, valid forms of reasoning in their most general characteristics exploit the information available in the premises, assumed to be true in an arbitrary given model, to draw a conclusion, guaranteed to be also true in that model. Preserving this assumed truth of the premises is a complex process that may be modeled in various formal systems, but if their admitted inference rules are somehow violated in the process the conclusion of the inference is not guaranteed to be true. This common *de*ductive approach accounts for validity in forms or patterns of reasoning based on the stable meaning of the logical vocabulary, regardless of the class of models under consideration. It has constituted the methodological corner stone of the research program of natural language semantics, where ordinary language expressions are translated into logical expressions, their 'logical form', to determine their truth conditions in models as a function of their form and subsequently characterize their valid forms of reasoning (May 1985; Montague 1974; Dowty, Wall & Peters 1981). Some important formal methods of major schools in this research program are reviewed, mostly to present their conceptual foundations and discuss their impact on linguistic insights, while referring the reader for more technical expositions and formal details to the relevant current literature and articles 10 [this volume] (Newen & Schröder) *Logic and semantics*, 11 [this volume] (Kempson) *Formal semantics and representationalism*, 7 [Semantics: Theories] (Zimmermann) *Model-theoretic semantics*, 4 [Semantics: Noun Phrases and Verb Phrases] (Keenan) *Quantifiers*, 11 [Semantics: Theories] (Kamp & Reyle) *Discourse Representation Theory* and 12 [Semantics: Theories] (Dekker) *Dynamic semantics* (see also van Benthem & ter Meulen 1997; Gabbay & Guenthner 1983; Partee, ter Meulen & Wall 1990).

Excluded from consideration as *formal* methods in the sense intended here are other mathematical methods, such as statistical, *in*ductive inference systems, where the assumptions and conclusions of inferences are considered more or less likely, or various quantitative approaches to meaning based on empirical studies, or optimality systems, which ordinarily do not account for inference patterns, but rank possible interpretations according to a given set of constraints of diverse kinds. In such systems form does not directly and functionally determine meaning and hence the role of inference patterns, if any, is quite different from the core role in logical, deductive systems of reasoning which constitute our topic. Of course, as any well defined domain of scientific investigation, such systems too may be further formalized and perhaps eventually even axiomatized as a logical, formal system. But in the current state of linguistics their methods are often informal, appealing to semantic notions as meaning only implicitly, resulting in fragmented theories, which, however unripe for formalization, may still provide genuinely interesting and novel linguistic results.

In section 2 of this article the best known logical system of first order logic is discussed. It served as point of departure of natural language semantics, in spite of its apparent limitations and idealizations. In section 3 the classical definition of a formal system is specified with its associated notions of proof and theorem, and these are related to its early applications in linguistic grammars. The hierarchy of structural complexity generated by the various kinds of formal grammars is still seen to direct the current quest in natural language semantics for proper characterizations of cognitive complexity. Meta-logical properties such as decidability of the set of theorems are introduced. In section 4 the general notion of a semantic model with its definition of truth conditions is presented, without formalization in set-theoretic notation, to serve primarily in conceptually distinguishing contingent truth (at a world) in a model from logical truth in regardless which model to represent valid forms of reasoning. Completeness is presented as a desirable, but perhaps not always feasible property of logical systems that have attained a perfect harmony between their syntactic and semantic sides. Section 5 discusses how the syntactic and semantic properties of pronouns first provided a strong impetus for using formal methods in separate linguistic research programs, that have later converged on a more integrated account of their behavior, currently still very much under investigation. In section 6 we review a variety of proof theoretic methods that have been developed in logic to understand how each of them had an impact on formal linguistic theories later. This is where constraints on derivational complexity and resource bounded generation of expressions is seen to have their proper place, issues that have only gained in importance in contemporary linguistic research. Section 7 presents an overview of the semantic methods that have been developed in logic over the past century to see how they have influenced the development of natural language semantics as a flourishing branch of cognitive science, where formal methods provide an important contribution to their scientific methods. The final section 8 contains the conclusion of this article stating that the application of formal methods, deriving from logical theories, has greatly contributed to the development of linguistics as an independent academic discipline with an integrated, interdisciplinary research agenda. Seeking a continued convergence of syntactic and semantic methods in linguistic applications will serve to develop new insights in the cognitive capacity underlying much of human information processing.

2 First order logic and natural language

Many well known systems of first order logic (FOL), in which quantifiers may only range over individuals, i.e. not over properties or sets of individuals, have been designed to study inference patterns deriving from the meaning of the classical Boolean connectives of conjunction (... *and* ...), disjunction (... *or* ...), negation (*not* ...) and conditionals (*if* ... *then* ...) and biconditionals (... *if and only if* ...), besides the universal (*every N*) and existential (*some N*) quantifiers. Syntactically these FOL systems differed in the number of axioms, logical vocabulary or inference rules they admitted, some were optimal for simplicity of the proofs, others more congenial to the novel user, relying on the intuitive meaning of the logical vocabulary (Boolos & Jeffrey 1980; Keenan & Faltz 1985; Link 1991).

The strongly reformist attitudes of the early 20th century logicians Bertrand Russell, Gottlob Frege, and Alfred Tarski, today considered the great-grandfathers of modern logic, initially steered FOL developments away from natural language, as it was regarded as too ambiguous, hopelessly vague, or content- and context-dependent. Natural language was even considered prone to paradox, since you can explicitly state that something is or is not true. This is what is meant when natural language is accused of "containing its own truth-predicate", for the semantics of the predicate "is true" cannot be formulated in a non-circular manner for a perfectly grammatical, but self-referential sentence like *This statement is false*, which is clearly true just in case it is false. Similarly treacherous forms of self-referential acts with circular truth-conditions are found in simple statements such as *I am lying*, resembling the ancient Cretense Liar Paradox, and the syntactically overtly self-referential, but completely comprehensible *The claim that this sentence contains eleven words is false*, that lead later model theoretic logicians to develop innovative models of self-reference and logically sound forms of circularity, abandoning the need for rock bottom atomic elements of sets, as classical set theory had always required (Barwise & Etchemendy 1987).

Initially FOL was advocated as a 'good housekeeping' act in understanding elementary forms of reasoning in natural language, although little serious attention was paid on just how natural language expressions should be systematically translated into FOL, given their syntactic constituent structure. This raised objections of what linguists often called 'miraculous translation', appealing to the implicit intuitions on truth-functional meaning only trained logicians apparently had easy access to. Although this limited logical language of FOL was never intended to come even close to modeling the wealth of expressive power in natural languages, it was considered the basic Boolean algebraic core of the logical inference engine. The descriptive power of FOL systems was subsequently importantly enriched to facilitate the Fregean adagio of compositional translation by admitting lambda abstraction, representing the denotation of a predicate as a set A by a characteristic function f that tells you for each element d in the underlying domain D whether or not d is an element of that set A, i.e. $f_A(d)$ is true if and only if d is an element of the set A (Partee, ter Meulen & Wall 1990). Higher order quantification with quantifiers ranging over sets or properties, or sets of those *ad infinitum*, required a type structure, derived from the abstract lambda calculus, a universal theory of functional structure. Typing formal languages resembled in some respects Bertrand Russell's solution to avoid vicious circularity in logic (Barendregt 1984; Carpenter 1997; Montague 1974; Link 1991).

More complex connectives or other truth functional expressions and operators were added to FOL, besides situations or worlds to the models to analyze modal, temporal or epistemic concepts (van Benthem 1983; Carnap 1947; Kripke 1972; Lewis 1983; McCawley 1981). The formal methods of FOL semantics varied from classical Boolean full bi-valuation with total functions that ultimately take only true and false as values, to three or more valued models in which formulas may not always have a determined truth value, initially proposed to account for presupposition failure of definite descriptions that did not have a referent in the domain of the intended model. Weaker logical systems were also proposed, admitting fewer inference rules. The intuitionistic logics are perhaps the best known of these, rejecting for philosophical and perhaps conceptual reasons the classical law of double negation and the correlated rule of inference that allowed you to infer a conclusion, if its negation had been shown to lead to contradictions. In classical FOL the truth functional definition of the meaning of negation as set-theoretic complement made double negation logically equivalent to no negation at all, e.g. *It is not the case that every student did not hand in a paper* should at least truth-functionally mean the same as *Some student handed in a paper* (Partee, ter Meulen & Wall 1990). Admitting partial functions that allowed quantifiers to range over possible extensions of their already fixed, given range, ventured into for logic also innovative higher order methods, driven by linguistic considerations of pronoun resolution in discourse and various sophisticated forms of quantification found in natural language, to which we return below (Chierchia 1995; Gallin 1975; Groenendijk & Stokhof 1991; Kamp & Reyle 1993).

3 Formal systems, proofs and decidability

Whatever its exact language and forms of reasoning characterized as valid, any particular logical system must adhere to some very specific general requirements, if it is to count as a formal system. A *formal system* must consist of four components:
(i) a lexicon specifying the terminal expressions or *words*, and a set of non-terminal symbols or *categories*,
(ii) a set of *production rules* which determine how the well formed expressions of any category of the formal language may be generated,
(iii) a set of *axioms* or expressions of the lexicon that are considered primitive,
(iv) a set of *inference rules*, determining how expressions may be manipulated.

A formal system may be formulated purely abstractly without being intended as representation of anything, or it may be designed to serve as a description or simulation of some domain of real phenomena or, as intended in linguistics, modeling aspects of empirical, linguistic data.

A formal *proof* is the product of a formal system, consisting of (i) axioms, expressions of the language that serve as intuitively obvious or in any case unquestionable first principles, assumed to be true or taken for granted no matter what, and (ii) applications of the rules of inference that generate sequences of steps in the proof, resulting in its conclusion, the final step, also called a *theorem*. The *grammar* of a language, whether logical or natural, is a system of rules that generates all and only all the grammatical or well-formed sentences of the language. But this does not mean that we can always get a definite answer to the general question whether an arbitrary string belongs to a particular language, something a child learning its first language may actually need. There is no general decision procedure determining for any arbitrary given expression whether it is or is not derivable in any particular formal system (Arbib 1969; Davis 1965; Savitch, Bach & Marsh 1987). However, this question is provably *decidable* for sizable fragments of natural language, even if some form of higher order quantification is permitted (Nishihara, Morita & Iwata 1990; Pratt-Hartmann 2003; Pratt-Hartmann & Third 2006). Current research on generative complexity is focused on expanding fragments of natural language that are known to be decidable to capture realistic limitations on search complexity, in attempting to characterize formal counterparts to experimentally obtained results on human limitations of cognitive resources, such as memory or processing time. Automated theorem provers certainly assist people in detecting proofs for complex theorems or huge domains. People actually use smart, but still little understood heuristics in finding derivations, trimming down the search space of alternative variable assignments, for example, by marked prosody and intonational meaning. Motivating much of the contemporary research in applying formal methods to natural language is seeking to restrain the complexity or computational power of the formal systems to less powerful, learnable and decidable fragments. In such cognitively realistic systems the inference rules constrain the search space of valuation functions or exploit limited resources in linguistically interesting and insightful ways.

The general research program of determining the generative or computational complexity of natural languages first produced in the late 1950s the well known *Chomsky Hierarchy* of formal language theory, which classifies formal languages, their corresponding automata and the phrase-structure grammar that generate the languages as regular, context-free, context-sensitive or unrestricted rewrite systems (Arbib 1969; Gross & Lentin 1970; Hopcroft & Ullman 1979). Initially, Chomsky (1957, 1959) claimed that the rich structure of natural languages with its complex forms of agreement required the strength of unrestricted rewrite systems, or Turing machines. Quickly linguists realized that for grammars to be learnable and to claim to model in any cognitively realistic way our human linguistic competence, whether or not innate, their generative power should be substantially restricted (Peters & Ritchie 1973). Much of the contemporary research on resource-bounded categorial grammars and the economy of derivation in minimalist generative grammar, comparing formal complexity of derivations, is still seeking to distill universal principles of natural languages, considered cognitive constants of human information processing, linguistically expressed in structurally very diverse phenomena (Ades & Steedman 1982; Moortgat 1996; Morrill 1994, 1995; Pentus 2006; Stabler 1997).

4 Semantic models, validity and completeness

On the semantic side of formal methods, the notion of a *model M* plays a crucial role in the definition of truth-conditions for formulas generated by the syntax. The meaning of the Boolean connectives is considered not to vary from one model to a next one, as it is separated in the vocabulary as the closed class of expressions of the logical vocabulary. The conjunction (... *and* ...) is true just in case each of the conjuncts is, the disjunction (... *or* ...) is false only in the case neither disjunct is true. The conditional is only false in the case the antecedent (*if* ... clause) is true, but the consequent (*then* ... clause) is false. The bi-conditional (... *if and only if* ...) is true just in case the two parts have the same truth value. Negation (*not* ...) simply reverses the truth value of the expression it applies to. For the interpretation of the quantifiers an additional tool is required, a variable assignment function f, which assigns to each variable x in the vocabulary of variables a referent d, an element of the domain D of the model M. Proper names and the descriptive vocabulary containing all kinds of predicates, i.e. adjectives, nouns, and verbs, are interpreted by a function P, given with model M, that specifies who was the bearer of the name, or who had a certain property corresponding to a one place predicate, or stood in a certain relation for relational predicates in the given model M.

Linguists were quick to point out that in natural language at least conjunctions and disjunctions connect not only full clauses, but also noun phrases, which is not always reducible to a sentential connective, e.g. *John and Mary met* ≠ *John met and Mary met*. This kind of linguistic criticism quickly led to generalizations of Boolean operations in a logical system, where variable assignment functions are generalized and given the flexibility to assign referents of appropriate complex types in a richer higher order logic, but such complexities need not concern us here.

A formal semantic model M consists hence of: (i) a domain D of semantic objects, sometimes classified into types or given a particular internal structure, and (ii) a function P that assigns appropriate denotations to the descriptive vocabulary of the language interpreted. If the language also contains quantifiers, the model M comes equipped with a given variable assignment function g, often considered arbitrary, to provide a referent, which is an element of D, for all free variables. The given variable assignment function is sometimes considered to represent the current context in some contemporary systems that investigate context dependencies and indexicals. In FOL the universal quantifier *every x [N(x)]* is interpreted as true in the model M, if all possible alternative assignment functions g' to the variable x that it binds provide a referent d in the denotation of N. So not only the given variable assignment function g provides a d in the denotation of N, but all alternative assignments g' that may provide another referent, but could equally well have been considered the given one, also do. For the existential quantifier *some x [N(x)]* only one such variable assignment, the given one or another alternative variable assignment function, suffices to interpret the quantifier as true in the model M. An easy way to understand the effect of the interpretation of quantifiers in clauses is to see that for a universal *NP* the set denoted by N should be a subset of the set denoted by the *VP*, e.g. *every student sings* requires that the singers include all the students. Similarly, the existential quantifier requires that the intersection of the denotation of the *N* and the denotation of the *VP* is not empty, e.g. *some student sings* means that among the singers there is at least one student.

Intensional models generalize this elementary model theory for extensional FOL to characterize truth in a model relative to a possible world, situation or some other index, representing, for instance, temporal or epistemic variability. Intensional operators typically require a clause in its scope to be true at all or at only some such indices, mirroring strong, universal and existential quantifiers respectively. The domain of intensional models must be enriched with the interpretation of the variables referring to such indices, if such meta-variables are included in the language to be interpreted. Otherwise they are considered to be external to the model, added as a set of parameters indexing the function interpreting the language. Domains may also be structured as (semi)lattices or other partial orders, which has proven useful for the semantics of plurals, mass terms and temporal reference to events, but such further variations on FOL must remain outside the scope of the elementary exposition in this article.

To characterize logical truths, reflecting the valid reasoning patterns, one simply generalizes over all formulas true in all logically possible models, to obtain those formulas that must be true as a matter of necessity or form only, due to the meaning assigned to their logical vocabulary, irrespective of what is actually considered to be factually the case in the models. By writing out syntactic proofs with all their premises conjoined as antecedents of a conditional of which the conclusion is the consequent one may test in a semantic way the validity of the inference. If such a conditional cannot be falsified, the proof is valid and vice versa.

A semantic interpretation of a language, natural or otherwise, is considered *formal* only if it provides such precise logical models in which the language can be systematically interpreted. Accordingly, contingent truths, which depend for their truth on what happens to be the case in the given model, are properly distinguished from logical truths, which can never be false in any possible model, because the meaning of the logical vocabulary is fixed outside the class of models and hence remains invariable.

A logical system in which every proof of a theorem can be proven to correspond to a semantically valid inference pattern and vice versa is called a *complete* system, as FOL is. If a formal system contains statements that are true in every possible model but cannot be proven as theorems within that system by the admitted rules of inference and the given axiom base, the system is considered *incomplete*. Familiar systems of arithmetic have been proven to be incomplete, but that does not disqualify them from their sound use in practice and they definitely still serve as a valuable tool in applications.

5 Formalizing linguistic methods

Given the fundamental distinction between syntactic, proof-theoretic and semantic, model-theoretic characterizations of reasoning in theories that purport to model meaning and interpretation, the general question arises what (dis)advantages these two methodologically distinct approaches respectively may have for linguistic applications. Although in its generality this question may not be answerable in a satisfactory way, it is clear that at least in the outset of linguistics as its own, independent scientific discipline, quite different and mostly disconnected, if not antagonizing research communities were associated with the two strategies. This separation of minds was only too familiar to logicians from the early days of modern logic, where proof theorists and model theoretic semanticists often drew blood in their disputes on the priority, conceptual or otherwise, of their respective methods. Currently seeking convergence of research issues in syntax and semantics is much more en vogue and an easy go-between in syntactic and semantic methods has already proven to pay off in obtaining the best linguistic explanations and new insights.

One of the best examples of how linguistic questions could fruitfully be addressed both by syntactic and semantic formal methods, at first separately, but later in tandem, is the thoroughly studied topic of binding pronouns and its associated concept of quantifier scope. Syntacticians focused primarily on the clear configurational differences between free (1a) and bound pronouns (1b), and reflexive pronouns (1c), which all depend in different ways on the subject noun phrase that precedes and commands them in the same clause. Co-indexing was their primary method of indicating binding, though no interpretive procedure was specified with it, as meaning was considered elusive (Reinhart 1983a, 1983b).

(1) a. [Every student]$_i$ who knows [John/a professor]$_j$ loves [him]$_{*i, j}$.
    b. [Every student]$_i$ loves [[his]$_i$ teacher]$_{*i, j}$.
    c. [Every student]$_i$ who knows [John/a professor]$_j$ loves [himself]$_{i, *j}$.

This syntactic perspective on the binding behavior of pronouns within clauses had deep relations to constraints on movement as a transformation on a string, to which we return below. It limited its consideration of data to pronominal dependencies among clauses within sentences, disregarding the fact that singular universal quantifiers cannot bind pronouns across sentential boundaries (2a,b), but proper names, plurals and indefinite noun phrases typically do (2c).

(2) a. [Every student]$_i$ handed in a paper. [He]$_{*i, j}$ passed the exam.
    b. [Every student]$_i$ who handed in a paper [t]$_i$ passed the exam.

c. [John/A student/All students]$_i$ handed in a paper.
      [He/they]$_{i,j}$ passed the exam.

Semanticists had to understand how pronominal binding in natural language was in some respects similar, but in other respects quite different from the ordinary variable binding of FOL. From a semantic perspective the first puzzle was how ordinary proper names and other referring expressions, including freely referring pronouns, that were considered to have no logical scope and hence could not enter into scope ambiguities, could still force pronouns to corefer (3a), even in intensional contexts (3b).

(3) a. John/he loves his mother.
    b. John believes that Peter loves his mother.
    c. Every student believes that Peter loves his mother.

In (3a) the reference of the proper name *John* or the contextually referring free pronoun *he* fixes the reference of the possessive pronoun *his*. In (3b) the possessive pronoun *his* in the subordinate clause could be interpreted as dependent on *Peter*, but equally easily as dependent upon *John* in the main clause. If FOL taught semanticists to identify bound variables with those variables that were syntactically within the scope of a existential or universal quantifier, proper names had to be reconsidered as quantifiers having scope, yet referring rigidly to the same individual, even across intensional contexts. By considering quantifying in as a primary semantic technique to bind variables simultaneously, first introduced in Montague (1974), semanticists fell into the logical trap of identifying binding with configurational notions of linear scope. This fundamental connection ultimately had to be abandoned, when the infamous Geach sentence (4)

(4) Every farmer who owns a donkey beats it.

made syntacticians as well as semanticists realize that existential noun phrases in restrictive relative clauses of universal subject noun phrases could inherit, as it were, their universal force, creating for the interpretation of (4) cases of farmers and donkeys over which the quantifier was supposed to range. This is called *unselective binding*, introduced first by David Lewis (Lewis 1972, 1983), but brought to the front of research in semantic circles in Kamp (1981). Generalizing quantifying in as a systematic procedure to account also for intersentential binding of pronouns, as in (2), was soon also realized to produce counterintuitive results. This motivated an entirely new development of dynamic semantics, where the interpretation of a given sentence would partially determine the interpretation of the next sentence in a text and pronominal binding was conceptually once and for all separated from the logical or configurational notion of scope (Groenendijk & Stokhof 1991; Kamp & Reyle 1993). The interested reader is referred to article 12 [Semantics: Theories] (Dekker) *Dynamic semantics* and article 1 [Semantics: Noun Phrases and Verb Phrases] (Büring) *Pronouns* for further discussion and details of the resulting account.

6 Linguistic applications of syntactic methods

In logic itself quite a few different flavors of formal systems had been developed based on formal proof-theoretic (syntactic) or model-theoretic (semantic) methods. The best known on the proof-theoretic side are axiomatic proof theory (Jeffrey 1967), Gentzen sequent calculus (Gentzen 1934), combinatorial logic (Curry 1961), and natural deduction (Jeffrey 1967; Partee, ter Meulen & Wall 1990), each of which have made distinct and significant contributions in various developments in semantics. Of the more semantically flavored developments most familiar are Tarski's classical notion of *satisfaction* in models (Tarski 1956), the Lambek and other categorial grammars (Ajdukiewicz 1935; Bar Hillel 1964; van Benthem 1987, 1988; Buszkowski 1988; Buszkowski & Marciszewski 1988; Lambek 1958; Oehrle, Bach & Wheeler 1988), tightly connecting syntax and semantics via type theory (Barendregt 1984; van Benthem 1991; Carpenter 1997; Morrill 1994), Beth's tableaux method (Beth 1970), game theoretic semantics (Hintikka & Kulas 1985), besides various intensional logical systems, enriched with indices representing possible worlds or other modal notions, which each also have led to distinctive semantic applications (Asher 1993; van Benthem 1983; Cresswell 1985; Montague 1974). The higher order enrichment of FOL with quantification over sets, properties of individuals or properties of properties in Montague Grammar (Barwise & Cooper 1981; van Benthem & ter Meulen 1985; Montague 1974) at least initially directed linguists' attention away from the global linguistic research program of seeking to constrain the generative capacity and computational complexity of the formal methods in order to model realistically the cognitive capacities of human language users, as it focused everyone's attention on compositionality, type theory and type shifting principles, and adopted a fully generalized functional structure.

The next two sections selectively review some of the formal methods of these logical systems that have led to important semantic applications and innovative developments in linguistic theory.

An axiomatic characterization of a formal system is the best way to investigate its logic, as it matches its semantics to prove straightforwardly its soundness and completeness, i.e. demonstrating that every provable theorem is true in all models (*semantically valid*) and vice versa. For FOL a finite, in fact small number of logically true expressions suffice to derive all and only all valid expressions, i.e. FOL is provably complete. But in actually constructing new proofs an axiomatic characterization is much less useful, for it does not offer any reliable heuristics as guidance for an effective proof search. The main culprit is the rule of inference guaranteeing the transitivity of composition, i.e. to derive A → C from A → B and B → C requires finding an expression B which has no trace in the conclusion A → C. Since there are infinitely many possible such Bs, you cannot exhaustively search for it. The Gentzen sequent calculus (Gentzen 1934) is known to be equivalent to the axiomatic characterization of FOL, and it proved that any proof of a theorem using the transitivity of composition, or its equivalent, the so called Cut inference in Gentzen sequent calculus, may be transformed into a proof that avoids using this rule. Therefore, transitivity of composition is considered 'logically harmless', since the Gentzen sequent calculus effectively limits searching for a proof of any theorem to the expressions constituting the theorem you want to derive, called the *subformula* property. The inference rules in Gentzen sequent calculus are hence guaranteed to decompose the complexity of the expressions in a derivation, making the question whether an expression is a theorem decidable. But from the point of view of linguistic applications the original Gentzen calculus harbored another drawback as generative system. It allowed structural inference rules that permuted the order of premises in a proof or rebracketed any triple (associativity), making it hard to capture linguistically core notions of dominance, governance or precedence between constituents of a sentence to be proven grammatical. To restore constitutive order to the premises, the premises had to be regarded to create an linearly ordered sequence or n-tuple, or a *multiset* (in mathematics, a multiset (or bag) is a generalization of a set. A member of a multiset can have more than one instances, while each member of a set has only one, unique instance). This is now customary within the current categorical grammars deriving from Gentzen's system, reviewed below in the semantic methods that affected developments in natural language semantics (Moortgat 1997).

Perhaps the most familiar proof theoretic characterization of FOL is Natural Deduction, in which rules of inference systematically introduce or eliminate the connectives and quantifiers (Jeffrey 1967; Partee, ter Meulen & Wall 1990). This style of constructing proofs is often taught in introductory logic classes, as it does provide a certain intuitive heuristics in constructing proofs and closely follows the truth-conditional meaning given to the logical vocabulary, while systematically decomposing the conclusion and given assumptions until atomic conditions are obtained. Proving a theorem with natural deduction rules still requires a certain amount of ingenuity and insight, which may be trained by practice. But human beings will never be perfected to attain logical omniscience, i.e. the power to find each and every possible proof of a theorem. No actual success in finding a proof may mean either you have to work harder at finding it or that the expression is not a theorem, but you never know for sure which situation you are in (Boolos & Jeffrey 1980; Stalnaker 1999).

The fundamental demand that grammars of natural languages must realistically model the human cognitive capacities to produce and understand language has led to a wealth of developments in searching how to cut down on the generative power of formal grammars and their corresponding automata. Early in the developments of generative grammar, the unrestricted deletion transformation was quickly considered the most dangerously powerful operation in an unrestricted rewrite system or Turing machine, as it permitted the deletion of any arbitrary expressions that were redundant in generating the required surface expression (Peters & Ritchie 1973). Although deletion as such has still not been eliminated altogether as possible effect of movement, it is now always constrained to leave a trace or some other formal expression, making deleted material recoverable. Hence no expressions may simply disappear in the context of a derivation. The Empty Category Principle (ECP) substantiated this requirement further, stating that all traces of moved noun phrases and variables must be properly governed (Chomsky 1981; Haegeman 1991; van Riemsdijk & Williams 1986). This amounts to requiring them to be c-commanded by the noun phrase interpreted as binding them (c-command is a binary relation between nodes in a tree structure defined as follows: Node A c-commands node B iff A ≠ B, A does not dominate B and B does not dominate A, and every node that dominates A also dominates B.). Extractions of an adjunct phrase out a wh-island as in

(5) *How$_i$ did Mary ask whether someone had fixed the car t_i?

or moving *wh*-expressions out of a *that*-clause as in

(6) *Who$_i$ does Mary believe that t_i will fix the car?

are clearly ungrammatical, because they violate this ECP condition, as the traces t_i are co-indexed with and hence intended to be interpreted as bound by expressions outside their proper governance domain.

The classical logical notion of *quantifier scope* is much less restricted, as ordinarily quantifiers may bind variables in intensional context without raising any semantic problems of interpretation, as we saw above in (3c) (Dowty, Wall & Peters 1981; Partee, ter Meulen & Wall 1990). For instance, in intensional semantics the sentence (7)

(7) Mary believes that someone will fix the car.

has at least one so called 'de re' interpretation in which *someone* is 'quantified in' and assigned a referent in the actual world, of whom Mary believes that he will fix the car in a future world, where Mary's beliefs have come true. Such wide scope interpretations of noun phrases occurring inside a complementizer *that*-CP is considered in generative syntax a form of opaque or hidden movement at LF, regarded a matter of semantic interpretation, and hence external to grammar, i.e. not a question of derivation of syntactic surface word order (May 1985). Surface wide scope *wh*-quantifiers in such 'de re' constructions binding overt pronouns occurring within the intensional context i.e. within the *that*-clause are perfectly acceptable, as in (8).

(8) Of whom$_i$ does Mary believe that he$_i$ will fix the car?

Anyone intending to convey that Mary's belief regarded a particular person, rather than someone hypothetically assumed to exist, would be wise to use such an overt wide scope clause as in (8), according to a background pragmatic view that speakers should select the optimal syntactic form to express their thought and to avoid any possible misunderstanding.

This theoretical division of labor between tangible, syntactic movement to generate proper surface word order and intangible movement to allow disambiguation of the semantic scope of quantifiers has perhaps been the core bone of contention over many years between on the one hand the generative formal methods, in which semantic ambiguity does not have to be syntactically derived, and on the other hand, categorial grammar and its later developments in Montague grammar, which required full compositionality, i.e. syntactic derivation must determine semantic interpretation, disambiguating quantifier scope by syntactic derivation. In generative syntax every derivational difference had to be meaningful, however implicit this core notion remained, but in categorial grammars certain derivational differences could be provably semantically equivalent and hence meaningless, often denigratingly called the *problem of spurious ambiguities*. To characterize the logical equivalence of syntactically distinguished derivations required an independent semantic characterization of their truth conditions, considered a suitable task of logic, falling outside the scope of linguistic grammar proper, according to most generativists. This problem of characterizing which expressions with different derivational histories would be true in exactly the same models, hence would be logically equivalent, simply does not arise in generative syntax, as it hides semantic ambiguities as LF movement not reflected in surface structure, avoiding syntactic disambiguation of semantic ambiguities.

A much stronger requirement on grammatical derivations is to demand methodologically that all and only the constitutive expressions of the derived expression must be used in a derivation, often called *surface compositionality* (Cresswell 1985; Partee 1979). This research program is aiming to eliminate from linguistic theory anything that is not absolutely necessary. Chomsky (1995) claimed that both deep structure, completely determined by lexical information, and surface structure, derived from it by transformations, may be dispensed with. Given that a language consists of expressions which match sound structure to representations of their meaning, Universal Grammar should consist merely of a set of phonological, semantic, and syntactic features, together with an algorithm to assemble features into lexical expressions and a small set of operations, including *move* and *merge*, that constitute syntactic objects, the computational system of human languages. The central thesis of this minimalist framework is that the computational system is the optimal, most simple, solution to legibility conditions at the phonological and semantic interface. The goal is to explain all the observed properties of languages in terms of these legibility conditions, and properties of the computational system. Often advocated since the early 1990s is the *Lexicalist Hypothesis* requiring that syntactic transformations may operate only on syntactic constituents, and can only insert or delete designated elements, but cannot be used to insert, delete, permute, or substitute parts of words. This Lexicalist Hypothesis, which is certainly not unchallenged even among generativists, comes in two versions: (a) a weak one, prohibiting transformations to be used in derivational morphology, and (b) a strong version prohibiting use of transformations in inflection. It constitutes the most fundamentally challenging attempt from a syntactic perspective to approach surface compositionality as seen in the well-known theories of natural language semantics to which we now turn.

7 Linguistic applications of semantic methods

The original insight of the Polish logician Alfred Tarski was that the truth conditional semantics of any language must be stated recursively in a distinct metalanguage in terms of satisfaction of formulas consisting of predicates and free variables to avoid the paradoxical forms of self-reference alluded to above (Tarski 1956; Barwise & Etchemendy 1987). By defining satisfaction directly, and deriving truth conditions from it, a proper recursive definition could be formulated for the semantics of any complex expression of the language. For instance, in FOL an assignment satisfies the complex sentence S *and* S' if and only if it satisfies S and it also satisfies S'. For universal quantification it required an assignment f

to satisfy the sentence '*Every x sings*' if and only if for every individual that some other assignment f' assigns to the variable x, while assigning the same things as f to the other variables, f' satisfies *sings(x)*, i.e. the value of every such $f'(x)$ is an element in the set of singers. Tarski's definition of satisfaction is compositional, since for an assignment to satisfy a complex expression depends only on the syntactic composition of its constituents and their semantics, as Gottlob Frege had originally required (Frege 1892). Truth conditions can subsequently be stated relative to a model and an arbitrary given assignment, assigning all free variables their reference. Truth cannot be compositionally defined directly for '*Every x sings*' in terms of the truth of *sings(x)*, because *sings(x)* has a free variable x, so its truth depends on which assignment happens to be the given one. The Tarskian truth conditional semantics of FOL also provided the foundation for natural language semantics, limited to fragments that do not contain any truth or falsity predicate, nor verbs like *to lie*, nor other expressions directly concerned with veridicality. The developments of File Change Semantics (Heim 1982), Discourse Representation Theory (Kamp 1981; Kamp & Reyle 1993), Situation Theory (Barwise & Perry 1983; Seligman & Moss 1997) and dynamic Montague Grammar (Chierchia 1995; Groenendijk & Stokhof 1991), that all allowed free variables or reference markers representing certain use of pronouns to be interpreted as if bound by a widest scope existential quantifier, even if they occurred in different sentences, fully exploit this fundamental Tarskian approach to compositional semantics by satisfaction.

Other formal semantics methods for FOL were subsequently developed in the second half of the 20th century as alternatives to Tarskian truth-conditional semantics. Beth (1970) designed a tableaux method in which a systematic search for counterexamples to the assumed validity of a reasoning pattern seeking to verify the premises, but falsify its conclusion leads in a finite number of decompositional steps either to such a counterexample, if one exists, or to closure, tantamount to the proof that no such counterexample exists (Beth 1970; Partee, ter Meulen & Wall 1990). This semantic tableaux method provided a procedure to enumerate the valid theorems of FOL, because it only required a finite number of substitutions in deriving a theorem: (i) the expression itself, (ii) all of its constituent expressions, and (iii) certain simple combinations of the constituents depending on the premises. Hence any tableau for a valid theorem eventually closes, and the method produces a positive answer. It does not however constitute a decision procedure for testing the validity of any derivation, since it does not enumerate the set of expressions that are not theorems of FOL.

Game-theoretic semantics characterizes the semantics of FOL and richer, intensional logics in terms of rules for playing a verification game between a truth-seeking player and falsification seeking, omniscient Nature (Hintikka & Kulas 1985; Hintikka & Sandu 1997; Hodges 1985). Its interactive and epistemic flavor made it especially suitable for the semantics of interrogatives in which requests for information are acts of inquiry resolved by the answerer, providing the solicited information (Hintikka 1976). Such information-theoretic methods are currently further explored in the generalized context of dynamic epistemic logic, where communicating agents each have access to partial, private and publicly shared information and seek to share or hide information they may have depending on their communicative needs and intentions (van Ditmarsch, van der Hoek & Kooi 2007). Linguistic applications to the semantics of dialogue or multi-agent conversations in natural language already seem promising (Ginzburg & Sag 2000).

It was first shown in Skolem (1920) how second order methods could provide novel tools for logical analysis by rewriting any linear FOL formula with an existential quantifier in the scope of a universal quantifier into a formula with a quantification prefix consisting of existential quantifiers ranging over assignment functions, followed by only monadic (one place) universal quantifiers binding individual variables. The dependent first order existential quantifier is eliminated by allowing such quantification over second-order choice functions that assign the value of the existentially quantified dependent variable as a function of the referent assigned to the monadic, universally quantified individual variable preceding it. Linguistic applications using such Skolem functions have been given in the semantics of questions (Engdahl 1986) and the resolution of functional pronouns (Winter 1997). The general strategy to liberate FOL from the linear dependencies of quantifiers by allowing higher order quantification or partially ordered, i.e. branching quantifier prefixes, was linguistically exploited in the semantic research on branching quantifiers (Hintikka & Sandu 1997; Barwise 1979). From a linguistic point of view the identification of linear quantifier scope with bound occurrences of variables in their bracketed ranges never really seemed justified, since informational dependencies such as coreference of pronouns bound by an indefinite noun phrase readily cross sentential boundaries, as we saw in (2c). Furthermore, retaining perfect information on the referents already assigned to all preceding pronouns smells of unrealistic logical omniscience, where human memory limitations and contextual constraints are disregarded. It is obviously much too strong as epistemic requirement on ordinary people sharing their necessarily always limited, partial information (Seligman & Moss 1997). Game-theoretic semantics rightly insisted that a proper understanding of the logic of information *in*dependence and hence of the *lack* of information was just as much needed for natural language applications, as the logic of binding and other informational dependencies. Such strategic reconsiderations of the limitations of foundational assumptions of logical systems have prompted innovative research in logical research programs, considerably expanding the formal methods available in natural language semantics (Muskens, van Benthem & Visser 1997).

By exploiting the full scale higher order quantification of the type-theoretic categorial grammars Montague Grammar first provided a fully compositional account of the translation of syntactically disambiguated natural language expressions to logical expressions by treating referential noun phrases semantically on a par with quantificational ones as generalized quantifiers denoting properties of sets of individuals. This was accomplished obviously at the cost of generating spurious ambiguities *ad libitum*, giving up on the program of modeling linguistic competence realistically (van Benthem & ter Meulen 1985; Keenan & Westerståhl 1997; Link 1991; Montague 1974; Partee 1979). Its type theory, based only on two primitive types, *e* for individual denoting expressions and *t* for truth-value denoting expressions, forged a perfect fit between the syntactic categories and the function-argument structure of their semantics. For instance, all nouns are considered syntactic objects that require a determiner on their left side to produce a noun phrase and semantically denote a set of entities, of type <*e, t*>, which is an element in the generalized quantifier of type <<*e, t*>, *t* > denoted by the entire noun phrase. Proper names, freely referring pronouns, universal and existential NPs are hence treated semantically on a par as denoting a set of sets of individuals. This fruitful strategy led to a significant expansion of the fragments of natural languages that were provided with a compositional model-theoretic semantics, including many kinds of adverbial phrases, degree and measurement expressions, unusual and complex quantifier phrases, presuppositions, questions, imperatives, causal and temporal expressions, but also lexical relations that affected reasoning patterns (Chierchia 1995; Krifka 1989). Logical properties of generalized quantifiers prove to be very useful in explaining, for instance, not only which noun phrases are acceptable in pleonastic or existential contexts, but also why the processing time of noun phrases may vary in a given experimental situation and how their semantic complexity may also constrain their learnability. In pressing on for a proper, linguistically adequate account of pronouns in discourse, and for a cognitively realistic logic of information sharing in changing contexts, new tools that allowed for non-linear structures to represent information content play an important conceptually clarifying role in separating quantifier scope from the occurrence of variables in the linear or partial order of formulas of a logical language, while retaining the core model-theoretic insights in modeling inference as concept based on Tarskian satisfaction conditions.

8 Conclusions

The development of formal methods in logic has contributed essentially to the emancipation of linguistic research into an academic community where formal methods were given their proper place as explanatory tool in scientific theories of meaning and interpretation. Although logical languages are often designed with a particular purpose in mind, they reflect certain interesting computational or semantic properties also exhibited, though sometimes implicitly, in natural languages. The properties of natural languages that lend themselves for analysis and explanation by formal methods have increased steadily over the past century, as the formal tools of logical systems were more finely chiseled to fit the purpose of linguistic explanation better. Even more properties will most likely become accessible for linguistic explanation by formal methods over the next century. The issues of cognitive complexity, characterized at many different levels from the neurobiological, molecular structure detected in neuro-imaging to interactive behavioral studies, and experimental investigations of processing time provide a new set of empirical considerations in the application of formal methods to natural language. They drive experimental innovations and require an interdisciplinary research agenda to integrate the various modes of explanation into a coherent model of human language use and communication of information.

The current developments in dynamic natural language semantics constitute major improvements in expanding linguistic application to a wider range of discourse phenomena. The forms of reasoning in which context dependent expressions may change their reference during the processing of the premises are now considered to be interesting aspects of natural languages, that logical systems are challenged to simulate, rather than avoid, as our great-grandfathers' advice originally directed us to do. There is renewed attention to limit in a principled and empirically justified way the search space complexity to decidable fragments of FOL and to restrict the higher order methods in order to reduce the complexity to model cognitively realistic human processing power. Such developments in natural language will converge eventually with the syntactic research programs focusing on universals of language as constants of human linguistic competence.

9 References

Ades, Anthony E. & Mark J. Steedman 1982. On the order of words. *Linguistics & Philosophy* 4, 517–558.
Ajdukiewicz, Kazimierz 1935. Die syntaktische Konnexität. *Studia Philosophica* 1, 1–27. English translation in: S. McCall (ed.). *Polish Logic*. Oxford: Clarendon Press, 1967.
Arbib, Michael A. 1969. *Theories of Abstract Automata*. Englewood Cliffs, NJ: Prentice Hall.
Asher, Nicholas 1993. *Reference to Abstract Objects in Discourse*. Dordrecht: Kluwer.
Bar-Hillel, Yehoshua 1964. *Language and Information: Selected Essays on their Theory and Application*. Reading, MA: Addison-Wesley.

Barendregt, Hendrik P. 1984. *The Lambda Calculus*. Amsterdam: North-Holland.
Barwise, Jon 1979. On branching quantifiers in English. *Journal of Philosophical Logic* 8, 47–80.
Barwise, Jon 1989. *The Situation in Logic*. Stanford, CA: CSLI Publications.
Barwise, Jon & Robin Cooper 1981. Generalized quantifiers and natural language. *Linguistics & Philosophy* 4, 159–219.
Barwise, Jon & John Etchemendy 1987. *The Liar. An Essay on Truth and Circularity*. Oxford: Oxford University Press.
Barwise, Jon & John Perry 1983. *Situations and Attitudes*. Cambridge, MA: The MIT Press.
van Benthem, Johan 1983. *The Logic of Time: A Model-Theoretic Investigation into the Varieties of Temporal Ontology and Temporal Discourse*. Dordrecht: Reidel.
van Benthem, Johan 1986. *Essays in Logical Semantics*. Dordrecht: Reidel.
van Benthem, Johan 1987. Categorial grammar and lambda calculus. In: D. Skordev (ed.). *Mathematical Logic and its Applications*. New York: Plenum, 39–60.
van Benthem, Johan 1988. The Lambek calculus. In: R.T. Oehrle, E. Bach & D. Wheeler (eds.). *Categorial Grammars and Natural Language Structures*. Dordrecht: Reidel, 35–68.
van Benthem, Johan 1991. *Language in Action: Categories, Lambdas and Dynamic Logic*. Amsterdam: North-Holland.
van Benthem, Johan & Alice ter Meulen 1985. *Generalized Quantifiers in Natural Language*. Dordrecht: Foris.
van Benthem, Johan & Alice ter Meulen 1997. *Handbook of Logic and Language*. Amsterdam: Elsevier.
Beth, Evert 1970. *Aspects of Modern Logic*. Dordrecht: Reidel.
Boolos, George & Richard Jeffrey 1980. *Computability and Logic*. Cambridge: Cambridge University Press.
Buszkowski, Wojciech 1988. Generative power of categorial grammars. In: R.T. Oehrle, E. Bach & D. Wheeler (eds.). *Categorial Grammars and Natural Language Structures*. Dordrecht: Reidel, 69–94.
Buszkowski, Wojciech & Witold Marciszewski 1988. *Categorial Grammar*. Amsterdam: Benjamins.
Carnap, Rudolf 1947. *Meaning and Necessity*. Chicago, IL: The University of Chicago Press.
Carpenter, Bob 1997. *Type-Logical Semantics*. Cambridge, MA: The MIT Press.
Chierchia, Gennaro 1995. *Dynamics of Meaning: Anaphora, Presupposition, and the Theory of Grammar*. Chicago, IL: The University of Chicago Press.
Chomsky, Noam 1957. *Syntactic Structures*. The Hague: Mouton.
Chomsky, Noam 1959. On certain formal properties of grammars. *Information and Control* 2, 137–167.
Chomsky, Noam 1981. *Lectures on Government and Binding*. Dordrecht: Foris.
Chomsky, Noam 1995. *The Minimalist Program*. Cambridge, MA: The MIT Press.
Chomsky, Noam & George A. Miller 1958. Finite-state languages. *Information and Control* 1, 91–112.
Chomsky, Noam & George A. Miller 1963. Introduction to the formal analysis of natural languages. In: R.D. Luce, R. Bush & E. Galanter (eds.). *Handbook of Mathematical Psychology*, vol. 2. New York: Wiley, 269–321.
Cresswell, Max J. 1985. *Structured Meanings: The Semantics of Propostitional Attitudes*. Cambridge, MA: The MIT Press.
Curry, Haskell B. 1961. Some logical aspects of grammatical structure. In: R. Jakobson (ed.). *Structure of Language and its Mathematical Aspects*. Providence, RI: American Mathematical Society, 56–68.

Davidson, Donald & Gilbert Harman 1972. *Semantics of Natural Language*. Dordrecht: Reidel.
Davis, Martin 1965. *The Undecidable: Basic Papers on Undecidable Propositions, Unsolvable Problems and Computable Functions*. Hewlett, NY: Raven Press.
van Ditmarsch, Hans, Wiebe van der Hoek & Barteld Kooi 2007. *Dynamic Epistemic Logic*. Dordrecht: Springer.
Dowty, David, Robert Wall & Stanley Peters 1981. *Introduction to Montague Semantics*. Dordrecht: Reidel.
Engdahl, Elisabeth 1986. *Constituent Questions*. Dordrecht: Reidel.
Frege, Gottlob 1892. Über Sinn und Bedeutung. *Zeitschrift für Philosophie und philosophische Kritik* 100, 25–50. Reprinted in: G. Patzig (ed.). *Funktion, Begriff, Bedeutung. Fünf logische Studien*, 3rd edn. Vandenhoeck Hoeck & Ruprecht: Göttingen, 1969, 40–65. English translation in: P. Geach & M. Black (eds.). *Translations from the Philosophical Writings of Gottlob Frege*. Oxford: Blackwell, 1980, 56–78.
Gabbay, Dov & Franz Guenthner 1983. *Handbook of Philosophical Logic*, vol. 1–4. Dordrecht: Reidel.
Gallin, Daniel 1975. *Intensional and Higher-Order Modal Logic. With Applications to Montague Semantics*. Amsterdam: North-Holland.
Gentzen, Gerhard 1934. Untersuchungen über das logische Schließen I & II. *Mathematische Zeitschrift* 39, 176–210, 405–431.
Ginzburg, Johnathan & Ivan Sag 2000. *Interrogative Investigations: The Form, Meaning and Use of English Interrogatives*. Stanford, CA: CSLI Publications.
Groenendijk, Jeroen & Martin Stokhof 1991. Dynamic Predicate Logic. *Linguistics & Philosophy* 14, 39–100.
Gross, Maurice & Andre Lentin 1970. *Introduction to Formal Grammars*. Berlin: Springer.
Haegeman, Liliane 1991. *Introduction to Government and Binding Theory*. Oxford: Blackwell.
Heim, Irene R. 1982. *The Semantics of Definite and Indefinite Noun Phrases*. Ph.D. dissertation. University of Massachusetts, Amherst, MA. Reprinted: Ann Arbor, MI: University Microfilms.
Hintikka, Jaakko 1976. *The Semantics of Questions and the Questions of Semantics: Case Studies in the Interrelations of Logic, Semantics, and Syntax*. Amsterdam: North-Holland.
Hintikka, Jaakko & Jack Kulas 1985. *Anaphora and Definite Descriptions: Two Applications of Game-Theoretical Semantics*. Dordrecht: Reidel.
Hintikka, Jaakko & Gabriel Sandu 1997. Game-theoretical semantics. In: J. van Benthem & A. ter Meulen (eds.). *Handbook of Logic and Language*. Amsterdam: Elsevier, 361–410.
Hodges, Wilfrid 1985. *Building Models by Games*. Cambridge: Cambridge University Press.
Hopcroft, John E. & Jeffrey D. Ullman 1979. *Introduction to Automata Theory, Languages and Computation*. Reading, MA: Addison-Wesley.
Jeffrey, Richard 1967. *Formal Logic: Its Scope and Limits*. New York: McGraw-Hill.
Kamp, Hans 1981. A theory of truth and semantic representation. In: J. Groenendijk (ed.). *Formal Methods in the Study of Language*. Amsterdam: Mathematical Centre, 277–322.
Kamp, Hans & Uwe Reyle 1993. *From Discourse to Logic*. Dordrecht: Kluwer.
Keenan, Edward L. & Leonard M. Faltz 1985. *Boolean Semantics for Natural Language*. Dordrecht: Reidel.
Keenan, Edward & Dag Westerståhl 1997. Generalized quantifiers in linguistics and logic. In: J. van Benthem & A. ter Meulen (eds.). *Handbook of Logic and Language*. Amsterdam: Elsevier, 837–893.

Krifka, Manfred 1989. Nominal reference, temporal constitution and quantification in event semantics. In: R. Bartsch, J. van Benthem & P. van Emde Boas (eds.). *Semantics and Contextual Expressions*. Dordrecht: Foris, 75–115.

Kripke, Saul A. 1972. Naming and necessity. In: D. Davidson & G. Harman (eds.). *Semantics of Natural Language*. Dordrecht: Reidel, 253–355 and 763–769.

Lambek, Joachim 1958. The mathematics of sentence structure. *American Mathematical Monthly* 65, 154–170.

Lewis, David 1972. General semantics. In: D. Davidson & G. Harman (eds.). *Semantics of Natural Language*. Dordrecht: Reidel, 169–218.

Lewis, David 1983, *Philosophical Papers, vol. 1*. Oxford: Oxford University Press.

Link, Godehard 1991. Formale Methoden in der Semantik. In: A. von Stechow & D. Wunderlich (eds.). *Semantik. Ein internationales Handbuch der zeitgenössischen Forschung* (HSK 6). Berlin: de Gruyter, 835–860.

May, Robert 1985. *Logical Form: Its Structure and Derivation*. Cambridge, MA: The MIT Press.

McCawley, James D. 1981. *Everything that Linguists Have Always Wanted to Know About Logic But Were Ashamed to Ask*. Chicago, IL: The University of Chicago Press.

Montague, Richard 1974. *Formal Philosophy. Selected Papers of Richard Montague*. Edited and with an introduction by Richard H. Thomason. New Haven, CT: Yale University Press.

Moortgat, Michael 1996. Multimodal linguistic inference. *Journal of Logic, Language and Information* 5, 349–385.

Moortgat, Michael 1997. Categorial type logics. In: J. van Benthem & A. ter Meulen (eds.). *Handbook of Logic and Language*. Amsterdam: Elsevier, 93–179.

Morrill, Glyn 1994. *Type Logical Grammar. Categorial Logic of Signs*. Dordrecht: Kluwer.

Morrill, Glyn 1995. Discontinuity in categorial grammar. *Linguistics & Philosophy* 18, 175–219.

Muskens, Reinhard, Johan van Benthem & Albert Visser 1997. Dynamics. In: J. van Benthem & A. ter Meulen (eds.). *Handbook of Logic and Language*. Amsterdam: Elsevier, 587–648.

Nishihara, Noritaka, Kenichi Morita & Shigenori Iwata 1990. An extended syllogistic system with verbs and proper nouns, and its completeness proof. *Systems and Computers in Japan* 21, 96–111.

Oehrle, Richard T., Emmon Bach & Deirdre Wheeler 1988. *Categorial Grammars and Natural Language Structures*. Dordrecht: Reidel.

Partee, Barbara 1979. Semantics – mathematics or psychology? In: R. Bäuerle, U. Egli & A. von Stechow (eds.). *Semantics from Different Points of View*. Berlin: Springer.

Partee, Barbara, Alice ter Meulen & Robert Wall 1990. *Mathematical Methods in Linguistics*. Dordrecht: Kluwer.

Pentus, Mati 2006. Lambek calculus is NP-complete. *Theoretical Computer Science* 357, 186–201.

Peters, Stanley & Richard Ritchie 1973. On the generative power of transformational grammars. *Information Sciences* 6, 49–83.

Pratt-Hartmann, Ian 2003. A two-variable fragment of English. *Journal of Logic, Language & Information* 12, 13–45.

Pratt-Hartmann, Ian & Allan Third 2006. More fragments of language. *Notre Dame Journal of Formal Logic* 47, 151–177.

Reinhart, Tanya 1983a. *Anaphora and Semantic Interpretation*. London: Croom Helm.

Reinhart, Tanya 1983b. Coreference and bound anaphora: A restatement of the anaphora question. *Linguistics & Philosophy* 6, 47–88.

van Riemsdijk, Henk & Edwin Williams 1986. *Introduction to the Theory of Grammar*. Cambridge, MA: The MIT Press.

Savitch, Walter J., Emmon Bach & Wiliam Marsh 1987. *The Formal Complexity of Natural Language*. Dordrecht: Reidel.
Seligman, Jerry & Lawrence S. Moss 1997. Situation theory. In: J. van Benthem & A. ter Meulen (eds.). *Handbook of Logic and Language*. Amsterdam: Elsevier, 239–280.
Skolem, Thoralf 1920. Logisch-kombinatorische Untersuchungen über die Erfüllbarkeit oder Beweisbarkeit mathematischer Sätze nebst einem Theorem über dichte Mengen. *Videnskapsselskapets Skrifter 1, Matem-naturv. Kl.I* 4, 1–36.
Stabler, Edward 1997. Derivational minimalism. In: C. Retoré (ed.). *Logical Aspects of Computational Linguistics*. Berlin: Springer, 68–95.
Stalnaker, Robert 1999. *Context and Content Essays on Intentionality in Speech and Thought*. Oxford: Oxford University Press.
Tarski, Alfred 1956. *Logic, Semantics, Metamathematics: Papers from 1923 to 1938*. Oxford: Clarendon Press.
Winter, Yoad 1997. Choice functions and the scopal semantics of indefinites. *Linguistics & Philosophy* 20, 399–467.

Oliver Bott, Sam Featherston, Janina Radó and Britta Stolterfoht
15 The application of experimental methods in semantics

1 Introduction —— 387
2 The stumbling blocks —— 389
3 Off-line evidence for scope interpretation —— 394
4 Underspecification vs. full interpretation —— 398
5 On-line evidence for representation of scope —— 399
6 Conclusions —— 404
7 References —— 406

Abstract: The purpose of this paper is twofold. On the methodological side, we shall attempt to show that even relatively simple and accessible experimental methods can yield significant insights into semantic issues. At the same time, we argue that experimental evidence, both the type collected in simple questionnaires and measures of on-line processing, can inform semantic theories. The specific case that we address here concerns the investigation of quantifier scope. In this area, where judgements are often subtle and controversial, the gradient data that psycholinguistic experiments provide can be a useful tool to distinguish between competing approaches, as we demonstrate with a case study. Furthermore, we describe how a modification of existing experimental methods can be used to test predictions of underspecification theories. The program of research we outline here is not intended to be a prescriptive set of instructions for researchers, telling them what they should do; rather it is intended to illustrate some problems an experimental semanticist may encounter but also the profit of this enterprise.

1 Introduction

A wide range of data types and sources are used in the field of semantics, as is demonstrated by the related article 12 [this volume] (Krifka) *Varieties of semantic evidence* in this volume. The aim of this article is to show with an example

---

Oliver Bott, Sam Featherston, and Britta Stolterfoht, Tübingen, Germany
Janina Radó, Frankfurt a. M., Germany

https://doi.org/10.1515/9783110368505-015

research study series what sort of questions can be addressed with experimental tools and suggest that these methods can deliver valuable data which is relevant to basic assumptions in semantics. This text also attempts to address the constraints on and limits to such an approach. These are both methodological and theoretical: it has long been recognized that links between empirical measures and theoretical constructs require careful argumentation to establish.

The authors therefore have two aims: one related to experimental methodologies and the other to do with the value of processing data. They first seek to show that even relatively simple and accessible experimental methods can yield significant insights into semantic issues. They second wish to illustrate that experimental evidence such as that gathered in their eye-tracking study has the potential to inform semantic theory.

Semanticists have of course always sought confirmatory evidence to support their analyses. There is, on the one hand, fairly extensive use of computational techniques and corpus data in the field, and a growing body of experimental work on semantic processing, language acquisition, and pragmatics, but in the area of theoretical and formal semantics the experimental methods are less frequently employed.

Now there are good reasons for this. There are inherent factors related to the accessibility of the relevant measures why controlled data gathering techniques are still somewhat less frequent in this field than in some others. We shall discuss what these reasons are and demonstrate with a case study what constraints they place on empirical studies, particularly experimental studies. The example research program that we shall report is thus not simply a recipe for others for what should be done, rather it is an illustration of the difficulties involved, which aims to explore some of the boundaries of what is accessible to experimental studies.

The specific case that we address here concerns the investigation of quantifier scope, a perennial issue in semantics. Previous attempts to account for the complex data patterns to be found in natural languages have met with the difficulty that the causal factors and preferences need first to be identified before a realistic model can be developed. This requires as an initial step the capture and measurement of the relevant effects and their interactions, which is no trivial task.

The next section lays out a range of reasons why semanticists do not routinely seek to test the empirical bases of their theories with simple experiments. Section 3 reports the series of empirical investigations on quantifier scope carried out by Bott and Radó in on-going research. Section 4 lays out some of the theoretical background and importance of these studies for current theory (the underspecification debate). The final section takes as a starting point Bott and Radó (2009) to suggest how some of the problems noted in section 3 may be overcome with a more sophisticated experimental procedure.

2 The stumbling blocks

As Manfred Krifka notes in his neighbouring article 12 [this volume] (Krifka) *Varieties of semantic evidence*, a major problem with investigating meaning is that we cannot yet fully define what it is. This is indeed a root cause of difficulty, but here we shall attempt to illustrate in more practical detail what effects this has on attempts to conduct experiments in this field.

2.1 Specifying meaning without using language

The essential feature distinguishing experiment procedure is control. In language experiments we may distinguish three (sets of) variables: linguistic form, context, and meaning. In the typical experiment we will keep two of them constant and systematically vary the other. Much semantic research concerns the systematic interdependence of form, context, and meaning. These issues can be investigated for example by:
a) keeping form and context constant, manipulating meaning systematically, and measuring the *felicity* of the outcome (in judgements, or reaction times, or processing effort), or
b) manipulating (at least one of) form and context, and measuring perceived meaning.

The first requires the experimenter to *manipulate* meaning as a variable, which entails expressing meaning in a form other than language, (pictures, situation descriptions, etc); the second requires the experimenter to *measure* perceived meaning, which again normally demands reference to meanings captured in non-linguistic form. But precisely this expression of tightly constrained meaning in non-linguistic form is very difficult.

To show how this factor affects studies in semantics disproportionately, it is worth noting how this makes controlled studies in semantics more challenging than in syntax. Work in experimental syntax is often interested in addressing precisely those effects of form change which are *independent* of meaning. The variable meaning can thus be held constant, but this does not require it to be exactly specified. Thus only the syntactic analysis need be controlled, which makes empirical studies in syntax a whole parameter less difficult than those in semantics.

2.2 The boundaries of form, context, and meaning

A further problem of exact studies concerning meaning is that the three variables are not always clearly distinguished, in part because they systematically covary, but also in part because linguists do not always agree about the boundaries. This is particularly visible when we seek to identify where an anomaly lies. Views have changed over time in linguistics about the nature and location of ill-formedness (e.g. the discussion of the status of *I am lurking in a culvert* in Ross 1970) but the fundamental ambiguity is still with us. For example, Weskott & Fanselow (2009) give the following examples and judgements of syntactic and semantic well-formedness: (1a) is syntactically ill-formed (*), (1b) is semantically ill-formed (#), and (1c) is ill-formed on both accounts (*#).

(1) a. *Die   Suppe wurde gegen   versalzen.
       the   soup   was   against oversalted

    b. #Der   Zug   wurde gekaut.
       the   train   was   chewed

    c. *#Das Eis   wurde seit   entzündet.
       the   ice   was   since   inflamed

Our own judgements suggest that the structures in (1-a) and (1-c) have no acceptable syntactic analysis, and therefore no semantic analysis can be constructed – they are thus both syntactically and semantically ill-formed. Crucially, the semantic anomaly is dependent upon the syntactic problem; the lack of a recognizable compositional interpretation is a result of the lack of a possible structural analysis. We would therefore regard these examples as primarily syntactically unacceptable. This contrasts with (1-b), which we regard as well-formed on both parameters, being merely implausible, except in a small child's playroom, where a train being chewed is an entirely normal situation (cf. Hahne & Friederici 2002).

2.3 Plausibility

Such examples highlight another problem in manipulating meaning as an experimental variable: the human demand to make sense of linguistic forms. We associate possible meanings with things that we can accept as being true or plausible. So 'the third-floor appartment reappeared today', which is both syntactically and semantically flawless, will cause irrelevant experimental effects since subjects will find it difficult to fit the meaning into their mental model of the world. Zhou & Gao (2009) for example argue that participants interpret *Every robber robbed a bank* in the surface scope reading because it is more *plausible* that each robber robbed a different bank.

This links in to a wider discussion of the role of plausibility as a factor in semantic processing and as a filter on possible readings. Zhou & Gao (2009) claim that such doubly quantified sentences are ambiguous in Mandarin, since their experimental evidence suggests that both interpretations are built up in parallel, but one reading is subsequently filtered out by plausibility, which accounts for the contrary judgements in work on semantic theory (e.g. Huang 1982, Aoun & Li 1989).

2.4 Meaning as a complex measure

The meaning of a structure is not fixed or unique, even when linguistic, social, and discourse context are fixed. First, a single expression may have multiple readings, which compete for dominance. Often a specific relevant reading of a structure needs to be forced in an experiment. Some readings of theoretical interest may be quite inaccessible, though nevertheless real. This raises the issue of expert knowledge, which again contrasts with the situation in syntax. Syntactic well-formedness judgements are generally available and accessible to any native speaker and require no expertise. On the other hand, it can require specialist knowledge to 'get' some readings since the access to variant readings is usually via different analyses. This is a crucial point in semantics, since it reduces the likelihood that the intuitions of the naïve native speaker can be the final arbiter in this field, as they can reasonably be argued to be in syntax (Chomsky 1965). A fine example of this is from Hobbs & Schieber (1987):

(2) Two representatives of three companies saw most samples.

They claim that this sentence is five-ways ambiguous. Park (1995) however denies the existence of one of these readings (*three > most > two*). It is doubtful whether this question is solvable by asking naïve informants.

Even within a given analysis of a construction, the meaning may not be fully determined. Aspects of meaning are left unspecified, which means that two different perceivers can interpret a single structure in different ways. This too requires great care and attention to detail when designing experiments which aim to be exact.

2.5 The observer's paradox

A frequent aim in semantic experiments is to discover how subjects interpret linguistic input under normal conditions. A constant problem is how experimenters can access this information, because whatever additional task we instruct the subjects to carry out renders the conditions abnormal. For example, if we ask them to choose which one of a pair of pictures illustrates the interpretation that they have gathered, or even if we just observe their eye movements, the very presence of two pictures is likely to make them more aware that more than one interpretation is possible, thus biasing the results. Even a single picture can alter or trigger the accessibility of a reading.

2.6 Inherent meaning and inferred meaning

One last linguistic distinction which we should note here is that between the inherent meaning of an expression ("what is said") and the inferred meaning of a given utterance of an expression. This distinction is fundamental in the division of research into meaning into separate fields, but it is in practice very difficult to apply in experimental work, since naïve informants do not naturally differentiate the two. The recent 'literal Lucy' approach of Larson et al. (2010) is a promising solution to this problem; in this paradigm participants must report how 'literal Lucy', who only ever perceives the narrowly inherent meaning of utterances and makes no inferences, would understand example sentences. This distinction is particularly important when an experimental design requires a disambiguation, and extreme care must be taken that its content is not only inferred. For example, in (3), it is implicated that every rugby player broke one of their own fingers, but this is not necessarily the case. This example cannot thus offer watertight disambiguation.

(3) Every rugby player broke a finger.
    Implication: Every rugby player broke one of their own fingers.

2.7 Experimental measures and the object of theory

As a rule, semantic theory makes no predictions about semantic processing. Instead it concerns itself with the final stable interpretation which is achieved after a whole linguistic expression, usually at the sentence level, has been processed and all reanalyses, for example as a result of garden paths, have been resolved. It fundamentally concerns the stative, holistic result of the processing of an expression, indeed many theoretical approaches regard meaning as only coming about in a full sentence (cf. article 8 [this volume] (Meier-Oeser) *Meaning in pre-19th century thought*). But the processing of a sentence is made up of many steps which are incremental and which interact strongly with each other, partly predicting, partly parsing input as it arrives, partly confirming or revising previous analyses. Much of the experimental evidence available to us provides direct evidence only of these processing steps.

It thus follows that for many semantics practitioners much of the empirical evidence which we can gather concerns at best our *predictions* about what the sentence is going to mean, not really aspects of its actual meaning. The time course of our arriving at a particular reading, whether it be remote or readily accessible, has no direct implications for the theory, since this makes no predictions about processing speed (cf. Phillips & Wagers 2007). One aim of this article is to show that experimental techniques can deliver data which can contribute to theory building.

2.8 Categorical predictions and gradient data

Predictions of semantic theories typically concern the *availability* of particular interpretations. Experiments deliver more fine-grained data that reflect the relative preferences among the interpretations. Mapping these gradient data onto the categorical predictions, that is, drawing the line between still available and impossible readings is a non-trivial task. At the same time, the ability to distinguish preferences among the "intermediate" interpretations may be highly relevant for testing predictions concerning readings that fall between the clearly available and the clearly impossible.

2.9 Outlook

In the remainder of this paper we will discuss two ways in which systematically collected experimental data can contribute to semantic theorizing. We will use quantifier scope as an example of a phenomenon where results of psycholinguistic experiments can make significant contributions to the theoretical discussions. We will not attempt to review here the considerable psycholinguistic literature on the processing of quantifiers (for a comprehensive survey cf. article 9 [Semantics: Typology, Diachrony and Processing] (Frazier) *Meaning in psycholinguistics*). Instead we will concentrate on a small set of studies that show the usefulness of end-of-sentence judgements in establishing the available interpretations of quantified sentences. Then we will sketch an experiment to address aspects of the unfolding interpretation of quantifier scope which are of interest to theoretical semanticists as well.

3 Off-line evidence for scope interpretation

Semantic theories are typically based on introspective judgements of a handful of theoreticians. The judgements concern available readings of a sentence, possibly ranked as to how easily available these readings are. Not surprisingly, judgements of this sort are subtle and often controversial. For instance, the sentence *Everyone loves someone* has been alternately considered to only allow the wide-scope universal reading (e.g. Hornstein 1995; Beghelli & Stowell 1997) or to be fully ambiguous (May 1977, 1985; Hornstein 1984; Higginbotham 1985). Example (2) above illustrates the same point. Park (1995) and Hobbs & Shieber (1987) disagree about the number of available readings.

The data problem has been known for a long time. Studies as early as Ioup (1975) and VanLehn (1978) have used the intuitions of naïve speakers in developing an empirically motivated theory. However, it has been clear from the beginning that "obvious" tasks such as paraphrasing a presumably ambiguous doubly-quantified sentence or asking informants to choose a (preferred) paraphrase are rather complex and that linguistically untrained participants may not be able to carry them out reliably.

Another purely linguistic task has been problematic for a different reason. Researchers have tried to combine the quantified sentence with a disambiguating continuation, as in (4).

(4) Every kid climbed a tree.
    (a) The tree was full of apples.
    (b) The trees were full of apples.

Disambiguation of this type was used by Gillen (1991), Kurtzman & MacDonald (1993), Tunstall (1998) and Filik, Paterson & Liversedge (2004), for instance. Here the plural continuation is only acceptable if multiple trees are instantiated, that is, the wide-scope universal interpretation (every kid > a tree) is chosen, whereas the singular continuation is intended to only fit the wide-scope existential interpretation (a tree > every kid). Unfortunately the singular continuation fails to disambiguate the sentence, as Tunstall (1998) points out: *the tree* (4a) can easily be taken to mean *the tree the kid climbed*, thus making it compatible with the wide-scope universal interpretation as well (see also Bott & Radó 2007 and article 9 [Semantics: Typology, Diachrony and Processing] (Frazier) *Meaning in psycholinguistics*).

Problems of these kinds have prompted researchers to look for non-linguistic methods of disambiguation. Gillen (1991) used, among other methods, simple pictures resembling set diagrams. In her experiments subjects either drew diagrams to represent the meaning of quantified sentences, chose the diagram that corresponded to the (preferred) reading or judged how well the situation depicted in the diagram fitted the sentence. Bott & Radó (2007) tested a somewhat modified form of the last of these methods using diagrams like those in Fig. 15.1, to see whether they constitute a reliable mode of disambiguation that naïve informants can use easily. They found that participants consistently delivered the expected judgements both for scopally unambiguous quantified sentences (i.e. sentences where one scope reading was excluded due to an intervening clause boundary) and for ambiguous quantified sentences where expected preferences could be determined based on theoretical considerations and corpus studies. These results show that there is no a priori reason to exclude the judgements of non-linguist informants from consideration.

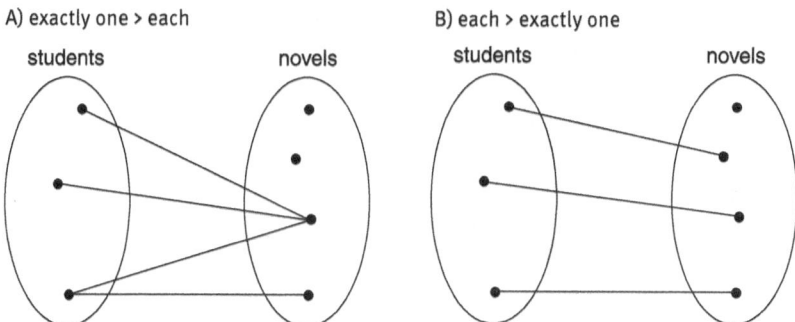

Fig. 15.1: Disambiguating diagrams for the sentence: "Exactly one novel was read by each student"

For informative experiments, however, we need to be able to derive testable hypotheses based on existing semantic proposals. Although semantic theories are not formulated to make predictions about processing, it is still possible to identify areas where different approaches lead to different predictions concerning the judgement of particular constructions. The interpretation of quantifiers provides an example here as well.

One possible way of classifying theories of quantifier scope has to do with the way different factors are supposed to affect the scope properties of quantifiers. In configurational models such as Reinhart (1976, 1978, 1983, 1995) and Beghelli & Stowell (1997), quantifiers move to/are interpreted in different structural positions.

A quantifier higher in the (syntactic) tree will always outscope lower ones. The absolute position in the tree is irrelevant; what matters is the position relative to the other quantifier(s). While earlier proposals only considered syntactic properties of quantifiers, Beghelli and Stowell also include semantic factors in the hierarchy of quantifier positions. Taking *distributivity* as an example, assuming that a +dist quantifier is interpreted in Spec,QP which is the highest position available for quantifiers, Q1 will outscope Q2 if only Q1 is +dist, regardless of what other properties Q1 or Q2 may have. An effect of other factors will only become apparent if neither of the quantifiers is +dist.

By contrast, the basic assumption in multi-factor theories of quantifier scope is that each factor has a certain amount of influence on quantifier scope regardless of the presence or absence of other factors (cf. Ioup 1975; Kurtzman & MacDonald 1993; Kuno 1991 and Pafel 2005). The effects of different factors can be combined, resulting in greater or lesser preference for a particular interpretation. Theories differ in whether one of the readings disappears when it is below some threshold, or whether sentences with multiple quantifiers are always necessarily ambiguous.

Let us assume that the two scope-relevant factors we are interested in are distributivity and discourse-binding, the latter indicated by the partitive NP *one of these N*, see (6). Crossing these factors yields four possible combinations: +dist/+d-bound, +dist/-d-bound, -dist/+d-bound, and -dist/-d-bound. In a configurational theory presumably there will be a structural position reserved for discourse-bound phrases. Let us consider the case where this position is lower than that for +dist, but higher than the lowest scope position available for quantifiers. Thus Q1 should outscope Q2 in the first two configurations, Q2 should outscope Q1 in the third, and the last one may in fact be fully scope ambiguous unless some additional factors are at play as well. Moreover, as configurational theories of scope have no mechanism to predict relative strength of scope preference, the first two configurations should show the same size preference for a wide-scope interpretation of Q1. In statistical terms, we expect an interaction: d-binding should have an effect when Q1 is -dist, but not when it is +dist.

In multi-factor theories, on the other hand, the prediction would usually be that the effects of the different factors should add up. That is, the difference in scope bias between a d-bound and a non-d-bound +dist quantifier should be the same as between a d-bound and a non-d-bound -dist quantifier. A given factor should be able to exert its influence regardless of the other factors present.

Bott and Radó have been testing these predictions in on-going work. In two questionnaire studies subjects read doubly-quantified German sentences and used magnitude estimation to indicate how well disambiguating set diagrams fitted the interpretation of the sentence. Experiment 1 manipulated distributivity and linear order and used materials like (5). Experiment 2 tested the factors distributivity and d-binding using sentences like (6).

(5) a. Genau   einen dieser Professoren haben alle Studentinnen   verehrt.
       Exactly one   these professors   have all   female students adored.
       All female students adored exactly one of these professors.

   b. Genau   einen dieser Professoren hat jede Studentin   verehrt.
      Exactly one   these professors   has each female students adored.
      Each female student adored exactly one of these professors.

   c. Alle Studentinnen   haben genau einen dieser Professoren verehrt.
      All   female students have exactly one these professors adored.
      All female students adored exactly one of these professors.

   d. Jede Studentin   hat genau einen dieser Professoren verehrt.
      Each female student has exactly one these professors adored.
      Each female student adored exactly one of these professors.

(6) a. Genau   einen Professor haben alle diese Studentinnen   verehrt.
       Exactly one   professor have all   these female students adored.
       All of these female students adored exactly one professor.

   b. Genau   einen dieser Professoren haben alle Studentinnen   verehrt.
      Exactly one   these professors   have all   female students adored.
      All female students adored exactly one of these professors.

   c. Genau   einen Professor hat jede dieser Studentinnen   verehrt.
      Exactly one   professor has each these female students adored.
      Each of these female students adored exactly one professor.

   d. Genau   einen dieser Professoren hat jede Studentin   verehrt.
      Exactly one   these professors   has each female student adored.
      Each female student adored exactly one of these professors.

Bott and Radó found clear evidence for the influence of all three factors. The distributive quantifier *jeder* took scope more easily than *alle*, d-binding of a quantifier and linear precedence both resulted in a greater tendency to take wide scope. Crucially, the effects were additive, which is compatible with the predictions of multi-factor theories but unexpected under configurational approaches.

These results show that even simple questionnaire studies can deliver theoretically highly relevant data. This is particularly important in an area like quantifier scope, where the judgements are typically subtle and not always accessible to introspection. Of course the study reported here cannot address all possible questions concerning the interpretation of quantified sentences like those in (5)–(6). It cannot for example clarify whether the processor initially constructs a fully specified representation of quantifier scope or whether it first builds only a underspecified structure which is compatible with both possible readings, an outstanding question of much current interest in semantics. The data that we have presented so far is off-line, in that it measures preferences only at the end of the sentence, when its content has been disambiguated. In section 5 we present an experimental design which allows investigation of the on-going (on-line) processing of scope ambiguities. In the next section we relate the semantic issue of underspecification to experimental data and predictions for on-line processing.

4 Underspecification vs. full interpretation

It is generally agreed that syntactic processing is *incremental* in nature (e.g. van Gompel & Pickering 2007) i.e. a full-fledged syntactic representation is assigned to every incoming word. Whether semantic processing is incremental in the strict sense, is far from being beyond dispute and is still an empirical question. To formulate hypotheses about the time-course of semantic processing, we will now look at the on-going debate in semantic theory on underspecification in semantic representations.

Underspecified semantic representations are a tool intended to handle the problem of ambiguity. The omission of parts of the semantic information allows one single representation to be compatible with a whole set of different meanings (for an overview of underspecification approaches, see e.g. Pinkal 1999; articles 9 [Semantics: Lexical Structures and Adjectives] (Egg) *Semantic underspecification* and 14 [Semantics: Typology, Diachrony and Processing] (Pinkal & Koller) *Semantics in computational linguistics*). It is thus an economical method of dealing with ambiguity in that it avoids costly reanalysis, used above all in computational applications.

Taking the psycholinguistic perspective, one would predict that constructing underspecified representations in semantically ambiguous regions of a sentence avoids processing difficulties in ambiguous regions and at the point of disambiguation (Frazier & Rayner 1990).

Underspecification can be contrasted with an approach that assumes strict incrementality and thus immediate full interpretation even in ambiguous regions. This would predict processing difficulties in cases of disambiguations to non-preferred readings. A candidate for a semantic processing principle guiding the choice of one specified semantic representation would be a complexity-sensitive one (for example: "Avoid quantifier raising" captured in Tunstall's *Principle of Scope Interpretation* 1998 and Anderson's 2004 *Processing Scope Economy*).

In the psycholinguistic investigation of coercion phenomena, the experimental evidence is interpreted along these lines. Processing difficulties at the point of disambiguation are taken as evidence for full semantic interpretation (see e.g. Piñango, Zurif & Jackendoff 1999; Todorova, Straub, Badecker & Frank 2000) whereas the lack of measurable effects is seen as support for an underspecified semantic representation (see e.g. Pylkkänen & McElree 2006; Pickering, McElree, Frisson, Chen & Traxler 2006).

Analogously, in the processing of quantifier scope ambiguities, experimental evidence for processing difficulties at the point of disambiguation will be interpreted as support for full interpretation. However, this need not be taken as final. If we look at underspecification approaches in semantics, non-semantic factors are mentioned which might explain (and predict) difficulties in processing local scope ambiguities (see article 9 [Semantics: Lexical Structures and Adjectives] (Egg) *Semantic underspecification*, section 6.4.1.). And these are exactly the factors which are assumed by multi-factor theories to have an impact on quantifier scope: syntactic structure and function, context, and type of quantifier. The relative weighting and interaction of these factors are not made fully explicit, however.

For the full picture, it would be necessary to examine not only the point of disambiguation but also the ambiguous part of the input, for it is there that the effects of these factors might be identified. Underspecification is normally only temporary, however, and a full interpretation will presumably be constructed at some stage (but see Sanford & Sturt 2002). This might be recognizable for example in behavioral measures, but the precise predictions of underspecification theory are not always clear. For example, it might be assumed that even representations which are never fully specified by the input signal (or context) do receive more specific interpretations at some later stage. This of course raises the question what domains of interpretation are relevant here (sentence boundary, utterance, ...). In the next section we present experimental work which may offer a starting point for the empirical investigation of such issues.

5 On-line evidence for representation of scope

The underspecification view would predict that relative scope should remain underspecified as long as neither interpretation is forced. Indeed there should not even be any preference for one reading. The results of the questionnaire studies reported in Section 3 already indicate that this view cannot be right: a particular combination of factors was found to systematically support a certain reading. Furthermore it is unlikely that the task itself introduced a preference towards one interpretation – although the diagram representing the wide-scope existential reading was somewhat more complex, this did not seem to interfere with participants' performance. The observed preferences must thus be due to the experimental manipulation. That is, even if all possible interpretations are available up to the point where disambiguating information arrives, there must be some inherent ranking of the various scope-determining factors that results in certain interpretations being more activated than others.

Off-line results such as those discussed above are thus equally compatible with two different explanations; one where quantifier scope is fully determined (at least) by the end of the sentence, and another one where several (presumably all combinatorially possible) interpretations are available but weighted differently. A different methodology is needed to find out whether there is any psycholinguistic support for an underspecified view of quantifier scope.

As it turns out, the currently existing results of on-line studies are no more able to distinguish the two alternatives than are offline studies. In on-line experiments a scope-ambiguous initial clause is followed by a second one that is only compatible with one scope reading. An indication of difficulty during the processing of the second sentence is typically taken as evidence that the disambiguation is incompatible with the (sole) interpretation that had been entertained up to that point. However, there is another way to look at such effects. When the disambiguation is encountered, the underspecified representation needs to be enriched to allow only one reading and exclude all others. It is conceivable that updating the representation may require more or less effort depending on the ultimate interpretation that is required.

This situation poses a dilemma for researchers investigating the interpretation of quantifier scope. If explicit disambiguation is provided we can only test how easily the required reading is available – the results don't tell us what other reading(s) may have been constructed. Without explicit disambiguation, however, reading time (or other) data cannot be interpreted, since we do not know what reading(s) the participants had in mind.

Bott & Radó (2009) approached this problem by tracking the eye-movements of participants while they read ambiguous sentences and then asking them to report the interpretation they computed. Although their results are only partly relevant for the underspecification debate, we will describe the experiment in some detail, since it provides a good starting point for a more conclusive investigation. We will then sketch a modification of the method that makes it possible to avoid some problems with the original study.

The scope-ambiguous sentences in Bott and Radó's study were instructions like those in (7):

(7) a. Genau   ein   Tier   auf jedem Bild   sollst   du   nennen!
       Exactly one   animal on each picture   should   you   name!
       Name exactly one animal from each picture!

   b. Genau   ein   Tier   auf allen Bildern sollst   du   nennen!
      Exactly one   animal on all   pictures should you   name!
      Name exactly one animal from all pictures!

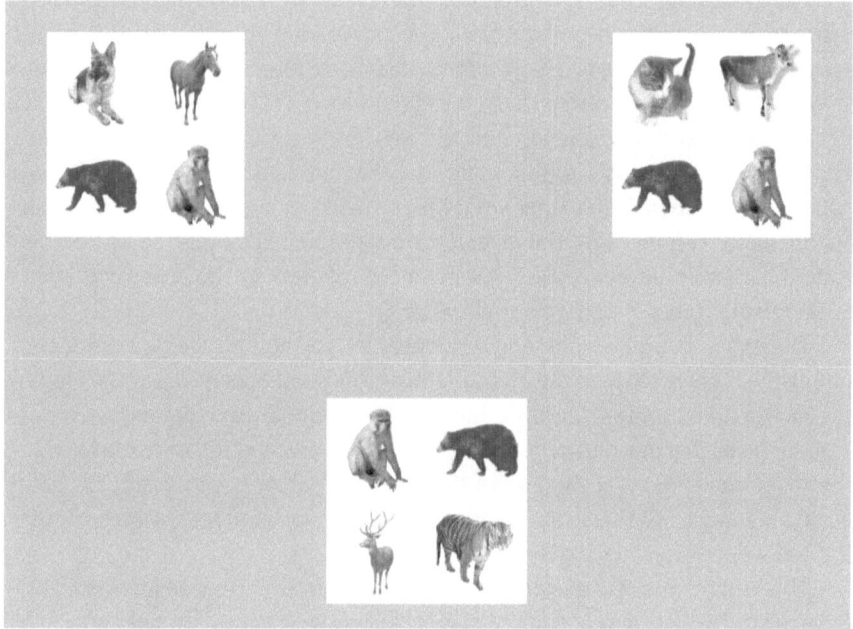

Fig. 15.2: Display following inverse linking constructions

The first quantifier (Q1) was always the indefinite *genau ein* "exactly one". The second (Q2) was either distributive (*jeder*) or not (*alle*). In one set of control conditions Q1 was replaced by a definite NP (*das Tier* "the animal"). In another set of control conditions the two possible interpretations of (7) (one animal that is present in all fields vs. a possibly different animal from each field on a display) were expressed by scope-unambiguous quantified sentences, as in (8).

(8) a. Name exactly one animal that is found on all pictures.
    b. From each picture name exactly one animal.

In each experimental trial participants first read one of these instruction sentences and their eye-movements were monitored. Then the instruction sentence disappeared and a picture display as in Fig. 15.2, replaced it. Participants inspected this and had to provide an answer within four seconds. The displays were constructed to be compatible with both possible readings: the wide-scope universal reading where the participant should select any one animal per field, but also the wide-scope existential reading where the one element common to all fields must be named (e.g. the monkey in Fig. 15.2). To make the quantifier *exactly one* felicitous, the critical displays always allowed two potential answers for the wide-scope existential interpretation.

The scope-ambiguous instructions were so-called inverse linking constructions, in which the two quantifiers are contained within one NP. It has been assumed (e.g. May & Bale 2006) that in inverse linking constructions the linearly second quantifier preferentially takes scope over the first. The purpose of the study was to test this prediction and to investigate to what extent the distributivity manipulation is able to modulate it. Based on earlier results (Bott & Radó 2007) it was assumed that *jeder* would prefer wide scope, which should further enhance the preference for the inverse reading. When *alle* occurred as Q2, there should be a conflict between the preferences inherent to the construction and those arising from the particular quantifiers.

The experimental setup made it possible to look at both the process of computing the relative scope of the quantifiers (eye-movement behavior while reading the instructions) and at the final interpretation (the answer participants gave) without providing any disambiguation. Thus the answers could be taken to reflect the scope preferences at the end of the sentence, whereas processing difficulty during reading would serve as an indication that scope preferences are computed at a point where no decision is yet required.

The off-line answers showed the expected effects. There was an overall preference for the inverse scope reading, which was significantly stronger with *jeder* than with *alle*. Crucially, the reading time data showed clear evidence of a conflict between the scope factors: there was a significant slow-down at the second quantifier in (7b). The effect was present already in first-pass reading times, suggesting that scope preferences were computed immediately. Bott and Radó interpret these results as strong indication that readers regularly disambiguate sentences during normal reading.

However, this conclusion may be too strong. In Bott and Radó's experiment participants had to choose a particular interpretation in order to carry out the instructions (i.e. *name an animal*). Although they did not have to settle on that interpretation while they were reading the instruction, they had to make a decision as to the preferred reading immediately after the end of the sentence. This may have caused them to disambiguate constructions that are typically left ambiguous during normal interpretation.

Moreover, the instructions used in the experiment were highly predictable in structure: they always contained a complex NP with two quantifiers (experimental items), a definite NP1 followed by a quantified NP2 (fillers A), or else an unambiguous sentence with two quantifiers. Although the content of NP1 (animal, vehicle, flag) and distributivity of Q2 was varied, the rest of the instruction was the same: *sollst du nennen* 'you should name'. This pattern was easy to recognize and may have resulted in a strategy of starting to compute the scope preferences as soon as the second NP had been received. To rule out this explanation Bott and Radó compared responses provided in the first and the last third of each experimental session and failed to find any indication of strategic behavior. Still the possibility remains that consistent early disambiguation in the experiment resulted from the task of having to choose a reading quickly in order to provide an answer. The ultimate test of underspecification would have to avoid such pressure to disambiguate fast.

We are currently conducting a modification of Bott and Radó's experiment that may not only avoid this pressure but actually encourage participants to delay disambiguation. In this experiment participants have to judge the accuracy of sentences like those in (9):

(9) a. Genau eine geometrische Form auf allen Bildern ist rechteckig.
    Exactly one geometrical shape on all pictures is rectangular.
    Exactly one geometrical shape on all pictures is rectangular.

   b. Genau eine geometrische Form auf jedem Bild ist rechteckig.
    Exactly one geometrical shape on each picture is rectangular.
    Exactly one geometrical shape on each picture is rectangular.

The experiment procedure is as before. The sentences will be paired with unambiguous displays supporting either the wide-scope universal or the wide-scope existential reading (Fig. 15.3.). In (9) full processing of the semantic content is not possible until the critical information (*rechteckig*) has been received. Since the display following the sentence is only compatible with one reading which the participant cannot anticipate, they are better off waiting to see which interpretation will be required for the answer. If underspecification is indeed the preferred strategy, there should be no difference in reading times across the different conditions, nor should there be any difficulty in judging any kind of sentence-display pair. Assuming immediate full specification of scope, however, we would expect the same pattern of results as in Bott and Radó's study: slower reading times in (9a) than in (9b) at the second quantifier, as well as slower responses to displays

A) wide scope existential disambiguation B) wide scope universal disambiguation

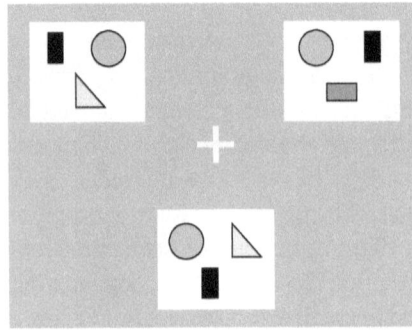
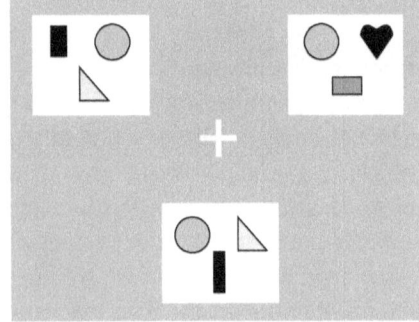

Fig. 15.3: Disambiguating displays in the proposed experiment

requiring the wide-scope existential interpretation, the latter presumably modulated by *distributivity* of Q2.

This experiment should be able to distinguish intermediate positions between the two extremes of complete underspecification and immediate full interpretation. It is conceivable, for instance, that scope interpretation is only initiated when the perceiver can be reasonably sure that they have received all (or at least sufficient) information. This would correspond to the same reading time effects (and same answering behavior) as predicted under immediate full interpretation, but the effects would be somewhat delayed. Another possibility is an initial underspecification of scope, but the construction of a fully specified interpretation at the boundary of some interpretation domain such as the clause boundary. That would predict a complete lack of reading time effects but answer times showing the same incompatibility effects as under versions of the full interpretation approach.

It is worth emphasizing how this design differs from existing studies. First, it looks at the ambiguous region and not just the disambiguation point. Second, it differs from Filik, Paterson & Liversedge (2004), who also measured reading times in the ambiguous region, but who used the kind of disambiguation that we criticized in section 3.

6 Conclusions

In this article we have attempted to show that experimentally obtained data can, in spite of certain complicating and confounding factors, be of relevance to semantic theory and provide both support for and in some cases falsification of its assumptions and constructs. In section 2 we noted that the field of theoretical semantics has made less use of experimental verification of its analyses and assumptions. We have seen that there are some quite good reasons for this and laid out what some of the problematic factors are. While some of these are shared to a greater or lesser degree with other branches of linguistics, some of them are peculiar to semantics or are especially severe in this case.

The main part of our paper reports a research program addressing the issue of relative scope in doubly quantified sentences. We present this work as an example of the ways in which experimental approaches can contribute to the development of theory. They also illustrate some of the practical constraints upon such studies. For example, we have seen that clear disambiguation is not always easy to achieve, in particular, it is difficult to achieve without biasing the interpretational choices of the experiment participant. The use of eye-tracking and fully ambiguous picture displays is a real advance on previous practice (Bott & Radó 2009).

Section 3 shows how experimental procedures which are simple enough for non-specialist experimenters can nevertheless yield evidence of value for the development of semantic theories: a carefully constructed and counter-balanced design can produce data of sufficient quality to answer outstanding questions with some degree of finality. In this particular case the configurational account of scope can be seen as failing to account for data that the multi-factor account succeeds in capturing. The unsupported account is demonstrated to need adaptation or development. Experimentation can make the field of theory more dynamic and adaptive; an account which repeatedly fails to capture evidence gathered in controlled studies and which cannot economically be extended to do so will eventually need to be reconsidered.

In section 5 we describe an experiment designed to provide evidence which distinguishes between two accounts (section 4) of the way that perceivers deal with ambiguity in the input signal: underspecification vs. full interpretation. This is an example of how processing data can under certain circumstances provide decisive evidence which distinguishes between theoretical accounts. It is of course often the case that theory does not make any direct predictions about psycholinguistically testable measures of processing. The collaboration of psycholinguists and semanticists may yet reveal testable predictious more often than has sometimes been assumed.

We therefore argue for experimental linguists and semanticists to cooperate more and take more notice of each other's work for their mutual benefit. Semanticists will gain additional ways to falsify theoretical analyses or aspects of them, which can deliver a boost to theory development. This will be possible, because experimenters can tailor experimental methods, tasks, and designs to their specific requirements.

Experimenters for their part will benefit by having the questioning eye of the semanticist look over their experimental materials, which will surely avoid many experiments being carried out whose materials fail to uniquely fulfill the requirements of the design. An example of this is the mode of disambiguation which we discussed in section 3. Further to this, experimenters will doubtless be able to derive more testable predictions from semantic theories, if they discuss the finer workings of these with specialist semanticists. We might mention here the example of semantic underspecification: can we find evidence for its psychological reality? Further questions might be: if some feature of an expression remains underdetermined by the input, how long can the representation remain underspecified? Is it possible for a final representation of a discourse to have unspecified features and nevertheless be fully meaningful?

We conclude, therefore, that controlled experimentation can provide a further source of evidence for semantics. This data can under certain circumstances give a more detailed picture of the states of affairs which theories aim to account for. This additional evidence could be the catalyst for some advances in semantic theory and explanation, in the same way that it has in syntactic theory.

7 References

Anderson, Catherine 2004. *The Structure and Real-time Comprehension of Quantifier Scope Ambiguity*. Ph.D. dissertation. Northwestern University, Evanstone, IL.

Aoun, Joseph & Yen-hui Audrey Li 1989. Scope and constituency. *Linguistic Inquiry* 16, 623–637.

Beghelli, Filippo & Tim Stowell 1997. Distributivity and negation: The syntax of *each* and *every*. In: A. Szabolcsi (ed.). *Ways of Scope Taking*. Dordrecht: Kluwer, 71–107.

Bott, Oliver & Janina Radó 2007. Quantifying quantifier scope. In: S. Featherston & W. Sternefeld (eds.). *Roots. Linguistics in Search of its Evidential Base*. Berlin: Mouton deGruyter, 53–74.

Bott, Oliver & Janina Radó 2009. How to provide exactly one interpretation for every sentence, or what eye movements reveal about quantifier scope. In: S. Winkler & S. Featherston (eds.). *The Fruits of Empirical Linguistics, Volume 1: Process*. Berlin: de Gruyter, 25–46.

Chomsky, Noam 1965. *Aspects of the Theory of Syntax*. Cambridge, MA: The MIT Press.

Filik, Ruth, Kevin B. Paterson & Simon P. Liversedge 2004. Processing doubly quantified sentences: Evidence from eye movements. *Psychonomic Bulletin & Review* 11, 953–959.

Frazier, Lyn & Keith Rayner 1990. Taking on semantic commitments: Processing multiple meanings vs. multiple senses. *Journal of Memory and Language* 29, 181–200.

Gillen, Kathryn 1991. *The Comprehension of Doubly Quantified Sentences*. Ph.D. dissertation. Durham University.

van Gompel, Roger P.G. & Martin J. Pickering 2007. Syntactic parsing. In: G. Gaskell (ed.). *The Oxford Handbook of Psycholinguistics*. Oxford: Oxford University Press. 455–504.

Hahne, Anja & Angela D. Friederici 2002. Differential task effects on semantic and syntactic processes as revealed by ERPs. *Cognitive Brain Research* 13, 339–356.

Higginbotham, James 1985. On semantics. *Linguistic Inquiry* 16, 547–594.

Hobbs, Jerry & Stuart M. Shieber 1987. An algorithm for generating quantifier scopings. *Computational Linguistics* 13, 47–63.

Hornstein, Norbert 1984. *Logic as Grammar*. Cambridge, MA: The MIT Press.

Hornstein, Norbert 1995. *Logical Form: From GB to Minimalism*. Oxford: Blackwell.

Huang, Cheng-Teh James 1982. *Logical Relations in Chinese and the Theory of Grammar*. Ph.D. dissertation. MIT, Cambridge, MA.

Ioup, Georgette 1975. *The Treatment of Quantifier Scope in Transformational Grammar*. Ph.D. dissertation. The University of New York, New York.

Kuno, Susumu 1991. Remarks on quantifier scope. In: H. Nakajima (ed.). *Current English Linguistics in Japan*. Berlin: Mouton de Gruyter, 261–287.

Kurtzman, Howard S. & Maryellen C. MacDonald 1993. Resolution of quantifier scope ambiguities. *Cognition* 48, 243–279.

Larson, Meredith, Ryan Doran, Yaron McNabb, Rachel Baker, Matthew Berends, Alex Djalali & Gregory Ward 2010. Distinguishing the said from the implicated using a novel experimental paradigm. In: U. Sauerland & K. Yatsushiro (eds.). *Semantics and Pragmatics. From Experiment to Theory*. Houndmills: Palgrave Macmillan.

May, Robert 1977. *The Grammar of Quantification*. Ph.D. dissertation. MIT, Cambridge, MA. Reprinted: Bloomington, IN: Indiana University Linguistics Club, 1982.

May, Robert 1985. *Logical Form: Its Structure and Derivation*. Cambridge, MA: The MIT Press.

May, Robert & Alan Bale 2006. Inverse linking. In: M. Everaert & H. van Riemsdijk (eds.). *Blackwell Companion to Syntax*. Oxford: Blackwell, 639–667.

Pafel, Jürgen 2005. *Quantifier Scope in German*. (Linguistics Today 84). Amsterdam: Benjamins.

Park, Jong C. 1995. Quantifier scope and constituency. In: H. Uszkoreit (ed.). *Proceedings of the 33rd Annual Meeting of the Association of Computational Linguistics*. Boston, MA: Morgan Kaufmann, 205–212.

Phillips, Colin & Matthew Wagers 2007. Relating structure and time in linguistics and psycholinguistics. In: M.G. Gaskell (ed.). *The Oxford Handbook of Psycholinguistics*. Oxford: Oxford University Press, 739–756.

Pickering, Martin J., Brian McElree, Steven Frisson, Lilian Chen & Matthew J. Traxler 2006. Underspecification and aspectual coercion. *Discourse Processes* 42, 131–155.

Piñango, Maria, Edgar Zurif & Ray Jackendoff 1999. Real-time processing implications of enriched composition at the syntax-semantics interface. *Journal of Psycholinguistic Research* 28, 395–414.

Pinkal, Manfred 1999. On semantic underspecification. In: H. Bunt & R. Muskens (eds.). *Computing Meaning*, Dordrecht: Kluwer, 33–55.

Pylkkänen, Liina & Brian McElree 2006. The syntax-semantics interface: On-line composition of meaning. In: M. A. Gernsbacher & M. Traxler (eds.). *Handbook of Psycholinguistics*. 2nd edn. New York: Elsevier, 537–577.

Reinhart, Tanya 1976. *The Syntactic Domain of Anaphora*. Ph.D. dissertation. MIT, Cambridge, MA.

Reinhart, Tanya 1978. Syntactic domains for semantic rules. In: F. Guenthner & S.J. Schmidt (eds.). *Formal Semantics and Pragmatics for Natural Language*. Dordrecht: Reidel, 107–130.

Reinhart, Tanya 1983. *Anaphora and Semantic Interpretation*. London: Croom Helm.
Reinhart, Tanya 1995. *Interface Strategies* (OTS Working Papers in Linguistics). Utrecht: Utrecht University.
Ross, John R. 1970. On declarative sentences. In: R. Jacobs & P. Rosenbaum (eds). *Readings in English Transformational Grammar*. Waltham, MA: Ginn, 222–272.
Sanford, Anthony J. & Patrick Sturt 2002. Depth of processing in language comprehension: Not noticing the difference. *Trends in Cognitive Neuroscience* 6, 382–386.
Todorova, Marina, Kathy Straub, William Badecker & Robert Frank 2000. Aspectual coercion and the online computation of sentential aspect. In: L. R. Gleitman & A. K. Joshi (eds.). *Proceedings of the 22nd Annual Conference of the Cognitive Science Society*. Mahwah, NJ: Lawrence Erlbaum Associates, 3–8.
Tunstall, Susanne L. 1998. *The Interpretation of Quantifiers: Semantics and Processing*. Ph.D. dissertation. University of Massachussetts, Amherst, MA.
VanLehn, Kurt A. 1978. *Determining the Scope of English Quantifiers*. Technical Report (AI-TR 483). Cambridge, MA, Artificial Intelligence Laboratory, MIT.
Weskott, Thomas & Gisbert Fanselow 2009. Scaling issues in the measurement of linguistic acceptability. In: S. Winkler & S. Featherston (eds.). *The Fruits of Empirical Linguistics, Volume 1: Process*. Berlin: de Gruyter, 229–246.
Zhou, Peng & Liqun Gao 2009. Scope processing in Chinese. *Journal of Psycholinguistic Research* 38, 11–24.

Index

19th century 182, 204, 208, 213, 217–234, 307

acceptability tests 321, 322, 342
ambiguity 5, 75, 79, 89–91, 112–115, 125, 149, 151, 158, 189, 195, 255–290, 310–326, 342, 344, 373–381, 390–405
argument linking 156, 157, 174, 178
Aristotelian syllogistic 243, 245, 246, 270
atomism 165, 167
attributive-referential distinction 77–79

behavioral effects 20, 306, 309, 325, 328
belief sentences 54, 62, 87, 91, 144, 146–148, 255

centrality of communication 91, 94
character-content 57, 80–82, 85, 134, 307
cognition 1, 29, 130, 175, 177, 193, 210, 238, 354
cognitive value 35–39, 58
communication 14–25, 45, 53–55, 104, 108, 117, 140–143, 188, 192, 205–209, 225, 233–237, 307–324
communicative
– behavior 22, 29, 30, 101, 1040, 308, 323, 325
– intention 14, 15, 22, 23, 29, 30, 101, 104, 111, 117, 307, 308, 380
completeness 170, 249, 365, 369, 374
compositionality 5–10, 12, 34, 40, 67, 69, 70, 80, 122–152, 197, 211, 250, 257, 258, 260, 261, 274, 277, 281, 284, 288, 290–293, 302, 308, 320, 347, 355, 374, 377, 378
concepts of meaning 10, 21–23, 40, 81, 143, 159–162, 165–172, 187, 189–213, 231, 233, 234, 284, 295, 310, 311, 316, 335, 362, 365
conceptual content 10, 35, 36, 144, 170, 299, 381
context 10–12, 19–29, 40–57, 86–88, 95–98, 112–117, 199, 226–234, 256–261, 268, 284–302, 310, 331, 332, 342–346, 389–391
– dependence 11, 56, 57, 134–136, 146, 151, 273, 284, 285, 289, 290, 293, 389

Cooperative Principle 22–25, 100–107, 117, 343
corpus-linguistic methods 13, 275, 333–335
Curry-Howard isomorphism 291, 292, 298

decidability 365, 368
decomposition 40, 156–160, 163–171, 173–178, 357, 379
– lexical 156–170, 174, 175, 177
de dicto / de re 74, 75, 79, 89, 90, 254, 255, 260
definite descriptions 33–36, 50–53, 57, 62–64, 68, 70, 73–80, 82–85, 88–91, 94, 243, 248, 251, 252, 266, 367
deixis 95, 98, 107, 243, 313
development of logic 50, 182, 183, 242–253, 256, 268, 270, 274, 275, 362, 364–366, 374, 381
direct reference 46, 48, 65–67, 69, 72, 73, 82, 85, 243, 256
disambiguation 98, 112, 115, 116, 149, 377, 392–406
Discourse Representation Theory 90, 98, 116, 267, 268, 286–290, 294–302, 364, 379
discourse 10–12, 95–98, 103–116, 186–197, 204–209, 223–237, 243, 259, 266–269, 274, 277, 286–289, 291, 317, 322, 341–346, 351, 363–368, 379–382, 391, 406
dynamic logic 242, 265–270
Dynamic Predicate Logic 268, 269, 288
Dynamic Semantics 11, 27, 90, 98, 115, 243, 250, 266, 267, 286, 288, 364–374

elicitation 321, 323, 341–346
eliciting translations 323, 342–345
ellipsis 273, 274, 295–297, 300–302
enrichment 8, 9, 27, 28, 144, 226, 297, 374
event-related potentials 330
extension 16, 34, 49, 50, 63, 71, 99, 124, 131–135, 187, 199, 206, 207, 221, 226, 242–260, 262–265, 274, 277, 292, 308, 316

fieldwork techniques 306, 312, 341, 388
fieldwork 310–318, 340–345, 346, 351, 354
first order logic 7, 38, 249, 261, 262, 311, 365–368, 380

formal languages 19, 40, 274–282, 284, 290, 302, 311, 367–369

generalized quantifiers 72, 261–265, 281, 294, 351, 352, 381

history of linguistics 221, 237, 307
history of semantics 159, 165, 182–238

idioms 17, 106, 149, 150, 309
illocutionary force 18–21, 24, 94, 95, 105–107
implicatures 21, 24–26, 28, 43, 103, 116, 144, 306, 307, 319, 322, 324
incrementality 288, 302, 398
indefinite descriptions 62, 64, 88–91
indexicality 26, 62, 76, 77, 80–82, 95
indirect sense 46, 48
inferential model of communication 15, 22–25
intensionality 16
intensional theory of types 260, 264
intension 3, 34, 49, 50, 63, 71, 124, 131, 134, 187, 206, 207, 226, 242, 243, 252, 253, 265, 308
intentionality 14–18, 22, 30, 203, 307
intersubjectivity 139, 140

lambda calculus 259, 276, 282, 291, 292, 367
language as logic 52, 211, 247, 253, 276–280, 366
learnability 136–138, 353, 381
lexicographic definitions 169
logical
– form 6, 26, 27, 38–41, 126, 199, 364
– tools 12, 242, 243, 270, 363, 380, 382
logic 16, 38, 40, 50–52, 63, 71, 72, 103, 124, 156, 182–224, 233, 242–270, 273–302, 311, 362, 364–367, 370–381

mode of presentation 33, 37–47, 52–58, 87, 88, 147, 250

necessity 34, 49, 84, 211, 213, 223, 250, 256, 265, 274, 371
nondescriptionality 82, 85, 87

observer's paradox 392
on-line evidence 387, 399–404

ontology 17, 183, 190, 252–258, 280, 285, 293
ordinary language 14, 15, 18–25, 220, 237, 364
ordo significationis 186, 191, 196, 199

philosophy 14–26, 33, 63, 73, 124, 136, 182–210, 217–237, 243–251, 274, 275, 290
physiological effects 328, 332
plausibility 41, 157, 282, 332, 344, 390, 391
pointing 40, 80, 98, 158, 185, 190, 209, 313–317
Port-Royal Logic 205–207
possible worlds 3, 10–12, 50, 51, 70–85, 102, 134, 243, 252–257, 264–270, 283–289, 321, 371, 374
pragmatics 8–10, 14–30, 43, 112–115, 145, 218, 243, 290, 301, 308, 364, 388
predicate logic 72, 156, 242–270, 275–283, 288, 290, 302, 311
presupposition 11, 69, 75–78, 94–117, 140, 141, 247, 252, 306, 319–326, 343–346, 356, 357, 367, 381
productivity 18, 138, 139
proofs 52, 249, 272, 275–295, 363–369, 371–376
proper names 34–44, 50–54, 62–64, 82–87, 90, 243, 248, 252, 256, 370–373, 381
propositional attitude 18, 46–49, 62–91, 116, 186, 250–255, 284, 323
psycholinguistics 169, 308, 393, 395

quantifier scope 151, 263–381, 387, 388, 393–403
quotation 136, 147–149, 236, 250

reasoning 18, 55, 145, 204–210, 233, 274, 275, 282, 362–382
reference 16, 26, 33–58, 62–85, 95–98, 124, 194, 196, 200, 201, 218, 242–256, 287–289, 307–317, 357, 373, 379
referential-attributive 77–79, 90
representationalism 63, 71, 218, 273, 275, 291, 302, 364
rigidity 50, 51, 84, 260

Salish 321, 343–357
scholastic tradition 183, 194–197, 203–206
scope interpretation 74, 75, 91, 300, 301, 377, 394–405

selectional restrictions 110, 156, 158, 161–164
semantic
– features 19, 140, 156–178, 189, 209, 218, 237, 243, 313, 326, 332, 343, 378, 406
– judgments 302, 317–343, 387–395
– models 63, 112, 200, 220, 265, 269, 273–290, 295, 302, 362–367, 369–382, 388
– primitives 7, 157, 159, 168–170, 175, 277, 298, 357
semantics
– 19th century 182, 208, 217–238, 307
– 20th century 94, 182, 217–238, 366, 379
– ancient 188, 193, 218, 362, 366
– cross-linguistic 12, 164, 221, 312, 340–357
– early modern 183, 203, 204–207, 372
– experimental 232, 308, 335, 382, 387–406
– grammars and 124, 134
– history of 159, 165, 182–218, 221–238
– lexical 160, 163, 238, 354
– medieval 123, 182–188, 192–198, 203
– recursive 128, 142, 162, 378
– two-dimensional 243, 250, 256, 315
– and logic 71, 182–184, 192–207, 218, 238, 242–270, 274–285, 288–293, 300–302, 311, 347–353, 362–367, 370–382
– in Britain 217, 219, 221, 232–237
– in France 217, 219, 220, 228–232
– in Germany 71, 217, 219, 221–230
semantics-pragmatics interface 8–10, 19, 308
sense 16, 33–58, 62–71, 81, 85, 107, 112, 204, 218, 242–252, 316
sentence meaning 2–12, 14–28, 40, 62–81, 98, 123–147, 151, 162, 183–211, 233–242, 246–253, 276, 285, 295, 306–327, 342–345, 391–395
significatio 191, 194–197, 203
speculative grammar 183, 201, 202

speech act 14, 15, 18–21, 25, 96, 105, 111, 190, 226, 248, 308, 325
speech community 64, 94–97, 109, 117
square of oppositions 246, 247, 263
substitutivity 65–74, 86, 140, 147
supposition 183, 195, 198–200, 211
syllogistic inference 244–246
syntax-semantics interface 177
syntax 18, 19, 122–177, 222–231, 246, 274–302, 307, 312, 341–355, 369–377, 389–391

truth 1–10, 19, 25–28, 34–50, 63–91, 112, 124–151, 174, 178, 186–210, 234, 243–269, 275–290, 308–333, 342–344, 363–379
– conditions 1–10, 12, 19–27, 63, 73, 112, 174, 178, 199, 243, 256, 268, 269, 277–290, 344, 363–379
– value judgments 35, 248, 317, 318, 342, 343
truth-conditional
– pragmatics 14, 15, 25–29, 112
– semantics 12, 94, 100, 218, 243, 267, 274, 280, 379
Type Logical Grammar 292–297
Type Theory with records 293–295, 302

underspecification 8, 9, 291, 294, 299, 357, 387, 388, 398–400, 403–406
universals 72, 252, 262, 340–356, 382
utterance meaning 10, 14–28, 40, 56, 80, 81, 95, 98–100, 103–105, 243, 307, 308, 327, 342–344, 364, 392

validity 42, 210, 363–371, 379
variation 53, 135, 142, 160, 237, 293, 309, 316, 340, 348–357
visual world paradigm 327

www.ingramcontent.com/pod-product-compliance
Lightning Source LLC
Chambersburg PA
CBHW031541300426
44111CB00006BA/137